Indian W

To,
A very wise man who
might find this book's wisdom
food for thought

With loads of regards to
Sagar ji. Enjoy the retirement

Rajeet & family.

Indian Wisdom

Monier Williams

Rupa . Co

Published by

Rupa • Co

7/16, Ansari Road, Daryaganj,
New Delhi 110 002

Offices at:
15 Bankim Chatterjee Street, Kolkata 700 073
135 South Malaka, Allahabad 211 001
PG Solanki Path, Lamington Road, Mumbai 400 007
36, Kutty Street, Nungambakkam, Chennai 600 034
Surya Shree, B-6, New 66, Shankara Park,
   Basavangudi, Bangalore 560 004
3-5-612, Himayat Nagar, Hyderabad 500 029

ISBN 81-7167-608-1

Typeset Copyright © Rupa & Co. 2001

Typeset by
Nikita Overseas Pvt Ltd, 19-A Ansari Road, New Delhi 110 002

Printed in India by
Gopsons Papers Ltd, A-14 Sector-60, Noida 201 301

Contents

INTRODUCTION   xix
LECTURE I   1
   The Hymns of the Veda   1
LECTURE II   28
   The Brahmanas and Upanishads   28
   The Upanishads   37
LECTURE III   52
   The Systems of Philosophy   52
   Buddhism   58
LECTURE IV   76
   The Nyaya   76
   The Vaiseshika   82
LECTURE V   96
   The Sankhya   96
   The Yoga   110
LECTURE VI   116
   The Purva-mimansa and Vedanta   116
   The Vedanta   120
LECTURE VII   137
   Irregular Systems and Eclectic School   137
   Jainism   138
   The Charvakas   142
   The Eclectic School Represented by the
     Bhagavad-gita   145
LECTURE VIII   169
   Smriti — The Vedangas   169
   I. The Vedangas   171

LECTURE IX   213

    II. The Smarta Sutras or Traditional Rules   213

    III. The Dharma-sastras or Law-books — Manu   232

LECTURE X   242

    The Dharma-shastras or Law-books — Manu   242

LECTURE XI   312

    The Law — Manu continued   312

    Achara, 'rules of conduct'   312

    Duties of Women and Wives   318

    Vyavahara, 'rules of government and judicature'   320

    Prayas-chitta, 'penance and expiation'   323

    Karma-phala, 'recompenses of acts'   324

    The Code of Yajnavalkya   327

    The eighteen principal Codes posterior to
       Manu and Yajnavalkya   337

    The Five Schools of Hindu Law   340

LECTURE XII   344

    IV. The Itihasa or Epic Poems — The Ramayana   344

    The Ramayana   373

LECTURE XIII   413

    The Itihasas or Epic Poems — The Mahabharata   413

LECTURE XIV   465

    The Indian Epics compared with each other and
       with the Homeric Poems   465

LECTURE XV   502

    The Artificial Poems. Dramas. Puranas.
       Tantras. Niti-shastras.   502

    The Artificial Poems   502

    The Dramas   518

    V. The Puranas   548

    The Tantras   562

    VI. The Niti-sastras   566

    The Two-headed Weaver   575

Index   583

Preface

To the Second Edition

The increasing interest felt in India and Indian literature has led to such a demand for the present work, that it was found necessary to begin printing a second edition almost immediately after the issue of the first. I have, therefore, been unable to avail myself of the suggestions contained in the reviews which have hitherto appeared. Nevertheless, a few unimportant alterations have been made in the present edition; and through the kindness of Professor W.D. Whitney, who lost no time in sending me some valuable notes, I have been able to improve the chapter on Astronomy at p. 197.

Being on the eve of quitting England for a visit to the principal seats of learning in India, I have for obvious reasons deferred addressing myself to the fuller treatment of those portions of Sanskrit literature of which I have merely given a summary in Lecture XV.

India, with all its immutability, is now making such rapid strides in education, that a Professor of Sanskrit at Oxford, if he is to keep himself up to the level of advancing knowledge and attainments, ought to communicate personally with some of those remarkable native Pandits whose intellects have been developed at our great Indian Colleges and Universities, and

vii

who owe their eminence in various branches of learning to
the advantages they have enjoyed under our Government.

In undertaking so long a journey my only motives are a
sense of what is due from me to the Boden Chair, a desire
to extend my sphere óf work, a craving for trustworthy
information on many obscure portions of Indian religious
literature not yet examined by European scholars, and a hope
that on my return, should health and strength be spared to
me, I may have increased my powers of usefulness within my
own province, and be enabled to contribute more than I have
yet effected towards making England and India better known
to each other, or at least towards making Oxford an attractive
centre of Indian studies, and its lecture-rooms, museums, and
libraries sources of accurate knowledge on Indian subjects.

Oxford, October 1875.

Preface

To the First Edition

The present volume[1] attempts to supply a want, the existence of which has been impressed upon my mind by an inquiry often addressed to me as Boden professor: — Is it possible to obtain from any one book a good general idea of the character and contents of Sanskrit literature?

Its pages are also intended to subserve a further object. They aim at imparting to educated Englishmen, by means of translations and explanations of portions of the sacred and philosophical literature of India, an insight into the mind, habits of thought, and customs of the Hindus, as well as a correct knowledge of a system of belief and practice which has constantly prevailed for at least three thousand years, and still continues to exist as one of the principal religions of the Non-Christian world[2].

---

1. The volume is founded on my official lectures.
2. See the caution, last line of p. xxxix, and p. 2. Although European nations have changed their religions during the past eighteen centuries, the Hindus have not done so, except very partially. Islam converted a certain number by force of arms in the eighth and following centuries, and Christian truth is at last creeping onwards and winning its way by its own inherent energy in the nineteenth; but the religious

It cannot indeed be right, nor is it even possible for educated Englishmen to remain any longer ignorant of the literary productions, laws, institutions, religious creed, and moral precepts of their Hindus fellow-creatures and fellow-subjects. The East and West are every day being drawn nearer to each other, and British India, in particular, is now brought so close to us by steam, electricity, and the Suez Canal, that the condition of the Hindu community — mental, moral, and physical — forces itself peremptorily on our attention. Nor is it any longer justifiable to plead the difficulty of obtaining accurate official information as an excuse for ignorance. Our Government has for a long period addressed itself most energetically to the investigation of every detail capable of throwing light on the past and present history of the Queen's Indian dominions.

A Literary survey of the whole of India, has been recently organized for the purpose of ascertaining what Sanskrit MSS., worthy of preservation, exist in public and private libraries. Competent scholars have been appointed to the task, and the result of their labours, so far as they have hitherto extended, has been published.

Simultaneously, an Archaeological survey has been ably conducted under the superintendence of Major-General A.

---

creeds, rites, customs, and habits of thought of the Hindus generally have altered little since the days of Manu, five hundred years B.C. Of course they have experienced accretions, but many of the same caste observances and rules of conduct (*acara, vyavahara,* see p. 239) are still in force; some of the same laws of inheritance (*daya,* p. 299) hold good; even a beggar will sometimes ask for alms in words prescribed by the ancient lawgiver (*bhiksham dehi,* Manu II. 49, Kulluka); and to this day, if a pupil absents himself from an Indian college, he sometimes excuses himself by saying that he has a *prayas-citta* to perform (see p. 307, and Trubner's Report of Professor Stenzler's Speech at the London Oriental Congress).

Cunningham, and we have most interesting results published and distributed by the Indian Governments in the shape of four large volumes, filled with illustrations, the last issued being the Report for the year 1871-72.

An Ethnological survey has also been set on foot in Bengal, and a magnificent volume with portraits from photographs of numerous aboriginal tribes, called *Descriptive Ethnology of Bengal*, by Colonel Dalton, was published at Calcutta in 1872. This was preceded by a valuable guide to the *Ethnology of India*, written by Sir George Campbell.

Even an Industrial survey has been partially carried out under the able direction of Dr. Forbes Watson, who proposes that a new Museum and Indian Institute shall be built and attached to the India Office.

Moreover, Sir George Campbell caused to be prepared, printed, and published, during his recent administration in Bengal, comparative tables of specimens of all the languages of India — Aryan, Dravidian, and aboriginal — the practical benefit of which requires no demonstration on my part.

But there are other official publications still more accessible to every Englishman who will take the trouble of applying to the proper authorities.

Those whose horizon of Eastern knowledge has hitherto been hopelessly clouded, so as to shut out every country beyond the Holy Land, have now a clear prospect opened out towards India. They have only to study the Report of the *Moral and Material Progress and Condition of India during 1872-73*, published by the India Office, and edited by Mr. C.R. Markham. At the risk of being thought impertinent, I must crave permission to record here an opinion that this last mentioned work is worthy of a better fate than to be wrapped in a blue cover, as if it were a mere official statement of dry facts and statistics. Its pages are full of valuable information on every subject connected with our Eastern

Empire — even including missionary progress — and the carefully drawn maps with which it is illustrated are a highly instructive study in themselves. The revelation the Report makes of what is being done and what remains to be done, may well humble as well as cheer every thoughtful person. But emanating as the volume does from the highest official, authority, it is in itself an evidence of great advance in our knowledge of India's needs, and in our endeavours to meet them, as well as an earnest of our future efforts for the good of its inhabitants.

The same must be said of Sir George Campbell's exhaustive Report on his own administration of Bengal during 1872-73. This forms a thick 8vo volume of about nine hundred pages, and affords a mine of interesting and valuable information[1].

Most significant, too, of an increasing interchange of Oriental and Occidental ideas and knowledge is the circumstance that almost every number of the *Times* newspaper contains able articles and interesting communications from its correspondents on Indian affairs, or records some result of the intellectual stir and ferment now spreading, as it has never done before, from Cape Comorin to the Himalaya mountains.

Another noteworthy indication of growing inter-community of thought between the East and West is the fact

---

1 Another very instructive publication, though of quite a different stamp from the official documents mentioned above, is M. Garcin de Tassy's Annual Review (*Revue Annuelle*) of the literary condition of India, which is every year kindly presented to me, and to many other scholars, by that eminent Orientalist. It is delivered annually in the form of a discourse at the opening of his Hindustani lectures. Though it deals more particularly with the development of Urdu and other linguistic studies, it gives a complete and reliable account of the intellectual and social movements now going on, and of the progress made in all branches of education and knowledge.

that every principal periodical of the day finds itself compelled
to take increasing account of the sayings and doings — wise
or unwise — of young Bengal, Madras, and Bombay. Our
attention is continually drawn by one or another publication
to the proceedings of native religious societies — such as the
Brahma-samaj, Sanatana-dharma-samaj, Dharma-sabha, &c.[1]
— or to the transactions of literary and scientific clubs and
institutions; while not unfrequently we are presented with
extracts from vernacular journals[2], or from the speeches of
high-minded Hindus, who occasionally traverse India, not as
Christian missionaries, but seeking, in a spirit worthy of
Christianity itself, to purify the Hindu creed and elevate the
tone of Indian thought and feeling. All this is a sure criterion
of the warm interest in Oriental matters now taking possession
of the public mind in Western countries.

But still more noteworthy as an evidence of increasing
personal intercourse between England and India is the presence
of Hindus and Muslims amongst us here. Many of the more
intelligent and enlightened natives, breaking through the
prejudices of caste and tradition that have hitherto chained
them as prisoners to their own soil, now visit our shores and
frequent our Universities to study us, our institutions, laws,

---

1. There appear to be two sections of the Brahma-samaj or Theistic
   society established in India. One clings to the Veda and seeks to
   restore Hinduism to the pure monotheism believed to underlie the
   Veda. These theists are followers of the late Rammohun Roy. The
   other society rejects the Veda and advocates an independent and
   purer theism. Its present leader is Keshab Chandra Sen.
2. The increase in the number of journals and newspapers in the
   vernacular languages, conducted with much ability and intelligence
   by native editors, is remarkable. An Urdu and Hindi paper called
   Mangala-samachara-patra, printed and published at Besvan, by
   Thakur Guru Prasad Sinh, is, through his kindness, regularly
   transmitted to me.

and literature. Some of them, too, have already received a thorough English education at Indian colleges. It is even asserted that they sometimes come amongst us knowing our language, our history, and our standard authors better than we know them ourselves. Be this as it may, thus much, at least, is clear that Englishmen and Hindus are at length holding out the right hand of fellowship to each other, and awaking to the consciousness that the duty of studying the past and present state — intellectual, moral, and physical — of their respective countries can no longer be evaded by educated men, whether in the East or in the West.

In truth, it cannot be too forcibly impressed upon our minds that good laws may be enacted, justice administered, the rights of property secured, railroads and electric telegraphs laid down, the stupendous forces of Nature controlled and regulated for the public good, the three great scourges of war, pestilence, and famine averted or mitigated — all this may be done — and more than this the truths of our religion may be powerfully preached, translations of the Bible lavishly distributed; but if, after all, we neglect to study the mind and character of those we are seeking to govern and influence for good, no mutual confidence will be enjoyed, no real sympathy felt or inspired. Imbued with the conciliatory spirit which such a study must impart, *all* Englishmen — whether resident in England or India, whether clergymen or laymen — may aid the caue of Christianity and good government, more than by controversial discussions or cold donations of guineas and rupees. Let us not forget that this great Eastern empire has been entrusted to our rule, not to be the *Corpus vile* of political and social experiments, nor yet for the purpose of extending our commerce, flattering our pride, or increasing our prestige, but that a vast population may be conciliated, benefited, and elevated, and the regenerating influences of Christianity spread through the length and breadth of the land. How, then, have we executed our mission? Much is now being done; but the results effected are mainly due to the growth of a more cordial feeling, and a better understanding between Christians, Hindus, Buddhists, and Musalmans. And these good results may be expected to increase if the true character of the three principal systems of religion opposed to Christianity, and now existing in India, British Burmah, and Ceylon, are fairly tested by an impartial examination of the written documents held sacred by each; if the points of contact between Christianity, Brahmanism, Buddhism, and Islam become better appreciated, and Christians while loyally devoting themselves — heart and soul, body and mind — to the extension of the one true faith, are led to search more candidly for the fragments of truth, lying buried under superstition and error.

Be it remembered, then, that Sanskrit literature, — bound up as it has ever been with all that is sacred in the religion and institutions of India — is the source of all trustworthy knowledge of the Hindus; and to this literature Englishmen must turn, if they wish to understand the character and mind and nearly two hundred millions (or about five-sixths) of India's population (see pp. xxi-xxx of Introduction).

Some departments of Sanskrit literature have been fully described of late years by various competent and trustworthy scholars. Good translations, too, of isolated works, and excellent metrical versions of the more choice poems have from time to time been published in Europe, or are scattered about in Magazines, Reviews, and ephemeral publications. But there has never hitherto, so far as I know, existed any one work of moderate dimensions like the present — accessible to general readers — composed by any one Sanskrit scholar with the direct aim of giving Englishmen who are not necessarily Sanskritists, a continuous sketch of the chief departments of Sanskrit literature, Vedic and Post-vedic, with accompanying translations of select passages, to serve as examples for comparison with the literary productions of other countries[1].

The plan pursued by me in my endeavour to execute a novel and difficult task in a manner likely to be useful to Oriental students, yet intelligible to general readers, and especially to those men of cultured minds who, not being Orientalists, are desirous of accurate information on subjects they can no longer ignore, will be sufficiently evident from a perusal of the lectures themselves, and their appended notes. To avoid misapprehension and exaggerated ideas of my scope and aim, as well as to understand the extent of my obligations to other scholars, let the reader turn to pp. 1-4 with notes, p. 15, note 2. I will merely add to what is there stated, that as Vedic literature has been already so ably elucidated by numerous scholars in Europe, and by Professor W.D. Whitney and others in America, I have treated this part of the subject as briefly as possible. Moreover, my survey of so vast and intricate a field of inquiry as Indian philosophy, is necessarily a mere sketch. In common with other European scholars, I am greatly indebted to Dr. Fitz-Edward Hall for his contributions to this and other departments of Sanskrit literature, and especially for his translation of Nehemiah Nilkantha's 'Rational Refutation of the Hindu Philosophical Systems.'

I should state that, although the present volume is intended to be complete in itself, I have been compelled to reserve some of the later portion of the literature for fuller treatment in a subsequent series of lectures.

It is possible that some English readers may have given so little attention to Indian subjects, that further preliminary

---

1. Great praise is, however, due to Mrs. Manning's valuable compilation called 'Ancient and Mediaeval India,' published by W.W. Allen and Co.

explanations may be needed by them before commencing the
perusal of the following pages. For their benefit I have written
an Introduction, which I hope will clear the ground sufficiently
for all.

Let me now discharge the grateful duty of tendering my
respectful thanks to the Governments of India for the patronage
and support they have again accorded to my labours. Let me
also acknowledge the debt I owe to two eminent Sanskritists
— Dr. John Muir of Edinburgh, and Professor E.B. Cowell
of Cambridge — for their kindness in reading the proof-sheets
of the present series of lectures. These scholars must not,
however, be held responsible for any novel theories
propounded by me. In many cases I have modified my
statements in accordance with their suggestions, yet in some
instances, in order to preserve the individuality of my own
researches, I have preferred to take an independent line of
my own. Learned Orientalists in Eurpoe and India who are
able adequately to appreciate the difficulty of the task I have
attempted will look on my errors with a lenient eye. As I shall
welcome their criticisms with gratitude, so I shall also hope
for their encouragement; for often as I have advanced in my
investigations, and have found an apparently interminable
horizon opening out before me, I have felt like a foolhardy
man seeking to cross an impassable ocean in a fragile coracle,
and so have applied to myself the well-known words of the
great Sanskrit poet:—

तितीर्षुर्दुस्तरं मोहादुडुपेनास्मि सागरम् ।।
Titirshur dustaram mohad udupenasmi sagaram

Oxford. May 1875.   M.W.

Introduction

In this Introduction[1] I shall endeavour, first, to explain how Sanskrit literature is the only key to a correct knowledge of the opinions and practices of the Hindu people; and, secondly, to show how our possession of India involves special responsibilities and opportunities with reference to the study of the three great systems of belief now confronting Christianity in the world — Brahmanism, Buddhism, and Islam.

To clear the ground let me review very briefly the past and present history of the great country whose teeming population has been gradually, during the past two hundred and fifty years, either drawn under our sway, or, almost against our will, forced upon our protection.

The name India is derived from the Greek and Roman adaptation of the word Hindu, which was used by the Persians for their Aryan brethren, because the latter settled in the districts surrounding the streams[2] of the Sindhu (pronounced

---

1. Some detached portions of the information contained in this Introduction were embodied in a lecture on 'The Study of Sanskrit in Relation to Missionary Work in India,' delivered by me, April 19, 1861, and published by Messris. Williams & Norgate. The lecture is still procurable.
2. Seven rivers (*sapta sindhavah*) are mentioned, counting the main river and the five rivers of the Panjab with the Sarasvati. In old Persian or Zand we have the expression Hapta Hendu. It is well known that a common phonetic interchange of initial *s* and *h* takes place in names of the same objects, as pronounced by kindred races.

by them *Hindhu* and now called Indus). The Greeks, who probably gained their first conceptions of India from the Persians, changed the hard aspirate into a soft, and named the Hindus *'Indoi* in Greek (Herodotus IV. 44, V.3). After the Hindu Aryans had spread themselves over the plains of the Ganges, the Persians called the whole of the region between the Panjab and Benares Hindustan or 'abode of the Hindus,' and this name is used in India at the present day, especially by the Musalman population[1]. The classical name for India, however, as commonly employed in Sanskrit literature and recognized by the whole Sanskritic race, more particularly in Bengal and the Dekhan, is *Bharata or Bharata-varsha* — that is to say — 'the country of king Bharata[2]', who must have ruled over a large extent of territory in ancient times (see pp. 414, 469 of this volume).

It will not, of course, be supposed that in our Eastern Empire we have to deal with ordinary races of men. We are not there brought in contact with savage tribes who melt away before the superior force and intelligence of Europeans. Rather are we placed in the midst of great and ancient peoples who, some of them tracing back their origin to the same stock as ourselves, attained a high degree of civilization when our forefathers were barbarians, and had a polished language, a cultivated literature, and abstruse systems of philosophy centuries before English existed even in name.

---

1. The name Hindustan properly belongs to the region between the Sutlej and Benares, sometimes extended to the Narmada and Mahanadi rivers, but not to Bengal or the Deccan.
2. Manu's name (II.22) for the whole central region between the Himalaya and Vindhya mountains is *Aryavarta,* 'abode of the Aryans,' and this is still a classical appellation for that part of India. Another name for India, occurring in Sanskrit poetry, is *Jambu-dvipa* (see p.470). This is restricted to India in Buddhist writings. Strictly, however, this is a poetical name for the whole earth (see p.470), of which India was thought to be the most important part. Bharata in Rig-veda I. xcvi. 3 may mean 'a supporter,' 'sustainer,' and *Bharata-varsha* may possibly convey the idea of 'a supporting land.'

The population of India, according to the census of 1872, amounts to at least 240 million[1]. An assemblage of beings so immense does not, of course, form one nation. India is almost a continent like Europe. From the earliest times its richness has attracted various and successive immigrants and invaders, Asiatic and European. Its inhabitants

---

1. Of these about 27 million belong to the native states. In the Bengal provinces alone, the number, according to the census of 1871-72, amounts to 66,856,859, far in excess of any previous estimate. Of these, only 19,857 are Europeans, and 20,279 Eurasians. A most exhaustive and interesting account of its details is given by Sir George Campbell in his Bengal Administration Report. This is the first real census of the country yet attempted. Sir William Jones in 1787 thought the population of Bengal, Behar, Orissa (with Benares also) amounted to 24,000,000; Colebrooke in 1802 computed it at 30,000,000; in 1844 it was estimated at 31,000,000; and of late years it was assumed to be about 40 or 41 million. Now it is found that the food-producing area of Bengal numbers 650 souls to the square mile, as compared with 422 in England, and 262 in the United Kingdom. The three Presidency towns number 644,405 inhabitants for Bombay (called by the natives *Mumbai*); 447,600 for Calcutta (Kalikata); and 397,522 Madras (*Chenna-pattanam*): but the suburbs have been calculated in the case of Bombay, making it come next to London as the second city in the Empire. If this had been done in Calcutta and Madras, the numbers for Calcutta (according to Sir G. Campbell's Report) would have been 892,429, placing it at the head of the three cities. Almost every one in India marries as a matter of course, and indeed as a religious duty (see p. 275 of this volume). No infants perish from cold and exposure. As soon as a child is weaned it lives on rice, goes naked for two or three years, and requires no care whatever. The consequent growth of population will soon afford matter for serious anxiety. The Hindus are wholly averse from emigration. Formerly there were three great depopulators — war, famine, and pestilence — which some regard as evils providentially permitted to exist in order to maintain the balance between the productive powers of the soil and the numbers it has to support. Happily, our rule in India has mitigated these scourges; but where are we to look for sufficient checks to excess of population?

differ as much as the various continental races, and speak languages equally distinct.

We have first the aboriginal primitive tribes, who, migrating from Central Asia and the steppes of Tartary and Tibet, entered India by successive incursions[1].

Then we have the great Hindu race, originally members of that primeval family who called themselves Arya or noble, and spoke a language the common source of Sanskrit, Prakrit, Zand, Persian, and Armenian in Asia; and of the Hellenic, Italic, Keltic, Teutonic and Slavonic languages in Europe. Starting at a later period than the primitive races, but like them from some part of the table-land of Central Asia — probably the region surrounding the sources of the Oxus, in the neighbourhood of Bokhara — they separated into distinct nationalities and peopled Europe, Persia, and India. The Hindu Aryans, after detaching themselves from the Persian branch of the family, settled in the Panjab and near the sacred river Sarasvati. Thence they overran the plains of the Ganges, and spread themselves over the region called Aryavarta (see p. xx, note 2), occupying the whole of Central India, coalescing with and, so to speak, Aryanizing the primitive inhabitants, and driving all who resisted them to the south or towards the hills.

But India, even after its occupation by the great Aryan race, appears to have yielded itself up easy prey to every invader. Herodotus (IV. 44) affirms that it was subjugated by Darius Hystaspes. This conquest, if it ever occurred, must have been very partial. The expedition of Alexander the Great to the banks of the Indus, about 327 B.C., is a familiar fact. To this invasion is due the first authentic information obtained by Europeans concerning the north-westerly portion of India and

---

1. These aboriginal tribes, according to the last census, amount to 14,238,198 of the whole population of India. For an account of them see p. 348, note 2, and p. 258, note 2, of this volume.

the region of the five rivers, down which the Grecian troops were conducted in ships by Nearchus. Megasthenes, the ambassador of Seleukos Nikator, during his long sojourn at Palibothra (see p. 254, note 1), collected further information, of which Strabo (see p. 311, note), Pliny, Arrian, and other availed themselves. The next immigrants who appear, after a long interval, on the scene are the Parsis. This small tribe of Persians (even now, according to the last census, not more than seventy thousand in number) were expelled from their native land by the conquering Muhammadans under the Khalif Omar in the seventh century. Adhering to the ancient religion of Persia — the worship, that is, of the Supreme Being under the symbol of fire — and bringing with them the records of their faith, the Zand-Avasta of their prophet Zoroaster (see p. 4, note 1), they settled down in the neighbourhood of Surat about 1100 years ago, and became great merchants and shipbuilders[1].

---

1. The Parsis appear to have settled first at Yazd in Persia, where a number of them still remain. The Zand-Avasta consists of 1. the *five Gathas,* or songs and prayers (in metres resembling Vedic), which alone are thought to be the work of Zoroaster himself, and form part of the *Yazna* (or *Yasna* = yajna), written in two dialects (the older of the two called by Haug the Gatha); 2. the *Vendidad,* a code of laws; 3. the *Yashts,* containing hymns to the sun and other deities. There is another portion, called the *Visparad,* also a collection of prayers. Peshotun Dustoor Behramjee Sunjana, in a note to his *Dinkard* (an ancient Pahlavi work just published at Bombay, containing a life of Zoroaster and a history of the Zorastrian religion), informs us that the Avasta has three parts: 1. Gatha, 2. Date, and 3. Mathre; 1. being in verse and treating of the invisible world, 2. in prose and giving rules of conduct, 3. comprising prayers and precepts and an account of the creation. The Hindu and Zoroastrian systems were evidently derived from the same source. Fire and the Sun are venerated in both; but Zoroaster (properly *Zarathustra Spitama*) taught that the Supreme Being created two inferior beings — Ormuzd (Ahura-mazda) the good spirit, and Ariman the evil. The former will destroy the latter. This daulistic principle is foreign to the Veda.

For two or three centuries we know little of their history. Like the Indo-Armenians[1], they never multiplied to any extent or coalesced with the Hindu population, but they well deserve notice for their busy active habits, in which they emulate Europeans.

Then came the Muhammadans (Arabs, Turks, Afghans, Moguls, and Persians), who entered India at different times[2].

---

1. The Armenians of India hold a position like that of the Parsis, but their numbers are less (about five thousand), and they are more scattered, and keep up more communication with their native country. There are often fresh arrivals; but some have been in India for centuries, and are dark in complexion. They are frequently merchants and bankers, and being Christian, generally adopt the European dress. They may be called the Jews of the Eastern Church: for, though scattered, they hang together and support each other. At Calcutta they have a large church and grammar-school. Their sacred books are written in ancient Armenian. Of the two modern dialects that spoken by S. E. of Ararat by the Persi-Armenians prevails among the Indo-Armenians.

2. Muhammad's successors, after occupying Damascus for about one hundred years, fixed their capital at Baghdad in 750, and thence their power extended into Afghanistan. The Arabs, however, never obtained more than a temporary footing in India. Under the Khalif Walid I, in 711, Muhammad Kasim was sent at the head of an army into Sinde, but the Muslims were expelled in 750; and for two centuries and a half India was left unmolested by invaders from the west. About the year 850, when the power of the Arabs began to decline in Asia, hardy tribes of Tartars, known by the name of Turks (not the Ottoman tribe which afterwards gained a footing in Europe, but hordes from the Altai mountains), were employed by the Khalifs to infuse vigour into their effeminate armies. These tribes became Muhammadans, and gradually took the power into their own hands. In the province of Afghanistan, Sabaktagin, once a mere Turkish slave, usurped the government. His son Mahmud founded an empire at Ghazni in Afghanistan, and made his first of thirteen incursions into India in the year 1000. During the thirteenth century the Mongol or Mogul hordes, under the celebrated Chengiz Khan, overthrew the Turkish or Tartar tribes; and in 1398 Timur, uniting Tartars and Mongols into

Though they now form about one-sixth (or, according to the
last census, about forty-one million) of the entire population,
a large number of them are supposed to be the descendants
of Hindus converted to Islam[1]. Politically they became supreme,

---

one army, made his well-known invasion of India. After desolating the
country he retired, but the sixth in descent from him, Baber (*Babar*),
conquered Afghanistan, and thence invading India about 1526, founded
the Mogul empire, which his grandson Akbar (son of Humayun)
established on a firm basis in 1556; a very remarkable man, Sher Shah
Suri, having previously usurped the empire of Hindustan, and raised
it to great prosperity. The power of the Moguls, which rapidly increased
under Akbar, Jahangir, and Shahjahan, until it culminated under
Aurangzib, began to decline under Shah 'Alam (Bahadur Shah), Jahandar
Shah, and Farrukh-siyar; and under Muhammad Shah, the fourth from
Aurangzib, took place the Persians invasion of Afghanistan and thence
of India, undertaken by Nadir Shah (A.D. 1738) to avenge on the
Afghans their inroads into Persia. Hence it appears that in all cases
the Muhammadan invaders of India came through Afghanistan, and
generally settled there before proceeding to conquer the Hindus. On
this account, and from the proximity of Afghanistan, it has followed
that the greater number of Muhammadan immigrants have been of
Afghan blood.

1. The total number of Muhammadans in the Bengal provinces alone
   is 20,664,775 — probably more than in any other country of the
   globe; so that if England had merely these provinces, she would stand
   at the head of all Muhammadan powers, ruling more Mussulmans
   than the present representative of the Khalifs himself (see p. xliii,
   note 1). The great bulk of Indian Muhammadans are Sunnis (see p.
   liii), very few Shi'as being found in Bengal, or indeed in any part of
   India (except Oude, and a few districts where there are descendants
   of Persian families). It is noteworthy that in Behar the mass of the
   people is Hindu, and singularly enough it is not in the great Mogul
   capitals of Bengal, such as Dacca, Gaur, and Murshidabad, that the
   Muslims are most numerous, but among the peasants and cultivating
   classes. Sir George Campbell has remarked that in Bengal the Musalman
   invasion found Hinduism resting on weak foundations. Its hold on
   the affections of the people was weak. The Aryan element was only
   able to hold its own by frequent importation of fresh blood from
   Upper India. Hence it happened that when the Muslim conquerors
   invaded the lower Delta with the sword and the Koran, they were

but they were never able to supplant the Hindus, as these had done their predecessors. Moreover, it was the policy of the Muhammadan conquerors to bend, in many points, to the prejudices of their Indian subjects. Hence the Muslims of India became partially Hinduized, and in language, habits, and character took from the Hindus more than they imparted[1].

Nor has the Hindu-Aryan element lost its ascendancy in India, notwithstanding the accession and admixture of European ingredients. The Portuguese, the Dutch, the Danes, the French have one after the other gained a footing on its shores, and their influence still lingers at isolated points[2].Last

---

not wholly unwelcome. They proclaimed equality among a people kept down by caste. Hence in Bengal great masses became Muhammadans, being induced to embrace Islam by the social elevation it gave them. In the North-west provinces and neighbourhood of the great Mogul capital Delhi, where the Hindus have always been more spirited and independent, there are only about four million Musalmans. In the Panjab, however, there are nearly nine million and a half.

One grand distinction between Islam and Hinduism is, that the former is ever spreading and seeking converts, whereas the latter, theoretically, can never do so. A Brahman is *born,* not *made.* Practically, however, any number of persons may form themselves into a new caste by community of occupation, and the Brahmans of the present day are ready to accept them as Hindus.

1. Hence it happens that the lower orders of Indian Muhammadans observe distinctions of caste almost as strictly as the Hindus. Many of them will eat and drink together, but not intermarry.
2. In later times there has been a constant immigration of Chinese into India, but only of the male sex. The Portuguese still hold three places in India, viz. Goa, Daman, and the island of Diu on the western coast. The Dutch once held Chinsura on the right bank of the Hooghly, and Negapatam on the coast of Tanjore; but about the year 1824 they made both over to us, receiving in return our possessions on the coast of Sumatra. Our cession of the coast of Sumatra was afterwards considered a blunder, to remedy which the formal transfer of Singapore to the British was effected in 1824 by Sir Stamford Raffles (a treaty being made with the neighbouring Sultan) as an

of all the English have spread themselves over the whole country, and at this moment our political supremacy is everywhere greater than that which once belonged to the Musalmans[1]. Yet the mass of the population is still essentially Hindu, and the moral influence of what may be called the Indo-Aryan race is still paramount.

---

intermediate port for our trade with China. The Danes once possessed Tranquebar and Serampore, both of which were purchased from them by us in 1844. In 1846 they ceded a small factory to us at Balasore, where the Portuguese also as well as the Dutch, held possessions in the early periods of European intercourse. The French still retain Pondicherry and Karical on the Coromandel coast, Chandernagore on the right bank of the Hooghly, Mahe on the Malabar coast, and Yanaon near the mouths of the Godavari.

1. Although our annexation of province after province cannot always be justified, yet it may be truly said that our dominion has been gradually forced upon us. Our first dealings with India were merely commercial. The trading corporation entitled 'Governors and Company of London Merchants trading to the East Indies' was formed in 1600. The first Court of Directors was held on the 23rd September 1600, and the first charter was dated by Queen Elizabeth on the 31st of December in that year. The first factory was built at Surat, near the mouth of the Tapty, north of Bombay, in 1613. In 1661 the island of Bombay was ceded to the British by Portugal, as the marriage portion of the Infanta Catharine, on her marriage with Charles II, but its final possession was withheld for four years. It was handed over by Charles to the East India Company in 1669. Another factory was built on the Hooghly above Calcutta in 1636; Madras came into the Company's possession in 1640, and they purchased Calcutta itself in 1698. The battle of Plassy, from which dates the real foundation of the British empire, was fought June 23, 1757.

There are still a large number of native states in India. According to the India Office Report they exceed 460. Some merely acknowledge our supremacy, like Nepal; but even this frontier country receives our Resident. Others are under a compact to govern well; others pay us tribute, or provide for contingents. Some have power of life and death, and some are obliged to refer capital cases to English

Nevertheless, however closely bound together this race may be by community of origin, of religion, of customs, and of speech, and however powerful the influence it may exert over the Non-Aryan population, differences distinguish the people of India as great as or even greater than those which once divided and still distinguish the whole continent of

courts of justice. Nearly all are allowed to adopt successors on failure of heirs, and their continued existence is thus secured. The Official Report classes them in twelve groups, thus: 1. The Indo-Chinese, in two subdivisions, comprising — A. the settled states, *Nepal* (whose chief minister and virtual ruler is Sir Jung Bahadur), *Sikkim* (whose king lives at two cities, Tumlung and Chumbi, and who has lately ceded some territory to us), *Bhutan* (a turbulent hill-district), and *Kuch Bahar;* B. the hill-tribes, of Chinese character and physiognomy. 2. The aboriginal *Ghond* and *Kole* tribes in *Chota Nagpur, Orissa,* the Central Provines, and the *Jaipur* (in Orissa) Agency. 3. The states among the *Himalayas,* from the western frontier of Nepal to Kashmir, ruled generally by Rajput chiefs. 4. The *Afghan* and *Beluchi* frontier tribes beyond the Indus. 5. The *Sikh* states in the *Sirhind* plain, occupying the classic ground between the Sutlej and the Yamuna, and once watered by the Sarasvati. 6. Three Muhammadan states, geographically apart, but having much in common, viz. *Rampur* (a district in Rohilkhand, representing the Rohilla state of the days of Warren Hastings), *Bhawalpur* (separated from the Panjab by the Sutlej), and *Khairpur* (or Khyrpur) in Sind. 7. *Malwa* and *Bundelkhand,* the former representing part of the Marathi power, and including the important state of Central India, viz. that of Gwalior, ruled over by Maharaj *Sindia;* the district governed by *Holkar;* the state of *Dhar,* ruled by the third Marathi family, called Puars; the Muhmmadan state of *Bhopal;* and Bundelkhand, including the district of *Rewah.* 8. The ancient sovereignties of *Rajputana,* including fifteen Rajput states (such as Udaipur, Jaipur, &c.), two Jat and one Muhammadan (Tonk). 9. The *Gujarati* native states, north of Bombay, the principal being that of Baroda, ruled over by the *Guikwar* or *Guicowar.* [*Gui* is for *gai,* 'a cow,' and *kwa*r or *cowar* (*kuwar*) is possibly a corruption of *kumar=kumara,* 'a prince;' but there is a Marathi word *Gayakya,* 'a cowherd.' He is of the herdsman caste, and descended from a Marathi general.] 10. The *Marathi* states south of Bombay, representing the remains of the Marathi power found by Shivaji. Of these *Satara* was annexed in 1848, but *Kolapur* remains; nineteen others are

Europe. The spirited Hindustatni, the martial Sikh, the ambitious Marathi, the proud Rajput, the hardy Gurkha[1], the

---

under our management owing to the minority of the chiefs. 11. The Muhammadan state of *Haidarabad* (or Hyderabad), in the Deccan, ruled over by the *Nizam*, at present a minor, the government being conducted by Sir Salar Jung and Shams-ul Umra. 12. The state of *Mysore,* whose old Raja remembered the siege of Seringapatam. He died in 1868, and was succeeded by a child for whom we are now governing the country. To this must be added the two neighbouring Malayalam states on the Malabar coast, called *Travancore* and *Cochin,* both of which are excellently governed by enlightened Rajas and good ministers. Here is a Muhammadan historian's account of the first settlement of the English in India: 'In the year 1020 (A.D. 1611) the Emperor of Delhy, Jahangir, the son of king Akbar, granted a spot to the English to build a factory in the city of Surat, in the province of Guzerat, which is the first settlement that people made on the shores of Hindustan. The English have a separate king, independent of the king of Portugal, to whom they owe no allegiance; but, on the contrary, these two nations put each other to death wheresoever they meet. At present, in consequence of the interference of the Emperor Jahangir, they are at peace with each other, though God only knows how long they will consent to have factories in the same town, and to live in terms of amity and friendship.' (Quoted in Sir George Campbell's *Modern India,* p. 23.) An excellent account of the rise of the British dominions in India is given by Professor W.D. Whitney in the Second Series of his Oriental and Linguistic Studies, procurable from Messrs. Trubner & Co.

1. The word *Gurkha* for *Gorkha* — a contraction of Sanskrit *Goraksha* — means 'cow-keeper.' The aborigines of Nepal are mostly of the Bhot or Tibetan family, and are therefore Buddhists; but tribes of Hindu immigrated into this mountainous region at different periods within memory, and obtained the sovereignty of the country. They were probably of the cowherd caste from the adjacent country of Oudh and from the district below the hills, known as *Gorakhpur.* 'The tutelary deity of Nepal is a form of Shiva, denominated *Gorakhnath,* whose priests are Yogis, and the same sect and worship had formerly equal predominance at Gorakhpur.' — Asiatic Researches, vol. xvii. p. 189.

calculating Bengali, the busy Telugu, the active Tamil, the patient Pariah differ *inter se* as much as or more than the vivacious Celt, the stubborn Saxon, the energetic Norman, the submissive Slav, the enterprising Englishman, and the haughty Spaniard.

Many causes have combined to produce these distinctions. Difference of climate has had its effect in modifying character. Contact with the aboriginal races and with Muhammadans and Europeans has operated differently in different parts of India. Even in districts where the Hindus are called by one name and speak one dialect they are broken up into separate classes, divided from each other by barriers of castes far more difficult to pass than the social distinctions of Europe. This separation constitutes, in point of fact, an essential doctrine of their religion. The growth of the Indian caste-system is perhaps the most remarkable feature in the history of this extraordinary people. Caste as a social institution, meaning thereby conventional rules which separate the grades of society, exists of course in all countries. In England, caste, in this sense, exerts no slight authority. But with us caste is not a religious institution. On the contrary, our religion, though it permits differences of rank, teaches us that such differences are to be laid aside in the worship of God, and that in His sight all men are equal. Very different is the caste of the Hindus. The Hindu theory, according to Manu (see p. 262), is that the Deity regards men as *unequal,* that he created distinct kinds of men, as he created varieties of birds or beasts: that Brahmans, Kshatriyas, Vaisyas, Sudras are born and must remain (at least in each separate existence) distinct from each; and that to force any Hindu to break the rules of caste is to force him to sin against God, and against nature. It is true, that the endless rules of caste in India principally hinge upon three points of mere social economy and order: 1. food and

its preparation[1], 2. Intermarriage[2], and 3. Professional pursuits[3];
but among a religious people, who regard these rules as sacred
ordinances of their religion, an offence against any one of
them becomes a great crime. It is a remarkable fact, that the
jails in India often contain hardened criminals, who have
fallen in our estimation to the lowest depths of infamy, but
who, priding themselves on the punctilious observance of
caste, have not lost one iota of their own self-respect, and
would resent with indignation any attempt to force them to
eat food prepared by the most virtuous person, if inferior to
themselves in the social scale.

A full account of the origin and development of caste —
of the strictness of its rules, and of the power it still exerts
as a religious rather than as a social institution — will be

---

1. The *preparation of food* is quite as vital a point as *eating together.*
   Food prepared by a person of inferior caste causes defilement. Some
   castes cook with their shoes on: but most Hindus would abhor food
   thus prepared, because leather causes defilement. Food cooked on
   board a boat or ship is supposed to destroy caste; thus, a boat
   proceeding down the Ganges sometimes stops to allow native
   passengers to cook their food on shore; perhaps, because wood is
   regarded as a conductor of defilement. It cannot, of course, be said
   that the rules of caste are *confined* to these three points. A Hindu's
   ideas about unclean animals are very capricious. He dreads the
   approach of a fowl to his house or person, as a source of
   contamination; but he does not mind ducks. Happily caste can no
   longer hold its own against necessity and advantage — against
   railroads and scientific inventions. (See the quotation at bottom
   of p. 241.)
2. See the note on the mixed castes, p. 240, and p. 255 with note.
3. It is the restriction of employments caused by caste which necessitates
   a large establishment of servants. The man who dresses hair feels
   himself degraded by cleaning clothes, and one who brushes a coat
   will on no account consent to sweep a room; while another who
   waits at table will on no consideration be induced to carry an
   umbrella.

found at pp. 240, &c. Moreover, for a description of the rise of Buddhism and its influence in the opposite direction the reader must refer to p. 59, &c.

It remains to point out that the very nature of the Hindu religious creed has been the source of great diversities among the people of India.

Every religion worthy of the name may be said to develop itself in three principal directions: 1. that of faith, 2. that of works and ritual, 3. that of doctrine or dogmatic knowledge; to one or other of which prominence is given according to peculiarities of mental bias or temperament. I have endeavoured to show at pp. 39 and 363 that the first two lines of development represent a religious exoteric or popular side, while the third exhibits its esoteric aspect, and is the only exponent of its more profound meaning.

Nothing can possibly be more simple than esoteric Hinduism. It is a creed which may be expressed by the two words — *spiritual Pantheism* (see p. 40). A pantheistic creed of the this kind is the simplest of all beliefs, because it teaches that nothing really exists but the one Universal Spirit; that the soul of each individual is identical with that Spirit, and that every man's highest aim should be to get rid for ever of doing, having, and being, and devote himself to profound contemplation, with a view to such spiritual knowledge as shall deliver him from the mere illusion of separate existence, and force upon him the conviction that he is himself part of the one Being constituting the Universe.

On the other hand, nothing can be more devoid of simplicity, nothing more multiform and capable of divergence into endless ramifications than the exoteric and popular side of the same creed. This apparent gulf between esoteric and exoteric Hinduism is bridged over by the simple substitution of the word *emanation* for *identification.*

Poplular Hinduism supposes that God may for his own purposes amuse himself by illusory appearances; in other words, that he may manifest himself variously, as light does in the rainbow, and that all visible and material objects, including superior gods (*isa, isvara, adhisa*), secondary gods (*deva*), demons (*daitya*), demi-gods, good and evil spirits, human beings, and animals, are *emanations* from him, and for a time exist separately from him, though ultimately to be reabsorded into their source. Both these aspects of Hinduism are fully explained at pp. 39 and 359-372 of the following Lectures. From the explanations there given, the multiform character and singular expansibility of the Hindu religious creed will be understood.

Starting from the Veda, it ends by appearing to embrace something from all religions, and to present phases suited to all minds[1]. It has its spiritual and its material aspect, its esoteric and exoteric, its subjective and objective, its pure and its impure. It is at once vaguely pantheistic, severely monotheistic, grossly polytheistic, and coldly atheistic. It has a side for the practical, another for the devotional, and another for the speculative. Those who rest in ceremonial observances find it all-satisfying; those who deny the efficacy of works, and make faith the one thing needful, need not wander from its pale; those who delight in meditating on the nature of God and man, the relation of matter to spirit, the mystery of separate existence, and the origin of evil, may here indulge their love of speculation. And this capacity for almost endless expansion and variety causes almost endless sectarian divisions even among those who worship

---

1. It is on this principle, I suppose, that Sir Mungoldas Nathooboy, K.S.I., of Bombay, is reported to have once argued with a zealous raw missionary that Hindus being Christians by nature needed not to be converted; adding, 'But I thank God that you English were converted to Christianity, or you would by this time have eaten up the world to the bone.'

the same favourite deity. And these differences are enhanced by the close intertwining of religion with social distinctions. The higher classes are supposed capable of a higher form of religion than the lower, the educated than the uneducated, men than women; just as the religions of Muhammadans and Christians are held (like their complexions) to be most suited to their peculiar constitutions, circumstances, and nationalities.

In unison with its variable characters, the religious belief of the Hindus has really no single succinct designation. We sometimes call it Hinduism and sometimes Brahmanism, but these are not names recognized by the natives.

If, then, such great diversities of race, spoken dialect, character, social organization, and religious belief exist among a teeming population, spread over an extent of territory so vast that almost every variety of soil, climate, and physical feature may be found there represented, the question fairly arises — How is it possible for us Englishmen, in the face of such differences, to gain any really satisfactory knowledge of the people committed to our rule? Only one key to this difficulty exists. Happily India, though it has at least twenty spoken languages (p. xxxvi), has one sacred and learned language and one literature, accepted and revered by all adherents of Hinduism alike, however diverse in race, dialect, rank, and creed. That language is Sanskrit and that literature is Sanskrit literature — the repository of *Veda,* or 'knowledge' in its widest sense; the vehicle of Hindu theology, philosophy, law, and mythology; the one guide to the intricacies and contradictions of Hinduism; the one bond of sympathy which, like an electric chain, connects Hindus of opposite characters in every district of India. Happily, too, the most important and interesting part of that literature are now accessible to all, both in the original and in good translations.

And here let me explain that the name Sanskrit as applied to the ancient language of the Hindus is an artificial designation for a *highly elaborated form* of the language originally brought by the Indian branch of the great Aryan race into India. This original tongue soon became modified by contact with the dialects of the aboriginal races who preceded the Aryans, and in this way converted into the peculiar language (*bhasha*) of the Aryan immigrants who settled in the neighbourhood of the seven rivers of the Panjab and its outlying districts (*Sapta Sindhavas* = in Zand *Hapta Hendu*).The most suitable name for the original language thus moulded into the speech of the Hindus is Hindu-i (= Sindhu-i), its principal later development being called Hindi[1], just as the Low German dialect of the Saxons when modified in England was called Anglo-Saxon. But very soon that happened in India which has come to pass in all civilized countries. The spoken language, when once its general form and character had been settled, separated into two lines, the one elaborated by the learned, the other popularized and variously provincialized by the unlearned. In India, however, from the greater exclusiveness of the educated few, the greater ignorance of the masses, and the desire of a proud priesthood to keep the key of knowledge in their own possession, this separation became more marked, more diversified, and progressively intensified. Hence, the very grammar which with other nations was regarded only as a means to an end, came to be treated by Indian Pandits as the end itself, and was subtilized into an intricate science,

---

1. It may be thought by some that this dialect was nearly identical with the language of the Vedic hymns, and the latter often gives genuine Prakrit forms (as *kuta* for *krita*); but even Vedic Sanskrit presents great elaboration scarcely compatible with the notion of its being a simple original dialect (for example, in the use of complicated grammatical forms like Intensives); and Panini, in distinguishing between the common language and the Vedic, uses the term *Bhasha* in contradistinction to *Chandas* (the Veda).

fenced around by a bristling barrier of technicalities. The language, too elaborated *pari passu* with the grammar, rejected the natural name of Hindu-i, or 'the speech of the Hindus,' and adopted an artificial designation, viz. *Sanskrita,* 'the perfectly constructed speech' (*sam= con, krita=factus,* ' formed'), to denote its complete severance from vulgar purposes, and its exclusive dedication to religion and literature; while the name *Prakrita* — which may mean 'the original' as well as 'the derived' speech — was assigned to the common dialect. This of itself is a remarkable circumstance; for although a similar kind of separation has happened in Europe, yet we do not find that Latin and Greek ceased to be called Latin and Greek when they became the language of the learned, any more than we have at present distinct names for the common dialect and literary language of modern nations.

The Sanskrit dramas afford a notable specimen of this linguistic elaboration on the one side, and disintegration on the other (see p. 526). The two forms of speech thus evolved may be compared to two children of the same parent — the one, called Sanskrit, refined by every appliance of art; the other, called Prakrit, allowed to run more or less wild.

The present spoken languages of India — Bengali, Uriya or Oriya (of *Odra-desa* Orissa, Marathi, Gujarati, and Hindi[1],

---

1. By Hindi I mean the speech of the Hindus as represented by the Prem Sagar, and the Ramayana of Tulasi Das. According to Dr. Fitz-Edward Hall, the Prem Sagar does not furnish a model of the most classical Hindi. There is certainly a modern literary Hindi which borrows largely from pure Sanskrit, and another which is so mixed with Arabic and Persian words as to receive another name, Hindustani Besides Hindi and Hindustani and the languages above named, there are Sindhi, Kashmiri, Nepalese, Assamese, Pushtu (of Afghanistan), Sinhalese (of Ceylon), Burmese, the five Dravidian and the half Dravidian Brahu-i. See Mr. Beames' valuable Comparative Grammar.

with its modifications — represent Prakrit[1] in its later stages
of decomposition, and variously modified by collision with
the primitive dialects of different localities.

It must not, however, be supposed that in taking this view
of the formation of Sanskrit, I mean to imply that it does not
also stand in a kind of parental relation to the spoken dialects.
Sanskrit, when too highly elaborated by the Pandits, became
in one sense dead, but in another sense it still breathes, and
lives in the speech of the people, infusing fresh life and vigour
into all their dialects[2]. For, independent of Sanskrit as the

---

1. The various kinds of Prakrit introduced into the Sanskrit dramas (the
   two principal forms of which — Maharashtri and Saurasen — are
   explained by *Vararuci* in his grammar, the *Prakrita-prakasha,* edited
   by Professor E.B. Cowell) represent the last stage of development
   in the direction of the modern vernaculars. The earlier form of the
   ancient spoken language, called *Pali* or *Magadhi,* has a grammar and
   extensive literature of its own, the study of which will be greatly
   facilitated by the Dictionary of Mr. R.C. Childers. Pali was introduced
   into Ceylon by Buddhist missionaries from Magadha when Buddhism
   began to spread, and is now the sacred language of Ceylon and
   Burmah, in which all their Buddhist literature is written. Singularly
   enough, it found a kindred dialect established in Ceylon, which had
   developed into the present Shinhalese. Pali is closely connected with,
   and was probably preceded by the language of the Rock Inscriptions
   of the second and third centuries B.C. The language of the Gathas,
   as found in the Lalita-vistara (see p. 60, note 1) of the Northern
   Buddhists of Nepal, is thought by some to be a still earlier form of
   the popular language; so that four separate stages of Prakrit, using
   that term generally for the spoken languages of the people which
   preceded the modern vernaculars, can be traced: 1. the Gathas; 2.
   the Inscriptions; 3. the Pali; 4. the Prakrit of the plays. (Professor
   E.B. Cowell's edition of Colebrooke's Essays, II. 21.)
2. The Sanskrit colleges founded at Benares, Calcutta, and other places,
   for the cultivation of the learned language and literature of the
   Hindus, are doing a good work; but, after all, the bearing of Sanskrit
   upon the vernaculars constitutes a point of primary importance. For
   we must not forget that the general diffusion of education throughout
   India must be chiefly effected through the medium of the vernacular
   dialects, and not merely through English. A knowledge of this fact

vernaculars probably were in their first origin, they all now draw largely from it, for the enrichment of their vocabulary[1].

If, then, the mere language of a people — the bare etymology of isolated words, and the history of the changes they have undergone in form and meaning — furnishes an excellent guide to its past and present condition, moral, intellectual, and physical, how much more must this be true of its literature! And here again we are met by the remarkable fact that India, notwithstanding all its diversities of race, caste, customs, creed, and climate, has to this day but one real literature, accepted by all alike — the common inheritance of all. In European countries, literature changes with language. Each modern dialect has its own literature, which is the best representative of the actual condition of the people to whom it belongs. To know the Italians, we need not study Latin, when the modern literature is at our command. But the literature of the Hindu vernacular dialects (except perhaps that of Tamil) is scarcely yet deserving of the name. In most cases it consists of mere reproductions of the Sanskrit[2]. To

---

has led to the establishment of Sir William Muir's new college at Allahabad (the 'Muir University College'), to which numerous vernacular schools will be affiliated. With reference to the study of the vernaculars and the spread of education by their means, let me recommend a perusal of Sir Charles Trevelyan's 'Original Papers on the Application of the Roman Alphabet to the Languages of India,' edited by me in 1859 (Longmans).

1. This applies even to the South-Indian languages — Tamil, Telugu, Kanarese, Malayalam, and Tulu; although these are not Aryan in structure, but belong rather to the Turanian or agglutinating family.

2. With regard to Hindustani (otherwise called Urdu), the proper language of the North-western districts and passing current, like French in Europe, over all India, it cannot be said to rank as a distinct language till the time of Timur, about A.D. 1400, when it was finally formed in his Urdu camp by blending Hindi with the Arabic and Persian of the Muhammadan invaders. Its prose literature, such as it is, certainly owes more to Arabic than to Sanskrit, and is quite modern. The productions of its greatest poet, Sauda, are not much more than a hundred years old.

understand the past and present state of Indian society — to unravel the complex texture of the Hindu mind; to explain inconsistencies otherwise inexplicable — we must trust to Sanskrit literature alone. Sanskrit is the only language of poetry, drama, law, philosophy — the only key to a vast and apparently confused religious system, and sure medium of approach to the hearts of the Hindus however unlearned, or however disunited. It is, in truth, even more to India than classical and patristic literature was to Europe at the time of the Reformation. It gives a deeper impress to the Hindu mind, so that every Hindu, however unlettered, is unconsciously affected by it, and every Englishman, however strange to the East, if only he be at home in Sanskrit literature, will rapidly become at home in every corner of our Indian territories.

These considerations will, I trust, justify my attempt to give some idea of the history and character of India's literature.

Let it be clearly understood, however, that the examples of Indian wisdom given in this volume generally present *the bright side of the picture only*. To make the sketch a faithful portrait of the reality, many dark lines and shadows must be introduced.

My reasons for giving prominence to all that is good and true in the Hindu system are stated in the note to p. 3 of Lecture I. Let me now add a few remarks to what is there asserted.

It appears to me high time that all thoughtful Christians should reconsider their position, and — to use the phraseology of our modern physicists — readjust themselves to their altered environments. The ground is now being rapidly cleared for a fair and impartial study of the writings of Eastern nations. The sacred books of the three great systems opposed to Christianity — Brahmanism, Buddhism, and Islam — are now at length becoming accessible to all; and Christians can

no longer neglect the duty of studying their contents[1]. All the
inhabitants of the world are being rapidly drawn together by

---

1. With regard to the books on which the three great false religions
   of the world rest, not only have we access to those of Brahmanism
   and Islam — viz. the Veda and the Koran — both in printed editions
   of the originals and in various translations (see pp. 6-9), but even
   the Buddhist sacred Canon — written in the ancient language called
   Pali (see p. xxxvii, note 1) — is now becoming accessible. Its name
   Tri-pitaka, ' three baskets or caskets,' denotes its distribution under
   three divisions, viz. A. *Sutra* (Pali *Sutta*), works containing the
   doctrinal and practical discourses of the great Buddha. B. *Vinaya*,
   ecclesiastical discipline, or works prescribing rules and penalties for
   the regulation of the lives of the monks (Bhikshukas, see p. 63). C.
   Abhidharma (Pali *Abhidhamma*), metaphysics and philosophy. These
   three classes of works were rehearsed at the first council by the
   Buddha's three pupils, *Ananda, Upali,* and *Kasyapa* respectively.
   A. has five subdivisions, viz. 1. *Digha-nikaya* (*dirgha-n°*), collections
   of long Sutras. 2. *Majjhima-nikaya-n°,* (madhyama-n°), collections of
   sutras of a midding lengh. 3. *Sanyutta-nikaya* (*Samyukta-n°*), groups
   of sutras. 4. *Anguttara-nikaya,* collections of other sutras. 5. *Khuddaka-
   nikaya* (*kshudraka-n°*), collections of short Sutras in fifteen different
   works, viz. 1. *Khuddaka-patha,* lesser readings, edited and translated
   in the 'Journal of the Royal Asiatic Society' by Mr. R.C. Childers; 2.
   Dhammapada, religious precepts (lit. verses or words, on Dharma);
   3. *Udana,* hymns of praise; 4. *Itivuttakam,* precepts in which Itivuttam,
   'it has been so said,' occurs; 5. *Sutta-nipata,* occasional Sutras; 6.
   Vimanavatthu, stories of celestial mansions; 7. *Petavatthu,* stories of
   Pretas; 8. *Thera-gatha;* 9. *Theri-gatha,* relating to elders among priests
   and priestesses; 10. *Jataka,* the Buddha's previous births; 11. *Maha-
   niddesa*, great commentary; 12. *Pati-sambhida,* exposition of the Patis;
   13. *Apadana,* heroic actions; 14. *Buddha-vansa,* history of Buddhas
   who preceded Gotama; 15. *Chariya-Pitaka* casket of rites and deeds.
   B. has five subdivisions: 1. *Parajika;* 2. *Pachittiya;* 3. *Chulavagga;* 4.
   Mahavagga; 5. Parivara.
   C. has seven subdivisions: 1. *Dhamma-san-gani;* 2. *Vibhan-ga;* 3.
   Kathavatthu; 4. *Puggala;* 5. *Dhatu;* 6. *Yamaka;* 7. *Pathana.*
   Of the fifteen works under the fifth subdivision of *Khuddaka-nikaya*
   of A, the *Dhamma-pada, Sutta-nipata,* and *Jataka* are the most
   important.

increased facilities of communication, and St. Paul's grand saying — that God has made all nations of men of one blood (Acts xvii. 26) — is being brought home to us more forcibly every day. Steam presses, as well as railroads and telegraphs, are doing a great work, and bringing about rapid changes. They are every day imposing upon us new duties and responsibilities in the opening out of hitherto unexplored regions. Surely, then, we are bound to follow the example of the great Apostle of he Gentiles, who, speaking to Gentiles, instead of denouncing them as 'heathen,' appealed to them as 'very God-fearing' and even quoted a passage from one of their own poets in support of a Christian truth (Acts xvii. 28);

The *Dhamma-pada,* or precepts of law — entirely in verse — has been edited by Dr. Fausböll, of Copenhagen, with parts of the commentary (*Artha-katha* or *Attha-katha*), and translated by Professor Weber (Indische Streifen, 1. 118) and by Professor Max Müller.

The *Sutta-nipata* has lately been translated by Sir M. Coomara Swamy (Trübner, 1874). It consists of maxims on doctrine and practice, in prose and verse — sometimes in the form of dialogues — possibly as old as the third Buddhist council, in Asoka's reign, 246 B.C. (see p. 64, note 1). They are compared to the discourses of Vasishtha, addressed to Rama, in the Vasishtha-ramayana (see p. 413).

The tenth work of the fifteen, viz. the *Jataka,* has been partially edited and translated by Fausböll (ten of the Jatakas very recently, Trübner, 1872; five others in 1861).

The above long list of works under A.B.C. constitutes the sacred Canon of the Southern Buddhist of Ceylon. The Tri-pitaka of the Northern Buddhists of Nepal has probably become corrupted and amplified in some of its details, though the names of the works — as far as has yet been ascertained — are in all likelihood the same. The *Sad-dharma-pundarika* and the *Lalita-vistara* (see p. 59, note) were once thought to belong to this Canon, but this is now held to be a mistake. In Burnouf's translation of the former (called by him *Lotus de la bonne loi*), a note was commenced on the difference between the Northern and South Tri-pitakas, but left unfinished in consequence of his untimely death.

and who, writing to Christians, directed them not to shut
their eyes to anything true, honest, just, pure, lovely, or of
good report, wherever it might be found, and exhorted them,
that if there be *any virtue,* and if there be *any praise,* they
were to think on these things (Phil. iv. 8). Surely it is time
we ceased to speak and act as if truth among Gentiles and
truth among Christians were two wholly different things.
Surely we ought to acknowledge and accept with gratitude
whatever is true and noble in the Hindu character, or in
Hindu writings, while we reflect with shame on our own
shortcomings under far greater advantages.

Nor ought we to forget the words of St. Peter, when —
looking down from our undoubted pre-eminence on the
adherents of false systems, such as Brahmans, Buddhists, Parsis,
Fetish-worshippers, and Muslims, wholly distinct from one
another and separated by vast chasms though they be — we
are accustomed to bracket them all together as if they were
equally far from the kingdom of God. To continue to label
them all, or even the first four, with the common label
Heathen[1], as if they were all to be placed in the same category

---

1. I lately read an able article, written by a Christian and a man of high
   culture, in which the term 'heathen' was applied to murderers and
   villains — I presume from the fact that the inhabitants of heaths and
   outlying districts are often lawless and benighted. Another author,
   speaking of certain ignorant vagabonds, says, 'These heathen,' &c.
   In point of fact, I believe that this is not an unusual application of
   the term, and such phrases as 'heathenish conduct,' 'heathenish
   idea,' are commonly current amongst us as opprobrious epithets. Are
   we, then, justified in still using this single term as a common label
   for *all* unbelievers in Christianity, however God-fearing and righteous
   (like Cornelius of old) they may be. We make an exception in favour
   of Muhammadans, forgetting that *corruptio optimi pessima.* True the
   translators of the Bible generally use 'heathen' as an equivalent for
   'Gentile nations;' but this rests on a false notion of some etymological
   affinity between the two words. The Greeks and Romans who called

as equally idolaters, seems, under the present altered circumstances of our increasing acquaintance with these systems, a proceeding wholly opposed to the spirit of that great Apostle, who, when addressing Gentiles, assured them that God had taught him not to call any man *common or unclean;* and declared that *God was no respecter of persons, but that in every nations he that feared Him and worked righteousness was accepted by Him* (Acts x. 35; see also Rom. ii. 10, 11, 14, 15, iii. 29).

If, then, it is becoming more and more a duty for all the nations of the world to study each other; to inquire into and compare each other's systems of belief; to avoid expressions of contempt in speaking of the sincere and earnest adherents of any creed; and to search diligently whether the principles and doctrines which guide their own faith and conduct rest on the one true foundation or not — surely we Englishmen, to whose rule India has been intrusted, have special opportunities and responsibilities in this respect. For in India the three great systems which now confront Christianity — viz. Brahmanism, Buddhism, and Islam — are all represented. Brahmanism is, of course, numerically the strongest; yet Muhammadans form, as we have seen (p. xxv), a sixth part of its population[1]. As to Buddhism, we have indicated that

---

the rest of the world 'Barbarians,' the Hindus who call all other persons 'Mlecchas,' and the Muslims who call all unbelievers in Muhammad 'Kafirs and Gabrs,' never have, so far as I know, applied these expressions to villains and criminals. It becomes a question whether, if we are to follow the example of the Founder of Christianity, we ought not to substitute some such term as 'Gentiles' or 'Unbelievers' or 'Non-Christian nations' for an epithet now become somewhat too opprobrious.

1. It may startle some to learn from p. xxv of this Introduction that England is the greatest Muhammadan power in the world, and that our Queen has probably more than double as many Muslim subjects as the ruler of the Turkish Empire. Roughly estimating the present

its relationship to Brahmanism was in some respects similar
to that of Christianity to Judaism; and although it is true that,
in contrast to Christianity, which, originating among Semitic
Jews afterwards spread among the Aryans of Europe, Buddhism
originated with the Aryans of India and afterwards spread
among Turanian races (see p. 5, note 1); still India was most
undoubtedly the original home of this most popular system
— the nominal creed of the majority of the human race.
Moreover, it may be gathered from a perusal of the dramas
(such as the Malati-madhava. p. 538), that Hinduism and
Buddhism coexisted and were tolerant of each other in India
till about the end of the eighth century of our era. A reference,
too, to pp. 138-142 will show that the Buddhistic philosophy
and Buddhistic ideas have left a deep impression on Hinduism,
and still linger everywhere scattered throughout our Eastern
Empire, especially among the Jainas[1] (see p. 138); and

---

population of the globe at thirteen hundred million, the Buddhists
along with the Confucianists (disciples of *Kung-fu-tsze*) and Tauists
(of *Laxu-tsze*) would comprise about 490 million; Christians, 360
million; Muslims or Muhammadans, 100 million; and Brahmanical
Hindus and Semi-Hindus, 185 million. Of other creeds, the Jews
comprise about 8 or 9 million; Jainas, Parsis, and Sikhs together
about 3 or 4 million. The Fetish-worshippers of Africa, America,
and Polynesia probably make up the remaining 153 million. The
census of 1872 showed that there were only 318,363 converts to
Protestant Christianity in all India. The religion of Christians,
Buddhists, and Muslims is missionary; that of Jews, Hindus and
Parsis, non-missionary. Without the missionary spirit there can be
no continued vitality and growth; and this spirit is part of the very
essence of Christianity, whose first missionary was Christ Himself.

1. According to the last census the number of Buddhists and Jainas
   in India amounts to nearly three million (2,629,200). Sir George
   Campbell's Report gives 86,496 as the number of Buddhists in the
   Bengal provinces. Although Jainism has much in common with
   Buddhism, it is nevertheless a very different system. The Jainas

Buddhism is to this day, as is well known, the faith of our fellow-subjects in Ceylon, Pegu, and British Burmah, being also found in outlying districts of India, such as Chittagong, Darjeeling, Assam, Nepal, Bhotan and Sikkim.

It is one of the aims, then, of the following pages to indicate the points of contact between Christianity and the three chief false religions of the world, as they are thus represented in India[1].

This common ground is to be looked for more in Brahmanism than in Buddhism, and even than in Islam. In proof of which I refer the reader to pp. 59-66 for a summary of Buddhism; to pp. 39, 361, and to p. 12, note 1, for a summary of Hinduism both popular and esoteric; to pp. 23, 250, for the Hindu account of the creation of the

---

always call themselves and are considered Hindus (see p. 142, note 1). According to Rajendralala, Mitra, the Jaina scriptures are comprised in fifty different works, collectively called the *Sutras*, and sometimes the *Siddhantas*, and classed in two different ways: 1st , under the two heads of *Kalpa-sutra* and *Agama*, five works coming under the former, and forty-five under the latter head: 2ndly, under eight different heads, viz. 1. eleven *An·gas*; 2. twelve *Upan·gas*: 3. four *Mula-sutra*; 4. five *Kalpa-sura*; 5. six *Cheddas*; 6. ten *Payannas*; 7. *Nandi-sutra*; 8. *Anuyoga-dvara-sutra*. Some of them have a four- fold commentary, under the names *Tika, Niryukti, Curni,* and *Bhashya,* constituting with the original the five-fold (*pancan·ga*) Sutra. They are partly in Sanskrit, partly in Magandhi Prakrit, and the total of the fifty works is said to amount to 600,000 Slokas (see Notices of Sanskrit MSS. No. VIII. p. 67).

1. Of course, the religion of ancient Persia, sometimes called Zoroastrianism — a most important and interesting creed (see p.4) — is also represented, but the Parsis are numerically insignificant (see note, p. xxiii).

world[1]; to pp. 34, 439, for that of the deluge; to pp. 6-8 for the Hindu and Muhammadan doctrine of revelation and inspiration; to p. 159, note 4, for the Hindu conception of original sin; to p. 369, note 3, for the Hindu theory of the gradual depravation of the human race; to p. 33, note 1, and to p. 276, for that of sacrifices and sacramental acts[2]; to pp. 273, 309, for that of the mystical efficacy of water in cleansing from sin[3]; to pp. 221, 271, for that of regeneration or second

---

1. Professor Banerjea ('Indian Antiquary,' Feb. 1875) thinks that the Hindu account of the creation of the world preserves traces of the revelation made in the Bible of the Spirit brooding on the surface of the waters; and that the theory of the Nagas, who were half serpents half men, dwelling in the lower regions (see p. 481), confirms the Biblical account of the Serpent, which was originally perhaps a species corresponding to the Naga, before the sentence was pronounced by which it became a creeping reptile. Compare the story of the eldest of the five sons of Ayus (of the lunar race), called Nahusha, cursed by Agastya to become a serpent, for excessive pride, in having, after gaining by penance the rank of Indra, compelled the Rishis to bear his litter on their backs, and then kicked some of them (Manu VII. 41; Vishnu-purana, p. 413; Maha-bh. V. 343).

2. The Hindus have two roots for 'to sacrifice,' *hu* (=an older *dhu*=) and *yaj*. The first is restricted to oblations of clarified butter in fire; the latter is applied to sacrificing, and honouring the gods with sacrifices generally. A third root, *su,* is used for offering libations with the juice of the Soma-plant, especially to the god Indra — the oldest form of sacrifice in India (note 1, p. 33). The idea of sacrifice is ingrained in the whole Hindu system. It is one of the earliest that appears in their religious works, and no literature — not even the Jewish — contains so many words relating to sacrifice as Sanskrit. It is remarkable that the food offered to the gods, when appropriated and eaten by the priests, and the rice distributed by them to the people, are called prasada (?=).

3. Bathing in sacred rivers — especially in the Ganges and at particular Tirthas, such as Haridvar, Prayaga — purifies the soul from all sin. Hence dying persons are brought to the river-side, leaves of the Tulasi plant being often put in their mouths. Hence also Ganges water (as other consecrated liquid) was used in the inauguration (*abhisheka*) of kings (see p. 578, and cf. Ramayana II. xv. 5) and in the administration of oath.

birth; to pp. 308, 309, for that of atonement and expiation; to pp. 358 for the Hindu theory of incarnation and the need of a Saviour; to p. 360 for that of the triple manifestation or Hindu Triad; to pp. 113, 272 (note 2), 275 for the Hindu and Muhammadan teaching as to the religious duties of prayer, ablutions, repetitions of sacred texts, almsgiving, penance, &c.; to p. 277, note 1, for the actual practice of these duties at the present day; to pp. 113-115 for the infliction of self-mortifications, fasting, &c.; and, lastly, to pp. 313, 492, 512-518 for examples of moral and religious sentiments.

Lest, however, it should be inferred that, while advocating perfect fairness and impartiality in comparing all four religious systems, I have aimed in the present work at lowering in the slightest degree the commanding position occupied by our own faith, or written anything to place Christianity in an unfavourable light in relation to the other systems of the world, I conclude this Introduction by adverting to some principal points which, in my opinion, constitute the distinctive features of our own religion, separating it decisively from all the other creeds as the only divine scheme capable of regenerating the entire human race.

It seems to me, then, that in comparing together these four systems — Christianity, Islam, Brahmanism, and Buddhism — the crucial test of the possession of that absolute divine truth which can belong to one only of the four, and which — if supernaturally communicated by the common Father of mankind for the good of all His creatures — must be intended to prevail everywhere, ought to lie in the answer to two questions: 1st, What is the ultimate object at which each aims? 2ndly, By what means and by what agency is this aim to be accomplished?

1. Let us begin with Buddhism, because as a religious system it stands lowest; not indeed deserving, or even claiming, to be called a religion at all in the true sense of the word

(see p. 62), though it is numerically the strongest of all the four creeds. With regard, then, to the first question:

The object aimed at by pure Buddhism is, as we have shown at p. 62, *Nirvana,* the being blown out like a flame — in other words — utter annihilation. It is true that the sramanas or Bhikshukas, 'ascetics and religious mendicants,' alone can be said to aim directly at Nirvana (see pp. 62). The upasakas or laymen think only of the effect of actions on the happiness or misery of future states of being. But, if personality and the remembrance of previous existences are not preserved, how can death be regarded in any other light than absolute extinction?

2. Brahmanism rises to a higher level, for here there is a theoretical craving after union with the Supreme Spirit, as the grand aim and object of the system (see p. 561). This union, however, really means identification with or absorption into the One only self-existing Being, as the river blends with the ocean; so that Brahmanism really ends in destroying man's personality, and practically, if not theoretically, lands its disciples in the same absolute extinction aimed at by Buddhists. In fact, the higher and more esoteric the teaching of both these systems, the more evidently do they exhibit themselves in their true colours as mere schemes for getting rid of the evils of life, by the extinction of all activity, individuality, self-consciousness, and personal existence.

3. Let us now turn to Islam. The end which Muhammad set before the disciples of the Koran was admission to a material paradise (*jannat*[1]), described as consisting of shaded gardens, abounding with delicious fruits, watered by flowing

---

1. Muslims believe there are seven (or eight) heavens representing degrees of felicity, and seven hells (*jahannam*), the seventh or deepest of which is for hypocrites, the sixth for idolaters, the third for Christians.

streams (*anhar*), filled with black-eyed Huris, and replete with exquisite corporeal enjoyments. It is certainly true that spiritual pleasures and the favour of God are also said to form part of its delights, and that the permanence of man's personality is implied. But a holy God is still immeasurably removed from His creatures, and intimate union with him, or even admission to His presence, is not the central idea of beatitude.

4. In contrast to Brahmanism, Buddhism, and Islam, the one object aimed at in Christianity is, emphatically, such as *access to* and *union with* a holy God as shall not only secure the permanence of man's own individual will, energy, and personality, but even intensify them.

Perhaps, however, it is in the answer to the second question that the great difference between the four systems is most apparent.

How, and by what means is the object aimed at by each system avowedly effected? In replying to this, let us reverse the order, and commence with our own religion.

1. Christianity asserts that it effects its aim through nothing short of an entire change of the whole man, and a complete renovation of his nature. The means by which this renovation is effected may be described as a kind of *mutual transfer or substitution,* leading to a reciprocal interchange and co-operation between God and man's nature acting upon each other. Man — the Bible affirms — was created in the image of god, but his nature became corrupt through a taint, derived from the fall of the first representative man and parent of the human race, which taint could only be removed by a vicarious death.

Hence, the second representative man — Christ — whose nature was divine and taintless, voluntarily underwent a sinner's death, that the taint of the cold corrupted nature transferred to him might die also. But this is not all. The great central truth of our religion lies not so much in the fact of Christ's

death as in the fact of His *continued life* (Rom. viii. 34). The
first fact is that He of His own free will died; but the second
and more important fact is that He rose again and lives
eternally, that He may bestow life for death and a participation
in His own divine nature in place of the taint which He has
removed.

This, then, is the reciprocal exchange which marks
Christianity and distinguishes it from all other religions —
an exchange between the personal man descended from a
corrupt parent, and the personal God made man and
becoming our second parent. We are separated from a rotten
root, and are grafted into a living one. We part with the
corrupt will, depraved moral sense, and perverted judgment
inherited from the first Adam, and draw re-creative force
— renovated wills, fresh springs of wisdom, righteousness,
and knowledge[1]— from the ever-living divine stem of the
second Adam, to which, by a simple act of faith, we are
united. In this manner is the grand object of Christianity
effected. Other religions have their doctrines and precepts
of morality, which, if carefully detached from much that is
bad and worthless, may even vie with those of Christianity.
But Christianity has, besides, all these, what other religions

---

1. It has been objected to in Christianity that it discourages increase
of knowledge; but the only knowledge it condemns is the empty
knowledge which 'puffeth up' (1 Cor. Viii, 1, 2). 'God is Light' or
knowledge itself. The more a Christian man becomes Godlike, the
more he aims at increase of light, whether in religion or science. It
is said of Christ that 'in Him are hid all the treasures of wisdom
and knowledge' (Col. ii. 3). Truth must be one, and all truth is
declared to come by Him, as well as grace (St. John i. 17). Other
religious systems, on the contrary, are interpenetrated with so much
that is false in every branch of knowledge, that a simple lesson in
geography tends to undermine every thoughtful person's faith in
such creeds.

have not — a personal God, ever living to supply the free grace or regenerating Spirit by which human nature is re-created and again made Godlike, and through which man, becoming once again 'pure in heart,' and still preserving his own will, self-consciousness, and personality, is fitted to have access to God the Father, and dwell in his presence for ever.

2. In Islam, on the contrary, Muhammad is regarded as the prophet of God and nothing more. He claimed no combination of divinity with humanity[1]. Even his human nature was not held to be immaculate, nor did he make any

---

1. He did not even pretend to be the founder of a new religion, but simply to have been commissioned to proclaim Islam and its cardinal doctrine — the unity of the Godhead — which dogma the Koran constantly affirms with great beauty of language (chap. ii. 256, xxiv. 36). God (Allah) in the Koran has one hundred names, indicative of his attributes, of which 'the merciful,' 'the compassionate' occur most frequently. But God, Muhammad maintained, begetteth not, nor is begotten. In chap. ii. of the Koran, we read: 'To god belongeth the east and the west; therefore whithersoever ye turn yourselves to pray, there is the face of God; for God is omnipresent and omniscient. They say, "God hath begotten children." God forbid.' Nevertheless, Muhammad did not deny that Christ was a prophet and apostle. He merely claimed to be a later and greater prophet himself. The Koran (lxi. 6) has the following: 'Jesus, the son of Mary, said, "O children of Israel, verily I am the apostle of God, sent unto you, confirming the law which was declared before me, and bringing good tidings of an apostle who shall come after me, whose name shall be Ahmad" (=Muhammad). But although thus arrogantly claiming to be the successor of Christ, any sharing (*shirk*) of god's divinity was utterly abhorrent from his whole teaching. He did not even rest his own claims on miracles (*ayat, karamat*), which he constantly excused himself from working. It is said that some doubters once asked him to give them a sign by turning the hill Safa into gold, but he declined to do so on the ground that God had revealed to him that if after witnessing the miracle, they remained incredulous,

pretence to mediatorial or vicarious functions. He died like any other man[1], and he certainly did not rise from the grave that his followers might find in him perpetual springs of

---

they would all be destroyed. The only sign of his mission to which he pointed was the Koran itself, declaring himself to be as untaught as a child just born (*ummiy*), or in other words a wholly unlettered person, to whom a composition in marvellously beautiful language was revealed. It is, however, quite true that Muhammad's biographers afterwards attributed various miracles to their prophet. For instance, it is handed down by tradition that taking a bar of iron he struck a huge rock with such force that it fell shivered to pieces, and the blow created a light which flashed from Medina to Madain in Persia. On the night called. *lailat ul mi'raj* he ascended to heaven from Jerusalem on a fabulous mule named Burak. He split the moon (by a miracle called *shakk ul kamar*). He put his fingers over empty vessels, and fountains of water flowed into them. He fed 130 men on the liver of a sheep. He fed a million people on a few loaves and a lamb, and many fragments were left. He once, by prayer to God, brought back the sun in the heavens when it had nearly set. On his entrance into Mecca (Makkah) he was saluted by mountains and trees, which said, 'Peace be to thee, O prophet of God!'

Here, again, in contrast to the above, it is to be noted that about ninety names are applied in the Bible to Christ Himself as the God-Man, and that Christians appeal to the personal Christ, as the one miracle of miracles, and to His personal resurrection as the sign of signs; while Christ Himself appealed to no book except the Old Testament; nor did he write any book or direct any book to be written; and attributed more importance to His own *personal* example, words, and works (erga) than to the wonders He performed, rebuking a constant craving after signs (shmeia.) We may also note that the artless unaffected simplicity and total absence of what may be called *ad captandum* glitter of style in the language of the New Testament, contrast remarkably with the studied magniloquence of parts of Muhammad's pretended revelation. See on the subject of miracles a valuable little work by the Rev. G. Renaud, called, 'How did Christ rank the proofs of His mission?' (Hatchards, 1872.)

1. He is supposed, however, not to have died a natural death, but to have been poisoned by a Jewess.

divine life and vivifying power, as branches draw sap and energy from a living stem. Nor do Muslims believe him to be the source of any re-creative force, capable of changing their whole being. Whatever the theory as to God's mercy propounded in the Koran, heaven is practically only accessible to Muslims through the strict discharge of religious duties which God as an absolute sovereign and hard task-master imposes[1]. If these religious exercises are really more than a lifeless form, the life-giving principle which animates them

---

1. Muhammad sets forth faith in Islam and in his own mission, repentance, the performance of prayer, fasting, alms, pilgrimages, and the constant repetition of certain words (especially parts of the Koran), as infallible means of obtaining paradise. In one place, suffering, perseverance, walking in the fear of God, and attachment to Him are insisted on. See Sale's Koran, xxix. 1-7, iv. 21, xviii. 31, xx. 71, xxi. 94, xxii. 14. xxiii. 1. Yet it must be admitted that the Koran elsewhere maintains that good works have no real meritorious efficacy in procuring paradise, and that the righteous obtain entrance there through God's mercy alone. Indeed, every action in Islam is done 'in the name of God, the merciful, the compassionate' (*b'ismillah ar-rahman ar-arhim*). But it must be noted that the Koran is by no means systematic or consistent. It was delivered in detached portions according to the exigences of the moment, and being often confused and contradictory, had to be explained and developed by traditional teaching. These traditions are called *Sunnah,* and a Sunni is one who obeys the laws of Muhammad founded not only on the Koran but on the traditions as interpreted by four great doctors or leaders of Islam, viz. Shafi-'i, Hanifa, Malik, and Hanbal, each of whom is the leader of a sect. It should be noted that the *Shi'as* — a name derived from *shi'at,* a party of persons forming a sect — are opposed to the Sunnis, like Protestants to Roman Catholics. They reject the traditions of the Sunnis, having separated from them about 363 years after Muhammad's Hijra (A. D. 985) under one of the 'Abbassi Khalifs (descendants of 'Abbas, Muhammad's uncle, who ruled as Khalifs over Baghdad and Persia from A. D. 749 to 1258). They do not call themselves Shi'as, but *'Adliyah,* 'the rightful society,' and deny the Khalifate of the first three successors of Muhammad, Abubakr, Omar,

is not supposed to come from Muhammad. Nevertheless, candour compels us to admit that in one notable point every true Muslim sets the Christian a good example. The word Islam means 'complete submission to the will of God,' and a Muslim is one who submits himself to that will without a murmur. The same candour, however, also suggests the inquiry whether the submission of the adherent of Islam may not be that of an abject slave, dreading the displeasure of a stern

---

and Othman (the first two being Muhammad's fathers-in-law and the third his son-in-law), who ruled at Medina. The Shi'as regard these three as usurpers of the successor ship (Khalifate), which they declare belonged only to another son-in-law, the fourth Khalif, 'Ali (husband of the prophet's daughter Fatima, and father of Hasan and Husain), whom they regard as the first of their true Imams, and who ruled with his sons at Kufa. The Turks, Egyptians, and Indian Muhammadans are mostly Sunnis, while the Persians are Shi'as. This doctrine of the Shi'as, which may be called the protesting form of Islam, is no doubt more spiritual than the original system of Muhammad. As it developed itself in Persia, it was influenced in some measure by the ancient religion of Zoroaster, which preceded it in that country. There the Shi'a tenets ultimately gave birth to a kind of spiritual philosophy called Sufi-ism — so similar to the Indian Vedanta (see p. 38 of this volume) that it is said to be based upon two ideas, viz. 1. Nothing really exists but God; all besides is illusion. 2. Union with God is the highest object of human effort (see p. 121 of this volume). The Shi'as keep with a great solemnity the anniversary of the murder of Husain, son of 'Ali, on a particular day in the Muharram (or first month of their lunar year). Hasan is supposed to have been poisoned by his wife, but Husain was killed at Karbala, by Yazid, son of the first Umayyad Khalif (commonly called Mu'aviya), who, instigated by Muhammad's favourite wife 'A-isha (daughter of Abubakr), opposed the succession of 'Ali's descendants, assumed the government, and transferred the Khalifate to Damascus. Hence the Shi'as perform pilgrimages to Karbala, rather than to Mecca. The *Wahabis* are a recent fanatical sect, founded by a man named Wahab. They may be described as puritanical reformers, seeking to bring Islam to its original purity.

master, rather than of a loving child depending on its Father for life and breath and all things.

3. As to Brahmanism, we must, in fairness, allow that, according to its more fully developed system, the aim of union with God is held to be effected by faith in an apparently personal god, as well as by works and by knowledge. And here some of the lines of Brahmanical thought seem to intersect those of Christianity. But the apparent personality of the various Hindu gods melts away, on closer scrutiny, into a vague spiritual essence. It is true that God becomes man and interposes for the good of men, causing a seeming combination of the human and divine — and an apparent interchange of action and even loving sympathy between the Creator and His creatures. But can there be any real interaction or co-operation between divine and human personalities when all personal manifestations of the Supreme Being — gods as well as men — ultimately merge in the Oneness of the Infinite, and nothing remains permanently distinct from Him? It must be admitted that most remarkable language is used of Krishna (Vishnu), a supposed form of the Supreme, as the source of all life and energy but if identified with the One God he can only, according to the Hindu theory, be the source of life in the sense of giving out life to reabsorb it into himself. If, on the other hand, he is held to be only an incarnation or manifestation of the Supreme Being in human form, then by a cardinal dogma of Brahmanism, so far from being a channel of life, his own life must be derived from a higher source into which it must finally be merged, while his claim to divinity can only be due to his possessing less of individuality as distinct from God than inferior creatures.

4. Finally, in Buddhism — as we have shown at p. 62 — the extinction of personality and cessation of existence, which is the ultimate aim of this system, is effected by suppression of the passions, self-mortification, and abstinence from action.

Buddha is no god, but only the ideal of what every man may become. He cannot, therefore, of course, be a source of even temporary life, when he is himself extinct. It is only in its high morality that Buddhism has common ground with Christianity. And can the only motive to the exercise of morality supplied by Buddhism — viz. on the one hand, the desire for non-existence; and, on the other, the hopes and fears connected with innumerable future existences — which existences are unconnected by conscious identity of being — be anything better than mere superstitious delusion?

It is refreshing to turn from such unsatisfying systems, however interspersed with wise and even sublime sentiments, to the living, energizing Christianity of European nations, however lamentably fallen from its true standard, or however disgraced by the inconsistencies and shortcomings of nominal adherents — possessors of its name and form without its power.

In conclusion, let me note one other point which of itself stamps our religion as the only system adapted to the requirements of the whole human race — the only message of salvation intended by God to be gradually pressed upon the acceptance of all His intelligent creatures, whether male or female, in all four quarters of the globe — I mean the position it assigns to women in relation to the stronger sex. It is not too much to affirm that the evils arising from the degradation of women, or at least the assumption of their supposed inferiority in the great religious systems of the East, constitute the principal bar to the progress and elevation of Asiatic nations. I refer the reader for evidence of this, as well as for fuller information on similar points, to pp. 283, 486 of the present volume.

It is, perhaps almost impossible as well as unreasonable, to expect the natives of India generally to look at such a question from a European stand-point. Nevertheless, those enlightened Hindus and philanthropic Englishwomen who are now interesting themselves in the spread of female education throughout the East, may adduce good authority from India's own sacred books for striving to elevate the wives of India to a higher position than that they occupy in the present day. They have only to quote such passages as those referred to at p. 488, note 1, 489, note 1, and p. 490 of this volume. To these may be added the remarkable definition of a wife given in Mahabharata. I. 3028 &c., of which I here offer a nearly literal version:

> A wife is half the man, his truest friend —
> A loving wife is a perpetual spring
> Of virtue, pleasure, wealth; a faithful wife
> Is his best aid in seeking heavenly bliss;
> A sweetly-speaking wife is a companion
> In solitude; a father in advice;
> A mother in all seasons of distress;
> A rest in passing through life's wilderness.

No wonder if, when sentiments like these are found in the sacred literature of India[1], a hope is dawning that inveterate prejudices may eventually give way, and that both Hindus and Muslims may one day be brought to confess that one of the most valuable results of Christianity is the co-ordination of the sexes, and one of its most precious gifts the restoration of woman to man, not only as the help most meet for him — not only as his best counsellor and companion — but as

---

1. Still more ancient and weighty authorities than the Mahabharata are the Taittiriya-brahmana III. 3, 3, 1 (see p. 30 of this volume), and Manu IX. 45, 130 (pp. 302 of this volume), which also assert that 'a wife is half of a man's self,' that 'a husband is one person with his wife,' and that 'a daughter is equal to a son.' The Ardha-nari form of Shiva (see p. 361, note 2) seems to point to the same truth.

his partner in religious privileges, and his equal, if not his superior, in religious capacities.

Modern Religious Sects of the Hindus.

Some account of these will be found in p. 138, note 1, and p. 364, note 1 of the present volume. They are fully described by Professor H. H. Wilson in vol. i. of his works edited by Dr. Rost. The three great sects are, A. The *Vaishnavas,* who worship Vishnu as the chief god of the Tri-murti (p. 360). B. The *Shaivas,* who exalt shiva. C. The Saktas, adorers of the female deity Devi (generally regarded as Shiva's wife). Each sect is distinguished by different practices, and sectarian marks on the forehead (called *Tilaka*). All three are subdivided into numerous sub-sects, each of which again has two classes of persons under it — the clerical or monastic, and the lay.

A. The *Vaishnavas* have six principal subdivisions, viz. 1. *Ramanujas* or *Sri-sampradayins,* founded by the reformer *Ramanuja,* who flourished in the South of India towards the latter part of the twelfth century; they have two perpendicular white lines drawn from the root of the hair to each eyebrow, and a connecting streak across the root of the nose. They draw their doctrines from Vedanta work, the Vishnu and other Puranas, and are remarkable for the scrupulous preparation and privacy of their meals. A sect called *Ramavats* differ little from them. 2. *Ramanandas,* founded by *Ramananda,* disciple of Ramanuj, and numerous in Gangetic India; they worship Ramachandra and Sita. 3. Followers of *Kabir,* the most celebrated of the twelve disciples of Ramananda, whose life is related in their favourite book the *Bhakta-mala.* He lived about the end of the fourteenth century, and is said to have been a Muslim by birth. The *Kabir-pathins* (or ° *panthis*) are found in Upper and Central India; they believe in one God, and do not observe all the Hindu ceremonies, yet pay respect to Vishnu (Rama) as a form of the Supreme Being. 4. *Vallabhacharyas* or *Rudra-sampradayins,* founded by *Vallabhacharya,* who was born in 1479, and had great success in controversies with the Shaivas. He left behind 84 disciples. They draw their doctrines from the Bhagavatapurana and works of Vallabha. 5. *Madhvas* or *Brahma-sampradayins,* founded by *Madhvacharya* (p. 138, note). They are found especially in the South of India, and although Vaishnavas, exhibit a leaning towards Shiva. 6. *Vaishnavas of Bengal,* founded by *Chaitanya,* regarded as an incarnation of Krishna. They are distinguished by *bhakti* or devotion to Krishna whose name they constantly repeat.

B. The *Shaivas* are generally distinguished by a horizontal Tilaka mark on the forehead, and by rosaries of Rudraksha berries. The temples dedicated to Shiva in his symbol of the Lin·ga (see p. 361, note 2) are numerous, but the doctrines of the great shaiva teachers, such as Shankara (p. 363, note 1), are too austere and philosophical for the mass of the people (p. 362). Earlier subdivisions of Shaivas are the *Raudras,* who have the Tri-shula (p. 362, note 2) marked on their foreheads; the *Ugras,* who have the Damaru on their arms; the *Bhaktas,* who have the Lin·ga on their foreheads; the *Jan·gamas,* who have that symbol on their heads; and the *Pashupatas* (p. 138, note), who have it marked on other parts of their bodies. Some more modern subdivisions are: 1. *Dandins* or mendicant staff-bearers; 2. *Das-nami-dandins,* divided into ten classes, each bearing a name of one of the ten pupils of the four disciples of Shankara; 3. *Yogins* (or Jogis), who cultivate absorption into Shiva by suppressions of breath, fixing the eyes, and eighty-four postures 4. *Jan·gamas,* called Lin·gavats (commonly Lin·ga-its), as wearing the Lin·ga on their person; 5. *Paramahansas,* who are solely occupied with meditating on Brahma; 6. *Aghorins or Aghora-pathins,* who propitiate Shiva by terrific and revolting austerities; 7. *Urdhva-bahus,* who extend one or both arms over the head and hold them in that position for years; 8. *Akasa-mukhins,* who keep their necks bent back looking up at the sky. The Shaivas sometimes carry a staff with a skull at the top, called *Khatvan·ga,*

C. The *Saktas* have two principal subdivisions, given pp. 563, 564. They aim at acquiring mystical powers by worshipping the Sakti.

Of the other sects named in p. 363, note 1, the *Ganapatyas* and *Sauryas* can scarcely now be regarded as important. The *Bhagavatas* are said to be a division of the Vaishnavas, and advocate faith in Bhagavat or the Supreme Being as the means of beatitude (according to Sandilya, p. 149, note 2). They are sometimes called *Pancha-ratras,* as their doctrine are taught in the *Narada-pancharatra.*

A form of Vishnu (Krishna), called *Viththal* or Vithoba, is the popular god at Pandharpur in Maharashtra, and the favourite of the celebrated Marathi poet Tukarama. The followers of Dadu *(Dadu-pathins),* a famous ascetic who lived at Jaipur about A.D. 1600, are also devoted to Vishnu.

With regard to the *Sikhs* (Sanskrit *Sishyah*), disciples of *Nanak Shah,* born near Lahore, A.D. 1469 (p. 363, note 1), this great reformer seems to have owed much to Kabir, who preceded him. Their *grantha* or sacred books are written in old Panjabi, and employ a modification of the Nagari character, called *Gurumukhi.* Their holy city is Amritsur.

Mendicant devotees who voluntarily undergo penances and austerities, and are variously called *Sannyasis* (often of the Saiva sect), *Vairagis* (often of the Vaishnava sect), *Yogis* (or Jogis, see p. 112), *Nagas* (for *Nagnas,* naked devotees), and *Fakirs* (which last name ought properly to be restricted to Muhammadans), form a large class in India.

There is an interesting sect of Syrian Christians in Travancore and Cochin, who have a bishop under the patriarch of Antioch, and trace back their foundation to St. Thomas, about A.D. 50, and to a colony which, 300 years afterwards immigrated from Syria.

Lecture I

The Hymns of the Veda

In the following Lectures I propose to offer examples of the most remarkable religious, philosophical, and ethical teachings of ancient Hindu authors, arranging the instances given in regular sequence according to the successive epochs of Sanskrit literature. In attempting this task I am conscious of my inability to do justice in a short compass to the richness of the materials at my command. An adequate idea of the luxuriance of Sanskrit literature can with difficulty be conveyed to occidental scholars. Perhaps, too, the severe European critic will be slow to acquiesce in any tribute of praise bestowed on compositions too often marked by tedious repetitions, redundant epithets, and far-fetched conceits; just as the genuine Oriental, nurtured under glowing tropical skies, cannot easily be brought to appreciate the coldness and severed simplicity of an educated Englishman's style of writing. We might almost say that with Hindu authors excellence is apt to be measured by magnitude, quality by quantity, were it not for the striking thoughts and noble sentiments which often reward the student who will take the trouble to release them from their surplusage of words; were it not also, that with all this tendency to diffuseness, it is certainly a fact that nowhere do we find the

1

art of condensation so successfully cultivated as in some departments of Sanskrit literature. Probably the very prolixity natural to Indian writers led to the opposite extreme of brevity, not merely by a law of reaction, but by the necessity for providing the memory with aids and restoratives when oppressed and debilitated by too great a burden. However that may be, every student of Sanskrit will certainly note in its literary productions a singular inequality both as to quantity and quality; so that in studying Hindu literature continuously we are liable to be called upon to pass from the most exuberant verbosity to the most obscure brevity; from sound wisdom to little better than puerile unwisdom; from subtle reasoning to transparent sophistry; from high morality — often expressed in impressive language worthy of Christianity itself — to precepts implying a social condition scarcely compatible with the lowest grade of culture and civilization.

Such being the case, it will be easily understood that, although my intention in these Lectures is to restrict myself to selections from the best writings only, it does not therefore follow that every example given will be put forth as a model of style or wisdom. My simple object is to illustrate continuously the development of Hindu thought; and it will conduce to a better appreciation of the specimens I offer if I introduce them by brief descriptions of the portions of literature to which they belong.

To give order and continuity to the subject it will be necessary to begin with that foundation of the whole fabric of Hindu religion and literature — the Veda.

Happily this word 'Veda' has now a familiar sound among Englishmen who take an interest in the history and literature of their Indian fellow-subjects, so that I need say but little on a subject which is really almost trite, or at least has been already elucidated by many clear and able writers. Indeed, most educated persons are beginning to be conscious of the duty of studying fairly and without prejudice the other religions of the world. For may it not be maintained that the traces of the original truth imparted to mankind should be diligently sought for in every religious system, however corrupt, so that when any fragment of the living rock is discovered[1], it may

1. Surely we should study to be absolutely fair in our examination of other religions, and avoid all appearance of a shadow of misrepresentation in our description of them, endeavouring to take a just and comprehensive view, which shall embrace the purest form of each false system, and not be confined to those corruptions, incrustations, and accretions which in all religions tend to obscure, and even to conceal altogether, what there is of good and true in them. Missionaries would do well to read 'An Essay on Conciliation in Matters of Religion, by a Bengal Civilian,' published in Calcutta in 1849. Let them also ponder the words of Sir William Jones, in his 'Discourse on the Philosophy of the Asiatics' (vol. iii. p. 242, &c., of his Works). This great Orientalist there maintains that our divine religion, the truth of which is abundantly proved by historical evidence, has no need of such aids as many think to give it by asserting that wise men of the heathen world were ignorant of the two Christian maxims which teach us to do to others as we would they should do unto us, and to return good for evil. The first exists in the sayings of Confucius, and the spirit of both may be traced in several Hindu precepts. One or two examples will be found in the Hitopadesa, and Sir W. Jones' is the following: *Su-jano na yati vairam para-hita-buddhir vinasha-kale' pi Chhede 'pi chandana-taruh surabhayati mukham kutharasya,* 'A good man who thinks only of benefiting his enemy has no feelings of hostility towards him even at the moment of being destroyed by him; (just as) the sandal-tree at the moment of being cut down sheds perfume on the edge of the axe.' Sir W. Jones affirms that this couplet was written three centuries BC. It is given by Boehtlingk in his 'Indische Spruche.' Professor Aufrecht, in his late article on the Sarn·gadhara-paddhati, mentions a similar verse in that Anthology attributed to an author Ravi-gupta. The Persian poet Sadi of Shiraz has a maxim taken from the Arabs, 'Confer benefits on him who has injured thee.' Again, 'The men of God's true faith grieve not the hearts e'en of their foes' (chap.ii. story 4). Hafiz is also quoted by Sir W. Jones thus:

'Learn from yon Orient shell to love thy foe,
And store with pearls the hand that brings thee woe.
Free, like you rock, from base vindictive pride,

(so to speak) at once be converted into a fulcrum for the upheaving of the whole mass of surrounding error? At all events, it may reasonably be conceded that if nothing true or sound can be shown to underlie the rotten tissue of decaying religious systems, the truth of Christianity may at least in this manner be more clearly exhibited and its value by contrast made more conspicuous.

If, then, a comparison of the chief religions[1] of the world, and an attempt to sweep away the incrustations which everywhere obscure the points of contact between them, is becoming every day more incumbent upon us, surely Brahmanism, next to Judaism and Christianity, has the first claim on our attention, both from its connection with the religion of ancient Persia (said to have acted on Judaism

---

> Imblaze with gems the wrist that rends thy side.
> Mark where yon tree rewards the stony shower
> With fruit nectareous or the balmy flowers.
> All nature calls aloud, "Shall man do less
> Than heal the smiter and the railer bless?'"

It Sarngadhara's Anthology a sentiment is given from the Mahabharata, which is almost identical with St. Matt. vii. 3.

1. These are eight in number, as shown by Professor Max Muller in his 'Science of Religion,' viz. 1. Judaism, 2. Christianity, 3. Brahmanism, 4. Buddhism, 5. Zoroastrianism, 6. Islam; and the systems of the Chinese philosophers, viz. 7. Confucius (a Latinized form of Kung-fu-tsze, 'the sage of the family of Kung'), 8. Lau-tsze ('aged master or sage'); and these eight rest on eight sets of books, viz. 1. the Old Testament, 2. the New Testament, 3. the Veda, 4. the Tri-pitaka, 5. the Zand-Avasta, 6. the Koran, 7. the five volumes or King (viz. Yi, Shu, Shi, Li-ki, Chun-tsiu) and the four Shu or books, some of which were written by the philosopher Mencius (Mang-tsze), 8. the Tau-te-King ('book of reason and virtue'); and are in seven languages, viz. 1. Hebrew, 2. Greek, 3. Sanskrit, 4. Pali, 5. Zand, 6. Arabic, and 7, 8. Chinese. Of these eight religions only four (the second, third, fourth, and sixth) are *numerically* important at the present day.

during the captivity), and from its close relationship to Buddhism, the faith of about thirty-one per cent of the human race[1]. Now it is noteworthy that the idea of a direct revelation, though apparently never entertained in a definite manner by the Greeks and Romans[2], is perfectly familiar, first, to the Hindus; secondly, to the Parsis, as representing the ancient Zoroastrian Persians; thirdly, to all the numerous races who have adopted the religion founded by Muhammad[3], and by

1. Rather more than two-thirds of the human race are still unchristianized (see note, p. xliii). Christianity and Buddhism, the two most prevalent religions of the world, and in their very essence the two most opposed to each other, though, at the same time, the two which have most common ground in their moral teaching, have both been rejected by the races which gave them birth; yet both, when adopted by other races, have acquired the greatest number of adherents. Christianity, originating with a Semitic race, has spread among Aryans; Buddhism, originating among Hindu Aryans, has spread chiefly among Turanian races. Buddhism was driven out of India into Ceylon and still continues there. Thence it passed into Burmah, Siam, Tibet, China, and Japan. It does not seem to have become established in China till the first century of our era, and did not reach Japan till much later. The form it has assumed in these countries deviates widely from the system founded by the great Indian Buddha, and its adoption by the masses of the people is after all more nominal than real. The ancient superstitious belief in good and evil spirits of all kinds (of the sun, wind, and rain; of the earth, mountains, rivers, trees, fields, &c., and of the dead) appears to prevail everywhere among the Chinese people, while the more educated are chiefly adherents of the old moral and philosophical systems taught by Kung-fu-tsze (Confucius) and Lau-tsze. The latter taught belief in one universal spirit called *Tau*, 'the way,' and his disciples are therefore styled Tau-ists.
2. Numa Pompilius is, however, supposed to have derived his inspirations from the prophetic nymph Aegeria; as the Greek poets are imagined to have owed theirs to the Muses.
3. The name of the great Arabian Pseudo-prophet popularly spelt Mohammed, means 'the highly praised' or 'praiseworthy.' We very naturally call the religion he founded Mohammedanism, but he laid no claim to be a founder. Islam is a word denoting 'submission to the will and ordinances of God,' whose absolute unity Mohammed claimed as a prophet to have been commissioned to proclaim.

him called Islam. Let us beware, however, of supposing that the Veda occupies exactly the position of a Bible to the Hindus, or that it is to them precisely what the Avasta is to the Parsis or the Koran to Muslims. Such a notion must lead to some confusion of thought in studying these very different religious systems. For the word Avasta probably signifies 'the settled test' delivered by Zoroaster (properly Zarathustra, and in Persian Zardusht), which was written down and accompanied with its commentary and paraphrases in Pahlavi[1]; as in the Hebrew sacred writings, the Old Testament was furnished with its accompaniments of Chaldee translations and paraphrases called Targums.

Again, the word Koran means emphatically 'the reading' or 'that which ought to be read by every one[2],' and is applied to a single volume, manifestly the work of one author, which according to Muhammad, descended entire from heaven in the night called Al Kadr[3], in the month called Ramazan, though alleged to have been revealed to him by the angel Gabriel at different times, and chapter by chapter. In fact, Muhammad affirmed that, being himself illiterate, he was specially directed and miraculously empowered by God to commit the revelation to writing for the spread of the true faith. (See Introd. xli-xliii.)

---

1. Pahlavi is a later Iranian dialect which followed on Zand and the old Persian of the inscriptions, and led to Parsi or Pazand and the Persian of Firdausi. The word Zand at first denoted commentary, and was afterwards applied to the language.

2. *qur'an*, 'reading,' is the verbal noun of the Arabic root *qura'a*, 'to read.' In the 96th chapter of the Koran the command is twice repeated, 'Read, in the name of thy Lord,' 'Read, by thy most beneficent Lord, who taught the use of the pen.'

3. That is, 'the night of *qadr* or power.' The 97th chapter of the Koran begins thus, 'Verily we sent down the Koran in the night of Al Kadr.' See Sale's translation.

The word Veda, on the other hand, means 'knowledge,' and is a term applied to divine *unwritten* knowledge, imagined to have issued like breath from the Self-existent[1], and communicated to no single person, but to a whole class of men called Rishis or inspired sages. By them the divine knowledge thus apprehended was transmitted, not in writing but through the ear, by constant oral repetition through a succession of teachers, who claimed as Brahmans to be its rightful recipients. Here, then, we have a theory of inspiration higher even than that advanced by the Pseudo-prophet Muhammad and his followers, or by the most enthusiastic adherents of any other religion in the world. It is very true that this inspired knowledge, though its very essence was held to be mystically bound up with Sabda or 'articulate sound' (thought to be eternal), was ultimately written down, but the writing and reading of it were not encouraged. It was even prohibited by the Brahmans, to whom alone all property in

---

1. In Manu I. 3 the Veda is itself called 'self-existent.' There are, however, numerous inconsistencies in the accounts of the production of the Veda, which seem not to have troubled the Brahmans or interfered with their faith in its divine origin. One account makes it issue from the Self-existent, like breath, by the power of A-drishta, without any deliberation or thought on his part; another makes the four Vedas issue from Brahman, like smoke from burning fuel; another educes them from the elements; another from the Gayatri. A hymn in the Atharva-veda (XIX. 54) educes them from Kala or 'Time.' The Satapatha-brahmana asserts that the Creator brooded over the three worlds, and thence produced three lights, fire, the air, and the sun, from which respectively were extracted the Rig, Yajur, and Sama-veda. Manu (I. 23) affirms the same. In the Purusha-sukta the three Vedas are derived from the mystical victim Purusha. Lastly, by the Mýmansakas the Veda is declared to be itself an eternal sound, and to have existed absolutely from all eternity, quite independently of any utterer or revealer of its texts. Hence it is often called *shruta*, 'what is heard.' In opposition to all this we have the Rishis themselves frequently intimating that the Mantras were composed by themselves.

it belonged. Moreover, when at last, by its continued growth, it became too complex for mere oral transmission, then this Veda resolved itself, not into one single volume, like the Koran, but into a whole series of compositions, which had in reality been composed by a number of different poets and writers at different times during several centuries.

There is this great difference, therefore, between the Koran and the Veda, that whereas the reading of the former is regarded as a sacred duty, and constantly practised by all good Muslims, the Veda, even after it had been committed to writing, became absolutely a sealed book to the masses of Hindus, and with the exception of some of the later Vedic works, called Upanishads, is to this day almost entirely unread even by the learned, however much it may be venerated and its divine authority as an infallible guide nominally upheld[1].

Of what, then, does this Veda consist? To conduce to clearness in arranging our examples we may regard it as separating itself into three quite distinct divisions, viz.

1. *Mantras* or prayer and praise embodied in texts and metrical hymns.
2. *Brahmana* or ritualistic precept and illustration written in prose.
3. *Upanishad,* 'mystical or secret doctrine' appended to the aforesaid Brahmana, in prose and occasional verse.

---

1. The absolute and infallible authority of the Veda is held to be so manifest as to require no proof, and to be entirely beyond the province of reason or argument. Manu even extends this to Smriti (II. 10), where he says, 'By *shruti* is meant the Veda, and by *smriti* the books of law; the contents of these must never be questioned by reason.' Nevertheless, the want of familiarity with the Mantras of the Rig-veda is illustrated by the native editions of Manu. That published in Calcutta with the commentary of Kulluka is a scholarlike production, but almost in every place where the Mantras of the Rig-veda are alluded to by Manu (as in VIII. 91, XI. 250, 252, 253, 254) errors disfigure the text and commentary.

To begin, then, with the Mantra portion. By this is meant those prayers, invocations, and hymns which have been collected and handed down to us from a period after the Indian branch of the great Indo-European race had finally settled down in Northern India, but which were doubtless composed by a succession of poets at different times (perhaps between 1500 and 1000 years B.C.). These compositions though very unequal in poetical merit, and containing many tedious repetitions and puerilities, are highly interesting and important, as embodying some of the earliest religious conceptions, as well as some of the earliest known forms, of the primitive language of that primeval Aryan race-stock from which Greeks, Romans, Kelts, Teutons, Russians, and Poles are all offshoots.

They are comprised in five principal Samhitas or collections of Mantras, called respectively Rik, Atharvan, Saman, Taittiriya, and Vajasaneyin. Of these the Rigveda-samhita — containing one thousand and seventeen hymns — is the oldest and most important, while the Atharva-veda-samhita is generally held to be the most recent, and is perhaps the most interesting. Moreover, these are the only two Vedic hyman-books worthy of being called separate original collections[1]; and to these, therefore, we shall confine our examples.

---

1. The Atharva-veda (admirably edited by Professors Roth and Whitney) does not appear to have been recognized as a fourth Veda in the time of Manu, though he mentions the revelation made to Atharvan and An·giras (XII33). In book XI, verse 264, he says, *Richo yajunshi chanyani samani vividhani cha, esha jneyas tri-vrid vedo yo vedainam sa veda-vit.* The Sama-veda and the two so-called Samhitas or collections of the Yajur-veda (Taittiriya and Vajasaneyin or Black and White) all borrow largely from the Rik, and are merely Brahmanical manuals, the necessity for which grew out of the complicated ritual gradually elaborated by the Hindu Aryans. A curious allusion to the Sama-veda occurs in Manu IV. 123 &c., 'The Rig-veda has the gods for its deities, the Yajur-veda has men for its objects, the Sama-veda

To what deities, it will be asked, were the prayers and hymns of these collections addressed? This is an interesting inquiry, for these were probably the very deities worshipped under similar names by our Aryan progenitors in their primeval home somewhere on the table-land of Central Asia, perhaps in the region of Bokhara, not far from the sources of the Oxus[1]. The answer is: They worshipped those physical forces before which all nations, if guided solely by the light of nature, have in the early period of their life instinctively bowed down, and before which even the more civilized and enlightened have always been compelled to bend in awe and reverence, if not in adoration.

To our Aryan forefathers in their Asiatic home God's power was exhibited in the forces of nature even more evidently than to ourselves. Lands, houses, flocks, herds, men, and animals were more frequently than in Western climates at the mercy of winds, fire, and water, and the sun's rays appeared to be endowed with a potency quite beyond the experience of any European country. We cannot be surprised, then, that these forces were regarded by our Eastern progenitors as actual manifestations, either of one deity in different moods

---

has the Pitris, therefore its sound is impure.' Kulluka, however, in his commentary is careful to state that the Sama-veda is not really impure, but only apparently so. This semblance of impurity may perhaps result from its association with deceased persons and its repetition at a time of A-shauca. The Sama-veda is really a mere reproduction of parts of the Rik, transposed and scattered about piece-meal, only seventy-eight verses in the whole Sama-veda being, it is said, untraceable to the present recension of the Rik. The greatest number of its verses are taken from the ninth Mandala of the Rik, which is in praise of the Soma plant, the Sama-veda being a collection of liturgical forms for the Soma ceremonies of the Udgatri priests, as the Yajus is for the sacrifices performed by the Adhvaryu priests.

1. Professor Whitney doubts this usual assumption (Lectures, p. 200).

or of separate rival deities contending for supremacy. Nor is it wonderful that these mighty agencies should have been at first poetically personified, and afterwards, when invested with forms, attributes, and individuality, worshipped as distinct gods. It was only natural, too, that a varying supremacy and varying honours should have been accorded to each deified force — according to the special atmospheric influences to which particular localities were exposed, or according to the seasons of the year when the dominance of each was to be prayed for or deprecated.

This was the religion represented in the Vedas and the primitive creed of the Indo-Aryans about twelve or thirteen centuries before Christ. The first forces deified seem to have been those manifested in the sky and air. These were at first generalized under one rather vague personification, as was natural in the earliest attempts at giving shape to religious ideas. For it may be observed that all religious systems, even the most polytheistic, have generally grown out of some undefined original belief in a divine power or powers controlling and regulating the universe. And although innumerable gods and goddesses, gifted with a thousand shapes, now crowd the Hindu Pantheon, appealing to the instincts of the unthinking millions whose capacity for religious ideas is supposed to require the aid of external symbols it is probable that there existed for the first Aryan worshippers a simpler theistic creed: even as the thoughtful Hindu of the present day looks through the maze of his mythology to the conception of one divine self-existing being, one all-pervading spirit, into whose unity all visible symbols are gathered, and in whose essence all entities are comprehended.

In the Veda this unity diverged into various ramifications. Only a few of the hymns appear to contain the simple conception of one divine self-existent omnipresent Being, and even in these the idea of one God present in all nature is somewhat nebulous and undefined[1]. Perhaps the most ancient and beautiful deification was that of Dyaus[2], 'the sky,' as Dyaush-pitar, 'Heavenly Father' (the Zeus or Ju-piter of the Greeks and Romans). Then, closely connected with Dyaus, was a goddess A-diti, 'the Infinite Expanse,' conceived of subsequently as the mother of all the gods. Next came a development of the same conception called Varuna, 'the Investing Sky,' said to answer to Ahura Mazda, the Ormazd of the ancient Persian (Zand) mythology, and to the Greek Ουρανος — but a more spiritual conception, leading to a

---

1. Though vaguely stated in the Veda, it was clearly defined in the time of Manu; see the last verses of the twelfth book (123-125): 'Him some adore as transcendently present in fire; others in Manu, lord of creatures; some as more distinctly present in Indra, others in pure air, others as the most high eternal Spirit. Thus the man who perceives in his own soul, the supreme soul present in all creatures, acquires equanimity towards them all, and shall be absorbed at last in the highest essence.' In the Purusha-sukta of the Rig-veda (X.90), which is one of the later hymns, probably not much earlier than the earliest Brahmana, the one Spirit is called Purusha. The more common name in the later system is *Brahman,* neut. (nom. *Brahma*), derived from root *brih,* 'to expand,' and denoting the universally expanding essence or universally diffused substance of the universe. For it is evident that this later creed was not so much monotheistic (by which I mean the belief in one god regarded as a personal Being external to the universe, though creating and governing it) as pantheistic; Brahman in the neuter being 'simple infinite being' — the only real eternal essence — which, when it passes into actual manifested existence, is called Brahma, when it develops itself in the world, is called Vishnu, and when it again dissolves itself into simple being, is called Siva; all the other innumerable gods and demigods being also mere manifestations of the neuter Brahman, who alone is eternal. This appears to be the genuine pantheistic creed of India to this very day.

2. From *dyu* or *dyo,* the the same as the Old German Tiu or Ziu, who, according to Professor Max Muller, afterwards became a kind of Mars (whence Tues-day). For Dyaush-pitar see Rig-veda VI. 51. 5.

worship which rose to the nature of a belief in the great Πατηρ ημων ο εν τοις ουρανοις. This Varuna again, was soon thought of in connection with another vague personification called Mithra (=the Persian *Mithra*), 'god of day.' After a time these impersonations of the celestial sphere were felt to be too vague to suit the growth of religious ideas in ordinary minds. Soon, therefore, the great investing firmament resolved itself into separate cosmical entities with separate powers and attributes. First, the watery atmosphere — personified under the name of Indra, ever seeking to dispense his dewy treasures (*indu*), though ever restrained by an opposing force or spirit of evil called Vritra; and, secondly, the wind — thought of either as a single personality named Vayu, or as a whole assemblage of moving powers coming from every quarter of the compass, and impersonated as Maruts of 'Storm-gods.' At the same time in this process of decentralization — if I may use the term — the once purely celestial Varuna became relegated to a position among seven secondary deities of the heavenly sphere called Adityas (afterwards increased to twelve, and regarded as diversified forms of the sun in the several months of the year), and subsequently to a dominion over the waters when they had left the air and rested on the earth.

Of these separately deified physical forces by far the most favourite object of adoration was the deity supposed to yield the dew and rain, longed for by Eastern cultivators of the soil with even greater cravings than by Northern agriculturists. Indra, therefore — the Jupiter Pluvius of early Indian mythology — is undoubtedly the principal divinity of Vedic worshippers, in so far at least as the greater number of their prayers and hymns are addressed to him.

What, however, could rain effect without the aid of heat? A force the intensity of which must have impressed an Indian mind with awe, and led him to invest the possessor of it with divine attributes. Hence the other great god of Vedic worshippers, and in some respects the most important in his connection with sacrificial rites, is Agni (Latin *Ignis*), 'the god of ire.' Even Surya, 'the sun' who was probably at first adored as the original source of heat, came to be regarded as only another form of fire. He was merely a manifestation of the same divine energy removed to the heavens, and consequently less accessible. Another deity, Ushas, 'goddess of the dawn,' was naturally connected with the sun, and regarded as daughter of the sky. Two other deities, the Ashvins, were fabled as connected with Ushas, as ever young and handsome, travelling in a golden car and precursors of the dawn. They are sometimes called Dasras, as divine physicians, 'destroyers of diseases;' sometimes Nasatyas, as 'never untrue.' They appear to have been personifications of two luminous points or rays imagined to precede the break of day. These, with Yama, 'the god of departed spirits,' are the principal deities of the Mantra portion of the Veda[1].

But here it may be asked, if sky, air, water, fire, and the sun were thus worshipped as manifestations of the supreme universal God of the universe, was not the earth also an object of adoration with the early Hindus? And it should be stated that in the earlier system the earth under the name of Prithvi, 'the broad one,' *does* receive divine honours, being thought of as the mother of all beings. Moreover, various deities were regarded as the progeny resulting from the fancied union of earth with Dyaus, 'heaven.' This imaginary marriage of heaven

---

1. It should be observed that there is no trace in the Mantras of the Tri-murti or Triad of deities (Brahma, Vishnu, and Shiva) afterwards so popular. Nor does the doctrine of transmigration, afterwards an essential element of the Hindu religion, appear in the Mantra portion of the Veda. Caste is only clearly alluded to in one hymn (the Purushasukta), generally allowed to be a comparatively modern composition.

and earth was indeed a most natural idea, and much of the later mythology may be explained by it. But it is remarkable that as religious worship became of a more selfish character, the earth, being more evidently under man's control, and not seeming to need propitiation so urgently as the more uncertain air, fire, and water, lost importance among the gods, and was rarely addressed in prayer or hymn.

It may conduce to a better appreciation of the succeeding hymns if it be borne in mind that the deified forces addressed in them were probably not represented by images or idols in the Vedic period, though, doubtless, the early worshippers clothed their gods with human form in their own imaginations[1].

I now commence my examples with a nearly literal translation of the well-known sixteenth hymn of the fourth book of the Atharva-veda, in praise of Varuna or 'the Investing Sky[2]:'

---

1. See Dr. Muir's Sanskrit Tests, v. p. 453.
2. Ably translated by Dr. Muir (Sanskrit Texts, vol. v. p. 63) and by Professor Max Muller. It may be thought that in giving additional translations of this and other hymns I am going over ground already well trodden; but it should be borne in mind that as the design of these Lectures is to illustrate *continuously* the development of Hindu knowledge and literature by a selection of good examples rendered into idiomatic English, I could not, in common justice to such a subject, exclude the best passages in each department of the literature merely because they have been translated by others. I here, however, once for all acknowledge with gratitude that, while making versions of my own, I have derived the greatest assistance from Dr. Muir's scholarlike translations and poetical paraphrases (given in his Texts), as well as from Professor Max Muller's works and those of Professor A. Weber of Berlin. It must be understood that my examples are not put forth as offering rival translations. They are generally intended to be as literal as possible consistently with the observance of English idiom, and on that account I have preferred blank verse; but occasionally they are paraphrases rather than translations, sentences

The mighty Varuna, who rules above, looks down
Upon these worlds, his kingdom, as if close at hand.
When men imagine they do ought by stealth, he knows it.
No one can stand or walk or softly glide along
Or hide in dark recess, or lurk in secret cell,
But Varuna detects him and his movements spies.
Two persons may devise some plot, together sitting
In private and alone; but he, the king, is there —
A third — and sees it all. This boundless earth is his,
His the vast sky, whose depth no mortal e'er can fathom.
Both oceans[1] find a place within his body, yet
In that small pool he lies contained. Whoe'er should flee
Far, far beyond the sky, would not escape the grasp
Of Varuna, the king. His messengers descend
Countless from his abode — for ever traversing
This world and scanning with a thousand eyes its inmates.
Whate'er exists within this earth, and all within the sky,
Yea all that is beyond, king Varuna perceives.
The winkings[2] of men's eyes, are numbered all by him.
He wields the universe, as gamesters handle dice.
May thy destroying snares cast sevenfold round the wicked,
Entangle liars, but the truthful spare, O king![3]

I pass from the ancient Aryan deity Varuna to the more
thoroughly Indian god Indra (see p. 13).

---

and words being here and there omitted or transposed, or fragments
joined together, so as to read like one continuous passage. In fact,
it will be seen that my main design has been to offer English versions
of the text for general readers and for those students and educated
men who, not being necessarily Sanskritists, are desirous of some
insight into Hindu literature.

1. That is, air and sea.
2. The winking of the eye is an especial characteristic of humanity,
   distinguishing men from gods; cf. Nala V. 25, Magha III. 42.
3. Compare Manu VIII. 82: 'A witness who speaks falsely is fast bound
   by the snares of Varuna.' These snares are explained by Kulluka to
   be 'cords consisting of serpents' (pashaih sarpa-rajjubhih).

The following metrical lines bring together various scattered texts relating to this Hindu Jupiter Pluvius[1]:

Indra, twin brother of the god of fire,
When thou wast born, thy mother Aditi
Gave thee, her lusty child, the thrilling draught
Of mountain-growing Soma — source of life
And never-dying vigour to thy frame.
Then at the Thunderer's birth, appalled with fear,
Dreading the hundred-jointed thunderbolt —
Forged by the cunning Tvashtri — mountains rocked,
Earth shook and heaven trembled. Thou wast born
Without a rival, king of gods and men —
The eye of living and terrestrial things.
Immortal Indra, unrelenting foe
Of drought and darkness, infinitely wise,
Terrific crusher of thy enemies,
Heroic, irresistible in might,
Wall of defence to us thy worshippers,
We sing thy praises, and our ardent hymns
Embrace thee, as a loving wife her lord.
Thou art our guardian, advocate, and friend,
A brother, father, mother, all combined.
Most fatherly of fathers, we are thine
And thou art ours; oh! let thy pitying soul
Turn to us in compassion, when we praise thee,
And slay us not for one sin or for many.
Deliver us to-day, to-morrow, every day.
Armed for the conflict, see! the demons come —
Ahi and Vritra, and a long array
Of darksome spirits. Quick, then, quaff the draught
That stimulates thy martial energy,

---

1. The texts which furnish the basis of these and the succeeding verses
   will be found in the 5th volume of Dr. Muir's work, and there will
   also be found a complete poetical sketch of Indra (pp. 126-139).

And dashing onward in thy golden car,
Drawn by thy ruddy, Ribhu-fashioned[1] steeds,
Speed to the charge, escorted by the Maruts.
Vainly the demons dare thy might; in vain
Strive to deprive us of thy watery treasures.
Earth quakes beneath the crashing of thy bolts.
Pierced, shattered, lies the foe — his cities crushed,
His armies overthrown, his fortresses
Shivered to fragments; then the pent-up waters,
Released from long imprisonment, descend
In torrents to the earth, and swollen rivers,
Foaming and rolling to their ocean home,
Proclaim the triumph of the Thunderer.

Let us, proceed next to the all-important Vedic deity Agni, 'god of fire,' especially of sacrificial fire. I propose now to paraphrase a few of the texts which relate to him:

Agni, thou art a sage, a priest, a king,
Protector, father of the sacrifice.
Commissioned by us men thou dost ascend
A messenger, conveying to the sky
Our hymns and offerings. Though thy origin
Be threefold, now from air and now from water,
Now from the mystic double Arani[2],
Thou art thyself a mighty god, a lord,
Giver of life and immortality,
One in thy essence, but to mortals three;
Displaying thine eternal triple form,
As fire on earth, as lightning in the air,
As sun in heaven. Thou art a cherished guest
In every household — father, brother, son,
Friend, benefactor, guardian, all in one.

---

1. The Ribhus (Greek 'orfeuss) were the celestial artists of the Veda.
2. Two pieces of the wood of the Ficus religiosa used for kindling fire.

Bright, seven-rayed god! how manifold thy shapes
Revealed to us thy votaries! now we see thee,
With body all of gold, and radiant hair
Flaming from three terrific heads, and mouths
Whose burning jaws and teeth devour all things.
Now with a thousand glowing horns, and now
Flashing thy lustre from a thousand eyes,
Thou'rt borne towards us in a golden chariot,
Impelled by winds, and drawn by ruddy steeds,
Marking thy car's destructive course, with blackness.
Deliver, mighty lord, thy worshippers.
Purge us from taint of sin, and when we die,
Deal mercifully with us on the pyre.
Burning our bodies with their load of guilt,
But bearing our eternal part on high
To luminous abodes and realms of bliss,
For ever there to dwell with righteous men.

The next deity is Surya, 'the Sun[1],' who, with reference
to the variety of his functions, has various names — such
as Savitri, Aryaman, Mitra, Varuna, Pushan, sometimes
ranking as distinct deities of the celestial sphere. As already
explained, he is associated in the minds of Vedic worshippers
with Fire, and is frequently described as sitting in a chariot
drawn by seven ruddy horses (representing the seven days
of the week), preceded by the Dawn. Here is an example
of a hymn (Rig-veda I. 50) addressed to this deity, translated
almost literally:

Behold the rays of Dawn, like heralds, lead on high
The Sun, that men may see the great all-knowing god.
The stars slink off like thieves, in company with Night,
Before the all-seeing eyes, whose beams reveal his presence,
Gleaming like brilliant flames, to nation after nation.

---

1. Yaska makes Indra, Agni, and Surya the Vedic Triad of gods.

With speed, beyond the ken of mortals, thou, O Sun,
Dost ever travel on, conspicuous to all.
Thou dost create the light, and with it dost illume
The universe entire; thou risest in the sight
Of all the race of men, and all the host of heaven.
Light-giving Varuna! thy piercing glance doth scan
In quick succession all this stirring, active world,
And penetrateth too the broad ethereal space,
Measuring our days and nights and spying out all creatures.
Surya with flaming locks, clear-sighted god of day,
Thy seven ruddy mares bear on thy rushing car.
With these thy self-yoked steeds, seven daughters of thy chariot,
Onward thou dost advance. To thy refulgent orb
Beyond this lower gloom and upward to the light
Would we ascend, O Sun, thou god among the gods.

As an accompaniment to this hymn may here be mentioned the celebrated Gayatri. It is a short prayer to the Sun in his character of Savitri or 'the Vivifier,' and is the most sacred of all Vedic text. Though not always understood, it is to this very day used by every Brahman throughout India in his daily devotions. It occurs in Rig-veda III. 62. 10[1], and can be literally translated as follows:

Let us mediate (or, we meditate) on that excellent glory of the divine Vivifier. May he enlighten (or stimulate)· our understandings. [*Tat Savitur varenyam bhargo devasya dhimahi, Dhiyo yo nah pracodayat.*]

May we not conjecture, with Sir William Jones, that the great veneration in which this text has ever been held by the Hindus from time immemorial, indicates that the more enlightened worshippers adored, under the type of the visible

---

1. Note that the Rishi or author was Vishvamitra, a *Kshatriya*.

sun, that divine light which alone could illumine their intellects?

I may here also fitly offer a short paraphrase descriptive of the Vedic Ushas, or Dawn:'

> Hail ruddy Ushas, golden goddess, borne
> Upon thy shining car, thou comest like
> A lovely maiden by her mother decked,
> Disclosing coyly all thy hidden graces
> To our admiring eyes; or like a wife
> Unveiling to her lord, with conscious pride, .
> Beauties which, as he gazes lovingly,
> Seem fresher, fairer each succeeding morn.
> Through years on years thou hast lived on, and yet
> Thou'rt ever young. Thou art the breath and life
> Of all that breathes and lives, awaking day by day
> Myriads of prostrate sleepers, as from death,
> Causing the birds to flutter from their nests,
> And rousing men to ply with busy feet
> Their daily duties and appointed tasks,
> Toiling for wealth or pleasure or renown.

Before leaving the subject of the Vedic deities I add a few words about Yama, 'the god of departed spirits.' It appears tolerably certain that the doctrine of metempsychosis has no place in the Mantra portion of the Veda[1], nor do the authors of the hymns evince any sympathy with the desire to get rid of all action and personal existence, which became so remarkable a feature of the theology and philosophy of the Brahmans in later times. But there are many indirect references to the immortality of the soul and a future life, and these become more marked and decided towards the end of the Rig-veda. One of the hymns in the last Mandala is addressed to the Pitris or fathers, that is to say, the spirits of departed ancestors who

---

1. In Mandala I. 164.32, *bahu-prajah* is explained by *bahu-janma-bhak*, 'subject to many births,' but it may mean 'having abundant offspring.'

have attained to a state of heavenly bliss, and are supposed to occupy three different stages of blessedness — the highest inhabiting the upper sky, the middle the intermediate air, and the lowest the regions of the atmosphere near the earth. Reverence and adoration are always to be offered them, and they are presided over by the god Yama, the ruler of all the spirits of the dead, whether good or bad. The earlier legends represent this god as a kind of first man (his twin sister being Yami) and also as the first of men that died. Hence he is described as guiding the spirits of other men who die to the same world. In some passages, however, Death is said to be his messenger, he himself dwelling in celestial light, to which the departed are brought, and where they enjoy his society and that of the fathers. In the Veda he has nothing to do with judging or punishing the departed (as in the later mythology), but he has two terrific dogs, with four eyes, which guard the way to his abode. Here are a few thoughts about him from various hymns in the tenth Mandala of the Rig-veda:

To Yama, mighty king, be gifts and homage paid.
He was the first of men that died, the first to brave
Death's rapid rushing stream, the first to point the road
To heaven, and welcome others to that bright abode.
No power can rob us of the home thus won by thee.
O king, we come; the born must die, must tread the path
That thou hast trod — the path by which each race of men,
In long succession, and our fathers, too, have passed.
Soul of the dead! depart; fear not to take the road —
The ancient road — by which thy ancestors have gone;
Ascend to meet the god — to meet thy happy fathers,
Who dwell in bliss with him. Fear not to pass the guards —
The four-eyed brindled dogs — that watch for the departed.
Return unto thy home, O soul! Thy sin and shame
Leave thou behind on earth; assume a shining form —
Thy ancient shape — refined and from all taint set free.

Let me now endeavour, by slightly amplified translations, to convey some idea of two of the most remarkable hymns in the Rig-veda. The first (Mandala X. 129), which may be compared with some parts of the 38th chap. of Job, attempts to describe the mystery of creation thus:

In the beginning there was neither nought nor aught,
Then there was neither sky nor atmosphere above.
What then enshrouded all this teeming Universe?
In the receptacle of what was it contained?
Was it enveloped in the gulf profound of water?
Then was there neither death nor immortality,
Then was there neither day, nor night, nor light, nor darkness,
Only the Existent One breathed calmly, self-contained.
Nought else than him there was — nought else above, beyond.
Then first came darkness hid in darkness, gloom in gloom.
Next all was water, all a chaos indiscreet.
In which the One lay void, shrouded in nothingness.
Then turning inwards he by self-developed force
Of inner fervour and intense abstraction, grew.
And now in him Desire, the primal germ of mind,
Arose, which learned men, profoundly searching, say
Is the first subtle bond, connecting Entity
With Nullity. This ray that kindled dormant life,
Where was it then? Before? or was it found above?
Were there parturient powers and latent qualities,
And fecund principles beneath, and active forces
That energized aloft? Who knows? Who can declare?
How and from what has sprung this Universe? the gods
Themselves are subsequent to its development.
Who, then, can penetrate the secret of its rise?
Whether 'twas framed or not, made or not made; he only
Who in the highest heaven sits, the omniscient lord,
Assuredly knows all or haply knows he not.

The next example is from the first Mandala of the Rig-veda (121). Like the preceding, it furnishes a good argument for those who maintain that the purer faith of the Hindus is properly monotheistic:

What god shall we adore with sacrifice? [1]
Him let us praise, the golden child that rose
In the beginning, who was born the lord —
The one sole lord of all that is — who made
The earth, and formed the sky, who giveth life,
Who giveth strength, whose bidding gods revere,
Whose hiding-place is immortality,
Whose shadow, death; who by his might is king
Of all the breathing, sleeping, waking world —
Who governs men and beasts, whose majesty
These snowy hills, this ocean with its rivers
Declare; of whom these spreading regions form
The arms; by whom the firmament is strong,
Earth firmly planted, and the highest heavens
Supported, and the clouds that fill the air
Distributed and measured out; to whom
Both earth and heaven, established by his will,
Look up with trembling mind; in whom revealed
The rising sun shines forth above the world.
Where'er let loose in space, the mighty waters
Have gone, depositing a fruitful seed
And generating fire, there *he* arose,
Who is the breath and life of all the gods,
Whose mighty glance looks round the vast expanse
Of watery vapour — source of energy,
Cause of the sacrifice — the only God
Above the gods. May he not injure us!
He the Creator of the earth — the righteous

---

1. In the text this question is repeated at the end of every verse. A literal translation will be found in Muir's Sanskrit Texts, vol. iv. p. 16.

Creator of the sky, Creator too
Of oceans bright, and far-extending waters.

Let me now give a few verses (not in regular order and
not quite literally translated) from the celebrated Purushasukta,
one of the most recent of the hymns of the Rig-veda (Mandala
X. 90). It will serve to illustrate the gradual sliding of Hindu
monotheism into pantheism, and the first foreshadowing of
the institution of caste, which for so many centuries has held
India in bondage:

The embodied spirit[1] has a thousand head,
A thousand eyes, a thousand feet, around
On every side enveloping the earth,
Yet filling space no larger than a span[2].
He is himself this very universe,
He is whatever is, has been, and shall be.
He is the lord of immortality.
All creatures are one-fourth of him, three-fourths
Are that which is immortal in the sky.
From him, called Purusha, was born Viraj,
And from Viraj was Purusha produced[3]
Whom gods and holy men made their oblation.
With Purusha as victim they performed
A sacrifice. When they divided him,
How did they cut him up? what was his mouth?
What were his arms? and what his thighs and feet?

---

1. According to the Upanishads and the Tattva-samasa the all-pervading
self-existent spirit is called Purusha, *puri shayanat,* from dwelling in
the body.

2. Dr. Muir translates (literally), 'He overpassed the earth by a space
of ten fingers.' The Katha Upanishad (II. 4. 12) says that Purusha,
'the soul,' is of the measure of a thumb (*an·gushtha-matrah*).

3. This is tantamount to saying that Purusha and Viraj are in substance
the same. Viraj, as a kind of secondary creator, is sometimes regarded
as male, sometimes as female. Manu (I.11) says that Purusha, 'the

The Brahman was his mouth, the kingly soldier[1]
Was made his arms, the husbandman his thighs,
The servile Shudra issued from his feet.

I close my examples of the Mantras with slightly amplified
versions of two hymns — one in praise of Time, personified
as the source of all things, taken from the Atharva-veda; the
other addressed to Night, from the Rig-veda[2].
The following is the hymn to Time (Tharava-veda XIX.
53). A few verses at the end are omitted, one or two lines
transposed, and a few inserted from the next hymn on the
same subject:

Time, like a brilliant steed with seven rays,
And with a thousand eyes, imperishable,
Full of fecundity, bears all things onward.
On him ascend the learned and the wise.
Time, like a seven-wheeled, seven-naved car, moves on.
His rolling wheels are all the worlds, his axle
Is immortality. He is the first of gods.
We see him like an overflowing jar;
We see him multiplied in various forms.
He draws forth and encompasses the worlds;
He is all future worlds; he is their father;
He is their son; there is no power like him.
The past and future issue out of Time,

first male,' was called Brahma, and was produced from the supreme
self-existent Spirit. In I. 32 he says that Brahma (see Kulluka's
commentary), having divided his own substance, became half male,
half female, and that from the female was produced Viraj, and that
from Viraj was born Manu — the secondary progenitor and producer
of all beings.

1. The second caste or Kshatriya is here called Rajanya. By 'husbandman'
in the next line is of course meant the third or Vaishya caste.
2. Both literally translated into prose by Dr. Muïr, Texts, vol. v. p. 408,
vol. iv. p. 498.

All sacred knowledge and austerity.
From Time the earth and waters were produced;
From Time, the rising, setting, burning sun;
From Time, the wind; through Time the earth is vast;
Trough Time the eye perceives; mind, breath, and name
In him are comprehended. All rejoice
When Time arrives — the monarch who has conquered
This world, the highest world, the holy worlds,
Yea, all the worlds — and ever marches on.

The hymn to Night is my last example. It is taken from
the tenth Mandala of the Rig-veda (127):

The goddess Night arrives in all her glory,
Looking about her with her countless eyes.
She, the immortal goddess, throws her veil
Over low valley, rising ground, and hill,
But soon with bright effulgence dissipates
The darkness she produces; soon advancing
She calls her sister Morning to return,
And then each darksome shadow melts away.
Kind goddess, be propitious to thy servants
Who at thy coming straightway seek repose,
Like birds who nightly nestle in the trees.
Lo! men and cattle, flocks and winged creatures,
And e'en the ravenous hawks, have gone to rest.
Drive thou away from us, O Night, the wolf;
Drive thou away the thief, and bear us safely
Across thy borders. Then do thou, O Dawn,
Like one who clears away a debt, chase off
This black, yet palpable obscurity,
Which came to fold us in its close embrace.
Receive, O Night, dark daughter of the Day,
My hymn of praise, which I present to thee,
Like some rich offering to a conqueror.

Lecture II

The Brahmanas and Upanishads

Having thus edeavoured to gain an insight into portions of the Vedic Mantras, turn we now to the second division of the Veda, called Brahamana, or ritualistic precept and illustration. This division stands to the Mantra portion in a relation somewhat resembling that of the Talmud to the Mosaic code and of the Hadis or Sunna to the Koran. There is, however, a noteworthy difference; for the Mosaic code alone contains the true revelation of divine law for the Jew, and the Koran is supposed to do the same for Muslims, whereas the Brahmanas are as much Veda and Sruti — as much revelation, according to the Hindu idea of revelation — as the Mantras.

In fact, in their relation to caste and the dominance of the Brahmans, these Brahmanas are even more important than the Hymns. When, however, we are asked to explain the contents of the Brahmanas, we find it difficult to define their nature accurately. It is usual to consider them as a body of ritualistic precepts distributed under two heads of *Vidhi* and *Artha-vada,* that is, rules and explanatory remarks. They are really a series of rambling and unsystematic prose compositions (the oldest of which may have been written seven or eight centuries B. C.), intended to serve as ceremonial directories for the use of the priests in the exercise of their craft, prescribing rules for the employment of the Mantras at sacrifices, speculating as to the meaning and effect of certain verses and metres, and giving detailed explanations of the origin, import, and conduct of the sacrifices, with the occasional addition of controversial remarks (*ninda*) and illustrations in the shape of legends and old stories. The great diffuseness of these compositions made them practically useless as directories to the ritual, until they themselves were furnished with guides in the form of Sutras or aphoristic rules to be afterwards described.

Each of the Samhitas or collections of Mantras has its own Brahmanas. Thus the Rig-veda has the Aitareyabrahmana and the Kaushitaki– (or San·khayana-) brahmana. The two collections of the Yajur-veda have the Taittiriya-brahmana and the Satapatha-brahmana[1], which last, belonging to the Vajasaneyi-samhita, is perhaps one of the most complete and interesting of these productions. The Sama-veda has eight Brahmanas, of which the best known are the Praudha or Panca-vinsa, the Tandya, and the Shad-vinsa. The Atharva-veda has also a Brahmana, called Go-patha[2].

Though much of the matter contained in these treatises is little better than mere silly sacerdotalism, yet they furnish valuable materials to any one interested in tracing out the growth of Brahmanism and many curious and interesting legends.

One of the most remarkable of these legends, as introducing the idea of human sacrifice, is called 'the Story of SunahSepa' in the Aitareya-brahmana[3] (Haug's edition, VII, 13; cf. Rig-veda I. 24, 12, &c., V. 2. 7). It has been well translated by

---

1. Edited, with the Vajasaneyi-samhiti, by Professor A. Weber of Berlin.
2. This Brahmana must be less ancient than others, as, according to some, the Atharva-veda was not recognized as a part of Shruti, 'revelation,' at the time of the composition of the more ancient Brahmanas.
3. Professor H. H. Wilson conjectured that this Brahmana was written about six centuries B. C. It is sometimes called Ashvalayana-brahmana.

more than one scholar. I here give a metrical epitome of part
of the story.

> King Harishchandra had no son; he asked
> Great Narada, the sage, 'What benefit
> Comes from a son?' then Narada replied —
> 'A father by his son clears off a debt[1],
> In him a self is born from self. The pleasure
> A father has in his own son exceeds
> All other pleasures. Food is life, apparel
> Is a protection, gold an ornament,
> A loving wife the best of friends, a daughter
> An object of compassion[2], but a son
> Is like a light sent from the highest heaven.
> Go then to Varuna, the god, and say —
> "Let but a son be born, O king, to me,
> and I will sacrifice that son to thee."'
> This Harishchandra did, and thereupon
> A son was born to him, called Rohita.
> One day the father thus addressed his son —
> 'I have devoted thee, my son, to him
> Who granted thee to me, prepare thyself
> For sacrifice to him.' The son said, 'No,'
> Then took his bow and left his father's home.

The story goes on to relate that Varuna, being disappointed
of his promised victim, punished Harishchandra by afflicting
him with dropsy. Meanwhile

> For six long years did Harishchandra's son
> Roam in the forest; there one day he met

---

1. A man is in debt to his forefathers till he has a son, because the
   happiness of the dead depends on certain ceremonies (called Shradha)
   performed by sons.
2. Those who have lived in the East will perhaps understand why the
   birth of a daughter is here described as a calamity.

A famished Brahman hermit, Ajigarta,
Half dead with hunger in the wilderness.
The hermit was attended by his wife
And three young sons; then Rohita addressed him —
'O Brahman, I will give a hundred cows
For one of these thy sons.' The father answered —
Folding his arms around his eldest boy —
'I cannot part with him.' The mother then
Clung to her youngest child and weeping said —
'I cannot part with him.' Then Sunahsepa,
Their second said, 'Father, I will go[1].'
So he was purchased for a hundred cows
By Rohita, who forthwith left the forest,
And taking him to Harishchandra said —
'Father, this boy shall be my substitute.'
Then Harishchandra went to Varuna
And prayed, 'Accept this ransom for my son.'
The god replied, 'Let him be sacrificed,
A Brahman is more worthy than a Kshatriya.'

Upon that, the sacrifice with the intended victim was prepared. Four great Rishis officiated as priests, but they

---

1. The Brahmana merely states that they agreed together upon selling the middle son. This idea of the voluntary offer of himself on the part of Sunahsepa may however be borrowed from the Ramayana, where the story is thus related (I. 61, 62):
Ambarisha, king of Ayodhya, performed a sacrifice, but the victim being stolen by Indra, he is told by the priest that either the victim itself must be recovered, or a human victim substituted in its place. Ambarisha wanders over the earth in search of the real victim, and meets at last with a Brahman named Richika, to whom he offers a hundred thousand cattle for one of his sons. Richika refuses to let his eldest son go, and his wife will not part with the youngest. Upon this the middle son, Sunahsepa, volunteers to go, and is accepted. When about to be offered up as a sacrifice he is saved by Vishvamitra, who teaches him a prayer to Agni, and two hymns to Indra and Vishnu.

could not find any one willing to bind the boy to the sacrificial post. His father Ajigarta, who had followed his son to the place of sacrifice, then came forward and said —

'Give me a hundred cows and I will bind him.'
They gave them to him, and he bound the boy.
But now no person would consent to kill him.
Then said the father, 'Give me yet again
Another hundred cows and I will slay him.'
Once more they gave a hundred, and the father
Whetted his knife to sacrifice his son.
Then said the child, 'Let me implore the gods,
Haply they will deliver me from death.'
So Sunahsepa prayed to all the gods
With verses from the Veda, and they heard him.
Thus was the boy released from sacrifice,
And Harishchandra was restored to health.

As a sequel to the preceding legend I extract the following. curious passages from the Aitareya-brahmana, Book II. (Haug, 1-8) not in order and not quite literally:

The gods killed a man for their victim. But from him thus killed the part which was fit for a sacrifice went out and entered a horse. Thence the horse became an animal fit for being sacrificed. The gods then killed the horse, but the part fit for being sacrificed went out of it and entered an ox. The gods then killed the ox, but the part fit for being sacrificed went out of it and entered a sheep. Thence it entered a goat. The sacrificial part remained for the longest time in the goat, thence it became pre-eminently fit for being sacrificed[1].

_____

1. This is curious as indicating that human sacrifice, if it prevailed to any extent, was superseded by the sacrifice of animals, here enumerated in the regular order of their fitness for sacrifice according to some supposed inherent efficacy in each class. Such sacrifices were held to be propitiatory, though one object of a Hindu's oblations

The gods went up to heaven by means of sacrifice. They were afraid that men and sages, after having seen their sacrifice, might inquire how they could obtain some knowledge of sacrificial rites and follow them. They therefore debarred them by means of the Yupa (or post to which the victim was fastened), turning its point downwards. Thereupon the men and sages dug the post out and turned its point upwards. Thus they became aware of the sacrifice and reached the heavenly world.

The following lines may serve to give an outline of another curious legend in the Aitareya-brahmana (Haug's edition, I. 23), written perhaps seven or eight centuries BC.:

The gods and demons were engaged in warfare.
The evil demons, like to mighty kings,
Made these worlds castles; then they formed the earth
Into an iron citadel, the air
Into a silver fortress, and the sky
Into a fort of gold. Whereat the gods

---

was to afford actual nourishment to the gods, food being a supposed necessity of their being. The Ashva-medha, or 'horse-sacrifice,' was a very ancient ceremony, hymns 162 and 163 in Mandala. I. of the Rig-veda being used at this rite. It was regarded as the chief of all animal sacrifices, and in later times its efficacy was so exaggerated that a hundred horse-sacrifices entitled the sacrificer to displace Indra from the dominion of heaven. Some think that the horse was not actually immolated, but merely bound to the post. Mr. Hardwick, in his valuable work, 'Christ and other Masters,' gives some interesting remarks on the five heads of Hindu sacrifices (vol. i. p. 324). The five heads are — 1. *Agni-hotra,* burnt-offerings and libations of butter on fire every morning and evening (see p. 275); 2. *Darshapurnamasa,* half-monthly sacrifices at new and full moon; 3. *Chaturmasya,* sacrifices every four months; 4. *Asva-medha* and *pashu-yajna,* sacrifices of animals; 5. *Soma-yajna,* offerings and libations of the juice of the Soma or moon-plant (to Indra especially). Goats are still offered to Kali, but Buddhism tended to abolish animal sacrifice in India.

Said to each other, 'Frame we other worlds
In opposition to these fortresses.'
Then they constructed sacrificial places,
Where they performed a triple burnt oblation.
By the first sacrifice they drove the demons
Out of their earthly fortress, by the second
Out of the air, and by the third oblation
Out of the sky. Thus were the evil spirits
Chased by the gods in triumph from the worlds.

I next give a metrical version of part of a well-known legend in the Satapatha-brahmana (Professor Weber's edition, I. 8. 1. 1.), which represents the Indo-Aryan tradition of the flood as it existed in India many centuries before the Christian era, perhaps not much later than the time of David:

There lived in ancient time a holy man,
Called Manu[1], who by penances and prayers
Had won the favour of the lord of heaven.
One day they brought him water for ablution;
Then, as he washed his hands, a little fish
Appeared and spoke in human accents thus —
'Take care of me and I will be thy saviour.'
'From what wilt thou preserve me?' Manu asked.
The fish replied, 'A flood will sweep away
All creatures, I will rescue thee from that.'
'But how shall I preserve thee?' Manu said.
The fish rejoined, 'So long as we are small
We are in constant danger of destruction;
For fish eats fish; so keep me in a jar;

---

1. According to the later mythology this Manu was not the first Manu, held to be the author of the well-known Code, but the seventh or Manu (Vaivasvata) of the present period, regarded as a progenitor of the human race, and represented as conciliating the favour of the Supreme Being by his piety in an age of universal depravity.

When I outgrow the jar, then dig a trench
And place me there; when I outgrow the trench,
Then take me to the ocean, I shall then
Be out of reach of danger.' Having thus
Instructed Manu, straightway rapidly
The fish grew larger; then he spake again —
'In such and such a year the flood will come;
Therefore construct a ship and pay me homage.
When the flood rises, enter thou the ship,
And I will rescue thee.' So Manu did
As he was ordered, and preserved the fish,
Then carried it in safety to the ocean;
And in the very year the fish enjoined
He built a ship and paid the fish respect,
And there took refuge when the flood arose.
Soon near him swam the fish, and to its horn
Manu made fast the cable of his vessel.
Thus drawn along the waters Manu passed
Beyond the northern mountain. Then the fish,
Addressing Manu, said, 'I have preserved thee;
Quickly attach the ship to yonder tree.
But, lest the waters sink from under thee;
As fast as they subside, so fast shalt thou
Descend the mountain gently after them.'
Thus he descended from the northern mountain.
The flood had swept away all living creatures;
Manu alone was left. Wishing for offspring,
He earnestly performed a sacrifice.
In a year's time a female was produced.
She came to Manu, then he said to her,
'Who art thou?' She replied, 'I am thy daughter.'
He said, 'How, lovely lady, can that be?'
'I came forth,' she rejoined, 'from thine oblations
Cast on the waters; thou wilt find in me
A blessing, use me in the sacrifice.'

> With her he worshipped and with toilsome zeal
> Performed religious rites, hoping for offspring.
> Thus were created men, called sons of Manu.
> Whatever benediction he implored
> With her, was thus vouchsafed in full abundance.

We shall see hereafter that the fish which figures in this story is declared, in the Mahabharata, to be an incarnation of Brahma, the creator, who assumed this form to preserve the pious Manu from perishing in the waters.

The Brahmanas express belief in a future life more positively than the Mantras. They also assert that a recompense awaits all beings in the next world according to their conduct in this. But the doctrine of transmigration, which became afterwards an essential element of the Hindu religion, is not developed[1]. There is a remarkable passage in the Satapatha-brahmana (X. 4. 3. 9), some idea of which may be gained from the following lines:

> The gods lived constantly in dread of death —
> The mighty Ender —so with toilsome rites
> They worshipped and performed religious acts
> Till they became immortal. Then the Ender
> Said to the gods, 'As ye have made yourselves
> Imperishable, so will men endeavour
> To free themselves from me; what portion then
> Shall I possess in man?' the gods replied,
> 'Henceforth no being shall become immortal
> In his own body; this mortal frame
> Shalt thou still seize; this shall remain thy own.
> He who through knowledge or religious works
> Henceforth attains to immortality
> Shall first present his body, Death, to thee.'

---

1. See the third of Professor Weber's Indische Streifen, and compare note 1, p. 72.

I add one other passage extracted from the Aitareya-brahmana (Dr. Haug's edition, III. 44):

The sun never sets nor rises. When people think to themselves the sun is setting, he only changes about (*viparyasyate*) after reaching the end of the day, and makes night below and day to what is on the other side. Then when people think he rises in the morning, he only shifts himself about after reaching the end of the night, and makes day below and night to what is on the other side. In fact, he never does set at all. Whoever knows this that the sun never sets, enjoys union and sameness of nature with him and abides in the same sphere. [*Atha yad enam pratar udetiti manyante ratrer eva tad antam itva atha atmanam viparyasyate, ahar eva avastat kurute ratrim parastat. Sa vai esha na kadachana nimrochati. Na ha vai kadacana nimrochaty etasya ha sayujyam sarupatam salokatam asnute ya evam veda.*]

We may close the subject of the Brahmanas by paying a tribute of respect to the acuteness of the Hindu mind, which seems to have made some shrewd astronomical guesses more than 2000 years before the birth of Copernicus.

The Upanishads

I come now to the third division of the Veda, called Upanishad, or mystical doctrine (*rahasya*). The title Upanishad (derived from the root *sad* with the prepositions *upa* and *ni*[1]) implies something mystical that underlies or is beneath the surface. And these Upanishads do in fact lie at the root of what may be called the philosophical side of Hinduism. Not only are they as much *shruti*, or revelation, as the Mantra and Brahmana,

---

1. According to native authorities *upa-ni-shad* means 'to set ignorance at rest by revealing the knowledge of the supreme spirit.'

but they are practically the only Veda of all thoughtful Hindus in the present day.

There appear, in real truth, to be two sides to almost every religious system. Perhaps the one religion of the world that offers the same doctrines both to the learned and unlearned is Christianity. Its deeper truths may be mysteries, but they are not restricted to any single class of men; they are open to the reception of all, and equally to be apprehended by all. The case is different with other religions. We know that the Greeks and Romans had their so-called mysteries reserved only for the initiated. Even the Koran is held to possess an exoteric or evident meaning called *zahr,* and an esoteric, deeper significance called *batn;* and in later times a mystical system of pantheistic philosophy called Sufi-ism was developed in Persia out of this esoteric teaching.

Very similar too is the Hindu idea of veda or sacred knowledge. It is said to possess two quite distinct branches. The first is called Karma-kanda, which embracing both Mantra and Brahmana, is for that vast majority of persons who are unable to conceive of religion except as a process of laying up merit by external rites. For these the one god, although really without form, assumes various forms with the sole object of lowering himself to the level of human understanding. The second branch of the Veda, on the other hand, is called Jnana-kanda, and is reserved for that select few who are capable of the true knowledge[1].

What then, it will be asked, is this true knowledge? The answer is that the creed of the man who is said to possess the true Veda is singularly simple. He believes in the unity of all being. In other words, that there is but one real Being in the universe, which Being also constitutes the universe.

---

1. The one implies action, the other cessation from all action. This division of the Veda is recognized by Manu, see XII. 88.

This, it will be said, is simple pantheism, but it is at least a pantheism of a very spiritual kind; for this one being is thought of as the great universal Spirit, the only really existing Soul, with which all seemingly existing material substances are identified, and into which the separate souls of men, falsely regarded as emanations from it, must be ultimately merged.

This, then, is the pantheistic doctrine everywhere traceable in some of the more ancient Upanishads, though often wrapped up in mystic language and fantastic allegory. A list of about 150 of these treatises has been given, but the absence of all trustworthy historical records in India, makes it impossible to fix the date of any of them with certainty. Some of the more ancient, however, may be as old as 500 years before Christ. These are appended to the Aranyakas — certain chapters of the Brahmanas so awe-inspiring and obscure that they were required to be read in the solitude of forests. Properly each Brahmana had its Aranyakas, but the mystical doctrines they contained were so mixed up with extraneous subjects that the chapters called Upanishads appear to have been added with the object of investigating more definitely such abstruse problems as the origin of the universe, the nature of deity, the nature of the soul, and the reciprocal connection of spirit and matter.

It is interesting to trace the rudiments of the later philosophy amid the labyrinth of mystic language, fanciful etymologies, far-fetched analogies, and puerile conceits, which bewilder the reader of the Upanishads. Moreover it is instructive to mark the connection of these treatises with the Brahmanas, manifested by the frequent introduction of legendary matter and allusions to sacrificial rites. The language of both, though occasionally archaic, is less so than that of the Mantras, and differs little from classical Sanskrit.

The following are some of the most important Upanishads: — the Aitareya Upanishad and Kaushitaki-

brahmana Upanishad[1] of the Rig-veda; the Taittiriya belonging
to the Taittiriya-samhita of the Yajur-veda; the Brihad-
aranyaka attached to the Satapatha-brahmana of the
Vajasaneyi-samhita of that Veda and the Isa or Isavasya
forming an actual part (the 40th chapter) of this latter
Samhita (this being the only instance of an Upanishad attached
to a Samhita rather than a Brahmana); the Chandogya and
Kena[2] belonging to the Sama-veda; the Prasna, Mundaka,
Mandukya, and Katha belonging to the Atharva-veda. In
some of these works (written generally in prose in the form
of dialogues with occasional variations in verse) striking
thoughts, original ideas, and lofty sentiments may be found
scattered here and there, as I hope now to show. I commence
my example with a nearly literal translation of about half
of a very short Upanishad — the Isa[3].

Whate'er exists within this universe
Is all to be regarded as enveloped
By the great Lord, as if wrapped in a vesture.
Renounce, O man, the world, and covet not
Another's wealth, so shalt thou save thy soul.
Perform religious works, so may'st thou wish
To live a hundred years; in this way only
May'st thou engage in worldly acts, untainted.
To worlds immersed in darkness, tenanted
By evil spirits, shall they go at death,
Who in this life are killers of their souls.
There is one only Being who exists
Unmoved, yet moving swifter than the mind;
Who far outstrips the senses, though as gods

---

1. Edited and translated for the Biblioteca Indica by Professor Cowell.
2. Also called Talava-kara, and also assigned to the Atharva-veda.
3. This has been well edited and translated into prose by Dr. Roer. Sir
   W. Jones translated the Isa, but by no means literally.

They strive to reach him; who himself at rest
Transcends the fleetest flight of other beings;
Who, like the air, supports all vital action.
He moves, yet moves not; he is far, yet near;
He is within this universe, and yet
Outside this universe; whoe'er beholds
All living creatures as in him, and him —
The universal Spirit — as in all,
Henceforth regards no creature with contempt.
The man who understands that every creature
Exists in God alone, and thus perceives
The unity of being, has no grief
And no illusion. He, the all-pervading,
Is brilliant, without body, sinewless,
Invulnerable, pure, and undefiled
By taint of sin. He also is all-wise,
The Ruler of the mind, above all beings,
The Self-existent. He created all things
Just as they are from all eternity.

Next we may pass to a few passages selected from different portions of the Brihad-aranyaka Upanishad — a long and tedious but important work:

In this universe there was not anything at first distinguishable. But indeed it was enveloped by Death, and Death is Voracity — that is to say — the desire to devour (I. 2. 1).

As the web issues from the spider, as little sparks proceed from fire, so from the one Soul proceed all breathing animals, all worlds, all the gods, and all beings (II. 1. 20).

Being in this world we may know the Supreme Spirit; if there be ignorance of him, then complete death ensues; those who know him become immortal (IV. 4. 14).

When a person regards his own soul as truly God, as the lord of what was and is to be, then he does not wish to conceal himself from that Soul (IV. 4. 15).

That Soul the gods adore as the light of lights (*jyotisham jyotih*) and as the immortal life (IV. 4. 16).

Those who know him as the life of life, the eye of the eye, the ear of the ear, and the mind of the mind, have comprehended the eternal pre-existing Spirit (IV. 4. 18).

By the mind is he to be perceived, in him there is no variation. Whoever sees variation in him obtains death after death (IV. 4. 19).

Infinitely full (or pervasive) is that Spirit (regarded as independent of all relation); infinite too is this Spirit (in his relations and attributes). From the infinite is drawn out the infinite. On taking the infinite from the infinite, there remains the infinite (V. 1).

'I am Brahma.' Whoever knows this, 'I am Brahma,' knows all. Even the gods are unable to prevent his becoming Brahma (I. 4. 10).

Man indeed is like a lofty tree, the lord of the forest. His hair is like the leaves, his skin the external bark. From his skin flows blood as sap from the bark; it issues from his wounded body like sap from a stricken tree. If a tree be cut down, it springs up anew from the root. From what root does mortal man grow again when hewn down by death? [Cf. Job xiv. 7-10] The root is Brahma, who is knowledge and bliss (III. 9. 28).

The Chandogya Upanishad of the Sama-veda has some interesting passages. In the seventh chapter occurs a dialogue between Narada and Sanat-kumara, in which the latter, in explaining the nature of God, asserts that a knowledge of the four Vedas, Itihasas, Puranas, and such works is useless without the knowledge of Brahma, the universal Spirit (VII. 1. 4):

The knowledge of these works is a mere name. Speech is greater than this name, Mind than Speech, Will than Mind, Sensation (or the capacity of feeling) is greater than Mind, Reflection is higher than Sensation, Knowledge than Reflection, Power than Knowledge, and highest of all stands Prana or Life.

As the spokes of a wheel are attached to the nave so are all things attached to Life[1].

This Life ought to be approached with faith and reverence, and viewed as an Immensity which abides in its own glory. That Immensity extends from above and from below, from behind and from before, from the south and from the north. It is the Soul of the universe. It is God himself. The man who is conscious of this divinity incurs neither disease, nor pain, nor death.

But lest the deity might from this description be confounded with space, it is afterwards stated that he is inconceivably minute, dwelling in a minute chamber of the heart; and lest this should lead to the notion of his being finite, he is afterwards to be the Envelope of all creation.

In another part of the work (VI. 10) human souls are compared to rivers:

These rivers proceed from the East towards the West, thence from the ocean they rise in the form of vapour, and dropping again they flow towards the South and merge into the ocean.

Again (VIII. 4), the supreme Soul is compared to a bridge which cannot be crossed by disease, death, grief, virtue, or vice:

Crossing this bridge, the blind cease to be blind, the wounded to be wounded, the afflicted to be afflicted, and on crossing this bridge nights become days; for ever refulgent is the region of the universal Spirit.

Here is a portion of a passage in the Chandogya Upanishad (VI. 2) which has some celebrity as containing the well-known Vedantist formula *ekam evadvitiyam:*

---

1. Cf. the hymn to Prana, Atharva-veda XI. 4 (Muir's Texts, vol. v. p. 394). It begins thus, 'Reverence to Prana, to whom this universe is subject, who has become the lord of all, on whom all is supported.' The text of this Veda has been edited in a masterly manner by Professors W. D. Whitney and R. Roth.

In the beginning there was the mere state of being — one only without a second. Some, however, say that in the beginning there was the state of non-being — one only without a second. Hence out of a state of non-being would proceed a state of being. But, of a truth, how can this be? How can being proceed out of non-being? In the beginning, then, there was the mere state of being — one only without a second. It willed[1], 'I shall multiply and be born.' It created heat. That heat willed, 'I shall multiply and be born.' It created water. The water willed 'I shall multiply and be born.' It created aliment. Therefore, wherever rain falls much aliment is produced. That deity willed, 'Entering these three divinities in a living form, I shall develop name and form.'

In the Mundaka Upanishad[2] there are some interesting passages. The following is from the second section of the second Mundaka (5):

Know him, the Spirit, to be one alone. Give up all words contrary to this. He is the bridge of immortality.

The following remarkable passage from the third Mundaka (1. 1-3) is quoted by the San·khyas in support of their doctrine of a duality of principle, but is also appealed to by Vedantists.

---

1. I follow Dr. Roer here. Subjoined are the divided Sanskrit words of the fragment taken from the original text :— *Sad eva idam agre asid, ekam eva advitiyam. Tad ha eke ahur asad eva idam agre asid, ekam eva advitiyam, tasmad asatah saj jayeta. Kutas tu khalu syad iti, katham asatah saj jayeta iti. Sat tv eva idam agre asid ekam eva advitiyam. Tad aikshata bahu syam prajayeya iti, tat tejo asrijata. Tat teja aikshata bahu syam prajayeya iti, tad apo asrijata. Ta apa aikshanta bahvah syama prajayemahi iti ta annam asrijanta. Tasmad yatra kva cha varshati tad eva bhuyishtham annam bhavati. Sa iyam devata aikshata, aham imas tisro devata jivena atmana anupravishya nama-rupe vyakaravani iti.*
2. The name Mundaka is derived from Mund, 'to shave,' because he who understands the doctrine of this Upanishad is 'shorn' of all error.

It rests on a Mantra of the Rig-veda (I. 164. 20), explained by Sayana in a Vedantic sense[1]:

Two birds (the Paramatman and Jivatman or supreme and individual souls) always united, of the same name, occupy the same tree (abide in the same body). One of them (the Jivatman) enjoys the sweet fruit of the fig (or fruit of acts), the other looks on as a witness. Dwelling on the same tree (with the supreme Soul), the deluded (individual) soul, immersed (in worldly relations), is grieved by the want of power; but when it perceives the Ruler, separate (from worldly relations) and his glory, then its grief ceases. When the beholder sees the golden-coloured maker (of the world), the lord, the soul, the source of Brahma, then having become wise, shaking off virtue and vice, without taint of any kind, he obtains the highest identity (Roer's edition, p. 305).

Here are two or three other examples from the same Upanishad:

As the spider casts out and draws in (its web), as from a living man the hairs of the head and body spring forth, so is produced the universe from the indestructible Spirit (I.1.7).

As from a blazing fire consubstantial sparks proceed in a thousand ways, so from the imperishable (Spirit) various living souls are produced, and they return to him too (II.1.1).

---

1. Subjoined is the Mantra:— *Dva suparna sayaja sakhaya samanam vriksham parishasvajate, Tayor anyah pippalam svadv atty an-asnann anyo abhichakasiti*, 'two birds associated together as friends inhabit the same tree. The one of them tastes the sweet fig, the other looks on without enjoying.' Shankara, commenting on the Upanishad, explains *sakhaya* by *samana-khyatau*, 'of the same name.' He also remarks that the Pippala or Asvattha, 'holy fig-tree,' having roots above and branches bent downwards, is allegorical, and that each tree, springing from an unperceived root, is emblematic of the body, which really springs from and is one with Brahma. In the Katha VI. 1 and Bhagavad-gita XV. 1-3 the same tree is said to typify the universe. It is supposed to be the male of the Vata or Banyan (Ficus Indica).

As flowing rivers are resolved into the sea, losing their names and forms, so the wise, freed from name and form, pass into the divine Spirit, which is greater than the great. He who knows that supreme Spirit becomes spirit (III.2. 8,9).

One of the most ancient and important Upanishads is the Katha. It enjoys considerable reputation in India, and is also well known by Sanskrit students in Europe. It opens with the story of Nachiketas.

He was the pious son of a sage who had given all his property to the priests, and who in a fit of irritation, devoted this son to Death.

Nachiketas is described as going to Death's abode, and there, having propitiated Yama, he is told to choose three boons. The youth chose for the first boon, that he might be restored to life and see his reconciled father once more; for the second, that he might know the fire by which heaven is gained. When asked to name the third boon, he addresses the god of death thus, —

Some say the soul exists after death, others say it does not exist. I request, as my third boon, that I may be instructed by thee in the true answer to this question.

Death tries to put him off, entreating, him to choose any other boon than this; but the youth persisting in his demand to be enlightened as to the mysteries of the next world, Yama at length gives way and enlarges upon the desired theme in the following manner (Valli, II):

The good, the pleasant, these are separate ends,
The one or other all mankind pursue;
But those who seek the good, alone are blest;
Who choose the pleasant miss man's highest aim.
The sage the truth discerns, not so the fool.
But thou, my son, with wisdom hast abandoned
The fatal road of wealth that leads to death.

Two other roads there are all wide apart,
Ending in widely different goals — the one
Called ignorance, the other knowledge — this,
O Nachiketas, thou dost well to choose.
The foolish follow ignorance, but think
They tread the road of wisdom, circling round
With erring steps, like blind men led by the blind.
The careless youth, by lust of gain deceived,
Knows but one world, one life; to him the Now
Alone exists, the Future is a dream.
The highest aim of knowledge is the soul;
This is a miracle, beyond the ken
Of common mortals, thought of though it be,
And variously explained by skilful teachers.
Who gains this knowledge is a marvel too.
He lives above the cares — the griefs and joys
Of time and sense — seeking to penetrate
The fathomless unborn eternal essence.
The slayer thinks he slays, the slain
Believes himself destroyed, the thoughts of both
Are false, the soul survives, nor kills, nor dies;
'Tis subtler than the subtlest, greater than
The greatest, infinitely small, yet vast,
Asleep, yet restless, moving everywhere
Among the bodies — ever bodiless —
Think not to grasp it by the reasoning mind;
The wicked ne'er can know it; soul alone
Knows soul, to none but soul is soul revealed.

In the third Valli (3,4, &c.) of the same Upanishad the
soul is compared to a rider in a chariot, the body being the
chariot, the intellect the charioteer, the mind the reins, the
passions or senses the horses, and the objects of sense the
roads. The unwise man neglects to apply the reins; in
consequence of which the passions, like unrestrained vicious

horses, rush about hither and thither, carrying the charioteer wherever they please[1].

In the fifth Valli (11) the following sentiment occurs:

As the sun, the eye of the whole world, is not sullied by the defects of the (human) eye or of external objects, so the inner soul of all beings is not sullied by the misery of the world.

I now add a few extracts from one of the most modern of these treatises, called Svetasvatara[2], which may serve to show how epithets of the Supreme Being are heaped together by the writers of the Upanishads without much order and often with apparent contradiction:

Him may we know, the ruler of all rulers,
The god of gods, the lord of lords, the greater
Than all the greatest, the resplendent being,
The world's protector, worthy of all homage.
Of him there is not cause nor yet effect.
He is the cause, lord of the lord of causes,
None is there like him, none superior to him,
His power is absolute, yet various,
Dependent on himself, acting with knowledge,
He the one god is hidden in all beings,
Pervades their inner souls and rules their actions,
Dwelling within their hearts, a witness, thinker,
The singly perfect, without qualities.

---

1. Compare Manu II. 88, 'In the restraint of the organs running wild among objects of sense, which hurry him away hither and thither, a wise man should make diligent effort, like a charioteer restraining restive steeds.' So Plato in the Phaedrus (54, 74) compares the soul to a charioteer (the reason) driving a pair of winged steeds, one of which (the will) is obedient to the rein, and tries to control its wild and vicious yoke-fellow (the appetite).
2. Of the Yajur-veda, though sometimes found (according to Colebrooke) in Atharva-veda collections. See Weber's Indische Studien I. 420-439.

He is the Universe's maker, he
Its knower, soul and origin of all,
Maker of time, endowed with every virtue,
Omniscient, lord of all embodied beings,
Lord of the triple qualities, the cause
Of man's existence, bondage and release,
Eternal, omnipresent, without parts,
All knowing, tranquil, spotless, without blame,
The light, the bridge of immortality,
Subtler than what is subtlest, many-shaped,
One penetrator of the universe,
All-blest, unborn, incomprehensible,
Above, below, between, invisible
To mortal eyes, the mover of all beings,
Whose name is Glory, matchless, infinite,
The perfect spirit, with a thousand heads,
A thousand eyes, a thousand feet, the ruler
Of all that is, that was, that is to be,
Diffused through endless space, yet of the measure
Of a man's thumb, abiding in the heart,
Known only by the heart, whoever knows him
Gains everlasting peace and deathlessness[1].

I close these extracts from the Upanishads by a metrical version of part of the first chapter of a short Upanishad called Maitrayani or Maitrayaniya, belonging to the Black Yajur-veda[2]:

---

1. Most of these epithets will be found in the following sections of the Svetasvatara Upanishad VI, 7, 8, 11, 17, 19, IV. 14, 17, 19, &c. Compare the extract from the Purusha-sukta given at p. 25.
2. Also called Maitrayani, Maitrayana, Maitri, and Maitri. Under the latter name it has been well edited and translated for the Bibliotheca Indica by Professor E. B. Cowell. It is in seven chapters, the first of which was translated into prose by Sir W. Jones, but without any name. My version is partly based on his, but I have consulted Professor Cowell's more accurate translation.

In this decaying body, made of bones,
Skin, tendons, membranes, muscles, blood, saliva,
Full of putrescence and impurity,
What relish can there be for true enjoyment? [1]
In this weak body, ever liable
To wrath, ambition, avarice, illusion,
To fear, grief, envy, hatred, separation
From those we hold most dear, association
With those we hate; continually exposed
To hunger, thirst, disease, decrepitude,
Emaciation, growth, decline, and death,
What relish can there be for true enjoyment?
The universe is tending to decay,
Grass, trees, and animals spring up and die.
But what are they? Earth's mighty men are gone,
Leaving their joys and glories; they have passed
Out of this world into the realm of spirits
But what are they? Beings greater still than these,
Gods, demigods, and demons, all have gone.
But what are they? For others greater still
Have passed away, vast oceans have been dried,
Mountains thrown down, the polar star displaced,
The cords that bind the planets rent asunder,
The whole earth deluged with a flood of water,
E'en highest angels driven from their stations.
In such a world what relish can there be
For true enjoyment? deign to rescue us;
Thou only art our refuge, holy lord[2].

---

1. Compare Manu VI. 77.
2. The following sentiment occurs in the text before the concluding
   line: *Andhodapana-stho bheka iva aham asmin samsare:*
       Living in such a world I seem to be
       A frog abiding in a dried-up well.

Compare some of the Stoical reflections of Marcus Aurelius, given by the Rev. F. W. Farrar in his 'Seekers after God:'

'Oil, sweat, dirt, filthy water, all things disgusting — so is every part of life.'

'Enough of this wretched life, and murmuring, and apish trifles.'

'All the present time is a point in eternity. All things are little, changeable, perishable.'

Lecture III

The Systems of Philosophy

I must now advert in a general way to the six systems of philosophy which grew out of the Upanishads. They are sometimes called the six Shastras or bodies of teaching, sometimes the Shad Darshanas or six Demonstrations. They are —

1. The Nyaya, founded by Gotama.
2. The Vaiseshika, by Kanada.
3. The Sankhya, by Kapila.
4. The Yoga, by Patanjali.
5. The Mimansa, by Jaimini.
6. The Vedanta, by Badarayana or Vyasa.

They are delivered in Sutras or aphorisms, which are held to be the basis of all subsequent teaching under each head[1].

---

1. These Sutras are often so brief and obscure as to be absolutely unintelligible without a commentary. They are commonly called 'aphorisms,' but really are mere memorial suggestions of the briefest possible kind, skilfully contrived for aiding the recollection of the teachers of each system. Probably the first to comment upon the Sutras thus delivered was the author of them himself. He was followed by a vast number of other commentators in succeeding generations (generally a triple set), and by writers who often embodied in

It is as impossible however to settle the date of any of them with certainty as it is to determine the period of the composition of any single work in Sanskrit literature. Moreover, it is scarcely practicable to decide as to which of the six systems of philosophy preceded the other in point of time. All we can say is, that about 500 years before the commencement of the Christian era a great stir seems to have taken place in Indo-Aryan, as in Grecian minds, and indeed in thinking minds everywhere throughout the then civilized world. Thus when Buddha arose in India, Greece had her thinker in Pythagoras, Persia in Zoroaster, and China in Confucius. Men began to ask themselves earnestly such questions as — What am I? whence have I come? whither am I going? How can I explain my consciousness of personal existence? What is the relationship between my material and immaterial nature? What is this world in which I find myself? Did a wise, good, and all-powerful Being create it out of nothing? or did it evolve itself out of an eternal germ? or did it come together by the combination of eternal atoms? If created by a Being of infinite wisdom, how can I account for the inequalities of condition in it — good and evil, happiness and misery? Has the Creator form, or is he formless? Has he any qualities or none?

Certainly in India no satisfactory solution of questions such as these was likely to be obtained from the prayers and hymns of the ancient Indo-Aryan poets, which though called Veda or 'knowledge' by the Brahmans, did not even profess to furnish any real knowledge on these points, but merely gave expression to the first gropings of the human mind,

---

treatises or compendiums of their own the tenets of the particular school to which they were attached. The most celebrated of all commentators is the great Shankara Acharya, a native of Malabar, who lived probably between 650 and 740 AD., and wrote almost countless works, including commentaries on the Upanishads, Vedanta-sutras, and Bhagavad-gita.

searching for truth by the uncertain light of natural phenomena[1].

Nor did the ritualistic Brahmanas contribute anything to the elucidation of such topics. They merely encouraged the growth of a superstitious belief in the efficacy of sacrifices and fostered the increasing dependence of the multitude on a mediatorial caste of priests, supposed to be qualified to stand between them and an angry god. Still these momentous questions pressed for solution, and the minds of men finding no rest in mere traditional revelation and no satisfaction in mere external rites, turned inwards, each thinker endeavouring to think out the great problems of life for himself by the aid of his own reason. Hence were composed those vague mystical rationalistic speculations called Upanishads, of which examples have been already given. Be it remembered that these treatises were not regarded as antagonistic to revelation, but rather as completory of it. They were held to be an integral portion of the Veda or true knowledge; and, even more — they so rose in the estimation of thoughtful persons that they ended by taking rank as its most important portion, its grandest and noblest utterance, the apex to which all previous revelation tended. Probably the simple fact was, that as it was found impossible to stem the progress of free inquiry, the Brahmans with true wisdom determined on making rationalistic speculation their own, and dignifying its first development in the Upanishads with the title of Veda. Probably, too, some of their number (like Javali) became themselves infected with the spirit of scepticism, and were not to be restrained from prosecuting free philosophical investigations for themselves.

---

1. The second alhorism of the Sankhya-karika states distinctly that Anusravika or knowledge derived from sruti — the revelation contained in the Veda — is ineffectual to deliver from the bondage of existence.

There are not wanting, however, evident indications that the Kshatriyas or second caste were the first introducers into India of rationalistic speculation. We shall presently point out that the great Buddha was Kshatriya, and the Chandogya Upanishad (V. 3) has a remarkable passage which, as bearing upon this point, I here abridge (Roer's edition, p. 315):

A youth called Shvetaketu (the son of a Brahman named Gautama) repaired to the court of the king of Panchala, Pravahana, who said to him, 'Boy, has thy father instructed thee?' 'Yes, sir,' replied he. 'Knowest thou where men ascend when they quit this world?' 'No, sir,' replied he. 'Knowest thou how they return?' 'No, sir,' replied he. 'Knowest thou why the region to which they ascend is not filled up?' 'No, sir,' replied he. 'Why then saidst thou that thou hadst been instructed?' The boy returned sorrowful to his father's house and said, 'The king asked me certain questions which I could not answer.' His father said, 'I know not the answers.' Then he, Gautama, the father of the boy, went to the king's house. When he arrived, the king received him hospitably and said, 'O Gautama, choose as a boon the best of all worldly possession.' He replied, 'O king, thine be all worldly possessions; tell me the answers to the questions you asked my son.' The king became distressed in mind (knowing that a Brahman could not be refused a request) and begged him to tarry for a time. Then he said, 'Since you have sought this information from me, and since this knowledge has never been imparted to any other Brahman before thee, therefore the right of imparting it has remained with the Kshatriyas among all the people of the world.'

This story certainly appears to favour the supposition that men of the caste next in rank to that of Brahmans were the first to venture upon free philosophical speculation. However that may be, it was not long before Brahmanism and rationalism advanced hand in hand, making only one compact, that however inconsistent with each other, neither should declare the other to be a false guide. A Brahman might be a rationalist, or both rationalist and Brahman might live together in harmony, provided both gave a nominal assent to the Veda, maintained the inviolability of caste, the ascendancy of Brahmans, and their sole right to be the teachers both of religion and philosophy. But if a rationalist asserted that any one might be a teacher, or might gain emancipation for himself irrespective of the Veda or caste observances, he was at once excommunicated as a heretic and infidel. It is evident that a spirit of free inquiry had begun to show itself even during the Mantra period and had become common enough in Manu's time. In the second book of his Laws (verse 11) it is declared:

The Brahman who resorting to rationalistic treatises (*hetu-shastra*) shall contemn the two roots of all knowledge (viz. *shruti* and *smriti*), that man is to be excommunicated (*vahish-karyah*) by the righteous as an atheist (*nastika*) and reviler of the Vedas.

Such heretics, however, soon became numerous in India by the simple law of reaction; for it may with truth be asserted that the Buddhist reformation, when it first began to operate, was the result of a reaction from the tyranny of Brahmanism and the inflexible rigour of caste. Like the return swing of a pendulum, it was a rebound to the opposite extreme — a recoil from excessive intolerance and exclusiveness to the broadest tolerance and comprehensiveness. It was the name for unfettered religious thought, asserting itself without fear of consequences and regardless of running counter to traditional usages, however ancient and inveterate.

According to this view, the lines of free inquiry which ended in the recognized schools of philosophy cannot be regarded as having sprung directly out of Buddhism; nor did the latter owe its origin to them. Buddhism and philosophy seem rather to have existed contemporaneously[1]. Buddhism

---

1. The Sankhya Sutras I. 27-47 refer to certain Buddhistic tenets, but, as remarked by Dr. Muir, these may be later interpolations, and so prove nothing as to the priority of Buddhism.

was for the bold and honest free-thinker who cared nothing for maintaining a reputation for orthodoxy, while the schools of philosophy were the homes of those rationalists who sacrificed honesty at the shrine of ecclesiastical respectability. Doubtless the orthodox philosopher usually went through the form of denouncing all Buddhist heretics; but except in the three points of a nominal assent to the Veda, adherence to caste, and a different term for final emancipation, two at least of the systems, viz. the *Vaiseshika* and *Sankhya,* went almost to the same length with Buddhism, even to the practical if not ostensible ignoring of a supreme intelligent creator. It is curious, too, that Gotama or Gautama, the name of the supposed orthodox Brahman founder of the *Nyaya,* was also a name of the heretical Kshatriya who founded Buddhism.

In fact, not the extremest latitudinarian of the present day could possibly be allowed such liberty of thought as was conceded to the free-thinkers of India, provided they neutralized their heterodoxy by nominally accepting the Veda, or at least its Upanishad portion, and conforming to *Hindu Dharma* — that is, to the duties of caste, involving of course the recognition of Brahmanical ascendancy.

It would be difficult then, I think, to refer Hindu rationalism to any one special person or school as its founder. Not that Kapila, Gautama, and the great Buddha of the sixth century B.C. were myths. Some men of vigorous intellect and enlightened views doubtless arose who gathered together and formulated the floating free thought of the day; and some one of them, like the Buddha, became a rallying point for the increasing antipathy to sacerdotal domination, a kind of champion of reason and liberator of mind from the tyranny of traditional opinions. It may without hesitation be affirmed that such leaders of rationalistic inquiry once lived in India. I commence, then, with a brief notice of the celebrated Buddha.

Buddhism

Some particulars in the life of the great Buddha are known with tolerable certainty. He is described as the son of a king, *Suddhodana*, who reigned in *Kapilavastu*, the capital of a country at the foot of the mountains of Nepal[1]. He was therefore a prince of the Kshatriya or military caste, which of itself disqualified him in the eyes of the Brahmans from setting up as a religious teacher. His proper family or tribal name was Sakya, and that of his race or clan Gautama or Gotama[2]; for it is well known that this great reformer never arrogated to himself an exclusive right to the title Buddha, 'enlightened,' or claimed any divine honours or even any special reverence. He is said to have entered on his reforming mission in the district of Magadha or Behar[3] about the year 588 B.C., but he taught that other philosophers (Budhas) and even numerous Buddhas — that is, perfectly enlightened men — had existed in previous periods of the world. He claimed

---

1. His mother's name was Maya or Maya-devi, daughter of king Suprabuddha. The Buddha had also a wife called Yasodhara and a son Rahula and a cousin Ananda.
2. Gautama is said to have been one of the names of the great Solar race to which king Suddhodana belonged. The titles Sinha and Muni are often added to Sakya, thus Sakya-sinha, 'the lion of the sakyas;' Sakyamuni, 'the Sakya-saint.' His name Siddhartha, 'one whose aims have been accomplished,' was either assumed, like Buddha, as an epithet in after life, or, as some say, was given by his parents, 'whose prayer had been granted,' something in the same manner as *Deva-datta,* Theodore. Shramana, meaning 'ascetic,' is sometimes affixed to Gautama. He is also styled Bhagavat, 'the adorable,' and Tatha-gata or Su-gata, 'one who has gone the right way.' Every Buddhist may be a *Shramana* (see p. 61) for the more rapid attainment of Nirvana.
3. He is said to have given lectures to his disciples in a garden belonging to a rich and liberal householder, named Sudatta or Anatha-pindada, in the city of Sravasti, somewhere in the district now called Oude, north of the Ganges.

to be nothing but an example of that perfection in knowledge to which any man might attain by the exercise of abstract meditation, self-control, and bodily mortification. Gentle, however, and unassuming as the great reforming Ascetic was, he aimed at the grandest practical results. He stood forth as the deliverer of a priest-ridden, caste-ridden nation — the courageous reformer and innovator who dared to attempt what doubtless others had long felt was necessary, namely, the breaking down of an intolerable ecclesiastical monopoly by proclaiming absolute free trade in religious opinions and the abolition of all caste privileges[1]. It may be taken as a fixed

---

1. Bauddhas or Buddhists believe that after immense intervals of time (Kalpas) men with perfect knowledge, entitled to be called supreme Buddhas, come into the world to teach men the true way to Nirvana, which gradually fades away from their minds in the lapse of ages and has again to be communicated by another perfect teacher. The Buddha foretold that one of his followers was to be the next supreme Buddha. An ascetic who has arrived at the stage when there is only one more birth, before attaining to the rank of a Buddha, is called by Buddhists Bodhisattva, 'one who has the essence of perfect wisdom in him.' Few, of course, attain to be supreme Buddhas — completely enlightened teachers — though all may ultimately reach Nirvana. Candidates for Nirvana are called Arhats, i.e. 'venerables.'

Dr. Muir, at the end of the second volume of his Texts, gives a most interesting metrical translation of part of the Lalita-vistara, a legendary history in prose and verse of the Buddha's life. The prose of this history is in Sanskrit but the Gathas or songs interspersed with it are in a kind of mixed dialect, half Sanskrit, half Prakrit. The passage translated describes Buddha as a deliverer and redeemer in terms which almost assimilate his character to the Christian conception of a Saviour. Professor Max Müller, in his Sanskrit Literature (p. 79), has drawn attention to a passage from Kumarila Bhatta, according to which the following words, claiming the functions of a kind of vicarious redeemer, are ascribed to Buddha :— 'Let all the evils (or sins) flowing from the corruption of the fourth or degenerate age (called Kali) fall upon me, but let the world be redeemed.' Bishop Claughton is reported to have said in a recent lecture, that there is nothing out of Christianity equal to Buddhism in a moral point of view.

law of human nature that wherever there arise extravagant claims to ecclesiastical authority on the one side, there will always arise Buddhas on the other — men who, like the Buddha of India, become rapidly popular by proclaiming general religious equality, universal charity and toleration, and whose followers develop their doctrines to a point beyond that intended by themselves. In fact, a sort of Buddhism capable of being pushed to the extremest point of Nihilism is a not unlikely terminus of all lines of uncontrolled thought, whose starting-point is the sense of freedom produced by the breaking loose of reason from the unnatural restraints which sacerdotal dogmatism delights to impose. It is a remarkable proof of the enchaining power of caste, that notwithstanding the popularity and attractive features of Buddhism, its universal toleration and benevolence, its recognition of the common brotherhood of mankind, its reverence for every form of organized existence — so that not only every human being, but every living creature however insignificant, has a right to respect and tender treatment — its inculcation of the virtues of self-sacrifice, purity, truthfulness, gentleness of speech, humility, patience, and courage — this wonderful system which originated in India and adapted itself so completely in most of its doctrines to Indian tastes and habits of thought, should have been in the end unsuccessful in its contest with Brahmanism.

But though the religion of India at the present day is certainly not Buddhism, yet it is equally certain that this rejected system has left a deep impress on the Hindu mind, and has much in common with Hinduism generally; while its attractiveness to the Oriental character is notably evidenced, by its having during a period of about two thousand four hundred years so commended itself to Eastern nations as to number at this moment, according to recent calculations, about four hundred and fifty-five million of nominal adherents.

Therefore, before quitting the subject of the great Indian reformer, it will not be irrelevant if I indicate briefly the principal points of his teaching.

Let me begin by directing attention to its most marked feature. The Buddha recognized no supreme deity[1]. The only god, he affirmed, is what man himself can become. In Brahmanism God becomes man; in Buddhism man becomes a god. Practically, however, Buddhists are subject to a formidable god in *Karman,* 'act.' But this is a god to be got rid of as soon as possible, for action leads to continual existence, carried on through innumerable bodies till acts are adequately rewarded or punished; and that all existence is an evil is a fundamental dogma of Buddhism. Hence the great end of the system is *Nirvana,* 'the being blown out' or non-existence. From this statement it might be supposed that all good actions as well as bad are to be avoided. But this is not exactly the case. Certain acts, involving abnegation of self and suppression of evil passions, are supposed very inconsistently to contribute to the great end of *Nirvana* or non-existence. According to the best authorities[2], the Buddha regarded men as divided into two classes — first, those who are still attached to the world and worldly life; secondly, those who by self-mortification are bent on being delivered from it. The first class are Upasakas or 'laymen,' the second are Shramanas or 'ascetics[3].' These last are rather monks or friars than priests. Of priests and

---

1. With Buddhist, as indeed with Brahmans, the gods are merely superior beings, subject to the same law of dissolution as the rest of the universe. Certainly the Buddha himself never claimed to be worshipped as a god, nor is he so worshipped, though his memory is revered and the relics of him are enclosed in shrines, and even a kind of prayer in his honour is uttered or turned round in a wheel to act as a charm. Strictly, a Buddhist never prays; he merely contemplates.
2. For a full account see the article 'Buddha' in Chambers' Cyclopaedia.
3. They are also called Shravakas as hearers of Buddha and Maha-shravakas as great hearers. When mendicants they are Bhikshus or Bhikshukas.

clergy in our sense the Buddhist religion has none. In real fact Buddhism ought not to be called a religion at all, for where there is no god there can be no need of sacrifice or propitiation or even of prayers, though this last is practised as a kind of charm[1] against diseases, worldly evils and malignant demons, and as having, like other acts, a kind of mechanical efficacy. Both classes, however, laymen and ascetics, must equally practise certain virtues to avoid greater misery, either in future births or in one of the 136 hells; for the passing through repeated births, even in the most degraded forms of life, is not sufficient punishment for the effacement of demerit without the endurance of terrific torments in numerous hells[2].

Ten moral prohibitions are given. Five are for all, viz. Kill not. Steal not. Commit not adultery. Lie not. Drink no strong drink. The other five are for the ascetics who have commenced the direct pursuit of *Nirvana,* viz. Eat no food out of season. Use no ornaments or perfumes. Abstain from luxurious beds. Abstain from dances, theatres, songs, and music. Receive no gold nor silver. Again, there are still more severe precepts for those who are not merely commencing a religious life, but have actually renounced the world. These persons are sometimes called Bhikshus or Parivrajakas, 'religious mendicants.' They must dress only in rags sewed together with their own hands, and covered with a yellow cloak. They must eat only one meal daily, and that before noon, and only

---

1. These Buddhist prayers are called Dharanis and are used, like the Brahmanical Mantras, as charms against evil of all kinds. It should be noted that Buddhists believe in a kind of devil or demon of love, anger, evil, and death, called Mara, who opposed Buddha and the spread of his religion. He is supposed to send forth legions of evil demons like himself.
2. See note 3, p. 70. There are also numerous Buddhist heavens. One of these, called Tushita, was inhabited by Sakya-muni as a Bodhisattva before he came into the world as a Buddha.

what may be collected from door to door in a wooden bowl. For a part of the year they must live in the woods with no other shelter than a tree, and with no furniture but a carpet on which they must sit, and never lie down during sleep. Besides these prohibitions and injunctions there are six transcendent perfections of conduct which lead to the other shore of Nirvana (Param-itas, as they are called), and which are incumbent on all, viz. 1. Charity or benevolence (*dana*). 2. Virtue or moral goodness (*sila*). 3. Patience and forbearance (*kshanti*). 4. Fortitude (*virya*). 5. Meditation (*dhyana*). 6. Knowledge (*prajna*)[1]. Of these, that which especially characterizes Buddhism is the perfection of benevolence and sympathy displayed towards all living beings, and carried to the extreme of avoiding injury to the most minute animalculae and treating with tenderness the most noxious animals. Even self-sacrifice for the good of such animals and of inferior creatures of all kinds is a duty. It is recorded of the Buddha himself that in former existences he frequently gave himself up as a substituted victim in the place of doves and other innocent creatures to satisfy the appetites of hawks and beasts of prey; and on one occasion, meeting with a famished tigress unable to feed her cubs, he was so overcome with compassion that he sacrificed his own body to supply the starving family with food[2].

These rules of conduct include many secondary precepts; for instance, not only is untruthfulness prohibited, but all offensive and bad language; not only is patience enjoined, but the bearing of injuries, resignation under misfortune, humility, repentance, and the practice of confessing sins, which last

---

1. Four others are sometimes added, making — 7. *Upaya*, 'expediency.' 8. *Bala*, 'power.' 9 *Pranidhi*, 'circumspection.' 10. *Jnana*, 'knowledge of universal truth.' See Lalita-vistara by Rajendralal Mitra, p. 7.
2. Modern Buddhism is not so tender to animals as Jainism, and in China animal food is eaten.

appears to have been regarded as possessing in itself some
kind of expiatory efficacy[1].

The following is an abridged version of Buddha's outburst
of joy at having achieved, by the knowledge of truth,
emancipation from the troubles of life and solved for himself
the great problem of existence[2]:

> See what true knowledge has effected here!
> The lust and anger which infest the world,
> Arising from delusion, are destroyed
> Like thieves condemned to perish. Ignorance
> And worldly longings, working only evil,
> By the great fire of knowledge are burnt up
> With all their mass of tangled roots. The cords
> And knots of lands and houses and possessions,
> And selfishness, which talks of 'self' and 'mine,'
> Are severed by the weapons of my knowledge.
> The raging stream of lust which has its source

---

1. In the edicts of Piya-dasi (Sanskrit Priya-darsi), supposed to be the
same as Ashoka, one of the Buddhist kings of Magadha, who lived
in the third century B.C., the people are commanded to confess their
sins publicly very five years. Four great Buddhist councils were held,
viz. 1. By Ajata-satru, king of Magadha after the Buddha's death
(which occurred, according to the opinion of the generality of
scholars, about 543 B.C.); 2. By Kalasoka, a century later; 3. By
Asoka, 246 or 247 B.C.; 4. By Kanishka, king of Kashmir, 143 B.C.
At the first council all the teachings and sayings of the Buddha, who
appears never to have written anything, were collected into three
sets of books, called Tri-pitaka, 'the three baskets or collections,'
which form the Buddhist sacred scriptures. These three collections
are — 1. The Sutra-pitaka, collected by Ananda, the Buddha's cousin,
containing all the maxims and discourses of Sakyamuni, and by no
means brief like the Brahmanical Sutras; 2. the Vinaya-pitaka, on
containing books on morals and discipline; 3 the Abhidarma-Pitaka,
on metaphysics and philosophy (see Introduction, xxxii. Note 1).
Professor Kern, in his recent learned dissertation on Buddha, makes
the date of Buddha's death 388 B.C.
2. The original text is given by Professor Banerjea, Dialogues, p. 198.

In evil thoughts, fed by concupiscence,
And swollen by sight's waters, are dried up
By the bright sun of knowledge; and the forest
Of trouble, slander, envy, and delusion,
Is by the flame of discipline consumed.
Now I have gained release, and this world's bonds
Are cut asunder by the knife of knowledge.
Thus I have crossed the ocean of the world,
Filled with the shark-like monsters of desire,
And agitated by the waves of passion —
Borne onward by the boat of stern resolve.
Now I have tasted the immortal truth —
Known also to unnumbered saints of yore —
That frees mankind from sorrow, pain, and death.

This imperfect sketch of Buddhism in its earliest and purest phase may conduce to the better understanding of the other lines of Indian rationalism, which differed from it in pretending to accept the authority of the Veda.

These lines were before described as six in number, but they are practically reducible to three, the *Nyaya,* the *Sankhya,* and the *Vedanta.* They all hold certain tenets in common with each other and to a certain extent also (especially the Sankhya) with heretical Buddhism.

A common philosophical creed, as we have already hinted, must have prevailed in India long before the crystallization of rationalistic inquiry into separate systems. If not distinctly developed in the Upanishads, it is clearly traceable throughout Manu[1]; and as it is not only the faith of every Indian philosopher at the present day, but also of the greater number of thinking Brahmans, whether disciples of any particular philosophical school or not, and indeed of the greater number of educated Hindus, whether nominal adherents of Vishnu or Shiva or to

---

1. See Manu XII, 12, 15-18.

whatever caste they may belong — its principal features may be advantageously stated before pointing out the chief differences between the six systems.

1. In the first place, then, rationalistic Brahmanism — as I propose to call this common faith — holds the eternity of soul, both retrospectively and prospectively[1]. It looks upon soul as of two kinds: a. the supreme Soul (called variously *Paramatman,* Brahman, &c.); b. the personal individuated soul of living beings (*jivatman*) [2]; and it maintains that if any entity is eternal it cannot have had a beginning, or else it must have an end. Hence the personal soul of every human being, just as the supreme Soul, has existed everlastingly and will never cease to exist[3].

2. In the second place this creed asserts the eternity of the matter or substance constituting the visible universe, or of that substance out of which the universe has been evolved; in other words, of its substantial or material cause[4]. It is very true that one system (the Vedanta) identifies soul with this

---

1. Plato appears to have held the same: Phaed. 51. And again: Phaed. 52. And again: Cicero expresses it thus: Id *autem nec nasci potest nec mori,* Tusc. Quaest. I. 23. Plato, however, seems to have given no eternity to individual souls, except as emanations from the divine; and in Timaeus 44 he distinguishes two parts of the soul, one immortal, the other mortal.

2. All the systems, as we shall see, are not equally clear about the existence of a supreme Soul. One at least practically ignores such a soul. With regard to the *Sutratman,* see the Lecture on the Vedanta. The Buddhist also believes that all souls have existed from the beginning of a cycle, but, in opposition to the Brahman, holds that their end is *Nirvana.*

3. The Muslims have two words for eternity: I. azl, 'that eternity which has no beginning' (whence God is called Azali, 'having no beginning') and 2. abd, 'that eternity which has no end.'

4. The term for substantial or material cause is *samavayi-karana,* literally, 'inseparable inherent on material cause;' in the Vedanta *upadana-karana,* is used. With regard to the word 'matter,' see note, p. 68.

substance by asserting that the world was not made out of gross particles of matter, but out of soul itself, as its illusory material cause; but to affirm that the universe is a part of the one only existing soul is of course equivalent to maintaining the eternal existence of both. In real truth a Hindu philosopher's belief in the eternity of the world's substance, whether that substance has a real material existence or is simply illusory, arises from that fixed article of his creed, 'Ex nihilo nihil fit,' *navastuno vastu-siddhih*. In other words, A-satah saj jayeta kutas, 'how can an entity be produced out of a nonentity?'[1]

Though the Greek philosophers are not very definite in their views as to the eternity of matter or its nature, yet they seem to have acquiesced generally in the independent existence of some sort of primordial substance. Plato appears to have held that the elements before the creation were shapeless and soulless, but were moulded and arranged by the Creator (Timaeus 27) out of some invisible and formless essence (Timaeus 24). Aristotle in one passage describes the views of older philosophers who held that primeval substance was affected and made to undergo changes by some sort of affections like the Sankhya Gunas, whence all the universe was developed: Metaph. I. 3. (See wilson's Sankhya-karika, p. 53.) Aristotle adds his own opinion, 'It is necessary there should be a certain nature — either one or more — out of which other entities are produced.'

1. 'Nothing is produced out of nothing.' All the ancient philosophers of Greece and Rome seem also to have agreed upon this point, as Aristotle affirms. Lucretius (I. 150) starts with laying down the same principle : — 'Principium hinc nobis exordia sumet Nullam rem e nihilo gigni divinitus unquam.' Aristotle, in the third chapter of the first book of his Metaphysics, informs us that Thales made the primitive substance out of which the universe originated water, Anaximenes and Diogenes made it air, Heracleitus made it fire, Empedocles combined earth, air, fire, and water. Anaximander, on the other hand, regarded the primordial germ as an indeterminate but infinite or boundless principle. Other philosophers affirmed something similar in referring everything back to a confused chaos.

3. In the third place, the soul, though itself sheer thought and knowledge, can only exercise thought, consciousness, sensation, and cognition, and indeed can only act and will when connected with external and material objects of sensation[1], invested with some bodily form[2] and joined to

---

Parmenides made Desire his first principle, and Hesiod, quoted by Aristotle, says poetically, —
'First indeed of all was chaos; then afterwards
Earth with her broad breast (cf. Sanskrit *prithivi*);
Then Desire who is pre-eminent among all the Immortals.'
Lastly, the Eleatics, like the Indian Vedantists, were thoroughly pantheistic, and held that the universe was God and God the universe; in other words, that God was or the only one existing thing. With all these accounts compare the Rig-veda hymn on the creation, translated on p. 23.

1. It is difficult to find any suitable word to express what the Hindus mean by material objects. There seems, in real truth, to be no proper Sanskrit word equivalent to 'matter' in its usual English sense. *Vastu,* as applied to the 'one reality,' is the term for the Vedantist's universal Spirit; *dravya* stands for soul, mind, time, and space, as well as the five elements; *murtti* is anything which has definite limits, and therefore includes mind and the four elements, but no *akasha,* 'ether;' *pradhana* is the original producer of the Sankhya system; *padartha* is used for the seven categories of the Vaiseshika. What is here meant is not necessarily a collection of material atoms, nor, again, that imperceptible substance propounded by some as lying underneath and supporting all visible phenomena (disbelieved in by Berkeley), and holding together the attributes or qualities of everything, but rather what is seen, heard, felt, tasted, and touched, which is perhaps best denoted by the Sanskrit word *vishaya,* the terms *samavayi-karana* and *upadana-karana* being generally used for the substantial or the material cause of the universe.

2. All the systems assign to each person two bodies: a. an exterior or gross body (*sthula-sharira*); b. an interior or subtle body (*sukshma-sarira* or *linga-sahrira*). The last is necessary as a vehicle for the soul when the gross body is dissolved, accompanying it through all its transmigrations and sojournings in heaven or hell, and never becoming separated from it till its emancipation is effected. The Vedanta

mind (*manas*), which last (viz. mind) is an internal organ of sense (*antah-karana*) [1] — a sort of inlet of thought to the soul — belonging only to the body, only existing with it, and quite as distinct from the soul as any of the external organs of the body [2]. The supreme Soul (variously called *Paramatman, Brahman,* neut., &c.) has thus connected itself in successive ages with objects and forms, becoming manifest either as Brahma the creator or in the form of other gods, as Vishnu and Siva (see note 1, p. 12), or again in the form of men.

4. Fourthly, this union of the soul with the body is productive of bondage, and in the case of human souls, of misery, for when once so united the soul begins to apprehend objects through the senses, receiving therefrom painful and pleasurable impressions. It also becomes conscious of personal

---

affirms the existence of a third body, called *karana-sharira* or causal body, described as a kind of inner rudiment or latent embryo of the body existing with the soul, and by some regarded as primeval ignorance united with the soul in dreamless sleep. The Platonists and other Greek and Roman philosophers seem to have held a similar doctrine as to a subtle material envelope investing the soul after death, serving as its vehicle. See Plato, Timaeus 17. This is like the idea of a deceased person's ghost or shade (umbra, imago, simulacrum). Cf. Virgil, Aeneid, VI. 390, 701.

1. *Manas* is often taken as the general term applicable to all the mental powers, but *Manas* is properly a subdivision of *antah-karana*, which is divided into '*Buddhi,* 'perception or intellection;' *Ahankara,* 'self-consciousness;' and *Manas,* 'volition or determination;' to which the Vedanta adds a fourth division, *Chitta,* 'the thinking or reasoning organ.'

2. This idea of the mind agrees to a great extent with the doctrine of Lucretius, stated in III. 94, &c.:

   'Primum animum dico (mentem quem saepe vocamus)
   In quo\consilium vitae regimenque locatum est,
   Esse hominis partem nihilo minus ac manus et pes
   Atque oculi partes animantis totius extant.'

The remainder of his description of the mind is very interesting in connection with the Hindu theory.

existence and individuality; then it commences to act but all action, whether good or bad, leads to bondage, because every act inevitably entails a consequence, according to the maxim, *Avasyam eva bhoktavyam kritam karma subhasubham,* 'the fruit of every action good or bad must of necessity be eaten.' Hence, if an act be good it must be rewarded, and if bad it must be punished[1].

5. Fifthly, in order to accomplish the entire working out of the these consequence or 'ripenings of acts' as they are called (karma-vipakah[2]), it is not enough that the personal soul goes to heaven or to hell. Merit or demerit, resulting from the inexorable retributive efficacy of former acts, continues clinging to the soul as grease does to a pot after it has been emptied. The necessity for removal to a place of reward or punishment is indeed admitted[3]; but this is not

---

1. In the Pancha-tantra (II. 135, 136) we read: 'An evil act follows a man, passing through a hundred thousand transmigrations; in like manner the act of a high-minded man. As shade and sunlight are ever closely joined together, so an act and the agent stick close to each other.'

2. Bad consequences are called *Dur-vipaka.* Some of these, in the shape of diseases, &c., are detailed by Manu (XI. 48-52). Thus any one who has stolen gold in a former life will suffer from whitlows on his nails, a drinker of spirits will have black teeth, and the killer of a Brahman, consumption. In the Sabda-kalp-druma, under the head of *Karma-vipaka,* will be found a long catalogue of the various diseases with which men are born as the fruit of evil deeds committed in former states of existence, and a declaration as to the number of births through which each disease will be protracted, unless expiations (*prayaschitta*) be performed in the present life, as described in the eleventh book of Manu.

3. The twenty-one hells (*Narakas*) are enumerated in Manu IV. 88-90. One is a place of terrific darkness; another a pit of red-hot charcoal; another a forest whose leaves are swords; another is filled with fetid mud; another is paved with iron spikes. These are not to be confounded with the seven places under the earth, of which Patala

effectual or final. In order that the consequences of acts may be entirely worked out, the soul must leave heaven or hell and return to corporeal existence. Thus it has to pass through innumerable bodies, migrating into higher, intermediate or lower forms, from a god[1] to a demon, man, animal, or plant, or even a stone, according to its various shades of merit or demerit[2].

---

is one, the abode of a kind of serpent demon. The Buddhists have one hundred and thirty-six hells in the interior of the earth, with regular gradations of suffering. Hindus and Buddhists have also numerous heavens. The former make six regions rising above earth, the seventh; viz. *bhur* (earth), *bhuvar, svar, mahar, janar, tapah, satya.*

1. The gods themselves are only finite beings. They are nothing but portions of the existing system of a perishing universe. In fact, they are represented as actually feeding on the oblations offered to them (see Bhagavad-gita III. 11); they go through penances (see Manu XI. 221); they are liable to passions and affections like men and animals, and are subject, as regards their corporeal part, to the same law of dissolution, while their souls obey the same necessity of ultimate absorption into the supreme soul. The following occurs in the Sankhya-karita (p. 3 of Wilson) : — 'Many thousands of Indras and other gods have, through time, passed away in every mundane age, for time cannot be overcome.' Muir's Texts, vol. v. p. 16.

2. According to Manu XII. 3, *Shubhashubha-phalam karma mano-vagdeha-sambhavam karma-ja gatayo nrinam uttamadhama-madhyamah.*, 'an act either mental, verbal, or corporeal bears good or evil fruit; the various transmigrations of men through the highest, middle, and lowest stages are produced by acts.' This triple order of transmigration is afterwards (XII. 40, &c.) explained to be the passage of the soul through deities, men, and beasts and plants, according to the dominance of one or other of the three Gunas goodness, passion, or darkness. And each of these three degress of transmigration has three sub-degrees. The highest of the first degree is Brahma himself, the lowest of the lowest is any *sthavara* or 'stationary substance,' which is explained to mean either a vegetable or a mineral; other lowest forms of the lowest degree are in an upward order worms, insects, fish, reptiles, snakes, tortoises, &c. Again, in VI. 61, 63, we read: Let the man who has renounced the

6. Sixthly, this transmigration of the soul through a constant succession of bodies, which is as much a fixed and peremptory doctrine of Buddhism as of Hinduism[1], is to be regarded as

---

world reflect on the transmigrations of men caused by the fault of their acts (*karma-dosha*); on their downfall into hell and their torments in the abode of Yama; on their formation again in the womb and the glidings of the soul through ten millions of other wombs. Again, in XII. 54, 55, &c.: Those who have committed great crimes, having passed through terrible hells for many series of years, at the end of that time pass through various bodies. A Brahman-killer enters the body of a dog, boar, ass, camel, bull, goat, sheep, stag, bird, &c. the violator of the bed of a Guru migrates a hundred times into the forms of grasses, shrubs, plants, &c. In I. 49, XI. 143-146, it is clearly implied that trees and vegetables of all kinds have internal consciousness (*antahsanjna*), and are susceptible of pleasure and pain. The Buddhists have also a triple series of transmigrations, borrowed doubtless from the Brahmans. The highest is called *Mahayana*, the lowest *Hina-yana*. Buddha is said to have pointed out to his followers a broom which he affirmed had formerly been a novice who had neglected to sweep out the assembly-hall.

1. The doctrine of metempsychosis, however, does not appear to have taken hold of the Hindu mind when the Mantras were composed. There seems at least to be no allusion to it in the Rig-veda, see note, p. 20. It begins to appear, though not clearly defined, in the Brahmanas, and is fully developed in the Upanishads, Darsanas, and Manu. A passage in the Satapatha-brahmana (XI. 6. 1. 1.), quoted by Professor Weber and Dr. Muir, describes animals and plants as revenging in a future state of existence injuries and death inflicted on them by men in this life.

In Greece and Rome the doctrine of transmigration seems never to have impressed itself deeply on the popular mind. It was confined to philosophers and their disciples, and was first plainly taught by Pythagoras, who is said to have asserted that he remembered his own previous existences. He was followed by Plato, who is supposed by some to have been indebted to Hindu writers for his views on this subject. In the Timaeus (72, 73) he affirms his opinion that those who have lived unrighteously and effeminately will, at their next birth, be changed to women; those who have lived innocently but frivolously will become birds; those who have lived without knowledge

the root of all evil. Moreover, by it all the misery, inequality of fortune and diversity of character in the world is to be explained[1]. For even great genius, aptitude for special work, and innate excellence are not natural gifts, but the result of habits formed and powers developed through perhaps millions of previous existences. So again, sufferings of all kinds — weaknesses, sicknesses, and moral depravity — are simply the consequences of acts done by each soul, of its own free will, in former bodies, which acts exert upon that soul an irresistible power called very significantly *Adrishta,* because felt and *not seen.*

Thus the soul has to bear the consequences of *its own acts only.* It is tossed hither and thither at the mercy of a force set in motion by itself alone, but which can never be guarded

---

of the truths of philosophy will become beasts; and those whose lives have been marked by the extreme of ignorance and folly will become fishes, oysters, &c. He sums up thus: Virgil, in the sixth book of the Aeneid (680-751), describes the condition of certain souls, which, after going through a sort of purgatory for a thousand years in the lower regions, again ascend to earth and occupy new bodies.   .
The Jews seem to have known something of the doctrine, if we may judge by the question proposed to our Lord.: 'Who did sin, this man (i. e. in a former life) or his parents, that he was born blind?' John ix. 2.

1. Among Greek philosophers, Aristotle, in the eleventh book of his Metaphysics (ch. 10), goes into the origin of evil, and his view may therefore be compared with that of Hindu philosophers. He recognizes good as a paramount principle in the world, but admits the power of evil, and considers matter as its prime and only source, much in the same way as the Gnostics and other early Christian philosophical sects, who, like Indian philosophers, denied the possibility of anything being produced out of nothing, and repudiated the doctrine that God could in any way be connected with evil. They, therefore, supposed the eternal existence of a sluggish, inert substance, out of which the world was formed by God, but which contained in itself the principle of evil.

against, because its operation depends on past actions wholly beyond control and even unremembered[1].

7. Seventhly and lastly, from a consideration of these essential articles of Hindu Rationalism it is plain that the great aim of philosophy is to teach a man to abstain from every kind of action; from liking or disliking, from loving or hating, and even from being indifferent to anything.

The living personal soul must shake off the fetters of action and getting rid of body, mind, and all sense of separate personality, return to the condition of simple soul.

This constitutes *Prama* or *Jnana*, the true measure of all existing difficulties — the right apprehension of truth — which, if once acquired by the soul, confers upon it final

---

1. The absence of all recollection of acts done in former states of existence does not seem to strike the Hindus as an objection to their theory of transmigration. Most of the systems evade the difficulty by maintaining that at each death the soul is divested of mind, understanding, and consciousness. See Mullens' Essay p. 386. The Garbha Upanishad (4) attributes the loss of memory to the pain and pressure suffered by the soul in the act of leaving the womb. The mythology, however, records cases of men who were gifted with the power of recollecting former existences. In the Phaedo of Plato (47) Cebes is described as saying to Socrates, 'According to that doctrine which you are frequently in the habit of advancing, if it is true, that all knowledge is nothing else than reminiscence it is surely necessary that we must at some former time have learned what we now remember. But this is impossible, unless our soul existed somewhere before it came into this human form.' Cicero, in Tusc. Quaest. I. 24, says, speaking of the soul, 'Habet primam memoriam, et eam infinitam rerum innumerabilium, quam quidem Plato recordationem esse vult superioris vitae.' Cf. Sakuntala, Act V. 104 'Can it be that the dim memory of events long past, or friendships formed in other states of being, flits like a passing shadow o'er the spirit?' Virgil (Aeneid VI. 714) wisely makes the souls who are to occupy new bodies upon earth throng the banks of Lethe that they may drink a deep draught of oblivion from its waters.

emancipation, whether called *Mukti, Moksha, Nihsreyasa, Apavarga,* or *Nirvana*[1]. This, in short, is the summum bonum of philosophical Brahmanism; this is the only real bliss — the loss of all personality and separate identity by absorption into the supreme and only really existing Being — mere life with nothing to live for, mere joy with nothing to rejoice about, and mere thought with nothing upon which thought is to be exercised[2].

Having thus attempted to set forth common tenets of Indian philosophy, I must next indicate the principal points in which the systems differ from each other[3].

---

1. *Nirvana,* ' the being blown out,' is, as we have seen, the Buddhist expression for liberation from existence. The other terms are used by rationalistic Brahmanism. Two of the Darsanas, however, as we have seen, practically ignore a supreme Being

2. Mr. Hardwick has well shown that the great boon conferred by the Gospel, in contradistinction to these false systems, is the recognition of man's responsible free agency and the permanence of his personality. 'Not to be' is the melancholy result of the religion and philosophy of the Hindus. See 'Christ and other Masters,' vol. i. p. 355. Christianity satisfies the deepest want of man's religious life, viz. to know and love God as a person. See Canon Liddon's 'Elements of Religion,' p. 36.

3. These were explained in lectures to my highest class only.

Lecture IV

The Nyaya

We begin with the Nyaya of Gotama or Gautama, with its supplement, the Vaiseshika, not because this is first in order of time (see p. 52), but because it is generally the first studies, and much of its terminology is adopted by the other systems[1].

The word Nyaya signifies 'going into a subject,' that is, investigating it analytically. In this sense of 'analysis,' Nyaya is exactly opposed to the word Sankhya, 'synthesis.' It is common to suppose that the Nyaya is chiefly concerned with

---

1. The Nyaya sutras, consisting of five books, with the commentary, were printed at Calcutta in 1828, under the title of Nyaya-sutra-vritti. Four of the five books were edited and translated by the late. Dr. Ballantyne. He also published the Nyaya compendium, called Tarka-sangraha. A favourite text-book of this system is the Bhasha-pariccheda, with its commentary, called Siddhanta-muktavali. This has been edited and translated by Dr. Roer. The Vaiseshika Sutras, consisting of ten books, have quite recently been edited and translated in a scholarlike manner by Mr. A.E. Gough, one of my most distinguished Boden scholars, and now Anglo-Sanskrit Professor in the Government College, Benares. Professor E.B. Cowell's edition of the Kusumanjali, a Nyaya treatise proving the existence of a God, is an interesting work.

logic; but this is merely one part of a single topic. The fact rather is that this system was intended to furnish a correct method of philosophical inquiry into *all the object and subjects* of human knowledge, including, *amongst others,* the process of reasoning and laws of thought. The Nyaya proper differs from its later development, the Vaiseshika, by propounding sixteen topics in its first Sutra. The first topic of these sixteen is *Pramana,* that is, the means or instruments by which *Prama* or the right measure of any subject is to be obtained. Under this head are enunciated the different processes by which the mind arrives at true and accurate knowledge.

The processes are declared in the third Sutra of the first book to be four, viz.

a. *Pratyaksha,* 'perception by the senses.' b. *Anumana,* 'inference.' c. *Upamana,* 'comparison.' d. *Shabda,* 'verbal authority' or 'trustworthy testimony,' including Vedic revelation.

The treatment of the second of these, viz. inference, possesses more interest for Europeans, as indicating that the Hindus have not, like other nations, borrowed their logic and metaphysics from the Greeks.

Inference is divided in Sutra I. 32 into five Avayavas or 'members.'

1. The *pratijna* or proposition (stated hypothetically).
2. The *hetu* or reason.
3. The *udaharana* (sometimes called *nidarsana*) or example (equivalent to the major premiss).
4. The *upanaya* or application of the reason (equivalent to the minor premiss).
5. The *nigamana* or conclusion (i.e. the *pratijna* or 'proposition' re-stated as proved).

This method of splitting an inference or argument into five divisions is familiarly illustrated by native commentators thus:

1. The hill is fiery; 2. for it smokes; 3. whatever smokes is fiery, as a kitchen-hearth (or, inversely, not as a lake, which is invariably without fire); 4. this hill smokes; 5. therefore this hill is fiery.

Here we have a combination of enthymeme and syllogism, which seems clumsy by the side of Aristotle's more concise method; the fourth and fifth members being repetitions of the second and first, which therefore appear superfluous. But it possesses some advantages when regarded, not as a syllogism, but as a full and complete rhetorical statement of an argument.

Perhaps the most noticeable peculiarity in the Indian method, stamping it as an original and independent analysis of the laws of thought, is the use of the curious terms, *Vyapti,* 'invariable pervasion' or 'concomitance;' *Vyapaka,* 'pervader' or 'invariably pervading attribute;' and *Vyapya,* 'invariably pervaded.' These terms are employed in making a universal affirmation or in affirming universal distribution; as, for example, 'Wherever there is smoke there is fire.' 'Wherever there is humanity there is mortality.' In such cases an Indian logician always expresses himself by saying that there is an invariably pervading concomitance of fire with smoke and of mortality with humanity.

Similarly, fire and mortality are called the pervaders (*Vyapaka*), smoke and humanity the pervaded (*Vyapya*). The first argument would therefore be thus briefly stated by a *Naiyayika:* 'The mountain has invariably fire-pervaded smoke, therefore it has fire.'

To show the importance attached to a right understanding of this technical expression *Vyapti,* and to serve as a specimen of a Naiyayika writer's style, I now make an abridged extract from Shankara-mishra's comment on the fourteenth Sutra of the first daily lesson of the third book of the Vaiseshika Sutras (Gough, p. 86):

It may be asked, What is this invariable concomitance? (*Nanu keyam vyaptih.*) It is not merely a relation of co-extension. Nor is it the relation of totality. For if you say that invariable concomitance is the connection of the middle term with the whole of the major term (*kritsnasya sadhyasya sadhana-sambandhah*), such connection does not exist in the case of smoke, &c. [for although fire exists wherever smoke exists, smoke does not always exist where fire exists, not being found in red-hot iron]. Nor is it natural conjunction; for the nature of a thing is the thing's proper mode of being. Nor is it invariable co-inherence of the major, which is absent only when there is absolute non-existence of that of which the middle is predicated; for volcanic fire must always be non-existent in a kitchen-hearth, though smoky. Nor is it the not being a subject of incompatibility with the predicate. Nor is it the possession of a form determined by the same connection as something else; as, for instance, the being fiery is not determined by connection with smoke, for the being fiery is more extensive. We proceed, then, to state that invariable concomitance is a connection requiring no qualifying term or limitation (*an-aupadhikah sambandhah*) [1]. It is an extensiveness co-extensive with the predicate (*sadhya-vyapaka-vyapakatvam*). In other words, invariable concomitance is invariable co-inherence of the predicate[2].

The second head or topic of the Nyaya is *Prameya,* by which is meant all the objects or subjects of *Prama* — those

1. Hence, 'the mountain is smoky because it has fire' is not *vyapti,* but *ati-vyapti,* because the upadhi or qualification *ardrendana-jata,* 'produced by wet wood,' must be added to make the argument correct. When the middle term (fire) and the major (smoke) are made co-extensive then the fault of *ati-vyapti* is removed.
2. It would be difficult to convey to a general reader any idea of the terseness with which the use of long compounds enables all this to be expressed in the original Sanskrit. Of course the obscurity of the style is proportionably great, and the difficulty of translation enhanced. Mr. Gough, however, is not responsible for every word of the above.

points, in short, about which correct knowledge is to be obtained. This topic includes all the most important subjects investigated by Indian philosophy. The Prameyas are twelve, as given in the ninth Sutra; thus —

1.Soul (*atman*). 2. Body (*sharira*) 3. Senses (*indriya*). 4. Objects of sense (*artha*). 5. Understanding or intellection (*buddhi*). 6. Mind (*manas*). 7. Activity (*pravritti*). 8. Faults (*dosha*). 9. Transmigration (*pretya-bhava*). 10. Consequences or fruits (*phala*). 11. Pain (*duhkha*). 12. Emancipation (*apavarga*).

In his first topic Gautama provides for hearing opposing disputants who desire to discuss fairly any of these Prameyas which form his second topic.

With regard to his fourteen other topics, they seem to be not so much philosophical categories as an enumeration of the regular stages through which a controversy is likely to pass. In India argument slides into wrangling disputation even more easily than in Europe, and these remaining topics certainly illustrate very curiously the captious propensities of a Hindu disputant, leading him to be quick in repartee and ready with specious objections in opposition to the most conclusive logic. There is, first, the state of *Samsaya,* or 'doubt about the point to be discussed.' Next, there must be a *Prayojana,* or 'motive for discussing it.' Next, *Drishtanta,* or 'familiar example,' must be adduced in order that *Siddhanta,* or 'established conclusion,' may be arrived at. Then comes an objector with his *Avayava,* or 'argument' split up, as we have seen, into five members. Next follows the *Tarka,* or 'refutation (*reductio ad absurdum*) of his objection' and the *Nirnaya,* or 'ascertainment of the true state of the case.' But this is not enough to satisfy a Hindu's passion for disputation. Every side of a question must be examined — every possible objection stated — and so a further *Vada,* or 'controversy,' takes place, which of course leads to *Jalpa,* 'mere wrangling,' followed by

Vitanda, 'cavilling;' *Hetv-abhasa,* 'fallacious reasoning[1];' *Chala,* 'quibbling artifices;' *Jati,* 'futile replies;' and *Nigraha-sthana,* 'the putting an end to all discussion' by a demonstration of the objector's incapacity for argument.

The above are Gotama's sixteen topics. After enumerating them he proceeds to state how deliverance from the misery of repeated births is to be attained; thus —

Misery, birth, activity, fault, false notions; on the removal of these in turn (beginning with the last), there is the removal also of that which precedes it; then ensues final emancipation.

That is to say, from false notions comes the fault of liking, disliking, or being indifferent to anything; from that fault proceeds activity; from this mistaken activity proceed actions involving either merit or demerit, which merit or demerit forces a man *nolens volens* to pass through repeated births for the sake of its reward or punishment. From these births proceed misery, and it is the aim of philosophy to correct the false notions at the root of this misery.

A Naiyayika commentator, Vatsyayana, thus comments on the foregoing statement (Banerjea, p. 185):

From false notion proceed partiality and prejudice; thence come the faults of detraction, envy, delusion, intoxication, pride, avarice. Acting with a body, a person commits injury, thefts, and unlawful sensualities — becomes false, harsh, and slanderous. This vicious activity produces demerit. But to do acts of charity, benevolence, and service with the body; to be truthful, useful, agreeable in speech, or given to repetition of the Veda; to be kind, disinterested, and reverential — these produce merit

---

1. As an example of fallacious argument may be taken the sixteenth Aphorism of the third book of the Vaiseshika Sutras, *yasmad vishani tasmad ashvah,* 'because this has horns, therefore it is a horse;' or the next Sutra, *yasmad vishani tasmad gauh,* ' because it has horns, therefore it is a cow,' which last is the fallacy of 'undistributed middle.'

(*dharma*). Hence merit and demerit are fostered by activity. This activity is the cause of vile as well as honourable births. Attendant on birth is pain. That comprises the feeling of distress, trouble, disease, and sorrow. Emancipation is the cessation of all these. What intelligent person will not desire emancipation from all pain? For, it is said, food mixed with honey and poison is to be rejected. Pleasure joined with pain is to be avoided.

I pass at once to the most important part of the Nyaya system, its supplement:

The Vaiseshika

We now come to the *Vaiseshika* development of the Nyaya, attributed to an author Kanada[1]. This is not so much a branch of this system as a supplement to it, extending the Nyaya to physical inquiries, which it does very imperfectly, it is true, and often with strange fancies and blunders; but, nevertheless, with occasional exactness and not infrequently with singular sagacity. It is certainly the most interesting of all the systems, both from its more practical character and from the parallels it offers to European philosophical ideas. It begins by arranging its inquiries under seven *Padarthas,* which, as they are more properly categories (i. e. an enumeration of certain general properties or attributes that may be predicated or affirmed of existing things[2]), are now the generally received categories

1. This was probably a mere nickname, meaning 'Feeder on Atoms.' He is also called Uluka. Gautama, the author of the Nyaya proper, had also a nickname, *Aksha-pada,* 'eye-footed,' having his eyes always fixed in abstraction on his feet, or supernaturally gifted with eyes in his feet, because too absent to see with those in his head.
2. Thus man is a substance, so also is a chair and a stone; whiteness, blackness, breadth, and length, though very different things, are yet all qualities &c.

of *Naiyayikas*. They are as follows: 1. Substance (*dravya*). 2. Quality or property (*guna*). 3. Act or action (*karman*). 4. Generality or community of properties (*samanya*). 5. Particularity or individuality (*visesha*). 6. Co-inherence or perpetual intimate relation (*samavaya*). 7. Non-existence or negation of existence (*abhava*)[1].

Kanada, however, the author of the Sutras enumerated only six categories. The seventh was added by later writers. This is stated in the fourth Sutra of book I; thus (Gough's translation, p. 4):

The highest good results from knowledge of the truth which springs from particular merit, and is obtained by means of the similarity and dissimilarity of the categories, substance, attribute, action, generality, particularity, co-inherence.

---

1. It is interesting to compare the ten Aristotelian categories. They are: 1. 'Substance.' 2. 'How much?' 'Quantity.' 3. 'Of what kind?' 'Quality.' 4. 'In relation to what?' 'Relation.' 5. 'Action.' 6. 'Passiveness' or 'Passivity.' 7. 'Where?' 'Position in space.' 8. 'When?' 'Position in time.' 9. 'Local situation' 10. 'Possession.' Mr. J.S. Mill, in his Logic, declares that this enumeration is both redundant and defective. Some objects are admitted and others repeated under different heads. 'It is like,' he says, 'a division of animals into men, quadrupeds, horses, asses, and ponies.' Action, passivity, and local situation ought not to be excluded from the category of relation, and the distinction between position in space and local situation is merely verbal. His own enumeration of all existing or describable things is as follows: 1. 'Feelings or states of consciousness.' Even the external world is only known as conceived by the mind. 2. 'The minds' which experience those feelings. 3. 'The bodies,' supposed to excite feelings or sensations. 4. 'The successions and co-existences, the likenesses and unlikenesses' between the feelings. Further, he shows that all possible propositions affirm or deny one or other of the following properties or facts: 1. Existence, the most general attribute. 2. Co-existence. 3. Sequence or Succession. 4. Causation. 5. Resemblance. See Chambers' Cyclopaedia, under the article 'Categories.'

The commentator adds:

In this place there is mention of six categories, but in reality non-existence is also implied by the sage as another category.

The seven categories are all subdivided.
Let us being with the first category of *Dravya* or 'substance.' The fifth Sutra makes the following enumeration of nine Dravyas:

Earth (*prithivi*), water (*apas*), light (*tejas*), air (*vayu*), ether (*akasha*), time (*kala*), space (*dish*), soul (*atman*), the internal organ, mind (*manas*) are the substances.

The commentator adds:

If it be objected, there is a tenth substance, darkness (*tamas*), why is it not enumerated? For it is recognized by perception, and substantially belongs to it, because it is possessed of colour and action; and because devoid of odour, it is not earth; and because it possesses dark colour, it is not water, &c.: we reply that it is not so, because it is illogical to imagine another substance, when it is necessarily produced by non-existence of light.

It should be stated that of these substances the first four (earth, water, light, and air) and the last (mind) are held to be atomic, and that the first four are both eternal and non-eternal — non-eternal in their various compounds, eternal in their ultimate atoms, to which they must be traced back[1].

---

1. According to the Platonic school, substances are ranged under two heads — a. perceptible by the mind and immovable; b. perceptible by the senses and in motion. Aristotle, in his Metaphysics (XI. 1.), seems to divide substances into three classes — a. those that are cognizable by the mind, immovable, unchangeable, and eternal; b. those cognizable by the senses and eternal; c. those cognizable by the senses and subject to decay, as plants and animals. In another place (VII. 8) he defines substance as the essence or very nature of

Next follows the second category of 'quality.' The sixth Sutra enumerates seventeen qualities or properties which belong to or are inherent in the nine substances:

Colour (*rupa*), savour (*rasa*), odour (*gandha*), tangibility (*sparsha*), numbers (*sankhyah*), extensions (*parimanani*), individuality (*prithaktva*), conjunction (*samyoga*), disjunction (*vibhaga*), priority (*parativa*), posteriority (*aparatva*), intellections (*buddhayah*), pleasure (*sukha*), pain (*duhkha*), desire (*iccha*), aversion (*dvesha*), volitions (*prayatnah*) are (the seventeen) qualities.

The commentator Shankara-mishra adds seven others, which, he says, are implied, though not mentioned, making twenty-four in all. They are:

Gravity (*gurutva*), fluidity (*dravatva*), viscidity (*sneha*), self-reproduction (*sanskara*, implying — *a.* impetus as the cause of activity; *b.* elasticity; *c.* the faculty of memory), merit, demerit, and sound.

In point of fact the Nyaya goes more philosophically and more correctly than the other systems into the qualities of all substances. The twenty-four which it enumerates may be regarded as separating into two classes, according as they are the sixteen qualities of material substances or the eight properties of soul. These eight are intellection, volition, desire, aversion, pleasure, pain, merit, and demerit.

---

a thing. Again, in illustration (IV. 8), he says that whatever may be the cause of being is a substance, as soul in an animal; and again, as many inherent parts in anything as define and indicate *what it is, e. g.* superficies, a line, number, and that essence of which the formal cause is the definition; and, thirdly, he says that earth, fire, water, &c., and all bodies and all animals consisting of these are substances. See the Rev. J.H. M'Mahon's useful translation, published by Bohn.

The third category, *Karman*, 'act' or 'action,' is thus divided in Sutra I. 1. 7:

Elevation (literally throwing upwards), depression (throwing downwards), contraction, dilatation, and going (or motion in general) are the (five kinds of) acts. [*Utkshepanam avakshepanam akuncanam prasaranam gamanam iti karmani.*]

The fourth category, *Samanya*, 'generality,' is said to be twofold, viz. higher (*para*) and lower (*apara*);the first being 'simple existence,' applicable to genus; the second being 'substantiality,' applicable to species.

The fifth category, *Visesha*, particularity,' belongs to the nine eternal substances of the first category, viz. soul, time, place, ether, and the five atoms of earth, water, light, air, and mind, all of which have an eternal ultimate difference, distinguishing each from the other.

The sixth category, *Samavaya*, 'co-inherence' or 'intimate relation,' is of only one kind. This relation appears to be that which exists between a substance and its qualities, between atoms and what is formed out of them, or between any object and the general idea connected with it, and is thought to be a real entity, every much in accordance with the Platonic realism of the Middle Ages. It is the relation between a jar and the earth which composes it, between a cloth and its threads, between the idea of round and any round thing, between a whole and its parts, between a genus of species and its individuals, between an act and its agents, between individuality and eternal substance.

In connection with this sixth category may be mentioned the Nyaya theory of causation. Sutra I. 2. 1, 2. states —

From non-existence of cause (*karana*) is non-existence of effect (*karya*), but there is not from non-existence of effect non-existence of cause.

In the Tarka-sangraha a cause is declared to be 'that which invariably precedes an effect which otherwise could not be,' and three kinds of cause are enumerated, viz.

a. Co-inherence cause, or that resulting from intimate and constant relation — perhaps best rendered by 'substantial cause' (*samavayi-karvana*), as threads are the substantial cause of cloth. This corresponds to the material cause of Aristotle. *b.* Non-substantial cause (*a-samavayi-karana*), as the putting together of the threads is of cloth. This corresponds to the formal cause. *c.* Instrumental cause (*nimitta-karana*), as the weaver's tools, the loom, or the skill of the weaver himself, &c. are of cloth. This corresponds to the efficient cause[1].

As to the seventh category of non-existence or negation, four kinds are specified, viz.

a. Antecedent (or the non-existence of anything before it began to exist, as a jar not yet made). *b.* Cessation of existence (as of a jar when it is smashed to pieces). *c.* Mutual non-existence (as of a jar in cloth). *d.* Absolute non-existence (as of fire in a lake).

Without dwelling longer on the seven categories we must briefly indicate how the views of the *Nyaya* and *Vaiseshika*,

---

1. Aristotle's four causes are — 1. Material cause, i.e. the matter from which anything is made, as marble of a statue, silver of a goblet. 2. Formal cause, i.e. the specific form or pattern according to which anything is made, as a drawing or plan is the formal cause of the building of a house. 3. Efficient cause, i.e. the origin of the principle of motion as the energy of a workman is the prime mover in producing any work. 4. Final cause, i.e. the purpose for which anything is made, the motive for its production, or the end served by its existence. According to Dr. Ballantyne (Lecture on the Nyaya, p. 23), Aristotle's final cause has a counterpart in the Naiyayika's *prayojana*, i.e. motive, purpose, or use. The writer in Chambers' Cyclopaedia, under the head of 'Cause,' shows that these causes of Aristotle and the Nyaya should rather be called the aggregate of *conditions* necessary to the production of any work of man.

as to the external world and the nature of soul, differ from those of the other systems. First, then, as to the formation of the world. This is supposed to be effected by the aggregation of *Anus* or 'atoms.' These are innumerable and eternal, and are eternally aggregated, disintegrated, and redintegrated by the power of Adrishta. According to Kanada's Sutras (IV. 1) an atom is 'something existing having no cause, eternal' (*sad akaranavan nityam*). They are, moreover, described as less than the least, invisible, intangible, indivisible, imperceptible by the senses; and — what is most noteworthy in distinguishing the Vaiseshika system from others — as having each of them a *Vishesha* or eternal essence of its own. The combination of these atoms is first into an aggregate of two, called *Dvy-anuka.* Three of them, again, are supposed to combine into a *Trasa-renu,* which, like a mote in a sunbeam, has just sufficient magnitude to be perceptible[1].

According to Colebrooke's statement of the Vaiseshika theory the following process is supposed to take place in the aggregation of atoms to form earth, water, light, and air:

Two earthly atoms concurring by an unseen peculiar virtue (*a-drishta*) or by the will of God, or by time, or by other competent cause, constitute a double atom of earth; and by concourse of three binary atoms a tertiary atom is produced, and by concourse of four triple atoms a quaternary atom, and so on to a gross, grosser, or grossest mass of earth; thus great

---

1. The binary compound only differs from the single atom by number, and not by measure, size, or perceptibility. Both are infinitesimal, and, being joined, can only produce an infinitesimal result (like multiplied fractions). It is the tertiary compound which first introduces magnitude and causes measure, just as a jar's measure is caused by that of its two halves. See Professor Cowell's translation of the Kusumanjali, p. 66.

earth is produced; and in like manner great water from aqueous atoms, great light from luminous, and great air from aerial[1].

From the Tarka-sangraha we may continue the account thus:

a. Earth possesses the property of odour, which is its distinguishing quality. It is of two kinds, eternal and non-eternal — eternal in the form of atoms (*paramanu-rupa*), non-eternal in the form of products (*karya-rupa*). The non-eternal character of aggregated earth is shown by the want of permanence in a jar when crushed to powder. When aggregated it is of three kinds, organized body (*sharira*), organ of sense (*indriya*), and unorganic mass (*vishaya*). The organ connected

---

1. As these Lectures were delivered before classical scholars I thought it superfluous, at the time of their delivery, to indicate all the obvious points of comparison between Indian and European systems. Reference might here, however, be made to the doctrines of Epicurus, especially as expounded by Lucretius, who begins his description of the coalescing of atoms or primordial seeds to form the world and various material objects thus:

'Nunc age, quo motu genitalia materiai
Corpora res varias gignant, genitasque resolvant
Et qua vi facere id cogantur, quaeve sit ollis
Reddita mobilitas magnum per inane meandi
Expediam.' (II. 61-64.)

Nearly the whole of the second book of Lucretius might be quoted. It is full of interest in connection with the Vaiseshika system. Cicero's criticisms on the Epicurean theory are also interesting in relation to this subject. In his De Natura Deorum (II. 37) he says, 'If a concourse of atoms could produce a world (*quod si mundum efficere potest concursus atomorum*), why not also a portico, a temple, a house, a city, which are much less difficult to form?' We might even be tempted to contrast some of the discoveries of modern chemists and physicists with the crude but shrewd ideas of Indian philosophers prosecuting their investigations more than 2000 years ago without the aids and appliances now at every one's command.

with it is the nose or sense of smell (*ghrana*), which is the recipient of odour. *b*. Water possesses the property of being cool to the touch. It is also of two kinds, eternal and non-eternal, as before. Its organ is the tongue or taste (*rasana*), the recipient of savour, which is one of the qualities of water. *c*. Light is distinguished by being hot to the feel[1]. It is similarly of two kinds, and its organ is the eye (*chakshus*), the recipient of colour or form, which is its principal quality. *d*. Air is distinguished by being sensible to the touch. It is similarly of two kinds, and is colourless. Its organ is the skin (*tvac*), the percipient of tangibility. *e*. Ether is the substratum of the quality of sound. It is eternal, one, and all-pervading. Its organ is the ear (*srotra*), the recipient of sound[2].

The great commentator Shankaracharya (quoted by Professor Banerjea, p. 62) states the process thus:

'At the time of creation action is produced in aerial atoms, which is dependent on A-drishta. That action joins its own atom with another. Then from binaries, by gradual steps, is produced the air. The same is the case with fire. The same with water. The same with earth. The same with organized bodies[3]. Thus is the whole universe produced from atoms[4].'

---

1. Light and heat are regarded by Naiyayikas as one and the same substance. Curiously enough, gold is described as mineral (*akara-ja*) light.
2. Professor H.H. Wilson has observed (Sankhya-karika, p. 122) that something like the Hindu notion of the senses and the elements partaking of a common nature is expressed in the dictum of Empedocles: 'By the earthy element we perceive earth; by the watery, water; by the aerial element, the air of heaven; and by the element of fire, devouring fire.' Plato, Repub. VI. 18, has the following: 'I regard it (the eye) as of all the organs of sense possessing most likeness to the sun.' See Muir's Texts V. 298.
3. In Manu (I. 75-78) and the Sankhya and the Vedanta the order of the elements is ether, air, light or fire, water, and earth. See p. 100,101.
4. Compare Cicero, De Natura Deorum II. 33, 'Since there are four sorts of elements, the continuance of the world is caused by their

With regard to the question whether God or the supreme Soul is to be regarded as having taken part in the bringing together and arranging of these atoms, it should be noted that although the name of *Ishvara* is introduced once into Gotama's Sutras[1], it is not found in Kanada's[2]. Probably the belief of both was that the formation of the world was simply the result of *Adrishta*, or 'the unseen force, which is derived from the works or acts of a previous world,' and which becomes in Hindu philosophy a kind of god, if not the only god (see p. 73). Later Naiyayika writers, however, affirm the existence of a supreme Soul, *Paramatman*, distinct from the *Jivatman*, or 'human soul;' and this supreme Soul is described as eternal, immutable, omniscient, without form, all-pervading, all-powerful, and, moreover, as the framer of the universe.

Thus the Tarka-sangraha states (Ballantyne, p. 12):

The seat of knowledge is the soul (*atman*). It is twofold, the living soul (*jivatman*) and the supreme soul (*paramatman*). The supreme soul is lord, omniscient, one only, subject to neither pleasure nor pain, infinite and eternal.

---

reciprocal action and changes (*vicissitudine*). For from the earth comes water; from water arises air; from air, ether; and then conversely in regular order backwards, from ether, air; from air, water; from water, earth, the lowest element.

1. The Sutra is IV. 5. 19, and is as follows. Some one suggests, 'God is the (sole) cause, because we see that the acts of men are occasionally unattended by their fruits' (*ishvarah karanam purusha-karmaphalya-darshanat*). The next Aphorism is an answer to this suggestion, and seems to assert that God was *not* the cause of the universe; thus, 'Not so, because in the absence of men's acts the fruit is not produced.' The next Aphorism runs thus: 'It (man's agency?) is not the (sole) cause, because that is caused by that.' The word 'sole,' however, is introduced by the commentator, and all three Aphorisms seem designedly obscure.

2. According to Banerjea, p. 62; but the commentators say it is implied in the third Sutra.

Indeed the Nyaya is held by some to be the stronghold of Theism.

As to the living individual souls of corporeal beings, the Nyaya view is that they are eternal, manifold[1], eternally separate from each other and distinct from the body, senses, and mind, yet capable of apprehension, volition (or effort), desire, aversion, pleasure, pain, merit, and demerit.

In the Vaiseshika Aphorisms (III. 2. 4) other characteristic signs (*lingani*) of the living soul are given, such as the opening and shutting of the eyes, the motions of the mind and especially life[2]. The commentator, in commenting upon this, describes the soul as the 'governor or superintendent over the body.' Here is the passage (Gough, p. 110):

Vitality is a mark of the existence of the soul; for by the word 'life' the effects of vitality, such as growth, the healing of wounds and bruises, are implied. For as the owner of a house builds up the broken edifice or enlarges a building which is too small, so the ruler of the body effects by food, &c., the increase and enlargement of the body, which is to him in the stead of a habitation, and with medicine and the like causes what is wounded to grow again and mutilated hands or feet to heal. Thus a superintendent of the body (*dehasya adhishthata*) is proved like a master of a house.

It should be added that souls are held to be infinite, ubiquitous, and *diffused everywhere throughout space,* so that a man's soul is as much in England as in Calcutta, though it can only apprehend and feel and act where the body happens to be.

---

1. According to the Vaiseshika-sutra III. 2. 20, *Vyavashato nana,* 'because of its circumstances (or conditions), soul is manifold.' The commentator adds, 'Circumstances are the several conditions; as, one is rich, another mean; one is happy, another unhappy; one is of high, another of low birth; one is learned, another read badly. These circumstances evince a diversity and plurality of souls.'
2. Plato (Phaedrus 52) defines soul as quoted by Cicero, Tusc. Quaest. I. 23.

The Nyaya idea of the mind or internal organ (*Manas*) is that it, like the soul, is a Dravya or 'eternal substance.' Instead, however, of being diffused everywhere like the soul, it is atomic, like earth, water, fire and air. Indeed, if it were infinite, like the soul, it might be united with all subjects at once, and all apprehensions might be contemporaneous, which is impossible. It is therefore regarded as a mere atom or atomic inlet to the soul, not allowing the latter to receive more than one thought or conception at a time. So in Nyaya-sutra. I. 3. 16, and in Vaiseshika VIII. 1. 22, 23, it is affirmed as follows:

'The characteristic of the mind is that it does not give rise to more than one notion simultaneously.' 'Ether, in consequence of its universal pervasion, is infinitely great, and so likewise is soul. In consequence of non-existence of that universal pervasion, the internal organ (mind) is an atom[1].'

In regard to the authority to be accorded to the Veda, the views of the Nyaya appear by no means unorthodox. Gautama, in his Aphorisms (II. 58-60, 68), declares plainly that the Veda is not false, that it is not chargeable either with self-contradiction or tautology, and that it is an instrument of true knowledge. Similarly, the third Aphorism of Kanada may be regarded as a kind of confession of faith in the Veda, intended apparently, like that of Gautama, to counteract imputations of heterodoxy.

In further proof of the Theism claimed for the Nyaya I here give a short passage from the Kusumanjali, a Naiyayika treatise by Udayana Acharya, which will serve as a specimen of the sort of arguments employed to prove the existence of a personal God (Ishvara) in opposition to atheistical objectors.

---

1. The theory propounded by Lucretius was that the mind is composed of exceedingly subtle atoms; he says (III. 180) of it, 'Esse aio persubtilem atque minutis Perquam corporibus factum constare.' As to ether, see note 2, p. 100.

This work has been ably edited and translated by Professor E.B. Cowell[1]. The following is merely the opening of the fifth chapter, with a portion of Hari-dasa's comment:

> An omniscient and indestructible Being is to be proved from the existence of effects, from the combination of atoms, from the support of the earth in the sky, from traditional arts, from belief in revelation, from the Veda, from its sentences, and from particular numbers.

Comment: The earth must have had a maker, because it is an effect like a jar. Combination is an action, and therefore the action which produced the conjunction of two atoms at the beginning of a creation must have been accompanied by the volition of an intelligent being. Again, the world depends upon some being who wills to hinder it from falling, like a stick supported by a bird in the air. Again, the traditional arts (*pada*) now current, as that of making cloth, &c., must have proceeded from an independent being. Again, the knowledge derived from the Veda is derived from a virtue residing in its cause, because it is true knowledge[2], (this virtue consisting in the Veda's being uttered by a fit person, and therefore necessarily implying a personal inspirer.)

From this brief statement of the distinctive features of the Nyaya school it is clear that this system, at least in its Vaiseshika cosmogony, is dualistic in the sense of assuming the existence of gross material *eternal atoms,* side by side either with *eternal souls* or with the supreme Soul of the universe. It sets

---

1. I have referred to his edition and to Dr. Muir's extracts in the appendix to the third volume of his Texts.
2. Those who wish to pursue the argument should consult Professor Cowell's translation. It is interesting to compare Cicero, De Natura Deorum (II. 34): 'But if all the parts of the universe are so constituted that they could not be better for use or more beautiful in appearance, let us consider whether they could have been put together by chance or whether their condition is such that they could not even cohere unless divine wisdom and providence had directed them (*nisi sensu moderante divinaque providentia*).'

itself against any theory which would make an impure and evil world spring from a pure and perfect spirit. Nor does it undertake to decide positively what it cannot prove dialectically, — the precise relation between soul and matter.

Lecture V

The Sankhya

The Sankhya[1] philosophy, though possibly prior in date, is generally studied next to the Nyaya, and is more peremptorily and categorically dualistic (*dvaitavadin*). It utterly repudiates the notion that impure matter can originate from pure spirit, and, of course, denies that anything can be produced out of nothing.

---

1. Kapila, the reputed founder of this school (sometimes fabled as a son of Brahma, sometimes as an incarnation of Vishnu and identified with the sage described in the Ramayana as the destroyer of the sixty thousand sons of Sagara, who in their search for their father's horse disturbed his devotions), was probably a Brahman, though nothing is known about him. See Mahabharat XII. 13703. The word *Kapila* means 'of a tawny brown colour,' and may possibly have been applied as a nickname, like Aksha-pada and Kanada. He is the supposed author of two works, viz. *a.* the original Sankhya Sutras, sometimes called *Sankhya-pravachana,* comprising 526 aphorisms in six books; *b.* a short work called the Tattva-samasa or 'Compendium of Principles' (translated by Dr. Ballantyne). The original Sutras are of course accompanied with abundant commentaries, of which one of the best known is the Sankhya-pravachana-bhashya, by Vijnana-bhikshu, edited with an able and interesting preface by Dr. Fitz-Edward Hall. A very useful and popular compendium of the doctrines of this system, called the Sankhya-karika, was edited and translated by Professor H.H. Wilson.

The following are Aphorisms, I. 78, 114-117, propounding its doctrine of evolution, which may not be altogether unworthy of the attention of Darwinians:

There cannot be the production of something out of nothing (*navastuno vastu-siddhih*); that which is not cannot be developed into that which is. The production of what does not already exist (potentially) is impossible, like a horn on a man (*nasad-utpado nri-shringavat*); because there must of necessity be a material out of which a product is developed; and because everything cannot occur everywhere at all times (*sarvatra sarvada sarvasambhavat*); and because anything possible must be produced from something competent to produce it[1].

'Thus,' remarks a commentator, 'curds come from milk, not water. A potter produces a jar from clay, not from cloth. Production is only manifestation of what previously existed.' Aphorism 121 adds, 'Destruction is a resolution of anything into its cause.'

---

1. See the note on the dogma *Ex nihilo nihil fit*, p. 67. We are also here reminded of Lucretius I. 160, &c.:

> *Nam si de Nihilo fierent ex omnibu's rebus*
> *Omne genus nasci posset; nil semine egeret;*
> *E mare primum homines, e terra posset oriri*
> *Squammigerum genus et volucres; erumpere caelo*
> *Armenta, atque aliae pecudes: genus omne ferarum*
> *Incerto partu culta ac deserta teneret:*
> *Nec fructus iidem arboribus constare solerent,*
> *Sed mutarentur: ferre omnes omnia possent.*

'If things proceed from nothing, everything might spring from everything and nothing would require a seed. Men might arise first from the sea, and fish and birds from the earth, and flocks and herds break into being from the sky; every kind of beast might be produced at random in cultivated places or deserts. The same fruits would not grow on the same trees, but would be changed. All things would be able to produce all things.'

In the Sankhya, therefore, instead of an analytical inquiry into the universe as actually existing, arranged under topics and categories, we have a synthetical system propounded, starting from an original primordial *tattva* or 'eternally existing essence[1],' called *Prakriti* (a word meaning 'that which evolves or produces everything else').

It is described by Kapila in his sixty-seventh Aphorism as 'a rootless root[2],' *amulam mulam,* thus:

---

1. It is usual to translate *tat-tva,* 'that-ness,' by principle; but such words as 'essence,' 'entity,' and in some cases even 'substance,' seem to convey a more definite idea of its meaning. It corresponds to the barbarous term 'quiddity' (from quid est?), discarded by Locke and modern English philosophers. Certainly 'nature' is anything but a good equivalent for *Prakriti,* which denotes something very different from matter or even the germ of mere material substances. It is an intensely subtle original essence wholly distinct from soul, yet capable of evolving out of itself consciousness and mind as well as the whole visible world. *Prakaroti iti prakriti* is given as its derivation in the Sarva-darshana-sangraha, p. 147, where *pra* seems to stand for 'forth,' not 'before.' The commentator on the Sankhya-karika (p. 4) uses the word *padartha* as applicable to all the twenty-five Tattvas. A Vedantist would not regard *tat-tva* as an abstract noun from *tat,* 'that' but would say it meant 'truth,' and in its etymology contained the essence of truth, viz. *tat tvam,* 'that art thou.'

2. In a passage in the Timaeus (34) Plato propounds a theory of creation in allegorical and not very intelligible language, which the reader can compare with the Sankhyan view: 'For the present, therefore, we ought to consider three things, that which is produced, that in which it is produced, and that from which a thing is produced, having a natural resemblance. And especially it is proper to compare that which receives to the mother, that from which it receives to the father, and the nature which is between these to the child. Then, as to this mother and receptacle of things created which are visible and altogether perceptible, we cannot term it either earth, air, fire, or water, nor any one of their compounds nor any of the elements from which they were produced, but a certain invisible and shapeless essence, which receives all things,' &c. Compare note 4, p. 66.

From the absence of a root in the root, the root (of all things) is rootless.

Then he continues in his sixty-eight Aphorism:

Even if there be a succession of causes (one before the other) there must be a halt at some one point; and so Prakriti is only a name for the primal source (of all productions).

Beginning, then, with this original eternal germ or element, the Sankhya reckons up synthetically, whence its name of 'Synthetic enumeration[1],' twenty-three other Tattvas or 'entities,' which are all productions of the first, evolving themselves out of it as naturally and spontaneously as cream out of milk or milk out of a cow.

The twenty-fifth entity is *Purusha,* 'the soul,' which is neither producer nor produced, but eternal, like Prakriti. It is quite distinct from the producing or produced elements and creations of the phenomenal world, though liable to be brought into connection with them. In fact, the object of the Sankhya system is to effect the liberation of the soul from the fetters in which it is involved by union with Prakriti. It does this by conveying the Prama or 'correct knowledge' of the twenty-four constituent principles of creation, and rightly discriminating the soul from them; its *Pramanas,* or 'means of obtaining the correct measure of existing things,' being reduced from four (see p. 77) to three, viz. *Drishta, Anumana,* and *Apta-vachana,* 'perception by the senses, inference, and credible assertion or trustworthy testimony.'

The third Aphorism of the Sankhya-karika thus reckons up the catalogue of all existing entities:

---

1. Hence Sir W. Jones called the Sankhya the Numeral philosophy. It has been compared partly with the metaphysics of Pythagoras, partly (in its Yoga) with the system of Zeno; also with that of Berkeley.

The root and substance of all things (except soul) is Prakriti. It is no production. Seven things produced by it are also producers. Thence come sixteen productions. Soul, the twenty-fifth essence, is neither a production nor producer.

Hence it appears that from an original *Prakriti* (variously called *Mula-prakriti,* 'root-principle;' *Amulammulam,* 'rootless root;' *Pradhana,* 'chief one,;' *A-vyakta,* 'unevolved evolver;' *Brahman,* 'supreme;' *Maya,* 'power of illusion'¹), seven other producers are evolved, and as so evolved are regarded as Vikaras or 'productions.' The first production of the original producer is *Buddhi,* commonly called 'intellect or intellectual perception' (and variously termed *Mahat,* from its being the *Great* source of the two other internal faculties, Ahankara, and Manas or 'self-consciousness and mind'). Third in order comes this *Ahankara,* the 'I-making' faculty, that is, self-consciousness or the sense of individuality (sometimes conveniently termed 'Ego-ism'), which produces the next five principles, called *Tanmatras* or 'subtle elementary particles,' out of which the grosser elements (*Maha-bhuta*) are evolved². These eight constitute the producers.

Then follow the sixteen that are productions only; and first in order, as produced by the *Tanmatras,* come the five grosser elements already mentioned, viz.

*a. Akasha*³, 'ether,' with distinguishing property of sound, or, in other words, the substraum of sound (which sound is the

---

1. According to Gaudapada's commentary on Sankhya-karika, 22.
2. These Tanmatras appear nearly to correspond to the of Plato (Theaet. 139), or rather to the 'elements of elements' (Theaet. 142), and to Empedocles.
3. Akasha, as shown elsewhere (see p. 124, note 3), must not be exactly identified with the modern 'ether,' though this word is usually taken as its nearest possible equivalent. In some of its properties and functions it more corresponds with the *inance,* 'vacant space,' of

vishaya or object for a corresponding organ of sense, the ear).
b. Vayu, 'air,' with the property of tangibility (which is the
vishaya for the skin). c. *Tejas* or *jyotis,* 'fire or light,' with the
property of form or colour (which is the *vishaya* for the eye).
d. *Aps,* 'water,' with the property of savour or taste (which is
the *vishaya* for the tongue). e. *Prithivi* or *bhumi,* 'earth,' with
the property of odour or smell (which is the vishaya for the nose).

Each of these elements after the first has also the property
or properties of the preceding besides its own.

Next follow the eleven organs produced, like the Tanmatras,
by the third producer, Ahankara, viz. the five organs of sense,
the five organs of action[1], and an eleventh organ standing
between these two sets, called *Manas,* 'the mind,' which is an
internal organ of perception, volition, and action.

The eight producers, then, with the five grosser elements
ether, air, fire, water, earth, and with the eleven organs,
constitute the true elements and constituent substances of the
phenomenal world. As, however, the most important of the
producers, after the mere unintelligent original germ, is the
third, called *Ahankara,* 'self–consciousness or individuality,'
it is scarcely too much to maintain that, according to the
Sankhya view, the whole world of sense is practically created

---

Lucretius. *quapropter locus eat intactus Inane, vacansque* (I. 335).
At any rate, one synonym of akasha is sunya. Cicero, De Nat.
Deorum II. 40, seems to identify *ether* with sky or space, which
stretches to the remotest point and surrounds all things. The Ramayan,
II. 110. 5, makes Brahma spring from ether, but the Epic and Puranic
accounts of akasha are very inconsistent. Some say that it was created
and is perishable, others that it was not created and is eternal. See
Muir's Texts IV. 119, Mahabharata XII. 6132.

1. The five organs of sense or perception (*buddhindriyani*) are, ear,
skin, eye, nose, tongue; those of action (*karmendriyani*) are, larynx,
hand, foot, and the excretory and generative organs.

by the individual Ego[1], who is, nevertheless, quite distinct from the soul, as this soul is supposed to possess in itself no real consciousness of separate individuality, though deluded by it.

It should also be noted that, according to the Sankhya theory, Prakriti, though a subtle elementary essence, is yet to be regarded as consisting of three ingredients or constituent principles in equipoise, called Gunas. These are *Sattva, Rajas,* and *Tamas,* 'goodness or purity, passion or activity, and darkness or ignorance.'

Thus Kapila (Aphorism 61) affirms as follows:

Prakriti is the state of equipoise (*Samyavastha*) of goodness, passion, and darkness.

Evidently, then, these three constituents of the primal elementary germ are really themselves elementary substances, and not qualities, although they are called Gunas and although such expressions as goodness, purity, &c. convey more the notion of a quality than of any actual substance. According to the Sankhya-pravachana-bhashya:

These Gunas are not like the 'qualities' of the Vaiseshika. They are substances possessing themselves qualities or properties, such as conjunction, disjunction, lightness, motion, weight &c. The word Guna, therefore, is employed because these three substances form the triple cord by which the soul, like an animal (*purusha-pashu*), is bound[2].

---

1. This idea of personal individual creation is what chiefly distinguishes the Sankhya from the pantheism of the Vedanta, which denies all real personal individuality. It has also led to the Sankhya system being compared to the theory of Berkeley.
2. Aristotle (Metaph. I. 3) describes primordial substance as undergoing changes through different affections, something after the manner of the Sankhya Gunas. See note 4, p. 66.

It is plain, indeed, that as one meaning of the word Guna
is 'rope' or 'cord,' the Sankhya three Gunas may be supposed
to act like a triple-stranded rope, binding and confining souls
in different degrees[1]. In point of fact, goodness, passion, and
darkness are imagined to be the actual substances of which
Prakriti is constituted, just as trees are the constituents of a
forest. Moreover, as they are the ingredients of Prakriti, so
they make up the whole world of sense evolved out of Prakriti.
Except, however, in the case of the original producer, they
are not conjoined in equal quantities. They form component
parts of everything evolved, but in varying proportions, one
or other being in excess. In other words, they affect everything
in creation unequally; and as they affect man, make him
divine and noble, thoroughly human and selfish, or bestial
and ignorant, according to the predominance of goodness,
passion, or darkness respectively. The soul, on the other hand,
though bound by the Gunas, is itself wholly and entirely free
from such constituent ingredients (*nir-guna*). It stands twenty-
fifth in the catalogue of Tattvas, and is to be wholly
distinguished from the creations evolved by the three evolvers,
Prakriti, Buddhi, and *Ahankara.* It has, in short, nothing
whatever in common with the world-evolver, Prakriti, except
eternal existence.

But although *Prakriti* is the sole originator of creation, yet,
according to the pure Sankhya, it does not create for itself,
but rather for each individual soul which comes into connection
or juxtaposition with it, like a crystal vase with a flower.
Souls, indeed, exist eternally separate from each other and

---

1. Manu states the doctrine of the three gunas very similarly (XII. 24,
   25, &c.) : 'One should know that the three Gunas (bonds or fetters)
   of the soul are goodness, passion, and darkness; (bound) by one or
   more of these, it continues incessantly attached to forms of existence.
   Whenever any one of the three Gunas predominates wholly in a
   body, it makes the embodied spirit abound in that Guna.'

from the world-evolver Prakriti; and with whatever form of body they may be joined, they are held to be all intrinsically equal, and each retains its individuality, remaining one and unchanged through all transmigrations[1]. But each separate soul is a witness of the act of creation without participating in the act. It is a looker on, uniting itself with unintelligent *Prakriti,* as a lame man mounted on a blind man's shoulders, for the sake of observing and contemplating the phenomena of creation, which *Prakriti* herself is unable to observe. In the Sankhya-karika (19) we read:

The soul is witness, solitary, bystander, spectator, and passive. For its contemplation of *Prakriti* the union of both takes place, as of the halt and blind; by that union a creation is formed.

It appears, too, that all Prakriti's performances are solely for the benefit of soul, who receives her favours ungratefully. Thus, in the Sankhya-karika 59, 60, we have the following:

As a female dancer, having exhibited herself to a spectator, desists from the dance, so does Prakriti desist, having manifested herself to soul. By various means Prakriti, endowed with qualities (*gunavat*), acting as a benefactress, accomplishes without profit to herself the purpose of soul, who is devoid of qualities (*aguna*) and makes no return of benefit.

In fact, Prakriti is sometimes reproached with boldness in exposing herself to the gaze of soul, who takes not interest

---

1. This *separate* eternal existence of innumerable individual souls is the great feature distinguishing the Nyaya and Sankhya from the Vedanta, which holds the oneness of all soul. And yet it would seem that each soul must be regarded as universally diffused both in Sankhya and Nyaya (see p. 92); for unless the soul is all-pervading it cannot be eternal. All Hindus hold that nothing can be eternal that is divisible into parts; and all things have parts except the infinite (soul) and the infinitesimal (atoms).

whatever in the sight. There is something to a European mind very unreal, cloudy, and unpractical in all this. Certainly no one can doubt that the Sankhya view of the soul is inferior to that of the Nyaya, which ascribes to it, when joined to mind, activity, volition, thought, and feeling (see p. 92). Obviously, too, its view of all existing things is even more atheistical than that of the earliest Naiyayikas. For if the creation produced by the Evolver, Prakriti, has an existence of its own independent of all connection with the particular Purusha to which it is joined, there can be no need for an intelligent Creator of the world or even of any superintending power[1].

Here are two or three of Kapila's Aphorisms bearing upon the charge of atheism brought against him. An objection is made that some of this definitions are inconsistent with the supposed existence of a supreme Lord (*Ishvara*). To this he replies in the ninety-second and following Aphorisms, thus:

(They are not inconsistent) because the existence of a supreme Lord is unproved (*Ishvarasiddheh*). Since he could not be either free (from desires and anxieties) or bound by troubles of any kind, there can be no proof of his existence. Either way he could not be effective of any creation. (That is, if he were free from anxieties he could have no wish to create; and if he were bound by desires of any kind, he would then be under bondage, and therefore deficient in power.)

The commentary of Gauda-pada on Sankhya-karika 61 ought, however, to be here quoted:

The Sankhya teachers say, 'How can beings composed of the three Gunas proceed from Isvara (God), who is devoid of Gunas? Or how can they proceed from soul, equally devoid of qualities?

---

1. I presume this is the reason why in a catalogue of MSS. just edited by Rajendralal Mitra the Sankhya is styled the Hylotheistic philosophy.

Therefore they must proceed from Prakriti. Thus from white threads white cloth is produced; from black threads, black cloth;' and so from Prakriti, composed of the three Gunas, the three worlds composed of the three Gunas are produced. God (Ishvara) is free from Gunas. The production of the three worlds composed of the Gunas from him would be an inconsistency.

Again, with reference to the soul, we have the following in Kapila's ninety-sixth Aphorism:

'There is a ruling influence of the soul (over Prakriti) caused by their proximity, just as the loadstone (draws iron to itself).' That is, the proximity of soul to Prakirit-impels the latter to go through the steps of production. This sort of attraction between the two leads to creation, but in no other sense is soul an agent or concerned in creation at all[1].

Notwithstanding these atheistical tendencies, the Sankhya evades the charge of unorthodoxy by a confession of faith in the Veda. Hence in Aphorism 98 we have —

The declaration of the meaning of the texts of the Veda is an authority, since the author of them knew the established truth.

And it should be noted that some adherents of the Sankhya maintain the existence of a supreme Soul[2], called Hiranya-garbha, and of a general ideal phenomenal universe with which that supreme Soul is connected and into which all the subcreations of inferior souls are by him gathered. Nor can it be affirmed that the Sankhya proper commits itself to a

---

1. It is stated in Kapila's fifty-eight Aphorism, quoted by Dr. Ballantyne, that the bondage of the soul caused by its union with Prakriti is after all merely nominal, and not real, because it resides in the mind, and not in the soul itself (*vanmatram na tu tattvam chitta-sthiteh*). See Mullens' Essay, p. 183.
2. Or, according to Professor E.B. Cowell, 'personified Sum of existence.' Elphinstone's India, p. 126, note.

positive denial of the existence of a supreme Being, so much as to an ignoring of what the founder of the school believed to be incapable of dialectic demonstration. As, however, the original World-evolver only evolves the world for the sake of the spectator, soul, this is practically an admission that there can be no realization of creation without the union of Prakriti with Purusha, the personal soul. In all probability Kapila's own idea was that every Purusha, though he did not himself create, had his own creation and his own created universe comprehended in his own person[1]. It may easily be supposed that this union of Purusha and Prakriti began soon to be compared to that of male and female; and it may be conjectured that the idea of the production of the universe by the male and female principles associating together, which was symbolized by the Ardha-nari form of Shiva, and which lies at the root of the whole later mythology of India, was derived mainly from the Sankhya philosophy.

It was not indeed to be expected that the uneducated masses could make anything of a metaphysical mysticism which could not be explained to them in intelligible language. How could they form any notion of a primordial eternal energy evolving out of itself twenty-three other elements or substances to form a visible world for the soul, described as apathetic, inactive, devoid of all qualities, and a mere indifferent spectator, though in close contact with the individual Evolver and deluded by its self-consciousness? But they could well understand the idea of a universe proceeding from Prakriti and Purusha as from mother and father. Indeed the idea of a union between the female principle, regarded as an energy, and the male principle, is of great antiquity in Hindu systems

---

1. Something after the manner of Berkeley, who held that the 'without' was all within, though he believed in the real existence of external objects produced by other minds and wills.

of cosmogony. In the Rig-veda and Brahmanas there are various allusions, as we have already seen, to a supposed union of Earth and Heaven, who together produce men, gods, and all creatures[1].

Buddhism, moreover, which represented many of the more popular philosophical ideas of the Hindus perhaps as early as the sixth century B.C., has more in common with the Sankhya philosophy than with any of the other systems.

Even the cosmogony of Manu, although a compound of various theories, presents a process of evolution very similar, as we shall see hereafter, to that of the Sankhya.

Again, the antiquity and prevalence of Sankhyan ideas is proved by the frequent allusions to them in the great Indian epic poem, called Mahabharata[2], and the permanence of their popularity till at least the first century of our era is indicated by the fact that the celebrated philosophical poem called Bhagavad-gita attempts to reconcile the Sankhya with Vedantist views[3].

Perhaps, however, the extensive prevalence of Sankhyan ideas in India is best shown by the later cosmogony and mythology. In those repositories of the popular Hindu creed, the Puranas and Tantras, Prakriti becomes a real Mother of the universe. It is true that in some of the Puranas there is occasional confusion and perversion of Sankhyan doctrines.

---

1. See Muir's Texts, vol. pp. 22, 23.
2. In the Sabha-parvan (Muir, vol. iv. p. 173) Krishna is described as undeveloped Prakriti, the eternal creator (*esha prakritir a-vyakta karta caiva sanatanah*). On the other hand, in the Vana-parvan (1622, &c., Muir, vol. iv. p. 195) the god Siva is declared to be the cause of the causes of the world (*loka-karana-karanam*), and therefore superior and antecedent to Pradhana and Purusha. Again, in Santi-parvan 12725, 12737, 13041, &c., the sons of Brahma are called Prakritayah.
3. See Lecture VII on the Eclectic School and Bhagavad-gita.

Thus, for example, in the Vishnu-purana I. 2. 22, we have the following:

'There was neither day nor night, neither sky nor earth; there was neither darkness nor light nor anything else. There was then the One, Brahma, the Male, possessing the character of Pradhana (*pradhanika*) [1].' And further on: 'The principles or elements, commencing with Mahat, presided over by Purusha and under the influence of Pradhana, generated an egg, which became the receptacle of Vishnu in the form of Brahma.'

But generally in the later mythology especially as represented by the Tantras, the Sankhya principle of Prakriti takes the form of female personifications, who are thought of as the wives or creative female energies of the principal male deities, to whom, on the other hand, the name Purusha, in the sense of the supreme Soul or the supreme Male, is sometimes applied[2]. This is especially the case with the Shakti or female energy of Shiva, worshipped by a vast number of persons as the true *Jagadamba*, or 'Mother of the universe.'

These proofs of the ancient popularity of the Sankhya and its influence on the later mythology may help us to understand that, although in modern times there are comparatively few students of the Sankhya among the Pandits of India, there is still a common saying current everywhere (which will be found in Mahabharata, Santi-parvan, 11676), *Nasti Sankhya samam jnanam nasti Yoga-samam balam,* 'there is no knowledge equal to the Sankhya and no power equal to the Yoga.'

---

1. Compare the Rig-veda hymn, translated at p. 22 of this book.
2. Vishnu or Krishna is called Purushottama, and the name Purusha is equally given to Brahma and Shiva.

The Yoga

The Yoga, commonly regarded as a branch of the Sankhya, is scarcely worthy of the name of a system of philosophy, though it has undoubted charms for the naturally contemplative and ascetical Hindu, and lays claim to greater orthodoxy than the Sankhya proper by directly acknowledging the existence of Ishvara or a supreme Being[1]. In fact, the aim of the Yoga is to teach the means by which the human soul may attain complete union with the supreme Soul. This fusion (*laya*) or union of individual with universal spirit may be effected even in the body. According to Patanjali, the author of the system, the very word *Yoga* is interpreted to mean the act of 'fixing or concentrating the mind in abstract meditation,' and this is said to be effected by preventing the modifications of *Chitta* or the thinking principle [which modifications arise through the three Pramanas, perception, inference, and verbal testimony, as well as through incorrect ascertainment, fancy, sleep, and recollection], by the constant habit (*abhyasa*) of keeping the mind in its unmodified state — a state clear as crystal when uncoloured by contact with other substances — and by the practice of *Vairagya* — that is, complete suppression of the passions. This *Vairagya* is only to be obtained by *Ishvara-pranidhana* or the contemplation of the supreme Being, who is defined to be a particular Purusha or Spirit unaffected by works, afflictions, &c., and having the appellation *Pranava*

---

1. The Yoga was propounded by Patanjali (of whom nothing is known except that he was probably not the same person as the author of the Maha-bhashya) in Aphorisms called the Yoga-sutra, a work in four books or chapters, two of which, with some of the commentary of Bhoja-raja or Bhoja-deva, were translated by Dr. Ballantyne. Other commentators were Vachaspati-misra, Vijnana-bhikshu, and Nagoji-bhatta.

or *Om*. The repetition of this monosyllable is supposed to be attended with marvellous results, and the muttering of it with reflection on its meaning[1] is said to be conducive to a knowledge of the Supreme and to a prevention of all the obstacles to Yoga. The eight means of mental concentration are — 1. *Yama*, 'forbearance,' 'restraint.' 2. *Niyama*, 'religious observances.' 3. Asana, *'postures*[2].' 4. *Pranayama*, 'suppression of the breath' or 'breathing in a peculiar way.' 5. *Pratyahara*, 'restraint of the senses.' 6. *Dharana*, 'steadying of the mind.' 7. *Dhyana*, 'contemplation.' 8. *Samadhi*, 'profound meditation,' or rather a state of religious trance, which, according to the Bhagavad-gita (VI. 13), is most effectually attained by such practices as fixing the eyes intently and incessantly on the tip of the nose, &c.[3] The system of Yoga appears, in fact, to be a mere contrivance for getting rid of all thought, or at least for concentrating the mind with the utmost intensity upon nothing in particular. It is a strange compound of mental and bodily exercises, consisting in unnatural restraint, forced and painful postures, twistings and contortions of the limbs, suppressions of the breath, and utter absence of mind. But although the Yoga of Patanjali professes to effect union with the universal Spirit by means such as these, it should be observed that far more severe austerities and self-imposed physical mortifications are popularly

---

1. *Om* is supposed to be composed of the three letters A, U, M, which form a most sacred monosyllable (*ekakshara*), significant of the supreme Being as developing himself in the Triad of gods, Brahma, Vishnu, and Siva. See Bhagavad gita VIII. 13, and especially Manu II. 83, 84.
2. One of these postures is called *paryanka-bandhana or paryanka-granthi*, 'bed-binding' or 'bed-knot,' and is performed by sitting on the hams with a cloth fastened round the knees and back. See line 1 of the Mric-chakatika.
3. See the account of the Bhagavad-gita, p. 154 of this volume.

connected with the Yoga system. All Hindu devotees and ascetics, especially those who, as forming a division of the Shaiva sect, identify the terrific god Shiva with the supreme Being, are commonly called Yogins or Yogis, and indeed properly so called, in so far as the professed object of their austerities is union with the Deity[1].

The variety and intensity of the forms of austerity practised by such Yogis in India would appear to surpass all credibility were they not sufficiently attested by trustworthy evidence. A few illustrations may not be out of place here, or at least may be instructive, especially as bearing upon an interesting field of inquiry, viz. first, how is it that faith in a false system can operate with sufficient force upon Hindu to impel him to submit voluntarily to almost incredible restraints, mortifications of the flesh, and physical tortures? And secondly, how is it that an amount of physical endurance may be exhibited by an apparently weakly and emaciated Asiatic, which would be impossible in a European, the climate and diet in the one case tending to debilitate, in the other to invigorate?

In the Sakuntala (Act VII. verse 175) there is a description of an ascetic engaged in Yoga, whose condition of fixed trance and immovable impassiveness had lasted so long that ants had thrown up a mound as high as his waist without being disturbed, and birds had built their nests in the long clotted tresses of his tangled hair. This may be thought a mere flight of poetical fancy, but a Mohammedan traveller, whose narrative is quoted by Mr. Mill (British India, I. 355), once actually saw a man in India standing motionless with his face turned towards the sun. The same traveller, having occasion to revisit the same

---

1. The name Fakir or Faqir, sometimes given to Hindu devotees, ought to be restricted to Muslims. It is an Arabic word, meaning 'poor,' 'indigent.'

spot sixteen years afterwards, found the very same man in the very same attitude. Such men have been known to fix their gaze on the sun's disk till sight has been extinguished. This is paralleled by a particular form of austerity described in Manu VI. 32, where mention is made of the *Pancha-tapas*, a Yogi who, during the three hottest months (April, May, and June), sits between four blazing fires placed towards the four quarters, with the burning sun above his head to form a fifth. In fact, a Yogi was actually seen not long ago (Mill's India, I. 353) seated between four such fires on a quadrangular stage. He stood on one leg gazing at the sun while these fires were lighted at the four corners. Then placing himself upright on his head, with his feet elevated in the air, he remained for three hours in that position. He then seated himself cross-legged and continued bearing the raging heat of the sun above his head and the fires which surrounded him till the end of the day, occasionally adding combustibles with his own hands to increase the flames.

Again, in the Asiatic Monthly Journal for March, 1829, an account is given of a Brahman who, with no other apparatus than a low stool, a hollow bamboo, and a kind of crutch, poised himself apparently in the air, about four feet from the ground, for forty minutes. This actually took place before the governor of Madras. Nor does there appear to be any limit to the various forms of austerity practised by Hindu devotees. We read of some who acquire the power of remaining under water for a space of time quite incredible; of others who bury themselves up to the neck in the ground, or even below it, leaving only a little hole through which to breathe; of others who keep their fists clenched for years till the nails grow through the back of their hands; of others who hold one or both arms aloft till they become immovably fixed in that position and withered to the bone; of others who roll their bodies for thousands of miles to some place of pilgrimage; of others who sleep on beds of iron spikes. One man was seen at Benares (described in the Asiatic Researches, vol. v p. 49) who was alleged to have used such a bed for thirty-five years. Others have been known to chain themselves for life to trees; others, again, to pass their lives, heavily chained, in iron cages. Lastly, the extent to which some Indian ascetics will carry fasting far exceeds anything ever heard of in Europe, as may be understood by a reference to the rules of the lunar penance given by Manu (VI. 20, XI. 216-220). This penance is a kind of fast which consists in diminishing the consumption of food every day by one mouthful for the waning half of the lunar month, beginning with fifteen mouthfuls at the full moon until the quantity is reduced to 0 at the new moon, and then increasing it in like manner during the fortnight of the moon's increase.

Of course all these mortifications are explicable by their connection with the fancied attainment of extraordinary sanctity and supernatural powers.

As a conclusion to the subject of Yoga, I quote a remarkable passage from Professor Banerjea (Dialogues, pp. 69, 70):

The Yogi may not see or hear what passes around, — he may be insensible to external impressions, but he has intuition of things which his neighbours cannot see or hear. He becomes so buoyant, or rather so sublimated by his Yoga, that gravitation, or, as Bhaskaracharya calls it, the attractive power of the earth, has no influence on him. He can walk and ascend in the sky, as if he were suspended under a balloon. He can by this intuitive process inform himself of the mysteries of astronomy and anatomy, of all things in fact that may be found in any of the different worlds. He may call to recollection the events of a previous life. He may understand the language of the brute creation. He may obtain an insight into the past and future. He may discern the thoughts of others. He may himself vanish at pleasure, and, if he choose to do so, enter into his neighbour's body and take possession of his living skin.

By these and other doctrines of Hindu philosophy we are
often reminded that the human mind repeats itself according
to the sentiment expressed in Ecclesiastes i. 9, 'The thing that
hath been, it is that which shall be; and that which is done
is that which shall be done: and there is no new thing under
the sun.' Certainly almost all extravagant ideas now current
seem to have their counterpart, if not their source, in the East.
The practisers to self-imposed superstitious restraints and
mortifications, not to speak of the votaries of animal
magnetism, clairvoyance, and so-called spiritualism, will find
most of their theories represented or rather far outdone by
corresponding notions existing in this Yoga system invented
by the Hindus considerably more than 2000 years ago, and
more or less earnestly believed in and sedulously practised up
to the present day.

Lecture VI

The Purva-mimansa and Vedanta

Our next subject is the Mimansa of Jaimini[1], which is sometimes connected with the Vedanta, this latter being called the *Uttara-mimansa* or *Brahma-mimansa* — as founded on the Upanishads or latter part of the Vedas — while Jaimini's system is styled the *Purva-mimansa* or *Karma-mimansa,* as concerned with the Mantras and Brahmanas only. It is more usual, however, to indicate the opposition of the two systems to each other by calling the one Mimansa and the other Vedanta. In fact, Jaimini's system, like the Yoga, cannot suitably be called a subdivision of any

---

1. Jaimini, as usual, enunciated his doctrines in aphorisms. His work called the Mimansa-sutra or Jaimini-sutra is in twelve books. It has been partly edited and translated by Dr. Ballantyne. A commentary on it was written by Sabara-svamin, which is being published in the Bibliotheca Indica, and this again was commented on by the celebrated Mimansa authority, Kumarila (also styled Kumaril-bhatta, Kumarila-svamin), whose work was again followed by numerous other commentaries and treatises. A compendious explanation of the system, called *Jaiminiya-nyaya-mala-vistara,* was written by Madhavacarya. Jaimini must have been a learned Brahman, but nothing is known as to the date of his life

116

other system, for it is in real truth not a system of philosophy, but rather of *ritualism*. It does not concern itself, like the other systems, with investigations into the nature of soul, mind, and matter, but with a correct interpretation of the ritual of the Veda and the solutions of doubts and discrepancies in regard to Vedic texts caused by the discordant explanations of opposite schools. Its only claim to the title of a philosophy consists in its *mode* of interpretation, the topics being arranged according to particular categories (such as authoritativeness, indirect precept, &c.), and treated according to a kind of *logical method,* commencing with the proposition to be discussed, the doubt arising about it, the *Purva-paksha* or prima facie and wrong view of the question, the *Uttara-paksha* or refutation of the wrong view, and the conclusion. The main design of the whole system appears to be to make a god of ritualism. Hence it consists chiefly of a critical commentary on the Brahamana or ritual portion of the Veda in its connection with the mantras, the interpretation given being an exposition of the obvious literal sense and not of any supposed occult meaning underlying the text, as in the Upanishads and Vedanta. Jaimini was, in point of fact, the opponent of both rationalism and theism. Not that he denied a God, but the real tendency of his teaching was to allow no voice or authority to either reason or God. The Veda was to be everything. A supreme Being might exist, but was not necessary to the system. The Veda, said Jaimini, is itself authority and has no need of an Authorizer. His first Aphorism states the whole aim and object of his system, viz. a desire to know duty (*dhrama-jijnasa*). When amplified, it may be thus stated:

Understand, O student, that, after studying the Veda with a preceptor, a desire to know *Dharma* or duty is to be entertained by thee.

The fifth Aphorism asserts the strange doctrine of an original and perpetual connection between a word and its sense. It is thus paraphrased:

The connection of a word with its sense is contemporaneous with the origin of both. In consequence of this connection, the words of the Veda convey unerring instruction in the knowledge of duty.

But it is to be understood that *Dharma* or duty consists in the performance of the ritual acts prescribed by the Veda because they are so prescribed, without reference to the will or approval of any personal god, for Dharma is itself the bestower of reward. Some recent Mimansakas, however, maintain that Dharma ought to be performed as an offering to a supreme Being, and that it is to be so performed as a means of emancipation. Even a verse of the Bhagavad-gita is quoted in support of this view. Krishna regarded by his worshippers as a manifestation of the supreme lord of the universe, says to Arjuna —

Whatever thou doest, whatever thou eatest, whatever thou sacrificest, whatever thou givest away, whatever austerity thou practisest, do that as an offering to me (IX. 27). (See Lecture VII on the Eclectic School and Bhagavad-gita, p. 155 of this volume.)

Some singular speculations occur in Jaimini's system. As he maintains the inherent authority of the Veda, without any dependence on an eternal Authorizer or Revealer, so he asserts its own absolute eternity, and declares that only eternally pre-existing objects are mentioned in it. This theory is supported by affirming that sound is eternal, or rather that an eternal sound underlies all temporary sound. From Aphorism 18 we gather the following:

Sound must be eternal because its utterance [exhibition] is intended to convey a meaning to others. If it were not eternal it would not continue till the hearer had learned its sense, and thus he would not learn the sense, because the cause had ceased to exist.

If, on the other hand (says a commentator), it continues to exist for any period, however short, after ceasing to be perceived, it is impossible to assign any other instant at which there is any evidence of the discontinuance of its existence, whence its eternity is inferred[1].

This eternity of sound is further pretended to be established by the two following short passages, one from the Rig-veda (VIII. 64.6) and one from Smriti, with which I close this brief notice of the Mimansa:

'Send forth praises, O Virupa, with an eternal voice.'

'An eternal voice, without beginning or end, was uttered by the self-existent[2].

Let me conclude these remarks on the singular theory of the eternity of sound by observing that the Chinese are said to have a saying, 'The echoes of a word once uttered vibrate in space to all eternity.'

---

1. See Muir's Texts, vol. iii. pp. 53, 57; Dr. Ballantyne's Mimansa sutra, p. 23.
2. The whole text of the Rig-veda (VIII. 64. or 75. 6) is, *Tasmai nunam abhidyave vacha Virupa nityaya, vrishne chodasva sushtutim,* 'send forth praises to this heaven-aspiring and prolific Agni. O Virupa, with an eternal voice.' Nitya, though taken by the Mimansakas in the sense of 'eternal,' probably means only 'unceasing.' Dr. Muir's Texts, vol. iii. p. 51. The text from Smriti has only as yet been found in Mahabharata, Shanti-parvan 8. 533, *An-adi-nidhana nitya vag utsrishta svayam-bhuva.*

The Vedanta

Of orthodox systems there only remains the Vedanta of Vyasa or Badarayana[1]; but this is in some respects the most important of all the six both from its closer conformity to the pantheistic doctrines propounded in the Upanishads, on which treatises as forming the end of the Veda it professes to be founded, and from its greater adaptation to the habits of thought common among thinking and educated Hindus, as much in present as in former periods. The pantheism pervading the Upanishads and leading directly to the Vedanta system has already been illustrated by a selection of examples.

The following simple confession of a Vedantist's faith can be added from the Chandogya Upanishad (III. 14):

All this universe indeed is Brahma; from him does it proceed; into him it is dissolved; in him it breathes[2]. So let every one adore him calmly.

---

1. The reputed author of this system, Badarayana, is very loosely identified with the legendary person named Vyasa, who is supposed to have arranged the Vedas and written the Mahabharata, Puranas, and a particular Dharma-shastra or law-book. No doubt the name Vyasa, 'arranger,' was applied as a kind of title to various great writers or compilers, and in this sense it seems to have been given to the founder of the Vedanta system. He propounded his views, as usual, in Sutras, but Badarayana's Aphorisms are generally called Brahama-sutra, or sometimes Shariraka-sutra and the system itself is variously styled Brahma-mimansa and Sariraka-mimansa (investigation into the supreme Soul or embodied Spirit). The text of the Sutras and the celebrated commentary by Shankaracharya have been edited in the Bibliotheca Indica by Dr. Roer, and a portion translated by Professor Banerjea. Dr. Ballantyne also edited and translated a portion of the Sutras and commentary and a popular compendium called the Vedanta-sara. A vast number of other commentaries and treatises on the Vedanta exist.

2. This is expressed in the text by one compound, *taj-jalan*, interpreted as equivalent to *taj-ja, tal-la, tad-ana*. The whole text is *sarvam khalv idam brahma taj-jalan iti sana upasita*. The philosophy of the Sufis, alleged to be developed out of the Koran (see p. 38), appears to be a kind of pantheism very similar to that of the Vedanta.

Here, then, we have presented to us a different view of the origin of the world. In the Nyaya it was supposed to proceed from a concurrence of innumerable eternal atoms; in the Sankhya from one original eternal element called Prakriti; both operating independently, though associated with eternal souls and, according to one view, presided over by a supreme Soul. But in the Vedanta there is really no material world at all, as distinct from the universal Soul. Hence the doctrine of this school is called *A-dvaita*, 'non-dualism.' The universe exists but merely as a form of the one eternal essence. He is the all-pervading Spirit, the only really existing substance (*vastu*). Even as early as the Rig-veda the outlines of this pantheistic creed, which became more definite in the Upanishads and Vedanta, may be traced. The germ of the Vedanta is observable in the Purusha-sukta, as we have already shown by the example given at p. 25. The early Vedantic creed has the merit of being exceedingly simple. It is comprised in these three words, occurring in the Chandogya Upanishad (see p. 43-44), *Ekam evadvitiyam*, 'one only Essence without a second;' or in the following line of nine short words, *Brahma satyam jagan mithya jivo brahmaiva naparah*, 'Brahma is true, the world is false, the soul is only Brahma and no other.'

As the Nyaya has much in common with the practical philosophy of Aristotle, which gave to things and individuals, rather than to ideas, a real existence, so the Vedanta offers many parallels to the idealism of Plato[1]. Badarayana's very

---

1. Plato does not always state his theory of ideas very intelligibly, and probably modified them in his later works. He seems, however, to have insisted on the doctrine that mind preceded and gave rise to matter, or, in other words, that the whole material world proceeded from or was actually produced by the Creator according to the idea or pattern of a world existing eternally and for ever the same in his own mind. In the Timaeus (10) he says: 'To discover the Maker and Father of this universe is difficult, and when he has been discovered,

first Aphorism states the object of the whole system in one compound word, viz. *Brahma-jijnasa*, 'Brahma-inquisitiveness,' i.e. the desire of knowing Brahman (neut.), or the only really existing being.

Here we may quote a portion of Sankaracarya's commentary (Roer's edition, pp. 29 and 43):

The knower of Brahma attains the supreme good and supreme object of man (*param purushartham* summum bonum).

A really existing substance (*vastu*) cannot alternately be thus and not thus, cannot (optionally) be and not be. The knowledge of a substance just as it is in reality (i.e. true knowledge) is not dependent on a man's own personal notions (*na purusha-buddhy-apeksham*) [1]. It depends on the substance itself. To say of one and the same post that it is either a post or a man or something else is not true knowledge (*tattva-jnanam*). It is a false notion

_____

it is impossible to describe him to the multitude. According to which of two patterns did he frame the world? According to one subsisting for ever the same? Or according to one which was produced? Since, then, this universe is beautiful and its Artificer good, he evidently looked in modelling it to an eternal pattern.' Similarly, Plato seems to have held that the human mind has existing within it certain abstract ideas or ideal forms which precede and are visibly manifested in the actual concrete forms around us. For example, the abstract ideas of goodness and beauty are found pre-existing in the mind, and, as it were, give rise to the various good and beautiful objects manifested before our eyes. In the same manner all circular things must have been preceded by some ideal circular form existing as an eternal reality. For, according to Plato, these abstract ideas had a real, eternal, unchanging existence of their own, quite separate from and independent of the ever-varying concrete objects and appearances connected with them.

1. Shankara appears here to argue against a doctrine like that ascribed to Protagoras, 'the individual man is the standard of all things.'

(*mithya-jnanam*) [1]. That it is a post is alone the truth, because it is dependent on the substance itself (*vastu-tantratvat*). Thus the proving of an existing substance is dependent on the substance itself. Thus the knowledge of Brahma is dependent on the substance itself (not on the notion a man may form of Brahma), because it relates to a really existing substance (*bhuta-vastu-vishayatvat*).

In the second Aphorism Brahma[2] is defined to mean 'that from which the production of this universe results.'

Shankara adds a fuller definition, thus (Roer's edition, p. 38):

Brahma is that all-knowing, all-powerful Cause from which arises the production, continuance, and dissolution of the universe, which (universe) is modified by name and form, contains many agents and patients (*karti-bhoktri-samyukta*), is the repository (*ashraya*) of actions and effects, and in the form of its arrangement cannot be conceived even by the mind.

The Aphorisms which follow, as far as the 28th, proceed to define and describe the character of God as the supreme

---

1. One of Plato's causes of mistaken notion is that when two persons or things have been seen and their forms impressed on the mind, they are yet, owing to imperfect observation, mistaken the one for the other: 'It remains that I may form a false notion in this case, when knowing you and Theodorus and having the impression of both of you on that waxen tablet of the mind made by a seal ring as it were, seeing you both from a distance and not sufficiently distinguishing you, I fit the aspect of each to the impression of the other, changing them like those that put their shoes on the wrong feet': Theaet 122. Compare Benerjea's translation of the Brahma-sutra, p. 2.
2. The name *Brahman* is in fact derived from the root *brih or vrih,* 'to grow and expand,' and therefore means literally the one essence which grows or expands. *Vriksha*, 'a tree,' is from the same root.

Soul of the universe. I here give a summary[1] of the most interesting of them, with portions of the commentary:

That the supreme Being is omniscient follows from the fact that he is the source of the Veda (*shastra-yonistvat*). As from that Being every soul is evolved, so to that same Being does every soul return. How can souls be merged into Prakriti?[2] For then the intelligent would be absorbed in the unintelligent. He, the supreme Being, consists of joy. This is clear from the Veda, which describes him as the cause of joy; for as those who enrich others must be themselves rich, so there must be abundant joy with him who causes others to rejoice. Again, he, the one God, is the light (*jyotis*). He is within the sun and within the eye. He is the ethereal element (*akasha*)[3]. He is the life and the breath of life (*prana*). He is the life with which Indra identified himself when he said to Pratardana, 'I am the life, consisting of perfect knowledge. Worship me as the life immortal[4].'

From other portions of the Aphorisms it appears that the one universal essence called Brahma, is to the external world what yarn is to cloth, what milk to curds, what earth to a jar, and gold to a bracelet. He is both creator and

---

1. See Dr. Ballantyne's translation, and that of Professor Banerjea.
2. The Prakriti or Pradhana of the Sankhya system.
3. Professor Banerjea considers that the word 'ether' is not a good rendering for *akasha,* which pervades everything. There is akasha in our cups and within our bodies, which are surely not ethereal. One of the synonyms of akasha is *shunya,* and this may be compared in some respects to the 'inane' or space of Lucretius (I. 330):

   Nec tamen undique corporea stipata tenentur
   Omnia natura; namque est in rebus inane.

   'And yet all things are not on all sides held and jammed together in close and solid parts; there is a space (or void) in things.'
4. This is from the Kaushitaki-brahmana Upanishad, chapter 3. See Professor E.B. Cowell's translation.

creation[1], actor and act. He is also Existence, Knowledge, and Joy (*Sach-chid-ananda*), but is at the same time without parts, unbound by qualities (*nir-guna,* see p. 102), without action, without emotion, having no consciousness such as is denoted by 'I' and 'Thou[2],' apprehending no person or thing, nor apprehended by any, having neither beginning nor end, immutable, the only real entity.

This is surely almost tantamount to asserting that pure Being is identical with pure Nothing, so that the two extremes of Buddhistic Nihilism and Vedantic Pantheism, far as they profess to be apart, appear in the end to meet.

I add two or three extracts from Shankaracharya's comment on Sutra II. 1. 34[3].

It may be objected that God is proved not to be the cause of the universe. Why? From the visible instances of injustice (*vaishamya*) and cruelty (*nairghrinya*). Some he makes very happy, as the gods, &c.; some very miserable, as the brutes, &c.; and some in a middling condition, as men, &c. Being the

---

1. A true Vedantic spirit is observable in the Orphic hymns when they identify Zeus with the universe; thus, 'Zeus is the ether; Zeus is the earth; Zeus is the heaven; Zeus is all things.' Orphic. Fragm. IV. 363, VI. 366. Compare also Virgil, Aeneid VI. 724, &c.:

    'Principio caelum ac terras, camposque liquentes
    Lucentemque globum Lunae, Titaniaque astra,
    Spiritus intus alit, totamque infusa per artus
    Mens agitat molem et magno se corpore miscet.'

2. As shown by Professor Banerjea, Shankara compares the second person *Thou* with darkness, because there cannot be a real Thou. So Shankara affirms that 'Thou' and 'I' are as opposed as darkness and light. Plato speaks similarly of darkness and light in connection with nonentity and real entity. Sophist. 254.

3. Quoted by Professor Banerjea and Mr. Mullens and translated by them. Dialogues, p. 120, &c. Essay on Hindu Philosophy, p. 190. The Aphorism is, *Vaishamya-nairghrinye na sapekshatvat tathahi darshayati.*

author of such an unjust creation, he is proved to be subject
to passions like other persons — that is to say, to partiality and
prejudice — and therefore his nature is found wanting in
spotlessness. And by dispensing pain and ruin, he is chargeable
with malicious cruelty, culpable even among the wicked. Hence,
because of the instances of injustice and cruelty, God cannot
be the cause of the universe. To this we reply: Injustice and
cruelty cannot be charged upon God. Why? Because he did not
act independently (*sapekshatvat*). God being dependent
(*sapekshah*) creates this world of inequalities. If you ask on
what he is dependent, we reply, on merit and demerit
(*dharmadharmau*). That there should be an unequal creation,
dependent on the merit and demerit of the souls created, is no
fault of God. As the rain is the common cause of the production
of rice and wheat, but the causes of their specific distinctions
as rice and wheat are the varying powers of their respective
seeds; so is God the common cause in the creation of gods,
men, and others; but of the distinctions between gods, men,
and others, the causes are the varying works inherent in their
respective souls.

In commenting on the next Aphorism (35), he answers
the objection, 'How could there be previous works at the
original creation?' The objection and reply are thus stated[1]:

The supreme Being existed at the beginning, one without a
second (see p. 121). Hence, before the creation there could be
no works in dependence on which inequalities might be created.
God may be dependent on works after distinctions are made. But
before the creation there could be no works caused by varying
instruments, and therefore we ought to find a uniform creation
(*tulya srishtih*). We reply: This does not vitiate our doctrine,
because *the world is without beginning* (*anaditvat samsarasya*).
The world being without beginning, nothing can prevent works

---

1. The original Sutra is, Na karmavibhagad iti cen nanditvat.

and unequal creations from continuing in the states of cause and effect, like the seed and its plant (*vijankura-vat*).

Other objections to the Vedanta theory are thus treated by Shankara:

How can this universe, which is manifold, void of life, impure, and irrational, proceed from him who is one, living, pure, and rational? We reply: The lifeless world can proceed from Brahma, just as lifeless hair can spring from a living man. But in the universe we find him who enjoys and him who is enjoyed; how can he be both? We reply: Such are the changes of the sea. Foam, waves, billows, bubbles are not different from the sea. There is no difference between the universe and Brahma. The effect is not different from its cause. He is the soul; the soul is he. The same earth produces diamonds, rock-crystal, and vermilion. The same sun produces many kinds of plants. The same nourishment is converted into hair, nails, &c. As milk is changed into curds, and water into ice, so is Brahma variously transformed without external aids. So the spider spins its web from its own substance. So spirits assume various shapes.

Such a creed as this does not necessarily imply what the later Vedantists teach — that the world is all Maya, 'a mere illusion.' This illusion theory, now so popular among Indian philosophers, receives little countenance in the Upanishads, being rather imported from Buddhism. A true Vedantist, though he affirms that Brahma alone is real, allows a *vyavaharika*, 'practical existence' to souls, the world, and Ishvara, as distinguished from *paramarthika*, 'real,' and *pratibhasika*, 'apparent or illusory existence.' How, indeed, can it be denied that external things exist, when we see them before our eyes and feel them at every instant? But how, on the other hand, can it be maintained that an impure world is the manifestation of a pure spiritual essence? To avoid this difficulty, the supreme Spirit is represented as ignoring himself by a sort of self-imposed ignorance, in order to draw out from himself for his own amusement the separate individuated souls and various appearances, which, although really parts of his own essence, constitute the apparent phenomena of the universe. Hence the external world, the living souls of individual men, and even Ishvara, the personal God, are all described as created by a power which the Vedantist is obliged, for want of a better solution of his difficulty, to call A-vidya[1], generally translated 'Ignorance,' but perhaps better rendered by 'False knowledge' or 'False notion.'

Of this power there are two distinct forms of operation, viz. 1. that of envelopment (avarana), which, enveloping the soul, causes it to imagine that it is liable to mundane vicissitudes — that it is an agent or a patient; that it rejoices or grieves, &c. — as if a person under a delusion were to mistake a rope for a snake: 2. that of projection (vikshepa), which, affecting the soul in its state of pure intelligence, raises upon it the appearance of a world, producing first the five subtle elements and drawing out from them seventeen subtle bodies (also called linga-sharira, comprising the five organs of sense, the five organs of action, the five vital airs, with buddhi and manas), and the five gross elements in the same order as in the Sankhya (see p. 100). Hence the soul mistakes itself for a mere mortal, as it mistook the rope for a snake[2].

By reason of A-vidya, then, the Jivatman, or 'personal soul of every individual,' mistakes the world, as well as its own body and mind, for realities, just as a rope in a dark night might be mistaken for a snake. The moment the personal soul

---

1. Something like the 'Agnoia of Plato. See Banerjea's translation of the Sutras, p. 3.
2. See Ballantyne's Lecture on the Vedanta-sara, p. 25. Reference may also be made to the Vedanta-paribhasha, a text book of the most modern Vedantic school.

is set free from this self-imposed Ignorance by a proper
understanding of the truth, through the Vedanta philosophy,
all the illusion vanishes and the identity of the Jivatman and
of the whole phenomenal universe with the Paramatman, or
'one only really existing spirit,' is re-established[1].

Let me here introduce a version of part of a short Vedantic
tract in verse, called *Atma-bodha*, 'knowledge of soul,'
attributed to the great Shankaracharya. It is highly esteemed
as an exposition of Vedantic doctrines, and has therefore been
inserted by Dr. Haberlin in his anthology of shorter poems[2].
The following metrical lines may serve as a specimen of some
of the ideas contained in this well-known epitome of Hindu
pantheistic philosophy:

Knowledge alone effects emancipation.
As fire is indispensable to cooking
So knowledge is essential to deliverance (2).
Knowledge alone disperses ignorance,
As sunlight scatters darkness — not so acts;
For ignorance originates in works (3).
The world and all the course of mundane things
Are like the vain creation of a dream[3],
In which Ambition, Hatred, Pride, and Passion
Appear like phantoms mixing in confusion.
While the dream lasts the universe seems real,
But when 'tis past the world exists no longer (6).
Like the deceptive silver of a shell[4],
So at first sight the world deludes the man

---

1. See the passage from the Mundaka Upanishad, quoted p. 44.
2. There is also a Tamil version and commentary translated by the Rev.
   I. F. Kearns, Madras, 1867. I have consulted the Tamil commentary
   as given by Mr. Kearns.
3. Cf. Shakespeare's 'We are such stuff As dreams are made of, and our
   little life Is rounded with a sleep.' Tempest, Act iv. Scene 1.
4. That is, the mother-of-pearl oyster (*sukti*).

Who takes mere semblance for reality (7).
As golden bracelets are in substance one
With gold, so are all visible appearances
And each distinct existence one with Brahma (8).
By action of the fivefold elements[1]
Through acts performed in former states of being,
Are formed corporeal bodies, which become
The dwelling-place of pleasure and of pain (11).
The soul enwrapped in five investing sheaths[2]
Seems formed of these, and all its purity
Darkened, like crystal laid on coloured cloth (14).
As winnowed rice is purified from husk,
So is the soul disburdened of its sheaths
By force of meditation[3], as by threshing (15).
The soul is like a king whose ministers
Are body, senses, mind, and understanding[4].
The soul is wholly separate from these,
Yet witnesses and overlooks their actions (18).
The foolish think the Spirit acts, whereas
The senses are the actors, so the moon
Is thought to move when clouds are passing o'er it (19).

---

1. This is called Panchi-krita or Panchi-karana, the production of the
   body, and indeed of the whole world, by the action of the five
   elements (see p. 100), being a dogma of the Vedanta.
2. See the remarks, p. 133.
3. *Yukti* seems here to be equivalent to *yoga*. It may also mean 'argument,'
   'reasoning.'
4. The soul is supposed by Vedantists to have three conditions besides
   the conditions of pure intelligence, viz. waking, dreaming, and
   profound or dreamless sleep (*su-shupti*). While awake, the soul,
   associated with the body, is active and has to do with a real creation.
   While dreaming, it has to do with an unreal or illusory world. When
   profoundly and dreamlessly asleep, it is supposed to have retired by
   the channel of some of the pericardial arteries into the perfect repose
   of union with the supreme Soul. See Vedanta-sutra III. 2. 1-10.

When intellect and mind are present, then
Affections, inclinations, pleasures, pains
Are active; in profound and dreamless sleep
When intellect is non-existent, these
Exist not; therefore they belong to mind (22).
As brightness is inherent in the sun,
Coolness in water, warmness in the fire,
E'en so existence, knowledge, perfect bliss[1],
And perfect purity inhere in soul (23).
The understanding cannot recognize
The soul, nor does the soul need other knowledge
To know itself[2], e'en as a shining light
Requires no light to make itself perceived (27, 28).
The soul declares its own condition thus —
'I am distinct from body, I am free
From birth, old age, infirmity, and death.
I have no senses; I have no connection
With sound or sight or objects of sensation.
I am distinct from mind, and so exempt
From passion, pride, aversion, fear, and pain.
I have no qualities[3], I am without
Activity, and destitute of option[4],
Changeless, eternal, formless, without taint,
For ever free, for ever without stain.
I, like the boundless ether, permeate

---

1. Hence the Vedantist's name for the one universal Spirit, *Sac-cidananda.*
2. The celebrated Hindu maxim *Atmanam atmana pasya,* 'know (see) thyself by thyself,' or 'know the soul by the soul,' has, therefore, a deeper philosophical meaning than the still more celebrated Greek precept attributed to Thales.
3. The epithet *nir-guna,* 'quality-less,' so commonly applied to the supreme Being in India, will be better understood by a reference to p. 102.
4. *Nir-vikalpa* may perhaps be translated, 'destitute of all reflection,' or perhaps, 'free from all will.'

The universe within, without, abiding
Always, for ever similar in all,
Perfect, immovable, without affection,
Existence, knowledge, undivided bliss,
Without a second, One, supreme am I' (31-35).
The perfect consciousness that 'I am Brahma'
Removes the false appearances projected
By Ignorance[1], just as elixir, sickness (36).
The universal Soul knows no distinction
Of knower, knowledge, object to be known.
Rather is it enlightened through itself
And its own essence, which is simple knowledge (40).
When contemplation rubs the Arani[2]
Of soul, the flame of knowledge blazing up
Quickly consumes the fuel ignorance (41).
The saint[3] who has attained to full perfection
Of contemplation, sees the universe
Existing in himself, and with the eye
Of knowledge sees the All as the One Soul (46).
When bodily disguises[4] are dissolved,
The perfect saint becomes completely blended
With the one Soul, as water blends with water,
As air unites with air, as fire with fire (52).
That gain than which there is no greater gain,
That joy than which there is no greater joy,
That lore than which there is no greater lore,
Is the one Brahma — this is certain truth (53).
That which is through, above, below, complete,
Existence, wisdom, bliss[5], without a second[6],

---

1. *Avidya-vikshepan,* 'the projections of ignorance.' Seep p. 128.
2. See p. 18, note 2
3. Yogin, see p. 110.
4. *Upadhi,* a term for the illusive disguises assumed by Brahma.
5. *Sach-chid-anandam.*
6. *A-dvayam.*

Endless, eternal, one — know that as Brahma (55).
That which is neither coarse nor yet minute,
That which is neither short nor long, unborn,
Imperishable, without form, unbound
By qualities, without distinctive marks,
Without a name — know that indeed as Brahma (59).
Nothing exists but Brahma, when aught else
Appears to be, 'tis, like the mirage, false[1] (62).

With regard to the five sheaths (*pancha-kosa*) alluded to
in the fourteenth verse of the Atma-bodha, it must be noted
that in the Vedanta the individuated soul, when separated off
from the supreme Soul, is regarded as enclosed in a succession
of cases (*kohsa*) which envelope it and, as it were, fold one
over the other, 'like the coats of an onion[2].' The first or
innermost sheath is called the *Vijnana-maya-kosha* or 'sheath
composed of mere intellection,' associated with the organs of
perception. This gives the personal soul its first conception
of individuality. The second case is called the *Mano-maya* or
'sheath composed of mind,' associated with the organs of
action. This gives the individual soul its powers of thought
and judgement. The third envelope is called the *Prana-maya*
or 'breathing sheath,' i.e. the sheath composed of breath and
the other vital airs associated with the organs of action. The
fourth case is called the *Anna-maya* or 'covering supported
by food,' i.e. the corporeal form or gross body; the three
preceding sheaths when combined together, constituting the
subtle body. A fifth case, called *Ananda-maya* or 'that composed
of supreme bliss,' is also named, although not admitted by
all. It must be regarded as the innermost of all, and ought
therefore, when five are enumerated, to be placed before the
Vijnana-maya. Moreover, a collective totality of subtle bodies

---

1. *Mithya yatha maru-marichika.*
2. As remarked by Dr. Ballantyne, Lecture on the Vedanta-sara, p. 29.

is supposed to exist, and the soul, which is imagined to pass through these subtle bodies like a thread, is called the *Sutratman*, 'thread-soul' (occasionally styled the *Pranatman*), and sometimes identified with Hiranya-garbha.

Of course the Vedanta Theory, if pushed to its ultimate consequences, must lead to the neglect of all duties, religious and moral, of all activity, physical or intellectual, and of all self-culture. If everything be God, then you and he and I must be one. Why should any efforts be made for the advancement of self or for the good of others? Everything we have must be common property. According to the Brihad-aranyaka Upanishad (IV. 5):

Where there is anything like duality there one sees another, one smells another, one tastes another, one speaks to another, one hears another, one minds another, one regards another, one knows another; but where the whole of this is one spirit, then whom and by what can one see? whom and by what can one smell? whom and by what can one taste? to whom and by what can one speak? whom and by what can one hear? whom and by what can one mind? whom and by what can one regard? whom and by what can one know?

This Indian pantheism is paralleled by some phases of modern German thought, as described by Dean Mansel in the following extract from one of his Essays lately published:

With German philosophers the root of all mischief is the number two — Self and Not-self, Ego and Non-ego. The pantheist tells me that I have not a real distinct existence and unity of my own, but that I am merely a phenomenal manifestation, or an aggregate of many manifestations of the one infinite Being. If [then] we shrink from Nihilism, there remains the alternative of Pantheism. The instincts of our nature plead against annihilation and maintain, in spite of philosophy, that there must really exist something somewhere. Granting that something exists, why is that something to be called Ego? What qualities can it possess which shall make it *I* rather than *Thou*, or any one being rather than any other being? I am directly conscious of the existence of a self. But this consciousness is a delusion. This self is but the phenomenal shadow of a further self, of which I am not conscious. Why may not this also be a shadow of something further still? Why may there not be a yet more remote reality, which is itself neither self nor not-self, but the root and foundation, and at the same time the indifference of both? This ultimate existence, the one and sole reality, is then set up as the deity of philosophy, and the result is pure pantheism.

Perhaps it may not be out of place here to contrast with Indian ideas Aristotle's grand conception of the nature of God as propounded in the eleventh book of his Metaphysics[1]. In chapter vii of that book Aristotle says (not, however, quite in the order here given):

The principle of life is in God; for energy and mind constitutes life, and God is this energy. He, the first mover, imparts motion and pursues the work of creation as something that is loved. His course of life must be similar to what is most excellent in our own short career. But he exists for ever in this excellence, whereas this is impossible for us. His pleasure consists in the exercise of his essential energy, and on this account vigilance, wakefulness, and perception are most agreeable to him. Again, the more we examine God's nature the more wonderful does it appear to us. He is an eternal and most excellent Being. He is indivisible, devoid of parts, and having no magnitude, for God imparts motion through infinite time, and nothing finite, as magnitude is, can have an infinite capacity. He is a being devoid of passions and unalterable[2].

---

1. This work has been well translated by the Rev. J.H. M'Mahon.
2. Hence, according to the translator, Aristotle's idea of god is that he is a Being whose essence is love, manifested in eternal energy, the final cause of this energy being the happiness of his creatures, in which he himself participates for ever. Aristotle, again, warns his disciples against regarding God's nature through the medium of their

Before quitting the subject of the Vedanta philosophy it should be stated that in many points the Vedanta agrees with the Sankhya. The order of creation in both is nearly the same, though the 'Originant' in one case is *Prakriti,* in the other *A-vidya,* 'ignorance' (or 'false knowledge'). But even here an attempt is made by some to establish a community of ideas by identifying both *Prakriti* and *A-vidya* with *Maya* or 'illusion.' In both systems the gross elements proceed from subtle principles, imperceptible to sense, in the same order (see the Sankhyan account of the elements, p. 100). In both there is a subtle as well as a gross body[1]. The nature of the soul in being incapable of cognition without the help of the mind or internal organ (*antah-karana*) is described in nearly similar language by both. Again, this internal organ (*antah-karana*) is held by both to stand between the organs of perception and those of action, as an eleventh organ partaking of the nature of each (see p. 101). But while the Sankhya divides the internal organ into *Buddhi,* 'intellectual perception,' *Ahankara,* 'self-consciousness,' and *Manas,* 'the reasoning mind,' the first being the great source of the others (see p. 100), the Vedanta propounds a fourth division, viz. *Chitta* or 'the faculty of thought.' On the other hand, the Vedanta adds two Pramanas or 'instruments of true knowledge' (*An-upalabdhi,* 'non-perception' or 'negative proof,' and *Arthapatti,* 'inference from circumstances') to the four admitted by the Nyaya (see p. 77), while the Sankhya rejects the Nyaya *Upamana,* and retains as its only three Pramanas, *Pratyaksha, Anumana,* and *Shabda.*

own subjectivity. There is a celebrated passage in book XI, chap. viii, in which he says that traditions have been handed down representing the heavens as gods, and the divine essence as embracing the whole of nature; and these traditions, he affirms, are kept up to win over the multitude and secure obedience to the laws and for the sake of general expediency. On that account gods are described as existing in the form of man, or even as taking the shape of animals.

1. The gross body is sometimes called the nine-gated city of Brahma (*Brahma-pura*), from its being the abode of the soul and from its having nine openings.

Lecture VII

Irregular Systems and Eclectic School

Before passing to the Eclectic School I must notice briefly two heretical and irregular systems of philosophy, which probably grew out of Buddhism, or at least have much in common with it as well as with the six orthodox systems just described.

These two systems are, 1. that of the Jainas or Jains, 2. that of the Charvakas or Materialists. They are described in the celebrated Madhavacharya's work, called Sarva-darsana-sangraha, which is a concise description of various Hindu systems and sects, religious and philosophical, orthodox and heterodox, even including the science of applying quicksilver (*rasesvara*, regarded as a form of Shiva) or its preparations to various chemical and alchemical operations, and embracing also Panini's theory of grammar[1].

---

1. Madhava lived in the fourteenth century. He was elder brother of Sayana, and associated with him in the commentary on the Rig-veda. (By Mr. Burnell, however, in his preface to the Vansha-brahmana, he is identified with Sayana.) He was also prime minister in the court of Bukka I at Vijaya-nagara. He wrote many works (e.g. an introduction to the Mimansa philosophy, called Nyaya mala-vistara, a commentary on Parashara's law-book, the Kala-

Jainism

Madhava's account of the Jainas or Jains, whom he calls Arhatas (from *arhat,* 'venerable,' applied to a Jina or chief saint), comes third in his list of sects, and naturally follows his exposition of the Bauddha doctrines. Jainism is, in fact, the only representative of Buddhistic ideas now left in India, and has so much in common with them that, having already gained some insight into Buddhism, we need only notice a

---

nirnayas, &c.) besides the Sarva-darshana-sangraha, which treats of fifteen systems as follow: 1. *Charvaka-darhsana;* 2. *Bauddha-d°;* 3. *Arhata-d°* 4. *Ramanuja-d°* 5. *Purna-prajna-d°;* 6. *Nakulisha-pashupata-d°* 7. *Shavia-d°* 8. *Pratyabhijna-d°;* 9. *Rasesvara-d°;* 10. *Aulukya-d°;* 11. *Akshapada-d°;* 12. *Jaimini-d°;* 13. *Panini-d°;* 14. *Sankhya-d°;* 15. *Patanjala-d°.* The Vedanta is not included in the list. Ramanuja, the founder of the fourth, was a Vaishnava Reformer, who, according to H.H. Wilson, lived about the middle of the twelfth century. The fifth is the doctrine of Ananda-tirtha, surnamed Madhvacharya, and also called Madhya-mandira, his epithet *Purna-prajna* merely meaning 'one whose knowledge is complete.' The sixth is the system of a branch of the Maheshvaras, as shown by Professor E.B. Cowell (Colebrooks's Essays, I. pp. 431, 434). He conjectures that Shiva himself, called Nakulisa, may have been the supposed founder of this sect, and points out that the Pasupatas are worshippers of Shiva as *Pashu-pati,* 'master of all inferior creatures' (explained by some to mean 'lord of *pashu* or the soul entangled in the bonds of matter'). The eighth is like the sixth and that of the Maheshvaras, a form of Shaiva doctrine, but more pantheistic, the Shaivas maintaining that God is, in creating *Karmadi-sapeksha,* 'dependent on the acts &c. of individual souls,' while this eighth asserts that God's will is the only cause of creation; for it is said, 'He being independent (*nir-apekshah*) and regarding no face but his own, threw all existences as a reflection on the mirror of himself.' Hence *pratyabhijna* is defined as *pratimabhimu-khyena jnanam,* 'recognition as of a visible object or image.' The tenth is the Vaiseshika. See note, p. 82.

few of the distinctive features of a system which is certainly its near relation, if not its actual descendant[1].

The Jainas, who are still found in great numbers in various parts of India[2], are divided into two principal sects or parties, — 1. The Shvetambaras, 'clothed in white garments;' 2. the Dig-ambaras, 'sky-clad' or 'naked[3];' the latter, however, wear coloured garments, except while eating, and are required to carry peacocks' tails in their hands. These sects, though their doctrines rest on the same sacred books, called collectively Sutra[4], differ in some unimportant matters, such as the clothing or non-clothing of their images, the number of their heavens, &c. They both agree with the Buddhists in rejecting the Veda of the Brahmans. The principal point in the Jaina creed is the reverence paid to holy men, who, by long discipline, have raised themselves to divine perfection. The Jina or 'conquering saint,' who, having conquered all worldly desires, declares the true knowledge of the Tattvas, is with Jainas what the Buddha or 'perfectly enlightened saint' is with Buddhists. He is also called Jinesvara, 'chief of Jinas;' Arhat, 'the venerable;' Tirtha-kara or Tirthan-kara, 'the saint who has made the passage of the world;' Sarva-jna, 'omniscient;' Bhagavat, 'holy one.' Time

---

1. I have consulted Professor E.B. Cowell's appendix to Colebrooke on the Jainas, H.H. Wilson's essay, an article in Chambers' Cyclopaedia and in the 'Indian Antiquary' for September 1873, and a dissertation on the Jainas in Tamil by a learned Jain, named Sastram Aiyar, in the Rev. H. Bower's introduction to the Chintamani, Madras, 1868. Professor Kern regards the Jains as having originally formed one sect with the Buddhists.

2. They are most numerous in Gujerat and the west coast, but are found everywhere, especially in South Behar (Magadha), where they originated.

3. Also called Muktambaras. Vi-vasanas. A nickname for an ascetic of both sects is Lunchita-kesha, 'one who tears out his hair.'

4. See Introduction, p. xliv, note 1. They have also Puranas.

with Jainas proceeds in two eternally recurring cycles or
periods of immense duration, defying all human calculation:
1. the Utsarpini or 'ascending cycle;' 2. the Avasarpini or
'descending cycle.' Each of these has six stages. Those of the
Utsarpini period are bad-bad, bad, bad-good, good-bad, good,
good-good time. In the Avasarpini period the series begins
with good-good and goes regularly backwards. In the first
cycle the age and stature of men increases; in the other,
decreases. We are now in the fifth stage of the Avasaripini,
i.e. in 'bad' time. When the two cycles have run out, a Yuga
or 'age' is accompished. Twenty-four Jinas or 'perfect saints'
raised to the rank of gods have appeared in the present
Avasarpini cycle, twenty-four in the past Utsarpini, and twenty-
four will appear in the future[1]. The idols representing them
are always, like that of the Buddha, in a contemplative posture,
but have different animals, plants, and symbols accompanying
them (such as a bull, elephant, horse, ape, a lotus, the moon),
to serve as distinguishing characteristics. The first Jina of the
present cycle lived 8,400,000 years, and attained a stature
equal to the length of 500 bows (*dhanus*). The age and stature
of the second was somewhat less, and so in a descending scale.
The last two Jinas, Parsva-natha and Maha-vira, were probably

---

1. The names are all given in the Abhidhana-chintamani, a well-known
vocabulary of synonyms, by a learned Jain, named Hemachandra,
who is said to have lived in the twelfth century of our era. Those
of the present cycle are, 1. Rishabha or Vrishabha; 2. Ajita; 3.
Sambhava; 4. Abhi-nandana; 5. Sumati; 6. Padmaprabha; 7. Su-
parshva; 8. Chandra-prabha; 9. Pushpa-danta; 10. Sitala; 11. Shreyas
or Shreyansa; 12 Vasupujya; 13. Vimala; 14. Ananta; 15. Dharma;
16. Shanti; 17. Kunthu; 18. Ara; 19. Malli; 20. Muni-suvrata or Suvrata; 21 Nimi; 22. Nemi; 23. Parsva-natha or Parsva; 24; Vardhamana
or Maha-vira or Vira. The last of these dwindled to the size of an
ordinary man, and only lived forty, while the twenty-third lived a
hundred years.

real persons and are those principally revered by the Jainas of the present day[1], the first founder of the sect having been Parsva-natha, and its first active propagator, Maha-vira. In the same cycle there have lived twelve Chakra-vartins, 'Universal emperors,' nine divine personages called Bala-devas, nine called Vasudevas, and nine others called Prativasudevas, making a list of sixty-three divine persons in all[2].

With regard to the world, the Jainas affirm that, being formed of eternal atoms, it has existed and will exist eternally. They believe that it has three divisions, viz. lower, middle, and upper, and that there are numerous hells and heavens. All existing things are arranged under the two great Tattvas of Jiva, 'living soul,' and A-jiva, 'inanimate objects.' Of living souls there are three kinds: *a. Nitya-siddha,* 'ever perfect,' as the Jina; *b. Muktatman,* 'liberated soul;' *c. Baddhatma,* 'bound soul' or one bound by works and worldly associations. Material objects are sometimes classed under a Tattva called *Pudgala,* and some make seven, others nine Tattvas.

There are three 'gems' which together effect the soul's Moksha, 'liberation,' viz. a. right intuition (*samyag-darshana*); b. right knowledge (*samyag-jnana*); c. right conduct (*samyak-charitra*). This last consists in observing five duties or vows of self-restraint (*Vratas*), thus: 1. Do not kill or injure; which Jainas carry to so preposterous an extreme that they strain

---

1. Dr. Muir has kindly allowed me to read his abstract of Professor H. Kern's learned dissertation on the date of Buddha's death and the Ashoka inscriptions, written for a forthcoming number of the 'Indian Antiquary,' whence I gather that, notwithstanding the notable difference between the legends of Sakya-muni and Jina Maha-vira, there are also striking points of resemblance. Maha-vira is said to have been the son of Siddhartha, of the solar race, and to have died in 388 B.C. which is also Dr. Kern's date for the death of the Buddha Sakya-muni.

2. See their names in Hemachandra's third chapter.

water before drinking it, sweep the ground with a brush before treading on it, never eat or drink in the dark, and sometimes wear muslin before their mouths to prevent the risk of swallowing minute insects. Moreover, they never eat figs or any fruit containing seed, nor will they even touch flesh-meat with their hands. 2. Do not tell lies. 3. Steal not. 4. Be chaste and temperate in thought, word, and deed. 5. Desire nothing immoderately.

There are two classes of Jainas, as of Buddhists (see p. 61), viz. *Shravakas,* those who engage in lay or secular occupations, and *Yatis,* monks or ascetics, who are required to pluck out their hair or wear it cropped short. The latter are often collected in Mathas or 'monasteries,' being called *Sadhu* when not monastic. Jainas are sometimes called Syad-vadins, from their method of propounding seven modes of reconciling opposite views as to the possibility of anything existing or not existing (*sapta-bhanga-naya, syad-vada*). It should be noted that they accord a sort of modified worship to the Hindu gods (especially Brahma, Vishnu, Siva, and Ganesa, as subordinate to the Jinas); and are even observers of caste, and claim to be regarded as Hindus, though rejecting the Hindu Veda. In Western India the priests of Jaina temples are brahmans.

The Charvakas

Nothing is known about Charvaka, the Pyrrho and Epicurus of India and founder of the materialistic school. His system is the worst form of all heresies, and therefore honoured with the first place in Madhavacharya's Sarva-dar-sana-sangraha. In the Shanti-parvan of the Mahabharata (1410, &c.) there is a story of a Rakshasa named Charvaka, who, in the disguise of a mendicant Brahman, reviled Yudhishthira during his triumphant entry into Hastinapura, and uttered profane and heretical doctrines. He was, however, soon detected, and the real Brahmans, filled with fury, killed him on the spot. This legend may possibly rest on some basis of fact.

The creed of the Charvakas, who are sometimes called Lokayatas or Lokayatikas[1], is said to have been derived from the Varhaspatya Sutras (Aphorisms of Vrihaspati). They reject all the Pramanas, or 'sources of true knowledge,' except Pratyaksha, 'perception by the senses' (see p. 77); they admit only four Tattvas or 'eternal principles,' viz. earth, air, fire, and water, and from these intelligence (*chaitanya*) is alleged to be produced; they affirm that the soul is not different from the body; and, lastly, they assert that all the phenomena of the world are spontaneously produced, without even the help of Adrishta (see p. 73). I sum up their views with a version of a passage in the Sarva-darsana-sangraha (Ishvara-chandra Vidyasagara's edition, p. 6), setting forth the opinions of the Charvaka materialists according to the supposed teaching of Vrishaspati[2]. The sentiments, it will be perceived, are worthy of the most sceptical, materialistic, and epicurean of European writers:

No heaven exists, no final liberation,
No soul, no other world, no rites of caste,
No recompense for acts; the Agnihotra[3],

---

1. By some this name is given to a subdivision of the Charvakas. The name Charvaka is applied to any adherent of the materialistic school; see Vedanta-sara, 82-85.

2. I have consulted Professor E.B. Cowell's appendix to Colebrooke's Essay, and Dr. Muir's prose translation as given by him in his article on 'Indian Materialists' (Royal Asiatic Society's Journal, vol. xix, art. xi). He compares a passage in the Vishnu-purana III. 18, which contains similar sentiments. Cf. also the speech of the rationalistic Brahman Javali, addressed to Rama in the Ramayana.

3. See note, p. 34.

The triple Veda, triple self-command[1],
And all the dust and ashes of repentance —
These yield a means of livelihood for men,
Devoid of intellect and manliness.
If victims slaughtered at a sacrifice
Are raised to heavenly mansions[2],   why should not
The sacrificer immolate his father?
If offerings of food can satisfy[3]
Hungry departed spirits, why supply
The man who goes a journey with provisions?
His friends at home can feed him with oblations.
If those abiding in celestial spheres
Are filled with food presented upon earth,
Why should not those who live in upper stories
Be nourished by a meal spread out below?
While life endures let life be spent in ease
And merriment[4]; let a man borrow money
From all his friends and feast on melted butter.
How can this body when reduced to dust
Revisit earth? And if a ghost can pass
To other worlds, why does not strong affection
For those he leaves behind attract him back?

---

1. *Tri-danda,* 'control over thoughts, words, and actions,' denoted by the three Dandas or staves carried by ascetics. See Manu XII. 10, 11.
2. This, as Dr. Muir points out, refers to Manu. V. 42, where it is stated that animals duly sacrificed are conveyed to mansions of supreme felicity. Cf. Mahabharata, Ashvamedhika-parvan 793 &c.
3. This is a hit at the Shraddha, one of the most important of all Hindu religious acts, when oblations of cakes and libations of water are made to the spirits of deceased fathers, grandfathers, and progenitors. The strict observance of these ceremonies at regular intervals is at least an evidence of the strength of filial feeling among Hindus. Respect for parents and their memory has all the sanction of religion, and is even more insisted on as a religious duty than in Europe.
4. 'Let us eat and drink, for to-morrow we die,' 1 Cor. xv. See Dr. Muir's note. Compare such Horatian precepts as Epod. XIII. 3, &c.

The costly rites enjoined for those who die
Are a mere means of livelihood devised
By sacerdotal cunning — nothing more.
The three composers of the triple Veda
Were rogues, or evil spirits, or buffoons.
The recitation of mysterious words
And jabber[1] of the priests is simple nonsense.

The Eclectic School Represented by the Bhagavad-gita

As a fitting conclusion to the subject of Indian philosophy let
me endeavour to give some idea of one of the most interesting
and popular works in the whole range of Sanskrit literature,
called the Bhagavad-gita, the Song of Bhagavat — that is, the
mystical doctrines (Upanishadah[2]) sung by 'the adorable one'
— a name applied to Krishna when identified with the supreme
Being. This poem, abounding in sentiments borrowed from
the Upanishads, and commented on by the great Vedantic
teacher Shankaracarya, may be taken to represent the Eclectic
school of Indian philosophy. As the regular systems or
Darshanas were more or less developments of the Upanishads,
so the Eclectic school is connected with those mystical treatises
through the Svetasvatara Upanishad[3] of the Black Yajur-veda

---

1. Two curious Vedic words *jarbhari* and *turphari,* are given in the text
   as specimens of what I suppose modern scoffers might call 'Vedic
   slang.' They occur, as Dr. Muir points out, in Rig-veda. X. 106. 6,
   and Nirukta XIII. 5. For their explanation see Bohtlingk and Roth
   and my Sanskrit-English Dictionary.
2. At the end of each chapter the name of the chapter is given in the plural;
   thus, *Iti-sri-bhagavad-gitasu upanishatsu, &c.* See note 1, p. 149.
3. The name of this Upanishad is derived from a sage, Svetasvatara,
   who, at the end of the work (VI. 21), is said to have taught the

(see p. 48). This latter is doubtless a comparatively modern work, but whether composed before or after the Bhagavad-gita, certain it is that the design of both appears to be the same. They both aim at reconciling the conflicting views of different systems, and both do so by attempting to engraft the Sankhya and Yoga upon Vedanta doctrines[1]. Although, therefore, the order of creation and much of the cosmogony and other Sankhya views are retained in both, the paramount sovereignty of the supreme Soul of the universe (Brahma) as the source and ultimate end of all created things, and yet wholly independent of all such creations, is asserted by both.

Some extracts from the Svetasvatara, describing the character and attributes of this supreme Being, who is everything and in everything, have already been given at p. 45. The following are additional extracts from the first and third chapters (Roer, pp. 50, 55, 58):

This (absolute Brahma) should be meditated on as eternal and as abiding in one's own soul; for beside him there is nothing to be known (natah param veditavyam, hi kinchit). As oil in seeds (tileshu), butter in cream, water in a river, and fire in wood, so is that absolute Soul perceived within himself by a person who beholds him by means of truth and by austerity.

---

doctrine of Brahma to the most excellent of the four orders. It has been translated by Dr. Roer into English, and nearly all by Professor Weber into German (Indische Studien I. 422-429). The author must have been a Shaiva (not a Vaishnava, like the author of the Bhagavad-gita), as he identifies Rudra with the supreme Being. According to Wilson, Shveta, 'white,' Shvetasva, 'white-horsed,' Shveta-shikha, 'white-haired,' and Shvetalohita, 'white-blooded,' were names of four disciples of Shiva. Weber suspects here a mission of Syrian Christians, and thinks that both the Upanishad and the Gita, the latter especially, may have borrowed ideas from Christianity.

1. See Dr. Roer's introduction for a full explanation of this.

He is the eye of all, the face of all, the arm of all, the foot of all.

Thou art the black bee (*nilah patangah*), the green bird with red-coloured eye, the cloud in whose womb sleeps the lightning, the seasons, the seas. Without beginning thou pervadest all things by thy almighty power; for by thee are all the worlds created.

The following, again, is an example of a passage occurring in the fourth chapter (5), which is decidedly Sankhyan in its tone:

The one unborn (individual soul), for the sake of enjoyment, lies close to the One unborn (*Prakriti*), is a white, red and black colour [answering evidently to the three Sankhyan Gunas], which is of one and the same form, and produces a manifold offspring. Then the other unborn (or eternal soul) abandons her (*Prakriti*) whose enjoyment he has enjoyed.

Let us now turn to the Bhagavad-gita. The real author of this work is unknown. It was at an early date dignified by a place in the Mahabharata, in which poem it lies embedded, or rather inlaid like a pearl[1], contributing with other numerous episodes to the mosaic-like character of that immense epic. The Bhagavad-gita, however, is quite independent of the great

---

1. It has been interpolated into the Bhishma-parvan of the Maha-bharata and is divided into eighteen chapters or into three sections, each containing six lectures, commencing at line 830 of the twenty-fifth chapter of the Parva, and ending at line 1532. Such is the estimation in which the work is held both in Asia and Europe, that it has been translated into Hindi, Telugu, Kanarese, and other Eastern languages, and is also well known by European translations, of which that of Sir C. Wilkins, published in London in 1785, was the first. Mr. J.C. Thomson's edition and translation, published, with an elaborate introduction, by Stephen Austin in 1855, is, on the whole, a very meritorious production, and I am glad to acknowledge my obligations to it.

epic; and it cannot be questioned that its proper place in any arrangement of Sanskrit literature framed with regard to the continuous development and progress of Hindu thought and knowledge should be at the close of the subject of philosophy. The author was probably a Brahman and nominally a Vaishnava, but really a philosopher whose mind was cast in a broad and comprehensive mould. He is supposed to have lived in India during the first or second century of our era[1]. Finding no rest for his spirit in any one system of philosophy, as commonly taught in his own time, much less in the corrupt Brahmanism which surrounded him, he was led to make a selection from the various schools of rationalistic and dogmatic thought, so as to construct a composite theory of his own. This he did with great perspicuity and beauty of language, interweaving various opinions into one system by taking, so to speak, threads from the Sankhya, Yoga, and Vedanta, as well as from the later theory of Bhakti or 'faith in a supreme Being[2].' With these threads he weaves, as it were, a woof of many-coloured hues of thought, which are shot across a stiff warp of stern uncompromising pantheistic doctrines, worthy of the most decided adherent of the Vedanta school[3]. Of these cross threads

---

1. Some consider that he lived as late as the third century, and some place him even later, but with these I cannot agree.
2. The Aphorisms of Sandilya, the editing of which was commenced by Dr. Ballantyne and continued by Professor Griffith, his successor at Benares, deny that knowledge is the one thing needful, and insist on the subjection of knowledge to the higher principle of *Bhakti,* 'faith in God.' The first Aphorism introduces the inquiry into the nature of faith, thus, *Athato bhakti-jijnasa.* Professor Weber and others think that the introduction of *pistis* and *agape* into the Hindu system is due to the influence of Christianity.
3. The predominance of pantheistic doctrines, notwithstanding the attempt to interweave them with portions of the Sankhya and Yoga systems, is denoted by the fact that the Vedantists claim this poem as an exponent of their own opinions.

the most conspicuous are those of the Sankhya system, for which the author of the Gita has an evident predilection. The whole composition is skilfully thrown into the form of a dramatic poem or dialogue, something after the manner of the book of Job or a dialogue of Plato[1]. The speakers are the two most important personages in the Mahabharata, Arjuna and Krishna. Arjuna is perhaps the real hero of that epic. He is the bravest, and yet the most tender-hearted of the five sons of Pandu. The god Krishna, who is identified with Vishnu[2], and in this philosophical dialogue is held to be an incarnation of the supreme being himself, had taken human form as the son of Devaki and Vasudeva, who was brother of Kunti, wife of Pandu. Hence the god was cousin of the sons of Pandu, brother of Dhritarashtra, the sons of these brothers being of

---

1. It is, however, styled an Upanishad, or rather a series of Upanishads it reveals secret and mystical doctrines. For instance, at the close of the dialogue (XVIII. 63), Krishna says, 'I have thus communicated to you knowledge more secret than secret itself' (*iti me jnanam akhyatam guhyad guhyataram maya*).

2. Professor Weber (Indische Studien I. 400) thinks that Brahmans may have crossed the sea to Asia Minor at the beginning of the Christian era, and on their return made use of Christian narratives to fabricate the story of their deified hero, Krishna, whose very name would remind them of Christ. The legends of the birth of Krishna and his persecution by Kansa, remind us, says Weber, too strikingly of the corresponding Christian narratives to leave room for the supposition that the similarity is quite accidental. According to Lassen, the passages of the Mahabharata in which Krishna receives divine honours are later interpolations, and the real worship of Krishna is not found before the fifth or sixth century. Dr. Lorinser, as we shall presently see, thinks he can trace the influence of Christianity throughout the Bhagavad-gita. The legend of Shveta-dvipa in the Mahabharata (XII. 12703) certainly favours the idea of some intercourse with Europe at an early date. The legends relating to Krishna are found detailed at full in the tenth book of the Bhagavata-purana and its Hindi paraphrase, the Prem Sagar.

course related as cousins to each other. In the great war which arose between the two families, each contending for the kingdom of Hastina-pura[1], Krishna refused to take up arms on either side, but consented to act as the charioteer of Arjuna and to aid him with his advice. At the commencement of the Bhagavad-gita the two contending armies are supposed to be drawn up in battle array, when Arjuna, struck with sudden compunction at the idea of fighting his way to a kingdom through the blood of his kindred, makes a sudden resolution to retire from the combat, confiding his thoughts to Krishna thus (I. 28-33):

Beholding these my relatives arrayed
Before my eyes in serried line of battle,
Preparing for the deadly fray, my limbs
Are all relaxed, my blood dries up, a tremor
Palsies my frame, the hairs upon my skin
Bristle with horror, all my body burns
As if with fever, and my mind whirls round
So that I cannot stand upright, nor hold
The bow Gandiva slipping from my hand.
I cannot — will not fight — O mighty Krishna.
I seek not victory, I seek no kingdom.
What shall we do with regal pomp and power,
What with enjoyments or with life itself,
When we have slaughtered all our kindred here?

Krishna's reply to this speech is made the occasion of the long philosophical and theological dialogue which, in fact, constitutes the Bhagavad-gita, the main design of which undoubtedly is to exalt the duties of caste above all other obligations, including the ties of friendship and affection, but at the same time to show that the practice of these duties is

---

1. See the epitome of this great epic in a subsequent Lecture.

compatible with all the self-mortification and concentration of thought enjoined by the Yoga philosophy, as well as with the deepest devotion to the supreme Being, with whom Krishna claims to be identified[1]. As Arjuna belongs to the military caste, he is exhorted to perform his duties as a soldier. Again and again is he urged to fight, without the least thought about consequences, and without the slightest question as to the propriety of slaughtering his relations, if only he acts in the path of duty. Hence we have the following sentiments repeated more than once (III. 35, XVIII. 47, 48):

> Better to do the duty of one's caste[2],
> Though bad and ill-performed and fraught with evil,
> Than undertake the business of another,
> However good it be. For better far
> Abandon life at once than not fulfil
> One's own appointed work; another's duty
> Brings danger to the man who meddles with it.
> Perfection is alone attained by him
> Who swerves not from the business of his caste.

Remembering the sacred character attributed to this poem and the veneration in which it has always been held throughout India, we may well understand that such words as these must have exerted a powerful influence for the last 1800 years; tending, as they must have done, to rivet the fetters of caste-

---

1. There is a sect among the Hindus called Ganapatyas, who identify Ganapati or Ganesa with the supreme Being. Their doctrines are embodied in the Ganesa-purana, but they have a poem called the Ganesa-gita, which is identical in substance with the Bhagavad-gita, the name of Ganesa being substituted for that of Krishna.
2. Compare Sakuntala, verse 133, 'Verily the occupation in which a man is born, though it be in bad repute, must not be abandoned.' The words used (*saha-jam karma*) are the same as those in the Bhagavad-gita.

institutions which, for several centuries preceding the Christian era, notwithstanding the efforts of the great liberator Buddha, increased year by year their hold upon the various classes of Hindu society, impeding mutual intercourse, preventing healthy interchange of ideas, and making national union almost impossible.

Before proceeding to offer further examples, we may remark that as the Bhagavad-gita is divided into three sections, each containing six chapters, so the philosophical teaching is somewhat distinct in each section.

The first section dwells chiefly on the benefits of the Yoga system, pointing out, however, as we have already observed, that the asceticism of the Yoga ought to be joined with action and the performance of regular caste duties, and winding up with a declaration that the grand end and aim of all asceticism is to attain that most desirable pantheistic state which enables a man to see God in everything and everything in God. Arjuna is exhorted as a member of the soldier-caste to dismiss all doubt about the propriety of fighting and killing his relations, by an argument drawn from the eternal existence of the soul, which is nobly expressed thus (II. 121, &c.)[1]:

> The wise grieve not for the departed, nor for those who yet survive.
> Ne'er was the time when I was not, nor thou, nor yonder chiefs, and ne'er
> Shall be the time when all of us shall be not; as the embodied soul
> In this corporeal frame moves swiftly on through boyhood, youth, and age,

---

1. I have endeavoured to give a more literal version than the well-known one of Dean Milman, though I have followed him in some expressions.

So will it pass through other forms hereafter — be not
grieved thereat.
The man whom pain and pleasure, heat and cold affect not,
he is fit
For immortality; whatever is not cannot be, whatever is
Can never cease to be. Know this — the Being that spread
this universe
Is indestructible. Who can destroy the Indestructible?
These bodies that enclose the everlasting soul, inscrutable,
Immortal, have an end; but he who thinks the soul can be
destroyed,
And he who deems it a destroyer, are alike mistaken; it
Kills not, and is not killed; it is not born, nor doth it ever
die;
It has no past nor future — unproduced, unchanging, infinite;
he
Who knows it fixed, unborn, imperishable, indissoluble,
How can that man destroy another, or extinguish aught
below?
As men abandon old and threadbare clothes to put on others
new,
So casts the embodied soul its worn-out frame to enter other
forms.
No dart can pierce it; flame cannot consume it, water wet
it not,
Nor scorching breezes dry it — indestructible, incapable
Of heat or moisture or aridity, eternal, all-pervading,
Steadfast, immovable, perpetual, yet imperceptible,
Incomprehensible, unfading, deathless, unimaginable[1].

The duty of Yoga or 'intense concentration of the mind
on one subject' (viz. the supreme Being, here identified with
Krishna), till at last the great end of freedom from all thought,

---

1. Compare the passage from the Katha Upanishad, translated p. 47.

perfect calm, and absorption in the Deity are obtained, is enjoined with much force of language in the second and sixth books, from which I extract the following examples, translated nearly literally, but not quite according to the order of the text:

> That holy man who stands immovable,
> As if erect upon a pinnacle[1],
> His appetites and organs all subdued,
> Sated with knowledge secular and sacred,
> To whom a lump of earth, a stone, or gold[2],
> To whom friends, relatives, acquaintances,
> Neutrals and enemies, the good and bad,
> Are all alike, is called 'one yoked with God.'
> The man who aims at the supreme condition
> Of perfect yoking[3] with the Deity
> Must first of all be moderate in all things,
> In food, in sleep, in vigilance, in action,
> In exercise and recreation. Then
> Let him, if seeking God by deep abstraction,
> Abandon his possessions and his hopes,
> Betake himself to some secluded spot[4],
> And fix his heart and thoughts on God alone.
> There let him choose a seat, not high nor low,
> And with a cloth or skin to cover him,
> And Kusha grass beneath him, let him sit
> Firm and erect, his body, head and neck
> Straight and immovable, his eyes directed

---

1. *Kuta-sthah*. (VI. 8) may mean 'standing erect like a peak.'
2. Tersely expressed in Sanskrit by *sama-loshtasma-kancanah*. VI. 8.
3. I use these expressions as kindred words to the Sanskrit *Yukta* and *yoga*. 'Joined' and 'junction' are also cognate expressions.
4. Cf. Matt. Vi. 6, 'But thou, when thou prayest, enter into thy closet, and when thou hast shut thy door, pray to thy Father which is in secret.'

Towards a single point[1], not looking round,
Devoid of passion, free from anxious thought,
His heart restrained, and deep in meditation.
E'en as a tortoise draws its head and feet
Within its shell, so must he keep his organs
Withdrawn from sensual objects. He whose senses
Are well controlled attains to sacred knowledge,
And thence obtains tranquillity of thought.
Without quiescence there can be no bliss.
E'en as a storm-tossed ship upon the waves,
So is the man whose heart obeys his passions,
Which, like the winds, will hurry him away.
Quiescence is the state of the Supreme.
He who, intent on meditation, joins
His soul with the Supreme, is like a flame
That flickers not when sheltered from the wind.

I pass now to the second division of this poem, in which
the pantheistic doctrines of the Vedanta are more directly
inculcated than in the other sections. Krishna here in the
plainest language claims adoration as one with the great
universal Spirit, pervading and constituting the universe. I
extract portions from different parts of this section without
observing the order of the text, which contains much
tautology, as well as repetitions of similar ideas in different
language:

What'er thou dost perform, whate'er thou eatest,
Whate'er thou givest to the poor, whate'er
Thou offerest in sacrifice, whatever
Thou doest as an act of holy penance,

---

1. The text (VI. 13) says, 'fixing his eyes on the tip of his nose'
(*samprekshya nasikagram*). See p. 111.

Do all as if to me, O Arjuna (IX. 27)[1].
I am the ancient sage[2], without beginning,
I am the Ruler and the All-sustainer[3],

---

1. Compare 1 Cor. x. 31. 'Whether therefore ye eat, or drink, or whatsoever ye do, do all to the glory of God.' Dr. Lorinser, expanding the views of Professor Weber and others concerning the influence of Christianity on the legends of Krishna, thinks that many of the sentiments of the Bhagavad-gita have been directly borrowed from the New Testament, copies of which, he thinks, found their way into India about the third century, when he believes the poem to have been written. He even adopts the theory of a parallel in the names of Christ and Krishna. He seems, however, to forget that fragments of truth are to be found in all religious systems, however false, and that the Bible, though a true revelation, is still in regard to the human mind, through which the thoughts are transfused, a thoroughly Oriental book, cast in an Oriental mould, and full of Oriental ideas and expressions. Some of his comparisons seem mere coincidences of language, which might occur quite naturally and independently. In other cases, where he draws attention to coincidences of ideas — as, for example, the division of the sphere of self-control into thought, word, and deed in chap. XVII. 14-16, &c., and of good works into prayer, fasting and alms-giving — how could these be borrowed from Christianity, when they are also found in Manu, which few will place later than the fifth century B.C.? Thus a *Tridandin* (Manu XII. 10) is explained to mean 'a triple commander,' who commands his thoughts, words, and actions (see note 1, p. 144); the same division is found in Manu II. 192, 236. Professor Cowell has pointed out that it occurs still earlier than Manu, in the Black Yajur-veda VI. 1. 7, and its Aranyaka X. 1. 10, and in the Aitareya-brahmana III. 28. Plato also has the same in his Protagoras (p. 348), and it is found in the Zand Avasta (Gatha Ahunavaiti III. 3). Nevertheless, something may be said for Dr. Lorinser's theory. His German translation (1869) is rich in notes, pointing out parallels. See also the 'Indian Antiquary' for October 1873.
2. *Kavih puranah* VIII. 9. 'Kavi' in Vedic Sanskrit means 'wise,' and is an epithet applied to most of the gods, especially to Agni. The meaning 'poet' belongs to later Sanskrit.
3. *Sarvasya dhata* VIII. 9.

I am incomprehensible in form,
More subtle and minute than subtlest atoms[1];
I am the cause of the whole universe;
Through me it is created and dissolved;
On me all things within it hang suspended,
Like pearls upon a string[2]. I am the light
In sun and moon, far, far beyond the darkness[3];
I am the brilliancy in flame, the radiance
In all that's radiant, and the light of lights[4],
The sound in ether, fragrance in the earth,
The seed eternal of existing things[5],
The life in all, the father, mother, husband,
Forefather, and sustainer of the world,
Its friend and lord. I am its way[6] and refuge,
Its habitation and receptacle,
I am its witness. I am Victory
And Energy; I watch the universe
With eyes and face in all directions turned[7].
I dwell, as Wisdom, in the heart of all[8].
I am the Goodness of the good, I am
Beginning, Middle, End, eternal Time,

---

1. *Anor Aniyan* VIII. 9. Compare p. 88 of this volume.
2. VII. 7. Dr. Lorinser compares Rom. xi. 36, 'Of him, and through him, and unto him, are all things.' John i. 3, 'All things were made by him; and without him was not anything made that was made.'
3. *Prabhasmi sasi-suryayoh.* VII. 8. *Tamasah parastat* VIII. 9. Cf. 1 John 1. 5, 'God is light, and in him is no darkness at all.' See Rig-veda I. 50. 10.
4. *Jyotisham jyotih.* XIII. 17. Cf. Brihad-aranyaka Upanishad, quoted p. 41 of this volume.
5. *Sarva-bhutanam vijam* VII. 10, X. 39. Cf. John i. 3, 'All things were made by him.'
6. *Gati* IX. 18. Cf. John xiv. 6, 'I am the way.'
7. *Vishvato-mukha*, 'facing in all direction,' IX. 15.
8. *Jnanam, hridi sarvasya nishthitam* XIII. 17. Cf. 2 Cor. iv. 6.

The Birth, the Death of all[1]. I am the symbol A
Among the characters[2]. I have created all
Out of one portion of myself. E'en those
Who are of low and unpretending birth[3],
May find the path to highest happiness,
If they depend on me; how much more those
Who are by rank and penance holy Brahmans
And saintly soldier-princes like thyself.
Then be not sorrowful; from all thy sins
I will deliver thee[4]. Think thou on me,

---

1. Compare Rev. i. 17, 18, 'I am the first and the last; and have the
keys of hell and of death.' Mr. Mullens draws attention to parallel
descriptions of the supreme Ruler in the Greek Orphic hymns: 'Zeus
was the first and Zeus the last; Zeus is the head; Zeus, the centre;
from Zeus have all things been made; Zeus is the breath of all things;
Zeus is the sun and moon,' &c. See his Essay, p. 193, and cf. note
1, p. 116. Cf. Also an inscription said to exist in a temple of Athene.
2. *Aksharanam a-karo smi* X. 33. Compare Rev. i. 8, 'I am Alpha and
Omega.'
3. *Papa-yanayah,* 'base-born,' IX. 32. The text states who these are, viz.
Women, Vaisya, and Sudras. This is significant in regard to the Hindu
estimate of the female sex. A woman's religion is thought to consist
in obedience first to her father and then to her husband, with
attention to domestic duties. See Manu II. 67. But the joining of
Vaisyas with Sudras is curious (cf. p. 159. 6). Brahmans, Kshatriyas,
and Rajarshis, i.e. holy personages — half princes, half saints — are
by birth and rank fitted for religious exercises, and more likely to
reach heaven.
4. *Aham tvam sarva-papebhyo mochayishyami ma shuchah.* Cf.
Matt. ix. 2, 'Be of good cheer; thy sins be forgiven thee.' A sense
of original corruption seems to be felt by all classes of Hindus, as
indicated by the following prayer used after the Gayatri by many
religious persons:

Papo 'ham papa-karmaham papatma papa-sambhavah,
Trahi mam, pundarikaksha sarva-papa-hara Hare,

'I am sinful, I commit sin, my nature is sinful, I am conceived
in sin,
Save me, O thou lotus-eyed Hari, the remover of sin.'

Have faith in me, adore and worship me[1],
And join thyself in meditation to me;
Thus shalt thou come to me, O Arjuna;
Thus shalt thou rise to my supreme abode,
Where neither sun nor moon have need to shine,
For know that all the lustre they possess is mine[2].

I come now to chapter XI, called 'the Vision (or Revelation) of the Universal Form' (*vishva-rupa-darshanam*). Arjuna filled with awe at the discovery of the true nature of Krishna, acting as his charioteer, addresses him thus:

Most mighty Lord supreme, this revelation
Of thy mysterious essence and thy oneness
With the eternal Spirit, clears away
The mists of my illusions. Show me then
Thy form celestial, most divine of men[3],
If haply I may dare to look upon it.

To this Krishna replies:

Thou canst not bear to gaze upon my shape
With these thy human eyes, O son of Pandu,
But now I gift thee with celestial vision;
Behold me in a hundred thousand forms,
In phases, colours, fashions infinite.

---

1. The original is, *Manmana bhava mad-bhakto mad-yaji mam namaskuru* IX. 34. Cf. Prov. Xxiii. 26, 'My son, give me thine heart.'
2. *Na tad Bhasayate suryo na Shashankah.* XV. 6. *Yad aditya-gatam tejo yac ḍandramasi tat tejo viddhi mamakam* XV. 12. Cf. Rev. xxi. 23, 'The city had no need of the sun, neither of the moon, to shine in it: for the glory of God did lighten it.' Cf. also Mahabharata III. 1745, &c., *Na tatra suryah somo va dyotate na cha pavakah, Svayaiva prabhaya tatra dyotante punya-labdhaya,* 'there (in Indra's heaven) the sun shines not, nor the moon nor fire; there they (righteous men) shine by their own glory acquired by their own merit.'
3. *Purushottama,* 'most excellent of men,' a common name for Krishna.

Here follows the description of Krishna's supernatural transformation[1]:

Thus having said, the mighty Lord of all
Displayed to Arjuna his form supreme,
Endowed with countless mouths and countless eyes,
With countless faces turned to every quarter,
With countless marvellous appearances,
With ornaments and wreaths and robes divine,
With heavenly fragrance and celestial weapons.
It was as if the firmament were filled,
All in an instant, with a thousand suns,
Blazing with dazzling lustre, so beheld he
The glories of the universe collected
In the one person of the God of gods[2].

Arjuna, with every hair on his body bristling with awe, bows his head at this vision, and folding his hands in reverence, gives utterance to a passionate outburst of enthusiastic adoration, which I here abridge:

I see thee, mighty Lord of all, revealed
In forms of infinite diversity.
I see thee like a mass of purest light,
Flashing thy lustre everywhere around.
I see thee crowned with splendour like the sun,
Pervading earth and sky, immeasurable,

---

1. The idea of this, Dr. Lorinser considers borrowed from the Gospel narrative of the transfiguration. It is certainly very instructive to contrast the simplicity of the Gospel scene: "His face did shine as the sun, and his raiment was white as the light,' Matt. xvii. 2, Mark ix. 3.

2. In the Udyoga-parva of the Mahabharata (4419-4430) Krishna reveals his form in the same way to the assembled princes, who are obliged to close their eyes at the awful sight, while the blind Dhritarashtra is gifted with divine vision that he may behold the glorious spectacle (4437).

Boundless, without beginning, middle, end,
Preserver of imperishable law,
The everlasting Man[1]; the triple world
Is awe-struck at this vision of thy form,
Stupendous, indescribable in glory.
Have mercy, God of gods; the universe
Is fitly dazzled by thy majesty,
Fitly to thee alone devotes its homage.
At thy approach the evil demons flee,
Scattered in terror to the winds of heaven.
The multitude of holy saints[2] adore thee —
Thee, first Creator[3], lord of all the gods,
The ancient One[4], supreme Receptacle
Of all that is and is not, knowing all,
And to be known by all. Immensely vast,
Thou comprehendest all, thou art the All (XI. 40).
To thee earth's greatest heroes must return,
Blending once more with thy resplendent essence,
Like mighty rivers rushing to the ocean (XI. 28).
To thee be sung a thousand hymns of praise
By every creature and from every quarter,
Before, above, behind. Hail! Hail! Thou All!
Again and yet again I worship thee.
Have mercy, I implore thee, and forgive,
That I, in ignorance of this thy glory,
Presumed to call thee Friend; and pardon too

---

1. *Sanatanah, purushah* (XI. 18) may be translated 'the eternal Spirit.'
2. *Maharshis,* great saints and Siddhas, XI. 21. Cf. parts of the Te Deum. The Siddhas are semi-divine beings supposed to possess great purity, called Sadhyas in the earlier mythology (Manu I. 22). Siddhas and Sadhyas are sometimes confused, though mentioned separately in the text.
3. Cf. John viii. 58, 'Before Abraham was, I am.'
4. *Purushah puranah,* 'the most ancient person,' XI. 38. Cf. Daniel vii. 9, 'The Ancient of days did sit.'

Whate'er I have too negligently uttered,
Addressing thee in too familiar tones.
Unrivalled God of gods, I fall before thee
Prostrate in adoration, thou the Father
Of all that lives and lives not; have compassion,
Bear with me, as a father with a son,
Or as a lover with a cherished one.
Now that I see thee as thou really art,
I thrill with terror! Mercy! Lord of lords,
Once more display to me thy human form,
Thou habitation of the universe[1].

Many other remarkable passages might be adduced in connection with the first two divisions of the subject-matter of the Bhagavad-gita. I note the following:

He who has brought his members under subjection, but sits with foolish mind thinking in his heart of sensual things, is called a hypocrite (*mithyachara*). (III. 6. Cf. Matt. v. 28.)

Many are my births that are past; many are thine too, O Arjuna. I know them all, but thou knowest them not. (IV. 5. Cf. John viii. 14.)

For the establishment of righteousness am I born from time to time. (IV 8. Cf. John xviii. 37, 1 John iii. 3.)

I am dearer to the wise than possessions, and he is dear to me. (VI. 17. Cf. Luke xiv. 33, John xiv. 21.)

The ignorant, the unbeliever, and he of a doubting mind perish utterly. (IV. 40. Cf. Mark xvi. 16.)

In him are all beings, by him this universe was spread out. (VIII. 22. Cf. Acts xvii. 28.)

---

1. XI. 45, 46. Dr. Lorinser compares the awe of our Lord's disciples, Matt. xvii. 6, 'They fell on their face, and were sore afraid.' Also of Simon Peter, Luke v. 8, 'When Simon Peter saw it, he fell down at Jesus' knees, saying, Depart from me; for I am a sinful man, O Lord.'

Deluded men despise me when I have taken human form. (IX. 11. Cf. Jon i. 10.)

In all the Veda I am to be known. (XV. 15. Cf. John v. 39).

As many uses as there are in a reservoir filled with waters coming from all parts (for bathing, washing, or drinking), so many does a knowing Brahman find in all the Vedas. (II. 46. Mr. Thomson compares the various uses made of texts from our own sacred Scriptures.)

The next is suggestive of the doctrine that the condition of the soul for a future state is determined before death:

Whatever a man's state of mind be at the moment when he leaves the body to that condition does he always go, being made to conform to that. (VIII. 6. F. Eccles. xi. 3. This is the dying Sanskara which delays the passage to heaven.)

A similar passage occurs in the Chandogya Upanishad:

Man is a creature of intelligence (*Kratu-maya*), whatever ideas he forms in this life, he becomes so when he departs to another, therefore he should reflect (on God, III. 14. 1).

The next is a paraphrase of XVI. 12-16. It may be compared with Luke xii. 17-20:

Entangled in a hundred worldly snares,
Self-seeking men, by ignorance deluded,
Strive by unrighteous means to pile up riches.
Then, in their self-complacency, they say,
'This acquisition I have made to-day,
That I will gain to-morrow; so much pelf
Is hoarded up already, so much more
Remains that I have yet to treasure up.
This enemy I have destroyed, him also
And others in their turn I will dispatch.
I am a lord; I will enjoy myself;
I'm wealthy, noble, strong, successful, happy;

I'm absolutely perfect; no one else
In all the world can be compared to me.
Now I will offer up a sacrifice,
Give gifts with lavish hand and be triumphant.'
Such men, befooled by endless, vain conceits,
Caught in the meshes of the world's illusion,
Immersed in sensuality, descend
Down to the foulest hell of unclean spirits.

I add a few lines from chapter III, in which Krishna exhorts Arjuna to energetic action by an argument drawn from the example set by himself in his own everlasting exertions for the good of the world (cf. John v. 17). The order of the text is not observed in the following version, and the sentiment in lines 6, 7, is from chapter II. 47:

Perform all necessary acts, for action
Is better than inaction, none can live
By sitting still and doing nought; it is
By action only that a man attains
Immunity from action. Yet in working
Ne'er work for recompense; let the act's motive
Be in the act itself. Know that work
Proceeds from the Supreme. I am the pattern
For man to follow; know that I have done
All acts already, nought remains for me
To gain by action, yet I work for ever
Unweariedly, and this whole universe
Would perish if I did not work my work (III. 19).

The third division of the poem, comprising the six last chapters, aims particularly at interweaving Sankhya doctrines with the Vedanta, though this is done more or less throughout the whole work. It accepts the doctrine of a supreme presiding Spirit (called *Param Brahma or Adhyatmam*, XIII. 12, VIII. 1), as the first source of the universe, but asserts the eternal existence of Prakriti and Purusha — that is, of an original eternal element and soul — both emanating from the supreme Being (then regarded as *Para Prakriti,* 'supreme Prakriti'). It maintains the individuality and personality of souls, and affirms that the body (*kshetra*) and all the world of sense is evolved out of Prakriti by the regular Sankhyan process, through Buddhi, Ahankara, the five subtle elements, the five grosser elements, and the eleven organs, including mind. Thus, in XIII. 19 and in VII. 4-6, we read:

Learn that *Prakriti* and *Purusha* also are both of them without beginning. And know that the Vikaras, or 'productions,' and the Gunas (see p. 102) are sprung from Prakriti.

Earth, water, fire, air, ether, mind, intellect, and egoism, into these eight is my Prakriti divided. This Prakriti is the inferior one, but learn my superior Prakriti to be other than this. Understand that all things are produced from this other Prakriti.

Again, in   VII. 12-14, Krishna, speaking of the three Gunas, says:

Know that all the three Gunas, whether Sattva, Rajas, or Tamas (cf. p. 101), proceed only from me. I am not in them, but they in me.

All this universe, deluded by these three conditions consisting of the Gunas, does not recognize me, the imperishable Being, superior to them all.

For this divine illusion (*Maya,* i.e. 'illusory creation'), consisting of the three Gunas, caused by me, is difficult to be passed over. Those only are delivered from it who have recourse to me.

The eclecticism of the Bhagavad-gita will be sufficiently apparent from these examples. I close my brief survey of this celebrated poem by three or four passages (taken from chapter III. 27, chapter XIII. 29, 31), which form a fit conclusion to the subject, as they contain the gist of the whole argument, viz. that it is Arjuna's duty as a soldier to act like a soldier and to do the work of his caste, regardless of consequences; and that this may be done consistently with adhesion to the Vedantic dogma of the soul's real inactivity and state of passionless repose:

> All actions are incessantly performed
> By operation of the qualities
> Of Prakriti; deluded by the thought
> Of individuality, the soul
> Vainly believes itself to be the doer.
> The soul existing from eternity,
> Devoid of qualities, imperishable,
> Abiding in the body, yet supreme,
> Acts not, nor is by any act polluted.
> He who perceives that actions are performed
> By Prakriti alone, and that the soul
> Is not an actor, sees the truth aright.

Krishna's last advice may be thus summed up:

> Act then and do thine own appointed task,
> In every action my assistance ask,
> Do all with heart and soul absorbed in me,
> So shalt thou gain thine end and be from trouble free.

Arjuna's conclusion may be thus paraphrased:

> Eternal One! thy glory just beheld
> Has all illusion from my soul dispelled;
> Now by thy favour is my conscience clear,
> I will thy bidding do and fight without a fear.

To any one who has followed me in tracing the outline of this remarkable philosophical dialogue, and has noted the numerous parallels if offers to passages in our sacred Scriptures, it may seem strange that I hesitate to concur in any theory which explains these coincidences by supposing that the author had access to the New Testament or that he derived some of his ideas from the first propagators of Christianity. Surely it will be conceded that the probability of contact and interaction between Gentile systems and the Christian religion in the first two centuries of our era must have been greater in Italy than in India. Yet, if we take the writings and recorded sayings of three great Roman philosophers, Seneca, Epictetus, and Marcus Aurelius, we shall find them full of resemblances to passages in our Scriptures, while there appears to be no ground whatever for supposing that these eminent Pagan writers and thinkers derived any of their ideas from either Jewish or Christian sources. In fact, the Rev. F.W. Farrar, in his interesting and valuable work, 'Seekers after God,' has clearly shown that 'to say that Pagan morality kindled its faded taper at the Gospel light whether furtively or unconsciously, that it dissembled the obligation and made a boast of the splendour, as if it were originally her own, is to make an assertion wholly untenable.' He points out that the attempts of the Christian Fathers to make out Pythagoras a debtor to Hebraic wisdom, Plato an 'Atticizing Moses,' Aristotle a picker up of ethics from a Jew, Seneca a correspondent of St. Paul, were due 'in some cases to ignorance, and in some to a want of perfect honesty in controversial dealing.'

His arguments would be even more conclusive if applied to the Bhagavad-gita, the author of which was probably contemporaneous with Seneca. It must, indeed, be admitted that the flashes of true light which emerge from the mists of pantheism in the writings of Indian philosophers, must spring from the same source of light as the Gospel itself; but it may reasonably be questioned whether there could have been any actual contact of the Hindu systems with Christianity without a more satisfactory result in the modification of pantheistic and anti-Christian ideas. In order that the resemblances to Scripture in the writings of Roman philosophers may be compared with those just noted, I subjoin a few instances from 'Seekers after God,' and Dr. Ramage's 'Beautiful Thoughts:'

1. Seneca. 'God comes to men: nay, what is nearer, comes into men.' 'A sacred spirit dwells within us, the observer and guardian of all our evil and our good.' Cf. 1 Cor. iii. 16. 'Let him who hath conferred a favour hold his tongue.' 'In conferring a favour nothing should be more avoided than pride.' Cf. Matt. vi. 3. 'If you wish to be loved, love.' 'Expect from another what you do to another.' 'We are all wicked; therefore whatever we blame in another we shall find in our own bosom.' 'A good man is God's disciple and imitator and His true offspring, whom that magnificent Father doth, after the manner of severe parents, educate hardly.' 'God is nigh to thee, he is with thee, He is in thee.' 'Temples are not to be built for God with stones piled on high; He is to be consecrated in the breast of each.' 'What a foolish thing it is to promise ourselves a long life, who are not masters of even to-morrow!' 'Live with men as if God saw you.' 'Other men's sins are before our eyes; our own behind our back.' 'The greater part of mankind are angry with the sinner and not with the sin.' 'The severest punishment a man can receive who has injured another, is to have committed the injury.'

2. Epictetus. 'If you always remember that in all you do in soul or body God stands by as a witness, in all your prayers and your actions you will not err; and you shall have God dwelling with you.' 'How should a man grieve his enemy? By preparing himself to act in the noblest manner.' Cf. Rom. xii. 20.

3. Marcus Aurelius. 'The best way of avenging thyself is not to become like the wrong-doer.' 'Men exist for the sake of one another. Teach them or bear with them.' Cf. 2 Thess. iv. 15, Col. iii. 13. 'In the morning when thou risest unwillingly let these thoughts be present, "I am rising to the work of a human being. Why, then, am I dissatisfied if I am going to do the things for which I exist and for which I was brought into the world?" Dost thou not see the little birds, the ants, the spiders, the bees working together to put in order their several parts of the universe?' Cf. Prov. vi. 6.

Lecture VIII

Smriti — The Vedangas

Hitherto we have been engaged in describing briefly and illustrating by selected examples the three divisions of the Veda, viz. Mantra, Brahmana, and Upanishad, and the six Darsanas or systems of philosophy developed out of the third of these divisions. All three portions of the Veda come under the head of *Shruti*, 'audition,' or *Shruta*, — that which is directly heard or revealed — the eternal voice of divine knowledge heard[1] by certain holy men called Rishis, and by them orally transmitted; or if committed to writing then written down exactly as heard, without any intervention of human authorship. We now pass from Sruti and the six Darsanas to the second great head of Sanskrit literature, called *Smriti*, 'recollection' or that which is remembered and handed down by tradition (as distinguished from 'audition'). This is believed to be founded on Sruti,

---

1. The expression generally used is that the Rishis *saw* the hymns, *rishi* being fancifully connected with *drishi*, as if from root *drish*; but the terms *Shruti* and *Shruta*, taken in connection with the theory of the eternity of sound, indicate that the ear was the channel of communication.

'direct revelation,' as its primary basis, and only possesses authority in so far as it is in harmony with such revealed truth[1]. The very essence of Smriti may be said to include six principal subjects or departments, viz. I. *six Vedangas,* 'limbs for supporting the Veda,' or, in other words, helps to aid the student in reading, understanding and applying it to sacrificial rites (and hence called *Pravachana,* Manu III. 184): they are — 1. Kalpa, 'ceremonial directory,' comprising rules relating to the Vedic ritual and the whole complicated process of sacrifices, which rules are called Shrauta-sutra, because they are *Vedic,* and relate directly to the application of the Mantra and Brahmana portion of Shruti, being especially guides to the Brahmanas; 2. Shiksha, 'the science of pronunciation;' 3. Chandas, 'metre;' 4. Nirukta, 'exposition of difficult Vedic words;' 5. Vyakarana, 'grammar;' 6. Jyotisha, 'astronomy,' including arithmetic and mathematics, especially in connection with astrology. Of these Vedangas, 1. and 6. are for employing the Veda at sacrifices, 2. and 3. are for reading, 4. and 5. for understanding it. II. The *Smarta-sutra,* a comprehensive term for such rules as do not relate to *Shrauta* or *Vedic* ceremonies, which were usually on a grand scale and public in their character, but rather to religious acts of a private and personal kind, falling naturally under two divisions, viz. *a.* family or domestic rites (*grihya*) performed at stated periods; *b* conventional usages and every-day practices (*samayachara*); on which account these Smarta Sutras must be separated into two classes, *a.* Grihya-sutra, *b.* Samayacharika-sutra. III. The *Dharma-shastras* or 'Law-books,' and especially the *Laws of Manu,* and other so-called inspired law-givers — supposed to have grown out of the Smarta Sutras. IV. The *Itihasas* or 'legendary poems,' under which head I place as portions of Smriti the two great epic poems called Ramayana and Mahabharata, and then, for convenience, as following and

---

1. If *Veda-vahya,* it is declared to be *nishphala.* Manu XII. 95.

depending on these, but not as properly Smriti, the artificial poems (Kavyas) and erotic poems and the dramas, almost all of which in their subject-matter are closely connected with the two great epics. V. The *eighteen Puranas* or ancient legendary histories and traditions, with their train of eighteen inferior Puranas (*Upa-purana*) and subsequent Tantras. VI. The *Nitishastras* or ethical and didactic writings of all kinds, including collections of fables and moral precepts.

I propose now to take these six divisions of post-Vedic literature in order, beginning with I. the Vedangas.

I. The Vedangas

They are six in number. Let us consider them (not quite according to the Hindu order) in the following sequence: 1. *Kalpa;* 2. *Shiksha;* 3. *Chandas;* 4. *Nirukta;* 5. *Vyakarana;* 6. *Jyotisha.*

The Vedangas — *Kalpa,* 'ceremonial directory.'

In the first place, then, as regards *Kalpa;* this denotes, as we have seen, a kind of ceremonial directory or rubric put forth in the form of short aphoristic Sutras or rules, called *Shrauta,* because serving as guides for the application of the Mantra and Brahmana portion of Shruti to the conduct of sacrificial rites. There are Srauta Sutras for each of the five Samhitas of the Veda. Thus, for the Rig-veda there are the *Ashvalayana, Shankhayana,* and *Shaunaka* Shrauta Sutras; for the Sama-veda, the *Mashaka, Latyayana,* and *Drahyayana;* for the Taittiriya or Black Yajur-veda, the *Apastamba, Baudhayana, Satyashadha Hiranya-keshin, Manava, Bharadvaja, Vadhuna, Vaikhanasa, Laugakshi, Maitra, Katha,* and *Varaha;* for the Vajasaneyi or White Yajur-veda there is only the *Katyayana*[1]; for the Atharva-veda only the *Kaushika.*

---

1. Edited by Professor Weber to complete the series of his great edition of the White Yajur-veda with its Brahmana (the Satapatha).

I should remark here that the word Sutra (derived from the root *Shiv,* 'to sew') means properly 'string,' and that this name was applied to any series[1] of rules or aphorisms, either because they were, figuratively, strung together, or because they were written on leaves held together by strings[2]. It is perhaps essential to the true nature of a Brahmanical Sutra that it should be a rule or dogma expressed as briefly as possible. In the grammatical Sutras not a single letter is allowed which can by any contrivance be dispensed with, and moreover in these Sutras letters and syllables are often used symbolically, like algebraic signs, to indicate ideas which would otherwise require a whole sentence or more to express them at full. In the philosophical Sutras, as we have already seen, great brevity and a rigid economy of words is also practised, the aim being to furnish the shortest possible suggestive memorial sentences as an aid to the memory of both teacher and learners in an age when books were scarce and paper and printing unknown (see note, p. 52). This extreme conciseness is not always maintained, especially in later Sutra works, but it generally holds good that the older the Sutra the greater its curtness and elliptical obscurity, so that without a commentary or a key to their interpretation these ancient aphorisms are quite unintelligible. In later times, as books became more common, the necessity for elaborate and overstrained conciseness was gradually removed[3], and rules and aphorisms, though still strung together in Sutra style, were more fully and explicitly and even sometimes metrically stated[4]. In fact, these later Sutra works may be regarded as simple collections of

---

1. *Sutra* in the singular may denote a whole collection of rules.
2. This last is the theory of the late Professor Goldstucker.
3. This relaxation led at last to the very opposite extreme of prolixity, as in the Buddhist Sutras.
4. In some Sutra works there is an occasional admixture of Shlokas.

formulated precepts or dogmas adapted to serve as convenient manuals to particular systems of teaching whether in ritual, philosophy, law, or grammar. If Sanskrit scholars are asked to state the age of the oldest Sutra works, they are again obliged to confess their inability to fix any precise date. The most ancient are probably not older than the fifth or sixth century B.C., and the time of the compilation of the most recent is perhaps not far removed from the commencement of the Christian era. I have placed the Kalpa Sutras first because they are probably oldest, being closely connected with the Brahmana or ritual portion of Shruti, and thence called Shrauta.

The following translation of the first ten Sutras of Katyayana's Shrauta-sutra, which belong to the Satapatha-brahmana and White Yajur-veda (see Weber's edition), will give some idea of the nature of these rules. To make each aphorism intelligible, additional matter has to be introduced from the commentary of Yajnika-deva. This I have done parenthetically in the examples here given. I have also given the original text of the Sutras in italics:

1. Now, therefore, the right (of engaging in sacrificial acts is about to be laid down in the following rules). [*Athao 'dhikarah.*]

2. (Sacrificial) acts (like the Agni-hotra, &c.) are attended with recompence (such as the attainment of heaven, of wealth, of a son, &c.) [*Phalayuktani karmani.*]

3. (According to the prima facie view of the matter there must be a right) of all (creatures, e.g. of men, even though blind, dumb, lame, or deaf, or gods, of Rishis, and of animals, but not of plants, to engage in sacrificial acts), without distinction, (because all such creatures are capable of desiring recompence.) [*Sarvesham avisheshat.*]

4. But (according to the orthodox view, right belongs) to human beings (only), because (they only as the Veda declares, have) the power of undertaking (sacrificial acts, and not to gods, Rishis, and animals). [*Manushyanam varambha-samarthyat.*]

5. Cripples, those ignorant of the Veda, eunuchs, and Sudras (are to be) excepted. [*Anga-hinashrotriya-shandha-shudra-varjam.*]

6. (The right belongs) to Brahmans, Kshatriyas[1], and Vaishyas (but not to Shudras), according to the Vedic precept. [*Brahmana-rajanya-vaishyanam shruteh.*]

7. A woman also (has the right), since there is no difference (between her and her husband in regard to the desire for heaven). [*Stri chavisheshat.*]

8. And since it is so seen (in the Veda). [*Darshanach-cha.*]

9. (According to one view, the right belongs) to a man of the Rathakara[2] ('chariot-maker') caste, (so far as regards the rite) of placing the sacred fire (on the sacrificial ground, on the score of this caste being reckoned among the first three classes). {*Rathakarasyadhane.*]

10. (But according to the orthodox view) it is settled (that the Rathakara is not to be reckoned among the first three classes). [*Niyatam cha.*]

The Vedangas — Shiksha, 'phonetic directory.'

The next Vedanga in our list is *Shiksha* or the science of proper pronunciation, especially as teaching the laws of euphony peculiar to the Veda. This comprises the knowledge of letters, accents, quantity, the right use of the organs of articulation, and phonetics generally. One short comparatively modern treatise on phonetics, consisting in one recension of thirty-five and in another of fifty-nine verses (ascribed to Panini), and a chapter of the Taittiriya-ranyaka are regarded as the representatives of this subject; but the Vedic Pratishakhyas

---

1. The word *Rajanya* is used here and in the Purusha-sukta for Kshatriya, see p. 25.
2. This mixed caste, held to be the offspring of a Mahishya by a Karani, is also called Saudhanvana. It appears to have enjoyed some religious privileges, perhaps because the Ribhus were Ratha-karas, see note, p. 18. Cf. Rig-veda III. 60. 4.

and other works on Vedic phonetics may be included under it[1], and it will be convenient so to regard them. These Pratishakhyas are grammatical, or rather phonetic, treatises written in the Sutra style (some of them perhaps of a more recent date than Panini[2]), regulating the euphonic combination of letters and their peculiar pronunciation according to the practice of the different Shakhas, 'branches' of the Vedas, in those traditional versions of the Vedic texts handed down by different families. The Pratishakhyas do not undo words in the same way as the Vyakarana, but take actually formed words as they occur in the hymns, and teach the phonetic changes they undergo, the mode of pronouncing the accents, &c. In fact they show how the Pada text is converted by a process of euphonic combination into the Samhita.

Since the chief virtue of the Vedic texts was in their oral repetition, and since so much importance was attached to the proper pronunciation and accentuation of every syllable, it may be easily supposed that these phonetic manuals were of great value to persons who had to repeat Mantras every day as an essential part of their religious exercises. They probably served as guides and aids to the memory, both for teachers in instructing their pupils and for pupils in learning to recite the Veda. Four Pratisakhyas are extant, viz.: 1. one to the Shakala-Shakha of the Rig-veda, ascribed to Shaunaka[3]; 2. another to a Shakha of the Taittiriya or Black Yajur-veda[4];

---

1. A number of works bearing the name of *Siksha,* and dealing with phonetics and other kindred subjects, have been recently brought to notice. See Haug on *the Vedic Accent* (Munich, 1874.)
2. The late Professor Goldstucker, in his work on Panini, decides that all the Pratisakhyas must have been posterior to Panini; but this opinion is shared by few other scholars.
3. Edited and translated into French by M. Adolphe Regnier, and into German by Professor Max Muller.
4. Edited, with its commentary, and translated by Professor William D. Whiteny.

3. another to a Shakha of the Madhyandinas, of the family of the Vajasaneyins or 'followers of the White Yajur-veda,' whence this is called the Vajasaneyi-pratishakhya[1]; it is ascribed to an author, Katyayana, probably identical with the writer of the Varttikas or 'supplementary rules' to Panini; 4. an Atharva-veda-pratishakhya, called Shaunakiya Chaturadhyayika[2], 'Shaunaka's treatise in four chapters.' No Pratisakhya has yet been found to the Sama-veda.

The relative age of the Pratishakhyas in their present form is an open question. That to the Rig-veda has been by some confidently declared the oldest, though written in Shlokas with occasional admixture of other metres.

I here translate the fifth and sixth Sutras of this Pratishakhya, as they contain a statement of some of the points which form the subject of the work:

Heaviness (i.e. prosodial length), lightness (i.e. prosodial shortness), equality, shortness, longness, and prolation (of vowels), elision, augmentation, and change, original form, non-change of Visarga into a sibilant, regular order, the mixed tone, high tone, low tone, breath and sound[3], and both (combined), — all this must be accurately understood by one who reads (or repeats) the words of the Veda.

[*Gurutvam laghuta samyam hrasva-dirgha-plutani cha!*
Lopâgama-vikarsa-cha prakriti vikramah kramah!!
Svaritodatta-nichatvam shvaso nadas tathobhayam!
Etat sarvam cha vijneyam chhando-bhasham adhiyata!!]

The first Atharva-veda-pratishakhya states the subject of the treatise (Whitney, p. 9), and gives a fourfold division of all the parts of speech in its first Sutra, thus:

---

1. Edited and translated by Professor Weber in the 'Indische Studien.'
2. Also edited, with a most valuable English translation and notes, by Professor William D. Whitney.
3. We learn from the Atharva-veda-pratishakhya I. 12, 13, that in the surd consonants there is mere breath, and in the sonant, sound.

The two qualities of the four kinds of words — noun (*nama*), verb (*akhyata*), preposition (*upasarga*), and particle (*nipata*) — as euphonically joined and as separate words, are here the subject (*pratijnam*).

That is to say, the design of the Pratishakhya is to form a Samhita out of a Pada text. In fact, it supposes all the words of the Veda to be separated from each other (as they are in the Pad), and then teaches how they are to be euphonically connected, as they must be in the Samhita[1].

The second chapter introduces a number of rules of Sandhi, which will be familiar to the students of Panini's Grammar. The first Sutra consists of one word, which must be amplified thus (Whitney's edition, p. 72):

(The following rules are to be understood as of force when the separate words of the disjointed text are put together) in the Samhita [Samhitayam].

Then follow the rules, of which I subjoin three or four examples (II. 10, 11, 18, 19, III. 20):

Before sh, *n* becomes *n* [*na-karasya sha-kare nakarah*].

Also before a sonant palatal (as before *j*) [*cha-vargiye ghoshavati*].

After the preposition *ud*, there is elision of the letter *s* of the roots *stha* and *stambha* [*lopa udah stha-stambhoh sa-karasya*].

There is elision of R before *r* [*rephasya rephe*].

When *r* is elided (the preceding vowel is lengthened) [*ra-lope*].

---

1. In the *Krama* text the 1st word is recited with the 2nd, that is repeated with the 3rd, that with the 4th, &c. In the *Jata*, the 1st word and 2nd, 2nd and 1st, and 1st, and 2nd again; next the 2nd and 3rd, 3rd and 2nd and 2nd and 3rd and so on. In the *Ghana*, the 1st and 2nd, 2nd and 1st, 1st and 2nd again, 3rd; then 3rd, 2nd, 1st, 1st, 2nd, 3rd; then the 2nd begins a new Ghana.

The Vajasaneyi-pratishakhya (I. 27) gives a still more complete enumeration of the parts of speech, thus:

Words are made up of inflected verbal bases [i.e. bases having the personal endings, technically called *tin*] nouns derived from verbs by Krit affixes, nouns derived from nouns by Taddhita affixes and four kinds of compounds (Avyayi-bhava, Tatpurusha, Dvandva, Bahu-vrihi). [*Tin-krit-taddhita-chatushtaya-samasah shabda-mayam.* See Professor Max Muller's Ancient Sanskrit Literature, p. 164.]

The Vedangas — Chhandas, 'metre.'

This Vedanga is imperfectly represented by the *Chhandah-shastra* ascribed to Pingala or Pingala-naga, which may be as old as the second century B.C., and treats of Prakrit as well as Sanskrit metres, including only a few Vedic. Other works on metres are the Nidana-sutra in ten Prapathakas and the Shruta-bodha. In truth, prosody, like every other subject in Sanskrit literature, affords field for almost endless investigation. It is a complete study in itself, and its importance in the estimation of the Hindus is shown by the excessive cultivation and elaboration bestowed upon their whole metrical system. A knowledge of the metre of each hymn of the Veda was considered essential to the right use and proper recitation of the Mantras. Hence we find Sayana, in his introduction to the first hymn of the Rig-veda, quoting the following precept:

He who shall cause anyone to repeat (*adhyapayet*) or shall himself repeat (any hymn of the Veda) without having acquainted himself with the name of the Rishi to whom it was revealed, the metre (*chhandas*) in which it was written, the deity to whom it was addressed, and its right application (*yoga*), is the worst of sinners (*papiyan*).

Again, immediately afterwards, he adds:

Any one who makes use of (a hymn) without knowing the Rishi, the metre, the deity, the right interpretation according to the Brahmanas (*brahmanartha*), and the accents is called 'a Mantra-thorn' (*mantra-kantaka*, as destroying or obstructing its efficacy).

In the ninth verse of the Purusha-sukta of the Rig-veda (see p. 25) the metres are said to have sprung from Purusha himself, thus:

From that universal sacrifice sprang the Ric and Saman verses, the metres, and the Yajus (*chhandansi jajnire tasmad yajus tasmad ajayata*).

The Taittiriya-samhita VIII. 1. 1. 4. &c. describes the creation of several metres by Prajapati (Muir, vol. i. p. 15):

Prajapati desired 'may I be propagated.' He formed the Trivrit from his mouth. After it were produced the deity Agni, the metre Gayatri, &c.

In Manu IV. 99, 100, we have the following:

Let not a man repeat the Veda without clear pronunciation (of the letters, accents, &c., *svara-varnadi*, Kulluka). Let him always be careful to recite it as composed in metre (chhandas-kritam).

It is remarkable that in Panini's Grammar the usual name for the Veda is Chhandas (see p. 195).

From the importance thus assigned to the metrical structure of the hymns we shall be prepared to find frequent allusions to the subject of metres in the Brahmanas. In fact, these treatises attach a kind of mystical efficacy to their use, and whole chapters of the Upanishads enlarge on the same fanciful theme. The Gayatri is held in especial veneration, the most sacred text of the Rig-veda being in this metre. (See p. 20.)

The following passage is from the Satapatha-brahmana I. 2, 5, 6, &c. (Muir's Texts, vol. iv. p. 123):

The gods having placed Vishnu to the east surrounded him with metres (*chhandobhir abhitah paryagrihnan*); saying, 'On the south side, I surround thee with the Gayatri metre; on the west I surround thee with the Trishtubh metre; on the north I surround thee with the Jagati.' Having thus surrounded him with metres, they placed Agni on the east, and thus they went on worshipping and toiling. By this means they acquired this whole earth (*tena imam sarvam prithivim samavindanta*).

Again, in the fourteenth Brahmana of the Brihadaranyaka Upanishad we read (Roer, p. 254):

The *Richah, Yajunshi,* and *Samani* are eight syllables (*ashtav aksharani*); the second Pada (*padam*) of the Gayatri consists of eight syllables (*ashtaksharam*). This Pada of the Gayatri represents that nature of the three Vedas. Whoever knows this Pada of the Gayatri conquers all that is conquerable by the knowledge of the three Vedas.

Hence we cannot be surprised that some of the most sacred metres, especially the Gayatri, were in the end personified and invested with divine functions. Our present purpose and limits do not admit of our giving schemes of even the commonest forms of Sanskrit metre, whether Vedic or Post-vedic. They will be found enumerated in the third edition of my Sanskrit Grammar, pp. 388-392[1]. Le me merely observe that great licence is allowed in Vedic prosody, so that in the Gayatri, which may be regarded as consisting either of three divisions of eight syllables each (whence it is called *tri-pada*) or of six feet of four syllables each, the quantity of each

---

1. See also Colebrooke's Essay on Sanskrit and Prakrit metres and Professor Weber's articles in the 'Indische Studien.'

syllable is very irregular, although the second, fourth, and sixth feet generally contain two iambics.

Of Post-vedic metres we have so great a variety that it becomes necessary to arrange them under classes and orders, genera and species. In truth, the elaboration of every kind of complicated metre is carried to an extent quite beyond the ordinary practice of poetical composition in other languages. 'A Hindu poet,' says Dr. Yates, 'may proceed to any length he pleases, within the limits of *a thousand syllables to the half-line*,' or quarter-stanza. The Dandaka metre (of which a specimen occurs in the drama called Malati-madhava, Act V[1]) offers more than any other an almost incredible capability of expansion. It will admit, indeed, of the stanza extending 27 x 4 to 999 x 4 syllables. But the commonest form of metre, chiefly found in epic poetry — the Anushtubh or Shloka — is short and easy. It consists of four half-lines of eight syllables each or two lines of sixteen syllables each, the last two feet of each line being iambics (see my Sanskrit Grammar, p. 288). The Indra-vajra (with its Upendra-vajra variety) is also a common metre, and one of the most rhythmical. It nearly corresponds to one occurring in Horace's fourth Ode:

Vulcanus ardens urit officinas,
Trahuntque siccas machinae carinas.

But to make the Latin agree with the Sanskrit metre we must suppose the first syllable of *machinae* and of *urit* to be short. It might be represented in an English line thus, 'Down comes the rain and with it comes the thunder,' an emphasis being placed on the first syllable.

---

1. Beginning Prachalita-kari-kritti, &c. It has fifty-four syllables to the quarter-verse. This specimen is translated in the Asiatic Researches, vol. x. p. 456.

The Vedangas — *Nirukta,* 'exposition.'

The object of this Vedanga is etymological explanation or interpretation of difficult Vedic words. Doubtless, numerous works devoted to this object once existed, but all have perished except one, which is now the typical representative of the whole class[1]. This is a compilation, accompanied with an exposition, by an author named Yaska, who according to the best authorities, lived before Panini[2], probably about 400 years B.C., or about 1800 years before Sayana. His work consists first of three bare lists or catalogues of words in five chapters: viz. *a.* The *Naighantuka* in three chapters of synonyms or rather of collections of words said to have the same meaning as some one word of known signification given at the end, one such collection being called a Nighantu. The synonyms in each collection vary from two (III. 22) to one hundred and twenty-two (II. 14), and can scarcely be called synonyms in the strict sense. For example, when it is said that *vartate,* 'he turns;' *lotate,* 'he rolls;' *sarpati,* ' he creeps;' *sravati,* 'he flows;' *sransate,* 'he drops;' *plavate,* 'he swims;' *diyate,* 'he flies;' *patati,* 'he falls,' and 122 other words are all synonyms of *gamati,* 'he goes,' or *gati,* 'going,' this must be understood very widely as intending to include all forms and varieties of motion. Again, in I. 12, we have a collection of 101 words, which are all said to be synonyms of water (*udaka*), but it is obvious that the only attribute most of these have in common is, that they are varieties of fluids, including, for example, nectar (*amrita*) and clarified butter (*havis*). Seeing therefore, that many of the words brought together are old

---

1. No less than seventeen Nairuktikas or 'interpreters of the Veda' are mentioned by name as having preceded Yaska. See Dr. Muir's article on the interpretation of the Veda, p. 321.
2. Panini himself implies (IV. I. 112) that the name Yaska means a descendant of Yaska.

Vedic words of doubtful meaning, quite unknown to classical Sanskrit, and seeing that a complete explanation of the gradations and modifications of sense under each head of synonyms is wanting, the practical utility of these lists is of course very small indeed. *b.* The *Naigama,* a collection of 278 separate words (*padani*) occurring in the Veda (*nigama*), all in one chapter of three sections. *c.* The *Daivata* or 151 words relating to deities and religious or sacrificial acts, in one chapter of six short sections. Whether these collections were drawn up by Yaska himself or by some previous compiler is not certain, but there is no doubt that the second and most important part of the work, viz. the Nirukta or 'explanation' of the words in these lists, is his own composition. Although, therefore, the term Nirukta is sometimes applied to the lists of words, it more properly belongs to Yaska's explanation of them, which occupies twelve chapters. The first of the twelve is a kind of introduction, which contains some interesting discussions of philological questions and a sort of summary or sketch of grammar; the following two chapters are an imperfect exposition of the Naighantuka or 'lists of synonymous words,' the deficiency of which has been to a certain extent supplied by Durga, a commentator on Yaska; the next three chapters explain the Naigama or 'single Vedic words,' and the last six the Daivata or 'deities addressed in the hymns.' Thus the three collections with their explanations occupy seventeen chapters. The value of the work[1] consists in its being the oldest extant commentary on the Veda. When words are explained, Vedic passages are quoted in illustration, and the author often enters into curious etymological investigations, which possess great interest from their universally admitted antiquity, but are difficult to understand from the extreme brevity and obscurity of their style.

---

1. It has been ably edited by professor Roth.

I here abridge some valuable remarks from Dr. John Muir's article on the 'Interpretation of the Veda,' in the Royal Asiatic Society's Journal (vol. ii. new series, p. 320):

The Nirukta makes frequent reference to the Brahmanas, and alludes to various schools of Vedic interpretation which existed anterior to its author, such as the Niruktas or 'etymologists,' the Aitihasikas or 'legendary writers,' and the Yajnikas or 'ritualists.' Yaska supplies specimens of the mode of explaining the hymns adopted by different schools of interpreters. Thus we are told (Nirukta XI. 29, 31) that the Nairuktas understood Anumati, Raka, Sinivali, and Kuhu to be goddesses, while the Yajnikas took them for the new and full moons. The gods called Asvins were a great enigma. The Nirukta (XII. 1) gives the following answers to the question who they were: 'Heaven and Earth,' say some; 'Day and Night,' say others; 'the Sun and Moon,' say others; 'two Kings, performers of holy acts,' say the Aitihasikas. Again, Nirukta (VI. 13) tells us that Aurnabhava understood Nasatyau (an epithet of the Asvins) as 'true, not false.' Agrayana took it to mean 'leaders of truth' (*satyasya pranetarau*); while Yaska himself suggests that it may mean 'nose-born' (*nasika-prabhavau*). Again, we are informed (Nirukta III. 8) that some understood the five peoples (*pancha-janah*) mentioned in Rig-veda X. 53. 4 to be the Gandharvas, Pitris, gods, Asuras, and Rakshases; whilst Aupamanyava took them for the four castes and the Nishadas. So, again, Katthakya understood Narasansa to designate 'sacrifice,' but Shakapuni took it for a name of Agni (Nir. VIII. 4. 5). In like manner, Yaska's predecessors were not agreed as to what was meant by Vishnu's three steps in Rig-veda I. 22.17; Shakapuni maintaining that they were planted on the earth, the atmosphere, and the sky respectively; and Aurnabhava that the hill over which the sun rises, the meridian, and the hill where he sets, were the localities referred to. One of these predecessors (Kautsa) had the audacity to assert that Vedic exposition was useless, as the hymns were obscure, unmeaning, or mutually contradictory. As instances of obscurity he cites the texts in which the words *amyak* (Rig-veda I. 169. 3), *yadrishmin*

(V. 44. 8), *jarayayi* (VI. 12. 4), and *kanuka* (VIII. 66.4) occur. In regard to this charge, Yaska replies that it is not the fault of the post that the blind man does not see it. In the Nirukta-parisishta the 'four defined graders or stages of speech' referred to in Rig-vida I. 164. 45, are said to be explained by the Rishis as meaning the four mystic words, *om, bhuh, bhuvah, svar;* by the grammarians, as denoting nouns, verbs, prepositions, and particles; by the ritualists, as the hymns, liturgical precepts, Brahmanas, and ordinary language; by the etymologists, as the Rig, Yajush, Saman, and the current language; by others, as the speech of serpents, birds, reptiles, and the vernacular; by the spiritualists, as that of beasts, musical instruments, wild animals, and soul.

It is evident from the above remarks that great difference of opinion existed among expositors of the Veda even in Yaska's time, considerably more than 2000 years ago, and that the objections of sceptics and rationalists had to be met and answered by orthodox theologians like himself. He commences his own exposition thus (I. 1):

The traditional collection of words has been thus traditionally repeated. That must now be explained. They call this traditional collection the Nighantus. [*samamnayah samamnatah sa vyakhyatavyas tam imam samamnayam nighantava ity achakshate.*]

Perhaps as good an example of Yaska's condensed style as can be offered is a passage quoted and explained by Professor Goldstucker from Roth's edition, I. 3. It is interesting as showing that, for the better interpretation of the Veda, Yaska aimed at giving some sort of exposition of grammar and grammatical science as then understood:

(The ancient grammarian) Shakatayana says that prepositions when not attached (to nouns or verbs) do not express meanings; but Gargya says that they illustrate (or modify) the action which is expressed by a noun or verb, and that their senses are various (even when detached). Now they express that sense which inheres in them; that is, that which modifies the sense of a noun or verb. The preposition *a* is in the sense of limit; *pra* and *para* express the reverse of that; *adhi,* direction towards; *prati,* the reverse of that; *ati* and *su,* superiority; *nir* and *dur,* the reverse of these two; *ni* and *ava,* the act of taking down; *ud,* the reverse of these two, *sam,* combining together; *vi* and *apa,* the reverse of that; *anu,* similarity or being after; *api,* conjunction; *upa,* the being appended; *pari,* being all around; *adhi,* being above or supremacy: thus they express various meanings, and these must be taken into consideration. [*Na nirbaddha upasarga arthan nir-ahur iti Shakatayano, nama-khyatayos tu karmopasamyoga-dyotaka bhavanty uchchavachah padartha bhavantiti Gargyas, tad ya eshu padarthah prahur ime tam namakhyatayor artha-vikaranam; a ity arvag-arthe, pra parety etasya pratilomyam; abhity abhimukhyam, pratity etasya pratilomyam; ati su ity abhipujitarthe, nir dur ity etayoh pratilomyam; ny aveti vinigraharthiya, ud ity etayoh pratilomyam; sam ity ekibhavam, vy apety etasya pratilomyam; anv iti sadrishyaparabhavam; apiti samsargam; upety upajanam; pariti sarvato-bhavam; adhity uparibhavam aishvaryam vaivam uchchavachan arthan prahus ta upekshitavyah.*]

There is a still more interesting passage on the subject of derivation a little further on in the same chapter (I. 12):

So these four kinds of words have been enumerated, nouns (*naman*), verbs (*akhyata*), prepositions (*upasarga*), and particles (*nipata*).Sakatayana affirms that nouns are derived from verbs, and on this point there is an agreement of the etymologists (*nairukta-samayah*). But Gargya and some of the grammarians say that not all (nouns are derived from verbs). For if all nouns came from verbs, then whatever performs the same action ought to have the same name. Thus, if *ashva,* 'a horse,' were derived from the root *ash,* 'to pass through,' then every one who passes along a road ought to be called *ashva;* and if *trina,* 'a blade of grass,' were derived from the root *trid*, 'to pierce,' then everything that pierces ought to be called *trina*. Again, if all nouns were derived from verbs, then everything would have as many names as there are states with which it could be connected. Thus, *sthuna*, 'a post,' might be called *dara-shaya*, 'hole-sleeper,' because resting in a hole, or *san-jani*, 'joiner together,' because things are joined by being attached to it. [Yaska ends by taking the side of Shakatayan. See Professor Max Muller's Ancient Sanskrit Literature, p. 165.]

The thirteenth and fourteenth chapters commonly called the Nirukta-parishishta, are thought to be the work of a more recent author than Yaska. There are numerous classical glossaries by later lexicographers, e.g.:

The Amara-kosha (sometimes called Tri-kanda, 'having three chapters'), by the Baudhha Amara-sinha, probably not later than A.D. 500; the Abhidhana-ratna-mala, by Halayudha; the Abhidhana-chintamani, by the Jaina Hema-chandra; the Vishva-prakasha, by Maheshvara; the Dharani; the Medini; the Haravali, &c.

The Vedangas — Vyakarana, 'grammar.'

This word *Vy-a-karana* means literally 'undoing,' and is applied first to linguistic analysis and then generally to grammar, but especially to Panini's grammar[1]. It is the opposite to *Sanskarana*, 'putting together,' whence the formed language is called *Sanskrita*, 'constructed.' Strictly, the great Vyakarana of Panini can scarcely be regarded as a Vedanga, seeing that it only treats of the Vedic idiom exceptionally. The grammatical Sutras which preceded his time and which have nearly all

---

1. No Pandit would use Vyakarana except for Sanskrit grammar, and a man's Sanskrit scholarship is often summed up by describing him as knowing 'the Vyakaran.'

perished must have constituted the Vyakarana division of works ancillary to the study of the Veda[1]. Nevertheless, the grammar of Panini, which is the great standard of correct Sanskrit, is usually taken to represent this Vedanga, and as it is one of the most remarkable literary works that the world has ever seen, and as no other country can produce any grammatical system at all comparable to it, either for originality of plan or for analytical subtlety, a brief description of its characteristic features may be introduced here.

Little or nothing is known of Panini, the author of the grammar. He is described as a descendant of Panin and grandchild of an inspired legislator named Devala. His mother's name was Dakshi (whence he is called Daksheya), and Shalatura in the Gandhara country (Kandahar), north-west of Attock on the Indus, is said to have been his birth-place (whence his name Shalaturiya). He belonged, therefore, to the North-western or Western school. As, however, in later times he became more and more an object of reverence, he was at last actually canonized by his admirers, that is to say, exalted to the rank of a Rishi or inspired Muni. Hence he is fabled to have *seen* rather than composed his grammar, which was declared to have been supernaturally revealed to him, the first fourteen Sutras especially having been communicated, according to the legend, by the

---

1. Panini himself mentions several grammarians as having preceded him, such as Apisali, Kasyapa, Gargya, Galava, Chakravarmana, Bharadvaja, Shakatayana, Shakalya, Senaka, and Sphotayana. The Unadi-sutras (commented on by Ujjvala-datta), giving the affixes, commencing with *un*, for the formation of words whose meaning has deviated from accordance with their etymology, and whose root is not always clear, are thought by some to be anterior to Panini. Possibly he may have made a list of them himself. At any rate, he mentions the *affixes* in III. 3. 1, III. 4. 75. Shantanava's Phit-sutras on accent are probably later than Panini. They have been well edited by Professor Kielhorn. I believe Dr. Buhler has found part of a work which claims to be Shakatayana's grammar.

god Siva. It is of course quite impossible to fix with certainty at what period Panini lived. The late professor Goldstucker thought he had good grounds for deciding that the great grammarian preceded Buddha. This would place him in the sixth century B.C. Other scholars, whose opinions are entitled to respect, consider that an earlier date cannot be assigned to him than the middle of the fourth century B.C.

His work — perhaps the most original of all productions of the Hindu mind — is sometimes called the Ashtadhyayi, sometimes Ashtakam Paniniyam, because it consists of eight lectures (Adhyayas), each of which is again subdivided into four chapters (Padas). In these eight Adhyayas are contained 3996 Sutras or Aphorisms[1]. The first Adhyaya explains the technical terms used in the grammar and the rules for their interpretation and application[2]. A root is called Dhatu, and a crude base Pratipadika, but a root never appears without some appendage (*anubandha*) in the shape of indicatory syllables or letters (technically called *it*) which do not really form part of the root, but merely denote certain peculiarities in its inflection. conjugation, &c. Similar indicatory letters and syllables (*it*) are attached either at the beginning or end of all affixes, augments, &c. [3] The case affixes are called *sup,*

---

1. Three or four of these are supposed to be later additions. In the excellent odition of Professor Bohtlingk there are 3997, including the fourteen Shiva Sutras. Panini is also the supposed author of the oldest Dhatu-patha or dictionary of roots with their Anubandhas.
2. A rule giving the key to Panini's Sutras and their application is called a Paribhasha; one which explains the technical terms is a Sanjna.
3. For example, the root *nid* is called *nidi* to show that a nasal is inserted in conjugation, thus, *nindami, nindasi,* &c. The affix *maya* is called *mayat* to show that its feminine is *mayi.* Sometimes these *Its* or *Anubandhas* serve to distinguish two roots or affixes, which, although similar in sound, have different senses; for example, the root *da,* 'to give,' is called *dudan,* while *da,* 'to divide,' is called *dap;* the affix *vat,* meaning 'like,' is called *vati,* the affix *vat,* meaning 'possessed

and the personal endings or terminations of verbs *tin*. Between the latter and the root a conjugational syllable is inserted, called *vikarana*. The third chapter of the first Adhyaya treats of the proper use of the active voice (*Parasmai-pada*) and middle or reflexive voice (*Atmanepada*). The second Adhyaya explains compound words. The third, fourth, and fifth Adhyayas enumerate the various affixes and their meanings. Those belonging to verbs occupy the third Adhyaya; those affixed to nouns, the fourth and fifth. The sixth, seventh, and eighth Adhyayas treat of the changes which roots and affixes undergo by augments and substitutions of various kinds. For brevity and economy of words nothing can be more successful than the system in which all this immense and intricate subject is explained. The Sutras of Panini are indeed a perfect miracle of condensation, their main design apparently being to aid the memory of teachers rather than learners by the briefest possible suggestions. When a single letter can be saved every other consideration is sacrificed to this paramount object; and to attain a greater amount of abridgment than could be effected by the use of ordinary words an arbitrary symbolical language is coined, the key to which must be acquired before the rules themselves can be rendered intelligible[1]. Perhaps the closing Sutra of the whole work may be taken as the best instance of the consummate brevity attained. It consists of two letters, as follow: *a a*. This is said to mean:

Let short *a* be held to have its organ of utterance contracted, now that we have reached the end of the work in which it was necessary to regard it as otherwise.

---

of,' is called *vatup*. Sometimes the only use of these Anubandhas is to enable Pratyaharas to be formed; thus the case-ending of the accusative dual is called *aut* merely for the sake of forming the Pratyahara *sut*.

1. For example, *shyan* stands for the characteristic of roots of the fourth class, *yak* for the passive, *nic* for the causal, *san* for the desiderative, *yan* for the intensive.

Here is one from the sixth Adhyaya (1. 77): *Iko yan achi*. This, of course, is not Sanskrit, but a kind of grammatical algebra. *Ik* is a symbol standing for the four vowels *i, u, ri, lri,* and gifted with an imaginary genitive case *ikah* (here changed to *iko*). *Yan* is a symbol for the letters *y, v, r, l;* and *ac* (supposed to possess a locative case *achi*) represents all the vowels. The rule at full is:

The letters *y, v, r, l* take the place of *i, u, ri, lri,* short or long, respectively, when followed by any dissimilar vowel.

Moreover, an aphorism which stands at the head of a series and is hence called an *Adhikara* or 'governing rule' is never repeated, but must be supplied after the whole series till the influence (*anuvritti*) of this governing Sutra is supposed to cease, such cessation being called *nivritti*. Thus the seventy-fourth Sutra of the third chapter of Adhyaya I is *nichash-cha,* which must be interpreted thus:

And after a verbal base ending in the causal affix (*nich*) the Atmanepada must come when the result of the action returns to the agent.

Of course nearly all the matter necessary to make this rule intelligible has to be supplied from other rules, and especially from the Adhikara rule 12, which is separated by sixty-two intervening Sutras.

In short, a careful examination of Panini's grammar will dispose the student to appreciate Colebrooke's remark that 'the endless pursuit of exceptions and limitations so disjoins the general precepts, that the reader cannot keep in view their intended connection and mutual relation. He wanders in an intricate maze, and the clue of the labyrinth is continually slipping from his hand.'

In point of fact, however, this grammar ought not to be examined from a European point of view at all. We must not forget that an Indian Pandit's ideas of grammar are very different from our own. Europeans are apt to look on a grammar of any kind as a necessary evil, only to be tolerated because indispensable to the attainment of a desired end beyond. With us the grammar of a language is in most cases a mere passage to its literature, a dreary region to be traversed as soon as possible. A Pandit, on the other hand, regards grammar as we should regard the natural sciences. It is with him something to be studied and elaborated for its own sake. According to the late Professor Goldstucker, 'Panini's work is indeed a kind of natural history of the Sanskrit language[1].' It gives an account of the linguistic facts and phenomena as it finds them tracing them out as they occur without regard to any scientific or methodical arrangement of materials. Thus the prolongation of vowels is dealt with as a fact, and is followed out through a whole chapter in order to trace all the instances in which such a lengthening takes place, whether in declension or conjugation or the composition of words. Hence the rules of declension and conjugation do not follow each other in their usual order according to the European system, but are scattered about in a disjointed and often very perplexing manner, so that it becomes necessary to search for and put together Aphorisms in widely separated parts of the work to enable the statement of some grammatical law or process to be completed.

Panini's grammar was criticized and its deficiencies supplied by the celebrated Katyayana, who is called Varttika-kara, as author of the Varttikas or 'supplementary rules and annotations.' He must have lived some time after Panini, perhaps in the century following. Some, however, believe the two grammarians to have been contemporaneous. Katyayana again was criticized by his rival Patanjali, who generally supports

1. See Chambers' Cyclopaedia, article Panini.

Panini against the composer of the supplementary rules. To Patanjali we owe one of the most wonderful grammetical works that the genius of any country has ever produced, viz. the Mahabhashya or 'great commentary[1],' written not so much to explain Panini as to defend such of his Aphorisms as had been criticized by Katyayana. He was probably not the same person as the author of the Yoga philosophy. According to some, his mother's name was Gonika; he was born at Gonarda in the east of India, and he lived for some time in Kashmir, where his work was well known. According to Professor Goldstucker, he wrote between 140 and 120 B.C.[2]; but Professor Weber places him about 25 years after Christ. These three men, Panini, Katyayana, and Patanjali, compose

---

1. The whole of this great work has been lately edited by two Pandits at Benares. See the able article on it by Professor Weber in the last volume of the 'Indische Studien.' A copy has been kindly sent to me by Professor A.E. Gough. Patanjali's additions to the Varttikas are called *Ishtis* or Desiderata. He is also the author of many Karikas or memorial verses on grammar. A compendium of such verses was also made by Bharti-hari.

2. See the 'Indian Antiquary' for February 1873. See also an article on Patanjali in Chambers' Cyclopaedia, where it is well said that 'Patanjali's method is analogous to that of other classical commentaries; it establishes, usually by repetition, the correct reading of the text in explaining every important or doubtful word, in showing the connection of the principal parts of the sentence, and in adding such observations as may be required. Frequently Patanjali attaches his own critical remarks to the emendations of Katyayana, often in support of the views of the latter, but not seldom, too, in order to refute his criticisms and to defend Panini; while, again, at other times, he completes the statement of one of them by his own additional rules.' Ramkrishan Gopal Bhandarkar, writing in the 'Indian Antiquary' for October 1872, states his opinion that Patanjali lived when Pushpamitra was reigning at Patali-putra, and 'that he probably wrote the third chapter of his Bhashya between 144 B.C. and 142 B.C.' Professor Weber, however, controverts this conclusion.

the great Indian triumvirate of grammarians, from whose authority there is no appeal in anything which relates to Vyakarana. About one hundred and fifty grammarians and commentators followed in their footsteps, each criticizing or commenting on his predecessors. Among these may be mentioned Kaiyata or Kaiyyata, who commented on Patanjali in a work called the Bhashya-pradipa, and was himself commented on by Nagoji-bhatta in the Bhashya-pradipoddyota[1]. One of the best of the more modern commentaries on Panini is Vamana's Kashika Vritti, so called because composed at Kashi or Benares. A grammarian named Bhattoji-dikshita attempted to arrange the Aphorisms on a plan more in accordance with modern idea. His useful work is called the Siddhanta-kaumudi[2]. A second and greater simplification of Panini is the Madhyama-kaumudi, and a still greater is the Laghu-kaumudi of Varada-raja[3], which is in fact a kind of abridgment of the Siddhanta-kaumudi, current in the north-west of India.

Vopadeva, a grammarian who is said to have flourished about the latter half of the thirteenth century at the court of Hemadri, king of Deva-giri (Dowlatabad), wrote a grammar for beginners on a system of his own, called the Mugdha-bodha[4], which is much valued as an authority in Bengal, and referred to by many native commentators, such, for example, as Bharata-mallika or Bharata-sena, who therefore called his commentary on the Bhatti-kavya, Mugdha-bodhini.

---

1. This Nagaji-bhatta was also the author of a grammatical work called Paribhashendu-shekhara, lately edited at Bombay, with a translation, by Professor F. Kielhorn.
2. A new edition of this was published not long ago in India.
3. This was edited and translated by Dr. Ballantyne.
4. It has been edited like Panini by Professor Bohtlingk.

Vopadeva's arrangement and many of his technical terms and symbolical expressions (including the technical forms of his affixes) differ from those of Panini, and the only allusion to Vedic peculiarities is in the last Sutra of the work (XXVI. 229), which is as follows:

Manifold forms and irregularities are allowed in the Veda. [*Bahulam brahmani*, which corresponds to Panini's often repeated bahulam chandasi, II. 4. 39, II. 4. 73, &c. Cf. also Panini's *vyatyayo bahulam*, 'opposition to the usual rule is frequent in the Veda,' III. 1. 85.]

In fact, Vopadeva[1] does not aim at the completeness of Panini. He omits all notice of the accents, and his treatment of the laws of euphonic combination is by no means exhaustive. In his explanation of declension and conjugation he is more satisfactory, and he gives numerous useful examples and paradigms, but usually contents himself with general rules, and does not, like Panini, trouble himself to trace out minute particulars or examine into every corner of an intricate subject with a view to a careful search for all possible exceptions.

---

1. It is very necessary to know the commonest of Vopadeva's technical expressions, as they are not only occasionally used by some native commentators, but are also employed in some instances by European expounders, of Sanskrit grammar. They often deviate from Panini's system. For example, the memorial terminations, usually given for verbs are those of Vopadeva (VIII. 1); *dhu* stands for dhatu, 'a root;' *vri* for vriddhi; *kva* for the terminations of the singular; *vva* for bahu-vachana, those of the plural; *li* for linga, a nominal base; *lidhu* for nominal verbs; *suup* and *up* for the characteristic *u* of the eighth class of roots; *tum* and *chatum* instead of Panini's *tumun,* for the Kriti affix *tum* forming the infinitive; *sana* (not *sanach*) for the termination of the present participle Atmane; *sri* for the pronominals (called Sarva-nama by Panini); *samahara* for Panini's *pratyahara* (see my Sanskrit-English Dictionary). Nevertheless, Vopadeva adopts a great number of Panini's technical terms.

Professor Bohtlingk has given an analysis of the Mugdha-bodha in the preface to his excellent edition of the work. Vopadeva's first chapter explains technical terms; the second treats of euphonic laws; the third, of declension; the fourth, of the formation of feminines; the fifth, of the use of the cases; the sixth, of compound words; the seventh, of Taddhita affixes; the eighth, of technical terms applicable to verbs and of roots of the first class; the ninth and tenth, of roots of the second and third classes; the eleventh to the seventeenth, of roots of the fourth to the tenth classes, one chapter being devoted to each class; the eighteenth, of causal verbs; the nineteenth, of desideratives; the twentieth, of the intensives; the twenty-first, of nominals; the twenty-second, of the use of the Parasmai-pada; the twenty-third, of the use of the Atmane-pada; the twenty-fourth, of passives, impersonals, and reflexive verbs; the twenty-fifth, of the use of the tenses and moods; the twenty-sixth, of Krit affixes and of affixes added to roots to form participles, &c.

I conclude by observing that a popular grammar called the *Katantra* (or *Kalapa*) is being well edited for the Bibliotheca Indica by professor J. Eggeling.

The Vedangas—Jyotisha, 'astronomy.'

This Vedanga should rather be called 'the astronomical or astrological calendar.' Strictly speaking, it is represented by a short tract, consisting of thirty-six verses, in a comparatively modern style, to which scholars cannot assign a date earlier than 300 years B.C. According to the best authorities, no genuine Sutras on astronomy have as yet been discovered. The object of the Jyotisha Vedanga is to fix the most auspicious days and seasons for commencing sacrifices. This treatise, brief and unsatisfactory as it is, nevertheless deserves attention as embodying some of the most ancient astronomical ideas, among which may be mentioned the measure of a day by thirty

Muhuryas or hours of forty-eight minutes, the division of the zodiac into twenty-seven parts or lunar asterisms (the first of which is Krittika), and the traditional place of the solstitial points, from which the attempt has been repeatedly made (by Jones, Davis, Colebrooke, Pratt, and others) to deduce a date for the treatise itself, as well as for the whole Vedic literature.

The following is Colebrooke's translation of verses seven and eight of the Jyotisha tract[1], which verses have been the subject of much controversy in relation to their bearing on the determination of dates from a comparison of the present position of the solstitial points:

The sun and moon turn towards the north at the beginning of Shravishta (= Dhanishtha), but the sun turns towards the south in the middle of the constellation over which the serpents preside; and this (turn towards the south and towards the north) always happens in the months of Magha and Shravana. [*Prapadyete Shravishthadau surya chandramasav udak, Sarpardhe dakshinarkas tu, magha-shtavanagoh sada.*] In the northern passage an increase of day and decrease of night take place amounting to a Prastha (or thirty-two Palas) of water; in the southern, both are reversed (i.e. the days decrease and the night increase), and the different amounts, by the journey, to six Muhurtas. [*Gharma-vriddhir apam prasthah kshapa-hrasa udag-gatau, Dakshine tau viparyastau shan-muhurty ayanena tu.*]

Whatever may be the value of these verses in an astronomical point of view, it is clear that a superstitious belief

---

1. See Professor E.B. Cowell's new edition of Colebrooke's Essays, republished by his son, Sir T.E. Colebrooke, p. 98; and see especially Professor Whitney's valuable notes on this point (p. 126). The latter shows that the date derivable from the statement made in the Jyotisha has a necessary uncertainty of about four centuries (from the 14th to the 10th B.C.), and he claims that the actual uncertainty is still greater — that's, in fact, the statement is worth nothing as yielding any definite date at all. Weber had before pointed out that the difference of six Muhurtas between the longest and shortest day or night is accurate only in the extreme north-western corner of India.

in the importance of choosing auspicious days and lucky moments for the performance of rites and ceremonies, whether public or domestic, began to show itself very early in India, and that it grew and strengthened simultaneously with the growth of priestcraft and the elaboration of a complex ritual. The influence of the sun upon the atmosphere and soil made itself so manifest that it was only natural to infer that similar influences belonged to the moon, planets, and stars; and the personification and deification of all the most conspicuous luminaries which resulted from the supposed power inherent in their rays, of course intensified the superstitious feeling of dependence upon their favourable aspects for the success, not only of religious acts, but of all the affairs of life. Pernicious as such superstitious ideas were in their effect on the mind and all mental progress, they were nevertheless productive of good in impelling the acute Hindu to study the movements of the heavenly bodies, and stimulating him to undertake arithmetical and mathematical investigations. In all probability, astronomical and mathematical science had an independent origin in India. It is at least certain that they were cultivated with some success at a very early epoch, though of course very roughly in the absence of all optical and mechanical appliances. We have already given an example from the Aitareya-brahmana, which contains certain shrewd guesses at scientific truth in regard to the sun (see p. 37).

In some of the earliest hymns of the Veda the Nakshatras or lunar mansions[1] are mentioned in connection with the

---

1. For the twenty-seven Vedic Nakshatras see my Sanskrit-English Dictionary (also Appendix). The word *Nakshatra* at first meant a star or asterism in general; then it was applied to the selected series of asterisms through or near which the moon passes; and finally it was loosely used for the part of the moon's path, the 27th or 28th of the zodiac, marked by each asterism. In the later mythology the lunar mansions were fabled as the twenty-seven daughters of Daksha and wives of the moon.

moon (see Rig-veda. I. 50. 2). Moreover, some of the phases of the moon, such as *Anumati*, 'the moon one digit less than full,' *Raka*, 'the full moon,' *Kuhu* (or *Gungy*), 'the new moon,' and *Sinivali*, 'the first thin crescent preceding or following new moon,' are personified (see Rig-veda. II. 32. 8), so that we are justified in inferring that the movements of the moon in the zodiac and its use as the time-measurer and month-maker (*masa-krit*)[1] were studied and noted by the Hindus perhaps as early as 1400 years B.C. The twenty-seven lunar mansions implied a lunar division of the zodiac into twenty-seven equal parts of 13° 20' to each part. Such a division (into twenty-seven or twenty-eight parts) is shared by other Asiatic peoples, as the Arabs and Chinese, and the question where it originated has provoked much discussion, without leading to any definite and certain results[2]. The names of the Indian months have certainly been taken from the asterisms in which the moon was supposed to be full at different times of the year, and, what is still more significant, the names of some of these lunar asterisms have clearly been derived from ancient

---

1. This is a Vedic name of the moon. A root *ma*, 'to measure,' meaning also 'the measurer,' is first applied to the moon in Sanskrit and then to a lunation or period measured by one revolution of the moon. Something similar has happened in the cognate Aryan languages. At least we know that the words for 'month' are generally derived from the moon, our word 'month' being nothing out *moonth*. In Rig-veda X. 85. 2 occurs the following: *Atho nakshatranam esham upashte Soma ahitah,* Soma is deposited in the lap of these Nakshatras.'

2. The various opinions and the arguments by which they have been supported have been lately reviewed by Professor Whitney in his 'Oriental and Linguistic Studies,' vol. ii. pp. 341-421. He regards the matter as still unsettled. The solar signs of the zodiac and much of the later astronomy, with many astronomical terms (such as *hora* = *kendra* = *drikana,* the third of a zodiacal sign = *lipta,* the minute of a degree = were borrowed from the Greeks.

Vedic deities, like the Asvins[1], &c. In the Yajur-veda and Brahmanas occur the expressions Nakshatra-darsha dn Ganaka, applied to observers of the heavens, either as astronomers or astrologers[2]; and the adjustment of the lunar to the solar year by the insertion of a thirteenth or intercalary month (*mala-masa, malimlucha, adhimasa*, sometimes called *Purushottama*) is probably alluded to in an ancient hymn (Rig-veda I. 25. 8), and frequently in more recent parts of the Veda. (Vajasaneyi-samhita 22. 30, Atharva-veda. V. 6. 4, &c.)

Whatever conclusions we may arrive at as to the original source of the first astronomical ideas current in the world it is probable that to the Hindus is due the invention of algebra[3] and its application to astronomy and geometry. From them

---

1. The names of the months are Magha (from the Nakshatra *Magha*), Phalguna (from *Phalguni*), Chaitra (from *Chitra*), Vaishakha (from *Visakha*), Jjaishtha (from *Jyeshtha*), Ashadha (from *Ashadha*), Shravana (from *Shravana*), Bhadrapada or Bhadra (from *Bhadra-pada*), Ashvina (from *Asvini*), Karttika (from *Krittika*), Margasirsha, commonly called Agrahayana (from *Mriga-shiras*), Pausha (from *Pushya*). I have arranged these names so as to correspond as nearly as possible with our months, *Magha* representing January — February, and the others continuing in regular order; but practically the Hindu calendar generally begins with Vaishakha, this being considered the first month in the year.

2. Of course astronomy and astrology were mixed up together, and the progress of the former was impeded in India by its subservience to the latter.

3. The name Algebra (from the Arabic *al jabr*, 'the reduction of part to a whole or of fractions to integers') shows that Europe received algebra like the ten numerical symbols from the Hindus through the *Arabs*. The Sanskrit word for algebra, *Vija-ganita*, means 'calculation of seeds,' 'calculation of original or primary elements,' i.e. analysis. If the Greeks did not receive their first ideas of algebra from the Hindus, it may at least be taken as proved (from all that Colebrooke has so ably written on the subject), that the Hindus were certainly not indebted to the Greeks, but invented their system independently.

also the Arabs received not only their first conception of algebraic analysis, but also those invaluable numerical symbols and decimal notation now current everywhere in Europe, which have rendered untold service to the progress of arithmetical science. It will not, therefore, be irrelevant if I introduce here a short account of the chief Hindu astronomical and mathematical works with a few illustrative extracts.

By some authorities nine principal astronomical treatises, called Siddhantas, are named, viz. the *Braham-siddhanta, Surya-s°, Soma-s°, Vrihaspati-s°, Garga-s°, Narada-s°, Parashara-s°, Pulastya-s°, Vasishtha-s°;* by others five, viz. the *Paulisa-s°, Romaka-s°,*[1] *Vasishtha-s°, Saura-s°,* and *Brahama-s°* or *Paitamaha-s°,* and these five sometimes called collectively the *Pancha-siddhantika,* are said to be the original Siddhantas. Whether the Surya-s° is the same as the Saura-s° appears somewhat doubtful, but this treatise, fabled to have been revealed by Surya 'the Sun' himself, is perhaps the best known of all Hindu astronomical works both in India and Europe[2].

The earliest Hindu astronomer whose name has come down to us is Arya-bhata, who lived, according to Colebrooke, about the fifth century of our era. Others place him, or another astronomer of his name, in the third century. Arya-bhata is the author of three works, the Aryabhatiya, Dasa-gitika, and Aryashta-shata, and is said to have asserted a diurnal revolution of the earth on its axis, to have known the true theory of the causes of lunar and solar eclipses, and noticed the motion of the solstitial and equinoctial points[3]. Professor Kern has just published an edition of the *Aryabhatiya.*

---

1. This title Romaka-s° points to an exchange of ideas on astronomical subjects between India, Greece, and Rome.
2. It has been well edited by Dr. Fitz-Edward Hall, and there are two translations of it, one published in America with notes (by Professor Whitney), and another by Bapudeva Shastri.
3. According to Brahma-gupta, as quoted by the writer of the article Sanskrit Literature in Chambers' Cyclopaedia, which I have consulted.

After Arya-bhata came the astronomer Varaha-mihira, who lived about the sixth century of our era, and was born at Ujjayini. He wrote a work on nativities called Vrihaj-jataka, another well-known astrological work called Brihat-samhita (recently translated by Professor Kern[1], an extract from which is given p. 205), and a summary of the five original Siddhantas called Pancha-siddhantika.

Next to Arya-bhata and Varaha-mihira lived Brahma-gupta (probably towards the end of the sixth century), who wrote the Brahma-siddhanta, containing the chapters on arithmetic (*ganita*) and algebra (*kuttaka*[2]) in Colebrooke's Indian Algebra.

Fourth and last of celebrated astronomers and mathematicians came Bhaskara or Bhaskaracharya, who is supposed to have lived in the twelfth century and composed a well-known book called the Siddhanta-shiromani, containing the treatises on algebra (*Vija-ganita*)and arithmetic (*Lilavati*[3]) translated by Colebrooke.

I proceed now to select specimens of the contents of the above works. The first extract gives the Indian division of time taken from the Surya-siddhanta (I. 11–13), Bhaskara's Siddhanta-shiromani (I. 19, 20), and other works with their commentaries (Burgess, pp. 5, 6). It illustrates very curiously the natural taste of the Hindus for hyperbole, leading them to attempt almost infinite calculations of inconceivable periods in the one direction, and infinitesimal subdivisions of the most minute quantities in the other. Without any reliable chronology in regard to the precise dates of any great events

---

1. For the Journal of the Royal Asiatic Society.
2. *Kuttaka* properly means a 'pulverizer' or 'multiplier.'
3. *Lilavati*, 'delightful by its elegance,' is merely the name of the chapter on arithmetic (*pati-ganita*, divided, into *vyakta-ganita*, 'distinct computation,' and *avyakta-g°*, 'indistinct').The name is also applied to a supposed 'charming woman,' to whom instruction in arithmetic is given.

in their own history, they yet delight in a kind of chronology
or 'science of time,' making time past, present, and future a
subject of the most elaborate and minute computations. Hence
we find them heaping billions upon millions and trillions
upon billions of years, and reckoning up ages upon ages,
Aeons upon Aeon, with even more audacity than modern
geologists and astronomers. In short, an astronomical Hindu
ventures on arithmetical conceptions quite beyond the mental
dimensions of any one who feels himself incompetent to
attempt the task of measuring infinity. Here is the time-table
enumerating the subdivisions of what is called *real* and
unreal time:

'That which begins with respiration (*prana*) is called real
(*murta*) time; that which begins with atoms (*truti*) is called
unreal (*amurta*) time. Ten long syllables (*gurv-akshara*) make one
respiration (*prana, asu*); six respirations make one Vinadi (also
called *pala* or *vighatika* of twenty-four seconds); sixty
Vinadis=one Nadi or Nadika (also called *danda, ghati, ghatika*
of twenty-four minutes); sixty Nadis=one day (a sidereal day
and night); thirty sidereal days=one civil (*savana*) month; a civil
month consists of thirty sunrises; a lunar month of thirty lunar
days (*tithi*); a solar (*saura*) month is determined by the entrance
of the sun into a sign of the zodiac.' And now with regard to
unreal time: 'One hundred atoms (*truti*)=one speck (*tatpara*);
thirty specks=one twinkling (*nimesha*); eighteen twinklings=one
bit (*kashtha*); thirty bits=one minute (*kala*);thirty minutes=one
half-hour (*ghatika*); two half-hours=one hour (*kshana*); thirty
hours=one day.' This makes the atom 1/33750 of a second.

Considerable variations occur in Manu and the Puranas.
According to Manu (I. 64) thirty Kalas=one Muhurta or hour
of forty-eight minutes. The Vishnu-purana (Wilson, p. 22)
makes the atom=1/2110 of a second, and goes back beyond
an atom to a Paramanu or infinitesimal atom, which it
makes=1/38000 of a second. All, however, agree in dividing

the day into thirty hours, just as the month is divided into thirty Tithis or lunar days, and the year into three hundred and sixty days, an intercalary month being inserted once in five years, which is thought to be the most ancient Hindu method of computing time[1]. The Surya-siddhanta then proceeds, like Manu (I. 68. 71), to reckon up vast periods of time through ages[2] (*yuga*) and great ages (*maha-yuga*), till it arrives at an Aeon (*kalpa*), the total duration of which is said to be 4,320,000,000 years. In verse 24 we read (Burgess, p. 12):

One hundred times four hundred and seventy-four divine years passed while the All-wise was employed in creating the animate and inanimate creation, plants, stars, gods, demons, and the rest.

Further on we have the division of a circle, which corresponds with our own:

Sixty seconds (*vikala*) make a minute (*kala*), sixty minutes make a degree (*bhaga*), thirty degress make a sign (*rashi*), twelve signs make a revolution (*bhagana*).

The following is the measurement of the earth:

Twice 800 *yojanas* are the diameter of the earth; the square root of ten times the square of that is the earth's circumference.

According to Bhaskara the earth's diameter is 1581 *yojanas*, so that if the *yojana* is reckoned at about four and a half

---

1. Almanacs and horoscopes (*Janma-patra*) are called *Panchanga,* as treating of five things, viz. solar days, (commonly called Varas, from the days of the week, Aditya-v°, Soma-v°, Mangala-v°, Budha-v°, Guru-v°, Shukra-v°, Shani-v°), lunar days (Tithis), the twenty-seven Nakshatras, the twenty-seven Yogas, the eleven Karanas.
2. There are properly four Yugas or ages in every Mahayuga, viz. *Krita, Treta, Dvapara,* and *Kali,* named from the marks on dice, the Krita being the best throw of four points, and the Kali the worst of one point.

English miles (which is given as one estimate of its length, though its value varies), the calculation in both cases is not very far from accurate.

At the commencement of Surya-siddhanta, Chapter II, we have a strange theory of planetary motion (p. 47):

Forms of time (*kalasya murtayah*) of invisible shape (*adrishya-rupad*) stationed in the zodiac (*bhaganashritah*), called conjunction (*sighrochcha*), upper apsis (*mandochcha*), and node (*pata*), are causes of the motion of the planets. The planets attached to these Beings by cords of air are drawn away by them with the right and left hand, forward or backward, according to nearness, toward their own place. A wind, moreover, called Pravaha, impels them towards their own apices (*uchcha*); being drawn away forward and backward, they proceed by a varying motion.

In the previous Chapter (29, 34) the following statement occurs:

In an age (*yuga*) the revolutions of the sun, Mercury (*Budha*), and Venus (*Shukra*), and of the conjunctions of Mars (*Mangala, Bhauma*) Saturn (*Shani*), and Jupiter (*Vrihaspati*), moving eastward, are four million, three hundred and twenty thousand. Of the asterisms, one billion, five hundred and eight-two·million, two hundred and thirty-seven thousand, eight hundred and twenty-eight.

I next give a portion of a remarkable passage from Varaha-mihira's *Brihat-samhita* or 'complete system of natural astrology' (see Dr. Kern's translation, p. 433, of vol. iv. of the Royal Asiatic Society's Journal):

An astrologer ought to be of good family, friendly in his appearance, and fashionable in his dress; veracious and not malignant. He must have well-proportioned, compact, and full limbs, no bodily defect, and be a fine man, with nice hands, feet, nails, eyes, chin, teeth, ears, brows, and head, and with a deep and clear voice; for generally one's good and bad moral qualities are in unison with one's personal appearance. As to mathematical astronomy, he must know the divisions of the heaven and of time, in ages, years, half-years, seasons, months, half-months, days, watches, hours, half-hours, minutes, respirations, moments, subdivisions of a moment, &c., as taught in the five Siddhantas (see p. 201). He must know the reason why there are four kinds of months — the solar (*saura*), natural (*savana*), stellar (*nakshatra*), and lunar (*chandra*) months — and how it happens that there are intercalary months and subtractive days. He must know the beginning and end of the Jovian cycle of sixty years, of the lustrums, years, days, hours, and their respective lords. He must foretell the moment of commencement and separation, the direction, measure, duration, amount of obscuration, colour and place of the eclipses of sun and moon; also the future conjunctions and hostile encounters of the nine planets[1]. He must be skilful in ascertaining the distance of each planet from the earth, expressed in *yojanas;* further, the dimensions of their orbits and the distance of the places on earth, in *yojanas*. He ought to be clever in geometrical operations and in the calculation of time. If, moreover, he knows how to speak pithily, because he thoroughly understands all sorts of captious questions; if the science he expounds, by being put to the test by his own exertion and unceasing study, had become more refined — like gold is rendered purer by being put on the touchstone, by purification in fire, and by careful workmanship — then he may be said to be a scientific man. It has been said: 'How can one who solves no difficulty, nor answers any question, nor teaches his pupils, be styled a scientific man?' And thus it has been said by the great seer Garga: 'The king who does not honour a scholar accomplished in horoscopy and astronomy comes to grief.' 'As

---

1. The nine planets are the Sun and Moon, Mercury, Venus, Mars, Jupiter, Saturn, with Rahu and Ketu or the ascending and descending nodes.

the night without a light, as the sky without the sun, so is a king without an astrologer; like a blind man he erreth on the road.' 'No one who wishes for well-being should live in a country where there is no astrologer.' 'No one that has studied astrology can go to the infernal regions.' 'A person who, without knowing the science, exercises the profession of an astrologer is a wicked man and a disgrace to society. Consider him to be a mere star-gazer. But such a one as properly knows horoscopy, astronomy, and natural astrology, him ought the king to honour and his service he ought to secure.'

With regard to Colebrooke's translation of Bhaskara's work on algebra (*Vija-ganita*), the following extract is taken from the translator's introduction (p. xxii):

The motions of the moon and sun were carefully observed by the Hindus, and with such success that their determination of the moon's synodical revolution is a much more correct one than the Greeks ever achieved. They had a division of the ecliptic into twenty-seven and twenty-eight parts, suggested evidently by the moon's period in days, and seemingly their own. It was certainly borrowed by the Arabs[1]. They were particularly conversant with most splendid of the primary planets; the period of Jupiter being introduced by them, in conjunction with those of the sun and moon, into the regulation of their calendar in the form of the cycle of sixty years, common to them and the Chaldeans.

We may add that from certain expressions in Bhaskara's work (see p. 106, Banerjea's Dialogues, p. 69[2]), it is inferred that some idea of the laws of gravitation was formed by Hindu

---

1. The Arabs, however, appear to have adopted the division of the zodiac into twenty-eight segments. Professor Whitney thinks that the Arabs did not borrow their lunar zodiac from the Hindus. See p. 199 and the authorities there referred to.
2. See also the 'Indian antiquary' for July 1872, p. 224.

astronomers as early as the twelfth century of our era. The precession of the equinoctial points (*vishuvat, kranti-pata*), was well known to Bhaskara, and the effect of the moon in causing tides seems to have been suspected much earlier (cf. Raghu-vansha V. 61).

The points in which Hindu algebra appears particularly distinguished from the Greek are (Colebrooke, p. xvi):

In addition to a better and more comprehensive algorithm (or notation): 1st. The management of equations involving more than one unknown term. 2nd. The resolution of equations of a higher order, in which, if they achieved little, they had at least the merit of the attempt and anticipated a modern discovery in the solution of biquadratics. 3rd. General methods for the solution of indeterminate problems of first and second degrees, in which they went far, indeed, beyond Diophantus, and anticipated discoveries of modern algebraists. 4th. Application of algebra to astronomical investigation and geometrical demonstration, in which they hit on some matters re-invented in later times. One of their anticipations of modern discoveries is the demonstration of the noted proposition of Pythagoras concerning the square of the base of a rectangular triangle being equal to the squares of the two legs containing the right angle.

As to the notation or algorithm of algebra, Colebrooke remarks (p. x):

The Hindu algebraists use abbreviations and initials for symbols. They distinguish negative quantities by a dot, but, have not any mark, besides the absence of the negative sign, to discriminate a positive quantity. No marks or symbols indicating operations of addition or multiplication &c. are employed; nor any announcing equality or relative magnitude (greater or less)[1].

---

1. The sign of equality was first used by Robert Recorde (because, he said, 'No two things can be more equal than a pair of parallels'), and those of relative magnitude by Harriot, — Colebrooke.

But a factum is denoted by the initial syllable of a word of that import, subjoined to the terms which compose it, between which a dot is sometimes interposed. A fraction is indicated by placing the divisor under the dividend, but without a line of separation. The symbols of unknown quantity are not confined to a single one, but extend to ever so great a variety of denominations, and the characters used are initial syllables of the names of colours, excepting the first, which is the initial of *yavat-tavat* (applied to the *first* unknown quantity, i.e. 'so much' of the unknown as this coefficient number). Colour, therefore, means unknown quantity or the symbol of it. Letters are likewise employed as symbols, either taken from the alphabet or else initial syllables of words signifying the subjects of the problem. Initials of the terms for square and solid respectively denote those powers. An initial syllable is in like manner used to mark a surd root (see the next extract and succeeding examples).

The following is from the Vija-ganita (chap. vi):

This is analysis by equation comprising several colours. In this the unknown quantities are numerous, two and three or more, for which *yavat-tavat* and the several colours are to be put to represent the values. The have been settled by the ancient téachers of the science, viz. black (*kala*), blue (*nila*), yellow (*pila*), red (*lohita*), green (*haritaka*), white (*shveta*), variegated (*chitra*), tawny (*kapila*), tan-coloured (*pingala*), grey (*dhumra*), pink (*patala*), mottled (*savala*), blackish (*shyamala,*), another kind of black (*mechaka*), &c. Or letters (that is, *k* &c.) are to be employed as names of the unknown. [In practice the initial syllables of the above words are used thus, *ya, ka, ni, pi, lo.*]

I here give some of the Sanskrit equivalents for terms in arithmetic and algebra:

An absolute quantity which has specific form is *rupa* (applied in the singular to a unit, in the plural to an integer number, and often expressed by the first syllable *ru*). A surd or irrational number is *karani* (often denoted by the first syllable *ka*). A nought or cipher is *shunya, cha;* a fraction which has a cipher for its denominator *cha-hara;* minus *rina, kshaya* (negative quantity); plus *dhana, sva* (positive quantity). A result or product is *bhavita* (often expressed by the first syllable *bha;* hence the product of two unknown quantities is expressed by *ya. ka bha,* or *ka. ni bha;* so also the square of the first unknown quantity multiplied by the cube of the second is thus abbreviated, *ya va. ka. gha, bha*).

It may be interesting to note the system of numeration increasing in decuple proportion given in chapter II of the Lilavati. This method, with the invention of the nine numerical figures (*anka*) and of the nought (*shunya*) and of the decuple value assigned to each according to its position in the series, is thought to be of divine origin:

Unit (*eka*), ten (*dasa*), hundred (*shata*), thousand (*sahasra*), ten thousand (*ayuta*), a hundred thousand (*laksha,* commonly called 'a lac'), million (*prayuta*), ten million (*koti,* commonly called 'a krore'), a hundred million (*arbuda*), a thousand millions (*abja* or *padma*), ten thousand millions (*kharva*), a hundred thousand millions (*nikharva*), a billion or million of millions (*maha-padma*), ten billions (*shanku*), a hundred billions (*jaladhi* or *samudra*), a thousand billions (*antya*), ten thousand billions (*madhya*), a hundred thousand billions (*parardha*).

I add four specimens of problems from the Lilavati and Vijaganita (Colebrooke, pp. 24, 124, 191, 269, 272):

1. Out of a swarm of bees, one-fifth part settled on a Kadamba blossom; one-third on a Silindhra flower; three times the difference of those numbers flew to the bloom of a Kutaja. One bee, which remained, hovered about in the air. Tell me, charming woman, the number of bees.

2. How many are the variations of form of the (ten-armed) god Shambhu (Shiva) by the exchange of his ten attributes held

reciprocally in his several hands, viz. the rope (*pasha*), the hook for guiding an elephant (*ankusha*), the serpent, the hour-glass-shaped drum (*damaru*), the human skull, the trident (*trishula*), the club shaped like the foot of a bedstead (*khatvanaga*), the dagger, the arrow, the bow? And those of (the four-armed) Hari (Vishnu) by the exchange of the mace, the discus (*chakra*), the lotus, and the conch (*shankha*)? Answer 3,628,800; 24.

3. Eight rubies, ten emeralds, and a hundred pearls, which are in thy ear-ring, my beloved, were purchased by me for thee at an equal amount; and the sum of the rates of the three sorts of gems was three less than half a hundred: tell me the rate of each, auspicious woman..

4. What four numbers are such that the product of them all is equal to twenty times their sum? The answer to this last is: Here let the first number be *ya* 1; and the rest be arbitrarily put 5, 4, and 2. Their sum is *ya* 1, *ru* 11, and multiplied by 20, *ya* 20 *ru* 220. Product of all the quantities *ya* 40 Statements for equation, *ya* 40, *ru* 0. Hence by the first analysis, the value of
ya 20, *ru* 220
ya is found 11, and the numbers are 11, 5, 4, 2.

I should mention here that attached to each Veda there are certain works called *Parishishta* or 'Supplements,' intended to supply directions omitted in the Shrauta Sutras, &c. There are also the *Anukramani* or 'Indices,' giving the first words of every hymn, the metre, the names of the authors and of the deities addressed, the number of verses, &c.

There are also Upa-vedas or 'secondary Vedas,' which, however, have really little or no connection with either the Veda or Smriti. They are, 1. *Ayur-veda,* 'the science of life' or medicine (regarded as belonging to the Atharvaveda, and by some to the Rig-veda); 2. *Gandharva-veda,* 'the science of music' (as a branch of the Sama-veda); 3. *Dhanur-veda,* 'the science of archery' or military art (connected with the Yajur-veda); 4. *Sthapatya-veda,* 'the science of architecutre,' including the Shilpa-shastra:

As to 1, two great medical writers are *Charaka* and *Su-sruta,* whose works treat of anatomy, physiology, materia medica, pharmacy, surgery (*shalya*), toxicology (*visha*), omens, and the evil influence of planets and demons (*bhuta*) in causing diseases. (See Wilson's Essays, vol. i. pp. 269-276, 380-393.) Su-shruta's work, in six books, has been well edited at Calcutta by Sri Madhusudana Gupta. As to 2, Works on music treat of notes, scales, melodies, singing, musical instruments, and sometimes of dancing. Six primary modes or modifications of melody, called Ragas, are enumerated, which are personified, and each of them married to five or sometimes six Raginis. The chief musical works are the *San-gita-ratnakara,* by Sharnga-deva; the *Sangita-darpana,* by Damodara; and the *Sangita-damodara,* by Subhankara. As to 3, This science is by some ascribed to Vishvamitra, by others to Bhrigu. As to 4, Some assert that there are sixty-four treatises on the sixty-four Shilpas or 'mechanical arts,' such as architecture, sculpture, carpentry, jewellery, farriery, &c. The principal work on architecture is the *Mana-sara,* 'essence of measurement,' in fifty-eight chapters, giving rules for the construction of buildings, temples, ornamental arches (*torana*), &c. Other works, by celebrated Sthapatis or 'architects,' describe the soil suited for building and rites in honour of the Vastu-purusha, 'spirit presiding over sites.'

Lecture IX

II. *The Smarta Sutras or Traditional Rules*

In our classification of Smriti or Post-vedic literature, at the commencement of the last Lecture, we placed the Smarta Sutras under the second head, and pointed out that they were to a great extent the source of the subsequent law-books which form, in our arrangement, the third head of Smriti. We also observed that the term *Smarta-sutra* is a general expression for collections of aphoristic rules which are distinguished from the Shrauta-sutra, of the Kalpa Vedanga, because they do not relate to Srauta or Vedic ceremonies, but rather to *Grihya* or 'domestic rites' and *Samayachara* or 'conventional everyday practices.' Hence the Smarta Sutras are commonly subdivided into, a. *Grihya Sutras,* and b. *Samayacharika Sutras.* It will be desirable, therefore, before commencing our survey of Manu's celebrated Law-book, to advert briefly to these sources from which some of its materials were derived, and especially to the Grihya Sutras[1]. Of these there are collections of different schools attached to each Veda. Thus to the Rig-veda belong the

---

1. Probably, however, Manu owes more to the Samayacharika than to the Grihya Sutras, although these latter are now best known to us by printed editions. We find that the authors of Grihya Sutras have often the same name as the authors of law-books.

Ashvalayana[1] and *Sankhayana* Grihya Sutras; to the Sama-veda those of Gobhila[1]; to the Vajasaneyi-samhita or White Yajur-veda those of *Paraskara;* to the Taittiriya or Black Yajur-veda those of *Kathaka, Baudhayana, Bharadvaja, Apastamba*[2], the *Maitrayaniya, Manava* (which last have perished, though some of their Kalp-sutras have been preserved; see p. 213), &c.

In fact, every Brahmanical family or school (*charana*[3]) had probably its own traditional recension *sakha,* (p. 175) of the Mantra and Brahmana portion of the Vedas as well as its own Kalpa, Grihya, and Samayacharika Sutras; and even at the present day the domestic rites of particular families of Brahmans are performed in accordance with the Sutras of the Veda of which they happen to be adherents.

Since these Grihya and Samayacharika Sutras are older than Manu, they are probably as old as the sixth century B.C., but possibly the works we possess represent comparatively recent collections of the original texts..

It has been already pointed out that the Shrauta Sutras are a kind of rubric for the more public solemn sacrifices

---

1. There are also, as we have seen, Ashvalayana Shrauta-sutra under the head of 'Kalpa,' and probably each school had all three sets of Sutras complete, though they are seldom all preserved. The Ashvalayana Grihya Sutras and part of the Paraskara have been edited and translated into German by Professor Stenzler (Leipzig, 1864, 1865), and the former have also been edited by Pandits for the Bibliotheca Indica (Calcutta, 1869). The Gobhiliya Grihya Sutras are being edited for the Bibliotheca Indica.
2. The Apastambas appear to have preserved all three sets of Sutras complete, for there are also Apastamba Shrauta-sutra and Samayacharika-sutra. According to professor Bhandarkar there are numbers of Brahmans in the south of India who are adherents to the Black Yajur-veda and who receive *dakshina* or 'fees' from rich men for repeating it with the Apastamba Sutras.
3. A work called the *Charana-vyuha* gives catalogues of these schools.

(Jyotishtoma, Agnishtoma, Asva-medha &c.) enjoined by the Veda. The subject of the Grihya is rather that indicated by Manu when he says (III. 67):

Let the householder observe domestic rites with the sacred fire kindled at his marriage (called *Garhapatya*) according to rule, and perform the five devotional acts and the daily domestic oblations. [*Vaivahike' gnau kurvita grihyam karma yatha-vidhi Panca-yajna-vidhanam cha paktim (=pakam) chanvahikim grihi.*]

Indeed the word Grihya means 'household,' and these Sutras do in fact give rules for the five diurnal acts of domestic devotion called *Maha-yajna* (or *Pancha-yajna,* four of them being also *Paka-yajna,* Manu II. 86), as well as for the domestic ceremonies named *Sanskaras,* common to all the three higher classes, and not restricted to Brahmans. The twelve Sanskaras are described at p. 269. They are generally performed at the one domestic hearth, instead of with all the three fires (called collectively *Treta*) of the *Vitanas* or 'hearths used at public sacrifices.'

I proceed to give a brief account of Ashvalayana's Grihya Sutras of the Rig-veda, making one prefatory remark that the Hindu race affords perhaps the only example of a nation who, although apparently quite indifferent to the registering of any of the great facts of their political life, or even to the recording of any of the most remarkable events of their history — as, for example, the invasion of the Greeks under Alexander the Great — nevertheless, at a very early period, regulated their domestic rites and customs according to definite prescribed rules, which were not only written down, but preserved with religious care, and many of them are still in force. Moreover, as this race belongs to the same original race-stock as ourselves, the antiquity of their customs must of necessity invest them with great interest in our eyes.

The domestic oblations called Paka-yajna (Manu II. 86,

143) are distinguished from the Vaitanika[1] in the first two Sutras, thus (Stenzler's edition, I. 1. 2):

The Vaitanika oblations (performed with all the three sacred fires[2]) have been explained (in the Srauta-sutra), we will now describe those (performed with the) domestic (fire only). There are three kinds of Paka-yajna, viz. those that are offered in fire (such as oblations of butter, &c.); those that are presented without being offered in fire; those that are offered to the supreme Being (*Brahmani*) in the feeding of Brahmans (*Brahmana-bhojane*).

Book I. ii. enumerates the gods to whom oblations are to be offered, such as Agni, Indra, Soma, Heaven and Earth, Yama, Varuna, the Visve Devah (cf. Manu III. 90, 121), Brahman, &c. These, it will be observed, are generally Vedic

---

1. Kulluka, on Manu V. 84, derives *vitana* from *vitan*, 'to spread out,' and explains *Vaitanika* to be those Shrauta oblations which are performed when the Garhapatya fire is spread over both the Ahavaniya˙ and Dakshina hearths (*vaitanam shrauto homah garhapatya-kunda-sthan agnin ahavani-yadi-kundeshu vitatya kriyate*). See also Manu VI. 9. There is much difference of opinion as to the exact meaning of *paka-yajna*. Stenzler translates it by 'Koch-opfer,' and thinks it means an oblation offered on the domestic fire when the daily food is cooked. Some of the commentators, on the other hand, interpret *paka* by 'small,' 'simple,' and some by 'good.' In Manu II. 86 four Paka-yajnas or 'domestic oblations' are mentioned (which Kulluka explains by *Vaisvadeva-homa, bali, nitya-sraddha,* and *atithi-bhojana*), thus identifying them with four of the Maha-yajna, see p. 222. Seven different kinds of Paka-yajna will be found enumerated in my Sanskrit-English Dictionary.

2. In Manu III. 100, 185, five sacred fires are mentioned, and a Brahman who keeps them all burning, called a *Panchagni* (=*Agnihotrin*), is regarded as peculiarly pious. They are, 1. Dakshina (*Anvaharya-pachana* in the Brahmanas); 2. *Garhapatya;* 3. *Ahavaniya;* 4. *Sabhya;* 5. *Avasathya.* The three first fires are the most important and are collectively called *Treta.* Agnihotris are still met with in India.

deities. The third prescribes the mode of preparing the place where oblations are to be made:

The ceremonies of tonsure (*chaula*=*chuda-karman*), investiture with the sacred cord (*upanayana*), shaving the beard (*go-dana*) and marriage must be performed during the northern course of the sun (*udag-ayane*), in the light half of the month (*apuryamane pakshe*), and under an auspicious constellation (*kalyane nakshatre*).

These Sanskara ceremonies are then described (beginning with marriage), and whenever Mantras or texts of the Veda have to be repeated during the performance of each rite, the first word or words of the several texts are cited. Thus before the marriage ceremony an oblation of clarified butter is to be offered with repetition of the text: *Tavam Aryama bhavasi yat kaninam*, &c., 'thou art Aryaman in relation to maidens' (Rig-veda. V. 3. 2).

The fifth Chapter prescribes the due selection of a wife after proper inquiry as to family and condition. Sutra 3 says:

A man ought to marry a woman who is possessed of intelligence, beauty, good character, and auspicious marks, and who is free from disease. (Compare the directions Manu III. 4-10.)

The sixth Chapter specifies and describes the eight forms of marriage, called *Brahma, Daiva, Prajapatya, Arsha, Gandharva, Asura, Paishacha,* and *Rakshasa.* They are also enumerated by Manu (III. 21), but not quite in the same order, and by Yajnavalkya (I. 58, 61). Manu (III. 27-34) describes them more fully than Ashvalayana.

Book I. vii. prescribes a common marriage ceremony:

West of the (sacred) fire a stone (for grinding corn and condiments, such as is used by women in all households) is placed, and north-east a water-jar. The bridegroom offers an oblation, standing, looking towards the west, and taking hold of the bride's hands while she sits and looks towards the east.

If he wishes only for sons, he clasps her thumbs and says, 'I clasp thy hands for the sake of good fortune;' the fingers alone, if he wishes for daughters; the hairy side of the hand along with the thumbs, if he wishes for both (sons and daughters). Then, whilst he leads her towards the right three times round the fire and round the water-jar, he says in a low tone, "I am he, thou art she; thou art she, I am he; I am the heaven, thou art the earth; I am the Saman, thou art the Rich. Come; let us marry, let us possess offspring; united in affection, illustrious, well disposed towards each other (*sumanasyamanau*), let us live for a hundred years." Every time he leads her round he makes her to ascend the mill-stone, and says, 'Ascend thou this stone, be thou firm as a stone' (*ashmeva tvam sthira bhava*). Then the bride's brother, after spreading melted butter on the joined palms of her hands, scatters parched grains of rice on them twice. Then, after pouring the oblation of butter on the fire, some Vedic texts are recited. Then the bridegroom unlooses the two braided tresses of hair, one on each side of the top of the bride's head, repeating the Vedic text, 'I loose thee from the fetters of Varuna with which the very auspicious Savitri has bound thee' (Rig-veda X. 85. 24[1]). The he causes her to step seven steps towards the north-east quarter, saying to her, 'Take thou one step (*ekapadi bhava*) for the acquirement of sap-like energy (*ishe*); take thou two steps for strength (*urje dvipadi bhava*); take thou three steps for the increase of wealth (*rayas-poshaya*); take thou four steps for well-being (*mayobhavyaya*); take thou five steps for offspring (*prajabhyah*); take thou six steps for the seasons (*ritubhyah*); take thou seven steps as a friend (*sakha saptapadi bhava*[2]); be faithfully devoted to me; may we obtain many sons! May they attain to a good old age!' Then bringing both their heads into

---

1. The text in the original is *Pra tva munchami Varunasya pashad yena tvabadhnat Savita susevah*. It is from the well-known Surya-sukta (X. 85), describing the marriage ceremony of Surya, the youthful daughter of the Sun, united to Soma, the Moon.
2. Sakha is Vedic for Sakhi. See Scholiast on Panini IV. 1. 62.

close juxtaposition, some one sprinkles them with water from the jar. He should then remain for that night in the abode of an old Brahman woman whose husband and children are alive. When the bride sees the polar star and Arundhati and the seven Rishis, let her break silence and say, 'May my husband live and may I obtain children.'

In Book I. viii. 12, 13, 14, we have the following:

When he (the bridegroom) has completed the marriage ceremonial he should give the bride's dress to one who knows the Surya-sukta (Rig-veda X. 85), and food to the Brahmans; then he should make them pronounce a blessing on him. [*Charita-vratah surya-vide vadhu-vastram dadyat / annam brahmanebhyah / atha svasty-ayanam vachayita.*]

·Book I. ix. directs that after the marriage (*pani-grahana*) the first duty of the bridegroom is to attend to the kindling and maintaining of the household fire. The tenth Chapter prescribes the performance of the rite called *Sthalipaka,* which appears to have been an oblation of rice, &c., cooked in a kind of cauldron. The eleventh gives the rules for the ritual of animal sacrifice (*pashu-kalpa*), and the twelfth for the *Chaitya-yajna,* which seems to have been a ceremonial performed at monuments, accompanied with offerings, perhaps to the memory of deceased persons. The thirteenth, fourteenth fifteenth, sixteenth, and seventeenth Chapters prescribe certain domestic ceremonies connected with the birth and treatment of children, which are included under the Sanskaras enjoined in the second Book of Manu. They are as follows:

Garbha-lambhana, a rite performed on the first signs of conception, and *Punsavana,* one that takes place on the first indication of the conception of a living male (cf. Manu II. 27).

Samantonnayana, 'arranging the parting of the mother's hair,' observed in the fourth, sixth, or eight month of pregnancy.

Hiranya-madhu-sarpisham prasanam, 'feeding an infant with honey and clarified butter from a golden spoon' before cutting the navel-string at birth=*jata-karman* (Manu II. 29).

Anna-prashana, 'feeding an infant with rice' between the fifth and eighth month (Manu II. 34).

Chaula (=*chuda-karman*), 'tonsure' or shaving the hair except one lock on the crown, performed in the third year (cf. Manu II. 35).

In Book I. xix. we have precise directions in regard to investiture (*upanayana*) with the sacred thread (*yajnopavita*), — a ceremony of great importance, supposed to confer on the recipients (like the Christian rite of baptism) a second spiritual birth. This is enjoined for a Brahman in his eighth year, for a Kshatriya in his eleventh, and for a Vaisya in his twelfth, though the time may be extended in each case. These are therefore the three twice-born (*dvi-ja*) classed. (Cf. Manu II. 36-38.) The twenty-second gives rules for the guidance of the young Brahman as a Brahma-charin or 'student of the Veda' in the house of his preceptor after investiture by him. It begins thus:

'Thou art now a Brahma-cari, take care to wash out thy mouth daily with water (=*upa-sprish, ch-cam* in Manu II. 51, 53), do thy appointed work (*karma kura*), sleep not in the day-time (*diva ma svapsih,* cf. *divasvapna,* Manu VII. 47), obey thy preceptor, study the Veda (*Vedam adhishva*); every morning and evening go out to beg for alms; every evening and morning collect fuel for the fire.' The period of studentship is to last for twelve years or until the student has acquired a knowledge of the Vedas (*grahanantam;* cf. Manu III. 1, II. 53-60).

The fourth and fifth chapter of the second Book prescribe the Ashtaka and Anvashtakya Shraddha ceremonies.

The subject of Book II. vii. viii. is Vastu-pariksha, 'examination of soil and situation' before fixing on a site, or laying the foundation of a house, thus:

A piece of ground (should be chosen) which does not contain saline soil, and the title to which is not likely to involve legal disputes, and which is well stocked with plants and trees, and where there is plenty of Kusa grass and Virana (fragrant grass). All thorny shrubs and plants with milky sap should be rooted out. A hole should be dug knee-deep and filled again with the excavated earth. If the earth when restored to the hole appears more than enough to fill it, the soil is excellent; if just enough, it is fairly good; too little, it is bad. [*Adhike prashastam same varttam nyune garhitam,* VIII. 3.] At sunset the hole should be filled with water and allowed to stand all night. If in the morning it is still full of water, the soil is excellent; if it is moist, the soil is fairly good; if dry, bad. White, sweet-tasting, sandy soil is good for Brahmans, red for Kashatriyas, yellow for Vaishyas.

Book II. x. prescribes a solemn entrance into the new house (*griha-prapadana*), after having stored it with seed-grain. The owner is then to cause the adjacent land belonging to him to be ploughed up and sown at the right season, and standing at a particular spot with his back to the wind, he is to offer oblations, repeating a hymn of the Rig-veda (IV. 57), part of which I here translate freely:

May the land's Lord be present as our friend!
So shall we prosper[1]. May the god accord us
Cattle and horses, nourishment and food!
By gifts like these he manifests his favour.
God of the land! bestow on us sweet water.
To us may every herb be sweet as honey!
To us may sky and atmosphere and rain
Be kind! And may the god who owns the soil
Be gracious! may we fearlessly approach him!
For us may oxen plough auspiciously[2]!

---

1. Lit. 'with the Lord of land as our friend,' &c. [*Kshetrasya patina vayam hiteneva jayamasi.*]
2. *Shunam = sukham.*

May peasants labour happily! may ploughshares
Draw every furrow smoothly! may the ploughmen[1]
Follow the oxen joyfully! may he,
The rain-god, water happily the earth
With sweetest showers! may the god of air
And sun[2] bestow on us prosperity!

The first Chapter of the third Book prescribes the five
solemn offerings or devotional acts which every twice-born
man is required to perform every day. These correspond to
the five *Maha-yajnah* of Manu III. 69–71, sometimes called
the five Sacraments. They are acts of homage directed — 1.
to the gods; 2. to all beings; 3. to departed ancestors; 4. to
the Rishis or authors of the Veda; 5. to men (1. *deva-yajna*,
2. bhuta-y°, 3. pitri-y°, 4. brahma-y°, 5. ˌmanushya-y°). The
first is performed by an oblation (*homa*) to the gods offered
on the domestic fire; the second by an offering (*bali*) to
animals and all creatures; the third by pouring out water to
the spirits of the departed; the fourth by repetition of the
Veda; the fifth by gifts to men and hospitality to guests (cf.
Manu III. 81, &c., where, however, they are not given in the
same order).

The second and third Chapters treat of the fourth diurnal
act of devotion (*brahma-yajna*), and direct the twice-born
man how he is to conduct his private devotions, and how and
what he is to repeat to himself (*svadhyaya-vidhi*):

He is to go in an easterly or northerly direction outside his
place of abode, wearing his sacrificial cord (*yajnopavita*) over
his shoulder; he is first to bathe, and having rinsed out his mouth
(*achamya*), to sit down on Kusha grass placed so that the points
are directed towards the east (Manu II. 75), and to repeat the

---

1. *Kinashah.*
2. This is the native interpretation of Shuna-sira. See Wilson.

sacred syllable *om,* the three Vyahritis (*bhur, bhuvah, svar*), and the Savitri (or *Gayatri,* see p. 20; cf. Manu II. 75-77, 79). Then he is to repeat, for as long a time as he may think proper, portions of some of the Ric, Yajus, Saman, Atharvagiras, Brahmanas, Kalpas, Gathas, Narasansis, Itihasas, and Puranas[1] (see note, p. 276.)

With regard to this subject, see p. 276 of this volume.

Book III. vii. declares that if a twice-born man, being in good health, allows himself to fall asleep while the sun is setting, he is to pass the remainder of the night in an upright position, without uttering a word, and at sun-rise to repeat five verses, from the fourth to the eighth inclusive, of Rig-veda. X. 37, beginning, 'With whatever light, O sun, thou dispellest the darkness.' [*Yena surya jyotisha badhase tamo, &c.*] Again, if the sun should rise while he is asleep, he is to continue standing and silent during the day, and to repeat the last four verses of the same hymn (cf. Manu II. 219-222). The eight, ninth, and tenth Chapters prescribe the ceremonies to be performed by a twice-born man whose period of studentship with his preceptor is completed, and who is about to return (*samavartamana*) home, and become a householder:

He is to procure various articles for himself and his preceptor (at any rate for the latter), such as a necklace, two ear-rings, a suit of clothes, a parasol, a pair of shoes, a staff, a turban, perfumes, &c. (cf. Manu II. 245, 246). Having completed his studies and received permission from his preceptor to depart, and having inquired what fee (*artha*) he is to pay, he must perform an ablution (*snana*). He is then to make certain vows of purity, after which he becomes elevated to the condition of a Snataka (cf. Manu III. 4) or Brahman who, after purification, has passed from the first stage of life — that of a student — to the second stage or that of a householder (*griha-stha*).

---

1. The modern Brahma-yajna of pious Brahmans is based on this Sutra.

The fourth Book is perhaps the most interesting. In the first four Chapters it prescribes the funeral rites to be performed at the burning of dead bodies[1], and gives some directions as to the subsequent Shraddha ceremonies:

When a man dies, a piece of ground is to be excavated in a *Smasana* or 'burning-ground' south-west of his abode. His relations are to carry the fires and the sacrificial implements (*yojna-patrani*) to the excavated place. Those of them who are most advanced in years (*pravayasah*) are to walk behind in single file — the men separated from the women — bearing the corpse, the hair and nails of which have all been cut off or clipped, and leading the sacrificial cords hanging down (*adho-nivitah*), and their hair dishevelled — the elder in front, the younger behind. When they reach the prepared ground, the performer of the ceremony is to sprinkle water on it with a branch of the Shami tree, repeating Rig-veda X. 14. 9:

'Depart (ye evil spirits), slink away from here; the Fathers (his departed ancestors) have made for him this place of rest, distinguished (*vyaktam*) by days (*ahobhir*), waters (*adbhir*), and bright lights (*aktubhir*)[2].'

Then he is to deposit the fires around the margin of the excavated place — the Ahavaniya fire to the south-east, the Garhapatya to the north-west, and the Dakshina to the sourth-west (see note 2, p. 216). Then some one who understands what is required, is to collect a heap of fire-wood and pile it up inside

---

1. See the article 'Uber Todtenbestattung,' by Professor Max Muller in vol. ix of the Zeitschrift der Deutschen Morgenlandischen Gesellschaft, in which a portion of this division of the Asvalayana Grihya Sutras is translated into German. With regard to the importance of the following extracts as bearing upon Sati (*Suttee*), see p. 282 of this volume.

2. The meaning of this is not very clear. I understand it as denoting that the ground is open and well exposed to daylight and well sprinkled with water and surrounded with the fires.

the sacrificial ground (*antar-vedi*). Next, a layer of Kusa grass is to be spread over the heap along with the black skin of the goat and the clipped hair, and the dead body is to be placed upon it with the feet towards the Garhapatya fire and the head towards the Ahavaniya. North of the body his wife is to be made to lie down (on the funeral pile), along with the bow of the dead man if he was a soldier (*Kshatriya*). Then either her husband's brother (*devarah*), who is in the place of a husband to her (*patisthaniyah*), or a pupil, or an old servant causes her to rise up, repeating the words of Rig-veda X. 18. 8:

'Rise up, O woman (*udirshva nari*), come back to the world of life; thou art lying by a dead man; come back. Thou hast sufficiently fulfilled the duty of a wife and mother (*janitvam*) to the husband who wooed thee (*didhishos*) and took thee by the hand.' (See note 1, p. 283.)

Next the brother-in-law is to take back the bow, repeating Rig-veda X. 18.9:

'I take the bow out of the hand of the dead man for our own protection, for our glory, and for our strength; remain thou there, we will remain here as heroes, (so that) in all battles we may conquer our foes.'

Then he is to place the various sacrificial implements and portions of the sacrificial animal in the two hands and on different parts of the body of the corpse. This being done, he is to order the three-fires to be kindled (*agnin prajvalayati*). If the Ahavaniya fire reaches the dead man first, then his spirit is borne to heaven; if the Garhapatya, then his spirit is taken to the middle region (*antariksha-loka*); if the Dakshina, then it remains in the world of mortals (*manushya-loka*). When all three reach him together, this is the most auspicious sign of all. While the body is burning, portions of hymns of the Rig-veda (such as X. 14. 7, 8, 10, 11, X. 16. 1-4, X. 17. 3-6, X. 18. 11, X. 154. 1-5) are to be repeated.

The followings are examples of some of the verses:
Open thy arms, O earth, receive the dead

With gentle pressure and with loving welcome.
Enshroud him tenderly, e'en as a mother
Folds her soft vestment round the child she loves (X.
18. 11).
Soul of the dead! depart; take thou the path —
The ancient path — by which our ancestors
Have gone before thee; thou shalt look upon
The two kings, mighty Varuna and Yama,
Delighting in oblations; thou shalt meet
The Fathers and receive the recompense
Of all thy stored-up offerings above.
Leave thou thy sin and imperfection here;
Return unto thy home once more; assume
A glorious form. By an auspicious path
Hasten to pass the four-eyed brindled dogs —
The two road-guarding sons of Sarama;
Advance to meet the Fathers who, with hearts
Kindly disposed towards thee, dwell in bliss
With Yama; and do thou, O mighty god,
Intrust him to thy guards[1] to bring him to thee,
And grant him health and happiness eternal (X. 14. 7-11)[2].

When a dead body is burnt by one who knows and can repeat these verses properly, then it is certain that the soul (invested with a kind of subtle body[3]) rises along with the smoke to heaven (sahaiva dhumena svargam lokam etiti ha vijnayate).

---

1. These are the four-eyed watch-dogs mentioned before.
2. Part of this has been freely rendered in a version given p. 22.
3. The eighth Sutra of Chapter IV states that a hole ought to be dug north-eastward of the Ahavaniya fire and strewn with the plants Avaka and Shipala; and the commentator adds that the soul of the dead man, invested with its vehicular subtle body (called *ativahika* and sometimes *adhishthana* and distinct from the *linga* or *sukshma*, being *angyshtha-matra*, 'of the size of a thumb'), waits in this hole until the gross body is burnt, and then emerging, is carried with the smoke to heaven.

Then the performer of the ceremony is to repeat the verse
(Rig-veda X. 18.3)

We living men, survivors, now return
And leave the dead; may our oblations please
The gods and bring us blessings! now we go
To dance and jest and hope for longer life.

After this they are to move to a spot where there is a pool
of still water, dip themselves once, cast a handful of water into
the air, pronouncing the name of the dead man and that of his
family (e.g. 'O Devadatta Kashyapa, this water is for thee'); then
coming out of the water, they are to put on other clothes and
to sit down till the stars appear or else till the sun is quite
invisible, when they are to proceed homewards, the younger
ones walking first, the elder behind. Before entering the house
they are (for purification) to touch a stone, fire, cow-dung,
grains of barley, oil, and water. During one night they are not
to cook any food, but to eat only what is already prepared, and
for there nights they are not to touch anything containing salt.

Book IV. v. prescribes the gathering together the bones
and ashes of the deceased (*sanchayana,* Manu V. 59):

This is to take place after the tenth day of the dark half of
the month, on an odd day (i.e. the eleventh, thirteenth, fifteenth,
&c.), and under a single Nakshatra (i.e. not under one like
Ashadha, which is both *purva* and *uttara*).

The bones and ashes of a man are to be placed in an
undecorated funeral vase or long vessel (*alakshane kumbhe*), and
those of a woman in a female vase (of a fuller shape, supposed
to resemble the female figure). A hole is to be excavated and
the bones thus collected in a vessel are to be placed in it, while
Rig-veda X. 18. 10 is repeated:

'Go to thy mother Earth, the Widely-extended (*uru-
vyachasam*), the Broad, the Auspicious; may she be to thee like
a young maiden, soft as wool (*urna-mrada*), to pious person!

may she protect thee from the embrace of the goddess of corruption!' (*Nirriter upasthat.*)

Then earth is to be scattered over the excavation, and Rig-veda X. 18. 11. 12 are to be repeated (see p. 206 for verse 11). Lastly, a cover or lid is to be placed over the vase or long vessel and the hole is to be filled up with earth, so that the vessel is quite hidden from view, while Rig-veda X. 18. 13 is repeated:

'I raise up the earth around thee for a support, placing this cover on thee without causing injury. May the Fathers guard this funereal monument for thee! May Yama establish a habitation for thee there!'

This being accomplished, the relations are to return home, without looking about, and after they have performed an ablution they are to offer the first Shraddha to the deceased person separately (*ekoddishta*).

Book IV. vii. prescribes four kinds of *Sraddha*, i.e. offerings to deceased persons and Pitris or ancestors generally: 1. *Parvana*, 'monthly,' to ancestors for three generations on the days of conjunction or new moon (cf. Manu III. 282; those to ancestors generally being called *Nitya*, 'constant,' 'daily,' and others *Ashtaka*, as performed on the eighth day of certain months); 2. *Kamya*, 'voluntary,' peformed for some object of desire (as the obtaining of a son); 3. *Abhyudayika*, performed as tank-offerings on occasions of family rejoicing (as at the Sanskaras) or for increase of prosperity, &c. (*Vriddhi-purta*); 4. *Ekoddishta*, 'special,' having reference to one person recently deceased, and not to ancestors generally. It is repeated annually on the anniversary of his death. (Those which are occasional are sometimes called *Naimittika.*) To these funeral ceremonies Brahmans are to be invited. They are to be feasted, and gifts presented to them. The guests are to be made to sit down with their faces towards the North, and water is to be poured into their hands with Kusha grass and Sesamum seed (*tila,* cf. Manu III. 223). Cakes of rice (*pinda*), libations of water are to be offered with the auspicious exclamation *Svadha*. There is also another Shraddha called *Daiva*, in honour of the Vishve Devah, 'deities collectively,' or of a particular troop of deities, ten in number. Hence some distinguish eight kinds of Shraddha (see p. 278); and the Nirnaya-sindhu, twelve.

A fuller description of these solemn Shraddhas is given by Manu III. 123-286, and in verse 202 the meaning of the term Shraddha is explained as follows:

> Mere water (*vary api*) offered with faith (*shraddhaya*) to the Pitris in silver or plated (*rajatanvitaih*) vessels procures imperishable bliss (*akshayayopakalapate*).

I close my account of the Ashvalayana Grihya Sutras by remarking that the rules relating to funeral ceremonies in the fourth Book, of which an abstract has just been given, possess great interest in their connection with the eighteenth hymn of the tenth Mandala of the Rig-veda. Although the Sutras direct that the texts of this hymn are to be used, yet the rite must have undergone considerable modifications since the period when the hymn was composed.

It may be gathered from a study of the text of the hymn, that at the early period when the Aryan race first settled on the plains of Hindustan, there was not the same prolonged and elaborate observance of funeral rites, which in later times was converted into an excuse for the ostentatious and costly feasting of priests and guests (see p. 280). But there was no less solemnity in the conduct of the ceremonial, no less exhibition of grief for the dead in the tender treatment of his remains, and no less affectionate respect for his memory, — a feeling cherished as a religious duty, more tenaciously in India than in Europe.

We notice, too, even at that early epoch an evident belief in the soul's eternal existence and the permanence of its personality hereafter, which notably contrasts with the later ideas of transmigration, absorption into the divine essence, and pantheistic identification with the supreme Soul of the universe.

We learn also from this same hymn that the body in ancient times was not burnt but buried; nor can we discover the slightest allusion to the later practice of Sati or cremation of the widow with her husband.

The corpse of the deceased person was deposited close to a grave dug ready for its reception, and by its side his widow, if he happened to be a married man, seated herself, while his children, relatives, and friends ranged themselves in a circle round her. The priest stood near at an altar, on which the sacred fire was kindled, and having invoked Death, called upon him to withdraw from the path of the living, and not to molest the young and healthy survivors, who were assembled to perform pious rites for the dead, without giving up the expectation of a long life themselves. He then placed a stone between the dead body and the living relations, to mark off the boundary line of Death's domain, and offered up a prayer that none of those present might be removed to another world before attaining to old age, and that none of the younger might be taken before the elder. Then the widow's married female friends walked up to the altar and offered oblations in the fire; after which the widow herself withdrew from the inner circle assigned to the dead, and joined the survivors outside the boundary-line, while the officiating priest took the bow out of the hand of the deceased, in order to show that the manly strength which he possessed during life, did not perish with him, but remained with his family. The body was then tenderly laid in the grave with repetition of the words of the hymn already translated, 'Open thy arms, O Earth, receive the dead,' &c. (see p. 225). The ceremony was concluded by the careful closing of the

tomb with a stone slab. Finally a mound of earth was raised
to mark and consecrate the spot[1].

With regard to the Samayacharika Sutras, little remains
to add to what has already been stated. Not many collections
of this third class of Sutras (as distinguished from the Srauta
and Grihya) have been preserved. Were they better known
to us, we should probably find that they furnished materials
for Manu's compilation, even more than the Grihya Sutras
appear to have done. It is for this reason that, as introductory
to the Dharmashastras or Law-books, they are sometimes
called Dharmasutras. Since 'conventional, every-day practices'
constitute the proper subject of these Sutras, and it is clear
that conventional usages may often come under the head of
Grihya or 'domestic rites,' it may easily be understood that
the Samayacharika not infrequently go over the same ground
as the Grihya Sutras. For instance, we find them both giving
rules for the Sanskaras &c. (see p. 269). Perhaps the best
known Samayacharika Sutras are those of Apastamba belonging
to the Black Yajur-veda (see note 2, p. 214). An account of
these will be found in Professor Max Muller's 'Ancient Sanskrit
Literature' (p. 100, &c.), and in No. 732 of Rajendralala
Mitra's MSS. They commence as follows:

1. Therefore let us now explain the Samayacharika duties.
[*Athatah samayacharikan dharman vyakhyasyamah.*]

2. These agreements which were made by men who knew
the law are an authority. [*Dharma-jna-samayah pramanam.*]

3. And the Vedas (are an authority). [*Vedas-cha.*]

---

1. A fuller account of the whole rite will be found in Professor Stenzler's
'Rede uber die Sitte,' which I have consulted throughout.

III. *The Dharma-sastras or Law-books — Manu.*

At least forty-seven independent Law-books[1] are enumerated, and of these at least twenty are still extant and are mentioned by Yajnavalkya (I. 3-5), as follow:

1. That of Manu. 2. Yajnavalkya' (second in importance to Manu). 3. Atri. 4. Vishnu. 5. Harita. 6. Usanas. 7. Angiras. 8. Yama. 9. Apastamba. 10. Samvarta. 11. Katyayana. 12. Vrihaspati. 13. Para shara. 14. Vyasa. 15. Sankha. 16. Likhita. 17. Daksha. 18. Gotama or Gautama. 19. Shatatapa. 20. Vasishtha. There is also a Law-book, the joint production of Sankha and Likhita; and others ascribed to Narada, Bhrigu, &c. (see the end of Lecture X); and Kulluka, the commentator on Manu, mentions the names of Baudhayana, Medhatithi, Govinda-raja, &c.

Let us first endeavour to gain some idea of the character of the most celebrated and ancient of these books commonly called 'the Code of Manu.'

This well-known collection of laws and precepts is perhaps the oldest and most sacred Sanskrit work after the Veda and its Sutras. Although standing in a manner at the head of Post-vedic literature, it is connected with the Veda through these Sutras, as the philosophical Darshanas are through the Upanishads. Even if not the oldest of Post-vedic writings (see note 1, p. 236), it is certainly the most interesting, both as presenting a picture of the institutions, usages, manners, and intellectual condition of an important part of the Hindu race

---

1. Professor Stenzler enumerates forty-six, Dr. Roer forty-seven. The names of the authors of some of these law-books are the same as those of some of the Grihya Sutras, e.g. Apastamba, Paraskara, and Baudhayana. The same men may have been authors of both Sutras and Dharma-shastras.

at a remote period, and as revealing the exaggerated nature of the rules by which the Brahmans sought to secure their own ascendancy, and to perpetuate an organized caste-system in subordination to themselves. At the same time it is in other respects perhaps one of the most remarkable books that the literature of the whole world can offer, and some of its moral precepts are worthy of Christianity itself.

Probably the compilation we now possess is an irregular compendium of rules and maxims by different authors, which existed unwritten for a long period of time, and were handed down orally. An original collection is alluded to by commentators under the titles Vriddha and Vrihat, which is said to have contained 100,000 couplets, arranged under twenty-four heads in one thousands chapters; whereas the existing Code contains only 2685 verses. Possibly abbreviated versions of old collections were made at successive periods, and additional matter inserted, the present text merely representing the latest compilation.

At any rate we must guard against a supposition that the expression 'Code,' often applied to this collection, is intended to denote a systematic arrangement of precepts which existed as actual laws in force throughout one country. It is probable that the whole of India was never under one government. Some few powerful monarchs are known to have acquired sovereignty over very extensive territories, and were then called Chakra-vartins, but we must beware of imagining that Manu's Law-book is a record of national ordinances and institutions prevalent over the whole of such territories. No doubt ultimately it worked its way to acceptance with the entire Hindu community; and certainly in the end it not only secured for itself a high place in popular estimation and a degree of reverence only second to that accorded to the Veda, but it became, moreover, the chief authority as a basis of Hindu jurisprudence. Originally, however, its position must have been different. It merely represented certain rules and precepts (perhaps by different authors) current among a particular tribe, or rather school of Brahmans called Manavas, who probably lived in the North-western region between the rivers Sarasvati and Drishadvati (see p. 237-238), not far from Delhi and the scene of the great social conflict described in the Mahabharata[1]. This tribe seems to have belonged to the Taittiriyakas, 'adherents of the Black Yajur-veda;' and their Mantras, Brahmana and Srauta Sutras are still extant[2], but their Grihya and Samayacharika Sutras appear to have perished. In all probability, too, many of the rules, as we have them presented to us, were simply theoretical — inserted to complete an ideal of what ought to constitute a perfect system of religious, ceremonial, moral, political, and social duties. Who the real compiler and promulgator of the Institutes was, is not known. He was probably a learned Brahman of the Manava school.

We must, of course, make a due allowance for the mythical element in the Code, as, for instance, when a divine sage named Manu[3] (or Svayambhuva — 'sprung from the great self-existent Being') is made to say (I. 58-60) as follows:

---

1. The inference deducible from II. 17, 18, that the Manavas lived in the region of the earliest Aryan settlements, must have weight in determining the antiquity of the Code and its value as representing the ancient social life of the Hindus before their advance into the Deccan.

2. A counterpart of a MS. of a commentary on part of the Manava-kalpa-sutra has been edited by the late Professor Goldstucker.

3. This name of the supposed divine progenitor of all beings is derived from the root *man,* which means 'to think' or 'reason' (and especially according to the Hindu theory, 'to think upon and understand the Veda,' whence the desiderative form *Mimansa* from the same root, signifying 'investigation of the meaning of the Veda'). Bhrigu states (I. 61) that Manu sprang from Svayambhu, and that six other Manus descended from him; whereas Manu himself (I. 33-36) declares that

The god (Brahma) having framed this system of laws himself, taught it fully to me in the beginning. I then taught it to Marichi and the nine other sages, my offspring (of whom Bhrigu is one, cf. I. 35). Of these (my sons) Bhrigu is deputed by me to declare the Code to you (Rishis) from beginning to end, for he has learned from me to recite the whole of it. Then the great sage, Bhrigu, having been thus appointed by Manu to promulgate his laws, addressed all the Rishis with a pleased mind, saying, 'Listen!'

Manu, therefore, is supposed to speak in his own person as far as I. 60. After that, Bhrigu is the speaker, and the closing verse of the whole Code (XII. 126) describes it as *Manavam Shastram Bhrigu-proktam,* 'enunciated by Bhrigu;' while in XI. 243 Prajapati or Brahma himself is declared to have created it by the power of austerity (*tapasa*).

We need hardly, however, explain that these are merely ideal personages, introduced dramatically like Krishna in the Bhagavad-gita; or rather perhaps are later additions, designed to give an air of antiquity and divine authority to the teaching of the Code.

---

he was created by Virja, the male power produced by Brahma, and that being so created he produced the ten Maharshis or Prajapatis, who again produced seven Manus. The name, however, is generic. In every Kalpa or interval from creation to creation there exist fourteen successive Manus, whence each whole period is called a *Manv-antara,* described as innumerable in I. 80. In the present creation there have been as yet seven Manus: 1. Manu *Svayambhuva,* the supposed author of the Code, who produced the ten Prajapatis or 'patriarchs' for peopling the universe; 2. *Svarochisha;* 3. *Auttami;* 4. *Tamasa;* 5. *Raivata;* 6. *Chakshusha;* 7. *Vaivasvata;* son of the Sun, the Manu of the present period, regarded as a kind of Indian Adam or Noah (see note, p. 34). According to some, this last Manu was the author of the Code, and therefore, as progenitor of the Solar line of kings, a Kshatriya.

The work in its present form can scarcely, I think, be assigned to a date earlier or later than the fifth century B.C.[1] Strictly speaking, or at least according to European notions, it is, as I have already hinted, no orderly codification of national statutes and customs, but rather an unsystematic compilation from previous sources[2], which, by blending civil and criminal law with religious, moral, and ceremonial precepts, philosophical doctrines, and metaphysical theories,

---

1. Sir W. Jones held that Manu's book was drawn up in about the year 1280 B.C. Mr. Eliphinstone placed it 900 years B.C. Possibly some parts of it may represent laws and precepts which were current among the Manavas at the latter date, but no one would now assign so early a date to the actual compilation of the Code. Nor can it, I think, reasonably be placed later than the fifth century B.C. The gods mentioned are chiefly Vedic, and the fourfold caste system is that of the Purusha-sukta (see p. 25). There is no direct allusion to Buddhism, though many of Manu's precepts are decidedly Buddhistic, having frequent parallels in the Dhamma-pada, which indicate that Buddhistic ideas were gaining ground in the locality represented by the Code. Nor is there any allusion to Sati, nor to the worship of Vishnu and Siva, which from a statement of Megasthenes, may be inferred to have prevailed in India soon after Alexander's invasion. Nor is there any mention of the stories of the Mahabharata and Ramayana. At the same time the former Epic often contains verses identical with those of Manu. These are probably either taken from Manu or derived from a common source. Possibly, however, portions of the Mahabharata may be older than Manu. Certainly in III. 232 occur the words *Dharma-shastra, Akhyana, Itihasa, Purana,* and *Khila,* as titles of sacred works, and Kulluka explains *Itihasa* by *Maha-bharata,* but these words may refer to the older works, which were the sources of the present compilations.

2. An evidence in favour of the supposition that more than one person may have had a hand in the Code is deducible from the emphasis laid upon certain maxims which are especially ascribed to Manu himself, such, for example, as V. 41, 131; Vi. 54; VIII. 124, 168, 279, 339; IX. 158, 182, 239; X. 63, 78, all of which introduce some phrase like *Manur abravit.*

confounds the ordinances of government with the obligations of religion, domestic life, and private morals. It is in twelve Chapters or Books.

In verse 6 of Book II we have a statement as to the 'root' or basis of all law (*dharma-mulam*). This is declared to be (1) the whole Veda (*Vedo 'khilah*), (2) the traditional law (*Smriti*), (3) morality (*Shlam*) of those who know the Veda, and (4) the practices and customs (*acharah*), established from time immemorial, of good men. In matters indifferent a man is free to follow his own inclination (*atma-tushti*).

Again, in verses 107, 108 of Book I it is said:

In this (Code) appears the whole system of law, with definitions of good and bad actions, and the traditional practices (*achara*) of the four classes, which usages are held to be eternal (*sashvatah*, since they reach back to a period beyond the memory of man). Traditional practice (*achara*) is equivalent to supreme law (*parama dharmah*), since it is so pronounced by the Veda and by Smriti (*Smarta*).

This Law-book, therefore, is a metrical compendium of rules of Smriti, Shhla, and Achara, most of which had been previously collected and propounded under the name of Grihya and Samayacharika Sutras. At the end of Book I a summary of subjects is given, but we may more conveniently examine the contents of the twelve books under six-principal heads, viz. 1. Veda, 'sacred knowledge' and religion; 2. Vedanta or Atma-vidya, as terms for philosophy in general; 3. Achara; 4. Vyavahara; 5. Prayas-chitta; 6. Karma-phala.

It will be found that after eliminating the purely religious and philosophical precepts the greater number of rules propounded fall under the third head of *Achara*, 'established practices,' which are described (II. 17, 18) as *Sad-achara*, 'approved practices,' sanctioned by the Veda and Smriti, if they are those which prevailed between the two sacred rivers,

Sarasvati and Drishadvati, in the region called Brahmavarta. The word Achara is, in truth, a very wide term, including under it all the observances of caste, regarded as constituting the highest law and highest religion — such observances, for instance, as the division of a Brahman's life into four periods, the conduct of a student in the house of his preceptor, investiture with the sacred cord, the five diurnal devotional acts, the domestic ceremonies of marriage, funeral rites, the various modes of gaining subsistence (*vritti*), the rules of diet, the laws concerning women, and in short, all the observances of private morality and social economy[1].

The fourth head, *Vyavahara,* 'practices of law and kingly government,' embraces the procedure of legal tribunals and all the rules of judicature and civil and criminal law.

The fifth head of *Prayas-chitta,* 'penitential exercises,' comprehends all the rules of penance and expiation.

The sixth head, *Karma-phala,* 'recompenses or consequences of acts,' is concerned not so much with rules of conduct as with the doctrine of transmigration; the unavoidable effect of acts of all kinds being to entail repeated births through numberless existences until the attainment of final beatitude.

All these rules apply especially to the highest class, viz. Brahmans, whose ascendancy in the social scale is in fact the first Acara, which must be accepted as *paramo dharmah,* 'the highest law and highest religion.'

It is only natural that, since the precepts included under these six heads were framed by Brahmans, they should have been framed with especial reference to the life of Brahmans, the regulations for which engross six Books, and are besides

---

1. In Book V. 4 there is a curious passage which attributes Death's power over Brahmans to four causes, viz.1. omitting to repeat the Veda, 2. neglect of Achara' 3. idleness, 4. sins of diet.

introduced everywhere throughout the other six. But as the Brahman could not be supported in his priority of rank without the strong arm of the Kshatriya or military class, a large portion of the work is devoted to the definition of the Kshatriya's duties and an exaggerated delineation of the kingly character and office, while the Vaishyas and Shudras, though essential to Manu's Chaturvarnya or fourfold social system[1], and the mixed classes are little noticed. (See p. 256, &c.)

---

1. 'Caste' is quite a modern word, and is supposed to be a corruption of the Portuguese *casta*, 'a race.' Manu's word for the four classes is *varna*, 'colour,' which suggests some original distinction of colour as marking the dominant races. The later term for caste is *jati*, 'birth,' corrupted into *jat*. Of Manu's four castes the Brahmans alone remain, though the Rajputs claim to be descendants of the ancient Kshatriyas. The mixed castes of the present day are almost innumerable, each separate trade forming a separate one. In Bengal there ᷄ᷓe the Rajaks, 'washer-men,' the Tantis, 'weavers,' the Kansaris, 'braziers,' the Jaliyas, 'fishermen,' the Suris, 'spirit sellers;' besides low and servile castes, such as the Bagdis, Bediyas, Doms, Hadis. Moreover, we find castes within castes, so that even the Brahmans are broken up and divided into numerous races, which again are subdivided into numerous tribes, families, or sub-castes. There are the Kanyakubja Brahmans, the Sarasvats, the Gauda or Gaur (God), the Maithila, the Utkala, the Dravida, the Karnata, the Maharashtra, the Gurjara, &c., all of which races are subdivided into a greater or less number of the tribes and families, forming, as it were, sub-castes, which do not intermarry. It is said that in Bengal religion was once at so low an ebb that a king, named Adishura (Adishvara), sent to the Raja of Kanyakubja or Kanouj for some high-caste Brahmans to revive it. These were accordingly sent, and, having settled in Bengal, became divided into one hundred and fifty-six tribes, of which one hundred were called Varendra and fifty-six Radha or Rarh, as belonging to the district of Radha in the West of Bengal. Of the former eight, and of the latter six, are regarded as Kulina or 'noble.' Kulluka, the commentator on Manu, was a Varendra Brahman. The six Kulina Rarh tribes are called Banerjea (Bandyopadhyaya), Mukhurjea (Mukhopadhyaya), Chaturjea (Chattopadhyaya), Ganguli, Goshahal, Kanjalala. The caste which in Bengal now comes next in rank to the Brahman is the

Hence, after an account of the creation of the world in the first Book, the four stages of a Brahman's life are the first and only subjects treated of in regular order in the second, third, fourth, fifth, and sixth Books; the sixth being devoted to the duties of the last two stages of anchorite (*vana-prastha*) and religious mendicant (*bhikshu*). The fifth Book contains, moreover, rules and regulations about food, the killing of animals, purification after defilement, the duties of wives and the position of women generally. The seventh and eighth Books propound the rules of government and judicature, principally, of course, for the guidance of the second great class of Kshatriyas, from which the king was chosen. The ninth Book contains further precepts on the subject of women, husband and wife, their offspring, and the law of inheritance and division of property. At the end (242, &c.) there are additional rules of government for kings and a few precepts which have direct reference to the two remaining principal

---

Vaidya or Baidya, 'medical' (=Ambashtha, Manu X. 8); and the Kanouj Brahmans, when they settled in Bengal, brought with them a number of Kayasthas or 'writers,' from whom sprang the present numerous Kayastha or 'writer-caste,' subdivided into various tribes, such as Gos (Ghosha), Bose (Vasu), Mitra, De, Datta, Palita, Dasa, Sena, &c. After them come the Nava Sak or 'nine divisions,' viz. Gopa, Mali, Taili, Tantri, Modaka, Varaji ('betel-grower'), Kulala, Karmakara, Napita. See Professor Cowell's Colebrooke's Essays II. 169. The power of caste and the effect of contact with Europeans in weakening it, are illustrated by the following extract from Dr. Hunter's valuable work on Orissa: 'Elderly Uriyas have more than once deplored to me the hopeless degeneracy of their grown-up sons, many of whom have actually no objection to wearing English shoes. In 1870 a Uriya Brahman held the post of sub-inspector of police in Puri itself, within the shadow of Jagan-nath, although a leather belt formed part of his uniform. Five years ago a Brahman who accidentally touched leather would have had to choose between public expiation or degradation and expulsion from caste.' Vol. ii. p. 147.

castes — the Vaisyas and Sudras — the former comprising agriculturists and merchants; the latter, slaves and servants. The tenth Book treats of the mixed classes, arising out of intermarriage between the four original principal castes. It also describes the employments to which the several classes are restricted, and states the occupations permitted to Brahmans, Kshatriyas, Vaishyas, and Shudras in times of great exigency and distress. There are some verses at the end (122-129) which are interesting as treating directly of the duties and position of Sudras. The eleventh Book gives rules for expiation and penance (*prayas-chitta*), both for sins committed in this life — especially sins against caste — and for the effects of offences perpetrated in previous bodies, as shown in congenital diseases, &c. (XI. 48, 49). The twelfth continues the subject of the recompenses or consequences of acts (*karma-phala*), good or bad, as leading to reward in heaven or punishment in various hells (XII. 75, 76), and to triple degrees of transmigration (see p.309). It closes with directions as to the best means of obtaining final beatitude and absorption into the universal Essence.

From this outline of the contents of the so-called Code of Manu we may perceive that the most diversified topics are introduced, some of which are quite out of the province of a mere code of laws or even of a collection of social and moral precepts. In the next Lecture I propose examining the contents more in detail.

Lecture X

The Dharma-shastras or Law-books
— Manu continued

T he Code of the Manavas, which we have assigned in
its present form to about the fifth century B.C. (see
p. 236), and which for convenience we may call
'Manu's Law-book,' is a metrical version of the traditions
(*smriti*) of the Manavas, probably before embodied in their
Grihya and Samayacharika Sutras (p. 234), the metre being
Anushtubh or that of the common Sloka[1] (p. 181). My aim
in the present Lecture will be to analyze and arrange in a
connected manner the contents of the Code[2], offering prose

---

1. The use of the common Epic Shloka throughout the *whole* work is
   one reason for regarding it as Post-vedic, but we must not forget
   that the Anushtubh metre is found even in the Veda (see X. 85, X.
   90, &c.).

2. I have used the Calcutta edition which has the excellent commentary
   of Kulluka-bhatta. I have always consulted Sir W. Jones' translation,
   and I owe much to Dr. Johentgen's tract *Uber das Gestzbuch des
   Manu*. When Kulluka lived is not known, but he describes himself
   in his modest preface (written in the Shardula-vikridita metre) as a
   Brahman, the son of Bhatta-divakera, of the Varendra tribe of Gauda
   (Gaur) or Bengal, and as having fixed his abode at Benares. I did
   not read Mr. Talboys Wheeler's analysis till my own was completed.

translations of selected passages and pointing out in a general way the characteristic features of (1) its sacred knowledge and religion, (2) its philosophy, (3) its *Achara* or 'social rules and caste organization,' (4) its *Vyavahara* or 'criminal and civil laws and rules of government,' (5) its system of *Prayas-citta* or 'penance,' (6) its system of *Karma-phala* or 'future recompenses of acts done in this life.' In the next Lecture I propose to give specimens of the most striking passages, under the last four heads, in a metrical English version.

I. First, then, as to its religious teaching. We may notice that this generally agrees with the later Vedic period, especially that represented by the Purusha-sukta and some of the Brahmanas.

'Divinely revealed knowledge' in general is called *Veda* (IV. 125, &c.); sometimes *Trayi vidya* (IV. 125); sometimes *Brahman* (nom. neut. *brahma,* I. 23, II. 81, VI. 83, in which last passage this title is also applied to the Vedanta or Upanishads); sometimes *Shruti* (as distinguished from Smriti, II. 10); sometimes *Chandansi* (when the metrical Mantras are especially intended, IV. 95-97, III. 188); once *Arsha* (neut., XII. 106), and even *Vac* 'word,' described as a Brahman's weapon (XI. 33).

The three Vedas are mentioned by name in I. 23, IV. 123, 124, XI. 264, and their Samhita in XI. 77, 200, 258, 262. In I. 23 we read that Brahma milked out the triple Veda (*trayam brahma*), Rik, Yajus, and Saman from Fire, Air, and the Sun, for the complete performance of sacrifice; and in II. 77 he is said to have milked out the sacred text called Savitri (= Gayatri, p. 20) from the three Vedas[1]. The Brahmana portion of the Veda does not seem to be directly mentioned,

---

1. See note, p. 9. In XI. 265 the three Vedas are said to be included in the triliteral Om. In IV. 125, Om, the Vyahritis (viz. Bhuh, Bhuvah, Savar), and the Savitri text are described as extracted from the three

except under the name of Brahma, as distinguished from the
Mantra portion, called Chhandas (IV. 100). The eternity and
infallible authority of the Veda and the duty and expiatory
efficacy of a complete knowledge of all three Vedas (XI. 262)
are insisted on in the strongest language. In illustration, I here
give a version of a passage in Book XII. 94, &c.:

> The Veda is of patriarchs and men,
> And e'en of gods, a very eye eternal,
> Giving unerring light; it is beyond
> All finite faculties, nor can be proved
> By force of human argument — this is
> A positive conclusion. Codes of laws
> Depending on the memory of men —
> Not grounded on the Veda — heresies
> And false opinions, all are held to be
> Barren and worthless and involved in darkness.
> Whatever doctrine rests not on the Veda
> Must pass away as recent, false, and fruitless.
> The triple world and quadruple distinction
> Of classes and of Ashramas[1], with all
> That has been, is, and ever will be, all
> Are through the Veda settled and established.
> By this eternal Veda are sustained
> All creatures; hence we hold it as supreme —
> Chief instrument of happiness to man.
> Command of armies, regal dignity,

Vedas. In III. 185, a Brahman who understands the application of
some portion of the Yajur-veda is called *Tri-nachiketa*, and one skilled
in some part of the Rig-veda a *Tri-suparna*, though it is clear from
Kulluka's remarks that the exact meaning of these words was not
known in his time.

1. That is, the four orders or stages of life (of student, householder,
anchorite, and mendicant) into which a Brahman's life is divided.

Conduct of justice and the world's dominion
He merits who completely knows the Veda.
As with augmented energy the fire
Consumes e'en humid trees, so he who knows
This book divine burns out the taint of sin
Inherent in his soul through former works.
For he who apprehends the Veda's truth,
Whatever be his Order, is prepared
For blending with the great primeval Spirit,
E'en while abiding in this lower world.

The inferior relationship of the Sama-veda to the two others is remarkable. The Rig-veda is said to be most concerned with the gods, the Yajur-veda with the religious rites of men, and the Sama-veda with those of the Pitris (IV. 124). Hence the sound of the latter is described as impure (*a-suci*, see note, p. 9).

In unison with this, an order of precedence is prescribed in III. 145. The preference at a Shraddha is directed to be given to a priest called Bahv-rica (elsewhere Hotri), who has made the Rig-veda his special study; then to one who has studied all the branches (*Shakhanta-ga*) and especially the Yajur-veda, and who is called Adhvaryu; and lastly to a Sama-veda priest, who is styled Chhando-ga (= Udgatri).

It is clear that when the Code was compiled the Atharvaveda had not yet been generally accepted as a fourth Veda, though it must have existed, as there is express allusion (XI. 33) to the revelation[1] made to *Atharvan* and *Angiras*.

I annex three other remarkable examples of the estimation in which the Veda was held:

A Brahman by retaining the Rig-veda in his memory incurs no guilt, though he should destroy the three worlds (XI. 261).

---

1. Described by Kulluka as consisting of charms and incantations.

This Veda is the refuge (*sarana*) of those who do not understand it (*ajnanam*) as well as those who do (*vijanatam*), of those who seek heaven and of those who seek immortality (*anantyam*, VI. 84).

When there is (apparent) contradiction of two precepts in the Veda (*shruti-dvaidham*) both are declared to be law; both have been justly promulgated (*samyag-uktau*) by ancient sages as valid law. Thus, there is a Vedic precept, (enjoining the sacrifice to be performed) when the sun has risen, and before it has risen, and when neither sun nor stars are visible (*samayadhyushite*). Wherefore the oblation to fire (*yajnah* = *agni-hotra-homah*) may be made at all times (II. 14. 15).

The doctrine of the Upanishads is directly mentioned in VI. 29 and alluded to elsewhere, thus:

He should study the Upanishad portion of the Veda (*aupanishadih shrutih*) for the sake of attaining union with the universal Spirit.

Let the whole Veda be studied (or repeated) by a twice-born man along with the Upanishads. [*Vedah kritsno 'ahigantavyah sarahasyo dvijanmana*, II. 165; cf. also II. 140, XI. 262.]

He should continually repeat (*japet*) that part of the Veda (*brahma*) which is on the subject of sacrifice (*adhiyajnam*), and that relating to the deities (*adhidaivikam*), and that relating to soul (*adhyatmikam*), and that declared in the Upanishads (*Vedantabhihitam*, VI. 83).

The Kalpa Sutras are probably referred to in II. 140.

A knower of Nirukta (see p. 182) is reckoned among the Brahmans who compose a Parishad in XII. 111, but no reference is made to Yaska, nor is it likely that his work then existed (see p. 183).

In I. 11. 50 the name Brahman is applied to the supreme Being (= *Brahma*, Kulluka); in XII. 50 the Creator of the universe is called Brahma (see note, 1, p. 12); in XI. 243, XII. 121, Prajapati. In I. 6 the supreme Spirit is termed

Svayambhu, 'the Self-existent;' in I. 10, Narayana. In XII. 121 the names Vishnu and Hara occur; but generally the gods named belong more to the Vedic than to the Epic and Puranic period. For instance, in Book IX. 303 we have the following list of deities:

Of Indra, Surya, Vayu (or Maruta), Yama, Varuna, Chandra, Agni, and Prithivi, let the king emulate the power and conduct.

There is no allusion to the Post-vedic Tri-murti or popular worship of Brahma, Vishnu, and Shiva, nor to the still more recent worship of the Shakti — that is to say, 'the energy' represented by the wives of the deities, especially by Durga, wife of Siva. Nor, again, is there any recognition of that principle of *bhakti* or 'faith' in Krishna, as supreme Lord of the universe, which was a subsequent development of Hindu religious thought (p. 148).

The doctrine of transmigration is, however, fully stated, and, as a consequence of this, the hells described in the Code (IV. 88-90, XII. 75, 77), though places of terrible torture, resolve themselves into merely temporary purgatories, while the heavens (IV. 182, 260, VI. 32, II. 244) become only steps on the road to union with Brahma.

The three worlds (*trailokya, loka-traya*) alluded to in XI. 236, 261, are probably the heavens, atmosphere, and earth.

What must strike every one as singular in regard to the religion of the Code is the total absence of allusion to public and congregational services or teaching in temples. Public sacrifices mentioned, but the chief rites of religion were evidently of a domestic kind, and the priests, whatever their ancient functions may have been, were at the time of the composition of the Code more like domestic chaplains (see p. 260). Little, too, is said about idols[1] — certainly nothing

---

1. It is very doubtful whether idolatry was at all commonly practised at the time of the compilation of the Code. We have already seen

to countenance the adoration of them or to encourage
Brahmans to undertake the care of idol-temples, nor are there
directions as to offering rice, flowers, and perfumes at idol-
shrines, which oblations (*naivedya*) are commonly presented
before images in temples at the present day.

II. In the second place, as to the philosophy of Manu's
Law-book. It is plain from a passage already quoted (p. 56
of this volume), that a love for rationalistic speculations (*hetu-
shatra*) and a spirit of free scepticism were beginning to show
themselves in India at the time the Code was compiled; and
it is possible that Buddha's adherents, though not mentioned
by name, were pointed at with reprobation under the
designation *Nastikah*, 'atheists' (= *Charvaka*, Kulluka II. 11),
and *Pashandinah*, 'heretics' (= *Shakya-bhikshu-kshapanakadi*,
Kulluka IV. 30, I. 118). The Code itself may have been an
attempt to stem the current of opinion which was setting in
the direction of Buddhism and rationalistic Brahmanism. The
compiler, however, thought it necessary to adopt some of the
current philosophical theories, and accordingly we find them
interspersed throughout the work, though more directly stated
at the beginning and end. They are of that vague and misty
kind which probably prevailed at the period preceding the
crystallization of the various systems into distinct schools. The
words Sankhya, Yoga, Nyaya, Vaisheshika, and Mimansa do
not occur as designations of philosophical systems. We notice

---

that there is no satisfactory proof of the existence of idols in the
Vedic period. See p. 15 of this volume. In Manu III. 152 a Devalaka,
'attendant on an idol' (= *pratima-paricharaka*), is directed to be
shunned. Certainly in II. 176, the Brahman student is enjoined to
perform *devatabhyarchanam*, 'worship of the deities,' and this is
interpreted by Kulluka to mean *pratimadishu hari-haradi-deva-
pujanam*, 'doing homage to Vishnu and Shiva before images,' &c.,
but whether Manu really intended to denote *pratima* by *devata* is
questionable. In IX. 285, however, the accidental breaker of images
(*pratimanam bhedakah*) is directed to repair them and pay a fine.

indeed a strong leaning towards the Sankhyan line of thought, though we find only a confused statement of some leading ideas of that system, without any mention of its twenty-five Tattvas. The growth of pantheistic ideas, as foreshadowed in the Purusha-sukta of the Rig-veda (see p. 25), is also traceable. All existing things are said to emanate from Brahma, the one self-existent Spirit, to whom all things must also return. Atma-vidya, equivalent to Brahma-vidya and to the Vedanta doctrine, is directed to be studied in VII. 43, and Vedantic ideas pervade the whole twelfth Book, which, however, may possibly be due to later additions. Still more remarkable is the attention directed to be given to the study of Anvikshiki, 'logic' (VII. 43 = *tarka-vidya*); and although the Nyaya, and Mimansa had evidently not become schools, we find from XII. III that a Parishad or 'assembly of twelve Brahmans,' competent to decide on disputed points of law, includes a Haituka (*nyaya-jna*) and a Tarkin (= *mimansaka,* Kulluka). Moreover, in XII. 106, it is declared that he only understands the Veda who investigates it by the rules of Tarka (= *mimansadi-nyaya),* agreeably to Vedic doctrine — all of which precepts are, of course, inconsistent with the reprobation of Haitukas in II. 11, IV. 30; as well as with a precept in II. 10, where Sruti and Smriti are affirmed to be *a-mimansye,* 'not to be reasoned about.'

The cosmogony adopted presents us with a compound of both the Sankhya and Vedanta theories of creation before they had diverged into distinct systems. There is, however, in Book I a synthetical scheme advanced which, though a confusion of two separate statements, one made by Manu himself (I. 14, &c.), the other by Bhrigu (I. 74, &c.), certainly more accords with the Sankhyan doctrine than with any other (see p. 108). I here abridge the account, commencing I. 5:

This universe first existed only in darkness (*tamo-bhutam),* imperceptible, undefinable, as if immersed in sleep (*prasuptam).* Then the Self-existent (*Svayam-bhu,* described by the same epithet as the Sankhyan *Prakriti,* viz. *A-vyakta,* 'undiscerned' or 'undeveloped'), having willed to produce various beings from his own substance, first with a thought created the waters, and placed on them a productive seed or egg (*vija* or *anda*). Then he himself was born in that egg in the form of Brahma. Next he caused the egg to divide itself, and out of its two divisions framed the heaven above and the earth beneath. Afterwards, having divided his own substance, he became half male, half female (I. 32), and from that female produced Viraj (see note 3, p. 25), from whom was created Manu, the secondary progenitor of all beings. Then he (Brahma, according to Kulluka on I. 14) from the supreme Soul (*Atman*) drew forth *Manas* (= *Mahat* or *Buddhi,* 'Intellect,' as explained by Kulluka on I. 74, 75[1], in which passage *Manas* is the principle of thought and stands for both Buddhi and Ahankara). Next to that came Ahankara, and, after that, the Tan-matras or 'subtile principles of the elements.' From these seven active principles (called 'the seven Purushas,' I. 19) — viz. Mahat or Buddhi (called *Manas* in I. 14, 74, 75), Ahankara, and the five suble elements — were evolved the five gross or material elements (*maha-bhuta*), the organs of sense, and the whole world of sense. (Compare the Sankhyan doctrine at pp. 100-102.)

It is curious to compare Strabo XV. 59 (see p. 310).

All this confusion and obscurity in the account of the creation is symptomatic of diversity of authorship. Of the two narratives, that of Bhrigu is the simplest. But both (I. 14 and I. 74) make 'the principle of thought' the first product — that which is and is not (*sad-asad-atmakam*) — to which belongs a real existence, and yet not eternity, because it is a product; (see Sankhya-pravachana V. 56.) I now abridge what follows according to Bhrigu's statement:

---

1. But according to I. 14 (Kulluka) *Manas* must be distinguished from *Buddhi,* and regarded as a product of Ahankara, as in the Sankhya system.

The first Manu Svayambhuva produced six other Manus, and these seven Manus (see note 3, p. 234), each in his own period, were the creators of all things (I. 61-63).

In order to show the duration of a Manv-antara or Manu-period, the divisions of time from a moment to a day of Brahma (12,000,000 years) are specified (I. 64-73):

A Manu-period consists of seventy-one times the 12,000 years, which constitute an age of the gods (I. 79). Each Maha-yuga or great age of the world is subdivided into four Yugas or ages, viz. 1. Krita, 2. Treta, 3. Dvapara, and 4. Kali, each decreasing in excellence; and the life of man lasts for 400 years in the first, 300 years in the second, 200 years in the third, and 100 years in the present or Kali age[1].

In I. 87-101 the account of the creation is concluded by a description of the origin of the four castes from the mouth, arm, thigh, and foot of Brahma, and the preeminence assigned to Brahmans (see extracts, pp. 262, 263).

In the twelfth Book the leaning towards a Sankhyan line of thought is again conspicuous. In 24-38 we have a description of the three Gunas of the Sankhya, viz. Sattva, Rajas, and Tamas, all three of which are said to pervade, and one or other of which predominate in every mortal frame (see note p. 103). In XII. 24 it is asserted that these three form the constituent substances of *atman* (self or soul), and that the first developed principle — Mahat or Buddhi — is also pervaded by them. Again, the triple degrees of transmigration, highest, middle, and lowest, through gods, men, and beasts, are supposed to result from acts done under the dominance of these three Gunas (see note 2, p. 71). We have also the three Pramanas of the Sankhya philosophy clearly laid down in XII. 105:

---

1. We find it constantly implied in Hindu writings that the natural term of human life in the present age is 100 years.

Three means of attaining true knowledge or three standards of truth, viz. perception by the senses (*pratyaksha*), inference (*anumana*), and the Veda (*Shabda*) or various books founded on it — these three must be known thoroughly by one wishing for a clear idea of duty (see pp. 77, 99 of this volume).

Although, however, the germ of the Sankhya is clearly traceable, there is an evident commingling of pantheistic ideas, tending towards the Vedanta, in the frequent declaration that all existing things emanate from, and will ultimately be absorbed into Brahma, 'the universal Spirit.' The distinction between the Jivatman and Paramatman (see p. 66) is recognized in VIII. 91, which verse Kulluka explains by a reference to the Vedic allegory of the two birds (quoted p. 45 of this volume). Nevertheless, we miss in Manu what we find in the later philosophical schools, a clear definition of the subtle body, as composed of the subtle elements, and a plain statement of its relationship to the individual soul and of its accompanying the soul through all its transmigrations. The survival of this soul over the dissolution of the gross body is indeed plainly implied; but Manu's doctrine is that if a man has been wicked the soul clothed in a kind of body, composed of coarse and impure elements, undergoes along with it torment in hell for a time (XII. 21); whereas, if a man has been virtuous, the soul invested in a kind of ethereal and shining body (*kha-sharirin*), composed of pure elementary particles of air, wind, and fire, enjoys bliss in heaven with it for a certain period (IV. 243, III. 93, II. 82, XII. 20); after which both the wicked and the virtuous are born again.

Nor do we find any precise definition of Brahman (neut.) as pure absolute Spirit — the only really existing entity — according to the Vedanta doctrine. Brahma seems rather to be regarded as a kind of shining ethereal essence, out of which the universe was evolved and into which it becomes absorbed (cf. II. 28, IV. 232, VI. 79, 81, 85, XII. 123-125).

III. Thirdly, as to the Achara, 'rules and precepts of conduct,' and social legislation of the Manavas.

The organization of classes in I. 87-91 is so simple that this simplicity, if it be not merely theoretical, bears witness to the antiquity of a considerable portion of the Code. According to Book X. 3, 4, there are only four pure classes (*varnah*, p. 239), as follows:

The Brahman (or priestly class), the Kshatriya (or military class), and the Vaishya (or agricultural class) constitute the three twice-born (*dvi-jati* or *dvi-ja*) classes (as obtaining a second spiritual birth through investiture with the sacred thread, see p. 270); the Shudra (or servile class) is once-born (*eka-jati*), and constitutes the fourth class; there is no fifth class.

From priority of birth, from superiority of origin (in being sprung from the mouth of the Creator), from possession of the Veda (*niyamasya* [= *vedasya*] *dharanati*, i.e. from the right of studying teaching, and expounding it, and from a distinction in the reception of the sacrificial thread (as the most important of the twelve Sanskaras or 'purificatory rites,' specified in II. 27, &c.), the Brahman is the lord (*pradbhu*) of all the classes (X. 3. See p. 262).

The only allusion in the Veda to this fourfold division is in the Purusha-sukta (Rig-veda. X. 90. 12), which, as we have seen (p. 25), is one of its most recent hymns.

A similar division into classes or professions is found to have prevailed in almost all countries[1].

---

1. Megasthenes (according to Strabo's India, 39), the Greek ambassador of Seleukos Nikator (Alexander's successor between the Euphrates and Indus, B.C. 312) at the court of Sandrokottos (Chandra-gupta) in Pataliputra divided the Hindu people into seven classe, viz. philosophers, husbandmen, shepherds, tradesmen or artificers, soldiers, spies or overseers and councillors of state (see note 1, p. 268); perhaps because Herodotus divided the inhabitants of Egypt into seven, viz. priests, soldiers, cowherds, swineherds, tradesmen, interpreters, and

In the same tenth book of Manu, however, we have a more developed social system depicted, and a number of mixed castes (*varna-sankarah, sankara-jatiyah,* X. 12) are described as resulting from the intermarriage of the pure classes[1]:

---

pilots; but Diodorus and Plato made only five divisions, and Strabo only three. From Plato's Timaeus (6) it appears that a similar division of professions existed among the Athenians. Again, from a passage in Herodotus (I. 101), it is inferred that a similar distinction existed among the Medes. In Malcolm's History of Persia (I. 205) the Persian monarch Jamshid is said to have divided the Persians into four classes. Mr. Mill also points out an instructive passage in Plato's Republic (II. 11), in which, describing the simplest form of a political association, he makes it to consist of four or five classes of men: Finally, we read in Millar's Historical View of the English Government (I. 11) that the Anglo-Saxons were originally divided into four great classes — artificers and tradesmen, husbandmen, soldiers, and clergy.

1. Mr. W.F. Sinclair gives some interesting information (in the February and March numbers of the 'Indian Antiquary') in regard to the various subdivisions or sub-castes of Brahmans, and adds a list of forty mixed castes, now found in the Deccan. With regard to the Brahmans, he places at the head the *Chitpavan* (i.e. I presume, *Chittapavana,* 'heart-purifiers') or *Konkanasth* (= *Konkana-stha*) Brahmans, to whom the notorious Nana Sahib of Bithur belonged. Then come the *Desasth* (= *Desha-stha*) or *Rigvedi* Brahmans, who claim for themselves descent from the Rishis, and therefore the highest rank; then the *Yajur-vedi,* who are chiefly engaged in trade; and then the *Devrukh* (?), who are mostly agricultural. There are also in the Deccan *Telangi* (i.e. *Telingi,* from Sanskrit *tri-linga*) Brahmans, from the Karnatak, chiefly engaged in trade; Kanouj Brahmans (from Hindustan), who are often Sipahis in native regiments or *employees* upon the railways, and some other tribes. With regard to the forty mixed castes enumerated by Mr. Sinclair, I here subjoin some of them as given by him, with a few notes of my own — *Prabhus* (Sanskrit *pradhu*), who are the highest, and divided into *Kayasth* and *Patane* (?); *Sonars* (= *Suvarna-kara*) or goldsmiths, a subdivision of whom are the *Ratha-kara* Sonars, who claim to be of Brahman race (cf. note 2, p. 174); *Vanis* (Banias, Banians = Baniyas, Sanskrit *banik*), who are grocers and grain-dealers, and are

By unlawful intermarriage of the classes (*vyabhicharena varnanam*), by their marrying women who ought not to be married, and by neglect of their own duties, mixed classes are produced (X. 24).

These have a great variety of names, such as Murdha-vasikta, Mahishya, Karana or Kaya-stha, Ambashtha or Vaidya, Ayogava, Dhigvana, Pukkasa, Chandala (see p. 259) and are restricted to particular occupations. Still the superiority of the Brahmans in the Hindu lawyer's scheme is the hinge on which the whole social system turns. In fact, the state of society depicted is that of pure and umitigated Brahmanism — a state of things which, if it really admitted of the amount of Brahmanical arrogance described as existing, would more than account for the Buddhist reaction. The Brahmans are made to constitute the great central body around which all other classes and orders of beings revolve like satellites. Not only are they invested with the highest dignity and importance, but they are bound together, and their position secured by the most stringent rules; while the other three classes of soldiers, agriculturists, and servants are made powerless for combined resistance by equally stringent regulations, one class being separated from the other by insurmountable lines of demarcation.

---

distinguished by great reverence for animal life; *Bhatiyas* or cloth and cotton merchants; *Khattris,* who claim Rajput (= *Kshatriya*) descent, but are dealers in cloth, gold and silver lace, &c.; *Vaisyas,* who claim to be a remnant of the original Vaishyas, and are traders; *Marvadi,* merchants; *Simpis* or tailors; *Sutars* (= *Sutra-dhara*) or carpenters; *Sikalgars* (*Saiqal-gar*), turners and weapon-sharpeners; *Lohars* (= *Loha-kara*) or smiths; *Telis* (= *Taili,* from *Tailin*) or oilmen; *Koshtis* and *Salis* or weavers; *Kumbhars* (= *Kumbha-kara*) or potters; *Kolis,* who are Bhistis or water-bearers; *Parits* or washermen; *Lonaris* (= *Lavana-karin*) or preparers of salt and lime and charcoal; *Rangaris* (= *Ranga-karin*) or dyers; *Chambhars* (= *Charma-karin*) or leather-cutters and shoe-makers, &c.

We must, however, guard against supposing that a Brahman claimed to take the lead merely in the character of a priest. To understand more clearly the nature of Brahmanical ascendancy we must ask ourselves the question, What physical and moral forces led to the first movements which ended in the crystallization of social distinctions into the caste-system?

It seems probable, then, that the formation of hard lines of separation between the classes was more the result of gradual and natural adjustment than of preconcerted plan. There can be little doubt that when the Aryan Hindus came into India as immigrants and conquerors, they were without any systematic arrangement of classes. Their first seat was in the Panjab, around the five chief affluents of the Indus and in the neighbourhood of Delhi. This was a productive plain watered by rivers[1]. Hence it happened that, although in their primeval abode, somewhere in Central Asia, they were probably half nomad, half agricultural, they became, when fairly settled in Hindustan, a nation of agriculturists[2]. The soil, too, being

---

1. By degrees they spread themselves over the whole region called by Manu (II. 21, 22) Aryavarta, 'the abode of Aryas,' i.e. the great central plains (Madhya-desha), extending from the western to the eastern sea, and bounded on the north and south by the Himalaya and Vindhya mountains. Only in this region were the three first classes allowed to dwell, but Sudras might sojourn wherever they liked. (see Manu II. 21-24.)

2. The very name Arya is, as every one now knows, connected with the root 4 ri = ar, whence *aratrum*, 'a plough' (cf. Sanskrit *aritra*). It is curious to note how Brahmans, after their segregation as the dominant class, sought to depreciate agriculture. Manu (X. 84) says, 'Some think that agriculture (*krishi*) is an excellent thing, but it is a mode of existence blamed by the good, because the iron-mouthed ploughshare wounds the earth and the creatures living in it.' Mr. W.F. Sinclair informs us in the 'Indian Antiquary,' that in the Deccan the cultivators of the soil are by the modern races of Brahmans considered pure Shudras.

fertile, yielded more than enough to supply the necessities of the cultivators. Hence the surplus produce enabled a large non-agricultural population to spring up. Some of these applied themselves to trade and the improvement of mechanical arts; others were enabled to devote themselves to one of three occupations. 1. mental and religious culture; 2. military exercises; 3. domestic service[1]. It was, indeed, absolutely necessary that the cultivators who were called Vaishyas, because they 'settled down' on the soil and gradually acquired an hereditary right to its occupation[2], should have a class of military men above them, with leisure either to cultivate arms,

---

1. The same happened in the fertile plains of Egypt and Mesopotamia.
2. In modern times they are called Ryots, from the Arabic ra"iyat, 'protected people' (root 'to pasture, guard'). The Hindu term Vaishya is more expressive of their original condition. It is derived from the root *vis*, 'to enter into,' 'sit down on' 'settle down on,' occupy' (whence *vesha*, 'an abode'), cognate with *vicus*, 'a village,' and 'an abode,' and our affix 'wick' at the end of names of towns, denoting originally a settlement or station of cultivators. Hence the root *vish*, when used as a substantive, means 'a man of the people.' The Vaisyas were allowed to become merchants if they preferred trading to agriculture; but the only provision for classes of artisans and mechanics, is from the mixed classes. This indicates that Manu's division belong to an early period, before the industrial and mechanical arts had acquired much importance, though they must have been considerably advanced even in Vedic times (as shown by Dr. Muir, Texts V. 450-472). The Hindu village system of the present day seems to have been developed out of that represented in Manu's Code. Almost everywhere are found bodies of agriculturists who have settled on the soil from time immemorial, and formed themselves into little republics presided over by a half-elective, half-hereditary headman, and a number of village officials (properly twelve, e.g. watchman, accountant, priest, schoolmaster, doctor, barber, astrologer, &c.), the lands around the village forming a sort of jurisdiction, and disputes being settled by gatherings of the villagers under trees, while various low-caste menials who have no interest in the soil are attached to the community.

and so defend the land thus occupied from the attacks of other invaders, or to undertake the cares of government, and so protect property from the dangers incident to anarchy. These ultimately received the name *Kshatriya*. But in the earliest times, as represented by the Vedic hymns, they were called *Rajanya*, 'the kingly class.' (See the Purusha-sukta, translated p. 25, and see p. 26, note 1.) Doubtless, when this class first arose they must have constituted the most powerful order of society; and so, indeed, practically they must have always remained, notwithstanding the intellectual superiority of the Brahmanical class[1]. That the close interdependence of the two higher classes was recognized by the Brahmans themselves is shown by the following:

A Kshatriya cannot thrive without a Brahman, nor a Brahman without a Kshatriya. The Brahman and the Kshatriya when associated together prosper in this world and the next (IX. 322).

It was also necessary that there should be a class willing to perform personal domestic service. These were called Shudras; and this class was probably made up to some extent of the remnants of the Turanian tribes, who were conquered by the Aryan Hindus, and who were mostly driven southwards[2].

---

1. The name Kshatriya comes from *kshatra*, 'dominion,' which is probably from root 1 *kshi* 'to possess, rule.' It is fancifully derived from *kshatat tra*, 'preserving from injury,' in Raghu-vansa II. 53. Manu x. 119 says, 'While defending the Vaishyas by his arms (*shastrena vaishyan rakshitva*) he may raise from them the rightful revenue (*dharmyam aharayed balim*),' which was really taken from the soil in kind.

2. It may be questioned whether Shudra (though found in the Purusha-Sukta, Rig-veda X. 90. 12) is a genuine Sanskrit word. At least no satisfactory etymology is given for it, and this favours the idea of its denoting some pre-Aryan race. The fanciful derivation from *Shuch*, 'to grieve,' and *dru*, 'to run' is hardly worth noticing. Besides the Turanian races who partially blended with the Aryans there were

But, although servants they were neither slaves nor serfs. They merely occupied the lowest step in the social organization. It is true that in theory (X. 129) they were debarred from any superfluous accumulation of wealth, yet, in point of fact, they sometimes rose to affluence, and even became kings[1]:

As a Shudra, without censuring others, performs lawful acts, so, without being censured, he obtains exaltation in this world and the next (X. 128).

Again, the gradual assumption of superiority over the Kshatriyas, Vaishyas, and Shudras, by a class of men who

---

doubtless other aboriginal tribes who occupied the hills and outlying districts and who were called Mlecchas, as constituting those more barbarous and uncultivated communities who stood aloof and would not amalgamate with the Aryans. *Mlechcha-desha* is defined to be a country where the four classes do not dwell. In Manu X. 44 a number of degraded tribes are mentioned, such as Paundrakas, Odras, Dravidas, Kambojas, Yavanas, Shakas, Paradas, Chinas, Kiratas, &c. As these were probably powerful warlike tribes, they are declared by Manu to be outcaste Kshatriyas. It is clear that the mountaineer Kiratas were a martial race; nor could they have been greatly despised, for Arjuna lived among them and adopted their style of life in order to learn archery from Shiva, regarded as their god. See my account of the Kiratarjuniya and the 'Indian Antiquary' for June, 1874, p. 178. The most degraded outcastes were men called Chandalas (children of a Shudra man and a Brahmani); they were expelled from towns, where they could not even walk except by day; they wore only dead men's clothes, rusty iron ornaments, &c. (X. 51-56).

1. Professor Cowell, in a note to Elphinstone's India, p. 18, well shows that the condition of a Shudra was very superior to that of the helot, slave, and serf of the Greek, Roman, and feudal system. The Puranas record dynasties of Shudra kings, and even Manu notices these. In II. 238 it is said, 'A believer in Scripture may receive pure knowledge even from a Shudra.' In modern times cultivators of the soil in some places are regarded as Shudras. There are occasional passages in the Mahabharata depreciating caste and even Vedic knowledge in comparison with moral character; cf. the Raja-dharma of the Shanti-parvan 2955.

called themselves Brahmans[1], seems to have been due to the operation of a law of intellectual development, such as has been common among all nations in their progress towards civilization, in all periods of the world's history. Those who were intellectually superior took advantage of that growth of religious cravings which generally accompanies political growth, and formed themselves into a fraternity of religious teachers, who afterwards became priests. Religion, or a sense of dependence upon God and a desire to propitiate Him, has always formed a marked feature of the Hindu character. Hence in India, the fraternity of priests multiplied with unusual rapidity; so that a considerable number of the sacerdotal class were thrown out of employment and forced to engage in secular occupations. In this manner it came to pass that although all priests were properly Brahmans, all Brahmans were by no means necessarily priests. Nor was it likely that with the partial secularization of the Brahmans the complicated Vedic ceremonial could be long maintained. Some public sacrifices, such as the Agnishtoma, were still performed, but the more intricate rites enjoined by the Brahmans, and occasionally practised in ancient times, lasting for long periods, and requiring for their efficacious performance a staff of sixteen different orders of priests[2], fell into partial if not

---

1. According to some scholars the original meaning of *brahman* was 'prayer,' or rather 'devotional spirit pervading and filling the soul' (root *brih* or *vrih*). Hence it came afterwards to mean Veda, 'sacred knowledge,' in which sense it is often used by Manu. Similarly, *brahman* and *brahmana* meant originally 'a prayer-offerer,' and afterwards 'religious teacher,' the signification 'priest' not having been attached to these words till sacrificial ideas had fully developed themselves in the Hindu mind. It is a mistake to suppose that Brahmana and priest are convertible terms. Brahmans are rather 'men of the first class.'

2. See their names all given in my Sanskrit-English Dictionary under Ritv-ij, p. 181, col. 1.

entire desuetude. It was found, however, indispensable to the retention of power over the other classes that some sacerdotal offices should be maintained. In proportion, indeed, to the neglect of high ceremonial observances was there an increased strictness in exacting a knowledge of the Veda, and the discharge of domestic rites for which a priest's teaching and superintendence were required.

In II. 84, 85, it is declared that all Vedic rites, oblations to fire, and solemn sacrifices gradually pass away (*ksharanti*), but that the act of repeating the Veda, especially the repetition of the Gayatri with the four mystic syllables, is ten times better than the appointed sacrifice (see pp. 276, 277).

Manu is careful to assign distinct functions and titles to the priests qualified for these duties; thus we read:

Some Brahmans are intent on knowledge (of the supreme Spirit), others are intent on acts of austerity (*tapo-nishthah*), others on acts of austerity and repetition of the Veda combined, and others on sacrificial rites (III. 123).

He who is selected for the office of preparing the sacred fire, for conducting the Paka-yajna (see note 1, 216) and performing the Agnishtoma[1] and other sacrifices, is called the *Ritv-ij* of his employer (II. 143).

He who having invested his pupil with the sacred thread afterwards instructs him in the whole Veda, with the rules of ceremonial (*sakalpam*[2]) and the Upanishads, is called an *Acharya* (II. 140).

He who, for the sake of a livelihood, gives instruction in one part only of the Veda or in the Vedangas (such as grammar, &c.) is called an *Upadhyaya* or sub-teacher (II. 141).

---

1. The Agnishtoma is a protracted sacrifice of five days' duration, performed by one who is desirous of obtaining heaven. It is either a part or a modification of the Jyotishtoma, and in ancient times required sixteen priests.
2. That is, probably, 'the Kalpa Sutras.'

The Brahman who performs the Sanskara ceremonies on conception &c. according to rule, and who feeds the child with rice (*i.e* performs the *anna-prashanam* in the sixth month, see II. 23 and p. 220 of this volume), is called a Guru[1] (III. 142).

Manu, however, found it necessary to conciliate the Kshatriya class. The most exalted eulogies were lavished on kings; but Brahmans were to act as their advisers and to have much of the judicial authority and interpretation of the laws in their own hands, and were always theoretically superior in rank — a circumstance which led in the end to jealousies, feuds, and even internecine warfare between the first two classes. Certain privileges also naturally fell to the Vaisyas, and both they and the Kshatriyas were equally with the Brahmans entitled to the appellation *Dvi-ja,* 'twice-born.' Their whole status, however, depended upon various domestic rites, to the due conduct of which the superintendence of Brahmans was indispensable. Yet, in spite of the importance and dignity thus attached to the priestly office, a Brahman, according to Manu's Code, was by *birth* and *divine right* — not by profession or self-elevation — at the head of all creatures. He was born a Brahman and did not become one. He not only inherited superiority as his birthright, but was created a leader of mankind — a sort of deity in human shape — by the fiat of the great Creator himself.

---

1. The title Guru, however, appears to have been applied in a general way to all spiritual preceptors, cf. 269. It is sometimes used alone as a distinctive epithet of Prabha-kara, a teacher of the Mimansa, often named in conjunction with Kumarila, to denote whom the title Bhatta is generally employed in the same way. According to Yajnavalkya I. 34, a Guru is one who imparts the Veda, while an Acharya is one who invests with the Yajnopavita or 'sacred thread.' Similarly in the Panjab the teachers of the Granths (Granthis) are called Gurus.

He is declared, in Book I. 87, to have proceeded from the mouth of Brahma, as the Kshatriya did from his arm, the Vaishya from his thigh, and the Shudra from his foot. Manu's theory, in short, was that the distinction of caste and the inherent superiority of one class over the three others was as much a law of nature and a matter of divine appointment, as the creation of separate classes of animals, with insurmountable differences of physical constitution, such as elephants, lions, horses, and dogs.

That the Brahmans assumed a pre-eminence nothing short of divine, is clear from numerous passages. I select the following:

Since the Brahman sprang from the most excellent part, since he has the priority arising from primogeniture (*jyaishthyat*), and since he possesses the Veda, he is by right the lord (*prabho*) of this whole creation (I. 93. See also p. 253 of this volume).

A Brahman, whether learned or unlearned, is a mighty divinity (*daivatam mahat*), just as fire is a mighty divinity, whether consecrated (*pranita*) or unconsecrated (IX. 317).

Even when Brahmans employ themselves in all sorts of inferior occupations (*an-ishteshu*), they must under all circumstances be honoured, for they are to be regarded as supreme divinities (*paramam daivatam*, IX. 319).

From his high birth alone (*sambhavenaiva*) a Brahman is regarded as a divinity even by the gods (*devanam api*). His teaching must be accepted by the rest of the world as an infallible authority (*pramanam*), for the Veda (*brahma*) itself is the cause (of its being so accepted, XI. 84).

Consistently with the divine nature thus ascribed to the Brahman, he is declared to possess powers of the most tremendous and awe-inspiring character:

Let not a king, although fallen into the greatest distress (through a deficiency of revenue), provoke Brahmans to anger (by taking revenue from them), for they, if once enraged, could instantly (by pronouncing curses and mystical texts) destroy him with all his army and retinue.

Who, without bringing destruction on himself, can provoke those men, by whose imprecation (*abhishapena,* Kulluka) all-devouring fire was created, and by whom the undrinkable ocean was swallowed[1], and the wasted moon restored to its full size[2] (*apyayitah = paschat puritah,* IX. 313, 314)?

What king would gain increase of revenue by oppressing those who, if angry, could create other worlds and guardians of worlds (*loka-palan*), and could create new gods and mortals (IX. 315)?

A Brahman, well skilled in the law, need not make any representation to the king (if he has received an injury), for by his own power (*svaviryena*), he may punish (*shishyat*) those who

---

1. This seems to refer to the legend of Agastya, who is said to have swallowed the ocean and was afterwards raised to be regent of the star Canopus. Much, however, of the detail of this legend must be later.

2. This refers to the legend of Chandra, 'the Moon,' afflicted with consumption for fifteen days by his father-in-law, Daksha, because of his (the Moon's) partiality for Rohini, one of Daksha's daughters, some of whom had become his wives. On the Moon's repentance, his wasted strength and size were restored. Manu IX. 129 states that Daksha gave ten of his daughters to Dharma, thirteen to Kashyapa, and twenty-seven to Soma, the Moon. The legend of Daksha's daughters is found (like many other of Manu's allusions) in the Taittiriya-samhita, ii. 3, 5: 'Prajapati had thirty-three daughters — he gave them to king Soma; among them he only went to Rohini. The others jealous returned [to their father]: he went after them, he sought them again; but he [the father] did not give them again to him. He said to him, "Take an oath that you will go to them alike, then I will give them to you again." He took an oath; he gave them back to him. He only out of them went to Rohini. Him, the king [Soma], consumption attacked. This is the origin of the Raja-yakshma.'

injure him. His own power is stronger than the power of the king, therefore by his own might may a Brahman chastise (*nigrihniyat*) his foes. He may, without hesitation, make use of (as magical formularies) the sacred texts (*shrutih*) revealed to Atharvan and Angiras (*Atharvangirasih*, see note, p. 9); for the uttering of texts (*vak* = *abhicara-mantrochcharanam*) is the weapon (*sastram*) of a Brahman; with that he may destroy his foes (XI. 31-33).

The crime of striking and killing a Brahman involves, of course, terrible consequences, thus:

He who merely assails a Brahman with intent to kill him will continue in hell (*narakam*) for a hundred years, and he who actually strikes him, a thousand years (XI. 206. Compare also IV. 165, where it is said that the hell to which he will be consigned, and where he will be made to wander about incessantly, is called *Tamisra*, 'profound darkness').

As many particles of dust (*panshun*) as the blood of a Brahman absorbs from the soil, so many thousand of years must the shedder of that blood abide in hell (XI. 207).

The above may be thought an exaggeration of the powers and status claimed by the highest order of Hindu society, and doubtless the compiler of the Code often draws an ideal picture of a condition of things which never actually existed, and was never likely to exist; much in the same manner as we in England maintain that our king can do no wrong. Yet in the matter of the Brahman we are compelled to accept the colouring as, in the main, truthful. Only recently there appeared in a leading journal a report of a sermon preached by a converted Brahman, in which the preacher asserted that the Brahmans of the present day pretend to 'dethrone the Creator and put themselves in his place. Moreover, that he himself (the preacher) had claimed and received divine honours and had seen believers (among his own fellow-countrymen) greedily drink the water in which his feet had been washed[1].'

It may be asked how did the Brahman, laden with all this weight of dignity and theoretically debarred from all other occupations, except studying and teaching the Veda, and performing religious rites, contrive to support himself? The answer is that he took care to provide for his own material comforts[2] by making the efficacy of all repetitions of the Veda

---

1. The Rev. Narayan Seshadri (a Marathi name derived from the serpent-like folds of the serpent Sesha, Vishnu's seat), who preached on Easter Sunday, April 5, 1874 (in a Presbyterian Church in Kensington Park Road), a sermon, the report of which appeared in the next day's 'Daily News.' He embraced the Christian faith on September 13, 1843. He had to give up father, mother, three brothers, and three sisters. Such is the condition of Brahmanical society that a man must renounce all former associations when converted. I subjoin a further portion of the matter reported as preached. 'He had been emptied of Hindooism. This creed dealt largely in the marvellous; for instance, it is said that one great saint drank up all the ocean in three sips, and was afterwards seated among the constellations on account of this feat. But there was a philosophic as well as a popular form of Hindooism. There were atheistical and theistical forms, the latter having as many advocates in India as it had in this country, in Germany, and in the United States. He, dwelt at length on the pantheistic notion of Brahm, which ignored man's responsibility. Man's sins, in fact, became God's sins; and gradually the preacher had become convinced that this was blasphemy.'

2. This appears to hold good even in the present day; for Professor Ramkrishna Bhandarkar, writing in the 'Indian Antiquary' for May, 1874, remarks that repetition of the Veda for *dakshina* still prevails in Gujarat and to a much greater extent in the Marathi country and Tailangana. 'Numbers of Brahmans go about to all parts of the country is search of *dakshina,* and all well-to-do natives patronize them according to their means, by getting them to repeat portions of their Veda, which is mostly the Black Yajush, with Apastamb for their Sutra. Hardly a week passes here in Bombay in which no Tailanga Brahman comes to ask me for *dakshina.'*

and all sacrificial rites depend upon the gifts (*dakshinah*) with which they were accompanied:

A sacrifice performed with trifling presents (*alpa-dakshinah*) destroys the organs of sense, fame, heaven, life, reputation, offspring, cattle; therefore let no man undertake a sacrifice who has not plenty of money to make liberal gifts (XI. 40).

Let a man, according to his ability, give wealth to Brahmans who know the Vedas and keep apart from the world. By so doing he obtains heaven when he dies (XI. 6).

A king, even though dying (from want), must not receive taxes from a Brahman learned in the Vedas, nor must he allow such a Brahman dwelling in his country to pine away with hunger. Of that king in whose territory a Brahman learned in the Vedas wastes with hunger, the whole kingdom will in a short time be wasted with famine (VII. 133, 144).

All that exists in this universe is the Brahmans' property (I. 100).

Moreover, when the increase of the Brahmanical class compelled the secularization of many of its members, they were allowed to engage in the occupations of the other classes. This was at first only permitted under circumstances of exigency and distress. Some verses in XII. 71, X. 75, 76, 80-82, lay down the law on this point:

A Brahman who swerves from his own peculiar duty is, on departing this life, born again as a vomit-eating demon called Ulka-mukha (XII. 71).

Repetition (or study) of the Veda (*adhyayanam*), expounding it (or literally, teaching others to repeat it, *adhyapanam*), sacrificing (*yajanam*) and assisting others to sacrifice (*yajanam*), giving (*danam*) and receiving gifts (*pratigrahah*) are the six legitimate acts[1] (*shat-karmani*) of a Brahman. Of these six acts, three are

---

1. Called the 'six privileges.' A particular tribe of Konkan Brahmans is said to be excluded from these privileges because its members eat fish.

the means of his subsistence, viz. assisting at sacrifices, teaching
the Veda, and receiving presents from a pious giver (*visuddhat*).
These three privileges (*dharmah*) are limited to Brahmans, and
do not extend to Kshatriyas (X. 75-77). Hence a Brahman is
called *Tri-karman*,' 'one who engages in three acts.'

The most proper occupation for the Brahman is teaching
and expounding the Veda (*vedabhyasah*); for a Kshatriya,
defending the people; for a Vaishya, agriculture, keeping cattle,
and trade (*varta-karma*[1]). Yet a Brahman, unable to subsist by
his proper employment, may live by the duty of a soldier, for
that is the next in dignity. If it be asked, how is he to live if unable
to subsist by either of these occupations? The answer is that he
may adopt the mode of life of a Vaishya (X. 80-82. See also X.
101, 102. Cf. note 2, p. 257).

Here are some of the rules by which the whole existence
of a Brahman from the cradle to the grave was regulated:

Every Brahman was supposed to pass through four
Ashramas or 'Orders,' — that is to say, his life was divided
into four stages or periods according as he became successively,
1. Religious student (*brahma-charin*); 2. Householder (*griha-stha*); 3. Anchorite or hermit (*vanaprastha*); 4. Religious
mendicant (*bhikshu* or *parivrajaka* or *sannyasin*). For the
regulation of his life in the first two of these periods the most
minute instructions are spread over the 2nd, 3rd, 4th, and
5th Book with much wearisome detail and repetition[2].

---

1. This word *varta-karman*, as may be gathered from Kulluka's
   commentary on these verses, includes *krishi, go-raksha*, and *banijya*.
   The caste-division of Megasthenes (note 1, p. 253) separates these
   three.
2. It is interesting to find that Megasthenes (Strabo XV. 1,59), three
   centuries B.C., had noted that Brahmans, even from the time of
   conception, were under the care of learned men, and lived for thirty-
   seven years as philosophers before becoming householders.

To begin with the religious student. The young Brahman is to reside with his preceptor (*guru*) until he has gained a thorough knowledge of the three Vedas. This residence may continue for thirty-six years, or for half that time, or for a quarter of it, according to his capacity for acquiring the requisite instruction (cf. Grihya Sutras, p. 219, 220). He may be a student for life (*naishthika,* III. 1, II. 243).

He is of course to go through all the twelve Sanskaras or 'purificatory rites' (II. 27, &c.). They are supposed to purify a man from the taint of sin derived from his parents (*garbhikam enas*), and are enjoined, with certain variations, on all the three first classes alike; some being performed before the birth of a male child, and some during the first year after birth. I here enumerate them:

1. *Garbhadhana* or *Garbhu-lambhana,* 'the ceremony on conception' (p. 219); 2. *Punasavana* (p. 219); 3. *Simantonnayana* (p. 219); 4. *Jata-karman* (p. 220); 5. *Nama-karman* or *Nama-karana,* 'the ceremony of giving a name' on the tenth or twelfth day after birth (Manu II. 30); 6. *Nish-kramana,* 'taking out the child' in the fourth month to see the sun (II. 34); 7. *Anna-prasana* (p. 220); 8. *Chuda-karman* or *Chaula* (p. 220); 9. *Upanayana* (p. 220); 10. *Keshanta,* 'cutting off the hair,' performed on a Brahman in his sixteenth year, on a Kshatriya in his twenty-second, on a Vaishya in twenty-fourth (Manu II. 65); 11. *Samavartana,* performed on the student's return home after completing his studies with his preceptor (pp. 223, 273); 12. *Vivaha,* 'marriage.' This last is the principal purificatory rite for women; but they are allowed some of the others, provided there is an omission of the Mantras or Vedic texts, with which all the Sanskaras were accompanied (II. 66. 67).

It is noteworthy that marriage is the twelfth Sanskara, and hence a religious duty incumbent upon all, completing the purification and regeneration of the twice-born:

Of the above twelve rites, 1, 2, 3, and 10 are little observed. The other eight are more worthy of attention; 8 and 9 are of considerable legal importance even in the present day, and 7 is still practised. 7 and 12 are said to be the only rites allowed to Shudras. Other Sanskaras, practised in some parts of India, are mentioned, such as *Karna-vedha,* 'boring the ears;' and occasionally the imparting of the Savitri or 'sacred Vedic Text' (= Gayatri, p. 20), which ought to be performed at Upanayana, is reserved for a separate ceremony four days later.

But the most important of the above Sanskaras is *Upanayana,* 'investiture with the sacred cord,' already described in the Grihya Sutras (p. 219). This cord, which is a thin coil of three threads, commonly called the *Yajnopavita* or 'sacrificial threads,' is worn over the left shoulder and allowed to hang down diagonally across the body to the right hip, and the wearing of it by the three twice-born classes was the mark of their second birth[1]. A third birth is mentioned for Brahmans (II. 169):

The first births is from the natural mother; the second from the binding on of the girdle (*maunji-bandhane*); the third is at initiation into sacrificial rites (as the *jyotishtoma,* &c.), according to a precept of the Veda.

There was some difference in the kind of thread worn, according to the class of the wearer. In II. 44 we read:

The sacred cord of a Brahman must be of cotton (*karpasa*), so as to be put on over his head in a coil of three threads (*tri-vrit*); that of a Kshatriya of flax or hemp (*sana*); that of a Vaisya of wool (*avika*).

[In the previous two verses Manu intimates that a Brahman must also have a girdle (*mekhala*) either of Munja grass or of

---

1. It is still worn, but the word *Yajnopavita* for 'the sacred thread' has been corrupted into Jane-o. In Bengali it is called *Poita* for *Pavitra*.

Kusha grass. From II. 169, 170, it might be inferred that the girdle and sacrificial thread are equivalent, but II. 174 clearly distinguishes them. The leather mantle, thread, girdle, staff, and under clothing are, all five prescribed at the time of Upanayana, and the binding on of the girdle seems to complete the rite.]

The ceremony of investiture begins by the youth's standing opposite the sun and walking thrice round the fire. Then girt with the thread, he asks alms from the assembled company. This begging for alms still constitutes part of the rite, and indicates that the youth undertakes to provide himself and his preceptor (guru, acharya) with food (p. 219). The guru then initiates him into the daily use of the Savitri or holy prayer in the three-measured Gayatri (pp. 20, 180), preceded by three suppressions of breath (tribhih pranayamaih), the triliteral syllable Om, and three Vyahritis or mystical words, Bhur Bhuvah Svar[1], and admits him to the privilege of repeating the three Vedas, and of performing other religious rites, none of which are allowed before investiture (II. 171, 173). The Guru or Acharya is thus his spiritual father.

Purifications, ablutions, and libations (called Savanas) are enjoined on Vanaprasthas or 'hermits' (p. 285) at all the three Sandhyas[2], that is, at the three divisions of the day — sunrise,

---

1. The utterance of these three mystical words, meaning 'earth, the middle region, and heaven' (note 3, p. 70), together with the awful syllable Om (pp. 111, 243), is supposed to be attended with marvellous and mysterious effects (see II. 76, 79, 83, 84). Note the sacredness attached to the number three.

2. See Book VI. 22, 24, and compare Kulluka, savaneshu snayat, pratar-madhyandina-sayam savaneshu trishu devarshi-pitri-tarpanam kurvan. Sandhya often means 'twilight,' but is applied to morning and evening twilight and to the change from midday to afternoon. With reference to the Hindu and Mohammedan custom of performing religious rites three times a day, we may compare a passage in Daniel, who 'kneeled upon his knees three times a day, and prayed, and gave thanks before his god,' Dan. Vi. 10. And David says, 'Evening, and morning, and at noon, will I pray, and cry aloud,' Ps. lv. 17.

noon, and sunset — but on Brahma-charins and Griha-sthas at the two Sandhyas of sunrise and sunset only, when the Gayatri (p. 20) is by all means to be repeated. Thus, in II. 222, we have:

Let him constantly observe the two Sandhyas according to rule, sipping water, with all his organs controlled and with fixed attention, repeating the Gayatri prayer (*japyam*, which ought to be repeated).

The young Brahman is also every day to bathe; to offer oblations of water (*tarpana*) to the gods, holy sages (*Rishis*) generally, and departed ancestors (*Pitris*); to reverence the deities [according to Kulluka, *Devata* = *pratima*, the images of the deities]; and to offer an oblation of fuel to the sacred fire (II. 176). But in V. 88 he is forbidden to perform the regular offerings of water to deceased persons, till his studentship is completed. He is to abstain from meat, perfumes, unguents, sensuality, wrath, covetousness, dancing, music, gambling, detraction of others, falsehood, impurity of all kinds, and is never to injure any being (II. 177-179).

Every day, too, both morning and evening, he is to go round the neighbouring villages begging for food for himself and his preceptor and collecting fuel for the maintenance of the sacred fire (II. 187).

He is always to pay the most profound respect to his religious teacher (*guru*), as well as to his parents and to all persons older than himself:

By reverencing his mother he gains this terrestrial world; by reverencing his father, the middle word; by constant attention to his spiritual master (*guru*), the celestial world of Brahma (II. 233).

A youth who habitually salutes and constantly reveres the aged, prospers in four things, life, knowledge, fame, and strength (II. 121).

In short, even Christians may learn from Hindus, as indeed from Oriental nations generally[1], 'to love, honour, and succour their father and mother, to submit themselves to all their governors, teachers, spiritual pastors and masters, and to order themselves lowly and reverently to all their betters;' and, moreover, to extend the duty of 'hurting nobody by word or deed' to animals and the whole inferior creation[2].

On completing his studies the young Brahman is to give some valuable present to his preceptor. He is then to perform the proper Sanskara ceremony of ablution (*snana*) on the occasion of his solemn return to his own home (*samavartana*), as already described (see pp. 223, 269):

Let not a student who knows his duty make a present to his spiritual master before the ceremony on his return; but when, being permitted by his preceptor, he is about to perform the requisite ablution (*snasyan*), let him offer him some valuable article (*guru-artham,* such as a field, gold, a jewel, cow, horse, &c.) as a gift to the best of his ability (II. 245, 246).

The young Brahman's return to his own house is made an occasion of festivity; he is decked with flowers and receives a present of a cow (III. 3). He is then to select a wife of the same class with himself, endowed with auspicious marks (*lakshana*), and thereupon he enters the second Ashrama, and becomes a householder (*griha-stha*). Some curious directions for his guidance in choosing a wife are given (III. 8-10):

Let him not marry a girl with reddish hair, nor one with a superfluity of limbs (as, for instance, one with six fingers), nor one who is sickly, nor one with either too little or too much hair,

---

1. Notably from the Chinese as well as from the Hindus.
2. I am told, however, that, notwithstanding the strict rules of *a-hinsa*, the 'Society for Prevention of Cruelty to Animals' might find work to do in some parts of India.

nor one who talks too much, nor one who is red-eyed, nor one named after a constellation, a tree, or a river, nor one with a barbarous name (*antya* = *mlechcha*), or the name of a mountain, a bird, a snake, a slave, or any frightful object. But let him marry a woman without defective or deformed limbs, having an agreeable name, whose gait is like that of a flamingo (*hansa*) or elephant[1], whose hair and teeth are moderate in quantity, and whose whole body is soft.

We have seen that marriage is a Sanskara. Hence it is a religious duty and a purificatory rite (p. 269).

It is clear from III. 12-15, IX. 45, 101, that, as a general rule, a twice-born man is expected to have one wife only; but polygamy is not illegal, and he might take other wives of classes different from this own, being careful to settle their precedence according to the order of these classes (IX. 85). A Brahman might thus have four wives, one from his own class and one from each of the three classes below him; a Kshatriya three; and a Vaishya two. But the sons of inferior wives are degraded and called Apasadah (X. 10). Nevertheless, if there be four wives of a Brahman in the order of the classes, and sons are born to all four wives, there is a rule for dividing the inheritance between them (IX. 149).

Manu's eight forms of marriage are specified in the Grihya Sutras (see p. 217). Of these the first four, viz. that of Brahma (which is described as 'the gift of a daughter to a man learned in the Veda'), the Devas (*daiva*), Rishis (*arsha*), and Prajapatis (*prajapatya*), are the most approved for a Brahman. The Gandharva marriage ('from affection without any nuptial rite') and Rakshasa ('marrying a girl carried off as a prize in war') were allowable for Kshatriyas; the Asura and Paisacha were prohibited.

---

1. That is, having a kind of rolling gait, corresponding to Homer's *eilipous*.

A description has been given of one of the oldest marriage rites (p. 217), as well as of the ceremony on commencing residence in a new house (p. 221). The householder is to fulfil every day all his domestic religious duties (*grihyma karma*), some of which, such as the morning and evening oblation (*agnihotra, sayam-pratar-homa*), are to be performed with the fire of the nuptial ceremony maintained ever afterwards (*vaivahike 'gnau,* III. 67, see p. 31).

He is especially to perform the five *Maha-yajnah,* great devotional acts[1] (III. 70, &c.): viz. 1. towards the divine Rishis, by repetition and teaching of the Veda (*Brahma-yajna*); 2. towards departed fathers (*Pitri-yº*), by the Sraddha ceremonies; 3. towards the gods (*Deva-yº*), by oblations (*homa*[2]) to Fire, Prajapati, Heaven and Earth, Indra, Soma, &c. (85-89); 4. towards all creatures (*Bhuta-yº*), including

---

1. The Musalmans have also five principal devotional acts, but these are not all diurnal. They are — 1. Prayer (*namaz*) five times a day, practically reduced to three times, morning, midday, and evening. 2. Almsgiving (*zakat*). 3. Fasting (*roza*), especially keeping the great fast during the ninth month, Ramazan, once a year. 4. Pilgrimage to Mecca (*haj*) once in a lifetime. 5. Confession of faith (*shahadat*), i.e. repeating the *tawhid* or 'declaration of faith in the unity of God;' 'there is no god but God, and Muhammad is the apostle of God.' A Hajji is a pilgrim who has performed the Haj. There is no duty of pilgrimage among the five necessary devotional acts prescribed by Manu, but the Hindu system has, nevertheless, its Haj. Puri, in Orissa (the abode of Jagan-nath), is described by Mr. Hunter as the Jerusalem of India. It is really only one of the Indian Meccas. Other great places of pilgrimage (*Tirthas*) are Haridvar, in the Himalaya (one of the most celebrated), where the Ganges is supposed to have descended from the head of Shiva on to the earth; Chitrakut, in Bundelkhand, Rama's first abode after his banishment; Jvala-mukhi, in the Panjab, where Sati, wife of Shiva, burned herself, and her presence is thought to be denoted by gas flaming from the ground.
2. The *homa* or 'oblation of butter' was the peculiar offering to the god of fire, as the Soma juice was to Indra, the rain-god. See note, p. 32.

good and evil spirits supposed to people the air, by the *bali* or offering of rice-grains &c. generally scattered on the house-top or outside the door for animals to devour (91); 5. towards men, by hospitality (*Manushya-y°*). A description of all five has already been given (p. 222). The last four are sometimes called Paka-yajnas (II. 86). Of these five, the first, viz. repetition of the Veda (*Brahma-yajna, japa-y°, svadhyaya¹*, III. 81, II.

---

1. It seems to me that Sir. W. Jones' usual translation of this and similar words by *'reading* and *studying* the Veda,' conveys a somewhat wrong idea. The words generally used to denote the performance of the Brahma-yajna rather imply 'going over inaudibly to one's self,' 'repeating or muttering texts in a low tone of voice.' It is doubtful whether the Veda was ever read or studied as we should read a book in the present day. Neither the word Veda nor any of the words connected with it imply truth written down like our word 'Scripture;' and for a long period the writing of it was discouraged, if not prohibited. The very object of the long residence with a Guru (see p. 269) was to learn to repeat the sacred texts by heart, not to study them. Indeed, very little mention of writing is made in Manu. Even written evidence is not alluded to as it is in Yajnavalkya. In connection with the repetition of the Veda at the present day I here give the substance of an interesting article by Professor Bhandarkar in the 'Indian Antiquary' for May, 1874. Every Brahmanic family is devoted to the study of a particular Veda or Sakha of a Veda, and its family domestic rites are performed in accordance with the Sutra of that Veda. In Northern India the favourite Veda is the White Yajur-veda in its Madhyandina Shakha, but the study has almost died out except at Benares. (According to Mr. Burnell the Black Yajur-veda is the favourite in the Telugu country.) Brahmans of each Veda are divided into two classes — Grihasthas, who are devoted to worldly avocations, and Bhikshukas, who study the sacred texts and perform religious rites. Both classes have to repeat the Sandhya-vandana or 'morning and evening prayers' (see p. 271-272), which principally consists of the Gayatri (see p. 20), recited five, ten, twenty-eight, or a hundred and eight times. Besides these prayers, many perform daily the Brahman-yajna, incumbent on all alike on certain occasions. This for Rig-vedi Brahmans consists of — 1. Part of Rig-veda I. 1. 2. Aitareya-brahmana I. 1. 3. Portions of the Aitareya-aranyaka (1-5). 4. The

85, 86), and especially of the Gayatri text, is regarded as the most efficacious; and a peculiar virtue is attributed to its being repeated in a low tone or even mentally:

The Japa-yajna or 'repetition of the Veda' is declared to be ten times superior to the Vidhi-yajna (or appointed oblations at the changes of the moon, called *Darsa* and *Paurnamasa*, see note, p. 32); a hundred times superior, if it is muttered in a low voice (*upansu*); and a thousand times superior, if it is only mentally repeated (*manasah,* II. 85).

The four Paka-yajnas, even when accompanied with the Vidhi-yajna, are not together worth a sixteenth part of the Japa-yajna (II. 86).

---

opening text or a portion of the White Yajur-veda. 5. Of the Sama-veda. 6. Of the Atharva-veda. 7. Of the Ashvalayana Kalpa-sutra. 8. Of the Nighantu. 9. Of the Nirukta. 10. Of the Chandas. 11. Of the Jyotisha. 12. Of the Siksha. 13. Of Panini. 14. Of Yajnavalkya's Smriti. 15. Of the Mahabharata. 16. Of Kanada's Sutra. 17. Of Jaimini's Mimansa. 18. Of Badarayana's Vedanta-sutra. This course of Svadhyaya is based on Ashvalayana's Sutra III. 23 (given at p. 222 of this volume). No. 1 corresponds to his Rich; 4. 5, 6, to his Yajur, Saman, and Atharvangiras; 2, 3 to his Brahmanas &c. Those Bhikshukas who have studied the whole Veda follow Ashvalayana's precept *yavan manyeta tavad adhitya.* Some of them are also Yajnikas, skilled in the performance of sacred rites, and some are Vaidikas, whose sole occupation in life is to learn the Vedas by heart in the Samhita, Pada, Krama, Jata, and Ghana arrangement of the texts (see p. 176-177) without making a single mistake in the Sandhi changes or even in the accents. The Rig-vedis pronounce the accents differently from the Taittiriyas, while the Madhyandians indicate the accents by movements of the right hand. In addition to the Mantra portion of the Veda, the Rig-vedis learn to recite the Brahmana portion and the Vedangas, including the Kalpa and Grihya Sutras. At a public recitation the first place is given to Rig-vedis, the second to Yajur-vedis, and the third to Sama-vedis (cf. p. 244). As the Black and White Yajur-vedis are liable to quarrel about precedence, they are not generally invited to recital-meetings (*Mantra-jargaras*) together.

A Brahman becomes fit for beatitude by simple repetition of the Veda, whether he perform other rites or not; of this there is no doubt (II. 87).

Let him habitually repeat (*abhyaset = japet*) the Veda at the right season without weariness, for that is called his highest duty (*paro dharmah*); every other duty is called subordinate (*upadharmah*, IV. 147).

The filial piety of the Hindus is notably manifested in the importance attached to the *Shraddhas*, sometimes reckoned as twelve in number (the three principal being *Nitya*, 'daily;' *Parvana*, 'monthly;' *Ekoddishta*, 'special,' p. 228), consisting of an offering of water (*udaka-dana, tarpana*) and cakes of rice-meal, &c. (*pinda*) to a deceased father, grandfather, and great grandfather, and to forefathers and progenitors (*Pitris*) collectively, on which offerings they are supposed really to feed (III. 237). The custom was probably very ancient, as the Pitris are addressed with the utmost reverence in the Rig-veda (VI. 52. 4, VII. 35, 12, X. 14,7, 8, &c. See p. 21 of this volume).

The actual funeral, when the bodies of all deceased persons (except those of infants up to two years old, cf. p. 335-336) are burnt, is described at p. 224. The offering to deceased fathers at the Sraddha is the key to the Hindu law of inheritance. It furnishes the principal evidence of kinship, on which the title to participate in the patrimony is founded, no power of making wills being recognized in Manu or any other authoritative code of Hindu jurisprudence (see p. 297). The *Gotra* or family is in fact a corporate body bound together by what may be called *Sapindaship* (*Sapindata*) and *Samanodakaship* (*Samanodaka-bhava*, Manu v. 60). All who offer the funeral cake (*pinda*) and water (*udaka*) together are Sapindas and Samanodakas to each other, and a kind of intercommunion and interdependence is thus continually maintained between the dead and living members of a family

— between past, present, and future generations. Practically, however, the closeness of the interconnexion extends only to three generations on each side, so that if we imagine a clasp connecting two short chains of three links each, this will represent the householder uniting father, grandfather, and great grandfather, on the one side, with son, grandson, and great grandson on the other — in all seven persons connected by the Pinda (Manu V. 60). The first three are supposed to be dependent on the living paterfamilias for their happiness, and even for their support, through the constant offering of the sacred cakes and water; and he himself, the moment he dies, becomes similarly dependent on the three succeeding generations.

The connexion of *Samanodakaship* lasts longer, and ends only when the family names are no longer known (V. 60).

The object of such Shraddhas is twofold, viz. first, the re-embodying of the soul of the deceased in some kind of form after cremation of the corpse, or simply the release of the subtle body which is to convey the soul away (see p. 226). Secondly, the raising him from the regions of the atmosphere, where he would have otherwise to roam for an indefinite period among demons and evil spirits to a particular heaven or region of bliss. There he is eventually half deified among the shades of departed kinsmen. Manu, however, is not clear as to the precise effect of the Shraddha. He merely states that its performance by a son or the nearest male kinsman is necessary to deliver a father from a kind of hell called *Put*[1], and that the spirits of the departed (Pitris) feed on the offered food (III. 237).

---

1. See Manu IX. 138. Whence a son who performs the rites is called *Put-tra*, 'the rescuer from Put.' This explains the desire of every Hindu for the birth of a son rather than a daughter; but it seems inconsistent that the Sraddha should have an effect irrespective of deeds done during life.

Special Shraddhas such as these (p. 208), which form to this very day the most important religious rite among the Hindus, are accompanied with much feasting and costly gifts to the Brahmans invited to assist at their celebration[1] (III. 145). The performance of the first Shraddha is more particularly marked by largesses of all kinds, and sometimes, it is said, costs a rich man a sum equivalent to several thousand pounds[2]. It should take place the day after mourning expires, and then at intervals during twelve successive months, this monthly ceremony being called by Manu *Anvaharya* (III. 123). Afterwards it should be performed on all anniversaries of a father's death. Other Shraddhas are described at p. 228.

It is curious to learn from II. 150-168 Manu's idea of the persons to be excluded from these ceremonies (viz. thieves, spirit-drinkers, atheists, men with diseased nails or teeth, dancers, physicians, &c., see note, p. 303).

At some Shraddhas the old Dharma-shastras, Akhyanas, Itihasas, and Puranas were recited (III. 232, note, p. 236).

With reference to the subject of diet, it is clear from v. 15. 5, &c., that as a general rule the eating of flesh (*mansa*) and of fish (*matsya*) by twice-born men was prohibited; that the drinking of spirituous liquor was included among the five great sins (see p. 303); and that many other kinds of food, such as garlic, onions, leeks (*lasuna, grinjana, palandu*), mushrooms (*kavaka, chatraka*), and carnivorous birds (*kravyadah pakshinah,* V. II), were forbidden. But it is an argument for the antiquity of Manu's Law-book that it directs flesh-meat (*amisha*)to be eaten at some of these Shraddhas

---

1. In Book III. 145 we have *yatnena bhojayec chraddhe bahv-ricam veda-paragam,* see p. 229. Manu, however, discouraged too much feasting (*vistara*), and limited the number of guests, see III. 125, 126.
2. That of the Bengali millionaire, Ramdoolal Dey, cost £50,000, according to Mr. Wheeler.

(III. 123, IV. 131). I annex a few interesting passages which bear upon the killing of animals for sacrifice and the eating of flesh-meat under certain circumstances:

Never let a Brahman eat the flesh of cattle unconsecrated with Mantras, but let him eat it only when hallowed with texts of the Veda (IV. 36).

On a solemn offering to a guest (*madhu-parka*) at a sacrifice, and in holy rites to departed ancestors or to the gods — on these occasions and no other may cattle be slain (V. 41).

As many hairs as grow on any animal, so many similar deaths shall one who slays it unnecessarily (*vritha*) endure hereafter from birth to birth. By the Self-existent himself were animals created for sacrifice, which was ordained for the welfare (*bhutyai*) of all this universe; therefore slaughter of animals for sacrifice is no slaughter (V. 38, 39)[1].

In eating meat (*mansa-bhakshane*) and in drinking wine (*madye*) there is no crime (provided it be on a lawful occasion, V. 56).

Hospitality is enjoined on the householder, in the strongest language, as religious duty (see also p. 318):

No guest (*atithi*) who arrives in the evening, brought by the setting sun (*suryodhah*), must be dismissed. Whether he arrives in season or out of season, let him be allowed to sojourn in the house and be well entertained.

A Brahman sojourning in a house and not honoured takes to himself all the merit of the householder's good deeds (III. 100).

Let the householder not eat anything himself till he has made his guest eat. The honouring of a guest confers wealth, reputation, life, and heaven (III. 105, 106. Compare also IV. 29).

An oblation (of food) in the fire of a Brahman's mouth delivers (the offerer) from great guilt (III. 98).

---

1. This is another indication of the priority of at least part of Manu's Code to the general spread of Buddhism, which reformation led to the almost total abolition of animal sacrifice in India.

With regard to the householder's wife and the condition
of women as depicted by Manu, we may observe that their
position is one of entire subordination, amounting, in theory,
to a complete abnegation of what in these days would be
called 'women's rights.' But although it is certain that the
inferiority of woman is a fixed Oriental dogma which no
contact with Europeans is likely entirely to eradicate, yet it
must be borne in mind that the practice does not always
conform to the theory. The influence of Hindu mothers in
their own families, and the respect paid to them by their
children, have always been great; and it is one indication of
the antiquity of Manu's Code that, although some of its
precepts pronounce women unfit for independence, and
debarred from the study of the Veda, others concede to them
an amount of freedom to which they became strangers in
times subsequent to the influx of Mohammedan customs[1]. In
some cases a girl, if unmarried for three years, is even allowed
to choose her own husband[2], when she is called Svayam-vara
(IX. 90, 92). It is very true that Manu distinctly directs (V.
162, IX. 47, 65) that no second husband is to be allowed to
widows, but he nowhere alludes to that exaggerated devotion
which induced the Sati or 'devoted wife' to burn herself with
her husband's body — a custom which from about the time
of Alexander's invasion[3], more than 300 years B.C., till the

---

1. The seclusion of Hindu women is chiefly due to the introduction
   of Muslim customs when the Mohammedans invaded India.
2. Girls of the Kshatriya class sometimes chose their own husbands, as
   we know from the story of Nala and other episodes of the
   Mahabharata.
3. It is clear from Strabo XV. 30 and 62 that Sati prevailed in India
   about the time of Alexander. Strabo says that the Kathaei
   (= Kanyakubja or perhaps Kshatriya), a tribe in the Panjab, in order
   to prevent wives poisoning their husbands made a law that they
   should be burnt with them when they died and that some wives burnt
   themselves voluntarily. Compare also Diodorus Siculus (XIX. 33),

THE LAW-BOOKS — MANU   283

year 1829, has led to the sacrifice of innumerable lives, and
has left a blot on the annals of our own administration[1].

---

who describes how, after the battle between Antiochus and Eumenes,
one of the wives of the Indian general (*Keteus* = Ketu or Khatri?)
burnt herself, after contending with the other for the honour. But
Arrian makes no mention of any Sati. He only describes (VII. 2,3)
Kalanos how (perhaps = Sanskrit Kalyana), one of a sect of Indian
wise men who went naked, burnt himself upon a pile. The description
is like that of the self-cremation of the ascetic Sarabhanga in Ramayana
III. 9. Cf. Cicero, Tusc. Disp. II. 22 and de Divin. I. 23. The following
is a portion of the latter passage: 'Est profecto quiddam etiam in
barbaris gentibus praesentiens, atque divinans: siquidem and mortem
proficiscens Calanus Indus, cum adscenderet in rogum ardentem, O
praeclarum discessum, inquiet, e vita!' The idea of Sati seems to have
been borrowed by the Hindus from the Scythians (Herod. IV. 71).
A similar custom prevailed among the Thracians (Herod. V. 5). Cf.
also Propertius III. 13, 'Ardent victrices, et flammae pectora praebent,
Imponuntque suis ora perusta viris.' Madri, wife of Pandu, became
a Sati (Mahabharata, Adi-parva 4896). Compare Dr. Rost's edition
of Wilson's Works, vol. ii. pp. 270-309.

1. The practice of Sati was for a long time thought to be so intimately
connected with the religious belief of the Hindus, that our Government
did not venture to put a stop to it. It was known to be enjoined
in the Brahman-purana and Codes of Vyasa, Angiras, &c.; and such
authorities as Colebrooke (see his life by his son, p. 287) and H.H.
Wilson (in 1828) gave their opinion against interference, although
it was ascertained that neither the Veda nor Manu directed or even
hinted at concremation of the living wife with the dead husband.
To Raghu-nandan (according to Dr. F. Hall) is due the alteration of
the last word of a Rig-veda text (X. 18. 7, see p. 229) on which
the authority for Sati was made to rest: *Anasravo 'namivah su-ratna
a rohantu janayo yonim egre,* 'without tears, without sorrow, bedecked
with jewels, let the wives go up to the altar first,' where *agneh,* 'of
fire,' was substituted for *agre,* 'first.'(compare pp. 224, 229, 230.)
It is true that our Government adopted a middle course, and prohibited
the burning of the widow, except under strict regulations, and except
with her own full consent; and officials were to be present to see
the rules enforced; but I have been informed by a distinguished
friend (Mr. Seton-Karr) who held high offices in India, that, in

Indeed, the marriage of widows is even spoken of as practised, though reprehended (IX. 66-68); and a damsel given away in marriage may be re-betrothed, if her husband dies before she is actually married (69).

The following passages will be sufficient to fill up the picture of Hindu domestic life (see also p. 319-320):

Day and night must women be made to feel their dependence on their husbands. But if they are fond of worldly amusements (*vishayeshu sajjantyah*), let them be allowed to follow their own inclinations (IX. 2).

Even if confined at home by faithful guardians they are not (really) guarded; but those women who guard themselves by their own will (*atmanam atmana yas tu raksheyuh*) are well guarded (IX. 12).

Let not (a husband) eat with his wife, nor look at her eating (IV. 43).

Women have no business to repeat texts of the Veda (*nasti strinam kriya manstrair*), thus is the law established (X. 18).

Domestic rites are to be performed in common with a wife (*sadharano dharmah, patnya saha*), so it is ordained in the Veda (IX. 96).

No sacrifice is permitted to women separately (from their husbands), no religious observance (*vratam*), no fasting (*uposhitam*). As far as a wife obeys her husband so far is she exalted in heaven (V. 155).

A husband must continually be revered (*upacharyah*) as a god (*deva-vat*) by a virtuous wife (V. 154).

A virtuous wife who remains unmarried after the death of her husband goes to heaven, even though she have no son (V. 160).

---

consequence of our half-sanction, the number of widows actually returned as burnt, rose in one year to 800, while in other years (between 1815 and 1828) it varied from 300 to 600. Lord William Bentinck passed a law in 1829 (Reg. xvii) which suppressed the practice with entire success and without difficulty.

We have already indicated that in the third and fourth periods of his life a Brahman, according to Manu, is to become first an anchorite (*vanaprastha*) and then a religious mendicant (*bhikshu* or *parivrajaka*). It is indeed wholly improbable that all Brahmans conformed to this rule, but the second verse of the sixth Book prescribes that when the father of a family perceives his hair to be turning grey, or as soon as his first grandchild is born, and after he has paid his three debts[1], he is to retire to a forest and there as a hermit to practise austerities:

Having taken up his sacred fire (*agni-hotram*) and all the domestic utensils for making oblations to it, and having gone forth from the town to the forest, let him dwell there with all his organs of sense well restrained (VI. 4).

With many kinds of pure food let him perform the five Maha-yajnas or 'devotional rites' (VI. 5).

Let him also offer the Vaitanika oblations with the (three sacred) fires according to rule (see p. 216, also notes).

Let him roll backwards and forwards on the ground, or stand all day on tiptoe (*prapadaih*), let him move about by alternately standing up and sitting down, going to the waters to bathe at the three Savanas (sunrise, sunset, and midday, VI. 22. See last para of p. 271).

Let him practise the rules of the lunar penance (VI. 20. See p. 114).

In the hot weather let him be a Pancha-tapas (VI. 23. See p. 1 13).

Let him offer libations (*tarpayet*) to the gods and Pitris, performing ablutions at the three Savanas (VI. 24).

---

1. These three debts (*trini rinani*) are, 1. to the gods, 2. to the Pitris, 3. to the Rishis. The 1st is liquidated by sacrifices, the 2nd by begetting a son for performance of the Shraddha, the 3rd by repetition of the Veda.

Having consigned the three sacred fires (*vaitanan*) to his own person (by swallowing the ashes) according to prescribed rules, let him remain without fire, without habitation, feeding on roots and fruits, practising the vow of a Muni (.e. the *Mauna-vrata* of perpetual silence, VI. 25).

Book VI. 33 directs him for the fourth period of his life to wander about as a Bhikshu or Parivrajaka, 'religious mendicant' (*chaturtham ayusho bhagam parivrajet*). Here are a few rules for the regulation of this final stage of his existence, when he is sometimes called a *Sannyasin,* 'one who has given up the world;' sometimes a *Yati,* 'one who has suppressed his passions[1]:'

Let him remain without fire, without habitation (a-niketah); let him resort once a day to the town for food, regardless of

---

1. I find that some of M. Barth's remarks in the 'Revue Critique' for June 13, 1874, bear on what I have stated with regard to Manu's ordinances in the preceding pages: 'Si nous remontous plus haut, aux livres vediques, aux plus anciens comme aux plus modernes, nous trouvons la nation Indienne divisee en un grand nombre de petites principautes, ou domine le principe ethnique de la peuplade et du clan. Cette organisation qui n'avait certainment pas beaucoup change a l'epque du Buddha, s'accorde encore moins avec le systeme de Manu, qui suppose une certaine uniformite et l'existence de grand etats. La plupart de ces peuplades avaient sans doute un etate social analogue: de temps immemorial elles etaient divisees en 4 classes ... Mais il est difficile de preciser le degre de rigueur de cette division. Encore a ne epoque relativement recente (Chandog. Up. iv. 4. 2) la plus jalouse, et la plus fermee de ces classes, celle des Brahmanes, ne parait pas tres scrupuleuse quant a la purete du sang. Je ne puis donc voir autre chose dans la theorie officielle de la caste qu'une sorte de theme convenu don't il faut faire usage avec la plus grande prudence, theme don't la donnee fondamentale a du, parce qu'elle etait consacree par une tradition sainte, se preter successivement, et d'une façon plus ou moins artificielle a l'explication d'etats de societe bien differents.'

hardships, resolute, keeping a vow of silence (*muni*), fixing his mind in meditation (VI. 43).

With hair, nails and beard well clipped, carrying a bowl (*patri*), a staff (*dandi*), and a pitcher (*kusumbhavan*), let him wander about continually, intent on meditation and avoiding injury to any being (VI. 52).

In this manner, having little by little (*shanaih shanaih*) abandoned all worldly attachments (*sangan*), and freed himself from all concern about pairs of opposites[1] (*dvandva*), he obtains absorption into the universal Spirit (*brahmany avatishthate*, VI. 81).

IV. Let us now note, in the fourth place, the chief characteristics of Manu's ordinances of government and judicature (*vyavahara*), and a few of the most remarkable civil and penal laws and rules of evidence[2]. The treatment of these subjects, which ought to constitute the most important department of a code of laws, is only commenced by Manu in the second half of his work, and is chiefly comprised in one quarter of it, viz. the seventh, eighth, and ninth Books. As the state of society depicted in the first six Books is of a simple and primitive character, recognizing only four principal divisions of the people, so the only form of government prescribed in the seventh Book is of a paternal and patriarchal description. The king is to rule by divine right, and though a despot, to act like a father[3] towards his subjects (*varteta pitri-van nrishu*, VII. 80). That he was treated as a kind of divinity is evident:

The Creator created a king for the protection of the whole world by drawing forth eternal particles (*matrah shashvatih*)

---

1. Such as honour and dishonour (*manapamana*), joy and sorrow, &c.
2. I have here consulted Elphinstone's and Mill's India.
3. Compare Shakuntala, Act V: *Tvayi parisamaptam bandhu-krityam prajanam*, 'in thee (the king) is comprehended the whole duty of a kinsman towards thy subject.' Is said to be = Sanskr *dasapati*, 'lord of conquered races.'

from the essence of Indra, Anila (Wind), Yama (god of justice), Surya (Sun), Agni (Fire), Varuna, Chandra (Moon), and Kuvera (god of wealth, VII. 3, 4).

A king, even though a child, must not be treated with contempt, as if he were a mortal; he is a great divinity in human shape (VII. 8).

He is directed to appoint seven or eight ministers (VII. 54) and to consult them first apart, and then collectively, as a kind of council. His prime minister (VII. 58) is to be a Brahman[1], and in him he is to place implicit confdence (59). He is to have a standing army (VII. 102, 103), commander-in-chief (VII. 65), and an ambassador (*dutah*) of great knowledge and abilities (VII. 63). The following is very significant:

Determination not to retreat in battle (*sangrameshu anivartitvam*), protection of the people, and obedience (*shushrusha*) to Brahmans is the highest duty of kings and secures their felicity in heaven (VII. 88).

The king's mode of life and the distribution of his time are carefully regulated (VII. 145, &c.). He is to rise˙in the last watch of the night, then to hold a court, then to assemble his council and deliberate on the affairs of his kingdom and all the eightfold business of kings (VII. 154); after that, to engage in manly exercises, then to dine, taking care that his food is not poisoned (VII. 218), and then to regulate his family; after that, he is allowed some relaxation; then he is to review his troops; then to perform religious exercises; and lastly, being himself well armed, to receive the report of his

---

1. This rule was followed by Shivaji in the constitution of the Marathi empire, and the Peshwa or chief of the eight Pradhanas, 'principal ministers,' ultimately superseded Sivaji's weak successors and usurped the supremacy.

spies (*cara*), informers and secret emissaries (*pranidhi*), who are regarded as of great importance[1]. He is to conclude the day by a frugal meal and musical recreations, and to go to bed early (VII. 225)[2]. The rule for diplomacy and war show that India was divided into a number of unequal states. Intrigues are to be carried on with the leaders of the enemy, and negotiation is declared to be better than force. (VII. 197, 198). In battle the king is to set an example of personal bravery (VII. 87). The chief weapon is the bow (VII.74). Elephants, chariots, cavalry, and infantry form the *Chaturanga* or 'fourfold army[3],' and minute directions are given for its marching (VII. 187, &c.).

With regard to internal administration, it is clear from the Code that the country was partitioned into divisions

---

1. In IX. 256 a king is called *chara-chakshuh*, 'spy-eyed.'
2. The royal office was no sinecure. This is evident from the Mahabharata and Dasha-kumara-charita as well as from Manu. It appears that the day and night were each divided into eight portions of one hour and a half each, reckoned from sunrise, and thus distributed. Day — 1. the king being dressed is to audit accounts; 2. he is to pronounce judgments in appeals; 3. he is to breakfast; 4. he is to receive and make presents; 5. he is to discuss political questions with his ministers; 6. he is to amuse himself; 7. he is to review his troops; 8. he is to hold a military council. Night — 1. he is to receive the reports of his spies and envoys; 2. he is to dine; 3. he is to retire to rest after the perusal of some sacred work; 4 and 5. he is to sleep; 6. he is to rise and purify himself; 7. he is to hold a private consultation with his ministers and instruct his officers; 8. he is to attend upon the Purohita or 'family priest' for the performance of religious ceremonies (Wilson's Hindu Theatre, 1. 209). Megasthenes (Strabo XV. 1, 55) says that the Indian king may not sleep in the day-time, but continues the whole day judging causes. Compare Macaulay's account of the daily life of Frederic the Great (Essays, p. 805).
3. In VII. 185 a sixfold (*shad-vidha*) army is spoken of, the two other component parts being officers and attendants.

governed by vicegerents, to whom the king delegated his own despotic powers, and whose authority was again delegated to other subordinate governors, who again divided their power by committing it to other rulers of townships in a regular chain, the highest governor ruling over a thousand towns, the next over a hundred, the next over twenty, the next over ten (cf. St. Luke xix. 17), and the lowest ruling over one town:

Let the lord of one town (*gramikah*) notify of his own accord, and in due order, to the lord of ten towns (*grama-dasheshaya*) any crimes which have taken place in his own district, and the lord of ten to the lord of twenty; let the lord of twenty notify everything to the lord of a hundred, and the lord of a hundred to the lord of a thousand (VII. 116, 117).

Another important subject is revenue, which the monarch is to obtain from the following sources: 1. Taxes on the produce of land, which was probably held in common by village communities, though occasional grants may have been made to individuals, the king being theoretically the only absolute proprietor of the soil (*bhumer adhipatih*, VIII. 39)[1] 2. Taxes on the produce of labour. 3. Taxes on certain metals and commodities added to capital stock. 4. Taxes on purchases and sales. 5. A kind of poll-tax. 6. Another kind paid in labour.

With regard to 1, the usual proportion of produce taken by the king was a sixth part, but in times of necessity (as of war or invasion), he might even take a fourth of the crops. But, even though dying for want of money, he is never to

---

1. In later times a sort of middle-man, to whom the name *Zamindar* (introduced by the Mohammedans) is applied, acquired an ownership nearly absolute in the soil; or, at any rate, intervened between the Ryot or 'cultivator' and the king, receiving a share of the produce from the former and paying a stipulated proportion to the sovereign.

receive a tax from a Brahman conversant with the Veda (VII. 133) [1]. The following passages illustrate the above six heads of taxation:

1. A sixth, an eight, or a twelfth part of grain may be taken by the king (according to the goodness or badness of the soil, VII. 130).

The king who, without giving protection, takes a sixth part of the grain as tax (*bali*) is declared to draw upon himself all the sins of all his subjects (VIII. 308).

A military king (*kshatriyah*) who takes even a fourth part in a time of necessity (*apadi*) while protecting his subjects to the utmost of his ability is freed from all culpability (X. 118).

2. Moreover, he may take a sixth part of the annual increase of trees (*dru*), meat, honey, clarified butter, perfumes, medicinal herbs, liquids, flowers, roots, and fruits, of leaves (*patra*), pot-herbs (*shaka*), grass, wicker-work (*vaidala*), hides, earthenware vessels, and all articles made of stone (VII. 131, 132).

3. Of cattle and gold and silver (*hiranyayho*) added to the capital stock (*mulad adhikayoh*), a fiftieth part may be taken by the king (VII. 130).

Of old treasures and precious metals in the earth the king may take one half, because he protects his subjects and is the paramount lord of the soil (VIII. 39).

4. Having well considered the rates of purchase and sale, the length of transit (*adhvanam*), with cost of food &c. on the journey (*saparivyayam*),the profit gained, and expense of insurance (*yoga-kshemam*), let him make merchants pay taxes on their commodities (VII. 127).

---

1. In Shakuntala, Act II, Mathavya says to the king, 'Say you have come for the sixth part of their grain which they owe you for tribute.' The Mahabharata allows secularized Brahmans to be taxed. Strabo (XV. 1, 40) says, 'the whole land belongs to the king, but the Indians work it on condition of receiving the fourth part of the crops'.

5. The king should cause the lower classes (*prithag-janam* = *nikrishta-janam,* Kulluka) in his kingdom, who live by petty trading, to pay some small sum (per head) in the name of the annual tax (VII. 137).

6. The king should cause inferior artisans and artificers (such as blacksmiths, &c.) and men of the servile class (*shudran*), who support themselves by their own labour, to work for one day in every month (VII. 138).

As regards the administration of justice, this is also to be performed by the king in person, aided by Brahmans or else by a Brahman acting as his deputy, assisted by three others (VIII. 9, 10). In Book VII. 14 we read:

For the use of the king the great Creator (*Isvarah*) created in the beginning his own son Justice, composed of particles of his own divine essence, to act as the protector of all creatures (by wielding) the rod of punishment.

The terrible consequences of neglecting to wield this rod are described in VII. 20, &c. (see p. 320). The king is not to encourage litigation (*notpadayet karyam*, VIII. 43). Nevertheless, he is to be ready every day to decide causes in the court (*sabha*) when brought before him. The mode of conducting a trial is simple and patriarchal. In VIII. 23 we read:

Let the king, having seated himself on the judgment-seat, with his body suitably attired and his mind collected (*samahitah*), and having offered homage (*pranamya*) to the gods who are guardians of the world, commence the trial of causes (*karya-darshana*). (Cf. Strabo XV. 1, 55.)

The litigant parties are to be heard in person, and the plaintiff's accusation is to be made *viva voce*. The witnesses are to be examined by the judge, who is to observe their countenances carefully (VIII. 25, 26). In his decision the judge is to attend to local usage, established practice (*achara*), the decisions of former judges (VIII. 45, 46), and written codes of law (*shastra*, VIII. 3).

Let me pass on to notice the broad features of the civil and criminal code. It is, of course, very desirable that the distinction between civil and criminal laws should be clearly marked out. They are, however, mixed together very confusedly in the eighteen heads or divisions of law given by Manu (Book VII. 4-7) as follows:

The eighteen titles or branches of law are: 1. Recovery of debts (*rinadanam*); 2. deposits (*nikshepah*); 3. sale of property by one who is not the rightful owner (*asvami-vikrayah*); 4. engaging in business after joining partnership, association in trade (*sambhuya samutthanam*); 5. non-delivery of what has been given (*dattasyanapakarma*); 6. nonpayment of wages (*vetanasya adanam*); 7. breach of contract (*samvido vyatikramah*); 8. annulling of purchase or sale (*kraya-vikrayanushayah*); 9. disputes between the owner and tender of cattle or between master and servant (*vivadah svamipalayoh*); 10. the law respecting disputes about boundaries (*sima-vivada-dharmah*); 11, 12. the two kinds of assault, viz. blows and abuse, or assault with blows and assault with slander (*parushye-danda-vachike*); 13. theft and larceny (*steyam*); 14. robbery with violence (*sahasam*); 15. adultery (*stri-sangrahanam*); 16. the law regulating (the duties of) husband and wife (*stri-pun-dharmah*); 17. partition of patrimony or inheritance (*vibhagah*); 18. gambling with dice and betting on animals, such as fighting-cocks (*dyutam ahvayash cha.*).

The first nine of the above titles and the sixteenth and seventeenth belong to civil law; those from the eleventh to the fifteenth, and the eighteenth relate to criminal law; the tenth belongs partly to civil, partly to criminal. With reference to the whole arrangement of the subject, Mr. James Mill's History of India (vol. i. p. 195, &c.) has some valuable remarks, the substance of which I here give:

Though no arrangement would appear more natural than the division of laws into *civil* and *penal,* we find them here mixed together. Another obvious ground of division — the distinction between the laws about *persons* and the laws about *things* — which prevailed in Roman law and was transferred, rude as it was, to English, seems never to have occurred to Hindu lawyers in the time of Manu. The first nine of the heads in Manu's arrangement relate to contracts, but the division is rude and imperfect. It begins with 'Loans,' one of the most refined of contracts. The subject of 'purchase and sale' is divided into two parts, but one occupies the third place in the list, the other the eighth, and a number of heterogeneous subjects intervene. 'Partnership' occupies a middle place between two subjects, to neither of which it has any relation. 'Non-payment of wages' stands immediately before 'Breach of contact,' as a separate title, though it ought to be included under that head. In fact, this seventh head is so general that it comprehends the whole subject of contracts. When the subject of contracts is ended, the principal branches of criminal law are introduced. After these and some other topics follows the great subject of inheritance[1].

Under the head of *Civil Law* the most interesting of Manu's ordinances are on the important subject of *property,* whether acquired by possession or occupancy (*labha, bhukti, bhoga*), by purchase (*kraya*), by contract (*samvid, vyavahara*), by labour (*karma-yoga*), by donation (*pratigraha*), by inheritance (*daya*). I note the following:

He who has acquired any property through the sale of it (*vikrayat*) in the presence of a number (of buyers and sellers) justly obtains the right to that property by reason of having paid the purchase money (VIII. 201).

---

1. In consulting Mr. James Mill I have found that some of his statements must be taken with considerable qualification, prejudiced as he appears to have been against everything Hindu.

The property of infants who are heirs let the king hold in trust until the owner has completed his term of studentship or till he is of age (at sixteen, VIII. 27).

Let the king fix the rate of the sale purchase of all marketable commodities (*sarva-panyanam*), after having considered the distance (from which they have been imported), the remoteness of the place to which they are sent, the time they are kept, and the gain or loss upon them. Once in every five nights or once a fortnight he should fix the proper rate in the presence of those (who understand it, VIII. 401, 402).

A lost article, when found, should be guarded by trusty men. Any thieves convicted of stealing it should be condemned to be trampled to death by the royal elephant (VIII. 34).

It is evidence of a somewhat rude state of society that in certain cases a man is allowed to repent of a bargain and to have a contract annulled, thus:

When a man has bought or sold anything (not perishable, such as land or copper), and may afterwards repent, he may restore it or take it back within ten days (*antar-dashahat*, VIII. 222).

Marriage is regarded as a contract, but the same liberty of annulling is in this case not allowed:

If a man shall give away in marriage a girl who has any defects (*doshavatim*) without notifying, the king must fine him ninety-six Panas (*kuryad dandam shannavatim panan*, VIII. 224).

The repetition of the nuptial text (*panigrahanika mantrah*) are the settled mark (*niyatam lakshanam*) of a marriage contract. Of those texts (the one) repeated on (making) the seventh step (viz. *sakha saptapadi bhava*, see p. 200, 1. 7) is decided by the wise to be (the sign of) the completion (*nishtha*) of the contract (VIII. 227).

Throughout Eastern countries, especially in ancient times, the insecurity of property has led to two practices little resorted to by the peoples of modern Europe, viz. concealment of valuable articles and the habit of entrusting them for safety to the keeping of others. We can understand, therefore, the importance assigned in Manu's Law-book (Book VIII. 179, &c.) to the subject of 'deposits' or, according to legal phraseology, 'bailments.' This branch of law opens thus:

A wise man should make a deposit (*nikshepam nikshipet*) with a person of good family, of good conduct, acquainted with law, a speaker of truth, possessing numerous relations, wealthy and honourable (VIII. 179).

If a bailee (*nyasa-dharin*) fail to restore a deposit, and there are no witnesses, the judge is to cause secret agents (*pranidhi*) to deposit gold with him, and should he fail to redeliver it, he is to be made to pay (*dapyah*) the equivalent of both deposits (VIII. 181-184).

Another proof of a primitive state of society may be found in the rules respecting interest and the premium paid for the use of borrowed property. This is sometimes allowed to be paid in kind[1]; as, for instance, when grain, fruit, wool, animals, &c., have been borrowed, showing that coined money was still uncommon as a general circulating medium. (Compare the mention of *nanaka*, 'coin,' in the later Code of Yajnavalkyá II. 241.)

Interest on money (*kusida-vriddhih*) received all at once (and not by the month, &c.) must not exceed the double (of the sum lent)[2] on grain (*dhanye*), fruit (*sade*), wool (*lave*), and beasts of burden (*vahye*) it must not exceed five times the value (*pancata*, VIII. 151).

---

1. Compare Deut. xxiii. 19, 20, 'thou shalt not lend upon usury to thy brother; usury of money, usury of victuals, usury of anything that is lent upon usury: unto a stranger thou mayest lend upon usury,' &c.
2. Principal doubled by accumulated interest is called in *Marathi Damdupat*. Even now a village Mahajan will take from 50 to 75 per cent.

The rate of interest (*vriddhi*) is not only high, but varies according to the class of the man to whom anything is lent; but compound interest (*chakra-vriddhi*) is not approved (VIII. 153):

A money-lender (*vardhushikah*) may take two per cent (*dvikam satam*) as interest per month from a Brahman, three (*trikam*) from a Kshatriya, four (*chatushkam*) from a Vaishya, and five (*panchakam*) from a Shudra, in the order of the classes (VIII. 142).

In VIII. 156, 157, there is a law bottomry, which is interesting as showing that sea-voyages were undertaken in Manu's time.

The recovery of debts is enforced by stringent laws, and the debtor is not only made to pay what he owes, but an additional fine to the king, thus[1]:

When a debt has to be pad (*rine deye*) which is admitted to be just, the debtor owes a fine of five per cent (*panchakam shatam*) in addition, and ten per cent if it be repudiated (though it be just, VIII. 139).

The laws respecting herdsmen (*pashu-pala*) and their employers (*svamin*) are carefully laid down (VIII. 229, &c.). I note one instance (VIII. 232):

The herdsman himself must restore an animal that has been lost (*nashta*), or destroyed by vermin (*krimibhih*), or killed by dogs, or has perished by falling into a hole (*vishame*)

---

1. No sanction, however, is given by Manu to the later practice of *Dharna* or 'sitting at the door of a house to compel payment of a debt.' The person so sitting refuses to eat, and as long as he does so the debtor must abstain from food too, and if the suitor perishes the crime of his death falls on the debtor. Originally the person sitting in Dharna, either on his own behalf or that of another, was a Brahman. See H.H. Wilson's Glossary of Indian Terms.

through want of his having exerted himself to save it (*hinam purusha-karena*).

We may also observe that the hire of some kinds of agricultural labourers is directed to be paid in kind[1]:

That hired herdsman whose hire is paid with milk must be allowed by the owner of the cattle to milk the best cow out of ten (*dashato-varam*), unless he be paid with some other kind of food (VIII. 231).

The most important subject connected with property is the law of inheritance (*daya*), treated of in the ninth Book of Manu's Code. And here we cannot fail to be struck with the remarkable circumstance that Hindu law does not allow the owner of property any testamentary power[2]. Indeed, a proper word for 'will' or 'testament' does not exist in the Sanskrit language. It must be borne in mind that in a patriarchal state of society all family property was supposed to be held in common by a sort of joint ownership, the father or principal person in a household being regarded as a head partner.

In India, where customs become stereotyped for centuries, this primitive idea of a common title to the family property has continued to prevail up to recent times. The family is, as we have seen, a corporate society, whose bond of union is the sacred oblation offered in common by its living to its deceased members. On the death of a father the sons or nearest relatives succeed to the inheritance by simple right of *Sa-pindaship*, that is, by a right obtained through the

---

1. Payments in kind in aid of money wages are not unusual even in the present day. Even quite recently in British territory the land-tax was sometimes paid in kind, and is still so paid in some native states.
2. Our Government made this legal by the Hindu Wills Act (xxi. of 1870). Certain peculiar documents, however, resembling wills, but bearing other titles, were previously recognized by our courts.

common offering of rice-cakes (*pinda*) and of water &c. to a deceased father, grandfather, and great grandfather at the Shraddha ceremonies (see p. 278). It must be noted, however, that although the whole family has a joint-interest in the property, the estate cannot be divided during the lifetime of the parents, and even at their death the eldest son is allowed to take the father's place as chief manager of the family partnership, thus:

The eldest brother may take the paternal property (*pitryam dhanam*)entirely (into his own hands). The rest of the family (*sheshah*) may live under him (*tam upajiveyuh*) exactly as they lived under the father (IX. 105).

An eldest brother conducting himself as he ought (towards his younger brothers) is to be regarded by them as a mother and father (IX. 110).

Nevertheless, the brothers are allowed, if they like, to separate, and full directions are given in Book IX. 112 &c. for the partition of the family estate; a distinction being made according to merit as well as age, and some being, very unjustly according to our ideas, disqualified:

After the death of the father and mother, the brothers having assembled together may make a partition of the paternal property, but they have no power to do so during the lifetime of their parents (IX. 104).

Either let them live together (*sahavaseyuh*) or separately, from religious motives; since the number of religious rites (such as the five Maha-yajnah, see p. 275) are increased by separation of households, therefore separation is legal (IX. 111).

The portion taken out (of the estate) by the eldest son is a twentieth, along with the best of all the chattels; by the middles son, a fortieth; and by the youngest, an eighteenth (IX. 112).

A deduction (*uddhara*) being thus made, the remainder should be allotted among the brothers in equal shares; if no deduction is made they should share in the following manner: Let the eldest takes a double share and the next born a share and a half (if they excel in learning and merit), and let the younger sons have a share each (IX. 116, 117).

Those brothers who are addicted to vicious habits (such as gambling, licentiousness, &c.) forfeit a right (*narhanti*) to any share in the inheritance (IX. 214).

Impotent persons (*kliva*), those who have lost caste (*patita*), those who are blind, deaf, insane, paralyzed (*jada*), dumb, defective in limb or sense, are also debarred from sharing (IX. 201).

But a wise heir will in common justice supply all such persons with food and raiment (*grasacchadanam*) to the best of his ability. Otherwise he is guilty of a great crime (IX. 202).

It must be observed that women are generally excluded from a direct title to share in the division of property:

Three persons are declared to have no property of their own (*a-dhanah*), a wife, a son, and a slave. Whatever money they earn is his to whom they belong (VIII. 416).

Nevertheless, some marriage portions (*sulka*) or gifts received by a married woman at and after the nuptial ceremony, are regarded as her own peculiar property. These constitute what is still called (*Stri-dhana*[1], 'a woman's (separate) wealth or dower,' which, according to Manu, is sixfold:

Whatever was given over the nuptial fire (*adhy-agni*), whatever she receives while being led in procession from her father's to

---

1. Commonly written Stridhun. Mr. Herbert Cowell, in his Tagore Law Lectures for 1871 (p. 28), says, that although this property is supposed to belong exclusively to a wife, the husband has a concurrent power over it, so that he may use it in any exigency, without being held accountable for it. Stri-dhana is now, however, acquired 'by gift, by earnings, and by inheritance,' and the Dayabhaga lays down that the husband has power over the wife's earnings and 'any presents she may receive from any other but kindred.'

her husband's house (*adhyavahanikam*), a gift (from her husband) in token of affection (*priti*), and a similar gift received from her brother, from her mother, from her father, all these are declared to be a woman's own property (IX. 194).

Those young girls, too, who are unmarried (*kanyah*) at a father's death are directed (IX. 118) to receive an allotment out of the shares accruing to their brothers. The following also (IX. 130) is noteworthy:

A man's own son is even as himself, and a daughter is like a son. How, then (if he have no son), ought any one else than a daughter, who is part of his own person (*atmani tishthanti*), to inherit his own property?

I pass on to a brief notice of Manu's *Criminal Code*. The three most conspicuous features of his penal laws are exactly those which mark the earliest forms of criminal legislation, viz. severity, inconsistency, and a belief in the supposed justice of the *lex talionis*, the latter leading to punishments which in later times would be considered unjustifiably disproportionate to the offences committed, and sometimes barbarously cruel[1]. Thus:

With whatever member of the body a low-born man may injure a superior, that very member of his must be mutilated (VIII. 279).

_____

1. Mr. Mill on this point quotes Sir W. Jones, who is not, like himself, disposed to view everything Hindu in an unfavourable light. 'The cruel mutilations practised by the native powers are shocking to humanity.' We know what was said by our Lord about 'an eye for an eye and a tooth for a tooth,' Matt. v. 38. See Lev. xxiv. 20, Deut. xix. 21. Compare the laws of Draco and of the ancient Egyptians. Strabo (XV. 1. 54) says of the Hindus, 'he who has given false testimony suffers mutilation of the extremities and he who maims a limb is condemned to suffer maiming.'

A once-born man insulting (*kshipan*) twice-born men with abusive language (*vacha darunaya*) must have his tongue cut (VIII. 270).

Should be mention their name and caste with insulting expressions (as, 'Hallo! there, Yajnadatta, vilest of Brahmans', a red-hot iron spike ten fingers long is to be thrust into his mouth (VIII. 271).

Should he, through arrogance, attempt to instruct a Brahman in his duty (saying, 'you ought to do so and so'), the king is to have boiling oil poured into his mouth and ears (VIII. 272).

Thieves are to have their hands cut off, and then to be impaled on a sharp stake (IX. 276).

A goldsmith detected in committing frauds is to have his body cut to pieces with razors (IX. 292).

Perhaps the most objectionable feature in the penal code is not the cruel retaliation, which was probably more a matter of theory than actual practice, but the leniency with which Brahmans are directed to be treated. It will be observed that a graduated scale is prescribed according to the rank of the offender and the class to which he belongs, thus:

A king must never kill a Brahman, though he may be found guilty of all possible crimes (*sarva-papeshv api sthitam*); let him expel him from the kingdom unharmed in body and intact in all his property. There is no greater injustice on earth than the killing of a Brahman. The king, therefore, must not harbour a thought about putting him to death (VIII. 380, 381).

A Kshatriya insulting a Brahman must be fined a hundred Panas (*satam dandam arhati*); a Vaishya doing the same must pay one hundred and fifty or two hundred Panas; a Shudra doing the same must receive corporal punishment[1] (*badham arhati*, VIII. 267).

---

1. *Badha* might be rendered 'capital punishment,' but Kulluka explains it by 'the lash.'

Five great crimes (*maha-patakani*) are enumerated in Book XI. 54, which are described as entailing the highest degree of guilt, though certainly from a European point of view they cannot all be regarded as equally heinous:

1. Killing a Brahman (*brahma-hatya*); 2. drinking intoxicating liquor (*sura-pana*); 3. stealing gold from a Brahman (*steya*); 4. adultery with the wife of a Guru or spiritual teacher (*guru-anganagamah*); and 5. associating with any one guilty of such sins.

Severe penances voluntarily performed, rather than legal penalties judicially inflicted, are enjoined for some of these crimes (see p. 308); and they are declared in XI. 49 to involve rather singular consequences (*phala*) in future states of existence. Thus for 1. a man will suffer from consumption (*kshaya-rogitvam*) in a future life (see also XI. 73); for 2. he will have discoloured teeth; for 3. diseased nails (*kaunakhyam*)[1].

Moreover, in XII. 54-57, much more awful results are alleged to follow hereafter; inasmuch as those who are guilty of these great crimes are condemned to dwell for a vast number of years in terrible hells (*ghoran narakan*) before entering on new states of being. After protracted torture in one or other of these hells (see p. 246) a Brahman-slayer (*brahma-ha*) must enter the body of a dog, boar, ass, camel, bull, goat, sheep, stag, bird, or outcaste Chandala, according to the degree of his guilt; a spirit-drinker will become a worm, insect, moth, &c.; a gold-stealer will pass a thousand times into the bodies of spiders, snakes, noxious demons, &c. (Compare p. 310).

Some crimes in the second degree are the following:

Falsely asserting oneself to be of too high a caste, falsely accusing a Guru, forgetting texts of the Veda through neglect

---

1. For this reason it is directed in Book III. 153, 154, that consumptive persons and persons with diseased nails (*ku-nakhin*) and discoloured teeth (*syava-dantaka*) ought to be excluded from Sraddha.

of repeating them (*brahmojjhata*), giving false testimony (*kauta-sakshyam*), eating impure food, stealing deposits, incest, intercourse with women of the lowest class.

A long list of crimes in the third degree (*upapataka*) is given in XI. 59-66. Some of them are:

Killing a cow (*go-badhah*); neglect of repetition of the Veda (i.e. of the daily Brahma-yajna); neglect of the sacred fire; usury (*vardhu-shyam*); selling a tank or garden or wife or child; neglecting investiture (*vratyata*); superintendence over mines of any kind (*sarvakareshv adhi-karah*); cutting down green trees for fuel; performing religious rites for selfish motives (*atmartha*); reading infidel books (*asach-chhastradhi-gamanam*); addiction to music and dancing (*kausilavyasya kriya*); atheism (*nastikyam*).

For many of these crimes also voluntary penances constitute the only punishment. Thus the killer of a cow must undergo great hardships and make atonement by attending upon a herd, guarding them from injury, following them day and night in all weathers for three months, swallowing the dust raised by their hoofs, &c. (XI. 108-115).

Trial by ordeal (*divya*) is recognized by Manu, though the ten different forms of it are not all specified as in later works[1]:

Let him cause a man (whose veracity is doubted) to take hold of fire or dive under water (*apsu nimajjayet*), or touch the heads

---

1. These ten forms (some of which are given by Yajnavalkya, see p. 300) are — 1. *Tula*, 'the balance;' 2. *Agni*, 'fire;'3. *Jala*, 'water;' 4. *Visha*, 'poison;' 5. *Kosha*, 'drinking water in which an idol has been washed;' 6. *Tandula*, 'ejecting chewed rice-grains;' 7. *Tapta-masha*, 'taking a Masha weight of gold out of heated oil;' 8. *Phala*, 'holding a hot ploughshare;' 9. *Dharmadharma*, 'drawing concealed images of virtue and vice out of a vessel filled with earth;' 10. *Tulasi*, 'holding the leaves of holy basil.' This holy basil is said to be sacred to Vishnu.

of his wife and sons one by one. The man whom flaming fire burns not and water forces not up (*apo nonmajjayanti*), and who suffers no harm, must be instantly held innocent of perjury (VIII. 114. 115).

It remains to notice a few of the laws of evidence. Fearful denunciations are pronounced against those who deliver false testimony in a court of justice (VIII. 82). The strictest rules are also to be observed in selecting witnesses competent to give trustworthy evidence (see p. 322). At least three witnesses are required to establish a fact in dispute:

If a man is summoned (*kritavasthah*) by a creditor for a debt and denies it when questioned, he is to be proved guilty by three witnesses at least (*try-avaraih sakshibhih*) in the presence of a Brahman appointed by the king[1] (VIII. 60).

Witnesses are to deliver their testimony *viva voice*, and no directions are give about written documents, which makes it probable that this kind of evidence, though fully recognized by Yajnavalkya (see p. 333), was not received, or at least not usual, at the early epoch when Manu's Law-book was composed. If the testimony is contradictory, the judge is to decide by the majority of credible witnesses. If the number of witnesses is equal, he is to be guided by the testimony of those who are most distinguished for virtuous qualities (VIII. 73). A similar rule is propounded by Yajnavalkya (see p. 334). It is a noteworthy point that women are, as a rule, debarred from giving evidence, except for women (VIII. 68). Moreover, the distinctions between the credibility of witnesses must strike a European mind as somewhat extraordinary and whimsical. A man who has male offspring is thought more worthy of credence than a man who has female (VIII. 62),

---

1. Compare Yajnavalkya's rules about witnesses, which are a development of those of Manu. See p. 334.

perhaps because he is supposed to have a greater stake in the common weal. A hungry or thirsty and tired person is excluded from all right of bearing testimony (VIII. 67). The reason for the following is not very clear:

In cases of robbery with violence (*sahaseshu*), theft, and adultery (*steya-sangrahaneshu*), calumny and assault (*vag-dandayoh parushye*), a judge must not examine (the competence of) witnesses too strictly (*na pariksheta sakshinah*, VIII. 72).

The following precept is calculated, I fear, to diminish the favourable impression which the laws of the Manavas, taken together and regarded relatively to circumstances, must produce on a candid mind:

In certain cases a man stating a fact falsely from a pious motive (*dharmatah*), even though he knows the truth, is not excluded from heaven; such a statement they call divine speech.
Whenever the death of a Brahman, Kshatriya, Vaishya, or Shudra may result from speaking the truth, then an untruth may be told, for falsehood is in this case preferable to truth (VIII. 103, 104).

A similar precept occurs in Yajnavalkya's Code, but an expiation is there prescribed. (See the examples, p. 334.)

V. I now turn to some of the Prayas-chitta or 'penances' enjoined in the eleventh Book of Manu:

A twice-born man performing the *Prajapatya* penance (i.e. that called after Prajapati) must for three days eat only once in the morning, for three days only once in the evening, for three days food unsolicited (but given as alms), and for three days more nothing at all (XI. 211).

A twice-born man performing the penance called *Ati-kricchra* ('very severe') must eat, as before (i.e. as described in the last), a single mouthful (*grasam*) for three times three days, and for the last three days must fast entirely (XI. 213).

A Brahman performing the penance called *tapta-kricchra* ('hot and severe') must swallow hot water, hot milk, hot clarified butter, and hot air, each of them for three days successively, after bathing and keeping his organs of sense all restrained (XI. 214).

The act of fasting for twelve days, performed by one whose heart is restrained, and whose mind is attentive, is called the *Paraka* penance, which removes all guilt (XI. 215).

Eating for one day the excrement and urine of a cow mixed with milk, curds, clarified butter and water boiled with Kusa grass and fasting entirely for a day and night is the penance called *Santapana* (XI. 212).

This last penance is to be performed by any one who does any voluntary act causing loss of caste (*jati-bhransa-karam karma*); if the act be involuntary, the Prajapatya is to be performed. (See XI. 124.)

The *Panchagavya* penance consists in swallowing the five products of a cow mentioned above under the Santapana penance. This is declared to be a sufficient atonement for having stolen food, a carriage, bed, chair, roots, flowers, or fruit (XI. 165). A variety of other curious penances and expiations are enumerated:

A twice-born man having, through infatuation, drunk intoxicating liquor, may (as an expiation) drink the same liquor when boiling hot (*agni-varnam*). If his body is completely scalded by this process he is absolved from guilt (XI. 90).

When the divine knowledge (*brahma*) which is in his body (*kayagatam*) is once immersed in spirituous liquor, his Brahmanical rank departs and he descends to the condition of a Shudra (XI. 97).

He who says 'hush' (*hum*) to Brahman, or 'thou' to one who is his superior (in knowledge), must perform an ablution, eat nothing for the rest of the day, and appease the Brahman's anger by prostrating himself at his feet (XI. 204).

If a Brahman who has drunk the Soma-juice (at a Soma-sacrifice, see end of note 1, p. 9) smells the breath of a man who has been drinking spirituous liquor, he is absolved from the taint by thrice suppressing his breath under water and swallowing clarified butter (XI. 149).

One of the most severe penances is called *Chandrayana* or 'the lunar penance,' described in VI. 20, XI. 216-221. We have already given a short account of this (see p. 114), and have only here to note, as peculiar, some of the offences for which it is required to be performed:

The Chandrayana is declared to be an expiation for carrying off a man or woman, for seizing a field or house, and for taking without permission the water of a well or reservoir (XI. 163). It is also to be performed for acts which cause mixture of caste and exclusion from society (XI. 125).

The following will show that the greatest atoning efficacy is attached to a repetition of the Veda:

Having repeated (*japitva*) the Savitri (or Gayatri, see p. 20) three thousand times with a collected mind, and having drunk milk for one month in a cow-house, a Brahman is delivered from the guilt of receiving gifts from wicked persons (*asat-pratigrahat,* XI. 194).

Desiring to obtain absolution (*chikirshan apanodanam*) for all his sins great and small, he should repeat once a day for a year the text beginning *Ava* and that beginning *Yatkim chedam* (Rig-veda VII. 89. 5).

Having accepted a prohibited gift or eaten improper food, he is absolved by repeating for three days the texts (Rig-veda IX. 58) beginning *Tarat sa mandi dhavati* (XI. 252, 253).

Although he be guilty of many crimes (*bahv-enah*) he is absolved (*shudhyate*) by repeating (*abhyasya*) for a month the text beginning *Somarudra* (Rig-veda VI. 74.1, Atharva-veda VII. 42. 1) and the three texts beginning *Aryamanam varunam mitram,* &c. (Rig-veda IV. 2. 4), while performing ablution in a running stream (XI. 254).

By intently (*samahitah*) repeating three times the whole Samhita (and Brahman *Kulluka*) of the Rig, Yajur, and Sama-veda with their Upanishads (*sa-rahasya*), he is absolved from all his sins (XI. 262).

VI. The sixth and last head is that of *karma-phala*, 'acts-recompenses.' I select a few passages illustrative of the most characteristic of all Hindu doctrines — that of the soul's transmigration through three stages of being, until a complete recompense of its acts is effected.

Book XII. 3, 9, 11, 39, 40, declares that the triple order of transmigration through the highest, middle, and lowest stages, results from good or bad acts, words, and thoughts produced by the influence of the three Gunas, Sattva, Rajas, and Tamas (see note 2, p. 71); and that for sins of act, a man takes a vegetable or mineral form (*sthavaratam*); for sins of word, the form of a bird or beast; for sins of thought, that of a man of the lowest caste; but that a triple self-command (p. 156, note 1, p. 323) leads to emancipation from all births and final beatitude:

Those who are endowed with the Sattva Guna ('purity') take the form of gods (*devatvam*), those who are filled with Rajas ('passion') become men, and those who are overwhelmed with Tamas ('darkness and ignorance') become beasts (XII. 40).

But in XII. 41, 50 each of the three orders of transmigration is described as divided into a threefold scale of being, the gradations and subdivisions of which proceed on principles which are not very consistent or intelligible:

1. *a.* Highest highest — Brahma, the creator, Marichi, &c. *b.* Highest middle — Sacrificers (*yajvanah*), Rishis, incarnate deities (*devah* = *devatah vigrahavatyah*), regents of the stars, Pitris, Sadhyas, &c. *c.* Highest lowest — Ascetics, religious mendicants, Brahmans, demigods borne in heavenly cars (*vaimanikah*), those that preside over the lunar mansions, Daityas, &c. (XII. 48-50).

2. *a.*Middle highest — Gandharvas, Guhyakas, Yakshas, Apsaras, &c. *b.* Middle middle — Kings, Kshatriyas, the chaplains of kings (*purohitah*), &c. *c.* Middle lowest — Club-fighters (*jhallah*), prize-fighters (*mallah*), actors, those who live by the use of weapons, gamblers, and drinkers (XII. 45-47).

3. *a.* Lowest highest — Dancers, birds (*suparnah = pakshinah*), deceitful men, Rakshasa, Pishachas, &c. *b.* Lowest middle — Elephants, horses, Sudras, despicable Mlecchas, lions, tigers, boars. *c.* Lowest lowest — Vegetables and minerals (*shavarah = vrikshadayah*), worms, insects, fish, reptiles, tortoises, cattle, animals of various kinds (XII. 42-44).

It is curious to note the effect of apparently slight sins of commission and omission in degrading a man to lower conditions of being, or in exposing him to diseases:

Through speaking ill (*parivadat*) of his preceptor, a man will be born an ass; if he reviles him, a dog; if he uses his property without leave, a worm; if he envies him, an insect (II. 201).

If a man steal grain he shall be born a mouse; if brass, gander; if water, a water-duck; if honey, a gad-fly; if milk, a crow; if syrup, a dog; if ghee, a weasel (XII. 62).

A Brahman neglecting his own appointed caste duty (*dharmat svakat*) will be born as a vomit-eating demon; a Kshatriya, as a demon feeding on excrement and dead bodies; a Vaisya, as a demon feeding on putrid carrion (*Ulka-mukha, Kata-putana,* and *Maitraksha-jyotika,* XII. 71, 72).

A stealer of grain will be afflicted with dyspepsia (in a future existence); a stealer of the words (of the Veda, by repeating it without authority), with dumbness; a stealer of cloth, with leprosy; a horse-stealer, with lameness (XII. 51). Compare p. 303-304[1].

---

1. It may be interesting to annex to this Lecture a few of the statements of Megasthenes (300 years B.C.) about the Brahmans (Strabo XV. 1, 59): 'They practise the greatest austerities to prepare for death which they hold to be birth to a real and happy life they maintain

that nothing of what happens to men is good or bad; that the world was created and is perishable; that it is spheroidal; that the God who made and rules it pervades every part of it; that water was the first element created; that besides the four elements there is a fifth and that the earth is in the centre of the universe. Besides, like Plato, they weave many fables about the immortality of the soul and punishments in hell. As to the Hindus generally — they are ignorant of writing, have no written laws, and arrange everything from memory (XV. 53, 66). They do not employ slaves (54). They worship Jupiter Pluvius the river Ganges, and the gods of the country; those who live in the mountains worship Dionysos (= Shiva); those in the plains, Herakles (= Vishnu, XV. 58, 69); they never drink wine except at sacrifices (53). It is not permitted to any one to marry a person of another caste, nor to change from one business or trade to another, nor to engage in many pursuits, unless he belong to the caste of philosophers (XV. 49). These philosophers are of two kinds, Brachmanes and Garmanes (Brahmans and Shramanas or Buddhist ascetics, 59). Both practise endurance and will remain a whole day in one posture without moving (60. Cf. also XV. 61, 63).'

Lecture XI

The Law — Manu continued

I now endeavour to give, as literally as possible, a metrical version of some of Manu's most noteworthy precepts, selected from different parts of the Code, under the four heads of *Achara,* 'rules of conduct;' *Vyavahara,* 'rules of government and judicature;' *Prayas-chitta,* 'penance;' *Karma-phala,* 'rewards and punishments of acts.'

Achara, 'rules of conduct'

A Brahman from exalted birth is called
A god among the gods, and is a measure
Of truth for all the world, so says the Veda (XI. 84).

Knowledge[1], descending from her home divine,
Said to a holy Brahman, I am come
To be thy cherished treasure, trust me not
To scorners, but to careful guardians,
Pure, self-restrained, and pious; so in them

---

1. In II. 117 knowledge is divided into three parts — 1, *Laukika,* 'secular;' 2. *Vaidika,* 'Vedic;' 3. *Adhyatmika,* 'spiritual' or that which relates to soul.

I shall be gifted with resistless power (II. 114, 115).

The man with hoary head is not revered
As aged by the gods, but only he
Who has true knowledge; he, though young, is old (II. 156).

A wooden elephant, an antelope
Of leather, and a Brahman without knowledge —
These are three things that only bear a name (II. 157).

As with laborious toil the husbandman,
Digging with spade beneath the ground, arrives
At springs of living water, so the man
Who searches eagerly for truth will find
The knowledge hidden in his teacher's mind (II. 118).

With pain the mother to her child gives birth,
With pain the father rears him; as he grows
He heaps up cares and troubles for them both;
Incurring thus a debt he ne'er can pay,
Though he should strive through centuries of time (II. 227).

Think constantly, O son, how mayest please
Thy father, mother, teacher — these obey.
By deep devotion seek thy debt to pay.
This is thy highest duty and religion (II. 228).

Who finds around him only wicked sons,
When called by fate to pass the gloom of death,
Is like a man who seeks to cross a flood
Borne on a raft composed of rotten wood (IX. 161).

Even though wronged, treat not with disrespect
Thy father, mother, teacher, elder brother (II. 226).

From poison thou mayest take the food of life,
The purest gold from lumps of impure earth,
Examples of good conduct from a foe,
Sweet speech and gentleness from e'en a child,
Something from all; from men of low degree
Lessons of wisdom, if thou humble be (II. 238, 239).

Wound not another, though by him provoked,
Do no one injury by thought or deed,
Utter no word to pain thy fellow-creatures (II. 161).

Say what is true, speak not agreeable falsehood (IV. 138).
Treat no one with disdain[1], with patience bear
Reviling language; with an angry man
Be never angry, blessings give for curses (VI. 47, 48).

E'en as a driver checks his restive steeds,
Do thou, if thou art wise, restrain thy passions,
Which, running wild, will hurry thee away (II. 88).

When asked, give something, though a very trifle,
Ungrudgingly and with a cheerful heart,
According to thy substance; only see
That he to whom thou givest worthy be (IV. 227, 228).

Pride not thyself on thy religious works,
Give to the poor, but talk not of thy gifts.
By pride religious merit melts away,
The merit of thy alms by ostentation (IV. 236, 237).

None see us, say the sinful in their hearts;
Yes, the gods see them and the omniscient Spirit
Within their breasts. Thou thinkest, O good friend,
'I am alone,' but there resides within thee
A Being who inspects thy every act,
Knows all thy goodness and thy wickedness (VIII. 85, 91).

The soul is its own witness; yea, the soul
Itself is its own refuge; grieve thou not,
O man, thy soul the great internal Witness (VIII. 84).

---

1. In IV. 135 the householder is especially warned against treating with
   contempt a Brahman well versed in the Veda, a Kshatriya, and a
   serpent, because (says Kulluka) the first has the power of destroying
   him by his unseen power of magical texts and spells, the other two
   by their seen power (*drishta-saktya*). Cf. the passages relative to the
   power of the Brahmans, translated p. 263.

The Firmament, the Earth, the Sea, the Moon,
The Sun, the Fire, the Wind, the Night, and both
The sacred Twilights[1] and the Judge of souls[2],
The god of Justice, and the Heart itself —
All constantly survey the acts of men (VIII. 86).

When thou hast sinned, think not to hide thy guilt
Under a cloak of penance and austerity (IV. 198).

No study of the Veda nor oblation,
No gift of alms, nor round of strict observance
Can lead the inwardly depraved to heaven (II. 97).

If with the great Divinity who dwells
Within thy breast thou hast no controversy,
Go not to Ganges' water to be cleansed,
Nor make a pilgrimage to Kuru's fields (VIII. 92) [3].

Iniquity once practised, like a seed,
Fails not to yield its fruit to him who wrought it,
If not to him, yet to his sons and grandsons (IV. 173).

Contentment is the root of happiness,
And discontent the root of misery.
Wouldst thou be happy, be thou moderate (IV. 12).

Honour thy food, receive it thankfully,
Eat it contentedly and joyfully,
Ne'er hold it in contempt; avoid excess,
For gluttony is hateful, injures health,
May lead to death, and surely bars the road
To holy merit and celestial bliss (II. 54, 57).

Desire is not extinguished by enjoyment,
Fire is not quenched by offerings of oil,
But blazes with increased intensity (II. 94).

Shrink thou from worldly honour as from poison,

---

1. See the account of the Sandhyas, p. 272.
2. Yama, see p. 22.
3. See note 1, p. 275.

Seek rather scorn; the scorn'd may sleep in peace,
In peace awake; the scorner perishes (II. 162, 163).

Daily perform thy own appointed work
Unweariedly; and to obtain a friend —
A sure companion to the future world —
Collect a store of virtue like the ants
Who garner up their treasures into heaps;
For neither father, mother, wife, nor son,
Nor kinsman, will remain beside thee then,
When thou art passing to that other home —
Thy virtue will thy only comrade be (IV. 238, 239).

Single is every living creature born,
Single he passes to another world,
Single he eats the fruit of evil deeds,
Single, the fruit of good; and when he leaves
His body like a log or heap of clay
Upon the ground, his kinsmen walk away;
Virtue alone stays by him at the tomb
And bears him through the dreary trackless gloom
(IV. 240-242) [1].

Thou canst not gather what thou dost not sow;
As thou dost plant the tree so will it grow (IX. 40).

Depend not on another, rather lean
Upon thyself; trust to thine own exertions.
Subjection to another's will gives pain;
True happiness consists in self-reliance (IV. 160).

Strive to complete the task thou hast commenced;
Wearied, renew thy efforts once again;
Again fatigued, once more the work begin,
So shalt thou earn success and fortune win (IX. 300).

Never despise thyself, nor yet contemn

---

1. Dr. Muir has pointed out that the expression *tamas tarati dustaram*,
'he crosses the gloom difficult to be passed,' may be taken from
Atharva-veda IX. 5. 1, *tirtva tamansi bahudha mahanti.*

Thy own first efforts, though they end in failure;
Seek Fortune with persistency till death,
Nor ever deem her hard to be obtained (IV. 137).

Success in every enterprise depends
On Destiny[1] and man combined, the acts
Of Destiny are out of man's control;
Think not on Destiny, but act thyself (VII. 205).

Be courteous to thy guest who visits thee;
Offer a seat, bed, water, food enough,
According to thy substance, hospitably;
Naught taking for thyself till he be served;
Homage to guests brings wealth, fame, life, and heaven
(III. 106, IV. 29).

He who possessed of ample means bestows
His gifts on strangers while his kindred starve,
Thinks to enjoy the honey of applause,
But only eating poison dies despised —
Such charity is cruelty disguised (XI. 9).

He who pretends to be what he is not,
Acting a part, commits the worst of crimes,
For, thief-like, he abstracts a good man's heart (IV. 255).

Though thou mayest suffer for thy righteous acts,
Ne'er give thy mind to aught but honest gain (IV. 171).

So act in thy brief passage through this world
That thy apparel, speech, and inner store
Of knowledge be adapted to thy age,
Thy occupation, means, and parentage (IV. 18).

The man who keeps his senses in control,
His speech, heart, actions pure and ever guarded[2],
Gains all the fruit of holy study; he
Need neither penance nor austerity (II. 160).

---

1. See note 1, p. 323.
2. *Daiva* is here the Adrishta described p. 73.

But if a single organ fail, by that defect
His knowledge of the truth flows all away
Like water leaking from a leathern vessel (II. 99).

Contentment, patience under injury,
Self-subjugation, honesty, restraint
Of all the sensual organs, purity,
Devotion[1], knowledge of the Deity[2],
Veracity, and abstinence from anger,
These form the tenfold summary of duty (VI. 92).

Long not for death, nor hanker after life;
Calmly expect thy own appointed time,
E'en as a servant reckons on his hire (IV. 45).

This mansion of the soul, composed of earth,
Subject to sorrow and decrepitude,
Inhabited by sicknesses and pains,
Bound by the bonds of ignorance and darkness,
Let a wise man with cheerfulness abandon (VI. 77).

Quitting this body, he resembles merely
A bird that leaves a tree. Thus is he freed
From the fell monster of an evil world[3] (VI. 78).

Duties of Women and Wives

In childhood must a father guard his daughter;
In youth the husband shields his wife; in age
A mother is protected by her sons —
Ne'er should a woman lean upon herself (V. 148, IX. 3).

A faithful wife who wishes to attain
The heaven of her lord, must serve him here

---

1. Kulluka interprets *dhi* by 'knowledge of the sacred truth contained in the Sastras.'
2. *Vidya*, 'knowledge of the supreme Spirit,' — Kulluka.
3. *Kricchrad grahat = samsara-kashtad grahad iva.*

As if he were a god, and ne'er do aught
To pain him, whatsoever be his state,
And even though devoid of every virtue (V. 154, 156).

She who in mind, speech, body, honours him,
Alive or dead, is called a virtuous wife (V. 165).

Be it her duty to preserve with care
Her husband's substance; let her too be trusted
With its expenditure, with management
Of household property and furniture,
Of cooking and purveying daily food.
Let her be ever cheerful, skilled in all
Domestic work, and not too free in spending (V. 150).

Drink, bad companions, absence from her lord,
Rambling about, unseasonable sleep,
Dwelling in others' houses, let her shun —
These are six things which tarnish woman's fame (IX. 13).

Whatever be the character and mind
Of him to whom a woman weds herself,
Such qualities her nature must imbibe,
E'en as a river blending with the sea (IX. 22).

Women, united by the marriage tie
To men they love, in hope of virtuous offspring,
Worthy of honour, eminently blessed,
Irradiate the houses of their lords,
Like shining lights or goddesses of fortune (IX. 26).

Then only is a man a perfect man
When he is three — himself, his wife, his son —
For thus have learned men the law declared,
'A husband is one person with his wife' (IX. 45).

Fidelity till death, this is the sum
Of mutual duties for a married pair (IX. 101).

And if the wife survives, let her remain
Constant and true, nor sully her fair fame,
E'en by the utterance of another's name (V. 157).

Vyavahara, 'rules of government and judicature'

The Lord of all in pity to our needs
Created kings, to rule and guard us here;
Without a king this world would rock with fear (VII. 3).

A king, e'en though a child, must not be treated
As if he were a mortal; rather he
Is a divinity in human shape (VII. 8).

The king, his council, and the royal city,
The country[1], treasure, army, and ally,
These are the seven members of a realm (IX. 294).

Dread of the rod alone restrains the bad,
Controls the good, and makes a nation happy (VII. 15).

The king must therefore punish fearlessly;
Else would the strong oppress the weak, the bad
Would wrong the good, and pierce them as with iron[2];
The crow would eat the consecrated rice,
The dog the burnt oblation; ownership
And rights of property would be subverted;
All ranks and classes would become confused,
All barriers and bridges broken down,
And all the world turned wrong side uppermost
                                         (VII. 20, 21, 24).

But let the monarch, ere he wield his rod,
Consider place and time, the written law
Of justice, and the measure of his strength (VII. 16).

---

1. For *rashtra* (= *desha*) Yajnavalkya (I. 352) substitutes *jana*, 'the people.'
2. The literal translation of the text here is 'the stronger would roast the weaker like fish on a spit (*shule matsyan ivapakshyan durbalan balavattarah*).'

Gamesters and public dancers, heretics,
Revilers of the Veda, infidels,
Sellers of liquor, men who interfere
In others' duties and neglect their own,
All such he should expel from his domain (IX. 225).

To women, children, crazy men, and fools,
The old, the poor, the sickly, and infirm
Let him be never harsh; if they do wrong
Let them be bound or punished tenderly[1] (IX. 230).

That king is equally unjust who frees
The guilty or condemns the innocent.
The wicked he must treat like thorny weeds,
They must be rooted out with active arm;
The good and virtuous let him shield from harm
                                    (IX. 252, 253).

Let not a king or judge promote disputes,
But if a suit be tried, let him with fairness
Adjudicate between the disputants (VIII. 43).

When Goodness, wounded by Iniquity,
Comes to a court of justice, and the judge
Extracts not tenderly the pointed dart,
That very shaft shall pierce him to the heart (VIII. 12).

Justice destroyed will ruin the destroyer;
Preserved, it will preserve. Beware, O judge,
Lest outraged justice overthrow the world (VIII. 15).

E'en as a hunter tracks the lurking-place
Of some poor wounded deer by drops of blood,
So must a king by strict investigation
Trace out the source of violated justice (VIII. 44).

Let him with full deliberation weigh
The evidence, the place, the mode, the time,

---

1. The text says 'with a whip, twig, or rope.' It must be presumed that
the whip and twig are intended to be used in the case of children only.

The facts, the truth, and his own frame of mind,
Firmly adhering to the rules of law (VIII. 45).

Just men and men of sense, whate'er their caste,
And those who know their duty and are free
From love of gain, may tender evidence;
The opposite must not be witnesses (VIII. 63).

Kings, priests, religious students, anchorites,
All interested men, friends, boon companions,
Foes, criminals, diseased and perjured men,
Low artisans and dancers, lunatics,
Old men, and children, drunkards, vagabonds,
Thieves, starving wretches, irritated persons,
A single witness — these are all excluded (VIII. 64-67).

Let women act as witnesses for women;
The twice-born classes for the twice-born; slaves
For slaves, and only lowest men for outcastes (VIII. 68).

The court must not be entered by a witness,
Unless he speak the truth without reserve;
For equally does he commit a crime,
Who tells not all the facts, or tells them falsely (VIII. 13).

A witness who gives evidence with truth
Shall be absolved from every sin, and gain
Exalted glory here and highest bliss above (VIII. 81, 83).

Headlong in utter darkness shall the wretch
Fall into hell, who in a court of justice
Answers a single question falsely; he
Shall be tormented through a hundred births (VIII. 82, 94).

And all the merit of his virtuous acts
Shall be transferred to dogs. Therefore be true,
Speak the whole truth without equivocation (VIII. 90, 101).

Let no considerate witness take an oath
Lightly, or in a trifling matter; he
Who does so shall incur eternal ruin (VIII. 111).

Prayas-chitta, 'penance and expiation'

According to a man's sincerity
In penitent confession of his crime,
And detestation of the evil deed,
Shall he be pardoned and his soul released
From taint of guilt, like serpent from its skin (XI. 227, 228).

If he do wrong, 'tis not enough to say
I will not sin again; release from guilt
Depends on true contrition, which consists
In actual abstinence from sinful deeds (XI. 230).

Therefore, whatever fault a man commits,
Whether from ignorance or knowingly,
Let him, desiring quittance from his crime,
Beware how he offend a second time (IX. 232).

Revolving in his mind the certainty
Of retribution in a future state,
Let him be pure in thought, in word, in deed[1] (XI. 231).

By free confession, penitence, and penance,
By daily repetition of the Veda[2],
By the five holy acts[3], by giving alms,
By patience, and by bearing injuries,
The greatest sinner may obtain release (XI. 227, 245).

Whate'er is hard to cross, whate'er is hard
To have or do or be, may be attained
By penance — sins of heart and speech and act
May be burnt out; therefore be rich in penance
                                        (XI. 238, 241).

---

1. Here and in another example below further instances occur of
   Manu's triple division of 'thought, word, and deed' (see note, p. 156).
   The same triple division is frequent in Buddhistic writings.
2. *Khyapanena, anutapena, tapasa, adhyayena cha.*
3. That is, the five Maha-yajnas; see p. 275.

E'en as a clod of earth melts all away
Cast in a mighty lake, so every sin
Becomes effaced, merged in the triple Veda (XI. 263).

In penance all the bliss of gods and men
Is said to have its root, continuance, end[1] (XI. 234).

Karma-phala, 'recompenses of acts'

Innumerable souls, endued with form,
Issue like scintillations[2] from the substance
Of the great Self-existent, constantly
Impelling beings multiform to action (XII. 15).

Whate'er the act a man commits, whate'er
His state of mind, of that the recompense
Must he receive in corresponding body (XII. 81).

Action of every kind, whether of mind
Or speech or body, must bear fruit, entailing
Fresh births through multifarious conditions,
In highest, mean, and lowest transmigrations (XII. 3).

Souls gifted with the quality of goodness
Attain the state of gods; those filled with passion,
The state of men; and those immersed in darkness,
The state of beasts — this is the triple course (XII. 40).

Let all men ponder with attentive mind
The passage of the soul through diverse forms,
Of Brahma, gods and men, beasts, plants, and stones,
According to their good or evil acts,
And so apply their minds to virtue only (XII. 22, 42, 50).

Just in proportion as a vital soul
Addicts itself to sensuality,

---

1. A variety of penances will be found detailed at p. 306.
2. Compare the extracts from the Upanishads, pp. 41-42, 45-46.

In that degree its senses shall become
Intensely keen in future transmigrations (XII. 73).

Reflect thou on man's manifold transitions
And passages through forms of being, caused
By faults of action[1], and his headlong fall
Down to the lower regions; then the torments
Reserved for him by Yama; then in life
His partings from his loved ones and his meetings
With those he loves not; then the victory
Of sickness and decrepitude and death;
Then the soul's painful egress from the body,
And lastly its return to other forms,
Passing from womb to womb to undergo
Ten thousand millions of existences[2] (VI. 61-63).

Then do thou contemplate with fixed attention
The subtle essence of the Soul supreme,
Existing in the highest and the lowest —
Pervading every creature equally (VI. 65).

He who perceives the omnipresent God
Is nevermore enslaved by acts, but he
Who sees him not, can never be released (VI. 74).

Those who repeat their vicious acts are doomed
To misery, increasing more and more,
In forms becoming more and more debased (XII. 74).

They shall be born as despicable beasts,
Suffer the worst extremes of cold and heat,
Painful diseases, various kinds of terror (XII. 77, 80).

He who by firmness gains the mastery
Over his words, his mind, and his whole body,
Is justly called a triple-governor[3] (XII. 10).

---

1. *Aveksheta gatir nrinam karma-dosha-samudbhavah.*
2. *Yoni-koti-sahasreshu sritis-cha antar-atmanah.*
3. This is the Tri-dandin (see note 1, p. 156). It is noticeable that the
   Indian ascetic, who is described by Arrian (VII. 2) as exciting the

Exerting thus a threefold self-command
Towards himself and every living creature,
Subduing lust and wrath, he may aspire
To that perfection which the good desire (XII. 11).

Every created being which exists
And yet is not eternal[1], is in Soul.
He who with fixed abstraction sees himself
And all things in the universal Self[2]
Cannot apply his soul to wickedness (XII. 118).

This universal Soul is all the gods,
Is all the worlds, and is the only source
Of all the actions of embodied spirits (XII. 119).

He is their ruler, brighter than pure gold,
Subtler than atoms, imperceptible,
Except by minds abstracted, all-pervading,
Investing all with rudiments of matter,
Causing all beings to revolve like wheels
In regular and constant revolution
Through birth and growth, decay and dissolution
                                    (XII. 122, 124).

The man who sees by means of his own soul
The universal Spirit present there,
Present in every creature everywhere,

---

wonder of Alexander the Great by his *karteria*, is named *Dandamis*,
probably from the same root as *danda* (*dam*, 'to subdue,' in Intens).
By others he is called Mandanis (root *mand?*).

1. This seems to mean, as explained by Dr. Johaentgen, that to which
belongs a real existence and yet not eternity, because it is a product.
Cf. Sankhya-pravacana V. 56.

2. Dr. Johaentgen thinks that *Atman* in these passages is wrongly
translated 'the supreme soul.' He believes that it denotes 'the whole
self or soul' of man, regarded as an epitome of the universe, and
he refers in confirmation of his view to Tattva-samasa 56. See also
Manu VIII. 84, translated p. 314.

With perfect equanimity may wait
Till he has reached the state of bliss supreme —
Complete absorption in the eternal essence (XII. 125).

The Code of Yajnavalkya

The most important Law-book next to Manu is the Dharma-
sastra of Yajnavalkya, which with its most celebrated
commentary, the Mitakshara by Vijnanesvara, is at present the
principal authority of the school of Benares and Middle India.
It seems originally to have emanated from a school of the
White Yajur-veda in Mithila[1] or North Bihar, just as we have
seen (p. 233-234) that the Code of the Manavas did from a
school of the Black Yajur-veda in the neighbourhood of Delhi.
Book I. 2 makes the author say:

The chief of devout sages (Yajnavalkya), dwelling in Mithila,
having reflected for a moment, said to the Munis, 'Listen to the
laws which prevail in the country where the black antelope is
found' (cf. Manu II. 23).

Yajnavalkya's work[2] is much more concise than that of
Manu, being all comprised in three books instead of twelve,
which circumstance leads to the inference that it has suffered
even more curtailment at the hands of successive revisers of
the original text than the Code of the Manavas. Like that
Code, it seems to have been preceded by a Vriddha and a
Vrihad Yajnavalkya. The whole work, as we now possess it,

---

1. According to Dr. Roer, it is still the leading authority of the Mithila
   school, but Colebrooke names other works as constituting the chief
   texts of this school.
2. The edition I have used is the excellent one of Stenzler. I have
   consulted his preface and translation, and the translation of part of
   the Code made by Dr. Roer and W.A. Montriou, to which there is
   an instructive introduction.

is written in the ordinary Sloka metre. The first Book, consisting of 376 couplets, is chiefly on social and caste deities (*achara*); the second, consisting of 307 verses (which have been transferred almost word for word to the Agni Purana), is mainly on administrative judicature and civil and criminal law (*vyavahara*); the third, consisting of 335 verses, is principally on devotion, purification, expiation, penance (*prayas-chitta*), &c. The Mitakshara commentary follows the same arrangement, and is divided also into three parts.

As to the date of Yajnavalkya's Law-book, it has been conjecturally placed in the middle of the first century of our era. The period of its first compilation cannot, of course, be fixed with certainty, but internal evidence clearly indicates that the present redaction is much more recent than that of Manu's Law-book.

The following points have been noted by me:

1. Although Yajnavalkya's Code must have represented the customs and practices prevalent in a district (Mithila) situated in a different and more easterly part of India, yet nearly every precept in the first book, and a great many in the second and third, have their parallels in similar precepts occurring throughout the Code of the Manavas.

2. Although generally founded on Manu, it represents a later stage of Hindu development. Its arrangement is much more systematic. It presents fewer repetitions and inconsistencies, and less confusion of religion, morality, and philosophy, with civil and criminal law.

3. In Book I. 3 the sources of law are expanded beyond those stated by Manu; although afterwards in I. 7 Manu's fourfold Dharma-mulam (see p. 237) is adopted, thus:

'The Vedas, with the Puranas, the Nyaya, the Mimansa, the codes of law (*dharma-sastra*), and the (six) Vedangas are the fourteen repositories (*sthanani*) of the sciences (*vidyanam*) and of law (*dharmasya*, I. 3).

'The Veda (*shruti*), traditional law (*smriti*), the practices of good men (*sad-achara*), and one's own inclination, are called the root of law' (I. 7).

4. Those of its precepts which introduce new matter evince a more advanced Brahmanism and a stricter caste-organization; thus, for example, it is directed in I. 57 that a Brahman must not have a Shudra as a fourth wife, but only wives of the three higher classes, whereas in Manu (see p. 274) such a wife is permitted[1].

5. In I. 271, 272, there is an allusion to the shaven heads (*munda*) and yellow garments (*kashaya-vasas*) of the Buddhists, which marks a period subsequent to the establishment and previous to the expulsion of Buddhism. It must be admitted, however, that there is no mention of the Buddhists by name.

6. In II. 185 the king is recommended to found and endow monasteries and to place in them Brahmans learned in the Vedas.

7. In II. 241 mention is made of *Nanaka*, 'coined money,' both true and counterfeit (*akuta* and *kutaka*), whereas, although Manu speaks of weights of gold and silver, such as Shuvarnas, Palas, Nishkas, Dharanas, and Puranas (VIII. 135-137), it is very doubtful whether any stamped coin was current in his day.

8. Written accusations and defences (*lekhya*) are required to be made (II. 6, 7), and written documents (*likhitam*) are allowed as evidence (II. 22); and in I. 318 grants of land and copperplates, properly sealed, are mentioned.

9. The worship of Ganesa, as the remover of obstacles, is expressly alluded to in I. 270, and *Graha-yajna* or 'offerings to the planets' are directed to be made in I. 294.

10. In III. 110 the author of the Code (Yajnavalkya) speaks of an Aranyaka or Upanishad (of the White Yajur-veda), which he had himself received from the Sun, and of a Yoga-sastra, 'Yoga system of philosophy,' which he had himself delivered (to Patanjali[2]).

---

1. Later Codes limit Brahmans to wives of their own classes only.
2. See p. 110 of this volume. Patanjali, who flourished, according, to Lassen, about 200 B.C., is not, however, mentioned in the text.

Some of these points seem decisive as to the lapse of a considerable period between Manu and Yajnavalkya, and lead us to agree with those who hesitate to refer the latter Code, in its present form, to an earlier epoch than the first century of our era[1]. On the other hand, some of the facts stated incline us to attribute a greater antiquity to portions of the work than that usually assigned to it.

I proceed to give specimens of the three divisions of Yajnavalkya's Code.

I. The following are from the first Book on *Acara* or 'social customs and immemorial practices.' Attention should be directed to the parallels in Manu at the end of several of the translated passages. The mention of four Vedas and the efficacy atrributed to their repetition is noticeable:

Brahmans, Kshatriyas, and Vaisyas are called twice-born (*dvijah*), since they are born once from their mothers and a second time through the binding on the girdle (*Maunji-bandhanat,* I. 39. Cf. Manu II. 169, and see p. 270).

The Veda is more efficacious in effecting the final salvation of the twice-born (*dvijatinam nihsreyasa-karah parah*) than sacrifices, than penances, and even than good works (I. 40. Cf. Manu II. 166).

A twice-born man[2] who every day repeats the texts of the Rig-veda (*richah*) satiates the gods with honey and milk, and the fathers (*Pitrin*) with honey and butter (I. 41. Cf. Manu II. 107).

---

1. Some of Yajnavalkya's verses are found in the Pancha-tantra, the date of the oldest portions of which is usually referred to the fifth century of our era. In almost all Sanskrit works the introduction of apposite verses from older sources, for the illustration of the original text, is common.

2. These following five verses are more explicit than Manu in describing the efficacy of the Brahma-yajna or Japa-yajna (see p. 276). They are based on Satapatha-brahmana XI. 5, 6, 4-8, and on Ashvalayana Grihya-sutra III. 3. 2, &c.

He who every day to the best of his ability repeats the texts of the Yajur-veda (*yajunshi*) refreshes the gods with butter and nectar and the fathers with honey and butter (I. 42).

He who every day repeats the texts of the Sama-veda (*samani*) satiates the gods with Soma-juice and butter and the fathers as before (I. 43).

Twice-born men who every day to the best of their power repeat the texts of the Atharva-veda (*Atharvangirasah*, see p. 245) satiate the gods with marrow (*medasa*) and the fathers as before (I. 44).

He who every day to the best of his power repeats the sacred discussion (*vakovakyam*[1]), the Puranas, the Narasansis[2], the sacred songs (*gathikah*), the Ithihasas, and the sciences (*vidyah*), satiates the inhabitants of the skies (*divaukasah*) with flesh, milk, rice, and honey, and the fathers as before (I. 45, 46).

The precept that the twice-born can take a Shudra as a wife (cf. Manu III. 13, IX. 149) is not approved by me, since in that wife (*tatra*) he is himself born again (whence she is called *jaya*, according to Manu IX. 8).

Three wives in the regular order (of the first three classes) may belong to a Brahman, two to a Kshatriya, and one to a Vaishya. A Sudra must only have one of his own class (I. 56, 57).

Once every year (the following persons) are to be honoured with a respectful offering (*argha*): a Snataka (see p. 223), an Acharya (see p. 261), a king, a friend, and a son-in-law, but a sacrificing priest at every sacrifice[3] (I. 110. Cf. Manu III. 119).

---

1. This might be translated 'dialogue.' It appears from Satapatha-brahmana IV. 6, 9, 20, that some portions of Vedic tradition were called *vakovakyam* or. *brahmodyam*.
2. See this word in my Sanskrit-English Dictionary. Compare the directions as to the *brahma-yajna* in the Ashvalayana Grihya-sutra, translated p. 222 of this volume.
3. These six are also named in Paraskara's Grihya-sutra I. 1 (Stenzler) as worthy of the Argha.

A traveller is to be treated as a guest, and also a Brahman who knows the entire Veda. These two a householder, who wishes to obtain the world of Brahman, must especially honour (I. 111. Cf. Manu I. 120, 130).

The success of every action depends on destiny and on a man's own effort; but destiny is evidently nothing but (the result) of a man's act in a former state of existence (I. 348. Cf. Manu VII. 205 and p. 317 of this volume).

Some expect the whole result from destiny or from the inherent nature (or force of a thing); some expect it from the lapse of time; and some, from a man's own effort: other persons of wiser judgment expect it from a combination of all these (I. 349).

II. The following are from the second section of Yajnavalkya's Code on *Vyavahara* or 'the administration of justice:'

Every day should a king, reflecting on his reward equal to that of sacrifices, personally investigate lawsuits in regular order surrounded by assessors[1] (I. 359. Cf. Manu VIII. 1).

---

1. Colebrooke, in one of his Essays (Professor E.B. Cowell's edition, vol. ii. p. 490), gives an interesting account of the composition of an Indian court of justice, according to the rules of Hindu Law-books. The administration of justice, civil and criminal, is one of the chief duties of the Raja or sovereign. Hence the king's court takes precedence of all. He is assisted by learned Brahmans as assessors, one of whom acts as chief judge in his absence. It is not stationary, but follows him about. The second court, which is stationary, is that of the chief judge (*Pradvivaka*), appointed by the king, and assisted by three or more Brahman assessors, not exceeding seven. The third court is that of the inferior judges for local trials. Besides these, there are country courts or assemblies of townsmen (*Puga*), of traders, artisans, &c. (*Shreni*), and of kinsmen (*Kula*) for arbitration in small matters. The sovereign or supreme court (to which there is an appeal from all the others) is compared to a body consisting of various members, viz. 1. the king, 2. the chief judge, 3. the assessors, 4. the

A king, having duly corrected the castes, families, companies of artisans (*shreni*), schools, and communities of people that have swerved from the duty of their caste (*sva-dharmat,* cf. p. 151), should place them in the right path (I. 360. Cf. Manu VIII. 41).

Let the king, keeping himself free from anger and covetousness, try lawsuits along with learned Brahmans in accordance with the rules of written law (*dharma-sastranusarena,* II. 1. Cf. Manu VIII. 1).

He should appoint as judges men well versed in the study of the Veda, conversant with the laws, speakers of truth, impartial to friend and foe (II. 2).

When any one, injured by others in any way contrary to law or usage, makes a representation to the king, this is a proper subject for a lawsuit (*vyavahara-padam,* II. 5).

The charge, as made by the plaintiff, is to be put down in writing in presence of the defendant, marked with the year, month, half-month, day, names, caste, &c. (II. 6).

The answer to the charge is to be then written down in presence of the person who made the first representation; after which the plaintiff shall immediately cause to be committed to writing the proofs by which his accusation is supported (II. 6, 7).

Legal proof (*pramanam*) is of three kinds, viz. written documents (*likhitam*), actual possession (*bhuktih*), and

---

ministers of state, 5. the king's domestic priest, 6. the written law, 7. gold, fire and water (used for oaths and ordeals), 8. the accountant, 9. the scribe (*Kayashta*), 10. the keeper of things in dispute and the enforcer of judgments, 11. the messenger, 12. the moderator of the court. The audience or bystanders are also regarded as a component part of the court, any one duly qualified to interpose with a suggestion or advice being at liberty to do so. All this is illustrated in a most interesting manner by the ninth act of the drama called Mricchakatika, to which reference will be made in a subsequent Lecture. In the description of a court of justice there given, as Professor Cowell has remarked, the Sreshthin or 'chief of the merchants' and the Kayastha or 'scribe' seem to sit as assessors with the judge.

witnesses (*sakshinah*). In the absence of any one of these, some one of the ordeals (*divyanyatamam*) is enjoined (II. 22. Cf. Manu VIII. 114).

The scales (*tula*), fire, water, poison, drinking the water in which idols have been washed (*kosa*), these are the ordeals for the testing of innocence (II. 95. See note 1, p. 304).

There should be at least three witnesses, who act in accordance with the precepts of the Veda or traditional law and are of suitable caste (II. 69. Cf. Manu VIII. 60, and see p. 305 of this volume).

The judge should thus address the witnesses standing near the plaintiff (*vadin*) and defendant (*prativadin*), 'Whatever worlds are appointed for the worst criminals, for incendiaries, for murderers of women and children, these shall be the abode of him who gives false evidence' (*sakshyam anritam*, II. 73, 74. Cf. Manu VIII. 89).

Know that whatever merit has been acquired by thee through good actions in hundreds of former births shall become the property of him whom thou defeatest by false evidence[1] (II. 75. Cf. Manu VIII. 90).

In conflicting evidence (*dvaidhe*), that of the majority (*bahunam*) must be taken; in the case of an equality of testimony, that of the virtuous persons; when these disagree, then the statements of the most virtuous must be taken (II. 78. Cf. Manu VIII. 73).

Whenever the evidence of a witness might occasion the death of a person of whatever class, the witness may tell an untruth. To obtain expiation (*pavanaya*) after such false evidence twice-born men must offer an oblation (*caru*) to Sarasvati (II. 83. Cf. Manu VIII. 104, 105).

When a murder or robbery has occurred (*ghatite 'pahrite*), and no traces of it are found beyond the village, the blame must rest on the governor of the village (*grama-bhartuh*), and the village must pay (II. 271, 272).

---

1. In Manu the merit is said to be transferred to dogs, see p. 322.

When a Brahman is a thief, he must be marked with a hot iron and banished from the country (II. 270).

Housebreakers, stealers of horses and elephants, and those who commit murder with violence should be impaled (II. 273. Cf. Manu IX. 276, 280).

A stealer of clothes should have his hand cut off; cut-purses should have the thumb and fore-finger amputated (II. 274. Cf. Manu Ix. 277).

The highest fine should be imposed on any one who knowingly gives a thief or murderer food, shelter, fire, water, advice, implements, or money (II. 276. Cf. Manu IX. 278).

Whoever falsifies scales, an edict, measures or coins, or does business with them so falsified should be made to pay the highest fine (II. 240. Cf. Manu IX. 232).

One who falsely practises as a physician must pay the first fine, if his deception be practised towards animals; the middle fine, if towards men; the highest fine, if towards any of the king's officers (II. 242. Cf. Manu IX. 284).

Any one who adulterates medicine, or oil, or salt, or perfumes, or corn, or sugar, or other commodities, should be made to pay sixteen Panas (II. 245. Cf. Manu VIII. 203, IX. 286, 291).

The highest fine should be imposed on those who, knowing the rise or fall in prices, combine to make a price of their own to the detriment of workmen and artisans (II. 249).

It a king has imposed any fine unjustly, he must give thirty times the amount to Brahmans after having made an offering to Varuna (II. 307. Cf. Manu Ix. 244).

III. The third Book gives various rules for *Prayas-chitta*, 'penance, expiation, and purification.' Many of the laws are like those of Manu. It will suffice to note a few examples which have reference to funeral ceremonies:

A child under two years old must be buried, and no offering of water should be made to him. (The corpse of) any other deceased person should be accompanied by (a procession of) relations to the burning-place (*a-smasanati*, III. 1. See p. 224. Cf. Manu V. 68, 69, 103).

It is then to be burnt with common fire (*laukikagnina*) while they repeat the hymn to Yama (*yama-suktam*) and the sacred chant (*gatham*, III. 2).

It is usual (for the relatives) to pour out a libation of water once (to the deceased), uttering his name and family, (and then) remaining silent (see p. 227).

But religious students and outcastes are not allowed to offer the oblations of water (III. 5. Cf. Manu V. 88).

The funeral oblation is not allowed for heretics (*pashandin*), persons without any fixed station (*an-asritah*), thieves, women, who have killed their husbands, or who have lived an independent life (*kama-gah*), or have been drunkards or have committed suicide (*atma-tyaginyah*, III. 6. Cf. Manu V. 89, 90).

When the relatives have poured out water, have completed their ablutions, and have seated themselves on a spot covered with soft grass, (the elder ones) may repeat to the others some verses from the ancient Ithihasas, such as the following (III. 7):

> Does it not argue folly to expect
> Stability in man, who is as transient
> As a mere bubble and fragile as a stalk?
> Why should we utter wailings if a frame,
> Composed of five material elements,
> Is decomposed by force of its own acts,
> And once again resolved into its parts?
> The earth, the ocean, and the gods themselves
> Must perish, how should not the world
> Of mortals, light as froth, obey the law
> Of universal death and perish too (III. 8-11)?

After hearing verses of this kind they should return home, the younger ones leading the way, stopping solemnly outside the door of the house to chew leaves of the Nimb tree (*Nimba-patrani*, III. 12).

After they have rinsed out their mouths and touched fire, water, cow-dung, white mustard-seed, and placed their feet on a stone, they should enter the house slowly (III. 13. Cf. the account of the funeral procession in the Grihya-sutras, pp. 224-227).

Impurity caused by the ceremonies connected with touching a corpse (*shavam ashaucham*) lasts for either three nights or ten nights (III. 18. Cf. Manu V. 59, 64).

Those who preserve this Law-book diligently in their memories shall obtain reputation in this world and shall go to heaven (III. 330).

He who repeats only three verses out of this Law-book at a Shraddha causes perpetual satisfaction to his departed ancestors; of this there is no doubt. A Brahman may obtain merit, a Kshatriya may become victorious and a Vaisya may become rich in corn and money by preserving this book in his memory (III. 332, 333).

The eighteen principal Codes posterior to Manu and Yajnavalkya

A list of eighteen of the most important of these has been given at p. 232. They are all extant in some form or other, as described by Colebrooke[1]. Little or nothing is known about the authorship of any one of them. They have arisen from the necessity of framing new laws or modifying old ones to suit particular localities and particular periods. In order to invest them with antiquity and authority, they are all eighteen ascribed, like the Codes of Manu and Yajnavalkya, to various

---

1. See Professor E.B. Cowell's edition of his Essays, vol. i. pp. 468-470. The works or their abridgments, ascribed to these eighteen inspired lawgivers, have been all printed in Kolkata.

mythical inspired sages. The fact is, that although Manu and Yajnavalkya still form the basis of Hindu jurisprudence, many of their laws are regarded by more recent Hindu legislators as only intended for the first three ages of the world, and therefore as having no force, or superseded by others, in the present fourth and more degenerate Kaliyuga (see note 2, p. 204). Thus the author of the work ascribed to Narada[1] says:

Marriage with the widow of a deceased brother, the slaughter of cattle in entertaining guests, flesh-meat at funeral obsequies, and the entrance into the third order (or that of a Vanaprastha, 'hermit') are forbidden in the fourth age.

The following acts, allowed under certain circumstances by ancient law, are also forbidden in the fourth age.

Drinking any spirituous liquor, even at a religious ceremony[2]; the gift of a young married woman to another bridegroom if her husband should die while she is still a virgin; the marriage of twice-born men with women not of the same class; any intercourse with a twice-born man who has passed the sea in a ship; the slaughter of a bull at a sacrifice, &c.

And the author of Parashara's Code[3] affirms:

The laws of various ages are different. Manu's Law-book belongs to the Krita age, Gautama's to the Treta, that of Shankha and Likhita to the Dvapara, and Parashara's Code to the Kali age.

Many modern lawyers, regard the whole of Smriti, beginning with Manu, as one, and assert that the inconsistencies and contradictions it contains are all capable of explanation.

I here annex a few particulars relative to the eighteen principal Codes posterior to Manu and Yajnavalkya:

---

1. Quoted by Sir W. Jones, vol. viii. p. 153.
2. As, for example, the Sautramani.
3. Quoted by Professor Stenzler in his preface to Yajnavalkya.

1. That attributed to *Atri*, one of Manu's ten Prajapatis (I. 35), is in verse, and written in a perspicuous style. 2. That of *Vishnu* is also in verse, and is regarded as an excellent treatise, an abridgment of which is also extant. 3. That of *Harita*, on the contrary, is in prose, but has been abridged in a metrical form. 4. That of *Usanas* or Sukra is in verse, and an abridgment is extant. 5. A short treatise of about seventy verses is ascribed to *Angiras*, one of Manu's Prajapatis and Maharshis (I. 35). 6. A tract consisting of one hundred verses, commented on by Kulluka-bhatta, is mythically attributed to *Yama* (brother of Manu Vaivasvata), ruler of the world of spirits. 7. That of Apastamba is in prose, but an abridgment in verse also exists. 8. *Samvarta's* Code has also a metrical abridgment. 9. *Katyayana's* law-treatise is full and perspicuous. 10. *Vrihaspati's* has been abridged, and it is doubtful whether we possess the abridgment or the Code itself. 11. *Parashara's* treatise is regarded by some as the highest authority for the Kali or fourth age of the world. It has been commented on by Madhavacarya. 12. A law-treatise is ascribed to the celebrated *Vyasa*, son of Parashara. 13, 14. Two separate tracts in verse by *Shankha* and *Likhita* exist, but their joint treatise in prose is the one usually cited by Kulluka and others. It is supposed to be adapted to the Dvapara age. 15. A code in verse of no special interest is attributed to *Daksha*, one of Manu's ten Prajapatis (I. 35). 16. A prose treatise written in a clear style bears the name of *Gautama*. It is held to have been written for the Treta age. 17. Shatatapa's Code is chiefly on penance and expiation. There is an abridgment of it in verse. 18. The treatise attributed to Vasishtaha, another of Manu's Prajapatis (I. 35), is a mixture of prose and verse.

Of other codes ascribed to various mythical lawgivers in the Padma-purana &c. it will be sufficient to mention those of Marichi, Pulastya, Narada (Manu I. 35), Kashyapa, Vishvamitra, Gargya, Baudhayana, Paithinasi, Sumantu, Lokakshi, Kuthumi and Dhaumya.

Besides, there are a vast number of legal treatises and commentaries based on ancient codes by modern lawyers, whose works are current and more or less esteemed as authorities in different parts of India. They form five schools, of which I here give a brief account.

The Five Schools of Hindu Law

These are the schools of — 1. Bengal, 2. Benares, 3. Mithila (North Behar and Tirhut), 4. Madras (*Dravida*), and 5. Bombay (*Maharashtra*)[1]. There are certain books regarded as special authorities in each of these principal schools.

1. In Bengal both Manu and Yajnavalkya are of course held in great reverence as original sources of law. We have already noted that the best commentary on Manu is one called Manv-artha-muktavali, by Kulluka-bhatta (see p. 242). There is also a commentary by Medhatithi (partially lost, and completed by another author); another by Govinda-raja; another by Dharani-dhara, Bhaguri, and others. To Yajnavalkya belong at least four other commentaries besides the Mitakshara, viz. that of Apararka (which is the oldest of all); of Shula-pani (called the Dipa-kalika); of Deva-bodha, and of Visva-rupa. Sula-pani is also the author of a work on penance and expiation. The Mitakshara of Vijnaneshvara[2] is however, the principal commentary on Yajnavalkya (as before noticed). It is much studied in Bengal, but the chief authority in the Bengal school is a well-known work, somewhat different in

---

1. I have here consulted Mr. Herbert Cowell's Tagore Law Lectures, copies of which have always been kindly given to me by the Senate of the Calcutta University.
2. Vijnanesvara belonged to a sect of Sannyasins founded by Shankara-charya, and his commentary may have been written as early as the ninth century of our era.

character and principles, called the Daya-bhaga or 'treatise on inheritance,' ascribed to Jimuta-vahana[1], by some thought to have been a prince of the house of Silara, who either composed this work himself or caused it to be compiled rather earlier than the beginning of the sixteenth century. It should be stated that both the Mitakshara and Daya-bhaga are developments of, rather than commentaries on, Manu and Yajnavalkya. Although they profess to be based on these ancient books, they sometimes modify the laws there propounded to suit a more advanced social system. In other cases they discuss doubtful points and supply omissions; while they, in their turn, have been commented on by succeeding lawyers, whose works introduce still further modifications on various important points[2], thus:

Three principal commentaries on the Mitakshara are named, viz. the Subodhini of Vishveshvara-bhatta (thought by Colebrooke to be as old as the fourteenth century); a later work by Balam-bhatta; and a third (called the Pratitakshara) by Nanda-pandita (who was also the author of the work on adoption called Dattak-mimansa and of the Vaijayauti (see next page). The commentaries on the Daya-bhaga are numerous. Some of. these (published under the patronage of Prasanna Kumar Thakur) are, that of Shrikrishna-tarkalankara, which, with a treatise by the same author called Daya-krama-sangraha, is highly esteemed in Bengal; that of Shri-nathacharya-chudamani; that of Achyuta-chakravartin; and that of Maheshara. Before any of these ought to be placed the works of a celebrated

---

1. Translated by Colebrooke. Jimuta-vahana's work seems to have been called Dharma-ratna, and only the chapter on inheritance is preserved.
2. The certainty we feel as to the accuracy of the texts of all important Sanskrit works is due to the practice of writing commentaries, which always quote the words of the original, and so prevent changes. Again, the accuracy and genuineness of the best commentaries is secured by other commentaries on them.

Brahman (who lived at the beginning of the sixteenth century), named Raghu-nandana, in about twenty-seven books, on rites and customs and the times of their observance. His treatises, intended to comment on and support Jimuta-vahana, are called Smriti-tattva, Tithi-tattva, &c., the former including the Vyavahara-tattva and Daya-tattva[1].

2. As regards the school of Benares and Middle India it should be noted that the Mitakshara of Vijnanesvara is acknowledged as an authority, and studied by the adherents of this school, as it is to a certain extent by all five schools. But in the Benares school certain popular commentaries on the Mitakshara, such as the Vira-mitrao-daya of Mitra-mishra and the Vivada-tandava of Kamala-kara, have great weight.

3. In the Maithila school or that of Mithila (North Behar and Tirhut), besides the Code of Yajnavalkya with the Mitakshara, the Vivada-chintamani and Vyavahara-chintamani of Vachaspati Misra[2] are much studied; also the Vivada-ratnakara of Chandesvara (who lived about 1314) and the Vivada-chandra, composed by a learned female named Lakhima-devi, who is said to have set the name of her kinsman, Misaru-misra, to her own works.

4. In the Dravidian or South-Indian school besides the Mitakshara, as before, there is the Smriti-chandrika and Dattaka-chandrika of Devana-bhatta; Madhavacharya's commentary on Parashara's Code (called Parashara-smriti-vyakhya); and Nanda-pandita's commentary on Vishnu's Code (called Vaijayanti), and on Parashara's Code, and his treatise on the law of adoption called Dattaka-chandrika.

---

1. Printed in Kolkata in 1828. Raghu-nandana is often called Smarta-bhattacharya.
2. Often called Misra. His work has been translated by Prasanna Kumar Thakur, and printed in Kolkata in 1863. A copy was kindly sent to me by the translator.

5. In the Western school (of Bombay and Maharashtra), besides the Mitakshara, certain treatises by Nilakantha-bhatta, particularly one called Vyavahara-mayukha[1], have the most weight.

---

1. A translation of this by Mr. H. Borrodaile of the Bombay Civil Service was published at Surat at the Mission Press in 1827.

Lecture XII

IV. *The Itihasa or Epic Poems —*
The Ramayana[1]

In India, literature, like the whole face of nature, is on a gigantic scale. Poetry, born amid the majestic scenery of the Himalayas, and fostered in a climate which inflamed the imaginative powers, developed itself with Oriental luxuriance, if not always with true sublimity. Although the Hindu, like the Greeks, have only two great epic poems[2] — the Ramayana and Mahabharata — yet to compare these vast compositions with the Iliad and the Odyssey, is to compare the Indus and the Ganges, rising in the snows of the world's

---

1. A portion of the matter of this Lecture and of that on the Mahabharata was delivered by me as a public Lecture before the University of Oxford, on the 9th of May, 1862, and was afterwards published in a little work called 'Indian Epic Poetry,' which is now out of print.
2. I am here speaking of that form of epic poetry which may be called natural and spontaneous as distinguished from artificial. Whether the Indian Epics (Itihasas) or even the Iliad can be strictly said to answer Aristotle's definition of Epos, is another question. Artificial epic poems (Kavyas) are not wanting in later Sanskrit, and specimens will be given in a subsequent Lecture.

most colossal ranges, swollen by numerous tributaries, spreading into vast shallows or branching into deep divergent channels, with the streams of Attica or the mountain-torrents of Thessaly. There is, in fact, an immensity of bulk about this, as about every other department of Sanskrit literature, which to a European mind, accustomed to a more limited horizon, is absolutely bewildering.

Nevertheless, a sketch, however imperfect, of the two Indian Epics can scarcely fail to interest Occidental scholars; for all true poetry, whether European or Asiatic, must have features of resemblance; and no poems could have achieved celebrity in the East as these have done, had they not addressed themselves to feelings and affections common to human nature, and belonging alike to Englishmen and Hindus.

I propose, therefore, in the next three Lectures, to give a brief general idea of the character and contents of the Ramayana and Mahabharata[1], comparing them in some important particulars with each other, and pointing out the most obvious features of similarity or difference, which must strike every classical scholar who contrasts them with the Iliad and the Odyssey.

It is, of course, a principal characteristic of epic poetry, as distinguished from lyrical, that it should concern itself more with external action than internal feelings. It is this which makes Epos the natural expression of early national life. When centuries of trial have turned the mind of nations inwards, and men begin to speculate, to reason, to elaborate language and cultivate science, there may be no lack of refined poetry, but the spontaneous production of epic song is, at that stage of national existence, as impossible as for

---

1. A more complete analysis of the Ramayana and Mahabharata was given by me at the end of the little work called 'Indian Epic Poetry,' and will probably be reprinted with additions hereafter.

an octogenarian to delight in the giants and giant-killers of his childhood. The Ramayana and Mahabharata then, as reflecting the Hindu character in ancient times, may be expected to abound in stirring incidents of exaggerated heroic action.

Songs in celebration of great heroes were probably current in India quite as early as the Homeric poems in Greece. No mention, indeed, is made of Rama, Arjuna, and Yudhishthira in the hymns of the Rig-veda, but the deeds of Indra and other gods and heroes, who were supposed to protect the more civilized Aryas from the barbarous An-aryas, are there narrated and lauded, and it is in the songs composed in their praise that we may trace the foreshadowings of Indian epic poetry. Again, we know that Itihasas, or legendary narratives, were recited orally at the period when the Grihya Sutras and Manu were composed (see first few lines of p. 223; note, p. 236; and p. 280). Such narratives doubtless recounted the adventures of the popular heroes of the period, with all the warmth of colouring natural to writers whose imaginations were stimulated by an Eastern climate and environments; but it is scarcely credible that they could have achieved much popularity had they not rested on a basis of historical truth.

It is certainly likely that at some early date, not long after the first settlement of the Aryan races in the country of the five rivers, rival tribes of immigrants, called Kurus, advancing from that region towards the plains of Hindustan, contended for supremacy. It is, moreover, probable that soon after their final occupation of the Gangetic districts, a body of invaders headed by a bold leader, and aided by the warlike but uncivilized hill-tribes, forced their way southwards into the peninsula of India as far as Ceylon. The heroic exploits of the chieftains in both cases would naturally become the theme of epic poetry, and the wild Aborigines of the Vindhya and neighbouring hills would be poetically converted into monkeys[1], while the powerful pre-Aryan races of the south would be represented as many-headed ogres and bloodthirsty demons[2]. These races, who are called *An-arya*,

1. Strabo (XV. 29) relates that on a particular occasion a large number of monkeys came out of a wood and stood opposite the Macedonian troops, who seeing them apparently stationed in military array, mistook them for a real army and prepared to attack them as enemies.

2. We must be careful not to confound the great Dravidian races occupying the Madras Presidency and speaking Tamil, Telugu, Kanarese, and Malayalam, with the uncivilized aboriginal tribes found on the hills and in the jungles of India. The Dravidian races (probably symbolized by the Ravanas and Vibhishanas of epic poetry) were the precursors of the Sanskrit-speaking Aryans, and possibly had their origin in the same districts of Central Asia, whence they immigrated by the same mountain-passes into the Panjab and Northern India. They may have partially amalgamated with the advancing Aryans, but were mostly driven southwards. There they attained a considerable independent civilization. Their languages, although eventually more or less intermingled with Sanskrit words, are agglutinating (commonly called Turanian) in structure, and possess an extensive and important literature of their own. On the other hand, the hill-tribes and others (such as were symbolized by the monkey-armies of Hanuman) — the Gonds of Central India, the Bhils of the hills to the west of the Gonds, the Khonds or Kus of the eastern districts of Gondvana and the ranges south of Orissa, the Santhals and Kols of the hills to the west of Bengal, the Khasias and Garos of the eastern border — are the present representatives of numerous wild Tartar tribes who swarmed into India at various epochs, some of them probably coming from Chinese Tartary and Tibet, and taking the course of the Brahma-putra into Bengal. These speak an infinite number of different dialects and are almost all mutually unintelligible. If the term Turanian is to embrace races so widely separated by language and customs as the Dravidians and various hill-tribes of India, the sooner it is expelled from the vocabulary of philologists and ethnologists the better. At any rate, there must be two great classes of Turanian languages, the North and the South; the former comprising the three sisters Tungusic (or Mantchu), Mongol, and Turkish, besides Samoyedic and Finnish, while the

'ignoble,' in opposition to *Arya*, 'noble,' had been gradually driven southwards or towards the hills by the Aryan settlers. They probably made great resistance in the North at the time the Rig-veda was composed. They are there called Dasyus, Yatudhanas, &c., and described as monstrous in form, godless, inhuman, haters of Brahmans, disturbers of sacred rites, eaters of human and horse flesh (Rig-veda X. 87, 16; Muir's Texts II. 435). In the epic poems they are generally called Rakshasas or evil demons, the relentless enemies of gods and good men and of all sacred rites[1]. It is to the subjugation

---

latter takes in Tibetan, Siamese, Burmese, and the Dravidian languages; the monosyllabic Chinese standing, as it were, between the two. Perhaps the dialects of the Himalayan tribes have, of all hill-dialects, the best title to be ranked among the South Turanian class. Dr. Caldwell, in his valuable Comparative Grammar of the South-Indian Languages, has discussed the affiliation of the Dravidian family with great ability. He considers that the Dravidians were the first inhabitants of India, and that they were driven southwards by other invaders, who were afterwards subdued by the Aryans. The rude dialects of the more southern hill-tribes are partially connected with the Dravidian, especially the Tuda, Kota (two dialects of the Nilgiri hills), Gonds, and Khond (Ku). The Ramusies and most of the Korawars speak a patois of Telugu. The Male-arasars ('hill-kings') of the Southern Ghats speak partly corrupt Malayalam and corrupt Tamil. The Lambadies, or gypsies, speak a dialect of Hindustani. Among the barbarous tribes of the South are included the Vedars of the forests of Ceylon.

1. In one place (Ramayana III. i. 15) they are described as black, with woolly hair and thick lips. The following is from III. i. 22, &c.: 'Men devouring Rakshasas of various shapes and wild-beasts dwell in this vast forest. They harass the devotees in the settlements. These shapeless and ill-looking monsters testify their abominable character by various cruel and terrific displays of it. These base-born wretches (*an-arya*) perpetrate the greatest outrages. Changing their shapes and hiding in the thickets they delight in terrifying devotees. They cast away the sacrificial ladles and vessels (*shrug-bhandam*), pollute the cooked oblations, and defile the offerings with blood. They utter frightful sound in the ears of the faithful.' Viradha, a Rakshasa, is said

of these non-Aryan races by heroic Aryan leaders who were Kshatriyas, as well as the rivalry between different tribes of the settlers themselves, that we owe the circumstances out of which the two great Epics arose. Whether the celebrated Aryan warriors of the Ramayana and Mahabharata were identical with those of the Itihasas of which mention is made in the Grihya Sutras and in Manu (III. 232) cannot be proved; but this much is clear, that the exploits of the three Ramas, Arjuna, &c., became, soon after Manu's time, the theme of song, and that these heroes were in the first instance represented as merely men of great strength and prowess, whose powers, however extraordinary, were not more than human. The oral descriptions of their deeds and adventures by public reciters formed the original basis of the two great Epics, and were naturally the peculiar property of the Kshatriya and conquering class. Probably these narratives were in the first instance delivered in prose, which became gradually interspersed with the simplest form of metre, such as that called Anushtubh or Shloka[1].

It is easy indeed for the most cursory reader of the Ramayana and Mahabharata to trace a substratum or basis (*mula*) of simple heroic narration underlying the mass of

---

(Ramayana III. vii. 5; Muir II. 427) to be 'like a mountain-peak, with long legs, a huge body, a crooked nose, hideous eyes, a long face, pendent belly, &c., like Death with an open mouth.' The Nishadas of the Puranas, though described as dwarfish, have similar features, and are no doubt intended for the same race. In the same way, in describing races unknown to the Greeks, such as the Cyclopes, Laestrogones, Centauri, &c., Homer and other Grecian writers are given to exaggeration, and relate the most absurd fables.

1. The oldest part of the Mahabharata has a section entirely in prose (see note 1, p. 414). The invention of the Sloka is attributed to Valmiki, the reputed author of the Ramayana, with the object doubtless of establishing his claims to be regarded as one of the earliest and most ancient of Indian poets. This metre is found in the Veda.

more recent accretions. But to what date is this first frame-
work of the poems to be referred? And again — When
occurred that first process of brahmanizing which obscured
and transformed its original character? And lastly — When
was the structure completed and the whole work moulded
into a form similar to that we now possess?

With regard to the first of these questions, I have now
to submit five reasons in support of the view that the earliest
or pre-brahmanical composition of both Epics took place at
a period not later than the fifth century B.C., as follow:

1. The Ramayana records no case of Sati. In the Mahabharata, Madri, wife of Pandu, is made to immolate herself with
her husband[1], and the four wives of Vasu-deva and some of
Krishna's wives to the same[2]; but it is remarkable that none of
the numerous widows of the slain heroes are represented as
burning themselves in the same manner. This shows that the
practice of Sati was beginning to be introduced in the North-
west of India near the Panjab (where we know it prevailed about
300 years B.C.), but that it had not at the time of the earliest
composition of the Ramayana reached the more eastern districts.
But if one Epic records no Sati, and the other only rare cases
— notwithstanding the numerous opportunities for referring to
the practice afforded by the circumstances of the plot — it
follows that we ought to place the laying down of the first lines
of both compositions before the third century B.C., when we
know from Megasthenes that it prevailed generally even as far
east as Magadha.

2. The first construction, or so to speak, 'first casting' of the
stories of Rama and of the Pandavas as poems with definite plots,
seems to have been pre-buddhistic quite as clearly as it was pre-
brahmanical — by which I mean, that it took place anterior to
the actual establishment of Buddhism as a rival system. Only one

---

1. Adi-parvan 4896. See also 3030.
2. Mausala-parvan 194, 249.

direct mention of Buddha and Buddhism occurs in the Ramayana, and the verses in which it occurs (II. cviii. 30-38), and in which Buddha is compared to a thief, are admitted to be an interpolation and not part of the original poem. Nor can it be proved that any such direct reference occurs in the original Mahabharata. Nevertheless, there are numerous allusions (not bearing the stamp of later additions) in both Epics, especially the latter, to that development of rationalistic inquiry and Buddhistic scepticism, which we know commenced about 5000 years B.C.[1]

3. It is evident from the Asoka inscriptions that the language of the mass of the people in Hindustan in the third century B.C. was not pure Sanskrit. It consisted rather of a variety of provincial Sanskritic dialects, to which the general name of Prakrit is applied. If, then, the first redaction of these popular poems had taken place as late as the third century, is it likely that some forms of Prakrit would not have been introduced into the dialogues and allowed to remain there, as we find has been done in the dramas, the oldest of which — the Mricchakatika — can scarcely be much later than the second century B.C.? It is true that the language of the original story of both Epics, as traceable in the present texts, is generally simple Sanskrit, and by no means elaborate or artificial; but this is just what might have been understood by the majority of the people about five centuries B.C., before the language of the people had become generally prakriticized.

4. When the story of the poems was first put together in a continuous form, it is clear that the Deccan and more westerly and southerly regions of India had not been occupied by the Aryans. But we know from the Asoka inscriptions that the empire of the kings of Magadha and Palibothra in the third century radiated in all directions, as inscriptions are found in the Panjab, at Delhi, in Kuttack, and as far west as Gujarata.

---

1. Note particularly the infidel doctrins expressed by the Brahman Javali (see p. 393), and Book I. 12. of the Bengali recension of the Ramayana, where Shramanas, or Buddhist mendicants, are mentioned.

5. The Greek writer, Dion Chrysostomos, who was born about the middle of the first century, and was especially honoured by the emperor Trajan, mentions (Or. LIII. 555) that records existed in his time of epic poems, recited by the Hindus, which had been copied or translated from Homer. These statements, as Professor Lassen has shown (Ind. Alt. III. 346), must have been taken from the accounts of Megasthenes, who lived at the court of Chandra-gupta (see note p. 253). They indicate that poems resembling the Iliad were current in India at least as early as the third or fourth century B.C., though it by no means follows that the Hindu poets borrowed a single idea from Homer[1].

These points seem to merit consideration in fixing 500 B.C. as an approximate date for the first or pre-brahmanical and pre-buddhistic versions of the two poems. The names of the authors of these original versions appear to have perished, unless it be held (which seems highly improbable) that the story of Rama must be assigned to Valmiki from its very first existence as a Kavya.

We come next to the second stage of their construction. We have suggested the fifth century B.C. as the probable date

---

1. The passage in Dion Chrysostomos is as follows: (Reiske's Edit. P. 253). There seems too great a disposition among European scholars to regard the Hindus as destitute of all originality. I cannot but agree with Professor Lassen that Megasthenes was mistaken, though obviously the story of the great war between the rival tribes, and that of the carrying off of Sita by a South-Indian chief, have, of course, points of resemblance to the Iliad, which may have suggested the idea of plagiarism. The sufferings of king Dhrita-rashtra are like those of Priam, and the lamentations of the wives of the slain heroes after the battles between the Pandavas and Kauravas are like those of Hecuba and Andromache, while the martial deeds of Arjuna and Duryodhana resemble those of Achilles and Hector. According to Professor Weber the passage in Dion contains the earliest notice by other writers of the Indian epic poems. He is, moreover, of opinion that the Indian poets really took ideas from Homer.

of the rise of Brahmanism, as depicted in Manu (see p. 236), and with it of Buddhistic scepticism. The ambitious Brahmans who aimed at religious and intellectual supremacy, gradually saw the policy of converting the great national Epics, which they could not suppress, into instruments for moulding the popular mind in accordance with their own pattern. Possibly, too, they may have hoped to turn them into important engines for arresting the progress of Buddhistic rationalism. Accordingly, I conjecture that in the fourth century B.C. they commenced re-constructing and remodelling the two great Epics. They proceeded, in short, to brahmanize what was before the property of the Kshatriya or warrior caste. This process was of course committed to poets who were Brahmans, and was not completed all at once. Those songs which described too plainly the independence of the military caste, were modified, obscured by allegory, and rendered improbable by monstrous fable and mythological embellishments. Any circumstance which appeared opposed to the Brahmanical system, was speciously explained away, glossed over, or mystified[1]. If unbelievers, like Javali, were brought on the scene, it was only that their arguments might be refuted, and

---

1. Thus when Dasharatha kills a boy while hunting (see p. 388), the dying youth is made to explain that, although a hermit's son, he is no Brahman, thereby relieving the king from the guilt of Brahmanicide, which, according to Manu, was unpardonable either in this world or the next (Manu VIII. 381, XII. 55). Again, the account of the victory of the Kshatriya Rama-chandra over the Brahman Parashu-rama — the mythical champion of the sacerdotal caste — is surrounded with a haze of mysticism (see p. 367, note 2; p. 386); while the episode which relates at full Visvamitra's quarrel with the great saint Vasishtha, and the success of the former, though a Kshatriya, in elevating himself to a Brahman's rank, introduces the wildest hyperbole, with the manifest object of investing the position of a Brahman with unapproachable grandeur, and deterring others from attempts in the same direction (see p. 403).

their characters reprobated (see p. 394). The great Kshatriya dynasties were made to trace back their origin to Brahmanical sages (see p. 383). Kings were allowed to undertake nothing except under the direction of Brahman ministers[1]; while the great heroes themselves were not really Kshatriyas, or even human beings, but emanations of the Deity.

In the case of the Ramayana, the unity of the story was never broken by calling in the aid of more than one author, whose name was Valmiki, and who must have completed the task single-handed. Hence it never lost its character of a Kavya, or poem, with a clear and coherent plot. On the other hand, the brahmanizing of the story of the great war between the Pandavas and Kauravas seems to have attracted a succession of poets, who interwove their own compositions into the original texture of the work, so that its individuality, and even the name of its first author, disappeared under the constant accession of new matter. Hence we must suppose, in the case of the Mahabharata, more than one Brahmanical redaction and amplification, which need not be assumed for the completion of the Ramayana. Moreover, the great mass of ever-increasing materials under which the original story of the Pandavas became almost lost to view, and under which the title to the name Kavya merged in that of a rambling Itihasa, had to be adjusted and arranged by an imaginary compiler, called Vyasa.

The first orderly completion, then, of the two poems in their brahmanized form, may have taken place, I think in the case of the Ramayana about the beginning of the third century B.C., and in the case of the Mahabharata (the original story of which is possibly more ancient than that of the Ramayana) still later — perhaps as late as the second century B.C. The

---

1. King Dasaratha in the Ramayana is described as surrounded by Brahman ministers (see p. 378).

posteriority of the brahmanized Mahabharata may be supported by the more frequent allusions it contains to the progress of Buddhistic opinions, and to intercourse with the Yavanas or Greeks, who had no considerable dealings with the Hindus till two or three centuries after Alexander's invasion[1].

It is, however, necessary to refer the final construction of both poems in their present form to a third and still later epoch, and even to assign portions of them to the early centuries of our own era, if we are to accept as integral parts of the two Epics such a supplement to the Ramayana as the Uttara-kanda, and such additions to the Mahabharata as the Bhagavad-gita and Hari-vansha, as well as those later episodes which identify Rama and Krishna with the Supreme Being. And here again in this final construction of both poems, we must bear in mind, that the deification of Rama represents an earlier stage of Vishnu-worship than that of Krishna; and that the Ramayana, as now presented to us, contains far fewer recent additions than the Mahabharata.

---

1. A candid study of Professor Weber's writing, and especially of the reproduction of his views lately put forth in the 'Indian Antiquary,' has led me to modify to a certain extent the statements in my Lecture on 'Indian Epic Poetry,' delivered May 9, 1862; but I cannot agree in thinking that the work of Valmiki is to be referred to as late a date as the beginning of the Christian era. Nor can I concur in the opinion that the Ramayana is later than, and to a certain extent a copy of the Buddhist story of Rama, called Dasharatha-jataka, in which Rama is represented as the brother of Sita, and in which there are certain verses almost identical with verses in the present text of the Ramayana. Nor do I think that the great Indian Epic has been developed out of germs furnished by this or any other Buddhistic legends. Still less can I give in my adhesion to the theory that the Hindu Epics took ideas from the Homeric poems; or to the suggestion of Mr. Talboys Wheeler, that the story of the Ramayana was invented to give expression to the hostile feeling and contention between the Brahmans and Buddhists of Ceylon, alleged to be represented by the Rakshasa.

My reasons, therefore, for placing the first Brahmanical construction of the two Indian Epics in the third and second century B.C. respectively, and for commencing an account of epic poetry with the story of Rama, rather than with that of Pandavas, will be clear. It must be remembered, however, that the priority of one poem over the other cannot be made to rest on any certain chronological basis. Indeed, the Mahabharata describes a conflict between rude colonists in a district nearer to the earliest settlements of the Aryans, while the Ramayana is concerned with a more established kingdom (Kosala), and a more civilized and luxurious capital city (Ayodhya).

Before commencing our summary of either story it will be desirable to note more particularly when and how the doctrine of divine incarnation was imported into both poems, imparting to them that religious and sacred character which they have ever since retained, and which is a distinguishing feature in comparing them with the epic poetry of other nations. We know from the statements of Megasthenes, preserved in Strabc and Diodorus, that the worship of Vishnu in his heroic incarnations prevailed in Hindustan about 300 years before Christ (see note, p. 310). The deification of great men probably began with the desire of the Brahmans to incorporate the most eminent Kshatriya heroes into their system. It proceeded, however, from necessity rather than from any wish to do honour to the warrior caste. The Buddhistic movement in India had broken down the Brahmanical monopoly and introduced a rival principle. Some counteracting and equally popular expansion of religious creed seemed essential to the very existence of Brahmanism, and it became absolutely necessary to present the people with deities of their own as a counter-attraction to Buddhism. Hence the previously human heroes Rama and Krishna were exalted by the Brahmans to divine rank, and even Buddha himself was, in the end, adopted into their system and represented as one of the ten incarnations of the god Vishnu[1].

But the idea of divine incarnation had taken possession of the Hindu mind still earlier. It is probable that in that primeval country, where the ancestors of Greeks and Hindus had their common home, men satisfied their first religious instincts by idealizing and worshipping, under no defined form and without precise ritual, the principal forces and energies of nature — the air, the rain, the wind, the storm, the fire, the sun — the elements on which, as an agricultural and pastoral race, their welfare depended. This was the earliest religion of nature which the Aryan family carried with them when they first left their home, and which they cherished in their wanderings; and in this we may trace the germ of their subsequent religious systems. When they had settled down in new resting-places, their religious cravings naturally found utterance in prayers, hymns, and a simple form of ritual. Religion, or a sense of dependence on a higher Power, and a desire to realize his presence, grew with their growth and strengthened with their strength. But in all ages and countries the religion of the mass of mankind rapidly assumes an anthropomorphic character. A richly peopled mythology arose in India and Greece as naturally as poetry itself. The one was the offspring of the other, and was in fact the poetical expression of those high aspirations which marked the Aryan character. Soon the Hindu, like the Greek, unguided by direct revelation, personified and deified not only the powers of external nature, but all the internal

---

1. Heroism, undaunted bravery, and personal strength will always find worshippers in India. It is recorded that a number of Panjabi Hindus commenced worshipping the late John Nicholson, one of the bravest and noblest of men, under the name Nikkil Seyn. He endeavoured to put a stop to the absurdity, but they persisted in their worship notwithstanding.

feelings, passions, moral and intellectual qualities and faculties of the mind. Soon he began to regard every grand and useful object as a visible manifestation of the supreme Intelligence presiding over the universe, and every departed hero or benefactor as a mere reflection of the same all-wise and omnipresent Ruler. Hence, to give expression to the varied attributes and functions of this great Being, thus visibly manifested to the world, both Hindu and Greek peopled their pantheons with numerous divine and semi-divine creations, clothing them with male and female forms, and inventing in connexion with them various fanciful and often monstrous myths, fables, and allegories, which the undiscriminating multitude accepted as realities, without at all understanding the ideas they symbolized. In India we are able to trace back the development of these anthropomorphic ideas to their source in the Rig-veda, and thence follow them step by step through Manu, the epic poems, and Puranas. In the Rig-veda a god Vishnu is often named as a manifestation of the Solar energy, or rather as a form of the Sun; and the point which distinguishes him from the others is his striding over the heavens in three paces, supposed to symbolize the three stages of the Sun's daily course in his rising, culminating, and setting (see note, p. 367). Subsequently he takes a foremost place among the twelve Adityas, or twelve distinct forms of the Sun in the twelve months of the year. In the Brahmanas he is identified with sacrifice (*Yajna*), and one described as a dwarf (*Vamana;* Satapatha-brahmana XIV. 1, 1, 6, I. 2, 5, 5). In Manu, Brahman, the universal Soul, is represented as evolving his essence in the form of Brahma, the Creator of all things, and various other visible manifestations of the Deity are recognized, as in the Veda. In Book XII. 121, Vishnu and Hara (= Shiva) are mentioned as present in the human body, the former imparting movement to its muscles, the later bestowing strength.

In all this, however, there was not enough to satisfy the cravings of the human heart for a religion of faith in a personal god — a god sympathizing with humanity, and even with the lower forms of animal life, loving all his creatures, interested in their affairs, and ever at hand to assist them in their difficulties. Nor, on the other hand, was there sufficient to meet the demands of other constituent parts of man's complex nature for a religion of activity and good works; of austerity and subjugation of the passions; of contemplation and higher spiritual knowledge. Soon, therefore, the great Sprit of the universe began to be viewed still more anthropomorphically, through the medium of man's increasing subjectivity, as a Being who not only created man but condescended to human sympathies, and placed himself in the closest connexion with all his creatures, whether gods, men, or animals.

But first arose the inquiry why and how this great Being willed to create at all? To account for this it was conceived that when the universal and infinite Being Brahman (*nom.case of the neut. Brahman*) — the only really existing entity, wholly without form and unbound and unaffected by the three Gunas or by qualities of any kind (pp. 102, 125) — wished to create for his own entertainment the phenomena of the universe, he assumed the quality of activity (*rajas*) and became a male person as Brahma (*nom. case masc.*) the Creator. Next, in the progress of still further self-evolution, he willed to invest himself with the second quality of goodness (*sattva*) as Vishnu the Preserver, and with the third quality of darkness (*tamas*[1]) as Siva the Destroyer. This development of the doctrine of triple manifestation (*tri-murti*), which appears first in the

---

1. In the Kumara-sambhava II. 4, we have the following: *Namas trimurtaye tubhyam prak-srishteh kevalatamane Guna-traya-vibhagaya paschad bhedam upeyushe*, 'Hail to thee of triple form, who before creation wast simple Soul, and afterwards underwent partition for the distribution of the three Gunas.'

brahmanized version of the Indian Epics, had already been adumbrated in the Veda in the triple form of fire (see p. 18), and in the triad of gods, Agni, Surya, and Indra (see note, p. 19); and in other ways[1].

In fact the Veda, rather than Manu, was the source of the later incarnations (see notes, pp. 365-367). It was the Vedic Vishnu (connected with Surya, 'the Sun') who became Vishnu the world-preserver, while Rudra (connected with Indra and the Maruts), the god of tempests, became the world-dissolver Shiva. Under the latter form, the Supreme Being is supposed to pass from the operation of creation and preservation to that of destruction, these three separate acts being assigned to separate deities who are themselves finite, and obey the universal law of dissolution at the end of a Kalpa (see note, p. 368), when they again become merged in simple Soul (*kevalatman*). But as it was essential that even the god of dissolution should connect himself with humanity, and as, according to a fundamental dogma of Hinduism, all death leads to new life, all destruction to reproduction, it was natural that the latter operation should be chosen as the link of connexion, rather than the former. His function of destroyer is, therefore, interchanged with that of creator (note 2, p. 362); he himself is called Shiva, 'the Auspicious,' and his character is oftener typified by the reproductive Linga (without necessary implication of sensual ideas) than by any symbol of destruction. Under this image, in fact, he is generally worshipped in India[2]. Nevertheless,

---

1. The thirty-three gods (3 multiplied by 11) of the Rig-veda (*tribhir ekadashair devebhir yatam*, I. 34, 11, I. 45, 2) point to the same idea of triple manifestation.
2. Twelve celebrated Lingas were set up, about the tenth century, in twelve great shrines, in twelve chief cities of India, of which Somnath was one. The representation of the generative organ is not offensive to delicacy even when surrounded by the Yoni, or female symbol. Quite enough, however, is implied to account for the degeneration

he is also represented in human form, living in the Himalaya mountains along with his wife Parvati[1], sometimes in the act of trampling on and destroying demons, wearing round his black neck (*nila-kantha*) a serpent and a necklace of skulls, and furnished with a whole apparatus of external emblems (such as a white bull on which he rides, a crescent, a trident[2], tiger's skin, elephant's skin, rattle, noose, &c.), the exaggeration of which imparts a childish and grotesque character to Hindu symbolism when regarded from a European point of view. Again, Mahadeva, or the great deity Shiva, is sometimes connected with humanity in one other personification very different from that just noted, viz. that of an austere naked ascetic, with matted hair[3] (*Dig-ambara, Dhurjati*), living in a

---

of Siva-worship in modern times, as expressed in the works called Tantras and in the practices of the Saktas. The representation of Shiva as Ardhanari, half male, half female, symbolizes the unity of the generative principal. Some think the god Siva with the Linga (Phallus) was adopted by the Aryans from the aborigines. The word Shiva means 'auspicious,' and being first applied euphemistically to the god of tempests (Rudra) afterwards passed into the name of the god of destruction.

1. The *shakti* or active energy of a deity is personified as his wife, and those who worship the female principle are called Shaktas. Parvati, daughter of the mountain, and worshipped under the name Durga in Bengal, is the chief object of the adoration of Shaktas and Tantrikas.

2. This three-pronged symbol may denote creation, destruction, and regeneration. He has also three eyes (one of which is in his forehead), in allusion to either the three Vedas or time past, present, and future (whence he is called *Try-ambaka*), and five faces (whence his name *Panchanana*); the crescent moon also symbolizing his power over the measurement of time. He is sometimes said to manifest himself under eight forms — ether, air, fire, water, earth, sun, moon, the sacrificing priest (whence his name *Ashta-murti*). His black throat was caused by the deadly poison churned out of the ocean, which would have destroyed the universe had he not swallowed it.

3. The hair is so worn by Shiva-worshipping Yogis (see p. 112).

forest apart from his consort, abiding in one spot fixed and immovable (*Sthanu*) — teaching men by his own example, first, the power to be acquired by penance (*tapas*), mortification of the body[1], and suppression of the passions; and, secondly, the great virtue of abstract meditation (*samadhi*), as leading to the loftiest spiritual knowledge (*jnana*) and ultimately to union (*yoga*) or actual identification with the great Spirit of the universe (*Paramatman*)[2].

These three manifestations of Brahma, Vishnu, and Shiva, whose functions are sometimes interchanged[3], exhibit the

---

1. In Mahabharata, Sauptika-parvan 769, Brahma, the Creator, is represented as calling on Shiva to create living creatures; and the latter, to qualify himself for the task, undergoes a severe penance under water.

2. In the character of 'lord of abstract meditation,' Shiva is called *Yogesa, Yogin.* Indeed, in some of the Puranas the origin of the Yoga (see p. 112) is ascribed to Shiva. In Book I. 55 and III. 45-50 of the Kumara-sambhava, and in the opening invocation or Nandi of the Mrichchakatika, there is a description of Shiva's posture and whole appearance while engaged in profound meditation. He is seated on his hams in the posture called *paryanka-bandha.* (p. 111, note 2), with his breath suppressed and his vision fixed on his nose. While in this situation the god of love attempted to inspire him with affection for Parvati, daughter of Himalaya, in order that a son might be born to Shiva for the destruction of the Daitya Taraka, who had extorted, by his penances, so many boons from Brahma, that the whole universe had become subject to him. Shiva, indignant at the interruption of his austerities, reduced Kama (Love) to ashes by a flash from his eye. Parvati then herself followed Shiva's example, and commenced a course of penance, whereby she conciliated Shiva and became his wife. A son, Karttikeya, 'god of war,' was then born, who killed Taraka. This is the subject of the Kumara-sambhava. The use of ashes rubbed upon the body and of Rudraksha berries, to form rosaries, is of great importance in Shiva-worship.

3. Thus, Vishnu-worship (like Shiva-worship) is connected with the highest spiritual knowledge in the Bhagavad-gita. See also note 2, p. 362. In some parts of India a saint *Dattatreya* is revered as combining the Hindu Triad in himself.

three sides of Hinduism as developed in the epic poems, and
still more unfolded in the subsequent Puranas. The first is the
religion of activity and works, the second that of faith and
love, the third that of austerity, contemplation, and spiritual
knowledge. This last is regarded as the highest, because it aims
at entire cessation of action and total effacement of all personal
entity and identity by absorption into simple Soul.

In medieval times bitter rivalries and disputes sprung up
between the upholders of these doctrines expressed by the
worship of Brahma, Vishnu, and Shiva[1] respectively. Each sect

---

1. Brahma, 'the Creator,' however, is supposed to have done his work.
Hence the worship of this manifestation fell into desuetude, and only
in one place do traces of it continue, viz. Pushkara in Ajmir (Rajputana).
Even the worship of the other two manifestations began in time to
languish, until that of Shiva was revived by the great teacher and
reformer Shan-karacharya (sometimes described as an incarnation of
Shiva) in the eighth century; and that of Vishnu or Krishna by
Ramanuja in the twelfth, and by Vallabhacharya at the end of the
fifteenth. Shiva is now the favourite manifestation with Brahmans
and the better classes, as Krishna is with the others. Benares is a
stronghold of Shiva-worship (whence his name Kashi-natha), but
even there Krishna is the popular god of the lower orders. The chiefs
of many monasteries in the south of India are to this day called
Shankaracharyas. A popular festival, or rather fast (*upavasa, vrata*),
called Shiva-ratri, in honour of the god Shiva (under the form of
the Linga), is kept for a whole day and night, on the 14th of the
dark half of the month Magha (January — February). The spring
festival (*utsava*), commonly called Huli or Holi, celebrated a few
days before the full moon of Phalguna (February — March), and still
more popular than the last, is said to be in honour of Krishna and
the Gopis dancing round fires. Their frolics are commemorated in
a variety of sports and jokes. In some parts of India the Holi
corresponds to the Dola-yatra or 'swinging festival,' when figures
of Krishna and his favourite wife Radha are swung in an ornamented
swing. The Divali (*dipali*) or 'festival of lights,' at the end of Ashvin
and beginning of Kartik (September — October), is in honour of
Vishnu's wife Lakshmi. Those who worship Durga or Parvati, wife

was jealous of the superiority of his own system, and particular Puranas were devoted to the exaltation of the one god or the other. But in the present day the strife of sects has generally given way to universal toleration, and a liberal school of theology has arisen in India. Most thinking men among the educated classes, whatever may be the form of religion to which they nominally incline, regard the names Brahma, Rama, Krishna, and Shiva as mere convenient symbols for different manifestations of the one Supreme Being, who may be worshipped under different external forms and by separate methods, according to the disposition, circumstances, and preference (*ishti*) of his worshippers. They hold, in short, that there are three ways or means of salvation, 1. the way of works (*karman*), 2. that of faith (*bhakti*), 3. that of spiritual knowledge (*jnana*); and heaven, they assert, may be reached by any one of these three roads or by a combination of all. The second, however, represents the popular side of the Indian creed, as of all religions, false or true.

---

of Shiva, are called Shaktas (see not 1, p.361). Besides the three principal sects of *Shaivas, Vaishnavas,* and *Saktas,* three other inferior ones are often named, viz. the Ganapatyas or worshippers of Surya, 'the sun,' and the *Bhagavatas,* who are supposed to worship Bhagavat, 'the Supreme Being.' There are also the Sikhs of the Panjab, disciples of Guru Nanak Shah — born near Lahore — who in the reign of Baber, at the end of the fifteenth century, attempted to combine Hinduism with Islam, and promulgated about the time of our Reformation a book called the Adi Grantha, 'first Book' (prohibiting idol-worship and teaching the unity of the Godhead pantheistically), as a kind of new Veda. He was succeeded by nine other Gurus, each of whom was in some way remarkable. The tenth, Govind, added another 'Book' to the first, and, meeting with persecution under Aurangzeb, converted the Sikhs from peaceable disciples of a peculiar teacher into a military nation and enemies of the Mogul empire. The Sikh chiefs formed themselves into confederacies called Misals, over whom Runjit Sinh eventually became supreme.

It is as Vishnu, then, that the Supreme Being, according to the Hindus, exhibited his sympathy with human trials, his love for the human race, his respect for all forms of life, and his condescension towards even the inferior animals as integral parts of his creation. Portions of his essence, they assert, became incarnate in the lower animals, as well as in men, to rescue the world in great emergencies. Nine principal occasions have already occurred in which the god has thus interposed for the salvation of his creatures. A tenth has still to take place. These incarnations are briefly as follow[1]:

1. *Matsya*, the fish. In this Vishnu became a fish to save the seventh Manu, the progenitor of the human race, from the universal deluge[2]. (See the story told p. 439.)

2. *Kurma*[3], the tortoise. In this he descended to aid in recovering certain valuable articles lost in the deluge. For this purpose he stationed himself as a tortoise at the bottom of the ocean, that his back might serve as a pivot for the mountain Mandara, around which the gods and demons twisted the great serpent Vasuki. They then stood opposite to each other, and using the snake as a rope and the mountain as a churning-stick, churned the ocean[4] for the recovery of the Amrita or

---

1. It should be mentioned that the Bhagavata-purana gives twenty-two incarnations of Vishnu. Muir's Texts IV. 156.

2. The oldest version of this legend, which furnished the germ of the subsequent incarnation, is found in the Satapatha-brahmana, as given pp. 34-36 of this volume. The legend is also told in Mahabharata Vana-parvan 12747 &c., where the fish is represented as an incarnation of Brahma; and in the Bhagavata-purana VIII. 24, 7, where it is identified with Vishnu. Muir's Texts I. 208 &c.

3. In Satapatha-brahmana VII. 4, 3, 5, Prajapati (or Brahma) is said to have assumed the from of the tortoise: 'Having assumed the form of a tortoise, Prajapati created offspring. That which he created he made (*akarot*); hence the word *kurma*'. Muir's Texts IV. 27.

4. In this there appears to be an allegory, and the lesson that may be supposed to be taught is, that nothing valuable can be produced or recovered by man without great labour —without, as it were, stirring the lowest depths of his whole nature.

'nectar,' the goddess Lakshmi[1], and twelve other sacred things which had been lost in the depths.

3. *Varaha*, the boar. In this he descended to deliver the world from the power of a demon called Hiranyaksha, who had seized the earth and carried it down into the lowest depths of the sea. Vishnu, as a boar, dived into the abyss, and after a contest of a thousand years, slew the monster and raised the earth[2]. In the earlier legends the universe is represented as a mass of water, and the earth being submerged, was upheaved by the tusks of the divine boar. According to some, the object of this incarnation was to recover the lost Vedas. It is noticeable that the first three incarnations are all connected with the tradition of a universal deluge.

4. *Nara-singh*, the man-lion. In this he assumed the shape of a creature, half man, half lion, to deliver the world from the tyranny of a demon called Hiranya-kasipu, who had obtained a boon from Brahma that he should not be slain by either god or man or animal. Hence he became so powerful that he usurped the dominion of the three worlds, and appropriated the sacrifices made to the gods. When his pious son Prahlada praised Vishnu, the demon tried to destroy the boy, but Vishnu appeared out of a pillar in the form Nara-sinha and tore Hiranya-kasipu to pieces.

---

1. Goddess of beauty, and wife of Vishnu, a kind of Hindu Venus, Aphrodite (a, 'foam-born').
2. The germs of the fable in the earlier literature are very simple. In Taittiriya-brahmana I. 1,3,5, we read: 'This universe was formerly water. Prajapati, as a boar, plunged beneath. He found the earth below. Breaking off a portion of her he rose to the surface.' In Satapatha-brahmana XIV. 1, 2, 11, occurs the following: 'The earth was formely so large—*Emusha*, a boar, raised her up' (Muir's Texts IV. 27). In the Ramayana II. 110, Brahma, not Vishnu, is represented as taking the form of the boar: ' All was water only in which the earth was formed. Thence arose Brahma. He, becoming a boar, raised up the earth,' &c. See Muir's Texts I. 53, IV. 36, &c.

These first four incarnations are said to have taken place in the Satya or first age of the world.

5. *Vamana*, the dwarf. In the second or Treta age Vishnu descended as a dwarf, to deprive the demon Bali (who resembles Ravana and Kansa in the stories of Rama and Krishna) of the dominion of the three worlds. Vishnu presented himself before him as a diminutive man, and solicited as much land as he could step in three paces. When his request was granted he strided in two steps over heaven and earth, but out of compassion left the lower world or Patala in the demon's possession[1].

6. *Parasu-rama*, Rama with the axe. In this Vishnu was born as the son of the Brhaman Jamad-agni and descendant of Bhrigu, in the second age, to restrain the Kshatriyas from arrogating dominion over the Brahmanical caste. Parashu-rama is said to have cleared the earth twenty-one times of the Kshatriya class[2] (see p. 386).

---

1. The germ of this incarnation in the Rig-veda. I quote one passage: 'Vishnu strode over this (universe); in three places he planted his step' (I. 22, 17). Hence Vishnu is called *Tri-vikrama*. See also p. 358 of this volume and Muir's Texts, vol. iv. p. 63. An account of the Dwarf incarnation is given in Ramayana (Schlegel) I. 31, 2, and (Bombay ed.) I. 29, 2 &c. (Gorresio I. 32, 2). It is noticed in the Mahabharata, Shanti-parvan 12943 &c., Vana-parvan 484 &c.

2. Though now regarded as the mythical type of Brahmanism, arrayed in opposition to the military caste, he was probably, in the first instance, the hero of a quarrel caused by a Kshatriya's stealing a cow from a Brahman named Jamad-agni. In revenge, his son Parashu-rama slew the Kshatriya, upon which the other Kshatriyas murdered Jamad-agni, and a fierce contest ensued between his son and the murderers. All this points to the historical fact of constant struggles between the two leading classes, and it may be inferred from the circumstance that Parashu-rama is described as fighting with (and conquered by) Rama-chandra, as well as with Bhishma in the Maha-bharata, that the Kshatriyas held their own if they did not gain the upper hand. The story of Parashu-rama is told in the Vana-parvan

7. *Rama* (commonly called Rama-chandra[1], 'the mild or moon-like Rama'), the hero of the Ramayana, son of king Dasharatha of the Solar race, and therefore a Kshatriya. Vishnu took this form at the close of the second or Treta age, to destroy the demon Ravana (see p. 382).

8. *Krishna*, 'the dark god' — the most popular of all the later deities of India[2]. This incarnation of Vishnu, at the end of the Dvapara or third age of the world[3], as the eighth son

---

11071 &c., and in the Shanti-parvan 1707 &c.; also in the ninth book of the Bhagavata and in the Padma and Agni Puranas. In the Vana-parvan 8679, Parashu-rama is described as struck senseless by Rama-chandra. The Udyoga-parvan 7142 &c. relates the long single combat between Parasu-rama and Bhishma. They both repeatedly strike each other senseless. Ultimately they are persuaded by some Munis to leave off fighting. In Adi-parvan 272-280, the destruction of the Kshatriyas by Parashu-rama is said to have taken place between the Treta and Dvapara ages. Muir's Texts I. 447. Tradition ascribes the formation of the Malabar coast to Parashu-rama, who is said to have compelled the ocean to retire and to have caused fissures in the western Ghats by blows of his axe.

1. The addition of Chandra, to distinguish this Rama from the other two, is only found in the later literature (see note 1, p. 402).

2. Especially in Bengal. In the upper provinces (except at Mathura or Muttra, Krishna's own city), Oude, Behar, and the greater part of Hindustan Proper, the seventh incarnation, Rama-chandra, is principally worshipped. That Krishna-worship is comparatively modern is shown by the fact that in the old Buddhist Sutras the gods reverenced at the time Buddhism arose are named, viz. Brahma, Narayana, Shiva, Indra, &c., but not Krishna.

3. The Kali-yuga or fourth age of the world was supposed to commence at the death of Krishna. Hence the events of the Mahabharata must have taken place during the third or Dvapara age, and those of the Ramayana at the end of the second or Treta age. From the gambling scene in the Second Act of the Mrichchakatika, it is probable that the names of the four ages are connected with throws of dice; Krita being the best throw; Treta, the throw of three or the second best throw; and Dvapara, the throw of two or a worse throw; the worst

of Vasu-deva and Devaki of the Lunar race, was for the destruction of the tyrant Kansa, the representative of the principle of evil, corresponding to Ravana in the previous incarnation.

The details of the later life of Krishna have been interwoven with the later portions of the Mahabharata, but they do not belong to the plot, and they might be omitted without impairing

---

of all being Kali. The Hindu notion appears to have been that gambling prevailed especially in the Dvapara and Kali Yugas. In the episode of Nala, the personified Dvapara enters into the dice, and the personified Kali into Nala himself, who is then seized with the fatal passion for play. The Hindu idea of a succession of four Yugas or ages, in which a gradual deterioration of the human race takes place, has its counterpart among the Romans in the Golden, Silver, Brazen, and Iron ages, as described in Ovid's Metamorphoses (I. 89 &c.). But the Hindu system of mundane periods is more elaborately extended, and perhaps agrees better with modern scientific theories). A Maha-yuga or period of four ages comprises 12,000 years of the gods, which (according to the Vishnu-purana) are equal to 12,000 x 360 (the assumed number of days in an ordinary year), and therefore to 4,320,000 years of mortals, when another cycle of four ages in commenced. One thousand of these periods of four ages constitute a Kalpa or day of Brahma = 4,320,000,000 human years (comprising under it fourteen Manv-antaras or periods presided over by fourteen successive Manus), after which there is a universal collapse (pratisanchara, maha-pralaya) of all creation—including Brahma, Vishnu, Shiva, gods, demons, men, animals—into Brahman or simple being. In the present Kalpa or Aeon, six Manus have passed away, of whom the first was Svayambhuva, the present or seventh being Vaivasvata. Manu's account is confused, and some think the periods of his four Yugas are no more than 4800, 3600, 2400 and 1200 ordinary years respectively (Manu I. 69-71). There is no allusion to mundane periods in the Rig-veda, but there is in the Aitareya-brahmana (VII. 15). The present Kali-yuga is reckoned to have begun February 18th, 3102 B.C. at midnight, on the meridian of Ujjayini. Whitney's 2nd Series of Oriental Studies, p. 366; Muir's Texts I. 43; Weber's Indische Studien I. 286, 460.

its unity. He is certainly not the hero of the great Epic. He appears as a great chief who takes the part of the real heroes — the Pandavas[1] — and his claims to deification are often disputed. His earlier days and juvenile feats, though not found in the oldest parts of the Mahabharata, may be gathered from the Hari-vansa and Puranas, especially the tenth book of the Bhagavata-purana, from which we learn as follows:

Vasu-deva (a descedent of the Yadu who with Puru, as sons of Yayati, formed the two branches of the lunar dynasty) had two wives, Rohini and Devaki. The latter had eight sons, of whom the eighth was Krishna. It was predicted that one of these would kill Kansa, king of Mathura and cousin of Devaki. He therefore imprisoned Vasu-deva and his wife, and slew their first six children. The seventh, Bala-rama, was abstracted from Devaki's womb, transferred to that of Rohini, and thus saved. The eighth was Krishna, born with black skin and the mark called *Sri-vatsa* on his breast[2]. His father, Vasu-deva, escaped from Mathura with the child, and favoured by the gods, found a herdsman named Nanda — of the race of the Yadavas—whose wife, Yashoda, had just had a son, whom Vasu-deva conveyed to Devaki, after substituting his own son in its place. Nanda took the infant Krishna and settled first in Gokula or Vraja, and afterwards in Vrindavana, where Krishna and Bala-rama grew up together, roaming in the woods, and joining in the sports of the herdsmen's sons. While still a boy, Krishna destroyed the serpent Kaliya, and lifted up the mountain Govardhana on his finger to shelter the Gopis from the wrath of Indra, who, enraged by their love for

---

1. Later additions to the Mahabharata make the Pandavas also incarnations of certain deities.
2. The anniversary of the birth-day of Krishna, called Janmashtami, because his birth is said to have occurred on the eighth day of the month Bhadra (August—September), is celebrated as a great festival. Professor Weber has lately published some valuable information on this subject.

Krishna, tried to destroy them by a deluge. He is described as sporting constantly with these Gopis or shepherdesses, of whom a thousand became his wives, though only eight are specified, Radha being the favourite. Krishna built Dvaraka in Gujarat, and thither transported the inhabitants of Mathura after killing Kansa.

According to some, Krishna is not an incarnation of Vishnu, but Vishnu himself; in which case, *Bala-rama*, 'the strong Rama[1]', born at the end of the Dvapara or third age of the world, as son of Vasu-deva and Devaki, and elder brother of Krishna, is sometimes substituted for Krishna as the eighth incarnation of Vishnu.

9. *Buddha.* According to the Brahmans, Vishnu assumed the form of the great sceptical philosopher, in the fourth age of the world, to delude the Daityas or demons into neglecting

---

1. This third Rama, usually held to be the seventh son of Vasu-deva, and sometimes called *Halayudha*, 'armed with a plough-shaped weapon', sometimes *Musalin*, 'club-armed,' is the Hindu Hercules. In Mahabharata I. 7308 (as well as in the Vishnu-purana), he is said to have been produced from a white hair of Vishnu, as Krishna was from a black. Elsewhere he is said to be an incarnation of the great serpent Shesha, and in Anushasana-parvan 6163 he is regarded as a Naga, or semi-divine being, half man, half serpent; and at his death (recorded in Mausala-parvan 117), a large Naga is described as coming out of his mouth and entering the ocean. Diodorus Siculus, in his account of the Indians (II. 39), has the following: 'It is said that Hercules also (as well as, worshipped by the inhabitants of the mountains) lived amongst them; and, like the Greeks, they represent him with a club and lion's skin; and that in strength of body and bravery, he excelled all mortals, and purged the earth and sea from monsters. And that since he had numerous sons from his many wives, but only one daughter, when they were grown up, he divided the whole of India into equal parts, so that each of his sons should have a kingdom of his own, and his one daughter he made queen. And that he founded many cities, and among them the largest and most celebrated was Palibothra; and that after his death, he obtained divine honours.'

the worship of the gods, and thus exposing them to destruction.

10. *Kalki* or *Kalkin,* who is yet to appear at the close of the fourth of Kali age, when the world has become wholly depraved, for the final destruction of the wicked, for the re-establishment of righteousness upon the earth, and the renovation of all creation with a return to a new age of purity (*satya-yuga*). According to some, he will be revealed in the sky, seated on a white horse, with a drawn sword in his hand, blazing like a comet[1].

Looking more closely at these ten incarnations, we may observe that in the first three, Vishnu is supposed to be present in the body of animals, and in the fourth to take the form of a being half animal, half human. This last may be regarded as a kind of intermediate link, the object of which is to prevent too great abruptness in connecting the Deity with the higher forms of worldly existence. From the mixed manifestation of half a lion, half, a man, the transition is natural to that of a complete man. The divine essence passing into human forms commences with the smallest type of humanity, represented by a dwarf. Thence it rises to mighty heroes, who deliver the world from the oppression of evil demons and tyrants whose power increases with the deterioration of mankind during the four ages. In the tenth and final manifestation, which remains to be revealed, evil and wickedness are to be entirely rooted out. We see in all this the working of the Hindu idea of transmigration. Even in Manu's time it was an accepted dogma that the souls of men, popularly regarded as emanations from the Deity, might descend into the bodies of animals, or rise to those of higher beings. It was therefore an easy expansion of such a doctrine to imagine the divine Soul itself as passing

---

1. According to Vishnu-purana IV. 24, he is to be born as Kalki in the family of Vishnu-yashas, an ancient Brahman of Sambhala.

through various stages of incarnation for the delivery of the world from the effects of evil and sin, and for the maintenance of order in the whole cycle of creation.

Let me introduce here a curious legend from the Bhagavata-purana X. lxxxix, which is also told at the end of the Prem Sagar. I translate it (with a little amplification) as well illustrating the character of the three gods, Brahma, Vishnu, and Shiva, in their relationship to men:

The great sage Bhrigu, one of the ten Maharshis or primeval patriarchs created by the first Manu (I. 35), was asked which god was the greatest. He said he would endeavour to ascertain, and first went to Brahma; on approaching whom, he purposely omitted an obeisance. Upon this, the god reprehended him very severely, but was pacified by seasonable apologies. Next he entered the abode of Shiva, in Kailasa, and omitted to return the god's salutation. The vindictive deity was enraged, and would have destroyed the sage, but was conciliated by his wife Parvati. Lastly, he repaired to Vaikuntha, the heaven of Vishnu, whom he found asleep with his head on Lakshmi's lap. To make a trial of his forbearance, he boldly gave the god a kick on his breast, which awoke him. Instead of showing anger, however, the god arose, and on seeing Bhrigu, inquired tenderly whether his foot was hurt, and then proceeded to rub it gently. 'This,' said Bhrigu, 'is the mightiest god; he overpowers by the most potent of all weapons — sympathy and generosity.'

The Ramayana

I proceed now to give a brief account of Valmiki's[1] poem, the Ramayana (*Rama-ayana,* ' the goings or doings of Rama'),

---

1. Valmiki is thought to have been born in that part of India which corresponds to Kosala, the chief town of which was Ayodhya (reigned over by Dasharatha, Rama's father), and which was close to the

which in its present form consists of about 24,000 stanzas, mostly in the common heroic Anushtubh metre[1].

It should be noted in the first place that the purity of its text has been exposed to risks, which the longer Epic has escaped. Its story was more popular and attractive. It was shorter, and far less burdened with digressions; it had more unity of plot; its language was simpler and presented fewer difficulties. As a result of these circumstances it was more easily committed to memory. Hence it happened that, even after the final settlement of its text, it became orally current over a great

---

region of Videha, whose king, Janaka, was the father of Sita, and whose connexion with Yajnavalkya is described in the Brahmana of the White Yajur-veda, and in some of the Mahabharata legends. Valmiki himself is believed to have been an adherent of the Black Yajur-veda, and it is certain that the story of Rama was carefully preserved among the Taittiryakas, and that Valmiki interweaves their legends into his narrative. According to Mr. Cust (Calcutta Review XLV), Valmiki resided on the banks of the Jumna, near its confluence with the Ganges at Allahabad; and tradition has marked a hill in the district of Banda, in Bundelkund, as his abode. Some actually assert that he began life as a highway robber, but repenting of his misdeeds, betook himself to a hermitage, on this hill, where he eventually received Sita, the wife of Rama, when banished by her over-sensitive husband. There were born her two sons, Kusha and Lava (sometimes combined into one compound, thus — *Kushilavau*), who were taught to sing the poem descriptive of their unknown father's actions, and from whom are traced the proudest Rajput castes. The reviewer thinks it not unlikely that Valmiki may have been contemporaneous with the heroes whom he describes.

1. The metre in which the greater part of the Ramayana and Maha-bharata is written is the common Shloka (see my Sanskrit Grammar, 935), in which only five syllables out of sixteen in each line are really fixed. The others may be either long or short. The Indra-vajra variety of Trishtubh is however frequently used in the Mahabharata; and in the Ramayana, at the end of the chapters, we have often the Jagati (Grama. 937, 941). The former of these has eleven syllables to the half-line, the latter twelve; and the quantity of every syllable being fixed, there is less simplicity and freedom of style.

part of India. We know from the fourth chapter of the first book that it had its minstrels and reciters like in Greece, and variations in the wording of the narratives became almost unavoidable. In process of time, as written copies of the poem multiplied, the unfettered flow of the common heroic metre facilitated slight alterations and interpolations by transcribers who sometimes aimed at being poets themselves. Hence we have at least three versions of the text of the poem: one belonging to Benares and the North-west; another, which is generally, though not always, more diffuse and open to suspicion of interpolations, peculiar to Calcutta and Bengal Proper; and a third, to Western India (Bombay). These principal recensions, as well as all the known MSS., whatever may be their occasional variations[1], divide the poem into seven books, as follow:

1. *Bala-kanda,* the section relating to the boyhood of Rama.
2. *Ayodhya-k°,* descriptive of the transaction in Ayodhya and

---

1. Professor Weber shows that the variation now discovered in MSS. of the Ramayana in different parts of India are so great, that it is no longer possible to talk of three recensions only. With regard to the Bengal (Gauda) recension, it may be observed that in that part of India, where there is less demand for MSS., learned men have been their own scribes, and have always tampered more freely with original texts than the unlearned copyists of the North. In 1806 and 1810 Carey and Marshman published the text and translation of two books out of the seven which complete this recension; but here and there they have followed the northern. Twenty years afterwards Augustus William Schlegel published the text of two books of the northern version, with a Latin translation of the first; and after another interval of twenty years Signor Gorresio, a learned Italian scholar, published, at the expense of king Charles Albert, a very beautiful and accurate edition of the Bengal recension, with an Italian translation, which I have generally followed in my summary of the narrative. The remainder of that particular recension, the editing of which was commenced by Schlegel, was left unprinted. More than ten years have elapsed since editions of the more reliable recension, with commentary, were put forth at Calcutta and Bombay. That of the Ramayan which has appeared since, deserves, and has received, the greatest commendation.

the banishment of Rama by his father, king Dasaratha. 3. *Aranya-k°*, narrating events in the forest-abode of Rama after his banishment, including the carrying off of Sita by Ravana. 4. *Kishkindhya-k°*, detailing the occurrences at Kishkindhya, the capital city of Rama's ally Sugriva. 5. *Sundara-k°*, 'the beautiful section,' giving an account of the miracles by which the passage of the straits and the arrival of the invading armies in Lanka (Ceylon) were effected. 6. *Yuddha-k°*, describing the actual war with Ravana in Lanka, the victory over his armies and his destruction by Rama, the recovery of Sita, the return to Ayodhya,the reunion of the four brothers, and final coronation of Rama. 7. *Uttara-k°*, narrating the concluding events of the history of Rama after his coronation on returning to Ayodhya — his sensitiveness to the gossip and scandal of the citizens, his consequent banishment of Sita to the hermitage of Valmiki notwithstanding the absolute certainty of her blameless conduct during her captivity in Ravana's palace, the birth of his twin sons, Kusha and Lava, in the hermitage, his final reunion with her, and translation to heaven. All this supplement to the story has been dramatized by Bhava-bhuti in his Uttara-rama-charitra, and the whole previous history in his Maha-vira-charitra.

We have already noted that the seventh Book, as well as the introductory chapters of the first, giving a summary of the plot, and the passages identifying Rama with Vishnu or the Supreme Being (such as VI. cii. 12, Gorresio), are in all probability comparatively modern appendages.

No suspicion, however, of interpolations and variations avails to impair the sacred character of the poem in the eyes of the natives[1]. Some idea of the veneration in which it is

---

1. Weber has noted that in the Sarva-darshana-sangraha (p. 72, l. 15) a passage is quoted from the Skanda-purana which places the Mula-ramayana, 'original Ramayana,' as a Shastra after the four Vedas, the Bharata, and the Pancha-ratraka. Some of the Sargas in the Uttara-kanda have no comment as being *prakshipta*.

held may be formed from the verses at the end of the introductory chapter, which declare —

He who reads and repeats this holy life-giving Ramayana is liberated from all his sins and exalted with all his posterity to the highest heaven.

Brahma also, in I. 2, 40, is made to utter the following prophecy in the presence of the poet Valmiki:

As long as the mountains and rivers shall continue on the surface of the earth, so long shall the story of the Ramayana be current in the world. [*Yavat Sthasyanti girayah saritas-cha mahitale Tavad Ramayana-katha lokeshu pracharishyati.*]

The main story of the poem[1], although often interrupted by long episodes which have little bearing on the plot, flows in a far more continuous and traceable course than that of the Mahabharata. It may be divided into four principal parts or periods, corresponding to the chief epochs in the life of Rama. I. The account of his youthful days; his education and residence at the court of his father Dasharatha, king of Ayodhya; his happy marriage to Sita; and his inauguration as heir-apparent or crown-prince. II. The circumstances that led to his banishment; the description of this exile and residence in the forests of Central India. III. His war with the giants or demons of the south for the recovery of his wife Sita, carried off by their chief Ravana; his conquest and destruction of Ravana, and reunion with Sita. IV. His return

---

1. While writing my account of the Ramayana, I have consulted an able article on this poem in the Calcutta Review (XLV), to which I am under great obligations. The author of the article is my friend Mr. R.N. Cust, a late distinguished member of the Bengal Civil Service.

with Sita to Ayodhya; his restoration to the throne of his father; and his subsequent banishment of Sita[1].

The poem opens with a description of Ayodhya[2], and an eulogium on Dasharatha and his ministers, of whom the most eminent were the two prime ministers Vasishtha and Vamadeva. Besides these, there were eight other counsellors (*amatyah*), agreeably to the precept laid down by Manu (see p. 288 with note 1). These are of course all Brahmans, and direct the affairs of the government. King Dasharatha has no son (VIII. 1) — a serious calamity in India, where a son is needed for the due performance of the Sraddha (see p. 279 with note 1). The usual remedy for this misfortune was a great sacrifice, purposely cumbered with a most tedious and intricate ceremonial, not to be performed except by Brahmans, who received in return enormous gifts. The Rakshasas, were, of course, eagerly on

---

1. According to Professor Lassen the development of the story of Rama may be divided into four stages. The first construction of the poem did not carry the narrative beyond the banishment of Rama to the Himalaya and the circumstances which caused his wife Sita and his brother Lakshmana to follow him into exile. The second changed the place of banishment to the Godavari, and described the protection afforded to the hermits against the attacks of the aborigines. The third embraced the account of the first attempts to subdue the inhabitants of the Deccan. The fourth amplification, which resulted from the knowledge gained by the Hindus of the island of Ceylon, included the description of Rama's expedition against Lanka. See Ind. Alt. II. p. 505.

2. Although Ayodhya is the base of operations in the Ramayana, yet the poet carries us through a vast extent of country, conducting us now beyond the Sutlej into the Panjab, now across the Vindhya mountains into the Deccan, and now across the Narmada and Godavari to the most southern parts of India, even to the island of Ceylon. The geography of the poem, however, though far more interesting, and extending to wider points in every direction, than that of the Mahabharata, is not always to be trusted. The river Sarayu is now called the Gora.

the watch for any flaw, defect, or mistake. If any occurred, the whole ceremony was seriously obstructed, and its efficacy destroyed.

Rishyasringa, therefore, a celebrated sage, is married to Dasharatha's daughter Santa, and induced to assist at the celebration of a great Ashva-medha or horse-sacrifice.

The episode in which the story of this sage is told is very curious:

It so happened, that in the neighbouring kingdom of Anga, now known as Bhagulpore, in Bengal, there had been a great dearth, and the king, Lompada, had been assured that the only chance of obtaining rain was to entice the ascetic Rishyashringa from his retirement, and induce him to marry the king's daughter, or rather the adopted child of Lomapada, and real daughter of Dasharatha. This ascetic was the son of Vibhandaka, a sainted mortal of frightful powers, who had produced him apparently without a mother, and had brought him up alone in the wilderness, where he had never seen nor even heard of the fascinations of women. The plan was to send a party of young females, disguised as ascetics, and inveigle the great saint from his retreat. The description of the surprise and unsettlement of mind, the interruption of devotion, and heart's unrest, that befell the unhappy saint when he received his strange guests, is very singular. In the end, the ascetic is seduced from his hermitage, put on board a vessel on the Ganges, married to the king's daughter, and brought to Ayodhya, to conduct the sacrifice[1].

---

1. I have consulted here Mr. Cust's article in the Calcutta Review (XLV). He there remarks that 'we might laugh at the conceit of such a case being possible had not a modern traveller in the Levant, Mr. Curzon, assured us of the existence of a similar case in one of the convents of Mount Athos in the nineteenth century. He there found a monk in middle life who had never set eyes on women, nor had any notion of them beyond what could be formed from a black and hideous altar-picture of the Virgin Mary. The cruel traveller, by an accurate description of the many charms of the fair sisterhood, entirely destroyed the poor monk's peace of mind for the future.'

The horse-sacrifice[1], therefore, was successfully performed. We are told that no oblation was neglected, nor any mistake committed; all was in exact conformity to the Veda (I. xiii. 10). The queen Kausalya, mother of Rama, and the other two queens, Sumitra and Kaikeyi[2], remain with the slaughtered horse for one whole night (I. xiii. 36, 37). The gods, Brahma,

---

1. The horse chosen for this purpose was let loose and allowed to roam about for a year. If no one was able to seize it during this period, it was deemed fit for sacrifice; but the seizure was sometimes effected by the god Indra, whose tenure of heaven was imperilled by the great power acquired by those who completed many Ashva-medhas. Another year was consumed in preparations for the sacrifice. The description of the ceremony, in I. xiii, is curious. Twenty-one Yupas or sacrificial posts were erected, to which were tied various animals, and the horse. Near the latter the queens of Dasharatha watched for a whole night. The marrow (vapa) of the horse [patatrin = horse; according to the commentator, pura ashvanam pakshah santiti] was then taken out and dressed, and the horse itself cut up and offered in the fire, and the king, smelling the smoke of the burning flesh, became absolved from his sins. Various other sacrifices seem to have accompanied the Ashva-medha, such as the Chatushtoma, Jyotishtoma, Atiratra, Abhijit, &c. the Pravargya and Upasad are described in Aitareya-brahmana I. 18, 1, 23-25. Compare the Ashva-medha hymns of the Rig-veda (I. 162, 163) and the rules for this sacrifice given in Satapatha-brahmana XIII. and Katyayana's Sutras XX. 6, 78. An important part of the proceedings was the feasting and the largesses. King Dasharatha is described as giving to the priests a million cows, a hundred million pieces of gold, and four times as many pieces of silver.

2. Of Dasharatha's three wives, the chief, Kausalya, is said to have been of his own race and country (probably so called from Kosala, the country of Dasharatha); the second, Kaikeyi, was the daughter of Asva-pati, king of Kekaya, supposed to be in the Panjab (whence the king himself is sometimes called Kekaya); and the third, Sumitra, was probably from Magadha or Behar. The father of the last is said to have been a Vaishya. It is noticeable that Asva-pati, king of Kekaya, is mentioned in the Brahmana of the White Yajur-veda as nearly contemporary with Janaka, father of Sita.

Vishnu, and Shiva, along with Indra and his troop of Maruts, assemble to receive their shares of the sacrificial oblations, and being satisfied, promise four sons to Dasharatha (I. xiv. 9). The scene then changes to the abode of the gods, where a deputation of the deities waits on Brahma, and represents to him that the universe is in danger of being destroyed by the chief of the Rakshasas or evil demons, called Ravana, who from his island-throne in Ceylon menaces earth and heaven with destruction. His power is described as so great that —

Where he is, there the sun does not give its heat; the winds through fear of him do not blow; the fire ceases to burn; and the ocean, crowned with rolling billows, becomes motionless (I. xiv. 17).

The secret of this power lay in a long course of austerity[1], which, according to the Hindu doctrine, gained for him who

---

1. According to the Hindu theory (cf. p. 114), the performance of *tapas* or austerities of various kinds was like making deposits in the bank of heaven. By degrees an enormous credit was accumulated, which enabled the depositor to draw to the amount of his savings, without fear of his drafts being refused payment. The merit and power thus gained by weak mortals was so enormous, that gods as well as men were equally at the mercy of these all but omnipotent ascetics. Hence both Rishis and Rakshasas and even gods, especially Shiva (p. 361), are described as engaging in self-inflicted austerities, in order to set mere human beings an example, or perhaps not to be supplanted by them, or else not to be outdone in aiming at re-absorption into Brahma. In these cases it is incorrect (as remarked by Professor Banerjea) to translate *tapas* by 'penance,' if expiation for sin is thereby implied. It is simply self-inflicted pain and suffering, with a view to the acquisition of superhuman powers, or of final emancipation. The root *tap* signifies first 'to burn' and then 'to torment.' It is connected with Lat *tepeo*. Also with Greek root which last originally signified 'to burn,' not 'to bury,' dead bodies. As, however, 'penance' is derived from *poena*, 'pain,' it is perhaps a suitable equivalent for the Sanskrit *tapas*.

persevered sufficiently, however evil his designs, superiority to the gods themselves, and enabled Ravana to extort from the god Brahma this remarkable boon — that neither gods, genii, demons, nor giants should be able to vanquish him. As, however, in his pride, he scorned to ask security from man also, he remained vulnerable from this one quarter, if any mortal could be found capable of coping with him. While the discussion of the matter is carried on in heaven, Vishnu joins the conclave, and at the request of the other gods, promises to take the form of man that he may kill Ravana, and consents to become incarnate for this purpose, in the family of Dasharatha, king of Ayodhya (Oude), of the Solar Dynasty.

It should be stated here that, according to the legendary history of India, two lines of rulers were originally dominant in the north of India, called Solar and Lunar, under whom numerous petty princes held authority and to whom they acknowledged fealty. Under the Solar dynasty the Brahmanical system gained ascendancy more rapidly and completely than under the Lunar kings in the more northern districts, where fresh arrivals of martial tribes preserved an independent spirit among the population already settled in that district.

This Solar line, though practically commencing with Ikshvaku, is fabled to have derived its origin from the Sun, and even from an earlier source — the god Brahma himself. Perhaps the object of the Brahman poet or later constructor of the poem might have been to connect Rama in his then acknowledged character of an incarnation of Vishnu, with the solar Vishnu of the Veda (see p. 358). However this may have been, nothing shows more clearly than the legendary pedigree of Rama how the whole poem was subjected to a brahmanizing process. We see from it that the most powerful line of Kshatriya kings is thus made to owe its origin to Brahmanical sages of the greatest sanctity. I here abridge the genealogy:

Ikshvaku was the son of Manu Vaivasvata (i.e. the seventh Manu, or Manu of the present period). The latter was a son of Vivasvat or the Sun (commonly called Surya). The Sun again was a son of the Muni Kashyapa, who was the son of the Rishi Marichi, who was the son of Brahma. From Ikshvaku sprang the two branches of the Solar dynasty, viz. that of Ayodhya or Oude, which may be said to have commenced in Kakutstha, the grandson of Ikshvaku (as the latter's son Vikukshi, father of Kakutstha, did not reign), and that of Mithila, or Videha (North Behar and Tirhut), which commenced in another of Ikshvaku's sons, Nimi. Thirty-fifth in descent from Kakutstha came Sagara; fourth from him Bhagiratha; third from him Ambarisha; and fifteenth from him Raghu, who was father of Aja, who was father of Dasharatha. Hence we have the following order of names: Brahma, Marichi, Kashyapa, Vivasvat or Surya, Vaivasvata, Ikshvaku [Vikukshi], Kakutstha [...............], Sagar [..], Dilipa, Bhagiratha [..], Ambarish [...], Nala [.........], Raghu, Aja, Dasharatha, Rama.

The explains why Rama is variously called Kakutstha, Raghava, Dasharatha, Dasharathi, &c. [1]

We are thus brought to the real commencement of the story — the birth of Rama[2]. Four sons are born from the three

---

1. This list agrees with the usual one as exhibited in Prinsep's table; but there is considerable variation in the genealogy, as given in Ramayana II. cx. and in the Raghu-vansha. For instance, the son of Ikshvaku is said to be Kukshi, and his son Vikukshi; the son of Dilipa is Bhagiratha, and his son is Kakutstha, and his son is Raghu. In the Raghu-vansha, Raghu, father of Aja (V. 36), is said to be the son of Dilipa (III. 13).

2. In Schlegel's and the Bombay Ramayana, the horoscope of Rama's birth is given. His birthday is called *Rama-navami* (see p. 408, note 1), because he is said (I. xix. 1, 2, II. xv. 3) to have been born on the 9th Tithi of Chaitra, about the vernal equinox, Jupiter being in Cancer (*Karkata*). Weber thinks that the mention of the Zodiacal sign and the planet Jupiter is a proof of the late date to be assigned to the composition of the Ramayana, or at least of this passage, seeing

wives of Dasharatha; the eldest, Rama, possessing half the
nature of Vishnu, from Kausalya; the second, Bharata,
possessing a fourth part, from Kaikeyi; and the other two,
Lakshmana and Satru-ghna, sharing the remaining quarter
between them, from Sumitra. The brothers are all deeply
attached to each other; but Lakshmana (often called Saumitri)
is especially the companion of Rama, and Satru-ghna of
Bharata[1].

While yet striplings Rama and his brothers are taken by
Vishvamitra (see p. 403) to the court of Janaka, king of
Mithila or Videha[2]. He had a wonderful bow, once the property
of Shiva, and had given out, that the man who could bend
it should win his beautiful daughter Sita[3]. On the arrival of

that the Hindus obtained their knowledge of the signs and planets
from the Greeks, and these latter only completed their Zodiac in
the first century B.C. Weber, however, remarks that in the Ramayana
Ceylon is never called Tamraparni or Sinhala (by which name alone
it was known to the Greeks), but always *Lanka*.

1. Although in xix. the birth of Bharata is narrated after that of Rama,
   he is supposed to have been born after the twins; and we read in
   I. xv. that the divine nectar containing the essence of the god Vishnu
   was drunk by Sumitra next to Kaushalya. According to Schlegel,
   Bharata was eleven months junior to Rama, and the twins only three
   months. Probably the mother of Bharata was higher in rank than
   Sumitra, which would give him the precedence. Lakshmana was to
   Rama like another self (*Ramasya Lakshmano vahihprana invaparah,
   na cha tena vina nidram labhate, na tam vina mishtam annam
   upanitam ashnati*, I. xix. 20-22).

2. It is evident that Mithila (North Behar and Tirhut), situated quite
   towards the east, was an Aryan country at this time, for Janaka is
   described (Ram. I. 12) as conversant with all the Shastras and Vedas.
   He is a frequent interlocutor in the Brihad-aranyaka.

3. Called Sita because not born form a woman, but from a furrow (*sita*)
   while Janaka was ploughing (I. lxvi. 14). This has given rise to a
   theory that the story of Rama allegorizes the introduction of agriculture
   into the south of India. The name Sita occurs in Taittiriya-brahmana
   II. 3, 10, 1-3, as applied to the daughter of Savitir, or Prajapati, and

Rama and his brothers the bow is brought on an eight-wheeled platform, drawn by no less than 5000 men. Rama not only bends the bow, but snaps it asunder with a concussion so terrible that the whole assemby is thrown to the ground, and the earth quivers as if a mountain were rent in twain.

Sita thus becomes the wife of Rama, and she remained his one wife — the type of wife-like devotion. Rama also remained her faithful lord — the type of all that a husband ought to be in loving tenderness and fidelity[1].

On their way back to Ayodhya, Dasharatha and his sons are met by Parashu-rama, and here we have introduced the curious episode of the conflict between the second Rama and the previous incarnation of Vishnu — who suddenly appears on the scene (though not till various strange omens and awful portents had given notice of his approach) to challenge the young son of Dasharatha. The object of this digression, which is clearly not part of the original story, seems to be, that the ex-incarnation of Vishnu, as a Brahman, may, by acknowledging himself justly superseded by the Kshatriya incarnation, give a Brahmanical sanction to the deification of the second Rama; but much mythological mysticism is mixed up with the narrative, with the apparent design of obscuring the actual facts of the Kshatriya hero's victory, which could not, if stated in plain language, be otherwise than mortifying to Brahmanical pride. I here abridge the story as told in Ramayana I. lxxiv. &c. (Schlegel; Muir's Texts, vol. iv. pp. 176, 177):

---

is in love with the Moon, who on his part loves another daughter, Shraddha, but in the end is brought to love Sita. (See also Rig-veda IV. 57, 6, 7; Atharva-veda XI. 3, 12.) This is a variation of the older legend which represents Savitri as giving his daugher Surya in marriage to the Moon. This may account for the name *Rama-chandra*, 'moon-like Ram,' which was ultimately given to the hero of the Ramayana.

1. In this respect he contrasts very remarkably with the five Pandavas — the heroes of the Mahabharata—who had one wife between them as common property, besides others on their own private account.

When the king and his son Rama were returning home after the marriage of the latter to Sita, he was alarmed by the ill-omened sounds uttered by certain birds, which, however, were counteracted, as the sage Vasishtha assured the king, by the auspicious signs of his being perambulated by the wild animals of the forest. Then a hurricane shook the earth, uprooting the trees, and thick darkness veiled the sun. Finally, Parashu-rama appeared, fearful to behold, brilliant as fire, with his axe in his hand, and a bow on his shoulder. He was angry at the breaking of the bow of Shiva, of whom he was a disciple. Being reverently received, he proceeded to tell Rama, Dasharatha's son, that he had heard of his success in breaking Shiva's bow, and had brought another bow, once the property of Vishnu (I. lxxv. 13), which he asked Rama to bend, and fit an arrow on the string, adding, that if he succeeded in bending it, he (Parashu-rama) would challenge him to single combat. Rama replies that though his powers were slighted by his rival, he would give him a proof of his strength. Whereupon, he angrily snatches the bow from Parasu-rama, bends it, fits an arrow on the string, and tells his challenger that he will spare his life because he is a Brahman, but will either destroy his supernatural power of movement, or deprive him of the abode in bliss he had acquired by his austerities. The gods now arrive to be witnesses of the scene. Parashu-rama becomes disheartened, loses his strength, and entreats not to be deprived of his faculty of moving in the air (lest he should be unable to fulfil his promise, made to Kashyapa, to leave the earth every night). He then continues to say that by the bending of the bow he recognizes Rama's divinity, and that he regards defeat by the lord of the three worlds as no disgrace. The second Rama then shoots the arrow, and thereby in some mysterious manner destroys Parashu-rama's abode in the celestial world.

Dasharatha and his party now return to the capital, and preparations are made for the inauguration of Rama as successor to the throne, when Kaikeyi, mother of his brother Bharata, jealous of the preference shown to the son of Kausalya, demands of the king the fulfiment of a promise, made to her in former years, that he would grant her any two boons she asked. A promise of this kind in Eastern countries is quite inviolable; and the king being required to banish his favourite son Rama for fourteen years to the forest of Dandaka, and to instal Bharata, is forced to comply.

Rama, therefore, with his wife Sita and his brother Lakshmana, is banished. They establish themselves in the forest near the river Godavari[1]. Meanwhile the heartbroken king pines away in inconsolable anguish. Here occurs a touching episode (II. lxiii). The king, in the midst of his despondency, confesses that his present bereavement is a punishment for a deed of blood committed by himself accidentally in his youthful days. Thus it happened: (I translate as nearly as I can word for word, in a metre resembling the sixteen-syllable heroic verse of the original, omitting portions here and there):

> One day when rains refreshed the earth, and caused my heart to swell with joy,
> When, after scorching with his rays the parched ground, the summer sun
> Had passed towards the south; when cooling breezes chased away the heart,
> And grateful clouds arose; when frogs and pea-fowl sported, and the deer
> Seemed drunk with glee, and all the winged creation, dripping as if drowned,
> Plumed their dank feathers on the tops of wind-rocked trees, and falling showers
> Covered the mountains till they looked like watery heaps, and torrents poured

---

1. The Dandaka forest is described as beginning south of the Yamuna, and extending to the Godavari. The whole of that country was wilderness, inhabited by savage tribes (Rakshasa), and infested by wild beasts.

Down from their sides, filled with loose stones and red as
dawn with mineral earth,
Winding like serpents in their course; then at that charming
season I,
Longing to breathe the air, went forth, with bow and arrow
in my hand,
To seek for game, if haply by the river-side a buffalo
Or elephant or other animal might cross, at eve, my path,
Coming to drink. Then in the dusk I heard the sound of
gurgling water:
Quickly I took my bow, and aiming towards the sound, shot
off the dart.
A cry of mortal agony came from the spot, — a human voice
Was heard, and a poor hermit's son fell pierced and bleeding
in the stream.
'Ah! wherefore then,' he cried, 'am I a harmless hermit's son
struck down?
Hither to this lone brook I came at eve to fill my water-jar.
By whom have I been smitten? whom have I offended? Oh!
I grieve
Not for myself or my own fate, but for my parents, old and
blind,
Who perish in my death. Ah! what will be the end of the
that loved pair,
Long guided and supported by my hand? this barbed dart
has pierced
Both me and them.' Hearing that piteous voice, I Dasaratha,
Who meant no harm to any human creature, young or old,
became
Palsied with fear; my bow and arrows dropped from my
senseless hands;
And I approached the place in horror; there with dismay
I saw,
Stretched on the bank, an innocent hermit-boy, writhing in
pain and smeared

With dust and blood, his knotted hair dishevelled, and a
broken jar
Lying beside him. I stood petrified and speechless. He on
me
Fixed full his eyes, and then, as if to burn my inmost soul,
he said,
'How have I wronged thee, monarch? that thy cruel hand
has smitten me —
Me, a poor hermit's son, born in the forest: father, mother,
child
Hast thou transfixed with this one arrow: they, my parents,
sit at home
Expecting my return, and long will cherish hope — a prey
to thirst
And agonizing fears. Go to my father — tell him of my fate,
Lest his dread curse consume thee, as the flame devours the
withered wood.
But first in pity draw thou forth the shaft that pierces to my
heart,
And check the gushing life-blood, as the bank obstructs the
bounding stream[1].'
He ceased, and as he rolled his eyes in agony, and quivering
writhed
Upon the ground, I slowly drew the arrow from the poor
boy's side.
Then with a piteous look, his features set in terror, he
expired.
Distracted at the grievous crime, wrought by my hand
unwittingly;
Sadly I thought within myself, how best I might repair the
wrong.
Then took the way he had directed me towards the hermitage.

---

1. I have omitted the youth's statement that he is not a Brahman, but
begotten by a Vaisya on a Sudra woman (II. lxiii. 48, &c.).

There I beheld his parents, old and blind; like two clipped wingless birds
Sitting forlorn, without their guide, awaiting his arrival anxiously,
And, to beguile their weariness, conversing of him tenderly.
Quickly they caught the sound of footsteps, and I heard the old man say,
With chiding voice, 'Why hast thou lingered, child? Quick give us both to drink
A little water. Long forgetful of us, in the cooling stream
Hast thou disported; come in — for thy mother yearneth for her son.
If she or I in ought have caused thee pain, or spoken hasty words,
Think on thy hermit's duty of forgiveness; bear them not in mind.
Thou art the refuge of us refugeless — the eyes of thy blind sire.
Why art thou silent? Speak! Bound up in thee are both thy parents' lives.'
He ceased, and I stood paralysed — till by an effort resolutely
Collecting all my powers of utterance, with faltering voice I said,
'Pious and noble hermit; I am not thy son; I am the king:
Wandering with bow and arrow by a stream, seeking for game, I pierced
Unknowingly thy child. The rest I need not tell. Be gracious to me.'
Hearing my pitiless words, announcing his bereavement, he remained
Senseless awhile; then drawing a deep sigh, his face all bathed in tears,
He spake to me as I approached him suppliantly, and slowly said,
'Hadst thou not come thyself, to tell the awful tale, its load of guilt

Had crushed thy head into ten thousand fragments. This ill-fated deed

Was wrought by thee unwittingly, O king, else hadst thou not been spared,

And all the race of Raghavas had perished. Lead us to the place:

All bloody though he be, and lifeless, we must look upon[1] our son

For the last time, and clasp him in our arms.' Then weeping bitterly

The pair, led by my hand, came to the spot and fell upon their son.

Thrilled by the touch, the father cried, 'My child, hast thou no greeting for us?

No word of recognition: wherefore liest thou here upon the ground?

Art thou offended? or am I no longer loved by thee, my son?

See here thy mother. Thou wert ever dutiful towards us both.

Why wilt thou not embrace me? speak one tender word. Whom shall I hear

Reading again the sacred Shastra in the early morning hours?

Who now will bring me roots and fruits to feed me like a cherished guest?

How, weak and blind, can I support thy aged mother, pining for her son?

Stay! Go not yet to Death's abode — stay with thy parents yet one day,

To-morrow we will both go with thee on the dreary way. Forlorn

And sad, deserted by our child, without protector in the wood,

---

1. This is literally translated. It is well known that blind people commonly talk of themselves as if able to see.

Soon shall we both depart towards the mansions of the King
of death.'
Thus bitterly lamenting, he performed the funeral rites; then
turning
Towards me thus addressed me, standing reverently near —
'I had
But this one child, and thou hast made me childless. Now
strike down
The father: I shall feel no pain in death. But thy requital be
That sorrow for a child shall one day bring thee also to
the grave.'

After narrating this affecting incident of his early life, king
Dasharatha, struck with remorse, sickens and dies[1].

Soon afterwards the ministers assemble, and decide that
Bharata shall assume the government (II. lxxix), but he declines
to deprive his elder brother Rama of his rightful inheritance,
and declares his intention of setting out for the forest with
a complete army (chatur-anga) to bring Rama back, and his
determination to undergo in his place the appointed term of
fourteen years' exile in the forest (II. lxxix. 8,9).

After some trouble he discovers Rama's retreat at Chitra-
kuta[2]. There and then he breaks the sad news of his father's

---

1. His body is burnt with much pomp. We have already noted, as a
   proof of the antiquity of the poem, that his widows are not burnt
   with him (see p. 350).
2. The isolated hill Chitra-kuta is the holiest spot of the worshippers
   of Rama, and is crowded with temples and shrines of Rama and
   Lakshmana. Every cavern is connected with their names; the heights
   swarm with monkeys, and some of the wild-fruits are still called Sita-
   phal. It is situated on a river called the Pishuni, described as the
   Mandakini (II, xcv), fifty miles south-east of the town of Bandah in
   Bundelkund, lat. 25, 12, long. 80. 47. The river is lined with ghats
   and flights of stairs suitable for religious ablutions. It is worthy of
   note that at some holy places all distinctions of caste are laid aside
   by the Hindus.

death, and entreats him to return to Ayodhya and assume the
sovereignty (cii).

Next ensues a generous contest between the brothers;
Bharata imploring Rama to accept the throne, and Rama
insisting on the duty of fulfilling his father's vow (cvi, cvii).

Here occurs the episode in which the Brahman Javali,
who is a sort of impersonation of scepticism, tries in a brief
address (II. cviii) to instil atheistic and irreligious sentiments
into Rama, hoping to shake his resolution and induce him to
accept the kingdom. His speech, which is full of interest as
indicating the prevalence of infidel and materialistic doctrines
at the time when the brahmanized version of the Ramayana
was completed, may be thus abridged:

You ought not by abandoning your paternal kingdom to
enter upon a wrong road, beset with difficulties and troubles.
Permit yourself to be enthroned in Ayodhya. Dasharatha (your
father) is dead and is now nothing to you, nor you to him. Any
one who feels attachment for any other person is insane, since
no one is anything to any other. I grieve for those who swerve
not from virtue and justice; such persons suffer affliction here,
and when they die incur annihilation. Men are careful to offer
oblations to their progenitors, but what can a dead man eat? If
an oblation eaten here by one person, passes into the body of
another, then let a Shraddha be offered to a man who is travelling
abroad; he need not eat upon his journey (cf. the doctrine of
the Charvakas, p. 142). The books composed by theologians (in
which men are enjoined to) worship, give gifts, offer sacrifice,
practise austerities, abandon the world, are mere artifices to
draw forth gifts (dana-samvanana). Make up your mind (kuru
buddhim) that no one exists hereafter. Have regard only to what
is visible and perceptible by the senses (pratyaksham). Cast
everything beyond this behind your back (prishthatah kuru). (See
Dr. Muir's article on Indian Materialists, Journal of the Asiatic
Society, vol. xix. p. 303.)

Rama's reply, in which he indignantly rebukes Javali, is a noble vindication of religion and faith, but his reference to Buddhism and his designation of Buddha himself as a *Chora* or thief (II. cviii. 33) must be regarded as interpolations[1].

In the end Bharata desists from pressing his brother to accept the throne, but only consents to take charge of the kingdom as a deposit. He bears away Rama's shoes on his head in token of this (cxiii. 1), and takes up his abode outside Ayodhya, at Nandi-grama, until the return of the rightful king, never transacting any business without first laying it before the shoes (cxv). Before dismissing him, the forgiving Rama entreats him not to indulge angry feelings towards his mother for having caused the family calamities in these words:

Cherish thy mother Kaikeyi, show no resentment towards her (II. cxii. 27).

After Bharata's departure ten years of Rama's banishment pass in moving from one hermitage to another. In the description of the quiet life of the exiles we find that their morning and evening devotions are never omitted, and that Sita dutifully waits on her husband and brother-in-law, never eating till they have finished[2]. When they travel, Rama walks first, Sita in the middle, and Lakshmana behind (III. xv. 1). At length they move westward to visit the hermitage of the sage Agastya, near the Vindhya mountains. He advises Rama to live for the remainder of his exile in the neighbourhood of Jana-sthana at Panchavati on the Godavari[3] (xix). This district is infested by Rakshasas, and amongst others, by

---

1. Other allusions to rationalistic doctrines will be found scattered throughout the Ramayana.
2. This custom remains unaltered to the present day. Compare Manu Iv. 43: 'Let him not eat with his wife, nor look at her eating.'
3. A spot now known as Nasik, in the Bombay presidency.

Ravana's sister, Shurpa-nakha, who becomes smitten with love for Rama. He of course repels her, telling her that he is already married (xxiv. 1); but this only rouses the jealousy of Shurpa-nakha, who makes an attack on Sita, and so infuriates the fiery Lakshmana that he thoughtlessly cuts off her ears and nose[1] (xxiv. 22). Shurpa-nakha, smarting with pain and bent on revenge, repairs to her brother Ravana, the demon-monarch of Ceylon.

The description of Ravana (III. xxxvi; Bombay ed. xxxii) is as follows:

This mighty demon had ten faces, twenty arms, copper-coloured eyes, a huge chest, and bright teeth like the young moon. His form was as a thick cloud, or a mountain, or the god of death with open mouth. He had all the marks of royalty; but his body bore the impress of wounds inflicted by all the divine arms in his warfare with the gods. It was scarred by the thunderbolt of Indra, by the tusks of (Indra's) elephant Airavata, and by the discuss of Vishnu. His strength was so great that he could agitate the seas and split the tops of mountains. He was a breaker of all laws, and a ravisher of other men's wives. He once penetrated into Bhogavati (the serpent-capital of Patala), conquered the great serpent Vasuki, and carried off the beloved wife of Takshaka. He defeated Vaishravana (i.e. his own brother Kuvera, the god of wealth), and carried off his self-moving chariot called Pushpaka. He devastated the divine groves of Chitra-ratha, and the gardens of the gods. Tall as a mountain-peak he stopped with his arms the sun and moon in their course, and prevented their rising. The sun, when it passed over his residence, drew in its beams in terror. He underwent severe austerities in the forest of Gokarna for ten thousand years, standing in the midst of five fires (see p. 113) with his feet in the air; whence he was released by

---

1. It was from this circumstance that Panchavati is now called Nasik (*nasika*, 'the nose').

Brahma, and obtained from him (among other boons, see p. 382) the power of taking what shape he pleased[1].

The better to secure the mighty Ravana's co-operation, Surpa-nakha succeeds in inspiring him with a passion for Sita (III. xxxviii. 17), whom he determines to carry off. Having with difficulty secured the aid of another demon, Maricha, — who was the son of the Tadaka (I. xxvii. 8) formerly killed by Rama — Ravana transports himself and his accomplice in the aerial car Pushpaka to the forest near Rama's dwelling. Maricha then assumes the form of a beautiful golden deer, which so captivates Sita (III. xlviii. 11) that Rama is induced to leave her with Lakshmana, that he may catch the deer for her, or kill it. Mortally wounded by his arrow, the deer utters cries for help, feigning Rama's voice, which so alarms Sita that she persuades Lakshmana against his will to leave her alone and go to the assistance of his brother. Meanwhile Ravana approaches in the guise of a religious mendicant. All nature seems petrified with terror as he advances (III. lii. 10, 11); and when Sita's eyes fall on the stranger, she starts, but is lulled to confidence by his mendicant's dress, and offers

---

1. One cannot help comparing part of this description with Milton's portrait of Satan. The majestic imagery of the English poet stands out in striking contrast to the wild hyperbole of Valmiki. It appears from III. liii (Gorresio) that Ravana was the son of Vishravas, who was the son of the sage Pulastya, who was the son of Brahma. Hence Ravana was the brother of the god Kuvera (though by a different mother), and in verse 30 he calls himself his brother and enemy. Both he and Kuvera are sometimes called Paulastya. Vibhishana of Kumbha-karna were also brothers of Ravana, and, like him, propitiated Brahma by their penances, and, like him, obtained boons, but the boon chosen by Vibhishana was that he should never swerve from virtue, and by Kumbhakarna (whose size was gigantic and appetite voracious) that he should enjoy deep sleep for long periods of time. (See Mahabharata III. 15916.)

him food and water. Suddenly Ravana declares himself. Then throwing off his disguise he avows his intention to make her his queen. Sita's indignation bursts forth, but her wrath is powerless against the fierce Ravana, who takes her up in his arms, places her in his self-moving car, and bears her through the sky to his capital. As Sita is carried along, she invokes heaven and earth, mountains and streams (lv. 43). The gods and saints come to look on, and are struck with horror, but they stand in awe of the ravisher, and know that this is part of the plan for his destruction. All nature shudders, the sun's disk pales, darkness overspreads the heavens (lviii. 16-43). It is the short-lived triumph of evil over good. Even the great Creator Brahma rouses himself, and exclaims, 'Sin is consummated' (III. lviii. 17).

Arrived in the demon-city, Ravana forces Sita to inspect all the wonders and beauties of his capital (III. lxi), and then promises to make them hers, if she will consent to become his queen. Indignantly rejected, he is enraged, and delivers her over to the guardianship of a troop of Rakshasis or female furies, who are described as horrible in appearance, and cannibal in their propensities (III. lxii. 29-38). Tormented by them, she seems likely to die of despair, but Brahma in compassion sends Indra to her with the god of sleep[1], and a vessel containing celestial food (lxiii. 7,8) to support her strength.

Terrible is the wrath of the usually gentle Rama when on his return he finds that Sita is carried off by Ravana (lxix). He and Lakshmana at once set off on a long search, determined to effect her rescue. After many adventures, in the course of which they have a battle with a headless fiend called Kabandha, who opposes their progress, but is killed, and then restored to life by them (III. lxxiv), they make an

---

1. Similarly in the Odyssey (IV. 795) Minerva sends a dream to console and animate Penelope.

alliance with Sugriva, king of the monkeys (foresters), and assisted by Hanuman, one of the monkey-generals, and by Ravana's brother Vibhishana, invade Lanka, the capital of Ravana, in Ceylon (IV. lxiii).

To transport the army across the channel, a bridge is constructed under the direction of the monkey-general Nala, son of Vishva-karman:

Thousands of monkey bridge-builders, flying through the sky in every direction, tear up rocks and trees, and throw them into the water. In bringing huge crags from the Himalayas, some are accidentally dropped, and remain to this day monuments of the exploit. At length a pier[1] is formed twenty Yojanas long and ten wide (v. xcv. 11-15, by which the whole army crosses, Vibhishana taking the lead. The gods, Rishis, Pitris, &c., look on, and utter the celebrated prophecy —

'As long as the sea shall remain, so long shall this pier (setu) endure, and the fame of Rama be proclaimed[2].'

---

1. The god of the ocean at first objected to a regular embankment (V. xciv. 8), though a pier (described as a *setu*) was afterwards constructed: the line of rocks in the channel is certainly known in India as Rama-setu. In maps it is called 'Adam's bridge.' Everywhere in India are scattered isolated blocks, attributed by the natives to Rama's bridge-builders. More than this, the hill Govardhana, near Muttra, and the whole Kymar range in Central India are firmly believed to have arisen from the same cause

2. 'In the midst of the arm of the sea is the island Ramesurum (Ramesvara), or the pillar of Rama, of as great repute and renown as the pillars of the western Hercules. There to this day stands a temple of massive Cyclopean workmanship, said to have been built by the hero, the idol of which is washed daily with water from the Ganges. From the highest point is a commanding view of the ocean, and the interminable black line of rocks stretching across the gulf of Manaar. Thither, from all parts of India, wander the pilgrims, who are smitten with the wondrous love of travel to sacred shrines. From Chuteerkote (*Chitra-kuta*), near the Yamuna, it is roughly calculated to be one hundred stages. We have conversed with some who have

After various engagements, described with much wearisome exaggeration, the great battle between Rama and Ravana takes place:

The gods assemble to take the side of the former, and all the demons and evil spirits back their own champion (VI. lxxxvii. 8). Ravana is mounted on a magic car, drawn by horses having human faces (*manushya-vadanair hayaih*); and, in order that the two champions may fight on an equality, Indra sends his own car, driven by his charioteer Matali, for the use of Rama. Both armies cease fighting, that they may look on (xci. 2); but the gods and demons in the sky, taking the part of either warrior, renew their ancient strife[1]. The heroes now overwhelm each other with arrows. Rama cuts off a hundred heads from Ravana successively; but no sooner is one cut off than another appears in its place[2] (xcii.24), and the battle, which has already lasted seven days and seven nights without interruption, seems likely to be endlessly protracted, until Matali informs Rama that Ravana is not vulnerable in the head. Thereupon Rama shoots off the terrible arrow of Brahma[3], given to him by the sage Agastya, and the demon-king falls dead (xcii. 58).

---

accomplished the great feat: but many never return; they either die by the way, or their courage and strength evaporate in some roadside hermitage. Whatever may be its origin, there is the reefy barrier, compelling every vessel from or to the mouths of the Ganges, to circumnavigate the island of Ceylon.' Calcutta Review, XLV.

1. This is just what takes place in the Iliad before the great battle between Achilles and Hector, the gods taking their respective places on either side (II. XX). It is interesting to compare the simple Homeric narrative with the wild improbabilities of the Indian poem.
2. This reminds one of Hercules and the Hydra.
3. Here called *paitamaham astram,* and described as having the wind for its feathers, the fire and the sun for its point, the air for its body, and the mountains Meru and Mandara for its weight (VI. xcii. 45). It had the very convenient property of returning to its owner's quiver after doing its work. There appear to have been various forms of this unerring weapon.

Great portents and prodigies precede the fall of Ravana, and when the victory is consummated a perfect deluge of flowers covers the conqueror. The generous Rama causes magnificent obsequies to be performed over the body of his enemy, which is duly consumed by fire[1], and then places Vibhishana on the throne of Lanka (VI. xcvii. 15). Rama then sends Hanuman with a message to Sita, and Vibhishana brings her into his presence in a litter (*sivika*); but Rama allows her to come before him on foot, that she may be seen by all the army.

The monkeys crowd round her, admiring her incomparable beauty, the cause of so much toil, danger, and suffering to themselves[2]. On seeing her, Rama is deeply moved. Three feelings distract him — joy, grief, and anger (xcix. 19) — and he does not address his wife. Sita, conscious of her purity, is hurt by his cold reception of her, and bursts into tears, uttering only the words, *ha aryaputra*, 'alas! my husband!' Rama then haughtily informs her, that having satisfied his honour by the destruction of the demon who had wronged his wife, he can do no more. He cannot take her back, contaminated as she must certainly be (VI. c). Sita asserts her innocence in the most dignified and touching language, and directs Lakshmana to prepare a pyre, that she may prove her purity. She enters the flames, invoking Agni (ci); upon which all the gods with the old king Dasharatha appear, and reveal to Rama his divine nature[3], telling him that he is Narayana, and that Sita is Lakshmi (cii). Agni, the god of

---

1. Contrast this with Achilles' treatment of the fallen Hector.
2. The whole scene is very similar to that in Iliad III. 121, &c., where Helen shows herself on the rampart, and calls forth much the same kind of admiration.
3. He never appears to be conscious of it, until the gods enlighten him. (see VI. cii. 10, cxix.) This is not the case with Krishna in the Mahabharata. It is probable, as we have seen, that all these passages are later additions.

fire, then presents himself holding Sita, whom he places in Rama's arms unhurt[1]. Thereupon Rama is overjoyed, and declares that he only consented to the ordeal that he might establish his wife's innocence in the eyes of the world (ciii). Dasharatha then blesses his son, gives him good advice, and returns to heaven (civ); while Indra, at the request of Rama, restores to life all the monkeys killed during the war (cv).

Rama and Lakshmana, along with Vibhishana, Sugriva, and the allies, now mount the self-moving car Pushpaka, which is described as containing a whole palace within itself, and set out on their return to Ayodhya; Rama, to beguile the way as they travel through the sky, recounting to Sita all the scenes of their late adventures lying beneath their feet[2] (cviii). On their reaching the hermitage of Bharadvaja at Prayaga, the car is stopped; and the fourteen years of banishment having now expired (cix), Hanuman is sent forward to announce their return to Bharata. Rama and the three brothers are now once more reunited, and, accompanied by them and by Sita and the monkeys, who assume human forms (cxii. 28), he makes a magnificent entry into Ayodhya. He is then solemnly crowned, associates Lakshmana in the empire, and, before dismissing his allies, bestows on them splendid presents (cxii). Hanuman, at his own request, receives as a reward the gift of perpetual life and youth (cxii. 101). Every one returns happy and loaded with gifts to his own home, and Rama commences a glorious reign at Ayodhya (cxiii).

---

1. The whole description of Sita's repudiation by Rama is certainly one of the finest scenes in the Ramayana.

2. Kalidasa devotes nearly the whole of the thirteenth chapter of his Raghu-vansha to this subject, which he makes a convenient pretext for displaying his geographical and topographical knowledge, as in the Megha-duta. Bhava-bhuti does the same in the seventh act of his drama, Maha-vira-charitra; and Murari, the same in his play on the same subject.

Such is a brief sketch of the Ramayana, omitting the Uttara-kanda or supplementary chapters, which contain the concluding events in the life of Rama (see p. 375-376). Much of the story, exaggerated as its later details are, probably rests, as we have already pointed out, on a foundation of historical truth.

It is clear, too, that a moral lesson is intended to be conveyed by the whole narrative. Under the story of the conflict between the armies of the noble Rama and the barbarous races of the South, figured by the Rakshasas, there appears to lie a typical representation of the great mystery of the struggle ever going on between the powers of good and evil. With regard, however, to any other allegorical and figurative ideas involved, as, for example, that Rama is a mere impersonation of the Solar energy[1]; Sita, of agriculture or of civilization introduced into the South of India by immigrants from the North; the Rakshasas, of night, darkness or winter

---

1. Certainly Rama belongs to the Solar race of kings, but this points to the connection of the Epic Vishnu (of whom Rama came to be regarded as an incarnation) with the Solar Vishnu of the Veda. Professor Weber remarks that as Rama is at a later period called Rama-chandra, and is even in one place called Chandra alone, the mildness so conspicuous in his character might be explained by supposing that he was originally a kind of moon-genius, and that the legend in the Taittiriya-brahmana (see note 3, p. 384) representing the love of Sita (the field-furrow) for the Moon might be regarded by some zealous mythologists as the first germ of the story of the Ramayana; the beautifying ointment (*anga-raga*) which Anasuya, wife of Atri, poured over the limbs of Sita (III. 2), representing the dew spread over the furrow in which the moonlight is reflected. Weber, however, thinks that as the name Ram-chandra was not given to the second Rama till a late date (the first application of it occurring in Bhava-bhuti's Maha-vira-charitra III. 18), the converse is rather true, viz. that a poetical spirit among the Brahmans connected Rama with the Moon merely on account of the mildness of his character.

— whatever ingenuity there may be in any or all of these theories, it seems very questionable whether any such conceptions ever entered into the mind of the author of any part of the poem.

Time would fail, if we were to attempt even the briefest epitome of all the episodes in the Ramayana. I note two others in addition to those already given. That of Vishvamitra (I. 51-65), which is one of the most interesting, may be thus abridged[1]:

Vishvamitra, son of Gadhi, was a prince of the Lunar race, sovereign of Kanoj, and the district of Magadha. He had a tremendous conflict with the Brahman Vashishtha for the possession of the cow of plenty (Kamadhenu, also called Shavala), which no doubt typified the earth (go) or India. At the command of Vasishtha, the cow created hordes of barbarians, such as Pahlavas (Persians), Shakas (Scythians), Yavanas (Greeks), Kambojas, &c., by whose aid Vashishtha conquered Vishvamitra. Hence the latter, convinced of the superior power inherent in Brahmanism, determined to raise himself to that dignity, and in order to effect this object, increased the rigour of his austerities for thousands of years. The gods, who always had a hard struggle to hold their own against resolute ascetics, did what they could to interrupt him, and partially succeeded. Vishvamitra yielded for a time to the seductions of the nymph Menaka, sent by them to entice his thoughts towards sensual objects. A daughter (Sakuntala) was the result of this temporary backsliding. However, in the end, the obstinate ascetic was too much for the whole troop of deities. He obtained complete power over his passions, and when the gods, still refused to brahmanize him, he began creating new heavens and new gods, and had already manufactured a few stars, when the celestial host thought it prudent to concede the point, and make him a veritable Brahman.

---

1. The episode of Vishvamitra includes under it the story of Ambarisha given at p. 31 of this volume.

Another curious episode is the story of the Ganges (I. 36-44)[1]

Ganga, the personified Ganges, was the eldest daughter of Himavat, lord of mountains, her younger sister being Uma. Sagara, a king of Ayodhya, of the Solar race, had 60,000 sons, who were directed by their father to look for a horse which had been stolen by a Rakshasa at an Ashva-medha or horse-sacrifice. Having first searched the earth unsuccessfully, they proceeded to dig up the ground towards the lower regions. Meeting with the sage Kapila, they accused him of the theft, which enraged him to such a degree, that without more ado he reduced them all to ashes. Sagara's grandson some time afterwards found their remains, and commenced performing the funeral obsequies of his relatives, but was told that it was necessary for Ganga to water the ashes with her sacred stream. Neither Sagara, however, nor his grandson could devise any means for effecting the descent of the heavenly river. It was reserved for his great-grandson, by his austerities to bring down the sacred stream from heaven. In her descent she fell first with great fury on the head of Shiva, who undertook to break her fall.

Mr. Ralph Griffith has translated the description of this descent with great skill and taste. I subjoin a portion of his version (vol. i. p. 7194):

On Shiva's head descending first
A rest the torrents found,
Then down in all their might they burst
And roared along the ground.
On countless glittering scales the beam
Of rosy morning flashed,
Where fish and dolphins through the stream
Fallen and falling dashed.
Then bards who chant celestial lays,

1. The story is also told in the Mahabharata, Vana-parvan 9920, &c.

And nymphs of heavenly birth,
Flocked round upon that flood to gaze
That streamed from sky to earth.
The gods themselves from every sphere,
Incomparably bright,
Borne in their golden cars drew near
To see the wondrous sight.
The cloudless sky was all aflame
With the light of a hundred suns,
Where'er the shining chariots came
That bore those holy ones.
So flashed the air with crested snakes
And fish of every hue,
As when the lightning's glory breaks
Through fields of summer blue.
And white foam-clouds and silver spray
Were wildly tossed on high,
Like swans that urge their homeward way
Across the autumn sky.

Then, by further austerities, Bhagiratha forced the sacred river to flow over the earth, and to follow him thence to the ocean (therefore called Sagara), and thence to the lower regions (Patala), where she watered the ashes of Sagara's sons, and became the means of conveying their souls to heaven. Hence a common name for the Ganges is Bhagirathi.

Another name for the river Ganges is Jahnavi, because in its course it inundated the sacrificial ground of the sage Jahnu, who thereupon without any ceremony drank up its waters, but consented to discharge them again from his ears.

Notwithstanding the wilderness of exaggeration and hyperbole through which the reader of the Indian Epics has occasionally to wander, there are in the whole range of the world's literature few more charming poems than the Ramayana. The classical purity, clearness, and simplicity of

its style, the exquisite touches of true poetic feeling with
which it abounds, its graphic descriptions of heroic incidents
and nature's grandest scenes, the deep acquaintance it displays
with the conflicting workings and most refined emotions
of the human heart, all entitle it to rank among the most
beautiful compositions that have appeared at any period or
in any country. It is like a spacious and delightful garden;
here and there allowed to run wild, but teeming with fruits
and flowers, watered by perennial streams, and even its most
tangled thickets intersected with delightful pathways. The
character of Rama is nobly portrayed. It is only too
consistently unselfish to be human. We must, in fact, bear
in mind that the poet is bent on raising his hero to the rank
of a god. Yet though occasionally dazzled by flashes from
his superhuman nature, we are not often blinded or
bewildered by it. At least in the earlier portion of the poem
he is not generally represented as more than a heroic,
nobleminded, pious, and virtuous man — a model son,
husband, brother — whose bravery, unselfish generosity,
filial obedience, tender attachment to his wife, fraternal
affection, and freedom from all resentful feelings, we cannot
help admiring. When he falls a victim to the spite of his
father's second wife, he cherishes no sense of wrong. When
the sentence of banishment is pronounced, not a murmur
escapes his lips. In noble language he expresses his resolution
to sacrifice himself rather than allow his parent to break his
pledged word; and he persists in this determination,
notwithstanding the entreaties of his mother Kausalya, the
taunting remarks of his fiery brother Lakshmana, and his
own anxious fear for the safety of his wife Sita, who resolves
to accompany him. Again, after the death of his father, when
Bharata urges Rama to accept the government, and when all
the citizens add their entreaties, and the atheistical Javali his
sophistical arguments (see p. 394), Rama replies:

There is nothing greater than truth; and truth should be esteemed the most sacred of all things. The Vedas have their sole foundation in truth. Having promised obedience to my father's commands, I will neither, through covetousness nor forgetfulness nor blind ignorance, break down the barrier of truth (II. cix. 17).

As to Sita, she is a paragon of wife-like virtues. Her pleadings for permission to accompany her husband into banishment breathe such noble devotion to her lord and master, that I close my examples with a few extracts[1]:

A wife must share her husband's fate. My duty is to follow thee
Where'er thou goest. Apart from thee, I would not dwell in heaven itself.
Deserted by her lord, a wife is like a miserable corpse.
Close as thy shadow would I cleave to thee in this life and hereafter.
Thou art my king, my guide, my only refuge, my divinity.
It is my fixed resolve to follow thee. If thou must wander forth
Through thorny trackless forests, I will go before thee, treading down
The prickly brambles to make smooth thy path. Walking before thee, I
Shall feel no weariness: the forest-thorns will seem like silken robes;
The bed of leaves, a couch of down. To me the shelter of thy presence
Is better far than stately palaces, and paradise itself.
Protected by thy arm, gods, demons, men shall have no power to harm me.

---

1. I have translated these nearly literally, but not consecutively, in the sixteen-syllable metre of the original. The substance of them will be found in the text of Gorresio's Ramayana, vol. ii. p. 74, &c.

With thee I'll live contentedly on roots and fruits. Sweet or
not sweet,
If given by thy hand, they will to me be like the food of life.
Roaming with thee in desert wastes, a thousand years will
be a day;
Dwelling with thee, e'en hell itself would be to me a heaven
of bliss.

As if in support of the prophecy recorded in the beginning
of the work (see p. 340) the story of Rama down to the death
of Ravana and recovery of Sita, is still regularly recited every
year throughout a great part of India, at an annual festival
in the beginning of October, called Rama-lila[1]. Moreover,
Hindu writers never seem tired of working up the oft-repeated
tale into various forms. Hence the history of the adventures
of Rama, or at least some reference to them, is found in
almost every work of the subsequent literature. I conclude this
Lecture with instances:

---

1. On the day in the month Ashvin or beginning of October, when the
   Bengalis consign their images of Durga to the waters (i.e. at the
   Durga-puja, of which the 4th day is called Dashahara, and during
   which for a whole fortnight all business is suspended, and even
   thieves and rogues allow themselves a vacation), Hindus of other
   provinces perform the Rama-lila, a dramatic representation of the
   carrying off of Sita, concluding with the death of Ravana, of which
   that day is the anniversary. Rama's birth is celebrated on the 9th of
   the month Chaitra (April),called Rama-navami. The sequel of the
   story of Rama, as contained in the Uttara-kanda and Uttara-rama-
   charita, is not so popularly known. See an article in the 'Indian
   Antiquary' for May 1872, by the Rev. K.M. Banerjea. It is noteworthy
   that the Rama legends have always retained their purity, and, unlike
   those of Brahma, Krishna, Shiva, and Durga, have never been mixed
   up with indecencies and licentiousness. In fact, the worship of Rama
   has never degenerated to the same extent as that of some of these
   other deities.

In the Mahabharata (Vana-parvan 15872-16601) the Ramopakhyana is told very nearly as in the Ramayana, but there is no mention of Valmiki as its author, and no allusion to the existence of the great sister Epic. Markandeya is made to recount the narrative to Yudhi-shthira, after the recovery of Draupadi (who had been carried off by Jayad-ratha, as Sita was by Ravan), in order to show that there were other examples in ancient times of virtuous people suffering violence at the hands of wicked men. It is probable (and even Professor Weber admits it to be possible) that the Mahabharata episode was epitomized from the Ramayana, and altered here and there to give it an appearance of originality. There are, however, remarkable differences. The story in the Mahabharata, although generally treating Rama as a great human hero only, begins with the circumstances which led to the incarnation of Vishnu, and gives a detailed account of what is first mentioned in the Uttara-kanda of the Ramayana — the early history of Ravana and his brother. The birth of Rama, his youth, and his father's wish to inaugurate him as heir-apparent are then briefly recounted. Dasaratha's sacrifice, Rama's education, his winning of Sita, and other contents of the Bala-kanda are omitted. The events of the Ayodhya-kanda and much of the Aranya-kanda are narrated in about forty verses. A more detailed narrative begins with the appearance before Ravana of the mutilated Surpa-nakha (see p. 395), but many variations occur; for instance, Kabandha is killed, but not restored to life (see p. 397); the story of Savari is omitted, and there is no mention of the dream sent by Brahma to comfort Sita (see p. 397) [1]

---

1. These and other differences have led Professor Weber to suggest the inquiry whether the Maha-bharata version may not be more primitive than that of the Ramayan, and possibly even the original version, out of which the other was developed. 'Or ought we,' he asks, 'to assume only that the Mahabharata contains the epitome of an earlier recension of our text of the Ramayana; or should both texts, the Ramopakhyana and the Ramayana, be regarded as resting alike upon a common ground-work, but each occupying an independent stand-point?'

There are other references to, and brief epitomes of parts of the story of the Ramayana in the Mahabharata, e.g. in Vana-parvan 11177-11219; in Drona-parvan 2224-2246; in Santi-parvan 944-955; in Hari-vansa 2324-2359, 8672-8674, 16232. The story of Rama is also (as Professor Weber observes) referred to in the Mricchakatika (Act I); and although not mentioned in Kalidasa's dramas, it is alluded to in his Megha-duta (verses 1, 99); and in his Raghu-vansha — which is a kind of abridged Ramayana — the poet Valmiki is named (XV. 63, 64). Moreover, the Ramayan forms the basis of a Prakrit work called the Setu-bandha (ascribed to one Kalidasa, and mentioned in Dandin's Kavyadarsha I. 34), as well as of the Bhatti-kavya, or grammatical poem of Bhatti (written, according to Lassen, Ind. Alt. III. 512, in Valabhi-pura under king Sridhara-sena, between 530 and 545 of the Christian era), and of the two celebrated dramas of Bhava-bhuti, called Maha-vira-charitra and Uttara-rama-charitra (whose date is fixed by Lassen between 695 and 733). The last of these dramas quotes verses from the Ramayana in three places, one in the second and two in the sixth Act. Indeed, the dramatic literature which makes use of the adventures of Rama for the subject-matter of the plots of its plays is extensive. Besides the two dramas of Bhava-bhuti, there is the Hanuman-nataka or Maha-nataka, 'great drama,' in fourteen acts, fabled to have been composed by the monkey-chief Hanuman himself, who first wrote it on the rocks, and then to please Valmiki (lest it should throw his Ramayana into the shade), cast it into the sea, whence some portions were recovered in Bhoja's time and arranged by Mishra-damodara (probably about the tenth century). There is also the Anargha-raghava or Anarghya-raghava in seven acts by Murari; the Prasanna-raghava by Jaya-deva (probably not the author of the Gita-govinda); the Abhiramamani in seven acts by Sundara-mishra; the Champu-ramayana by Vidarbha-raja (or Bhoja) in five acts; the Raghavabhyudaya; the Bala-ramayana by Raja-sekhara; the Udatta-raghava; the Chalita-rama; (the last three quoted by the well-known work on the *Ars poetica* called *Sahitya-darpana*); the *Dutangada,* a short piece by Su-bhata, and others.

Other work mentioned by Weber as noticing the Ramayana are that of *Varaha-mihira* — written between 505 and 587 of our era — which takes for granted that Rama was honoured as a demigod about that time; the *Satrunjaya-mahatmya* written in Valabhi under king Shiladitya about A.D. 598; the *Vasava-datta* of Subandhu (about the beginning of the seventh century, Weber's Indische Streifen I. 373, 380), in which mention is made of the Sundara-kanda as a section of the Ramayana; the *Kadambari* of Bana (written a little later, Indische Streifen I. 354), in which repeated reference is made to the great Epic (I. 36, 45, 81); the *Sapta-sataka* of Hala (35, 316), on which Weber has written a treatise; the *Prachanda-pandava* of Raja-sekhara (about the end of the tenth century); the *Dasa-rupa* of Dhananjaya (I. 61, about the same date); the *Sapta-sati* of Govardhana (32, about the tenth century or later); the *Damayanti-katha* of Trivikrama-bhatta (11); the *Raja-tarangini* (I 166); Sarngadhara-paddhati (Bohtlingk, Ind. Spr. 1586), &c.

The eighteen Puranas (which are to a great extent drawn from the two great Epics) contain, of course, numerous allusions to the Ramayana, and sometimes relate the whole story. The *Agni-purana* has an epitome of the seven Books in seven chapters. The *Padama* and *Skanda* also devote several chapters to the same subject. The *Vishnu-purana* has also a section (IV. 4) about Rama, and in III. 3 describes Valmiki as the Vyasa of the 24th Dvapara. The *Brahmanda-purana* — a confused medley of various subjects — has a *Ramayana-mahatmya,* and in this Purana is also contained the well known Adhyatma-ramayana, 'Spiritual Ramayana,' divided into seven Books, bearing the same titles as those of Valmiki's Ramayana. Its object is to show that Rama was a manifestation of the Supreme Spirit, and Sita (identified with Lakshmi), a type of Nature.

This Adhyatma-ramayana contains two chapters, held to be especially sacred: 1. The *Rama-hridaya* or first chapter, in which the inner or hidden nature of Rama is explained and his identification with Vishnu, as the Supreme Spirit, is asserted; 2. the *Rama-gita* or fifth chapter of the seventh Book, in which the author, who is evidently a Vedantist, sets forth the advantages of giving up all works in order to meditate upon and become united with the Supreme Spirit.

There is also a remarkable work called *Vasishta-ramayana* (or *Yoga-vasishtha* or *Vasishtham Maha-ramayanam*) in the form of an exhortation with illustrative narratives addressed by Vasishtha to his pupil, the youthful Rama, on the best means of attaining true happiness, and considered to have been composed as an appendage to the Ramayan by Valmiki himself.

We ought also here to mention the celebrated Hindi Ramayan by the poet Tulasi-dasa (Tulsi-das). This poem is so well known and so greatly esteemed in some parts of India, that it is sometimes affirmed that there are three epic poems called Ramayana: 1. that of Valmiki, 2. that attributed to Vyasa called Adhyatma-ramayana, 3. the Hindi Epic by Tulasi-dasa.

I conclude the list by noting the following comparatively modern artificial poems on the same subject: 1. the *Raghavapandaviya* by Kavi-raja, a very singular production, much admired and imitated by later Indian writers, being nothing less than a poem worded with such dexterous 'double-entendre,' that it may serve as an epitome of either the Ramayana or Maha-bharata; 2. the *Raghava-vilasa* by Vishva-natha (author of the Sahitya-darpana); 3. the *Rama-vilasa* by Rama-charana; 4. another *Rama-vilasa* by Hari-natha (in imitation of the Gita-govinda); 5. the *Ramachandra-charitra-sara* by Agni-vesa; 6. the *Raghu-nathabhyudaya* mentioned by Professor Weber[1].

With regard to the composition called *Champu*, this is a kind of highly artificial style in alternations of prose and verse (*gadya* and *padya*).

---

1. The story of the Ramayana and Mahabharata, as given in full by Mr. Talboys Wheeler in his History of India, is most interesting and instructive, although it does not profess to be an analysis made by himself from the original Sanskrit.

Lecture XIII

The Itihasas or Epic Poems —
The Mahabharata

I pass on now to the Mahabharata — probably by far the longest epic poem that the world has ever produced. Its main design is to describe the great contest between the descendants of king Bharata[1]. He was the most renowned monarch of the Lunar dynasty, and is alleged to have reigned in the neighbourhood of Hastinapur or ancient Delhi, and to have extended his authority over a great part of India, so that

---

1. The title of the poem is *Mahabharatam,* a compound word in the neuter gender, the first member of which, *maha* (for *mahat*), 'great,' and the second, *bharata,* 'relating to Bharata.' The title of a book is often in the neuter gender, some word like *kavyam,* 'a poem,' being understood. Here the word with which Mahabharatam agrees may be either *akhyanam,* 'a historical poem,' or *yuddham,* 'war.' It is curious that in the *Sangraha-parva,* or introductory summary (l. 264), the word Mahabharata is said to be derived from its large size and great weight, because the poem is described as outweighing all the four Vedas and mystical writings together. Here is the passage: — *Ekatash chaturo Vedan Bharatam chaitad ekatah Pura kila suraih sarvaih sametya tulaya dhritam, Chaturbhyah sarahasyebhyo Vedebhyo hy adhikam yada, Tada prabhriti loke 'smin [mahattvada bharavattvaccha] Maha-bharatam uchyate.*

413

India to this day is called by the natives Bharat-varsha. The great Epic, however, is not so much a poem with a single subject as a vast cyclopaedia or thesaurus of Hindu mythology, legendary history, ethics, and philosophy. The work, as we now possess it, cannot possibly be regarded as representing the original form of the poem. Its compilation appears to have proceeded gradually for centuries. At any rate, as we have already indicated (pp. 354, 356), it seems to have passed through several stages of construction and reconstruction, until finally arranged and reduced to orderly written shape by a Brahman or Brahmans, whose names have not been preserved[1]. The relationship which the original Brhaman compiler bore to the scattered legends and lays of India, many of them orally transmitted until transferred to the Maha-bharata, was similar to that borne by Pisistratus to the Homeric

---

1. Professor Lassen, in his 'Indische Alterthumskunde' (II. 499, new edition), considers that it may be proved from an examination of the Introduction to the Mahabharata that there were three consecutive working-up (*bearbeitung*) of that poem by different authors. The first or oldest version, called simply *Bharata,* which contained only 24,000 verses, began with the history of Manu, the progenitor of the Kshatriya or military class (Adi-parvan 3126), and a short section — describing the pedigree of Vyasa, and how he appeared at the Snake-sacrifice, and how, at the request of Janamejaya, he commissioned Vaishampayana to relate the story of the strife between the Pandavas and Kauravas (I. 2208, &c.) — might have formed the introduction (*einleitung*) to this oldest Bharata. The second reconstruction or recasting of the poem — thought by Professor Lassen to be identical with the Itihasa mentioned in Ashvalayana's Grihya-sutras, and recited at Shaunaka's Horse-sacrifice — took place about 400 B.C. It began with the history of king Vasu, whose daughter Satyavati was mother of Vyasa; and the section called *Paushya* (I. 661), the antiquity of which is indicated by its being almost entirely in prose, might have served as its introduction. The section called *Pauloma* (I. 851) probably formed the commencement of the third reconstruction of the great Epic, which he considers must have preceded the era of Ashoka.

poems. But the Hindus invest this personage, whoever he was, with a nimbus of mystical sanctity, and assert that he was also the arranger of various other celebrated religious works, such as the Vedas and Puranas. He is called Vyasa, but this is, of course, a mere epithet derived from the Sanskrit verb *vy-as*, meaning 'to dispose in regular sequence,' and therefore would be equally applicable to any compiler[1].

Many of the legends are Vedic, and of great antiquity; while others, as we have already pointed out, are comparatively

---

1. *Vivyasa Vedan yasmat sa tasmad Vyasa iti smritah* (I. 2417). Similarly the name Homerus is thought by some to come from and it may seem strange that the compilation of wholly different works composed at very different epochs, such as the Vedas, Mahabharata, and Puranas undoubtedly were, should be attributed to the same person; but the close relationship supposed by learned natives to subsist between these production, will account for a desire to call in the aid of the same great sage in their construction. The following passage from the Vedartha-prakasaa of Madhava Acharya (who lived in the fourteenth century) commenting on the Taittiriya Yajur-veda (p. 1), translated by Dr. Muir in his Sanskrit Texts, vol. iii. p. 47, attributes the actual composition of the Mahabharata to the sage Vyasa, and gives a remarkable reason for his having written it: — 'It may be said that all persons whatever, including women and Shudra, must be competent students of the Veda, since the aspiration after good (*ishtam me syad iti*) and the deprecation of evil are common to all mankind. But it is not so. For though the expedient exists, and women and Sudras are desirous to know it, they are debarred by another cause from being competent students of the Veda. The scripture (*shastra*) which declares that those persons only who have been invested with the sacrificial cord are competent to read the Veda, intimates thereby that the same study would be a cause of unhappiness to women and Shudras (who are not so invested). How then are these two classes of persons to discover the means of future happiness? We answer, from the Puranas and other such works. Hence it has been said: Since the triple Veda may not be heard by women, Sudras, and degraded twice-born men, the Mahabharata (*Bharatam akhyanam*) was, in his benevolence, composed (*kritam*) by the Muni.'

modern — probably interpolated during the first centuries of the Christian era. In fact, the entire work, which consists, of about 220,000 lines in eighteen Parvans or sections, nearly every one of which would form a large volume, may be compared to a confused congeries of geological strata. The principal story, which occupies little more than a fifth of the whole, forms the lowest layer; but this has been so completely overlaid by successive incrustations, and the mass so compacted together, that the original substratum is not always clearly traceable. If the successive layers can ever be critically analysed and separated, the more ancient from the later additions, and the historical element from the purely fabulous, it may be expected that light will be thrown on the early history of India, religious, social, and political — a subject still veiled in much obscurity, notwithstanding the valuable researches of Professor Lassen and others.

I now give the names of the eighteen sections or Books which constitute the poem, with a brief statement of their contents:

1. *Adi-parvan*, 'introductory Book,' describes how the two brothers, Dhrita-rashtra and Pandu, are brought up by their uncle Bhishma; and how Dhrita-rashtra, who is blind, has one hundred sons — commonly called the Kuru princes — by his wife Gandhari; and how the two wives of Pandu — Pritha (Kunti) and Madri — have five sons, called the Pandavas or Pandu princes.

2. *Sabha-parvan* describes the great *Sabha* or 'assembly of princes' at Hastina-pura, when Yudhi-shthira, the eldest of the five Pandavas, is persuaded to play at dice with Shakuni and loses his kingdom. The five Pandavas and Draupadi, their wife, are required to live for twelve years in the woods.

3. *Vana-parvan* narrates the life of the Pandavas in the Kamyaka forest. This is one of the longest books, and full of episodes such as the story of Nala and that of the Kiratarjuniya.

4. *Virata-parvan* describes the thirteenth year of exile and the adventures of the Pandavas while living disguised in the service of king Virata.

5. *Udyoga-parvan.* In this the preparations for war on the side of both Pandavas and Kauravas are described.

6. *Bhishma-parvan.* In this both armies join battle on Kuru-kshetra, a plain north-west of Delhi. The Kauravas are commanded by Bhishma, who falls transfixed with arrows by Arjuna.

7. *Drona-parvan.* In this the Kuru forces are commanded by Drona, and numerous battles take place. Drona falls in a fight with Dhrishta-dyumna (son of Drupada).

8. *Karna-parvan.* In this the Kurus are led by Karna. Other battles are described. Arjuna kills Karna.

9. *Shalya-parvan.* In this Salya is made general of the Kuru army. The concluding battles take place, and only three of the Kuru warriors, with Duryodhana, are left alive. Bhima and Duryodhana then fight with clubs. Duryodhana, chief and eldest of the Kurus, is struck down.

10. *Sauptika-parvan.* In this the three surviving Kurus make a night attack on the camp of the Pandavas and kill all their army, but not the five Pandavas.

11. *Stri-parvan* describes the lamentations of queen Gandhari and the other wives and women over the bodies of the slain heroes.

12. *Shanti-parvan.* In this Yudhi-shthira is crowned in Hastina-pura. To calm his spirit, troubled with the slaughter of his kindred, Bhishma, still alive, instructs him at great length in the duties of kings (*raja-dharma* 1995-4778), rules for adversity (*apad-dharma* 4779-6455), rules for attaining final emancipation (*moksha-dharma* 6456 to end).

13. *Anushasana-parvan.* In this the instruction is continued by Bhishma, who gives precepts and wise axioms on all subjects, such as the duties of kings, liberality, fasting, eating, &c., mixed up with tales, moral and religious discourses, and metaphysical disquisitions. At the conclusion of his long sermon Bhishma dies.

14. *Ashvamedhika-parvan.* In this Yudhi-shthira, having assumed the government, performs an Asva-medha or 'horse-sacrifice' in token of his supremacy.

15. *Ashramavasika-parvan* narrates how the old blind king Dhrita-rashtra, with his queen Gandhari and with Kunti, mother of the Pandavas, retires to a hermitage in the woods. After two years a forest conflagration takes place, and they immolate themselves in the fire to secure heaven and felicity.

16. *Mausala-parvan* narrates the death of Krishna and Bala-rama, their return to heaven, the submergence of Krishna's city Dvaraka by the sea, and the self-slaughter in a fight with clubs (*musala*) of Krishna's family — the Yadavas — through the curse of some Brahmans.

17. *Mahaprasthanika-parvan* describes the renunciation of their kingdom by Yudhi-shthira and his four brothers, and their departure towards Indra's heaven in Mount Meru.

18. *Svargarohanika-parvan* narrates the ascent and admission to heaven of the five Pandavas, their wife Draupadi, and kindred.

Supplement or *Hari-vansha-parvan,* a later addition, recounting the genealogy and birth of Krishna and the details of his early life.

The following is a more complete and continuous account of the story of the poem, which is supposed to be recited by Vaishampayana, the pupil of Vyasa, to Jana-mejaya, great-grandson of Arjuna.

We have seen that the Ramayana commences by recounting the genealogy of the Solar line of kings, of whom Rama was one. The heroes of the Mahabharata are of the other great race, called Lunar. Here, however, as in the Solar race, the Brahman compiler was careful to assign the origin of the second great dynasty of kings to a noted sage and Brahman. I epitomize the genealogy as essential to the comprehension of the story:

Soma, the Moon, the progenitor of the Lunar race, who reigned at Hastina-pur, was the child of the Rishi *Atsri,* and had

a son named *Budha,* who married Ila or Ida, daughter of the
Solar prince Ikshvaku, and had by her a son, *Aila* or *Pururavas.*
The latter had a son by Urvashi, named *Ayus,* from whom came
Nahusha, the father of *Yayati.* The latter had two sons, *Puru*[1]
and *Yadu,* from whom proceeded the two branches of the Lunar
line. In the line of *Yadu* we need only mention the last three
princes, *Sura, Vasu-deva*[2], and *Krishna* with his brother *Bala-*
rama. Fifteenth in the other line — that of *Puru* — came
Dushyanta, father of the great *Bharata,* from whom India is
called Bharata-varsha. Ninth from Bharata came *Kuru,* and
fourteenth from him *Shantanu.* This Santanu had by his wife
Satyavati, a son named *Vichitra-virya. Bhishma* (also called
Santanava, Deva-vrata, &c.), who renounced the right of
succession and took the vow of a Brahmachari[3], was the son of
Shantanu by a former wife, the goddess Ganga, whence one of
his names is Gangeys. *Satyavati* also had, before her marriage
with Shantanu, borne *Vyasa* to the sage Parashara; so that *Vichitra-*
virya, Bhishma, and *Vyasa* were half-brothers[4]; and *Vyasa,*
although he retired into the wilderness, to live a life of
contemplation, promised his mother that he would place himself
at her disposal whenever she required his services. Satyavati had
recourse to him when her son Vichitra-virya died childless, and

---

1. This name *Puru* (nom. case *Purus*) is probably the original of Porus,
   whose country in the Panjab, between the Hydaspes and Acesines,
   was conquered by Alexander the Great.
2. Pritha or Kunti, wife of Pandu, and mother of three of the Pandu
   princes, was a sister of Vasu-deva, and therefore aunt of Krishna.
3. I. e. perpetual celibacy. *Adya-prabhriti me brahmacharyam bhavishyati;*
   Aputrasyapi me loka bhavishyanty akshaya divi (I. 4060).
4. Parasara met with Satyavati when quite a girl, as he was crossing
   the river Yamuna (Jumna) in a boat. The result of their intercourse
   was a child, Vyasa, who was called Krishna, from his swarthy
   complexion, and Dvaipayana, because he was brought forth by
   Satyavati on an island (*dvipa*) in the Yamuna. (See Mahabharata I.
   2416, 2417, and 4235.)

requested him to pay his addresses to Vicitra-virya's two widows, named Ambika and Ambalika. He consented and had by them respectively two children *Dhrita-rashtra,* who was born blind, and *Pandu,* who was born with a pale complexion[1]. When Satyavati begged Vyasa to become the father of a third son (who should be without any defect), the elder wife, terrified by Vyasa's austere appearance, sent him one of her slave-girls, dressed in her own clothes; and this girl became the mother of Vidura (whence he is sometimes called Kshattri[2]).

Dhrita-rashtra, Pandu and *Vidura* were thus brothers, sons of Vyasa, the supposed author or compiler of the Mahabharata. Vyasa after this retired again to the woods; but, gifted with

---

1. The mother of Pandu was also called Kausalya; and this name (which was that of the mother of Rama-chandra) seems also to be applied to the mother of Dhrita-rashtra. Paleness of complexion, in the eyes of a Hindu, would be regarded as a kind of leprosy, and was therefore almost as great a defect as blindness. The reason given for these defects is very curious. Ambika was so terrified by the swarthy complexion and shaggy aspect of the sage Vyasa (not to speak of the *gandha* emitted by his body), that when he visited her she closed her eyes, and did not venture to open them while he was with her. In consequence of this assumed blindness her child was born blind. Ambalika, on the other hand, though she kept her eyes open, became so colourless with fright, that her son was born with a pale complexion (I. 4275-4290). Pandu seems to have been in other respects good-looking — *Sa devi kumaram ajijanat pandu-lakshana-sampannam dipyamanam vara-shriya.*

2. Vyasa was so much pleased with this slave-girl that he pronounced her free, and declared that her child, Vidura, should be *sarva-buddhimatam varah,* 'the most excellent of all wise men.' Kshattri, although described in Manu as the child of a Sudra father and Brahman mother, signifies here the child of a Brahman father and Shudra mother. Vidura is one of the best characters in the Maha-bharata, always ready with useful advice (*hitopadesha*) both for the Pandavas and for his brother Dhrita-rashtra. His disposition leads him to side with the Pandu princes and warn them of the evil designs of their cousins.

divine prescience, appeared both to his sons and grandsons whenever they were in difficulties, and needed his advice and assistance.

The two brothers, Dhrita-rashtra and Pandu, were brought up by their uncle Bhishma[1], who until they were of age, conducted the government of Hastinapur[2]. Dhrita-rashtra was the first-born, but renounced the throne, in consequence of his blindness. The other brother, Vidura, being the son of a Shudra woman, could not succeed, and Pandu therefore, when of age, became king (I. 4361). Meanwhile Dhrita-rashtra married Gandhari, also called Saubaleyi or Saubali, daughter of Subala, king of Gandhara. When she first heard that her future husband was blind, she from that moment showed her respect for him, by binding her own eyes with a handkerchief, and always remaining blindfolded in his presence[3]. Soon afterwards a Svayamvara was held by king Kuntibhoja, and his adopted daughter, Pritha or Kunti, then chose Pandu for her husband. She was really the child of a Yadava prince, Sura, who gave her to his childless cousin Kuntibhoja; under whose care she was brought up:

One day, before her marriage, she paid such respect and attention to a powerful sage named Durvasas, a guest in her father's house, that he gave her a charm and taught her an incantation, by virtue of which she might have a child by any god she liked to call into her presence. Out of curiosity, she

---

1. They were all three thoroughly educated by Bhishma. Dhrita-rashtra is described as excelling all others in strength (I. 4356), Pandu as excelling in the use of the bow, and Vidura as pre-eminent for virtue and wisdom (4358).
2. Hastinapur is also called Gajasahvaya and Nagasahvaya.
3. *Sa patam adaya kritva bahu-gunam tada Babandha netre sve rajan pativrata-parayana* (I. 4376). She is described as so devoted to her husband that *Vacha' pi purushan anyan suvrata nanvakirtayat.*

invoked the Sun, by whom she had a child, who was born clothed in armour[1]. But Pritha (Kunti), fearing the censure of her relatives, deserted her offspring, after exposing it in the river. It was found by Adhiratha, a charioteer (*suta*), nurtured by his wife Radha; whence the child was afterwards called Radheya, though named by his foster-parents Vasu-shena. When he was grown up, the god Indra conferred upon him enormous strength, and changed his name to Karna[2].

After Pandu's marriage to Pritha, his uncle Bhishma wishing him to take a second wife, made an expedition to visit Shalya, king of Madra, and prevailed upon him to bestow his sister Madri upon Pandu, in exchange for vast sums of money and jewels. Soon after this second marriage Pandu undertook a great campaign, in which he subjugated so many countries, that the kingdom of Hastina-pur became under him as glorious and extensive as formerly under his ancestor Bharata (I. 4461). Having acquired enormous wealth, he distributed it to Bhishma, Dhrita-rashtra, and Vidura, and then retired to the woods to indulge his passion for hunting, living with his two wives as a forester on the southern slope of the Himalayas. The blind Dhrita-rashtra, who had a very useful charioteer named Sanjaya, was then obliged, with the assistance of Bhishma as his regent, to assume the reins of government.

We have next an account of the supernatural birth of Dhrita-rashtra's sons:

One day the sage Vyasa was hospitably entertained by queen Gandhari, and in return granted her a boon. She chose to be

---

1. The Sun afterwards restored her kanyatva (I. 4400).
2. He is also called Vaikartana, as son of Vikartana or the Sun, and sometimes Vrisha. Karna is described (4405) as worshipping the Sun till his back became warm (a-*prishtha-tapat,* i.e. 'till after midday,' when the sun began to shine behind him). Compare Hitop. book II. v. 32.

the mother of a hundred sons. After two years she produced a mass of flesh, which was divided by Vyasa into a hundred and one pieces, as big as the joint of a thumb. From these in due time the eldest, Dur-yodhana, 'difficult to be subdued' (sometimes called Su-yodhana, see p. 426, note 5), was born. At his birth, however, various evil omens took place; jackals yelled, asses brayed, whirlwinds blew, and the sky seemed on fire. Dhrita-rashtra, alarmed, called his ministers together, who recommended him to abandon the child, but could not persuade him to take their advice. The miraculous birth of the remaining ninety-nine sons then occurred in due course[1]. There was also one daughter, called Duhsala (afterwards married to Jayad-ratha).

Next follows the description of the supernatural birth of the five reputed sons of Pandu:

One day, on a hunting expedition, Pandu transfixed with five arrows a male and female deer. These turned out to be a certain sage and his wife, who had assumed the form of these animals. The sage cursed Pandu, and predicted that he would die in the embraces of one of his wives. In consequence of this curse, Pandu took the vow of a Brahmachari[2], gave all his property to the Brahmans, and became a hermit.

Thereupon his wife Pritha (also called Kunti), with his approval, made use of the charm and incantation formerly given to her by Durvasas, and had three sons, Yudhi-shthira Bhima, and Arjuna, by the three deities, Dharma, Vayu, and Indra respectively:

Yudhi-shthira was born first, and at the moment of his birth a heavenly voice was heard to utter these words, 'This is the most virtuous of men. Bhima, the son of Pritha and Vayu, was born on the same day as Duryodhan. Soon after his birth, his mother

---

1. Their names are all detailed at I. 4540.
2. The *brahmacharya-vrata,* or vow of continence.

accidentally let him fall, when a great prodigy — indicative of the vast strength which was to distinguish him — occurred; for the body of the child falling on a rock shivered it to atoms. On the birth of Arjuna auspicious omens were manifested; showers of flowers fell[1], celestial minstrels filled the air with harmony, and a heavenly voice sounded his praises and future glory.

Madri, the other wife of Pandu, was now anxious to have children, and was told by Pritha (Kunti) to think on any god she pleased. She chose the two Asvins (see p. 14), who appeared to her, and were the fathers of her twin sons Nakula and Sahadeva. While the five princes were still children, Pandu, forgetting the curse of the sage whom he had killed in the form of a deer, ventured one day to embrace his wife Madri, and died in her arms. She and Pritha (Kunti) then had a dispute for the honour of becoming a Sati (see p. 350), which ended in Madri burning herself with her husband's corpse (I. 4896). Pritha and the five Pandu princes were then taken by certain Rishis, or holy men — companions of Pandu — to Hastina-pur, where they were presented to Dhrita-rashtra, and all the circumstances of their birth and of the death of Pandu narrated. The news of the death of his brother was received by Dhrita-rashtra with much apparent sorrow; he gave orders for the due performance of the funeral rites, and allowed the five young princes and their mother to live with his own family. The cousins were in the habit of playing together:

In their boyish sports the Pandu princes excelled the sons of Dhrita-rashtra, which excited much ill feeling; and Duryodhana, spiteful even when a boy, tried to destroy Bhima by mixing poison in his food, and then throwing him into the water when

---

1. Showers of flowers are as common in Indian poetry as showers of blood; the one indicating good, the other portending evil.

stupefied by its effects (I. 500). Bhima, however, was not drowned, but descended to the abode of the Nagas (or serpent-demons), who freed him from the poison (5052), and gave him a liquid to drink which endued him with the strength of ten thousand Nagas. From that moment he became a kind of Hercules.

Then Duryodhana, Karna, and Shakuni[1] devised schemes for destroying the Pandu princes, but without success.

The characters of the five Pandavas are drawn with much artistic delicacy of touch, and maintained with general consistency throughout the poem[2]. The eldest, Yudhi-shthira, is the Hindu ideal of excellence — a pattern of justice, integrity, calm passionless composure, chivalrous honour, and cold heroism[3]. Bhima is a type of brute courage and strength: he is of gigantic stature, impetuous, irascible, somewhat vindictive, and cruel even to the verge of ferocity, making him, as his name implies, 'terrible.' It would appear that his great strength had to be maintained by plentiful supplies of food; as his name Vrikodara, 'wolf-stomached,' indicated a voracious appetite; and we are told that at the daily meals of the five brothers, half of the whole dish had to be given to Bhima (I. 7161). But he has the capacity for warm unselfish

---

1. Sakuni was the brother of Gandhari, and therefore maternal uncle (*matula*) of the Kaurava princes. He was the counsellor of Duryodhana. He is often called Saubala, as Gandhari is called Saubali.
2. Complete consistency must not be expected in such a poem as the Mahabharata, which was the growth of several centuries. The act of the five Pandavas, described p. 429-430 cannot be reconciled with their usual probity and generosity, though committed under great provocation. Bhima appears to have been most in fault, which is so far consistent.
3. Yudhi-shthira, 'firm in battle,' was probably of commanding stature and imposing presence. He is described as *Maha-sinha-gati*, 'having a majestic lion-like gait,' with a Wellington-like profile (*Pralambojjvala-charu-ghona*) and long lotus-eyes (*kamalayataksha*).

love, and is ardent in his affection for his mother and brothers. Arjuna rises more to the European standard of perfection. He may be regarded as the real hero of the Mahabharata[1], of undaunted bravery, generous[2], with refined and delicate sensibilities, tender-hearted, forgiving, and affectionate as a woman, yet of superhuman strength, and matchless in arms and athletic exercises. Nakula and Sahadeva are both amiable, noble-minded, and spiritual[3]. All five are as unlike as possible to the hundred sons of Dhrita-rashtra, commonly called the *Kuru* princes, or *Kauravas*[4], who are represented as mean, spiteful, dishonourable, and vicious.

So bad indeed are these hundred brothers, and so uniformly without redeeming points that their characters present few distinctive features. The most conspicuous is the eldest, Duryodhana[5], who, as the representative of the others, is painted in the darkest colours, and embodies all their bad

---

1. Strictly, as in the Iliad, there is no real hero kept always in view.
2. Perhaps it may be objected that some of Arjuna's acts were inconsistent with this character. Thus he carried off Subhadra, the sister of Krishna, by force. It must be borne in mind, however, that Krishna himself encourages him to this act, and says, *Prasahya haranam Kshatri-yanam prasasyate* (I. 7927). Compare p. 436.
3. The five Pandu princes are known by various other names in the Maha-bharata, some of which it may be useful here to note. Yudhi-shthira is also called Dharma-raja, Dharma-putra, and sometimes simply Rajan. His charioteer was called Indrasena. Bhima's other names are Bhimasena, Vrikodara, Bahushalin. Arjuna is also called Kiritin, Phalguna, Jishnu, Dhananjaya, Bibhatsu, Savyasachin, Pakashasani, Guda-kesha, Shveta-vahana, Nara, Vijaya, Krishna, and sometimes *par excellence* Partha, though Bhima and Yudhi-shthira, as sons of Pritha, had also this title. Nakula and Sahadeva are called Madreyau (as sons of Madri), and sometimes Yamau (the twins).
4. This name, however, is occasionally applied to the Pandavas, as they and the sons of Dhrita-rashtra were equally descendants of Kuru.
5. 'Difficult to conquer,' cf. p. 456. The names of all are given in Adiparvan 4541. Duhshasana is one of the most conspicuous.

qualities. When the Mahabharata (like the Ramayana) is regarded as an allegory, then Duryodhana (like Ravana) is a visible type of the evil principle in human nature[1] for ever doing battle with the good and divine principle, symbolized by the five sons of Pandu.

The cousins, though so uncongenial in character, were educated together at Hastina-pur, the city of Dhrita-rashtra, by a Brahman named Drona[2], who found in the Pandu princes apt pupils. From him the five sons of Pandu acquired 'intelligence and learning, lofty aims, religious earnestness, and love of truth.' All the cousins were equally instructed in war and arms; but Arujna, by the help of Drona, who gave him magical weapons, excelled all, distinguishing himself in every exercise, 'submissive ever to his teacher's will, contented, modest, affable, and mild,' and both Bhima and Duryodhana learnt the use of the club from their cousin Bala-rama (I. 5520).

Their education finished, a tournament was held, at which all the youthful cousins displayed their skill in archery, in the management of chariots (ratha-charya), horses, and elephants, in sword, spear, and club exercises, and wrestling. The scene is graphically described (I. 5324):

An immense concourse of spectators cheered the combatants. The agitation of the crowd was like the roar of a mighty ocean.

---

1. There are certainly many points in his character, as well as in that of Ravana, which may be compared to Milton's conception of Satan. Perhaps his intimacy with the Asura Charvaka may be intended to mark him out as a type of heresy and infidelity, as well as of every other bad quality. In the case of Ravana it is remarkable that he gained his power by penances, and that he is described as well-read in the Veda (Ram. VI. xciii. 58). Some Rakshasas, such as Vibhishana, Atikaya, are described as religious (Ram. VI. lxxi. 31). Cf. Manu VII. 38.

2. Drona appears to have kept a kind of school to which all the young princes of the neighbouring countries resorted (I. 5220). He married Kripi, sister of Kripa, and had by her a son, Ashvatthaman.

Arjuna, after exhibiting prodigies of strength, shot five separate arrows simultaneously into the jaws of a revolving iron boar, and twenty-one arrows into the hollow of a cow's horn suspended by a string. Suddenly there was a pause. The crowd turned as one man towards a point in the arena, where the sound of a warrior striking his arms in defiance[1] rent the sky like a thunder-clap, and announced the entrance of another combatant. This proved to be a warrior named *Karna*, who entered the lists in full armour, and after accomplishing the same feats in archery, challenged Arjuna to single combat. But each champion was required to tell his name and pedigree; and Karna's parentage being doubtful (see p. 421-422), he was obliged to retire, 'hanging his head with shame like a drooping lily.'

Karna, thus publicly humiliated, became afterwards a conspicuous and valuable ally of the Kurus against his own half-brothers. His character is well imagined. Feeling keenly the stain on his birth, his nature was chastened by the trial. He exhibited in a high degree fortitude, chivalrous honour, self-sacrifice, and devotion. Especially remarkable for a liberal and generous disposition[2], he never stooped to ignoble practices like his friends the Kurus, who were intrinsically bad men.

The tutor's fee (*Gurv-artha*, see pp. 223, 273, Manu II. 245 Raghu-vansa V.17) which Drona required of his pupils for their instruction was, that they should capture Drupada, king of Panchala, who was his old schoolfellow, but had insulted him by repudiating his friendship (I. 5446):

They therefore invaded Drupada's territory and took him prisoner; but Drona generously spared his life, and gave him

---

1. So in Vishnu-purana, p. 513: 'Krishna having dived into the pool struck his arms in defiance, and the snake-king, hearing the sound, came quickly forth.'
2. He is often to this day cited as a model of liberality. Hence his name, Vasu-shena.

back half his kingdom. Drupada, however, burning with resentment, endeavoured to procure the birth of a son, to avenge his defeat and bring about the destruction of Drona. Two Brahmans undertook a sacrifice for him, and two children were born from the midst of the altar, out of the sacrificial fire, a son, Dhristha-dyumna, and a daughter, Krishna or Draupadi, afterwards the wife of the Pandavas (see p. 433).

After this, Yudhi-shthira was installed by Dhrita-rashtra as Yuva-raja or heir-apparent, and by his exploits soon eclipsed the glory of his father Pandu's reign.

The great renown gained by the Pandu princes excited the jealousy and ill-will of Dhrita-rashtra, but won the affections of the citizens. The latter met together, and after consultation declared that, as Dhrita-rashtra was blind, he ought not to conduct the government, and that as Bhishma had formerly declined the throne, he ought not to be allowed to act as regent. They therefore proposed to crown Yudhi-shthira at once. When Duryodhana heard of this, he consulted with Karna, Sakuni, and Duhshasana, how he might remove Yudhi-shthira out of the way, and secure the throne for himself:

Urged by Duryodhana, Dhrita-rashtra was induced to send the Pandava princes on an excursion to the city of Varanavata, pretending that he wished them to see the beauties of that town, and to be present at a festival there. Meanwhile Duryodhana instigated his friend Purochana to precede them, and to prepare a house for their reception, which he was to fill secretly with hemp, resin, and other combustible substances, plastering the walls with mortar composed of oil, fat, and lac (*laksha, jatu*). When the princes were asleep in this house, and unsuspicious of danger, he was to set it on fire. The five Pandavas and their mother left Hastina-pur amid the tears and regrets of the citizens, and in eight days arrived at Varanavata, where, after great demonstrations of respect from the inhabitants, they were conducted by Purochana to the house of lac. Having been warned by Vidura, they soon discovered the dangerous character of the structure, and with the assistance of a miner (*khanaka*) sent by Vidura, dug an underground passage, by which to escape from the interior (I. 5813). Then they devised a counterplot, and agreed together that a degraded outcaste woman (*nishadi*) with her five sons should be invited to a feast, and stupefied with wine. Bhima was then to set fire to the lac-house in which they were all assembled (see note, p. 425). This was done. Purochana was burnt, as well as the woman with her five sons, but they themselves escaped by the secret passage (*surunga*). The charred bodies of the woman and her sons being afterwards found, it was supposed that the Pandava princes had perished in the conflagration, and their funeral ceremonies were actually performed by Dhrita-rashtra. Meanwhile they hurried off to the woods; Bhima the strong one, carrying his mother and the twins, and leading his other brothers by the hands when through fatigue they could not move on. Whilst his mother and brothers were asleep under a fig-tree, Bhima had an encounter with a hideous giant named Hidimb, whom he slew[1]. Afterwards he married Hidimba, the sister of this monster, and had a son by her named Ghatotkacha.

By the advice of their grandfather Vyasa, the Pandava princes next took up their abode in the house of a Brahman at a city called Ekachakra. There they lived for a long time in the guise of mendicant Brahmans, safe from the persecution of Duryodhana. Every day they went out to beg for food as alms (*bhiksha, bhaiksha*), which their mother Kunti divided at night, giving half of the whole to Bhima as his share (cf. P. 425). While resident in the house of the Brahman, Bhima delivered his family and the city of Ekachakra from a fierce giant (or Rakshasa) named Baka (or Vaka), who forced the citizens to send him every day a dish of food by a man whom

---

1. This forms the subject of a celebrated episode, edited by Bopp.

he always devoured as his daintiest morsel at the end of the repast[1].

The turn had come to a poor Brahman to provide the Rakshasa with his meal. He determined to go himself, but lamented bitterly the hardness of his fate. Upon this, his wife and daughter addressed him in language full of the deepest pathos, each in turn insisting on sacrificing herself for the good of the family. Lastly, the little son, too young to speak distinctly, ran with beaming eyes and smiling face to his parents, and in prattling accents said, 'Weep not, father; sigh not, mother.' Then breaking off and brandishing a pointed spike of grass, he exclaimed, 'With this spike will I kill the fierce man-eating giant.' His parents, hearing this innocent prattle of their child, in the midst of their heart-rending anguish felt a thrill of exquisite delight. In the end Bhima, who overheard the whole conversation, undertook to convey the meal to the monster, and, of course, speedily despatched him (I. 6202).

After this Vyasa appeared to his grandsons, and informed them that Draupadi, the daughter of Drupada, king of Panchala, was destined to be their common wife[2]:

In real fact she had been in a former life the daughter of a sage, and had performed a most severe penance, in order that a husband might fall to her lot. Shiva, pleased with her penance, had appeared to her, and had promised her, instead of one, five

---

1. This story forms a touching episode, which has been printed by Bopp, and translated by Milman.
2. Polyandry is still practised among some hill-tribes in the Himalaya range near Simal, and in other barren mountainous regions, such as Bhotan, where a large population could not be supported. It prevails also among the Nair (Nayar) tribe in Malabar. Our forefathers, or at least the ancient Britons, according to Caesar, were given to the same practice: 'Uxores habent deni duodenique inter se communes,' &c. De Bello Gallico, V. 14.

husbands. When the maiden replied that she wanted only one husband, the god answered, 'Five times you said to me, Grant me a husband; therefore in another body you will obtain five husbands' (I. 6433, 7322). This Rishi's daughter was thereupon born in the family of Drupada as a maiden of the most distinguished beauty, and was destined to be the wife of the Pandavas[1].

---

1. Vyasa, who is the type and representative of strict Brahmanism, is made to explain at length the necessity for the marriage of Draupadi to five husbands (which is called a *sukshma-dharma*, I. 7246). He also gifted Drupada with divine intuition (*chakshur divyam*) to perceive the divinity of the Pandavas and penetrate the mystic meaning of what otherwise would have been a serious violation of the laws and institutions of the Brahmans (7313). Hence Drupada became aware of his daughter's former birth, and that Arjuna was really a portion of the essence of Indra (*Shakrasyansha*), and all his brothers portions of the same god. Draupadi herself, although nominally the daughter of Drupada, was really born, like her brother Dhrishta-dyumna out of the midst of the sacrificial fire (*vedi-madhyati*, I. 6931; see p. 429), and was a form of Lakshmi. In no other way could her supernatural birth, and the divine perfume which exhaled from her person, and was perceived a league off (*krosha-matrat pravati*), be accounted for. Vyasa at the same time explained the mysterious birth of Krishna and Baladeva; — how the god Vishnu pulled out two of his own hairs, one white and the other black, which entered into two women of the family of the Yadavas (Devaki and Rohini), and became, the white one Baladeva, the black one Krishna (I. 7307; Vishnu-purana V. 1). The Markandeya-purana (ch. 5) shows how the five Pandavas could be all portions of Indra, and yet four of them sons of other gods. When Indra killed the son of Tvashtri (or Vishvakarma as Prajapati, the Creator), his punishment for this *brahmahatya* was that all his *tejas*, 'manly vigour,' deserted him, and entered Dharma, the god of justice. The son of Tvashtri was reproduced as the demon Vritra, and again slain by Indra; as a punishment for which his *bala*, 'strength,' left him, and entered *Maruta*, 'the Wind.' Lastly, when Indra violated Ahalya, the wife of the sage Gautama, his *rupa*, 'beauty,' abandoned him, and entered the Nasatyau or Ashvins. When Dharma gave back the *tejas* of Indra, Yudhi-shthira was born; when the Wind gave up Indra's *bala*, Bhima was born; and when the Ashvins restored the *rupa* of Indra, Nakula and Sahadeva were born. Arjuna was born as half the essence of Indra. Hence, as they were all portions of one deity, there could be no harm in Draupadi becoming the wife of all five.

In obedience to the directions of their grandfather, the five Pandavas quitted Ekachakra, and betook themselves to the court of king Drupada, where Draupadi was about to hold her Svayamvara:

An immense concourse of princely suitors with their retainers, came to the ceremony; and king Drupada eagerly looked for Arjuna among them, that, strengthened by that hero's alliance, he might defy Drona's anger. He therefore prepared an enormous bow, which he was persuaded none but Arjuna could bend, and proposed a trial of strength, promising to give his daughter to any one who could by means of the bow shoot five arrows simultaneously through a revolving ring into a target beyond. An amphitheatre was erected outside the town, surrounded by tiers of lofty seats and raised platforms, with variegated awnings. Magnificent palaces, crowded with eager spectators, overlooked the scene. Actors, conjurors, athletes, and dancers exhibited their skill before the multitude. Strains of exquisite music floated in the air. Drums and trumpets sounded. When expectation was at its height, Draupadi in gorgeous apparel entered the arena, and the bow was brought. The hundred sons of Dhrita-rashtra strained every nerve to bend the ponderous weapon, but without effect. Its recoil dashed them breathless to the ground, and made them the laughing-stock of the crowd.

Arjuna now advanced, disguised as a Brahman. I here translate a portion metrically (I. 7049, &c.):

A moment motionless he stood and scanned
The bow, collecting all his energy.
Next walking round in homage, breathed a prayer
To the Supreme Bestower of good gifts;
Then fixing all his mind on Draupadi
He grasped the ponderous weapon in his hand,
And with one vigorous effort braced the string.
Quickly the shafts were aimed; they flew;
The mark fell pierced; a shout of victory

Rang through the vast arena; from the sky
Garlands of flowers crowned the hero's head,
Ten thousand fluttering scarfs waved in the air,
And drum and trumpet sounded forth his triumph.

I need not suggest the parallel which will at once be drawn by the classical scholar between this trial of archery and a similar scene in the Odyssey.

When the suitors found themselves outdone by a mere stripling in the coarse dress of a mendicant Brahman, their rage knew no bounds. A real battle ensued:

The Pandu princes protected Drupada, and enacted prodigies. Bhima tore up a tree, and used it as a club. Karna at last met Arjuna in single combat, rushing on him like a young elephant. They overwhelmed each other with showers of arrows, which darkened the air. But not even Karna could withstand the irresistible onset of the godlike Arjuna, and he and the other suitors retired vanquished from the field, leaving Draupadi as the bride of Arjuna.

Arjuna having been chosen by Draupadi, the five brothers returned with her to their mother, who being inside the house, and fancying that they had brought alms, called out to them, 'Share it between you' (*bhunkteti sametya sarve*, I. 7132). The words of a parent, thus spoken, could not be set aside without evil consequences; and Drupada, at the persuasion of Vyasa, who acquainted him with the divinely ordained destination of his daughter[1], consented to her becoming the common wife of the five brothers. She was first married by the family-priest Dhaumya to Yudhi-shthira

---

1. See note 1, p. 432. Drupada at first objected. Yudhi-shthira's excuse for himself and his brothers is remarkable; *Purvesham anupurvyena yatam vartmanuyamahe* (I. 7246).

(I. 7340), and then, according to priority of birth, to the other four[1].

The Pandavas, being now strengthened by their alliance with the powerful king of Panchala, threw off their disguises; and king Dhrita-rashtra thought it more politic to settle all differences by dividing his kingdom between them and his own sons. He gave up Hastina-pur to the latter, presided over by Duryodhana, and permitted the five Pandavas to occupy a district near the Yamuna (Jumna), called Khandava-prastha, where they built Indra-prastha (the modern Delhi), and, under Yudhi-shthira as their leader, subjugated much of the adjacent territory by predatory incursions (I. 6573).

One day, when Arjuna was bathing in the Ganges, he was carried off by the serpent-nymph Ulupi, daguther of the king of the Nagas, whom he married (I. 7809). Afterwards he married Chitrangada, daughter of the king of Manipura, and had a child by her named Babhru-vahana (I. 7883).

Wandering for twelve years in the forests, to fulfil a vow, Arjuna came to Prabhasa, a place of pilgrimage in the west of India, where he met Krishna[2], the details of whose early

---

1. She had a son by each of the five brothers — Prativindhya by Yudhi-shthira; Sutasoma by Bhima; Shrutakarman by Arjuna; Shatanika by Nakula; Srutasena by Sahadeva (I. 8039). Arjuna had also another wife, Subhadra, the sister of Krishna, with whom he eloped when on a visit to Krishna at Dvaraka. By her he had a son, Abhimanyu. He had also a son named Iravat by the serpent-nymph Ulupi. Bhima had also a son, Ghatotkacha, by the Rakshasi Hidimba (see p. 430); and the others had children by different wives (Vishnu-purana, p. 459). Arjuna's son Abhimanyu had a son Parikshit, who was father of Janamejaya. Parikshit died of the bite of a snake; and the Bhagavata-purana was narrated to him between the bite and his death.
2. See note 1, p. 432. I enumerate some of the other names by which Krishna is known in the Mahabharata, as follows: Vasudeva, Keshava, Govinda, Janardana, Damodara, Dasharha, Narayana, Hrishikesa, Purushottama, Madhava, Madhu-sudana, Achyuta. (See V. 2560). In the Draupadi-harana (75) Krishna and Arjuna are called Krishnau.

life have already been given (p. 370), and who here first
formed a friendship with Arjuna, and took him to his city
Dvaraka, where he received him as a visitor into his own
house (I. 7905). Soon afterwards, some of the relatives of
Krishna celebrated a festival in the mountain Raivataka, to
which both Arjuna and Krishna went There they saw Bala-
rama, elder brother of Krishna (p. 370), in a state of intoxication
(*kshiva*)[1] with his wife Revati; and there they saw Subhadra,
Krishna's sister. Her beauty excited the love of Arjuna, who,
after obtaining Krishna's leave, carried her off (see note 1,
p. 435) and married her (I. 7937). In the twelfth year of his
absence he returned with her to Indra-prastha.

The Pandavas and all the epole of Indra-prastha then lived
happily for some time under the rule of Yudhi-shthira, who,
elated with his conquests, undertook, assisted by Krishna, to
celebrate the Rajasuya, a great sacrifice, at which his own
inauguration as paramount sovereign was to be performed.

A great assembly (*sabha*) was accordingly held:

Various princes attended, and brought either rich presents
or tribute (II. 1264). Among those who came were Bhishma,
Dhrita-rashtra and his hundred sons, Subala (king of Gandhara),
Sakuni, Drupada, Salya, Drona, Kripa, Jayad-ratha, Kuntibhoja,
Sishu-pala, and others from the extreme south and north (Dravida,
Ceylon, and Kashmir, II. 1271)[2]. On the day of the inauguration
(*abhisheka*) Bhishma, at the suggestion of the sage Narada,
proposed that a respectful oblation (*argha*) should be prepared
and offered in token of worship to the best and strongest person
present, whom he declared to be Krishna. To this the Pandavas

---

1. Compare Megha-duta, verse 51, where Bala-rama's fondness for
   wine is alluded to. See also Vishnu-purana V. 25.
2. The details in this part of the poem are interesting and curious. As
   shown by Professor H.H. Wilson, they throw light on the geographical
   divisions and political condition of India at an early epoch.

readily agreed; and Sahadeva was commissioned to present the offering. Shishu-pala (also called Sunitha), however, opposed the worship of Krishna; and, after denouncing him as a contemptible and ill-instructed person (II. 1340), challenged him to fight[1], but Krishna instantly struck off his head with his discus called Su-darshana[2].

After this, Dhrita-rashtra was persuaded to hold another assembly (*sabha*) at Hastina-pur; and Vidura was sent to the Pandavas, to invite them to be present (II. 1993). They consented to attend; and Yudhi-shthira was easily prevailed on by Duryodhana to play with Shakuni. By degrees Yudhi-shthira staked everything — his territory, his possessions, and last of all Draupadi. All were successively lost; and Draupadi, then regarded as a slave, was treated with great indignity by Duhshasana. He dragged her by the hair of the head into the assembly; upon which Bhima, who witnessed this insult, swore that he would one day dash Duhshasana to pieces and drink his blood[3] (II. 2302). In the end a compromise was agreed upon. The kingdom was given up to Duryodhana for twelve years; and the five Pandavas, with Draupadi, were required to live for that period in the woods, and to pass the thirteenth concealed under assumed names in various disguises.

---

1. Duryodhana also, in a subsequent part of the Mahabharata, evinces scepticism in regard to the divine nature of Krishna (V. 4368).

2. The story of Shishu-pala and his destruction by Krishna form the subject of the celebrated poem of Magha. The particulars of the narrative as told in this book of the Mahabharata are given by Dr. Muir in his Sanskrit Texts, vol. iv. The Vishnu-purana identifies Shishu-pala with the demons Hiranya-kashipu and Ravana (Wilson, p. 437).

3. This threat he fulfilled. The incident is noticeable as it is the subject of the well-known drama by Bhatta-narayana called Veni-samhara, 'braid-binding,' which describes how the braided hair torn by Duhshasana was again bound together by Bhima, who is made to say *Svayam aham sam-harami*, 'I myself will again bind the braid together.' See Sahitya-darpana, p. 169.

They accordingly retired to the Kamyaka forest, and took
up their abode on the banks of the Sarasvati.

While they were resident in the forest, various episodes
occurred, thus:

Arjuna went to the Himalaya mountains to perform severe
penance, and thereby obtain celestial arms. After some time
Shiva, to reward him and prove his bravery, approached him as
a Kirata or wild mountaineer living by the chase, at the moment
that a demon named Muka, in the form of a boar, was making
an attack upon him. Shiva and Arjuna both shot together at the
boar, which fell dead, and both claimed to have hit him first.
This served as a pretext for Shiva, as the Kirata, to quarrel with
Arjuna, and have a battle with him. Arjuna fought long with the
Kirata[1] but could not conquer him. At last he recognized the
god, and threw himself at his feet. Shiva, pleased with his bravery,
gave him the celebrated weapon Pashupata, to enable him to
conquer Karna and the Kuru princes in war (III. 1650, 1664).

Many legends were also repeated to console and amuse
the Pandu princes in their time of exile. For instance, we have
here introduced (III. 12746-12804) the epic version of the
tradition of the Deluge (the earliest account of which occurs
in the Satapatha-brahmana, see p. 34 of this volume), as
follows:

Manu, the Hindu Noah (not the grandson of Brahma, and
reputed author of the Code, but the seventh Manu, or Manu
of the present period, called Vaivasvata, and regarded as one
of the progenitors of the human race, Manu I. 61, 62), is
represented as conciliating the favour of the Supreme Being by

---

1. This forms the subject of a celebrated poem by Bharavi called the
Kiratarjuniya. Shiva was regarded as the god of the Kiratas, who
were evidently a race of aborigines much respected by the Hindus
for their bravery and skill in archery.

his austerities in an age of universal depravity. A fish, which
was an incarnation of Brahma (cf. p. 365), appeared to him
whilst engaged in penance on the margin of a river, and accosting
him, craved protection from the larger fish. Manu complied,
and placed him in a glass vessel. Having outgrown this, he
requested to be taken to a more roomy receptacle. Manu then
placed him in a lake. Still the fish grew, till the lake, though
three leagues long, could not contain him. He next asked to
be taken to the Ganges; but even the Ganges was soon too
small, and the fish was finally transferred to the ocean. There
he continued to expand, till at last, addressing Manu, he warned
him of the coming Deluge.

Manu, however, was to be preserved by the help of the fish,
who commanded him to build a ship and go on board, not with
his own wife and children, but with the seven Rishis or patriarchs;
and not with pairs of animals, but with the seeds of all existing
things. The flood came; Manu went on board, and fastened the
ship, as directed, to a horn in the fish's head. He was then drawn
along[1] — (I translate nearly literally):

Along the ocean in that stately ship was borne the lord of
men, and through
Its dancing, tumbling billows, and its roaring waters; and the
bark,
Tossed to and fro by violent winds, reeled on the surface
of the deep,
Staggering and trembling like a drunken woman. Land was
seen no more,
Nor far horizon, nor the space between; for everywhere
around

---

1. There is still a later accout of the Deluge in the Bhagavata-purana,
   where the fish is represented as an incarnation of Vishnu. The god's
   object in descending as a fish seems to have been to steer the ship.
   In the Assyrian account (as interpreted by Mr. G. Smith) sailors and
   a helmsman are taken on board.

Spread the wild waste of waters, reeking atmosphere, and
boundless sky.
And now when all the world was deluged, nought appeared
above the waves
But Manu and the seven sages, and the fish that drew the
bark.
Unwearied thus for years on years the fish propelled the ship
across
The heaped-up waters, till at length it bore the vessel to the
peak
Of Himavan; then, softly smiling, thus the fish addressed the
sage:
Haste now to bind thy ship to this high crag. Know me the
lord of all,
The great creator Brahma, mightier than all might —
omnipotent.
By me in fish-like shape hast thou been saved in dire
emergency.
From Manu all creation, gods, Asuras, men, must be
produced;
By him the world must be created — that which moves
and moveth not.

Another tale told in this section of the poem (III. 16619),
&c.) may be cited for its true poetic feeling and pathos —
qualities in which it is scarcely excelled by the story of Admetus
and Alcestis. I subjoin the briefest epitome:

Savitri, the beautiful daughter of a king Ahsvapati, loved
Satyavan, the son of an old hermit, but was warned by a seer
to overcome her attachment, as Satyavan was a doomed man,
having only one year to live. But Savitri replies[1]:

---

1. I translate as closely as I can to the original. This and other select
specimens of Indian poetry have been more freely and poetically
translated by Mr. R. Griffiths.

Whether his years be few or many, be he gifted with all grace
Or graceless, him my heart hath chosen, and it chooseth not
again,

The king's daughter and the hermit's son were therefore
married, and the bride strove to forget the ominous prophecy;
but as the last day of the year approached, her anxiety became
irrepressible. She exhausted herself in prayers and penances,
hoping to stay the hand of the destroyer; yet all the while dared
not reveal the fatal secret to her husband. At last the dreaded
day arrived, and Satyavan set out to cut wood in the forest. His
wife asked leave to accompany him, and walked behind her
husband, smiling, but with a heavy heart. Satyavan soon made
the wood resound with his hatchet, when suddenly a thrill of
agony shot through his temples, and feeling himself falling, he
called out to his wife to support him.

Then she received her fainting husband in her arms, and sat
herself
On the cold ground, and gently laid his drooping head upon
her lap;
Sorrowing, she call'd to mind the sage's prophecy, and
reckoned up
The days and hours. All in an instant she beheld an awful
shape
Standing before her, dressed in blood-red garments, with a
glittering crown
Upon his head: his form, though glowing like the sun, was
yet obscure,
And eyes he had like flames, a noose depended from his
hand; and he
Was terrible to look upon, as by her husband's side he stood
And gazed upon him with a fiery glance. Shuddering she
started up
And laid her dying Satyavan upon the ground, and with her
hands

Joined reverently, she thus with beating heart addressed the
Shape:
Surely thou art a god, such form as thine must more than
mortal be!
Tell me, thou godlike being, who thou art, and wherefore
art thou here?
The figure replied that he was Yama, king of the dead; that
her husband's time was come, and that he must bind and take
his spirit:
Then from her husband's body forced he out and firmly with
his cord
Bound and detained the spirit, clothed in form no larger
than a thumb[1].
Forthwith the body, reft of vital being and deprived of
breath,
Lost all its grace and beauty, and became ghastly and
motionless.

After binding the spirit, Yama proceeds with it towards the
quarter of which he is guardian — the south. The faithful wife
follows him closely. Yama bids her go home and prepare her
husband's funeral rites; but she persists in following, till Yama,
pleased with her devotion, grants her any boon she pleases,
except the life of her husband. She chooses that her husband's
father, who is blind, may recover his sight. Yama consents, and
bids her now return home. Still she persists in following. Two
other boons are granted in the same way, and still Savitri follows
closely on the heels of the king of death. At last, overcome by
her constancy, Yama grants a boon without exception. The
delighted Savitri exclaims —

Nought, mighty king, this time hast thou excepted: let my
husband live;
Without him I desire not happiness, nor even heaven itself;

---

1. Compare note 3, 226 of this volume.

Without him I must die. 'So be it! Faithful wife,' replied the
king of death;
'Thus I release him;' and with that he loosed the cord that
bound his soul.

During the residence of the five brothers in the forest,
Jayad-ratha attempted to carry off Draupadi, while they were
absent on a shooting excursion. This resembles in some respects
the story of Sita's forcible abduction by Ravana in the Ramayana
(III. 15572), which story, therefore, is here told (15945. See
p. 409-410 of this volume).

In the thirteenth year of exile, the Pandavas journeyed to
the court of king Virata, and entered his service in different
disguises:

Yudhi-shthira called himself a Brahman and took the name
of Kanka (23); Arjuna named himself Vrihan-nala, and pretending
to be a eunuch (*tritiyam prakritim gatah*), adopted a sort of
woman's dress, putting bracelets on his arms and ear-rings in his
ear, in order, as he said, to hide the scars caused by his bow-
string. He undertook in this capacity to teach dancing, music,
and singing to the daughter of Virata and the other women of
the palace, and soon gained their good graces (IV. 310).

One day when Virata and four of the Pandavas were absent,
Duryodhana and his brothers made an expedition against Virata's
capital, Matsya, and carried off some cattle. Uttara the son of
Virata (in the absence of his father) determined to follow and
attack the Kuru army, if any one could be found to act as his
charioteer. Vrihan-nala (Arjuna) undertook this office, and
promised to bring back fine clothes and ornaments for Uttara
and the other women of the palace (IV. 1226). When they
arrived in sight of the Kuru army, the courage of Uttara, who
was a mere youth, failed him. Vrihan-nala then made him act
as charioteer while he himself (Arjuna) undertook to fight the
Kauravas. Upon that great prodigies occurred. Terror seized
Bhishma, Duryodhana, and their followers, who suspected that

Vrihan-nala was Arjuna in disguise, and even the horses shed tears[1] (IV. 1290). Duryodhana, however, declared that if he turned out to be Arjuna, he would have to wander in exile for a second period of twelve years. Meanwhile Arjuna revealed himself to Uttara, and explained also the disguises of his brothers and Draupadi. Uttara, to test his veracity, inquired whether he could repeat Arjuna's ten names, and what each meant. Arjuna enumerated them (Arjuna, Phalguna, Jishnu, Kiritin, Svetavahana, Bibhatsu, Vijaya, Krishna, Savyasacin, Dhananjaya), and explained their derivation[2] (IV. 1380). Uttara then declared that he was satisfied, and no longer afraid of the Kuru army (IV. 1393).

Arjuna next put off his bracelets and woman's attire, strung his bow Gandiva, and assumed all his other weapons, which had been concealed in a Sami tree. They are described as addressing him suppliantly, and saying, 'We are your servants, ready to carry out your commands' (IV. 1421). He also removed Uttara's standard and placed his own ape-emblazoned banner in front of the chariot. Then was fought a great battle between Arjuna and the Kauravas. In the end the whole Kuru army fled before him, and all the property and cattle of Virata was recovered. Arjuna told Uttara to conceal the real circumstances of the battle, but to send messengers to his father's capital announcing his victory, which so delighted Virata that he ordered the whole city to be decorated.

Not long afterwards Virata held a great assembly, at which the five Pandavas attended, and took their seats with the other princes. Virata, who did not yet know their real rank, was at first angry at this presumption (IV. 2266). Arjuna then revealed who they were. Virata was delighted, embraced the Pandavas, offered them all his possessions, and to Arjuna his

---

1. Compare Homer, Iliad XVII. 426.
2. See Arjuna's other names in note 3, p. 426.
3. Compare note 1, p. 449.

daughter Uttara in marriage. Arjuna declined, but accepted
her for his son Abhimanyu (IV. 2356).

A council of princes was then called by Virata, at which
the Pandavas, Krishna, and Bala-rama were present, and a
consultation was held as to what course the Pandavas were
to take:

Krishna, in a speech advised that they should not go to war
with their kinsmen until they had sent an ambassador to
Duryodhana, summoning him to restore half the kingdom. Bala-
rama supported Krishna's opinion, and recommended conciliation
(*saman*), but Satyaki, in an angry tone, counselled war (V. 40).
Drupada supported him, and recommended that they should
send messengers to all their allies, and collect forces from all
parts. The upshot was that the family-priest of Drupada was
despatched by the Pandavas as an ambassador to king Dhrita-
rashtra at Hastina-pur, to try the effect of negotiation.

Meanwhile Krishna and Bala-rama returned to Dvaraka.
Soon afterwards Duryodhana visited Krishna there, hoping to
prevail on him to fight on the side of the Kuru army.

On the same day Arjuna arrived there also, and it happened
that they both reached the door of Krishna's apartment, where
he was asleep, at the same moment. Duryodhana succeeded in
entering first, and took up his station at Krishna's head. Arjuna
followed behind, and stood reverently at Krishna's feet. On
awaking, Krishna's eyes first fell on Arjuna. He then asked them
both the object of their visit. Duryodhana thereupon requested
his aid in battle, declaring that although Krishna was equally
related to Arjuna, yet that, as he (Duryodhana) had entered the
room first, he was entitled to the priority. Krishna answered that,
as he had seen Arjuna first, he should give Arjuna the first choice
of two things. On the one side, he placed himself, stipulating
that he was to lay down his weapons and abstain from fighting.
On the other, he placed his army of a hundred million (*arbuda*)

warriors, named Narayanas. Arjuna, without hesitation, chose Krishna; and Duryodhana, with glee, accepted the army, thinking that as Krishna was pledged not to fight, he would be unable to help the Pandavas in battle (V. 154).

Duryodhana next went to Bala-rama and asked his aid; but Bala-rama declared that both he and Krishna had determined to take no part in the strife[1]. Krishna, however, consented to act as Arjuna's charioteer, and soon afterwards joined Yudhi-shthira, who with his brothers was still living in the country of Virata. Various attempts at negotiation followed, and before any actual declaration of war the Pandavas held a final consultation, at which Arjuna begged Krishna to undertake the office of a mediator. Krishna consented and departed for Hastina-pura:

Midway he was met by Parashu-rama and various Rishis, who informed him of their resolution to be present at the coming congress of Kuru princes. On reaching Hastina-pura, Krishna retired to rest in the house of Vidura. In the morning he performed all the appointed religious ceremonies, dressed himself, put on the jewel Kaustubha (V. 3343), and set out for the assembly. Then followed the great congress. The Rishis, headed by Narada, appeared in the sky, and were accommodated with seats. Krishna opened the proceedings by a speech, which commenced thus: 'Let there be peace (sama) between the Kurus and Pandavas.' Then, looking towards Dhrita-rashtra, he said, 'It rests with you and me to effect a reconciliation.' When he had concluded a long harangue, all remained riveted and thrilled by his eloquence (V. 3448). None ventured for some time to reply, except Parashu-rama, the sage Kanva, and Narada, who all advocated harmony and peace between the rival cousins. At length Duryodhana spoke, and flatly refused to give up any territory: 'It was not our fault,' he said, 'if the Pandavas were

---

1. Compare Megha-duta, verse 51, where Bala-rama is described as *Bandhu-pritya samara-vimukhah.*

conquered at dice.' Upon that Krishna's wrath rose, and addressing
Duryodhana, he said, 'You think that I am alone, but know that
the Pandavas, Andhakas, Vrishnis, Adityas, Rudras, Vasus, and
Rishis are all present here in me. Thereupon flames of fire, of
the size of a thumb, settled on him. Brahma appeared on his
forehead, Rudra on his breast, the guardians of the world issued
from his arms, Agni from his mouth. They Adityas, Sadhyas,
Vasus, Ashvins, Maruts with Indra, Vishvadevas, Yakshas,
Gandharvas, and Rakshasas were also manifested out of his
body; Arjuna was produced from his right arm; Bala-rama from
his left arm; Bhima, Yudhi-shthira, and the sons of Madri from
his back; flames of fire darted from his eyes, nose, and ears; and
the sun's rays from the pores of his skin[1] (V 4419-4430). At this
awful sight, the assembled princes were compelled to close their
eyes; but Drona, Bhishma, Vidura, Sanjaya, the Rishis, and the
blind Dhrita-rashtra were gifted by Krishna with divine vision
that they might behold the glorious spectacle of his identification
with every form (cf. p. 160 of this volume). Then a great
earthquake and other portents occurred, and the congress broke
up. Krishna having suppressed his divinity, re-assumed his human
form and set out on his return. He took Karna with him for some
distance in his chariot, hoping to persuade him to take part with
the Pandavas as a sixth brother. But, notwithstanding all Krishna's
arguments, Karna would not be persuaded; and, leaving the
chariot, returned to the sons of Dhrit-rashtra (V. 4883).

Meanwhile Bhishma consented to accept the generalship
of the Kuru army (V. 5719). Though averse from fighting
against his kinsmen, he could not as a Kshatriya abstain from
joining in the war, when once commenced[2].

---

1. This remarkable passage, identifying Vishnu with everything in the
   universe, is probably a later interpolation.
2. Bhishma, though really the grand-uncle of the Kuru and Pandu
   princes, is often styled their grandfather (*pitamaha*); though really
   the uncle of Dhrita-rashtra and Pandu, is sometimes styled their
   father. He is a kind of Priam in caution and sagacity, but like a hardy
   old veteran, ever consents to leave the fighting to others.

Before the armies joined battle, Vyasa appeared to his son
Dhrita-rashtra, who was greatly dejected at the prospect of the
war, consoled him, and offered to confer sight upon him, that
he might view the combat. Dhrita-rashtra declined witnessing
the slaughter of his kindred, and Vyasa then said that he would
endow Sanjaya (Dhrita-rashtra's charioteer) with the faculty of
knowing everything that took place, make him invulnerable, and
enable him to transport himself by a thought at any time to any
part of the field of battle (VI. 43-47).

The armies now met on Kuru-kshetra, a vast plain north-
west of modern Delhi; the Kuru forces being commanded by
Bhishma, and the Pandavas by Dhristhta-dyumna, son of
Drupada (VI. 832). While the hosts stood drawn up in battle-
array, Krishna, acting as Arjuna's charioteer, addressed him
in a long philosophical discourse, which forms the celebrated
episode called Bhagavad-gita (VI. 830-1532), an epitome of
which is given at pp. 147-166 of this volume.

And now as the armies advanced a tumult filled the sky;
the earth shook; 'Chafed by wild winds, the sands upcurled
to heaven, and spread a veil before the sun.' Awful portents
occurred; showers of blood fell[1]; asses were born from cows,
calves from mares, jackals from dogs. Shrill kites, vultures,
and howling jackals hung about the rear of the marching
armies. Thunder roared in the cloudless sky. Then darkness
supervened, lightnings flashed, and blazing meteors shot across
the darkened firmament; yet,

> The mighty chiefs, with martial ardour fired,
> Scorning Heaven's portents, eager for the fray,
> Pressed on to mutual slaughter, and the peal
> Of shouting hosts commingling, shook the world.

---

1. So Jupiter rains blood twice in the Iliad, XI. 53 and XVI. 459. We
have also the following in Hesiod, Scut. Herc. 384:

There is to a European a ponderous and unwieldy character about Oriental warfare, which he finds it difficult to realize; yet the battle-scenes, though exaggerated, are vividly described, and carry the imagination into the midst of the conflict. Monstrous elephants career over the field, trampling on men and horses, and dealing destruction with their huge tusks; enormous clubs and iron maces clash together with the noise of thunder; rattling chariots dash against each other, thousands of arrows hurtle in the air, darkening the sky; trumpets, kettle-drums, and horns add to the uproar; confusion, carnage, and death are everywhere.

In all this, however, there is nothing absolutely extravagant; but when Arjuna is described as killing five hundred warriors simultaneously, or as covering the whole plain with dead and filling rivers with blood; Yudhi-shthira, as slaughtering a hundred men 'in a mere twinkle' (*nimesha-matrena*); Bhima, as annihilating a monstrous elephant, including all mounted upon it, and fourteen foot-soldiers besides, with one blow of his club; Nakula and Sahadeva, fighting from their chariots, as cutting off heads by the thousand, and sowing them like seed upon the ground; when, moreover, the principal heroes makes use of mystical god-given weapons, possessed of supernatural powers, and supposed to be themselves celestial beings[1] — we at once perceive that the utter unreality of such

---

1. About a hundred of these weapons are enumerated in the Ramayana (I. xxix), and constant allusion is made to them in battle-scenes, both in the Ramayana and Mahabharata. Arjuna underwent a long course of austerities to obtain celestial weapons from Siva (see p. 438). It was by the terrific *brahmastra* that Vasishtha conquered Vishvamitra, and Rama killed Ravana. Sometimes they appear to be mystical powers exercised by meditation, rather than weapons, and are supposed to assume animate forms, and possess names and faculties like the genii in the Arabin Nights, and to address their owners (see p. 443). Certain distinct spells, charms, or prayers had to be learnt

scenes mars the beauty of the description. Still it must be borne in mind that the poets who brahmanized the Indian Epics gifted the heroes with semi-divine natures, and that would be incredible in a mere mortal is not only possible but appropriate when enacted by a demigod[1]. The individual deeds of prowess and single combats between the heroes are sometimes graphically narrated. Each chief has a conch-shell (*sankha*) for a trumpet, which, as well as his principal weapon, has a name, as if personified[2]. Thus we read:

Arjuna blew his shell called Deva-datta, 'god-given,' and carried a bow named Gandiva. Krishna sounded a shell made of the bones of the demon Pancajana and hence called Panchajanya, Bhima blew a great trumpet named Paundra, and Yudhi-shthira sounded his, called Ananta-vijaya, 'eternal victory.'

The first great single-combat was between Bhishma and Arjuna. It ended in Arjuna transfixing Bhishma with innumerable arrows, so that there was not a space of two fingers' breadth on his whole body unpierced.

---

for their due use (*prayoga*) and restraint (*samhara*). See Rama. I xxix, xxx, where they are personified; also Raghu-vansha V. 57 (*Samamohanam nama astram adhatsva prayoga-samhara-vihhakta-mentram*). When once let loose, he only who knew the secret spell for recalling them, could bring them back; but the *brahmastra* returned to its possessor's quiver of its own accord.

1. Aristotle says that the epic poet should prefer impossibilities which appear probable to such things as though possible appear improbable (Poetics III. 6). But previously, in comparing epic poetry with tragedy, he observes, 'the surprising is necessary in tragedy, but the epic poem goes further, and admits even the improbable and incredible, from which the highest degrees of the surprising results' (III. 4).

2. Trumpets do not appear to have been used by Homer's heroes. Whence the value of a Stentorian voice. But there is express allusion in II. XVIII. 219 to the use of trumpets at sieges.

Then Bhishma fell from his chariot; but his body could not touch the ground, surrounded as it was by countless arrows (VI. 5658). There it remained, reclining as it were on an arrowy couch (*shara-talpe shayana*). In that state consciousness returned, and the old warrior became divinely supported. He had received from his father the power of fixing the time of his own death[1], and now declared that he intended retaining life till the sun entered the summer solstice (*uttarayana*). All the warriors on both sides ceased fighting that they might view this wonderful sight, and do homage to their dying relative (VI. 5716). As he lay on his arrowy bed, his head hanging down, he begged for a pillow; whereupon the chiefs brought soft supports, which the hardy old soldier sternly rejected. Arjuna then made a rest for his head with three arrows, which Bhishma quite approved, and soon afterwards asked Arjuna to bring him water. Whereupon Arjuna struck the ground with an arrow, and forthwith a pure spring burst forth, which so refreshed Bhishma that he called for Duryodhana, and in a long speech begged him before it was too late, to restore half the kingdom to the Pandavas (VI. 5813).

After the fall of Bhishma, Karna advised Duryodhana to appoint his old tutor Drona — who was chiefly formidable for his stock of fiery arrows and magical weapons[2] — to the command of the army (VII. 150). Several single combats and general engagements (*sankula-yuddham, tumula-yuddham*), in which sometimes one party, sometimes the other had the advantage, took place. Here is an account of a single combat (VII. 544):

> High on a stately car
> Swift borne by generous coursers to the fight,
> The vaunting son of Puru proudly drove,

---

1. Compare Kiratarjuniya III. 19.
2. These *agneyastra* were received by Drona from the son of Agni, who obtained them from Drona's father, Bharadvaja.

Secure of conquest o'er Subhadra's son.
The youthful champion shrank not from the conflict.
Fierce on the boastful chief he sprang, as bounds
The lion's cub upon the ox; and now
The Puru chief had perished, but his dart
Shivered with timely aim the upraised bow
Of Abhimanyu[1]. From his tingling hand
The youthful warrior cast the fragments off,
And drew his sword, and grasped his iron-bound shield;
Upon the car of Paurava he lept
And seized the chief — his charioteer he slew,
And dragged the monarch senseless o'er the plain[2].

Amongst other battles a great fight was fought between
Ghatotkacha and Karna, in which the former as a Rakshasa
(son of the Rakshasi Hidimba and Bhima) assumed various
forms, but was eventually slain (VII. 8104). This disaster filled
the Pandavas with grief, but the fortunes of the day were
retrieved by Dhrishta-dyumna (son of Drupada), who fought
with Drona, and succeeded in decapitating his lifeless body,
— not, however, till Drona had laid down his arms and saved
Dhrishta-dyumna from the enormous crime of killing a
Brahman and an Acharya, by transporting himself to heaven
in a glittering shape like the sun. His translation to Brahma-
loka was only witnessed by five persons, and before leaving
the earth he made over his divine weapons to his son
Ashvatthama. The loss of their general Drona caused the
flight of the whole Kuru army (VII. 8879), but they appointed
Karna general, in his place, and renewed the combat:

---

1. The name of Arjuna's son by Subhadra.
2. The translation of this and the short passage at p. 448 is a slightly
   altered version of some spirited lines by Professor H.H. Wilson,
   given in vol. iii. of his collected works edited by Dr. R. Rost.

In this engagement so terrible was the slaughter that the rivers flowed with blood, and the field became covered with mutilated corpses (VIII. 2550, 3899). Numbers of warriors bound themselves by oath (samshap-taka) to slay Arjuna, but were all destroyed, and an army of Mlechchas or barbarians with thirteen hundred elephants, sent by Duryodhana against Arjuna, were all routed by him (4133).

Then Bhima and Duhshasana joined in deadly conflict. The latter was slain, and Bhima, remembering the insult to Draupadi, and the vow he made in consequence (see p. 437), cut off his head, and drank his blood, on the field of battle (4235).

Then occurred the battle between Karna and Arjuna:

Arjuna was wounded and stunned by an arrow shot off by Karna, and seemed likely to be defeated had not the wheel of Karna's chariot come off. This obliged Karna to leap down, and his head was then shot off by one of Arjuna's arrows[1] (VIII. 4798). His death struck terror into the Kuru army, which fled in dismay, while Bhima and the Pandu party raised a shout of triumph that shook heaven and earth.

On the death of Karna, Shalya, king of Madra, was appointed to the command of the Kuru army, then much reduced in numbers (IX. 327). Another general engagement followed, and a single combat between Shalya and Bhima with clubs or maces, in which both were equally matched (IX. 594). Here is a version of the encounter:

Soon as he saw his charioteer struck down,
Straightway the Madra monarch grasped his mace,

---

1. This arrow is called in the text Anjalika (VIII. 4788). The arrows used in the Mahabharata are of various kinds, some having crescent-shaped heads. It may be useful to subjoin a list of words for arrow, which occur constantly in the description of battles: sara, vana, ishu, shayaka, patrin, kanda, vishikha, naracha, vipatha, prishatka, bhalla, tomara (a kind of lance), shalya (a dart), ishika, shilimukha.

And like a mountain firm and motionless
Awaited the attack. The warrior's form
Was awful as the world-consuming fire,
Or as the noose-armed god of death, or as
The peaked Kailāsa, or the Thunderer
Himself, or as the trident-bearing god,
Or as a maddened forest elephant.
Him to defy did Bhima hastily
Advance, wielding aloft his massive club.
A thousand conchs and trumpets and a shout,
Firing each champion's ardour, rent the air.
From either host, spectators of the fight,
Burst forth applauding cheers: 'The Madra king
Alone,' they cried, 'can bear the rush of Bhima;
None but heroic Bhima can sustain
The force of Shalya.' Now like two fierce bulls
Sprang they towards each other, mace in hand.
And first as cautiously they circled round,
Whirling their weapons as in sport, the pair
Seemed matched in equal combat. Shalya's club,
Set with red fillets, glittered as with flame,
While that of Bhima gleamed like flashing lightning.
Anon the clashing iron met, and scattered round
A fiery shower; then fierce as elephants
Or butting bulls they battered each the other.
Thick fell the blows, and soon each stalwart frame,
Spattered with gore, glowed like the Kinshuka,
Bedecked with scarlet blossoms; yet beneath
The rain of strokes, unshaken as a rock
Bhima sustained the mace of Shalya, he
With equal firmness bore the other's blows,
Now like the roar of crashing thunder-clouds
Sounded the clashing iron; then, their clubs
Brandished aloft, eight paces they retired,
And swift again advancing to the fight,

Met in the midst like two huge mountain-crags
Hurled into contact. Nor could either bear
The other's shock; together down they rolled,
Mangled and crushed, like two tall standards fallen.

After this a great battle was fought between Yudhi-shthira
and Shalya, who was at first aided and rescued by Asvatthaman,
but was eventually killed (IX. 919).

The Kauravas after suffering continual reverses, rallied
their scattered forces for a final charge, which led to a complete
rout and general slaughter, Duryodhana, Ashvatthaman (son
of Drona), Krita-varman (also called Bhoja), and Kripa (see
note 2, p. 427) being the only chiefs of the Kuru army left
alive[1]. Nothing remained of eleven whole armies (IX. 1581).
Duryodhana, wounded, disheartened, and alarmed for his
own safety, resolved on flight:

On foot, with nothing but his mace, he took refuge in a lake,
hiding himself under the water, and then, by his magical power,
supporting it so as to form a chamber around his body[2]. The
Pandavas informed of his hiding-place, came to the lake, and
Yudhi-shthira commenced taunting Duyodhana, 'Where is your
manliness? where is your pride? where your valour? where your
skill in arms, that you hide yourself at the bottom of a lake? Rise
up and fight; perform your duty as a Kshatriya' (IX 1774).
Duryodhana answered, that it was not from fear, but fatigue, that
he was lying under the water, and that he was ready to fight them
all. He entreated them, however, to go and take the kingdom, as
he had no longer any pleasure in life, his brothers being killed.

---

1. Sanjaya was taken by Dhrishta-dyumna, and would have been killed
   had not Vyasa suddenly appeared and demanded that he should be
   dismissed unharmed (compare p. 419).
2. So interpret *astambhayat toyam mayaya* (IX. 1621) and *vishtabhya
   apah sva-mayaya* (1680, 1739). Duryodhana is described as lying
   down and sleeping at the bottom of the lake (1705).

Yudhi-shthira then continued his sarcasms, till at last, thoroughly roused by his goading words (*vak-pratoda*), Duryodhana rose up out of the lake, his body streaming with blood and water (IX. 1865).

It was settled that a single combat with clubs should take place between Duryodhana and Bhima; and when Bala-rama heard that his two pupils (see p. 428) were about to engage in conflict, he determined to be present, that he might ensure fair play[1].

Then followed the great club-fight (*gada-yuddha*):

The two combatants entered the lists and challenged each other, while Krishna, Bala-rama, and all the other Pandavas sat round as spectators. The fight was tedious, the combatants being equally matched. At last Bhima struck Duryodhana a blow on his thighs, broke them, and felled him to the ground. Then reminding him of the insult received by Draupadi, he kicked him on the head with his left foot (IX. 3313). Upon this Bala-rama started up in anger, declaring that Bhima had fought unfairly (it being a rule in club-fights that no blow should be given below the middle of the body), and that he should ever after be called *Jihma-yodhin* (unfair-fighter), while Duryodhana should always be celebrated as *Riju-yodhin* (fair-fighter).

Bala-rama thereupon returned to Dvaraka, and the five Pandavas with Krishna entered the camp of Duryodhana, and took possession of it and its treasures as victors (IX. 3492).

The three surviving Kuru warriors (Ashvatt haman, Kripa, and Krita-varman), hearing of the fall of Duryodhana, hastened to the place where he was lying. There they found him

---

1. An interesting episode about the *mahatmya* of Tirthas, and especially of those on the sacred Sarasvati (IX. 2006), is inserted in this part of the poem. The story of the Moon, who was afflicted with consumption, on account of the curse of Daksha, is also told (2030), as well as the celebrated legend of Vashishtha and Vishvamitra (2296, see p. 403).

weltering in his blood (IX. 3629), but still alive. He spoke to them, told them not to grieve for him, and assured them that he should die happy in having done his duty as a Kshatriya. Then leaving Duryodhana still lingering alive with broken thighs on the battle-field, they took refuge in a forest.

There, at night, they rested near a Nyagrodha-tree, where thousands of crows were roosting. Ashvatthaman, who could not sleep, saw an owl approach stealthily and destroy numbers of the sleeping crows (X. 41). This suggested the idea of entering the camp of the Pandavas by night and slaughtering them while asleep (*supta*[1]). Accordingly he set out for the Pandu camp, followed by Kripa and Krita-varman. At the gate of the camp his progress was arrested by an awful figure, described as gigantic, glowing like the sun, dressed in a tiger's skin, with long arms, and bracelets formed of serpents. This was the deity Shiva[2]; and after a tremendous conflict with him, Ashvatthaman recognized the god, worshipped and propitiated him (X. 251).

Ashvatthaman then directed Kripa and Krita-varman to stand at the camp-gate and kill any of the Pandu army that attempted to escape (X. 327). He himself made his way alone and stealthily to the tent of Dhrishta-dyumna, who was lying there fast asleep. Him he killed by stamping on him, declaring that one who had murdered his father (Drona, see p. 452) — a Brahman and an Acharya — not worthy to die in any other way (X. 342). After killing every one in the camp and destroying the whole Pandu army (except the five Pandavas themselves with Satyaki and

---

1. Hence the name *sauptika* applied to this section of the poem. Compare Homer's narrative of the night adventures of Diomed and Ulysses in the camp of the Trojans (Iliad X).

2. The description of Shiva in this passage is remarkable. Hundreds and thousands of Krishnas are said to be manifested from the light issuing from his person. Many of Shiva's names also are enumerated as follow: Ugra, Sthanu, Shiva, Rudra, Sharva, Ishana, Ishvara, Girisha, Varada, Deva, Bhava, Bhavana, Sitikantha, Aja, Sukra, Daksha-kratu-hara, Hara, Vishvarupa, Virupaksha, Bahurupa, Umapati (X. 252).

Krishna who happened to be stationed outside the camp), Asvatthaman joined his comrades, and they all three proceeded to the spot where Duryodhana was lying. They found him just breathing (*kinchit-prana*), but weltering in his blood and surrounded by beasts of prey. Ashvatthaman then announced that he was avenged, as only seven of the Pandu army were now left; all the rest were slaughtered like cattle (X. 531). Duroyodhan hearing this, revived a little, and gathering strength to thank them and say farewell, expired; his spirit rising to heaven and his body entering the ground (X. 536).

Thus perished both armies of Kurus and Pandavas.

Dhrita-rashtra was so overwhelmed with grief for the death of his sons, that his father Vyasa appeared to him and consoled him by pointing out that their fate was pre-destined, and that they could not escape death. He also declared that the Pandavas were not to blame; that Duryodhana, though born from Gandhari, was really a partial incarnation of Kali[1] (*Kaler ansa*), and Sakuni of Dvapara (see p. 368, note 3).

Vidura also comforted the king with his usual sensible advice, and recommended that the funeral ceremonies (*preta-karyani*) should be performed. Dhrita-rashtra then ordered carriages to be prepared, and with the women proceeded to the field of battle (XI. 269).

There he met and became reconciled to the five Pandavas, but his wife Gandhari would have cursed them had not Vyasa interfered. The five brothers next embraced and comforted their mother Pritha, who with the queen Gandhari, and the other wives and women, uttered lamentations over the bodies of the slain heroes, as one by one they came in sight on the field of battle (XI. 427-755).

Finally, the funeral obsequies (*sraddha*) were performed at the command of Yudhi-shthira (XI. 779), after which he, with his brothers, entered Hastina-pura in triumph.

---

1. So also Shakuni is said to be an incarnation of Dvapara (XVIII. 166).

All the streets were decorated; and Brahmans offered him congratulations, which he acknowledged by distributing largesses among them (XII. 1410). Only one person stood aloof. This turned out to be an impostor, a friend of Duryodhana — a Rakshasa named Charvaka — who in the disguise of a mendicant reviled him and the Brahmans. He was, however, soon detected; and the real Brahmans, filled with fury and uttering imprecations, killed him on the spot (see p. 142).

After this incident, Yudhi-shthira, seated on a golden throne, was solemnly crowned (XII. 1443).

Nevertheless, restless and uneasy, and his mind filled with anguish at the slaughter of his kindred, he longed for consolation (*shanti*), and Krishna recommended him to apply to Bhishma, who still remained alive on the field of battle, reclining on his soldier's bed (*vira-shayana*), surrounded by Vyasa, Narada, and other holy sages. Accordingly Yudhi-shthira and his brothers, accompanied by Krishna, set out for Kuru-kshetra, passing mutilated corpses, skulls, broken armour, and other evidences of the fearful nature of the war. This reminded Krishna of the slaughter caused by Parashu-rama, who cleared the earth thrice seven times of the Kshatriya caste (see p. 367). His story was accordingly narrated to Yudhi-shthira (XII. 1707-1805). They then approached Bhishma lying on his couch of arrows (*shara-samstara-shayinam*), and Krishna entreated him to instruct Yudhi-shthira, and calm his spirit.

Upon that Bhishma, who had been lying for fifty-eight nights on his spiky bed (XIII. 7732), assisted by Krishna, Narada, Vyasa, and other Rishis, commenced a series of long and tedious didactic discourses (contained in the Santi-parvan and Anushasana-parvan[1]).

---

1. In XII. 1241 we have some curious rules for expiation (*prayash-chitta*), and at 1393 rules for what to eat and what to avoid (*bhakshya-bhakshya*). Some of the precepts are either taken from or founded on Manu. For instance, compare 6071 with Manu II. 238. Many of the moral verses in the Hitopadesha will be found in the Shanti-parvan; and the fable of the three fishes is founded on the story at 4889. For the contents of the Ashvamedhika, Ashramavashika, and Mausala Parvans, see p. 417-418.

Then having finished instructing his relatives, he bade them farewell, and asked Krishna's leave to depart. Suddenly the arrows left his body, his skull divided, and his spirit, bright as a meteor, ascended through the top of his head to the skies (XIII. 7765). They covered him with garland and perfumes, carried him to the Ganges, and performed his last obsequies.

And here a European poet would have brought the story to an end. The Sanskrit poet has a deeper knowledge of human nature, or at least of Hindu nature.

In the most popular of India dramas (the Sakuntala) there occurs this sentiment[1]:

'Tis a vain thought that to attain the end
And object of ambition is to rest.
Success doth only mitigate the fever
Of anxious expectation: soon the fear
Of losing what we have, the constant care
Of guarding it doth weary.

If then the great national Epic was to respond truly to the deeper emotions of the Hindu mind, it could not leave the Pandavas in the contented enjoyment of their kingdom. It had to instil a more sublime moral — a lesson which even the disciples of a divine philosophy are slow to learn — that all who desire rest must aim at union with the Infinite. Hence we are brought in the concluding chapters to a sublime description of the renunciation of their kingdom by the five brothers, and their journey towards Indra's heaven in the mountain Meru. Part of this (XVII. 24, &c.) I now translate:

When the four brothers knew the high resolve of king Yudhi-shthira,
Forthwith with Draupadi they issued forth, and after them a dog

---

1. See my translation of this play, 4th edition, p. 124 (recently published by W.H. Allen &c Co., 13, Waterloo Place).

Followed: the king himself went out the seventh from the
royal city,
And as all the citizens and women of the palace walked behind;
But none could find it in their heart to say unto the king,
'Return.'
And so at length the train of citizens went back, bidding adieu.
Then the high-minded sons of Pandu and the noble Draupadi
Roamed for union with their faces towards the east; their
hearts
Yearning for union with the Infinite; bent on abandonment
Of worldly things. They wandered on to many countries,
many a sea
And river. Yudhi-shthira walked in front, and next to him
came Bhima,
And Arjuna came after him, and then, in order, the twin
brothers.
And last of all came Draupadi, with her dark skin and lotus-
eyes —
The faithful Draupadi, loveliest of women, best of noble
wives —
Behind them walked the only living thing that shared their
pilgrimage —
The dog — and by degrees they reached the briny sea. There
Arjuna
Cast in the waves his bow and quivers[1]. Then with souls well-
disciplined
They reached the northern region, and beheld with heaven-
aspiring hearts
The mighty mountain Himavat. Beyond its lofty peak they
passed
Towards a sea of sand, and saw at last the rocky Meru, king
Of mountains. As with eager steps they hastened on, their
souls intent
On union with the Eternal, Draupadi lost hold of her high
hope,
And faltering fell upon the earth.

---

1. Arjuna had two celebrated quivers, besides the bow named Gandiva,
given to him by the god Agni. See Kiratarjuniya XI. 16.

One by one the others also drop, till only Bhima, Yudhi-shthira, and the dog are left. Still Yudhi-shthira walks steadily in front, calm and unmoved, looking neither to the right hand nor to the left, and gathering up his soul in inflexible resolution. Bhima, shocked at the fall of his companions, and unable to understand how beings so apparently guileless should be struck down by fate, appeals to his brother, who, without looking back, explains that death is the consequence of sinful thoughts and too great attachment to worldly objects; and that Draupadi's fall was owing to her excessive affection for Arjuna; Sahadeva's (who is supposed to be the most humble-minded of the five brothers) to his pride in his own knowledge; Nakula's (who is very handsome) to feelings of personal vanity; and Arjuna's to a boastful confidence in his power to destroy his foes. Bhima then feels himself falling, and is told that he suffers death for his selfishness, pride, and too great love of enjoyment. The sole survivor is now Yudhi-shthira, who still walks steadily forward, followed only by the dog:

When with a sudden sound that rang through earth and heaven the mighty god
Came towards him in a chariot, and he cried, 'Ascend, O resolute prince.'
Then did the king look back upon his fallen brothers, and address'd
These words unto the Thousand-eyed in anguish — ' Let my brothers here
Come with me. Without them, O god of gods, I would not wish to enter
E'en heaven; and yonder tender princess Draupadi, the faithful wife,
Worthy of endless bliss, let her too come. In mercy hear my prayer.'

Upon this, Indra informs him that the spirits of Draupadi and his brothers are already in heaven, and that he alone is permitted to ascend there in bodily form. Yudhi-shthira now stipulates that his dog shall be admitted with him. Indra says sternly, 'Heaven has no place for men accompanied by dogs (*shvavatam*);' but Yudhi-shthira is unshaken in his resolution, and declines abandoning the faithful animal. Indra remonstrates — 'You have abandoned your brothers and Draupadi; why not forsake the dog?' To this Yudhi-shthira haughtily replies, 'I had no power to bring them back to life: how can there be abandonment of those who no longer live?'

The dog, it appears, is his own father Dharma in disguise (XVII. 88[1]). Reassuming now his proper form, he praises Yudhi-shthira for his constancy, and they enter heaven together. There, to his surprise, he finds Duryodhana and his cousins, but not his brothers or Draupadi. Hereupon he declines remaining in heaven without them. An angel is then sent to conduct him to the lower regions and across the Indian Styx (*Vaitarani*) to the hell where they are supposed to be. The scene which now follows may be compared to the Nekyomanteia in the eleventh book of the Odyssey, or to parts of Dante.

The particular hell to which Yudhi-shthira is taken is a dense wood, whose leaves are sharp swords, and its ground paved with razors (*asi-patra-vana*, see p. 70, note 3). The way to it is strewed with foul and mutilated corpses. Hideous shapes flit across the air and hover over him. Here there is an awful sensation of palpable darkness. There the wicked are burning in flames of blazing fire. Suddenly he hears the voices

---

1. So I infer from the original, which, however, is somewhat obscure. The expression is *dharma-svarupi bhagavan*. At any rate, the dog was a mere phantom created to try Yudhi-shthira, as it is evident that a real god is not admitted with Yudhi-shthira to heaven.

of his brothers and companions imploring him to assuage their torments, and not desert them. His resolution is taken. Deeply affected, he bids the angel leave him to share their miseries. This is his last trial. The whole scene now vanishes. It was a mere illusion, to test his constancy to the utmost. He is now directed to bathe in the heavenly Ganges; and having plunged into the sacred stream, he enters the real heaven, where at length, in company with Draupadi and his brothers, he finds that rest and happiness which were unattainable on earth.

Lecture XIV

The Indian Epics compared with each other and with the Homeric Poems

I proceed to note a few obvious points that force themselves on the attention in comparing the two great Indian Epics with each other, and with the Homeric poems. I have already stated that the episodes of the Mahabharata occupy more than three-fourths of the whole poem[1]. It is, in fact, not one poem, but a combination of many poems: not a *Kavya*, like the poem of Valmiki, by one author, but an Itihasa by many authors. This is one great distinctive feature in comparing it with the Ramayana. In both Epics there is a leading story; about which are collected a multitude of other stories; but in the Mahabharata the main narrative only acts as a slender thread to connect together a vast mass of independent legends, and religious, moral, and political precepts; while in the Ramayana the episodes, though numerous, never break the

---

1. Although the Mahabharata is so much longer than the Ramayana as to preclude the idea of its being, like that poem, the work of one or even a few authors, yet it is the number of the episodes which, after all, causes the disparity. Separated from these, the main story of the Mahabharata is not longer than the other Epic.

solid chain of one principal and paramount subject, which is ever kept in view. Moreover, in the Ramayana there are few didactic discourses and a remarkable paucity of sententious maxims.

It should be remembered that the two Epics belong to different periods and different localities. Not only was a large part of the Mahabharata composed later than the Ramayana, parts of it being comparatively modern, but the places which gave birth to the two poems are distinct (see p. 355). Moreover, in the Ramayana the circle of territory represented as occupied by the Aryans is more restricted than that in the Mahabharata. It reaches to Videha or Mithila and Anga in the East, to Surashtra in the South-west, to the Yamuna and great Dandaka forest in the South. Whereas in the Mahabharata (as pointed out by Professor Lassen) the Aryan settlers are described as having extended themselves to the mouths of the Ganges in the East, to the mouth of the Godavari on the Koromandel coast, and to the Malabar coast in the West; and even the inhabitants of Ceylon (Sinhala) bring tribute to the Northern kings. It is well known that in India different customs and opinions frequently prevail in districts almost adjacent; and it is certain that Brahmanism never gained the ascendancy in the more martial north which it acquired in the neighbourhood of Oude[1], so that in the Mahabharata we have far more allusions to Buddhistic scepticism than we have in the sister Epic. In fact, each poem, though often running parallel to the other, has yet a distinct point of departure; and the

---

1. Professor Weber (Ind. Stud. I. 220) remarks that the north-western tribes retained their ancient customs, which those who migrated to the east had at one time shared. The former (as represented in the Mahabharata) kept themselves free from those influences of hierarchy and caste, which arose among the inhabitants of Ayodhya (in the Ramayana) as a consequence of their intermingling and coming more in contact with the aborigines.

Mahabharata, as it became current in various localities, diverged more into by-paths and cross-roads than its sister. Hence the Ramayana is in some respects a more finished composition than the Mahabharata, and depicts a more polished state of society, and a more advanced civilization. In fact, the Mahabharata presents a complete circle of post-Vedic mythology, including many myths which have their germ in the Veda, and continually enlarging its circumference to embrace the later phases of Hinduism, with its whole train of confused and conflicting legends[1]. From this storehouse are drawn much of the Puranas, and many of the more recent heroic poems and dramas. Here we have repeated many of the legends of the Ramayana, and even the history of Rama himself (see p. 409). Here also we have long discourses on religion, politics, morality, and philosophy, introduced without any particular connexion with the plot. Here again are most of the narratives of the incarnation of Vishnu, numberless stories connected with the worship of Shiva, and various details of the life of Krishna. Those which especially bear on the modern worship of Krishna are contained in the supplement called Hari-vansha, which is itself a long poem — consisting of 16,374 stanzas[2] — longer than the Iliad and Odyssey combined[3]. Hence the religious system of the Mahabharata

---

1. It should be noted, that the germs of many of the legends of Hindu epic poetry are found in the Rig-veda. Also that the same legend is sometimes repeated in different parts of the Mahabharata, with considerable variations; as, for example, the story of the combat of Indra — god of air and thunder — with the demon Vritra, who represents enveloping clouds and vapour. See Vana-parvan 8690 &c.; and compare with Shanti-parvan 10124 &c. Compare also the story of the 'Hawk and Pigeon,' Vana-parvan 10558, with Anushasana-parvan 2046.
2. The Hari-vansha bears to the Mahabharata a relation very similar to that which the Uttara-kanda, or last Book of the Ramayana, bears to the preceding Books of that poem.
3. The Iliad and Odyssey together contain about 30,000 lines.

is far more popular, liberal, and comprehensive than that of the Ramayana. It is true that the god Vishnu is connected with Krishna in the Mahabharata, as he is with Rama in the Ramayana, but in the latter Rama is everything; whereas in the Mahabharata, Krishna is by no means the centre of the system. His divinity is even occasionally disputed[1]. The five Pandavas have also partially divine natures, and by turns become prominent. Sometimes Arjuna, sometimes Yudhishthira, at others Bhima, appears to be the principal orb round which the plot moves[2]. Moreover, in various passages Siva is described as supreme, and receives worship from Krishna. In others, Krishna is exalted above all, and receives honour from Siva[3]. In fact, while the Ramayana generally represents one-sided and exclusive Brahmanism[4], the Mahabharata reflects the multilateral character of Hindusim; its monotheism and polytheism, its spirituality and materialism, its strictness and laxity, its priestcraft and anti-priestcraft, its hierarchical intolerance and rationalistic philosophy, combined. Not that there was any intentional variety in the original design of the work, but that almost every shade of opinion

---

1. As by Sisu-pala and others. See p. 436-437 with notes.
2. In this respect the Mahabharata resembles the Iliad. Achilles is scarcely its hero. Other warriors too much divide the interest with him.
3. In the Bhagavad-gita Krishna is not merely an incarnation of Vishnu; he is identified with Brahma, the Supreme Spirit, and is so in numerous other places. It is well known that in Homer the supremacy of one god (Jove), and due subordination of the other deities, is maintained.
4. Some free thought, however, has found its way into the Ramayana; see II. cviii (Schl.); VI. Lxii. 15 (Gorr., Bomb. Lxxxiii. 14); VI. Lxxxiii. 14 (Calc.). It is remarkable that in the Ramayana the same gods are appealed to by Rama and Ravana, just as by Greeks and Trojans in the Iliad; and Hanuman, when in Lanka, heard the Brahma-ghosha in the morning. Ramay. V. xvi. 41. This has been noticed by Weber.

found expression in a compilation formed by gradual accretion through a long period.

In unison with its more secular, popular, and *human* character, the Mahabharata has, as a rule, less of mere mythical allegory, and more of historical probability in its narratives than the Ramayana. The reverse, however, sometimes holds good. For example, in Ramayana IV. xl. we have a simple division of the world into four quarters or regions, whereas in Mahabharata VI. 236 &c. we have the fanciful division (afterwards adopted by the Puranas) into seven circular Dvipas or continents, viz. 1. Jambu-dvipa or the Earth, 2. Plaksha-dvipa, 3. Shalmali-dvipa, 4. Kusha-dvipa, 5. Krauncha-dvipa, 6. Shaka-dvipa, 7. Push-kara-dvipa; surrounded respectively by seven oceans in concentric belts, viz. 1. the sea of salt-water (*lavana*), 2. of sugar-cane juice (*ikshu*), 3. of wine (*sura*), 4. of clarified butter (*sarpis*), 5. of curdled milk (*dadhi*), 6. of milk (*dugdha*), 7. of fresh water (*jala*); the mountain Meru, or abode of the gods, being in the centre of *Jambu-dvipa*, which again is divided into nine Varshas or countries separated by eight ranges of mountains, the Varsha called *Bharata* (India) lying south of the Himavat range[1].

Notwithstanding these wild ideas and figments, the Mahabharata contains many more illustrations of real life and of domestic and social habits and manners than the sister Epic. Its diction again is more varied than that of the Ramayana.

---

1. The eight ranges are Nishadha, Hema-kuta, Nishadha on the south of Meru; Nila, Shveta, Shringin on the north; and Malyavat and Gandha-madana on the west and east. Beyond the sea of fresh water is a circle called 'the land of gold,' and beyond this the circle of the Lokaloka mountains, which form the limit of the sun's light, all the region on one side being illuminated, and all on the other side of them being in utter darkness. See Raghu-vansha I. 68. Below the seven Dvipas are the seven Patalas (see p. 480), and below these are the twenty-one Hells (note 3, 70).

The bulk of the latter poem (notwithstanding interpolations and additions) being by one author, is written with uniform simplicity of style and metre (see p. 374, note 1); and the antiquity of the greater part is proved by the absence of any studied elaboration of diction. The Mahabharata, on the other hand, though generally simple and natural in its language, and free from the conceits and artificial constructions of later writers, comprehends a greater diversity of composition, rising sometimes (especially when the Indra-vajra metre is employed) to the higher style, and using not only loose and irregular, but also studiously complex grammatical forms[1] and from the mixture of ancient legends, occasional archaisms and Vedic formations.

In contrasting the two Indian poems with the Iliad and the Odyssey, we may observe many points of similarity. Some parallel passages have been already pointed out. We must expect to find the distinctive genius of two different people (though both of the Aryan race) in widely distant localities, colouring their epic poetry very differently, notwithstanding general features of resemblance. The Ramayana and Mahbharata are no less wonderful than the Homeric poems as monuments of the human mind, and no less interesting as pictures of human life and manners in ancient times, yet they bear in a remarkable degree the peculiar impress ever stamped on the productions of Asiatic nations, and separating them from European. On the side of art and harmony of proportion, they can no more compete with the Iliad and the Odyssey than the unnatural outline of the ten-headed and twenty-armed Ravana can bear comparison with the symmetry of a

---

1. Thus jivase (I. 732) kurmi (III. 10943, and Ramay. II. xii. 33), dhita for hita (Hari-vansha 7799), parinayamasa for parinayayamasa, ma bhaih for bhaishih, vyavasishyami for vyavasayami. The use of irregular grammatical forms is sometimes due to the exigency of the metre.

Grecian statue. While the simplicity of the one commends itself to the most refined classical taste, the exaggerations of the other only excites the wonder of Asiatic minds, or if attractive to European, can only please imaginations nursed in an Oriental school.

Thus, in the Iliad, time, space, and action are all restricted within the narrowest limits. In the Odyssey they are allowed a wider, though a not too wide, cycle; but in the Ramayana and Mahabharata their range is almost unbounded. The Ramayana, as it traces the life of a single individual with tolerable continuity, is in this respect more like the Odyssey than the Iliad. In other points, especially in its plot, the greater simplicity of its style, and its comparative freedom from irrelevant episodes, it more resembles the Iliad. There are many graphic passages in both the Ramayana and Mahabharata which, for beauty of description, cannot be surpassed by anything in Homer. It should be observed, moreover, that the diction of the Indian Epics is more polished, regular, and cultivated, and the language altogether in a more advanced stage of development than that of Homer. This, of course, tells to the disadvantage of the style on the side of nervous force and vigour; and it must be admitted that in the Sanskrit poems there is a great redundance of epithets, too liberal a use of metaphor, simile, and hyperbole, and far too much repetition, amplification, and prolixity.

In fact, the European who wishes to estimate rightly the Indian Epics must be prepared not to judge them exclusively from his own point of view. He should bear in mind that to satisfy the ordinary Oriental taste, poetry requires to be seasoned with exaggeration.

Again, an Occidental student's appreciation of many passages will depend upon his familiarity with Indian mythology, as well as with Oriental customs, scenery, and even the characteristic idiosyncrasies of the animal creation in the East. Most of the similes in Hindu epic poetry are taken from the habits and motions of Asiatic animals, such as elephants and tigers[1], or from peculiarities in the aspect of Indian plants and natural objects. Then, as to the description of scenery, in which Hindu poets are certainly more graphic and picturesque than either Greek or Latin[2], the whole appearance of external nature in the East, the exuberance of vegetation, the profusion of trees and fruits and flowers[3], the glare of burning skies, the freshness of the rainy season, the fury of storms, the serenity of Indian moonlight[4], and the gigantic mould in which natural objects are generally cast — these and many other features are difficult to be realized by

1. Thus any eminent or courageous person would be spoken of as 'a tiger of a man.' Other favourite animals in similes are the lion (*sinah*), the ruddy goose (*cakravaka* or *rathanga*) the buffalo (*mahisha*), the boar (*varaha*), the koel or Indian cuckoo (*kokila*), the heron (*kraunca*), the ox (*gavaya*, i.e. *bos gavaeus*), &c. &c. A woman is sometimes said to have a rolling gait like that of an elephant. It should be noted, however, that similes in the Indian Epics, though far too frequent, are generally confined to a few words, and not, as in Homer, drawn out for three or four lines.

2. The descriptions of scenery and natural objects in Homer are too short and general to be really picturesque. They want more colouring and minuteness of detail. Some account for this by supposing that a Greek poet was not accustomed to look upon nature with a painter's eye.

3. The immense profusion of flowers of all kinds is indicated by the number of botanical terms in a Sanskrit dictionary. Some of the most common flowers and trees alluded to in epic poetry are, the *chuta* or mango; the *ashoka* (described by Sir William Jones); the *kinshuka* (butea frondosa, with beautiful red blossoms); the tamarind (*amlika*); the jasmine (of which there are many varieties, such as *malati, jati, yuthika*, &c.); the *kuruvaka* (amaranth); the sandal (chandana); the jujube (*karkandhu*); the pomegranate (*dadima*); the kadamba (*nipa*); the tamarisk (*pichula*); the *vakula, karnikara, shpringata*, &c.

4. See the beautiful description of night in Ramayana (Gorr.) I. xxxvi. 15.

a European. We must also make allowance for the difference in Eastern manners; though, after conceding a wide margin in this direction, it must be confessed that the disregard of all delicacy in laying bare the most revolting particulars of certain ancient legends which we now and then encounter in the Indian Epics (especially in the Mahabharata) is a serious blot, and one which never disfigures the pages of Homer, notwithstanding his occasional freedom of expression. Yet there are not wanting indications in the Indian Epics of a higher degree of civilization than that represented in the Homeric poems. The battle-fields of the Ramayana and Mahabharata, though spoiled by childish exaggerations and the use of supernatural weapons, are not made barbarous by wanton cruelties[1]; and the descriptions of Ayodhya and Lanka imply far greater luxury and refinement than those of Sparta and Troy.

The constant interruption of the principal story (as before described) by tedious episodes, in both Ramayana and Mahabharata, added to the rambling prolixity of the story itself, will always be regarded as the chief drawback in Hindu epic poetry, and constitutes one of its most marked features of distinction. Even in this respect, however, the Iliad has not escaped the censure of critics. Many believe that this poem is the result of the fusion of different songs on one subject, long current in various localities, intermixed with later interpolations, something after the manner of the Mahabharata. But the artistic instincts of the Greeks required that all the parts and appendages and more recent additions should be blended into one compact, homogeneous, and symmetrical

---

1. There is something savage in Achilles' treatment of Hector; and the cruelties permitted by Ulysses, in the 22nd Book of the Odyssey, are almost revolting. Compare with these Rama's treatment of his fallen foe Ravana, in the Yuddha-kanda.

whole. Although we have certainly in Homer occasional digressions or parentheses, such as the description of the 'shield of Achilles,' the 'story of Venus and Mars,' these are not like the Indian episodes. If not absolutely essential to the completeness of the epic conception, they appear to arise naturally out of the business of the plot, and cause no violent disruption of its unity. On the contrary, with Eastern writers and narrators of stories, continuity is often designedly interrupted. They delight in stringing together a number of distinct stories — detached from each other, yet connected like the figures on a frieze. They even purposely break the sequence of each; so that before one is ended another is commenced, and ere this is completed, others are interwoven; the result being a curious intertwining of stories within stories, the slender thread of an original narrative running through them all. A familiar instance of this is afforded by the well-known collection of tales called 'Hitopadesha,' and by the 'Arabian Nights.' The same tendency is observable in the composition of the epic poems — far more, however, in the Mahabharata than in the Ramayana.

Passing on to a comparison of the plot and the personages of the Ramayana with those of the Iliad, without supposing, as some have done, that either poem has been imitated from the other, it is certainly true, and so far remarkable, that the subject of both is a war undertaken to recover the wife of one of the warriors, carried off by a hero on the other side; and that Rama, in this respect, corresponds to Menelaus, while in others he may be compared to Achilles, Sita answering to Helen, Sparta to Ayodhya, Lanka to Troy. It may even be true that some sort of analogy may be traced between the parts played by Agamennon and Sugriva, Patroclus and Lakshmana, Nestor and Jambavat[1]. Again,

---

1. Jambavat was the chief of the bears, who was always giving sage advice.

Ulysses[1], in one respect, may be compared to Hanuman; and Hector, as the bravest warrior on the Trojan side, may in some points be likened to Indrajit, in others to the indignant Vibhishana[2], or again in the Mahabharata to Duryodhana, while Achilles has qualities in common with Arjuna. Other resemblances might be indicated; but these comparisons cannot be carried out to any extent without encountering difficulties at every step, so that any theory of an interchange of ideas between Hindu and Greek epic poets becomes untenable. Rama's character has really nothing in common with that of Menelaus, and very little with that of Achilles; although, as the bravest and most powerful of the warriors, he is rather to be compared with the latter than the former hero. If in his anger he is occasionally Achillean, his whole nature is cast in a less human mould than that of the Grecian hero. He is the type of a perfect husband, son, and brother. Sita also rises in character far above Helen, and even above Penelope[3], both in her sublime devotion and loyalty to her husband, and her indomitable patience and endurance under suffering and temptation. As for Bharat and Lakshmana, they are models of fraternal duty; Kaushalya of maternal tenderness; Dasharatha of paternal love: and it may be affirmed generally that the whole moral tone of the Ramayana is certainly above that of the Iliad. Again, in the Iliad the subject is really the anger of Achilles; and when that is satisfied the drama closes. The fall of Troy is not considered necessary to the completion of the plot. Whereas in the

1. When any work had to be done which required peculiar skill or stratagem, it was entrusted to Polumetis Odysseus.
2. Hector, like Vibhishana, was indignant with the ravisher, but he does not refuse to fight on his brother's side.
3. One cannot help suspecting Penelope of giving way to a little womanly vanity in allowing herself to be surrounded by so many suitors, though she repudiated their advances.

Ramayana the whole action points to the capture of Lanka and destruction of the ravisher. No one too can read either the Ramayana or Mahabharata without feeling that they rise above the Homeric poems in this — that a deep religious meaning appears to underlie all the narrative, and that the wildest allegory may be intended to conceal a sublime moral, symbolizing the conflict between good and evil, and teaching the hopelessness of victory in so terrible a contest without purity of soul, self-abnegation, and subjugation of the passions.

In reality it is the religious element of the Indian Epics that constitutes one of the principal features of contrast in comparing them with the Homeric. We cannot of course do more than indicate here the bare outlines of so interesting a subject as a comparison between the gods of India, Rome, and Greece. Thus:

Indra[1] and Shiva certainly offer points of analogy to Jupiter and Zeus; Durga or Parvati to Juno; Krishna to Apollo; Shri to Ceres; Prithivi to Cybele; Varuna to Neptune, and, in his earlier character, to Uranus; Sarasvati, goddess of speech and the arts, to Minerva; Karttikeya or Skanda, god of war, to Mars[2]; Yama to Pluto or Minos; Kuvera to Plutus; Vishvakarman to Vulcan; Kama, god of love, to Cupid; Rati, his wife, to Venus[3]; Narada

---

1. Indra is, as we have already seen (p. 13), the Jupiter Pluvius who sends rain and wields the thunderbolt, and in the earlier mythology is the chief of the gods, like Zeus. Subsequently his worship was superseded by that of Krishna and Shiva.
2. It is curious that Karttikeya, the war-god, is represented in Hindu mythology as the god of thieves — I suppose from their habit of sapping and mining under houses. (See Mrich-chhakatika, Act III.) Indian thieves, however, display such skill and ingenuity, that a god like Mercury would appear to be a more appropriate patron. Karttikeya was the son of Shiva, just as Mars was the offspring of Jupiter.
3. In one or two points Lakshmi may be compared to Venus.

to Mercury[1]; Hanuman to Pan; Ushas, and in the later mythology Aruna, to Eos and Arurora; Vayu to Aeolus; Ganesha, as presiding over the opening and beginning of all undertakings, to Janus; the Ashvini-kumaras[2] to the Dioscuri Castor and Pollux.

But in Greece, mythology, which was in many respects fully systematized when the Homeric poems were composed[3], never passed certain limits, or outgrew a certain symmetry of outline. In the Iliad and the Odyssey, a god is little more than idealized humanity. His form and his actions are seldom out of keeping with this character. Hindu mythology, on the other hand, springing from the same source as that of Europe, but, spreading and ramifying with the rank luxuriance of an Indian forest, speedily outgrew all harmony of proportions, and surrounded itself with an intricate undergrowth of monstrous and confused allegory. Doubtless the gods of the Indian and Grecian Epics preserve some traces of their common origin, resembling each other in various ways; interfering in human concerns, exhibiting human infirmities, taking part in the battles of their favourite heroes, furnishing them with celestial arms, or interposing directly to protect them.

But in the Ramayana and Mahabharata, and in the Puranas to which they led, the shape and operations of divine and

---

1. As Mercury was the inventor of the lyre, Narada was the inventor of the Vina or lute.
2. These ever-youthful twin sons of the Sun, by his wife Sanjna, transformed into a mare (*ashvini*), resemble the classical Dioscuri, both by their exploits and the aid they render to their worshippers (see p. 14).
3. Herodotus says (Euterpe, 53) that 'Homer and Hesiod *framed* the Greek Theogony, gave distinctive names to the gods, distributed honours and functions to them, and described their forms.' I conclude that by the verb Herodotus did not mean to imply that Homer *invented* the myths, but that he gave system to a mythology already current; see, however, Grote's History of Greece, I. 482 &c.

semi-divine beings are generally suggestive of the monstrous, the frightful, and the incredible. The human form, however idealized, is seldom thought adequate to the expression of divine attributes. Brahma is four-faced; Shiva, three-eyed and sometimes five-headed; Indra has a thousand eyes; Karttikeya, six faces; Ravana, ten heads; Ganesha has the head of an elephant. Nearly every god and goddess has at least four arms, with symbols of obscure import exhibited in every hand[1]. The deeds of heroes, who are themselves half gods, transport the imagination into the region of the wildest chimera; and a whole pantheon presents itself, teeming with grotesque fancies, with horrible creations, half animals half gods, with man-eating ogres, many-headed giants and disgusting demons, to an extent which the refined and delicate sensibilities of the Greeks and Romans could not have tolerated[2].

\ Moreover, in the Indian Epics the boundaries between the natural and supernatural, between earth and heaven, between the divine, human, and even animal creations, are singularly vague and undefined; troops of deities and semi-divine personages appear on the stage on every occasion. Gods, men, and animals are ever changing places. A constant communication is kept up between the two worlds, and such is their mutual interdependence that each seems to need the other's help. If distressed mortals are assisted out of their difficulties by divine interposition, the tables are often turned, and perturbed gods, themselves reduced to pitiful straits, are forced to implore the aid of mortal warriors in their conflicts

---

1. The Roman god Janus (supposed to be for Dianus and connected with *dies*) was represented by two and sometimes four heads.
2. It is true that Homer now and then indulges in monstrous creations; but even the description of Polyphemus does not outrage all probability, like the exaggerated horrors of the demon Kabandha, in the 3rd Book of the Ramayana (see p. 397).

with the demons[1]. They even look to mortals for their daily
sustenance, and are represented as actually *living on the
sacrifices* offered to them by human beings, and at every
sacrificial ceremony assemble in troops, eager to feed upon
their shares. In fact, sacrifice with the Hindus is not merely
expiatory or placatory; it is necessary for the *food* and *support*
of the gods. If there were no sacrifices the gods would starve
to death (see Introduction, p. xlvi, note 1). This alone will
account for the interest they take in the destruction of demons,
whose great aim was to obstruct these sources of their
sustenance. Much in the same way the spirits of dead men
are supposed to depend for existence and happiness on the
living, and to be fed with cakes of rice and libations of water
at the Sraddha ceremonies.

Again, not only are men aided by animals which usurp
human functions, but the gods also are dependent on and
associated with birds and beasts of all kinds, and even with
plants. Most of the principal deities are described as using
animals for their Vahanas or vehicles. Brahma is carried on
a swan, and sometimes seated on a lotus; Vishnu is borne on
or attended by a being, half eagle, half man (called Garuda);
Lakshmi is seated on a lotus or carries one in her hand; Shiva
has a bull for his vehicle or companion; Karttikeya, god of
war, has a peacock[2]; Indra has an elephant; Yama, god of
death, has a buffalo (*mahisha*[3]); Kama-deva, a parrot and
fish[4]; Ganesha, a rat[5]; Agani, a ram; Varuna, a fish; Durga,

---

1. Indra does so in the Shakuntala and Vikramorvashi.
2. *Karttikeya* is represented as a handsome young man (though with
   six faces). This may account for his being associated with a peacock.
3. Perhaps from its great power.
4. A parrot often figures in Indian love-stories. He is also associated
   with a kind of crocodile as his symbol (whence his name *Makara-
   dhvaja*). Such an animal is kept in tanks near his temples.
5. Supposed to posses great sagacity.

a tiger. The latter is sometimes represented with her husband on a bull, Shiva himself being also associated with a tiger and antelope as well as with countless serpents. Vishnu (Hari, Narayana) is also represented as the Supreme Being sleeping on a thousand-headed serpent called Shesha (or Ananta, 'the Infinite').

This Shesha is moreover held to be the chief of a race of Nagas or semi-divine beings, sometimes stated to be one thousand in number, half serpents half men, their heads being human and their bodies snake-like. They inhabit the seven Patalas[1] or regions under the earth, which, with the seven

---

1. Patala, though often used as a general term for all the seven regions under the earth, is properly only one of the seven, called in order, *Atala, Vitala, Sutala, Rasatala, Talatala, Mahatala,* and *Patala;* above which are the seven worlds (Lokas), called *Bhu* (the earth), *Bhuvar, Svar, Mahar, Janar, Tapah,* and *Brahma* or *Satya* (see note 3, p. 70); all fourteen resting on the heads of the great serpent. The serpent-race who inhabit these lower regions (which are not to be confounded with the Narakas or hells, note 3, p. 70) are sometimes regarded as belonging to only one of the seven, viz. Patala, or to a portion of it called Naga-loka, of which the capital is Bhogavati. They are fabled to have sprung from Kadru, wife of Kashyapa, and some of the females among them (Naga-kanyas) are said to have married human heroes. In this way Ulupi became the wife of Arjuna (p. 435, note 1), and, curiously enough, a tribe of the Rajputs claims descent from the Nagas even in the present day. A particular day is held sacred to the Nagas, and a festival called Naga-panchami is kept in their honour about the end of July (Shravana). Vasuki and Takshaka are other leading Nagas, to whom a separate dominion over part of the serpent-race in different parts of the lower regions is sometimes assigned. All the Nagas are described as having jewels in their heads. Their chiefs, Shesha, Vasuki, and Takshaka, are said to rule over snakes generally, while Garuda is called the enemy of Nagas (*Nagari*); so that the term Naga sometimes stands for an ordinary serpent. The habit which snakes have of hiding in holes may have given rise to the notion of peopling the lower regions with Nagas. The Rev. K.M. Banerjea has a curious theory about them (see p. xlvi. of this volume).

superincumbent worlds, are supposed to rest on the thousand heads of the serpent Sesha, who typifies infinity — inasmuch as, according to a common myth, he supports the Supreme being between the intervals of creation, as well as the worlds created at the commencement of each Kalpa (note 3, p. 368). Again, the earth is sometimes fabled to be supported by the vast heads and backs of eight male and eight female mythical elephants, who all have names[1], and are the elephants of the eight quarters. When any one of these shakes his body the whole earth quakes (see Ramayana I. xli).

In fact, it is not merely in a confused, exaggerated, and overgrown mythology that the difference between the Indian and Grecian Epics lies. It is in the injudicious and excessive use of it. In the Ramayana and Mahabharata, the spiritual and the supernatural are everywhere so dominant and overpowering, that anything merely human seems altogether out of place.

In the Iliad and Odyssey, the religious and supernatural are perhaps scarcely less prevalent. The gods are continually interposing and superintending; but they do so as if they were themselves little removed from men, or at least without destroying the dramatic probability of the poem, or neutralizing its general air of plain matter-of-fact humanity. Again, granted that in Homer there is frequent mention of the future existence of the soul, and its condition of happiness or misery hereafter, and that the Homeric descriptions of disembodied spirits correspond in many points with the Hindu notions on the

---

1. The eight names of the male elephants are given in the Amara-kosha, thus: Airavata, Pundarika, Vamana, Kumuda, Anjana, Pushpa-danta, Sarva-bhauma, Suratika. Four are named in Ramayana (I. xli), Viru-paksha, Maha-padma, Saumanas, and Bhadra. Sometimes these elephants appear to have locomotive habits, and roam about the sky in the neighbourhood of their respective quarters (see Megha-duta 14).

same subject[1] — yet even these doctrines do not stand out with such exaggerated reality in Homer as to make human concerns appear unreal. Nor is there in his poems the slightest allusion to the soul's pre-existence in a former body, and its liability to pass into other bodies hereafter — a theory which in Hindu poetry invests present actions with a mysterious meaning, and gives a deep distinctive colouring to Indian theology.

Above all, although priests are occasionally mentioned in the Iliad and the Odyssey, there is wholly wanting in the Homeric poems any recognition of a regular hierarchy, or the necessity for a mediatorial caste of sacrificers[2]. This, which may be called the sacerdotal element of the Indian Epics, is more or less woven into their very tissue. Brahmanism has been at work in these productions almost as much as the imagination of the poet; and boldly claiming a monopoly of all knowledge, human and divine, has appropriated this, as it has every other department of literature, and warped it to its own purposes. Its policy having been to check the development of intellect, and keep the inferior castes in perpetual childhood, it encouraged an appetite for

---

1. See the following passages, which bear on the existence of the after death as in Hades: Il. XXIII. 72, 104: Od. XI. 213, 476; XX. 355; XXIV. 14. It is curious that the Hindu notion of the restless state of the soul until the Shraddha is performed (see p. 279) agrees with the ancient classical superstition that the ghosts of the dead wandered about as long as their bodies remained unburied, and were not suffered to mingle with those of the other dead. See Odyss. XI. 54: Il. XXIII. 72; and cf. Aen. VI. 325: Lucan I. II: Eur. Hec. 30.

2. A king, or any other individual, is allowed in Homer to perform a sacrifice without the help of priests. See Il. II. 411; III. 392. Nevertheless we read occasionally of a 'sacrifice-viewer,' who prophesied from the appearance of the flame and the smoke at the sacrifice. See Il. XXIV. 221: Odyss. XXI. 144; XXII. 319.

exaggeration more insatiable than would be tolerated in the most extravagant European fairy-tale. This has been done more in the Ramayana than in the Mahabharata; but even in the later Epic, full as it is of geographical, chronological, and historical details, few assertions can be trusted. Time is measured by millions of years, space by millions of miles; and if a battle has to be described, nothing is thought of it unless millions of soldiers, elephants, and horses are brought into the field[1].

This difference in the religious system of Europe and India becomes still more noteworthy, when it is borne in mind that the wildest fictions of the Ramayana and Mahabharata are *to this very day* intimately bound up with the religious creed of the Hindus. It is certain that the more intelligent among them, like the more educated Greeks and Romans, regarded and still regard the fictions of mythology as allegorical. But both in Europe and Asia the mass of the people, not troubling themselves about the mystical significance of symbols, took emblem and allegory for reality. And this, doubtless, they are apt to do still, as much in the West as in the East. Among European nations, however, even the ductile faith of the masses is sufficiently controlled by common sense to prevent the fervour of religious men from imposing any great extravagance on their credulity; and much as the Homeric poems are still admired, no one in any part of the world now dreams of placing the slightest faith in their legends, so as to connect them with religious opinions and practices. In India a complete contrast in this respect may be observed. The myths of the Indian Epics are still closely interwoven with *present* faith. In fact, the capacity of an uneducated Hindu for accepting and admiring the most monstrous fictions is apparently unlimited. Hence the absence of all history in the

---

1. Cf. extract from Aristotle's Poetics, p. 484, note 1, of this volume.

literature of India. A plain relation of facts has little charm for the ordinary Hindu mind.

Even in the delineation of heroic character, where Indian poets exhibit much skill, they cannot avoid ministering to the craving for the marvellous which appears to be almost inseparable from the mental constitution of Eastern peoples.

Homer's characters are like Shakespeare's. The are *true* heroes, if you will, but they are always *men;* never perfect, never free from human weaknesses, inconsistencies, and caprices of temper. If their deeds are sometimes praeterhuman, they do not commit improbabilities which are absolutely absurd. Moreover, he does not seem to delineate his characters; he allows them to delineate themselves. They stand out like photographs, in all the reality of nature. We are not so much told what they do or say[1]. They appear rather to speak and act for themselves. In the Hindu Epics the poet gives us too long and too tedious descriptions in his own person; and, as a rule, his characters are either too good or too bad. How far more natural is Achilles, with all his faults, than Rama, with his almost painful correctness of conduct! Even the cruel vengeance that Achilles perpetrates on the dead Hector strikes us as more likely to be true than Rama's magnanimous treatment of the fallen Ravana. True, even the heroes sometimes commit what a European would call crimes; and the Pandavas were certainly guilty of one inhuman act of treachery. In their anxiety to provide for their own escape from a horrible death, they enticed an outcaste woman and her five sons into their

---

1. Aristotle says that 'among the many just claims of Homer to our praise, this is one — that he is the only poet who seems to have understood what part in his poem it was proper for him to take himself. The poet, in his own person, should speak as little as possible.... Homer, after a few preparatory lines, immediately introduces a man, a woman, or some other character; for all have their character.' (Poetics III. 3.)

inflammable lac-house, and then burnt her alive (see p. 429-430). But the guilt of this transaction is neutralized to a Hindu by the woman being an outcaste; and besides, it is the savage Bhima who sets fire to the house. Rama and Lakshmana again were betrayed into a deed of cruelty in mutilating Shurpanakha. For this, however, the fiery Lakshmana was responsible. If the better heroes sin, they do not sin like men. We see in them no portraits of ourselves. The pictures are too much one colour. There are few gradations of light and shadow, and little artistic blending of opposite hues. On the one side we have all gods or demigods; on the other, all demons or fiends. We miss real human beings with mixed characters. There is no mirror held up to inconsistent humanity. Duryodhana and his ninety-nine brothers are too uniformly vicious to be types of real men. Lakshmana has perhaps the most natural character among the heroes of the Ramayana, and Bhima among those of the Mahabharata. In many respects the character of the latter is not unlike that of Achilles; but in drawing his most human heroes the Indian poet still displays a perpetual tendency to run into extravagance.

It must be admitted, however, that in exhibiting pictures of domestic life and manners the Sanskrit Epics are even more true and real than the Greek and Roman. In the delineation of women the Hindu poet throws aside all exaggerated colouring, and draws from nature. Kaikeyi, Kaushalya, Mandodari (the favourite wife of Ravana[1]), and even the hump-backed Manthara (Ramayana II. viii), are all drawn to the very life. Sita, Draupadi, and Damayanti engage our affections and our interest far more than Helen, or even than Penelope. Indeed, Hindu wives are generally perfect patterns

---

1. What can be more natural than Mandodari's lamentations over the dead body of Ravana, and her allusions to his fatal passion for Sita in Ramayana VI. 95 (Gorresio's ed.)?

of conjugal fidelity; nor can it be doubted that in these delightful portraits of the Pativrata or 'devoted wife' we have true representations of the purity and simplicity of Hindu domestic manners in early times[1]. We may also gather from the epic poems many interesting hints as to the social position occupied by Hindu women before the Muhammadan conquest. No one can read the Ramayan and Mahabharata without coming to the conclusion that the habit of secluding women, and of treating them as inferiors, is, to a certain extent, natural to all Eastern nations, and prevailed in the earliest times[2]. Yet various passages in both Epics clearly establish the fact, that women in India were subjected to less social restraint

---

1. No doubt the devotion of a Hindu wife implied greater inferiority than is compatible with modern European ideas of independence. The extent to which this devotion was carried, even in little matters, is curiously exemplified by the story of Gandhari, who out of sympathy for her blind husband never appeared in public without a veil over her face (see p. 421). Hence, during the grand sham-fight between the Kuru and Pandu princes, Vidura stood by Dhrita-rashtra, and Kunti by Gandhari, to describe the scene to them (see p. 427).

2. It was equally natural to the Greeks and Romans. Chivalry and reverence for the fair sex belonged only to European nations of northern origin, who were the first to hold 'inesse foeminis sanctum aliquid' (Tac. Germ. 8). That Hindu women in ancient times secluded themselves, except on certain occasions, may be inferred from the word *asuryam-pashya,* given by Panini as an epithet of a king's wife ('one who never sees the sun') — a very strong expression, stronger even than the *parda-nishin* of the Muhammadans. It is to be observed also that in the Ramayana (VI. xcix. 33) there is clear allusion to some sort of seclusion being practised; and the term *avarodha,* 'fenced or guarded place,' is used long before the time of the Muhammadans for the women's apartments. In the Ratnavali, however, the minister of king Vatsa, and his chamberlain and the envoy from Ceylon, are admitted to an audience in the presence of the queen and her damsels; and although Rama in Ramayana VI. 99 thinks it necessary to excuse himself for permitting his wife to expose herself to the gaze of the crowd, yet he expressly (99, 34)

in former days than they are at present, and even enjoyed considerable liberty[1]. True, the ancient lawgiver, Manu, speaks of women as having no will of their own, and unfit for independence (see p. 284 of this volume); but he probably described a state of society which it was the aim of the priesthood to establish, rather than that which really existed in his own time. At a later period the pride of Brahmanism, and still more recently the influence of Muhammadanism, deprived women of even such freedom as they once enjoyed; so that at the present day no Hindu woman has, *in theory,* any independence. It is not merely that she is not her own mistress: she is not her own property, and never under any circumstances, can be. She belongs to her father first, who gives her away to her husband, to whom she belongs *for ever*[2].

---

enumerates various occasions on which it was allowable for a woman to show herself unveiled. I here translate the passage, as it bears very remarkably on this interesting subject. Rama says to Vibhishana — 'Neither houses, nor vestments, nor enclosing walls, nor ceremony, nor regal insignia (*raja-satkara*), are the screen (*avarana*) of a woman. Her own virtue alone (protects her). In great calamities (*vyasaneshu*), at marriages, at the public choice of a husband by maidens (of the Kshatriya caste), at a sacrifice, at assemblies (*samsatsu*), it is allowable for all the world to look upon women (*strinam darshanam sarvalaukikam*).'

Hence Shakuntala appears in the public court of king Dushyanta; Damayanti travels about by herself; and in the Uttara-rama-charita, the mother of Rama goes to the hermitage of Valmiki. Again, women were present at dramatic representations, visited the temples of the gods, and performed their ablutions with little privacy; which last custom they still practise, though Muhammadan women do not.

1. In Maha-bh. I. 4719 we read: *An-avritah kila pura striya asan kama-cara-viharinyah svatantrah,* &c.

2. Hence when her husband dies she cannot be remarried, as there is no one to give her away. In fact, the remarriage of Hindu widows, which is now permitted by law, is utterly opposed to all modern Hindu ideas about women; and many persons think that the passing of this law was one cause of the mutiny of 1857. It is clear from

She is not considered capable of so high a form of religion
as man[1], and she does not mix freely in society. But in ancient
times, when the epic songs were current in India, women
were not confined to intercourse with their own families; they
did very much as they pleased, travelled about, and showed
themselves unreservedly in public[2], and if of the Kshatriya
caste, were occasionally allowed to choose their own husbands
from a number of assembled suitors[3]. It is clear, moreover,
that, in many instances, there was considerable dignity and
elevation about the female character, and that much mutual

the story of Damayanti, who appoints a second Svayamvara, that in
early times remarriage was not necessarily improper; though, from
her wonder that the new suitor should have failed to see through
her artifice, and from her vexation at being supposed capable of a
second marriage, it may be inferred that such a marriage was even
then not reputable.

1. See, however, the stories of Gargi and Maitreyi (Brihad-aranyaka
Upanishad, Roer's transl. pp. 198, 203, 242). No doubt the inferior
capacity of a woman as regards religion was implied in the epic
poems, as well as in later works. A husband was the wife's divinity,
as well as her lord, and her best religion was to please him. See Sita's
speech, p. 407 of this volume; and the quotation from Madhava
Acharya (who flourished in the fourteenth century), p. 415, note.
Such verses as the following are common in Hindu literature: *Bharta
hi paramam narya bhushanam bhushanair vina*, 'a husband is a wife's
chief ornament even without (other) ornaments.' Manu says (V. 151),
*Yasami dadyat pita tv enam bhrata vanumate pituh, Tam shushrusheta
jivantam samsthitam cha na langhayet*. See p. 318 of this volume.
In IV. 198, Manu classes women with Sudras.

2. Especially married women. A wife was required to obey her husband
implicitly, but in other respects she was to be independent (*svatantryam
arhati*, Maha-bhar. I. 4741).

3. The Svayamvara, however, appears to have been something
exceptional, and only to have been allowed in the case of the
daughters of kings or Kshatriyas. See Draupadi-svayamvara 127;
Maha-bhar. I. 7926.

affection prevailed in families. Nothing can be more beautiful and touching than the pictures of domestic and social happiness in the Ramayana and Mahabharata. Children are dutiful to their parents[1] and submissive to their superiors; younger brothers are respectful to elder brothers; parents are fondly attached to their children, watchful over their interests and ready to sacrifice themselves for their welfare; wives are loyal, devoted, and obedient to their husband, yet show much independence of character, and do not hesitate to express their own opinions; husbands are tenderly affectionate towards their wives, and treat them with respect and courtesy; daughters and women generally are virtuous and modest, yet spirited and, when occasion requires, firm and courageous; love and harmony reign throughout the family circle. Indeed, in depicting scenes of domestic affection, and expressing those universal feelings and emotions which belong to human nature in all time and in all places, Sanskrit epic poetry is unrivalled even by Greek Epos. It is not often that Homer takes us out of the battle-field; and if we except the lamentations over the bodies of Patroclus and Hector, the visit of Priam to the tent of Achilles and the parting of Hector and Andromache, there are no such pathetic passages in the Iliad as the death of the hermit-boy (p. 387), the pleadings of Sita for permission to accompany her husband into exile (p. 407), and the whole ordeal-scene at the end

---

1. Contrast with the respectful tone of Hindu children towards their parents, the harsh manner in which Telemachus generally speaks to his mother. Filial respect and affection is quite as noteworthy a feature in the Hindu character now as in ancient times. It is common for unmarried soldiers to stint themselves almost to starvation-point, that they may send home money to their aged parents. In fact, in proportion to the weakness or rather total absence of the *national* is the strength of the *family* bond. In England and America, where national life is strongest, children are less respectful to their parents.

of the Ramayana. In the Indian Epics such passages abound, and, besides giving a very high idea of the purity and happiness of domestic life in ancient India, indicate a capacity in Hindu women for the discharge of the most sacred and important social duties.

We must guard against the supposition that the women of India at the present day have altogether fallen from their ancient character. Notwithstanding the corrupting example of Islamism, and the degrading tendency of modern Hinduism, some remarkable instances may still be found of moral and even intellectual excellence[1]. These, however, are exceptions, and we may rest assured, that until Asiatic women, whether Hindu or Muslim, are elevated and educated, our efforts to raise Asiatic nations to the level of European will be fruitless[2]. Let us hope that when the Ramayan and Mahabharata shall no longer be held sacred as repositories of faith and storehouses of trustworthy tradition the enlightened Hindu may still learn from these poems to honour the weaker sex; and that Indian women, restored to their ancient liberty and raised to a still higher position by becoming partakers of the 'fulness of the blessing' of Christianity, may do for our Eastern empire what they have done for Europe — soften, invigorate, and dignify the character of its people.

I close my present subject with examples of the religious and moral teaching of the two Indian Epics. A few sentiments and maxims, extracted from both poems, here follow:

---

1. In some parts of India, especially in the Marathi districts, there is still considerable freedom of thought and action allowed to women.
2. Manu gives expression to a great truth when he says (III. 145), *Sahasram tu pitrin gauravenatirichyate,* 'a mother exceeds in value a thousand fathers.'

A heavy blow, inflicted by a foe[1],
Is often easier to bear, than griefs,
However slight, that happen casually.

> Ramayana (ed. Bomaby) II. lxii. 16.

To carry out an enterprise in words
Is easy, to accomplish it by acts
Is the sole test of man's capacity.

> Ramayana (ed. Gorresio) VI. lxvii. 10.

Truth, justice, and nobility of rank
Are centred in the King; he is a mother,
Father, and benefactor of his subjects.

> Ramayana (ed. Bombay) II. lxvii. 35.

In countries without monarchs, none can call
His property or family his own;
No one is master even of himself.

> Ramayana (ed. Gorresio) II. lxix. 11.

Where'er we walk, Death marches at our side;
Where'er we sit, Death seats himself beside us;
However far we journey, Death continues
Our fellow-traveller and goes with us home.
Men take delight in each returning dawn,
And with admiring gaze, behold the glow
Of sunset. Every season, as it comes,
Fills them with gladness, yet they never reck
That each recurring season, every day
Fragment by fragment bears their life away.
As drifting logs of wood may haply meet

---

1. Though some of these translations were made years ago from Bohtlingk's admirable collection of Indische Spruche, I have since been assisted in my renderings of many examples by Dr. Muir's 'Religious and Moral Sentiments freely translated from Indian writers,' lately printed at Edinburgh, with an appendix and notes. I may not have succeeded so well as Dr. Muir, but rhymeless metre may have enabled me to keep somewhat closer to the original.

On Ocean's waters, surging to and fro,
And having met, drift once again apart;
So fleeting is a man's association
With wife and children, relatives and wealth,
So surely must a time of parting come.

> Ramayana (ed. Bombay) II. cv. 24-27.

Whate'er the work a man performs,
The most effective aid to its completion —
The most prolific source of true success —
Is energy without despondency.

> Ramayana (ed. Bomaby) V. xii. 11.

Fate binds a man with adamantine cords,
And drags him upwards to the highest rank
Or downward to the depths of misery.

> Ramayana (ed. Bombay) V. xxxvii. 3

He who has wealth has strength of intellect;
He who has wealth has depths of erudition;
He who has wealth has nobleness of birth;
He who has wealth has relatives and friends;
He who has wealth is thought a very hero;
He who has wealth is rich in every virtue.

> Ramayana (ed. Bombay) VI. lxxxiii. 35, 36.

Time is awake while mortals are asleep,
None can elude his grasp or curb his course,
He passes unrestrained o'er all alike.

> Maha-bh. I. 243.

Thou thinkest; I am single and alone —
Perceiving not the great eternal Sage
Who dwells within thy breast. Whatever wrong
Is done by thee, he sees and notes it all.

> Maha-bh. I. 3015.

Heaven, Earth, and Sea, Sun, Moon, and Wind, and Fire,
Day, Night, the Twilights, and the Judge of souls,
The god of justice and the Heart itself,

All see and note the conduct of a man[1].

Maha-bh. I. 3017.

A wife is half the man, his truest friend,
Source of his virtue, pleasure, wealth — the root
Whence springs the line of his posterity.

Maha-bha. I. 3028.

An evil-minded man is quick to see
His neighbour's faults, though small as mustard-seed;
But when he turns his eyes towards his own,
Though large as Bilva[2] fruit, he none descries.

Maha-bh. I. 3069.

If Truth and thousands of Horse-sacrifices
Were weighed together, Truth would weigh the most[3].

Maha-bh. I. 3095.

Death follows life by an unerring law;
Why grieve for that which is inevitable?

Maha-bh. I. 6144.

Conquer a man who never gives by gifts;
Subdue untruthful men by truthfulness;
Vanquish an angry man by gentleness;
And overcome the evil man by goodness[4].

Maha-bh. III. 13253.

Triple restraint of thought and word and deed,
Strict vow of silence, coil of matted hair,
Close shaven head, garments of skin or bark,

---

1. Compare Manu VIII. 86, p. 314 of this volume.
2. This is the Aegle Marmelos (*Bel*) or Bengal Quince, bearing a large fruit. It is esteemed sacred to Maha-deva. Compare St. Matthew vii. 3, 4.
3. Hitopadesa IV. 135.
4. See Rom. xii. 21. Compare the Pali Rajovada Jataka (Fausböll's Ten Jatakas, p. 5), *Akkodhena jine kodham, Asadhum sadhuna jine, Jine kadariyam danena, Sachchena alika-vadinam.* See also Dhammapada 223.

Keeping of fasts, ablutions, maintenance
Of sacrificial fires, a hermit's life,
Emaciation — these are all in vain,
Unless the inward soul be free from stain.

Maha-bh. III. 13445.

To injure none by thought or word or deed,
To give to others, and be kind to all —
This is the constant duty of the good.
High-minded men delight in doing good,
Without a thought of their own interest;
When they confer a benefit on others,
They reckon not on favours in return[1].

Maha-bh. III. 16782, 16796.

An archer shoots an arrow which may kill
One man, or none; but clever men discharge
The shaft of intellect, whose stroke has power
To overwhelm a king and all his kingdom.

Maha-bh. V. 1013.

Two persons will hereafter be exalted
Above the heavens — the man with boundless power
Who yet forbears to use it indiscreetly,
And he who is not rich and yet can give[2].

Maha-bh. V. 1028.

Sufficient wealth, unbroken health, a friend,
A wife of gentle speech, a docile son,
And learning that subserves some useful end —
These are a living man's six greatest blessings.

Maha-bh. V. 1057.

Good words, good deeds, and beautiful expressions
A wise man ever culls from every quarter,
E'en as a gleaner gathers ears of corn.

Mah-bh. V. 1126.

---

1. Compare St. Luke vi. 35.
2. Compare St. Mark xii. 41-44.

The gods defend not with a club or shield
The man they wish to favour — but endow him
With wisdom; and the man whom they intend
To ruin, they deprive of understanding[1];
So that to him all things appear distorted.
Then, when his mind is dulled and he is ripe
To meet his doom, evil appears to him
Like good, and even fortunate events
Turn to his harm and tend to his destruction.

                         Maha-bh. V. 1122, 2679.

To curb the tongue and moderate the speech,
Is held to be the hardest of all tasks[2].
The words of him who talks too volubly
Have neither substance nor variety.

                               Maha-bh. V. 1170.

Darts, barbed arrows, iron-headed spears,
However deep they penetrate the flesh,
May be extracted; but a cutting speech,
That pierces, like a javelin, to the heart,
None can remove; it lies and rankles there.

                               Maha-bh. V. 1173.

Repeated sin destroys the understanding,
And he whose reason is impaired, repeats
His sins. The constant practising of virtue
Strengthens the mental faculties, and he
Whose judgment stronger grows, acts always right.

                               Maha-bh. V. 1242.

Bear railing words with patience, never meet
An angry man with anger, nor return
Reviling for reviling, smite not him
Who smites thee; let thy speech and acts be gentle.

                         Maha-bh. V. 1270, 9972.

---

1. *Quos Deus vult perdere prius dementat.*
2. St. James iii. 8.

If thou art wise, seek ease and happiness
In deeds of virtue and of usefulness;
And ever act in such a way by day
That in the night thy sleep may tranquil be;
And so comport thyself when thou art young,
That when thou art grown old, thine age may pass
In calm serenity. So ply thy task
Throughout thy life, that when thy days are ended,
Thou may'st enjoy eternal bliss hereafter.

Maha-bh. V. 1248.

Esteem that gain a loss which ends in harm;
Account that loss a gain which brings advantage.

Maha-bha. V. 1451.

Reflect that health is transient, death impends,
Ne'er in thy day of youthful strength do aught
To grieve thy conscience, lest when weakness comes,
And thou art on a bed of sickness laid,
Fear and remorse augment thy sufferings.

Maha-bh. V. 1474.

Do naught to others which if done to thee
Would cause thee pain; this is the sum of duty.

Maha-bh. V. 1517.

How can a man love knowledge yet repose?
Would'st thou be learned, then abandon ease.
Either give up thy knowledge or thy rest.

Maha-bh. V. 1537.

No sacred lore can save the hypocrite,
Though he employ it craftily, from hell;
When his end comes, his pious texts take wing,
Like fledglings eager to forsake their nest.

Maha-bh. V. 1623.

When men are ripe for ruin, e'en a straw
Has power to crush them, like a thunderbolt.

Maha-bh. VII. 429.

By anger, fear, and avarice deluded,
Men do not strive to understand themselves,
Nor ever gain self-knowledge. One is proud
Of rank, and plumes himself upon his birth,
Contemning those of low degree; another
Boasts of his riches, and disdains the poor;
Another vaunts his learning, and despising
Men of less wisdom, calls them fools; a fourth
Piquing himself upon his rectitude,
Is quick to censure other peoples' faults.
But when the high and low, the rich and poor,
The wise and foolish, worthy and unworthy,
Are borne to their last resting-place — the grave —
When all their troubles end in that last sleep,
And of their earthly bodies naught remains
But fleshless skeletons — can living men
Mark differences between them, or perceive
Distinctions in the dust of birth or form?
Since, all are, therefore, levelled by the grave,
And all must sleep together in the earth —
Why, foolish mortals, do ye wrong each other?

Maha-bh: XI. 116.

Some who are wealthy perish in their youth,
While others who are fortuneless and needy,
Attain a hundred years; the prosperous man
Who lives, oft lacks the power to enjoy his wealth.

Maha-bh. XII. 859.

A king must first subdue himself, and then
Vanquish his enemies. How can a prince
Who cannot rule himself, enthral his foes?
To curb the senses, is to conquer self.

Maha-bh. XII. 2599.

Who in this world is able to distinguish
The virtuous from the wicked, both alike

The fruitful earth supports, on both alike
The sun pours down his beams, on both alike
Refreshing breezes blow, and both alike
The waters purify? Not so hereafter —
Then shall the good be severed from the bad;
Then in a region bright with golden lustre —
Centre of light and immortality —
The righteous after death shall dwell in bliss[1].
Then a terrific hell awaits the wicked —
Profound abyss of utter misery —
Into the depths of which bad men shall fall
Headlong, and mourn their doom for countless years.

Maha-bh. XII. 2798.

He who lets slip his opportunity,
And turns not the occasion to account,
Though he may strive to execute his work,
Finds not again the fitting time for action.

Maha-bh. XII. 3814.

Enjoy thou the prosperity of others,
Although thyself unprosperous; noble men
Take pleasure in their neighbour's happiness.

Maha-bh. XII. 3880.

Even to foes who visit us as guests
Due hospitality should be displayed;
The tree screens with its leaves, the man who fells it[2].

Maha-bh. XII. 5528.

What need has he who subjugates himself
To live secluded in a hermit's cell?

---

1. Compare St. Matthew xiii. 43, xxv. 46.
2. This verse occurs in Hitopadesha I. 60. Cf. Rom. xii. 20. Professor
   H.H. Wilson was induced to commence the study of Sanskrit by
   reading somewhere that this sentiment was to be met with in Sanskrit
   literature.

Where'er resides the self-subduing sage,
That place to him is like a hermitage.

Maha-bh. XII. 5961.

Do good today, time passes, Death is near.
Death falls upon a man all unawares,
Like a ferocious wolf upon a sheep.
Death comes when his approach is least expected.
Death sometimes seizes ere the work of life
Is finished, or its purposes accomplished.
Death carries off the weak and strong alike,
The brave and timorous, the wise and foolish,
And those whose objects are not yet achieved.
Therefore delay not; Death may come to-day.
Death will not wait to know if thou art ready,
·Or if thy work be done. Be active now,
While thou art young, and time is still thy own.
This very day perform to-morrow's work,
This very morning do thy evening's task.
When duty is discharged, then if thou live,
Honour and happiness will be thy lot,
And if thou die, supreme beatitude[1].

Maha-bh. XII. 6534.

The building of a house is fraught with troubles,
And ne'er brings comfort; therefore, cunning serpents
Seek for a habitation made by others,
And creeping in, abide there at their ease.

Maha-bh. XII. 6619.

Just as the track of birds that cleave the air
Is not discerned, nor yet the path of fish
That skim the water, so the course of those
Who do good actions, is not always seen.

Maha-bh. XII. 6763, 12156.

---

1. The order of the text has been slightly changed in this translation,
and a few liberties taken in the wording of it.

Let none reject the meanest suppliant
Or send him empty-handed from his door.
A gift bestowed on outcasts or on dogs
Is never thrown away or unrequited.

Maha-bh. XIII. 3212.

Time passes, and the man who older grows
Finds hair and teeth and eyes grow ever older.
One thing alone within him ne'eer grows old —
The thirst for riches and the love of gold.

Maha-bh. XIII. 3676, 368a.

This is the sum of all true righteousness —
Treat others, as thou would'st thyself be treated.
Do nothing to thy neighbour, which hereafter
Thou would'st not have thy neighbour do to thee.
In causing pleasure, or in giving pain,
In doing good, or injury to others,
In granting, or refusing a request,
A man obtains a proper rule of action
By looking on his neighbour as himself[1].

Maha-bh. XIII. 5571.

No being perishes before his time,
Though by a hundred arrows pierced; but when
His destined moment comes, though barely pricked
By a sharp point of grass, he surely dies[2].

Maha-bh. XIII. 7607.

Before infirmities creep o'er thy flesh;
Before decay impairs thy strength and mars
The beauty of thy limbs; before the Ender,
Whose charioteer is sickness, hastes toward thee,
Breaks up thy fragile frame and ends thy life[3],

---

1. Comapre St. Matthew xxii. 39. Luke vi. 31.
2. This occurs also in Hitopadesha II. 15.
3. Compare Eccles. xii. 1.

Lay up the only treasure: do good deeds;
Practise sobriety and self-control;
Amass that wealth which thieves cannot abstract,
Nor tyrants seize, which follows thee at death,
Which never wastes away, nor is corrupted[1].

Maha-bh. XIII. 12084.

Heaven's gate is very narrow and minute[2],
It cannot be perceived by foolish men,
Blinded by vain illusions of the world.
E'en the clear-sighted who discern the way,
And seek to enter, find the portal barred
And hard to be unlocked. Its massive bolts
Are pride and passion, avarice and lust.

Maha-bh. XIV. 2784.

Just heaven is not so pleased with costly gifts,
Offered in hope of future recompense,
As with the merest trifle set apart
From honest gains, and sanctified by faith[3].

Mah-bh. XIV. 2788.

---

1. Compare St. Matthew vi. 19, Job xxi. 23.
2. Compare St. Matthew vii. 14.
3. Compare St. Matthew vi. 1-4, St. Mark xii. 43, 44.

Lecture XV

The Artificial Poems. Dramas. Puranas.
Tantras. Niti-shastras.

I can only notice very briefly the remaining classes of
Indian writings which follow on the Ramayana and Mahabharata. In their religious bearing, as constituting part of
Smriti, and as chiefly drawn from the two great Epics, the
eighteen Puranas possess the next claim on our attention. It
will be convenient, however, to introduce here an enumeration
of some of the more celebrated artificial poems and dramas,
which are connected with the Epics, adding a few explanations
and examples, but reserving the fuller consideration of these
and other departments of Sanskrit literature to a future
opportunity.

The Artificial Poems

Some of the best known of the artificial poems are:

1. The *Raghu-vansha* or 'history of Raghu's race,' in nineteen
chapters, by Kalidasa, on the same subject as the Ramayana, viz.
the history of Rama-chandra, but beginning with a longer account
of his ancestors; 2. the *Kumara-sambhava,* by Kalidasa, on the

'birth of Kumara' or Karttikeya, god of war, son of Siva and Parvati — originally in sixteen cantos, of which only seven are usually edited, though nine more have been printed in the *Pandit* at Benares; 3. the *Megha-duta*, 'cloud-messenger,' also by Kalidasa — a poem of 116 verses, in the Mandakranta metre (well edited by Professor Johnson), describing a message sent by a banished Yaksha to his wife in the Himalayas; a cloud being personified and converted into the messenger; 4. the *Kiratarjuniya*, 'battle of the Kirata and Arjuna,' by Bharavi, in eighteen cantos, on a subject taken from the fourth chapter of Mahabharata III, viz. the penance performed by Arjuna, one of the Pandava princes, and his combat with Siva disguised as a Kirata or wild mountaineer (see p. 438); 5. the *Sishupala-badha* or 'destruction of Sishupala,' a poem in twenty cantos, by Magha, on a subject taken from the seventh chapter of the Sabha-parvan of the Mahabharata, viz. the slaying of the impious Sisu-pala by Krishna at a Rajasuya sacrifice performed by Yudhi-shthira (see p. 437); 6. the *Naishadha* or *Naishadhiya,* by Sri-harsha[1], on a subject drawn from an episode in the sixth chapter of the Vana-parvan of the Mahabharata, viz. the history and adventures of Nala, king of Nishadha.

The above six are sometimes called Maha-kavyas, 'great poems,' not with reference to their length (for they are generally short), but with reference to the subject of which they treat. To these may be added:

7. The *Ritu-samhara* or 'collection of the seasons,' a short but celebrated poem by Kalidasa, on the six seasons of the year (viz. *Grishma,* the hot season; *Varsha,* the rain; *Sharad,* autumn;

---

1. He is supposed to have lived about the year 1000 (cf. note, p. 544). This Sri-harsha was the greatest of all sceptical philosophers, and wrote a book called *Khandana-khanda-khadya* for the refutation of all other systems. It is alluded to in Naishadha VI. 113 (Premachandra's commentary). The commentator Narayana does not seem to have understood this. There are some philosophical chapters in the Naishadha.

Hemanta, the cold season; *Sisira,* the dewy season; *Vasanta,* the spring); 8. the *Nalodaya* or 'rise of Nala,' an artificial poem, also ascribed to one Kalidasa, but probably not the composition of the celebrated poet of that name, on much the same subject as the Naishadha, and describing especially the restoration of the fallen Nala to prosperity and power; 9. the *Bhatti-kavya,* 'poem of Bhatti,' according to some the work of Bhartri-hari or his son, on the same subject as the Ramayana, written at Valabhi (Ballabhi) in the reign of Sridhara-sena (probably the king who reigned in Gujarat from about A.D. 530-544); its aim being to illustrate the rules of Sanskrit grammar, as well as the figures of poetry and rhetoric, by introducing examples of all possible forms and constructions, as well as of the Alankaras (see p. 508); it is divided into two great divisions, viz. *Shabda-lakshana,* 'illustration of grammar,' and *Kavya-lakshana,* 'illustration of poetry' together comprising twenty-two chapters; 10. the *Raghava-pandaviya,* on artificial poem by Kavi-raja, giving a narrative of the acts of both the descendants of Raghu and Pandu, in such language that it may be interpreted as a history of either one or the other family; 11. the *Amaru-shataka* or *Amaru-satak,* 'hundred verses of Amaru,' on erotic subjects, to which a mystical interpretation is given, especially as they are supposed to have been composed by the great philosopher Shankaracharya, when, according to a popular legend, he animated the dead body of king Amaru, his object being to become the husband of his widow, that he might argue on amatory subjects with the wife of a Brahman, named Mandana; 12. the *Gita-govinda* or 'Krishna in his character of Govinda (the Cow-finder or Herdsman) celebrated in song,' by Jaya-deva, a lyrical or erotic poem, thought to have been composed about the twelfth or thirteenth century of our era; it was written nominally to celebrate the loves of Krishna and the Gopis, especially of Krishna and Radha; but as the latter is supposed to typify the human soul, the whole poem is regarded as susceptible of a mystical interpretation.

Some of these poems, especially the Raghu-vansha, Kumara-sambhava, Megha-duta, and Ritu-samhara of Kalidasa (who, according to native authorities, lived a little before the commencement of the Christian era, but is now placed in the third century[1]), abound in truly poetical ideas, and display great fertility of imagination and power of description; but it cannot be denied that even in these works of the greatest of Indian poets there are occasional fanciful conceits, combined with a too studied and artificial elaboration of diction, and a constant tendency to what a European would consider an almost puerile love for alliteration and playing upon words (*wort-spiel*). Some of the other poems, such as the Kiratarjuniya, Shishupala-badha, Nalodaya, Naishadha, and Bhatti-kavya, are not wanting in occasional passages containing poetical feeling, striking imagery, and noble sentiment; but they are artificial to a degree quite opposed to European cannons of taste; the chief aim of the composers being to exhibit their artistic skill in bringing out the capabilities of the Sanskrit language, its ductility, its adaptation to every kind of style from the most diffuse to the most concise, its power of compounding words, its intricate grammatical structure, its complex system of metres, and the fertility of its resources in the employment of rhyme, rhythm, and alliteration. In fact, there is nothing in the whole range of Greek or Latin or any other literature that can be compared with these poems. Nearly every verse in them presents a separate puzzle — so that when one riddle is solved, little is gained towards the solution of the next — or exhibits rare words, unusual grammatical forms, and intricate compounds, as it were twisted together into complicated verbal knots, the unravelment of which can only be effected by the aid of a native commentary.

---

1. Professor Weber places him either in the third or sixth century.

Of course, in such cases the sense, and even the strict grammatical construction are sometimes sacrificed to the display of ingenuity in the bending and straining of words to suit a difficult metre or rhyme; and this art is studied as an end in itself, the ideas to be conveyed by the language employed being quite a secondary matter. To such an extreme is this carried, that whole verses are sometimes composed with the repetition of a single consonant[1], while in other cases a string of epithets is employed, each of which will apply to two quite distinct words in a sentence, and thus be capable of yielding different senses, suited to either word, according to the will of the solver of the verbal puzzle.

Again, stanzas, are sometimes composed so as to form fanciful shapes or figures, such as that of a lotus (*padama-bandha*); or so that the lines or parts of the lines composing the verses, whether read horizontally, diagonally, or perpendicularly, or in opposite directions, will yield significant and grammatical sentences of some kind, the sense being a matter of subordinate consideration. This is called the Fanciful-shape (*chitra*) ornament.

The formation of the octopetalous *Lotus-stanza* is described in Shitya-darpana x. p. 268. One of the commonest of these artificial stanzas, called *Sarvato-bhadra,* is a verse so contrived

---

1. English, in fear, would be quite unequal to such a task as the production of a verse like the following from the Kiratarjuniya (XV. 14) —

   Na nonanunno nunnono nana nananana nanu
   Nunno nunnonanunneno nanena nunnanunnanut

   Or the following from Magha (XIX. 114) —

   Dadadoduddaduddadi dadadodudadidadoh
   Duddadam dadade dudde dadadadadadodadadah

   Though in Latin we have something similar in Ennius, O *Tite tute Tati tibi tanta tyranne tulisti.* It must be admitted, however, that the celebrated nursery stanza beginning *Peter Piper picked a peck of pepper* is an effort in the same direction.

that the same syllables occur in each Pada of the verse, whether read backwards or forwards, or from the centre to each extremity, while all the Padas together read the same either downwards or upwards, whether the reader commence at the centre or each extremity. An example of this verse occurs in Kiratarjuniya XV. 25.

Still more complicated forms are occasionally found, as described by Dr. Yates in his edition of the Nalodaya.

Thus we have the *muraja-bandha,* a stanza shaped like a *drum;* the *khadga-bandha,* like a *sword;* the *dhanu-bandha,* like a *bow;* the *srag-bandha,* like a *garland;* the *vriksha-bandha,* like a *tree;* the *gomutrika,* like a *stream of cow's urine,* in uneven or undulating lines.

The art, too, of inventing and employing an almost endless variety of rhetorical figures called Alankaras, 'ornaments of speech,' for the sake of illustrating the various sentiments, feelings, and emotions depicted in dramatic and erotic poetry, is studied to a degree quite unknown in other languages, the most refined subtlety being shown in marking off minute gradations of simile, comparison, metaphor, &c. There are numerous works on this subject — which may be called a kind of *Ars poetica* or *rhetorica* — some of the best known of which are:

1. The *Sahitya-darpana,* 'mirror of composition,' by Vishvanatha-kavi-raja (said to have lived in Dacca about the fifteenth century), giving rules and canons for literary composition from simple sentences to epic poems and dramas, illustrated by examples from standard authors, especially dramatic (see p. 521, note). 2. The *Kavyadarsha,* 'mirror of poetry,' by Dandin. 3. The *Kavya-prakasa,* 'illumination of poetry,' by Mammata (the commentary to which, by Govinda, is called Kavya-pradipa). 4. The Dasha-rupaka, 'description of the ten kinds of dramatic composition called Rupakas,' by Dhananjaya (p. 520, note). 5.

The *Kavyalankara-vritti,* 'explanation of the ornaments of poetry,' by Vamana. 6. The *Sarasvati-kanthabharana,* 'necklace of the goddess of speech,' by Bhoja-deva. 7. The *Shringara-tilaka,* 'mark of love,' a work by Rudra-bhatta, describing and illustrating by examples the various emotions, feelings, and affections of lovers, male and female (*nayaka* and *nayika*), as exhibited in dramas, &c. 8. The *Rasa-manjari,* 'cluster of affections,' a wok on the Rasas[1], by Bhanu-datta, of much the same character as the last.

I add here a brief description of some of the commonest Alankaras. They are divided into two classes: A. *Shabdalankara,* those produced by the mere sound of words; B. *Arthalankara,* those arising from the meaning. The tenth Books of the Sahitya-darpana and Bhatti-kavya are devoted to the illustration of this subject.

Examples of A. are, 1. *Anuprasa,* a kind of alliteration or repetition of the same consonants, although the vowels may be dissimilar, e.g. *Sama-lingam angan.* 2. *Yamaka,* more perfect alliteration or repetition of vowels and consonants, e.g. *Sakalaih sakalaih.* Various kinds of Yamaka will be found in Bhatti-kavya X. 2-21; and in Kiratarjuniya XV. 52 there is a *Maha-yamaka.*

Examples of B. are, 1. *Upama,* comparison or simile (the subject of comparison is called *upameyam,* sometimes *prastuta, prakrita, prakranta, vastu, vishaya;* while the object to which it is compared is called *upamanam,* sometimes *a-prastuta, a-prakrita,* &c.). It is essential to an *Upama* that the *upameya,* the *upamana,* and common attribute (*samanya-dharma*) should be all expressed, and the complete subordination of the *upamana* to the *upameya* preserved; thus 'her face is like the moon in charmingness,'

---

1. There are ten Rasa or 'feeling,' enumerated as exemplified in dramatic composition: 1. *Sringara,* love; 2. *Vira,* heroism; 3. *Bibhatsa,* disgust; 4. *Raudra,* anger; 5. *Hasya,* mirth; 6. *Bhayanaka,* terror; 7. *Karuna,* pity; 8. *Adbhuta,* wonder; 9. *Shanta,* calmness; 10. *Vatsalya,* parental fondness. Some authors only allow 1-8.

where 'her face' is the *upameya;* 'moon,' the *upamana;* and 'charmingness,' the common quality. If the latter is omitted it is a *luptopama* (see Bhatti-kavya X. 30-35). 2. *Utpreksha,* a comparison in which the *upamana* is beginning to encroach on the upameya and to assume equal prominence. It is thirty-two-fold, under two classes, one called *vachya* when a word like *iva* is expressed, as 'her face shines as if it were a moon;' the other *pratiyamana* when *iva* is understood (cf. Bhatti-k. X. 44). 3. *Rupaka,* 'superimposition,' consisting in the superimposition (*aropa*) of a fancied form over the original subject, the *upameya* and *upamana* being connected as if possessing equal prominence, and their resemblance implied rather than expressed; thus 'moon-face,' 'her face is the moon' (Bhatti-k. X. 28). 4. *Atishayokti,* hyperbole, exaggeration, pleonasm (Bhatti-k. X. 42), in which the *upameya* is swallowed up in the *upamana,* as when 'her moon' is used for 'her face,' or 'her slender stem' for 'her figure.' 5. *Tulya-yogita,* in which the *upamana* or *upameya* is connected with the common quality, as 'a snow-white flower' (Bhatti-k. X. 61; Kumara-s. I. 2). 6. *Drishtanta,* exemplification by comparing or contrasting similar attributes (Magha II. 23). 7. *Dipaka,* 'illuminator,' i.e. using an illustrative expression, placed either in the beginning (*adi*), middle (*madhya*), or end (*anta*) of a verse to throw light on a description (Bhatti-k. X. 22-24; Kumara-s. II. 60). 8. *Vyaja-stuti,* artful or indirect eulogy in which praise is rather implied than directly expressed (Bhatti-k. X. 59). 9. *Slesha* (*lit.* coalescence), paronomasia, using distinct words which have identity of sound, the meaning being different; thus *vidhau* may mean 'in fate' if it comes from *vidhi,* or 'in the moon' if from *vidhu.* 10. *Vibhavana,* description of an effect produced without a cause (Kumara-sambhava I. 10.). 11. *Viseshokti,* description of a cause without its natural effect. 12. *Arthantara-nyasa,* transition to another matter, i.e. the turning aside to state a general truth as an illustration of a particular case (Bhatti-k. X. 36; Kiratarjuniya VII. 15). 13. *Arthapatti,* inference of one fact from another. 14. *Sara,* climax. 15. *Karana-mala,* series of causes. 16. *Vyatireka,* contrast or dissimilitude. 17. *Akshepa,* hint. 18. *Sahokti,* a hyperbolical description of simultaneous action connected by the word *saha.* 19. *Parikara,* employment of a number of significant epithets. 20. *Samsrishti,* conjunction, i.e. the employment of more than one figure in the same verse independently of each other (Bhatti-k. X. 70). When there is a commixture or combination of more than one figure, it is called *Shankara;* especially when they are combined as principal and subordinates (*angangi-bhava*).

To give examples from all the artificial poems enumerated (pp. 502, 503) would be wearisome. It will be sufficient to select a passage from Kalidasa's Raghu-vansha, and a few of the moral sentiments scattered through the Kiratarjuniya and the Shishupala-badha. I first translate Raghu-vansha X. 16-33. The inferior gods are supposed to be addressing Vishnu as the Supreme Being (cf. a similar address in Kumara-sambhava II):

Hail to thee, mighty lord, the world's creator,
Supporter and destroyer, three in one —
One in thy essence, tripartite in action[1]!
E'en as heaven's water — one in savour — gains
From different receptacles on earth
Diversity of flavours, so dost thou,
Unchangeable in essence, manifest
Changes of state in diverse qualities[2].
Unmeasured and immeasurable, yet
Thou measurest the world; desireless, yet
Fulfilling all desire; unconquered and
A conqueror; unmanifested, yet
A manifester; uniformly one,
Yet ever multiform from various motives.
Thy manifold conditions are compared
To those of clearest crystal, which reflects

---

1. See p. 359.
2. See p. 359, note 1.

Varieties of hue from diverse objects.
Though ever present in the heart, thou art
Held to be infinitely distant; free
From passion, yet austere in self-restraint;
Full of all pity, yet thyself untouched
By misery; the ever ancient one,
Yet never growing ancient; knowing, all,
Yet never known; unborn, yet giving birth
To all; all-ruling, yet thyself unruled;
One in thyself, yet many in thy aspects.
Men hymn thy praises in seven songs; and say
Thou liest sleeping on the earth's seven seas[1];
Thy face is seven-flamed fire, and thou thyself
The sole asylum of the world's seven spheres[2].
From the four mouths of thee, portrayed as four-faced,
Proceeds the knowledge of life's fourfold objects,
Time's quadruple divisions through four ages[5],
Man's fourfold distribution into castes.
On thee abiding in man's heart, the source
Of light, with minds and senses all subdued,
The pious meditate in hope of bliss.
Of thee the mystic nature who can fathom?
Unborn, yet taking birth; from action free,
Yet active to destroy thy demon-foes;
Seeming asleep, yet ever vigilant;
Possessing senses fitted for enjoyment,
Yet in all points restrained; protecting all
Thy creatures, yet apparently indifferent.
The ways which lead to everlasting bliss,
Though variously distinguished in the Veda,
Converge to thee alone; e'en as the streams
Of Ganga's waters to their ocean home.
Thou art the only way, the only refuge

---

1. See p. 469.   2. See p. 480.   3. See p. 368, note 3.

Of all whose hearts are fixed on thee, whose acts
Are centred in thee, and whose worldly longings,
Checked and suppressed, have passed away for ever.
Thy greatness is displayed before our eyes
In this thy world and these thy mighty works;
Yet through the Veda and by inference
Alone can thy existence be established[1].
How then can we, the finite, tell thy essence?
Since merely by the thought of thee thy creatures
Are purified, much more have other acts
Which have thee for their object, full reward.
As jewels lying deep in ocean's bed,
And fires deep hidden in the solar orb
Are far beyond the reach of mortals, so thy deeds
Exceed our praises. Naught is unattained
By thee, and naught is unattainable;
Yet love, and love alone, for these thy worlds
Moves thee to act, leads to thy incarnations[2].
That in the celebration of thy praises
Our voices are restrained, deign to ascribe
This to our limited capacities,
Not to the limitation of thy glory.

I next translate some moral sentiments and wise sayings
from the Kiratarjuniya of Bharavi.

Those who wish well towards their friends disdain
To please them by fair words which are not true (I.2).
Better to have a great man for one's foe
Than court association with the low (I.8).
As drops of bitter medicine, though minute,
May have a salutary force, so words
Though few and painful, uttered seasonably,

---

1. This is an allusion to the three Pramanas of the Sankhya, viz.
   Pratyaksha, Anumana, and Apta-vachana or Shabda; see p. 99.
2. See p. 358.

May rouse the prostrate energies of those
Who meet misfortune with despondency (II. 4).
Do nothing rashly, want of circumspection
Is the chief cause of failure and disaster.
Fortune, wise lover of the wise, selects
Him for her lord who ere he acts, reflects (II. 30).
He who with patience and deliberation
Prepares the ground whence issue all his actions,
Obtains, like those who water seeds and roots,
An ample harvest of autumnal fruits (II. 31).
The body's truest ornament consists
In knowledge of the truth; of sacred knowledge
The best embellishment is self-control;
Of self-control the garniture is courage,
Courage is best embellished by success (II. 32).
In matters difficult and dark, concealed
By doubt and disagreement of opinion,
The Veda, handed down by holy men,
Explained with clearness, and well put in practice,
Like a bright lamp throws light upon the way,
Guiding the prudent lest they go astray (II. 33).
To those who travel on the rugged road
Trodden by virtuous and high-minded men,
A fall, if pre-ordained by destiny,
Becomes equivalent to exaltation;
Such falls cause neither evil nor distress,
The wise make failures equal to success (II. 34).
Would'st thou be eminent, all passion shun,
Drive wrath away by wisdom; e'en the sun
Ascends not to display his fullest light
Till he has chased away the mists of night (II. 36).
That lord of earth, who equable in mind,
Is on occasion lenient and kind,
Then acts in season with severity,
Rules like the sun by his own majesty (II. 38).

The man who every sacred science knows,
Yet has not strength to keep in cheek the foes
That rise within him, mars his Fortune's fame
And brings her by his feebleness to shame (II. 41).
Be patient if thou would'st thy ends accomplish,
For like to patience is there no appliance
Effective of success, producing surely
Abundant fruit of actions, never damped
By failure, conquering impediments (II. 43).
If the constituent members of a state
Be in disorder, then a trifling war
May cause a ruler's ruin, just as fire
Caused by the friction of the dried-up branches
Of one small tree, may devastate a mountain (II. 51).
Success is like a lovely woman, wooed
By many men, but folded in the arms
Of him alone who free from over-zeal
Firmly persists and calmly perseveres (III. 40).
The drops upon a lovely woman's face
Appear like pearls; no marks avail to mar,
But rather to her beauty add a grace (VII. 5).
The noble-minded dedicate themselves
To the promotion of the happiness
Of others — e'en of those who injure them.
True happiness consists in making happy (VII. 13, 28).
Let not a little fault in him who does
An act of kindness, diminish aught its value (VII. 15).
If intercourse with noble-minded men,
Though short and accidental, leads to profit,
How great the benefit of constant friendship! (VII. 27.)
As persons though fatigued forbear to seek
The shelter of the fragrant sandal-trees,
If deadly serpents lurk beneath their roots,
So must the intercourse of e'en the virtuous,
If vicious men surround them, be avoided (VII. 29).
A woman will not throw away a garland,

Though soiled and dirty, which her lover gave;
Not in the object lies a present's worth,
But in the love which it was meant to mark (VIII. 37).
To one who pines in solitude apart
From those he loves, even the moon's cool rays
Appear unbearable; for in affliction
Even a pleasant object heightens grief (IX. 30).
Wine is averse from secrecy; it has
A power to bring to light what is concealed —
The hidden qualities both good and bad (IX. 68).
True love is ever on the watch, and sees
Risks even in its loved one's happiness (IX. 70).
Youth's glories are as transient as the shadow
Of an autumnal cloud; and sensual joys,
Though pleasant at the moment, end in pain (XI. 12).
Soon as a man is born, an adversary
Confronts him, Death the Ender; ceaseless troubles
Begin; his place of birth — the world —
Must one day be abandoned; hence the wise
Seek the full bliss of freedom from existence (XI. 13).
Riches and pleasure are the root of evil;
Hold them not dear, encourage not their growth;
They are aggressors hard to be subdued,
Destroyers of all knowledge and of truth (XI. 20).
To one united with a much-loved object
The empty turns to fulness; evil fortune
Brings festive joys; and disappointment, gain;
But not to him who lives in separation —
He in the midst of friends feels solitary;
The pleasant causes grief; and life itself,
Before so dear, pains like a piercing shaft (XI. 27, 28).
The enemies which rise within the body,
Hard to be overcome — thy evil passions —
Should manfully be fought; who conquers these
Is equal to the conqueror of worlds (XI. 32).
Why give thyself to pleasure? this day's joys

Are thought upon tomorrow, then like dreams
They pass away and are for ever lost (XI. 34).
Who trusts the passions finds them base deceivers;
Acting like friends, they are his bitterest foes;
Causing delight, they do him great unkindness;
Hard to be shaken off, they yet desert him (XI. 35).
The clear and quiet minds of prudent men,
Though ruffled on the surface and disturbed
Like the deep waters of the ocean, fear
To pass the limits of self-mastery (XI. 54).
The friendship of the bad is like the shade
Of some precipitous bank with crumbling sides,
Which falling buries him who sits beneath (XI. 55).
The natural hostility of beasts
Is laid aside when flying from pursuers;
So also when calamities impend
The enmity of rivals has an end (XII. 46).

The following are from Book II. of the Shishupala-badha
of Magha (I translate nearly literally):

Alliance should be formed with friendly foes,
Not with unfriendly friends; of friend and foe
The test is benefit and injury (37) [1].
He who excites the wrath of foes and then
Sits down inactively, is like a man
Who kindles withered grass and then lies near
While a strong wind is blowing from beyond (42).
He who by virtue of his rank, his actions,
And qualities, effect no useful purpose,
Is like a chance-invented word; his birth
Is useless, for he merely bears a name (47).
A man of feeble character resembles
A reed that bends with every gust of wind (50).

---

1. This verse occurs also in Hitopadesha IV. 16.

Soft words, intended to alleviate,
Often foment the wrath of one enraged,
Like drops of water poured on burning butter (55).
A rambling speech whose meaning is confused,
Though long, is spoken easily; not so
A clear, connected, logical discourse (73).
Two only sources of success are known —
Wisdom and effort; make them both thine own
If thou would'st rise and haply gain a throne (76).
Science is like a couch to sapient men;
Reclining there, they never feel fatigue (77).
A subtle-witted man is like an arrow,
Which rending little surface, enters deeply;
But they whose minds are dull, resemble stones,
Dashing with clumsy force, but never piercing (78).
The foolish undertake a trifling act
And soon desist, discouraged; wiser men
Engage in mighty works and persevere (79).
The undertaking of a careless man
Succeeds not, though he use the right expedients;
A clever hunter, though well placed in ambush,
Kills not his quarry if he fall asleep (80).
A monarch's weapon is his intellect;
His minister and servants are his limbs;
Close secresy of counsel is his armour;
Spies are his eyes; ambassadors, his mouth (82).
That energy which veils itself in mildness
Is most effective of its object; so
The lamp that burns most brightly owes its force
To oil drawn upwards by a hidden wick (85).
Wise men rest not on destiny alone,
Nor yet on manly effort, but on both (86).
Weak persons gain their object when allied
With strong associates; the rivulet
Reaches the ocean by the river's aid (100).
A good man's intellect is piercing, yet

Inflicts, no wound; his action are deliberate,
Yet bold; his heart is warm, but never burns;
His speech is eloquent, yet ever true (109).

The Dramas

If we bear in mind that the nations of modern Europe can
scarcely be said to have possessed a dramatic literature before
the fifteenth century of the present era, the antiquity of the
extant Hindu plays, some of which may be traced back to about
the first or second century of our era, will of itself appear a
remarkable circumstance. But to the age of these dramas must
be added their undoubted literary value as repositories of much
true poetry, though of an Oriental type. They are also valuable
as representing the early condition of Hindu society, and as
serving to illustrate some of its present peculiarities; for
notwithstanding the increasing intercourse with Europe, India,
like other Eastern countries, is slow in delivering itself from
subjection to the stereotyped laws of tradition which appear
to be stamped on its manners and social practices.

In all likelihood the germ of the dramatic representations
of the Hindu, as of the Greeks, is to be sought for in public
exhibitions of dancing, which consisted at first of simple
movements of the body, executed in harmony with singing
and music. Indeed, the root *nat*, and the nouns *natya* and
nataka, which are now applied to dramatic acting, are probably
mere corruptions of *nrit*, 'to dance,' *nritya*, 'dancing,' and
nartaka, 'a dancer.' Of this dancing various styles were gradually
invented, such as the *Lasya* and *Tandava*[1], to express different
actions or various sentiments and emotions.

---

1. The *Tandava* is a boisterous dance regarded as the peculiar invention
   of Shiva; the *Lasya* is said to have been invented by Parvati; the
   Rasamandala is the circular dance of Krishna.

Very soon dancing was extended to include pantomimic gesticulations accompanied with more elaborate musical performances, and these gesticulations were aided by occasional exclamations between the intervals of singing. Finally, natural language took the place of music and singing, while gesticulation became merely subservient to emphasis in dramatic dialogue.

When we come to actual dramatic writing we are obliged to confess that its origin, like that of epic poetry, and of nearly every department of Sanskrit composition, is lost in remote antiquity. There is evidence that plays were acted in India as early as the reign of Ashoka, in the third century B.C. At that period intercourse between India and Greece had certainly commenced, but it does not appear that the Hindus borrowed either the matter or form of any of their dramas from the Greeks. (See Lassen's Ind. Alt. II. 507.)

Semitic nations have never inclined towards theatrical representations. The book of Job is a kind of dramatic dialogue. The same may be said of parts of the Song of Solomon, and there is occasional dialogue in the Makamat of *al Hariri* and Thousand and One Nights; but neither the Hebrews nor Arabs seem to have carried dramatic ideas beyond this point. Among the Aryans, on the other hand, as well as among the Chinese, the drama appears to have arisen naturally. At least, its independent origin in Greece and India — both of which countries also gave birth independently to epic poetry, grammar, philosophy, and logic — can scarcely be called in question, however probable it may be that an interchange of ideas took place in later times. In fact, the Hindu drama, while it has certainly much in common with the representations of other nations, has quite a distinctive character of its own which invests it with great interest.

At the same time the English reader, when told that the author of the earliest Hindu drama which has come down to

us — the *Mrich-chhakatika* or 'Clay-cart' — probably lived
in the first or second century of the Christian era, will be
inclined to wonder at the analogies it offers to our own
dramatic compositions of about fifteen centuries later. The
dexterity with which the plot is arranged, the ingenuity with
which the incidents are connected, the skill with which the
characters are delineated and contrasted, the boldness and
felicity of the diction are scarcely unworthy of our own great
dramatists. Nor does the parallel fail in the management of
the stage-business, in minute directions to the actors and
various scenic artifices. The asides and aparts, the exits and
the entrances, the manner, attitude and gait of the speakers,
their tones of voice, tears, smiles and laughter are as regularly
indicated as in a modern drama.

A great number of other ancient plays besides 'the Clay-
cart' are extant, and many of the most celebrated have been
printed. To classify these Hindu dramas according to European
ideas, or even to arrange them under the general heads of
tragedy and comedy, is impossible. Indeed, if a calamitous
conclusion be necessary to constitute a tragedy, Hindu plays
are never tragedies[1]. They are rather mixed representations,
in which happiness and misery, good and evil, right and
wrong, justice and injustice are allowed to blend in confusion
until the end of the drama. In the last act harmony is restored,
tranquillity succeeds to agitation, and the minds of the
spectators, no longer perplexed by the ascendency of evil are
soothed and purified by the moral lesson deducible from the
plot, or led to acquiesce in the inevitable results of Adrishta
(see p. 74). Such dramatic conceptions are, in truth, exactly
what might be expected to prevail among a people who look
upon no occurrence in human life as really tragic, but regard

---

1. A rule states that the killing of a hero is not to be hinted at. This
   does not always hold good. No one, however, is killed on the stage.

evil and suffering of all kinds as simply the unavoidable consequences of acts done by each soul, of its own free will, in former bodies.

Nevertheless, to invest the subject of dramatic composition with dignity, a great sage is, as usual (compare p. 414), supposed to be its inventor. He is called Bharat, and is regarded as the author of a system of music, as well as of an Alankara-shastra containing Sutras or rules. His work is constantly quoted as the original authority for dramatic composition[1]. On Bharata's Sutras followed various treatises which laid down minute precepts and regulations for the construction and conduct of plays, and subjected dramatic writing to the most refined and artificial rules of poetical and rhetorical style.

Beside the *Dasha-rupaka, Kavya-prakasha, Kavyadarsha,* and *Sahitya-darpana,* &c., mentioned at pp. 507, 508, others are named which treat of dramatic composition as well as of ornaments (*alankara*) and figures of rhetoric. For example: the *Kavyalankara-vritti,* by Vamana; the *Alankara-sarvasva,* by Bhama; the *Alankara-kaustubha,* by Kavi Karana-purka; the *Kuvalayananda,* by Apyaya [or Apya]-dikshita; the *Chandraloka,* by Jaya-deva; and a work on music, singing, and dancing, called the *Sangita-ratnakara,* by Sarngadeva, thought by Wilson to have been written between the twelfth and thirteenth centuries.

These treatises classify Sanskrit plays very elaborately under various subdivisions; and the Sahitya-darpana — a favourite authority[2] — divides them into two great classes, viz. 1.

---

1. Dr. Fitz-Edward Hall has a MS. of the work in 36 Books, of which 18, 19, 20, and 34 were printed at the end of his Dasha-rupa. Dr. Heymann is now editing the whole work.
2. The Sahitya-darpana is in ten sections, treating of the nature and divisions of poetry, the various powers of a word, varieties of style, ornaments of style and blemishes (*dosha*). I have here consulted the late Dr. Ballantyne's translation of part of it, published at Benares.

Rupaka, 'principal dramas,' of which there are ten species; 2. *Upa-rupaka,* 'minor or inferior dramas,' of which eighteen are enumerated. The trouble taken to invent titles for every variety of Hindu play, according to far more subtle shades of distinction than those denoted by our drama, melodrama, comedy, farce and ballet, proves that dramatic composition has been more elaborately cultivated in India than in European countries. The ten species of *Rupaka* are as follow:

1. The *Nataka,* or 'principal play,' should consist of from five to ten acts (*anka*), and should have a celebrated story (such as the history of Rama) for its plot (*vastu*). It should represent heroic or godlike characters, and good deeds; should be written in an elaborate style, and be full of noble sentiments. Moreover, it should contain all the five 'joints' or 'junctures' (*sandhi*)[1] of the plot; the four kinds of action (*vritti*); the sixty-four members (*anga*) or peculiar properties; and the thirty-six distinctive marks (*lakshana*). The hero or leading character (*nayaka*) should be of the kind described as high-spirited but firm[2], being either a royal sage of high family (as Dushyanta in the Sakuntala), or a god (as Krishna), or a demigod (*divyadivya*), who, though a god (like Rama-chandra), thinks himself a man (*narabhimani,* see note 3, p. 400). The principal sentiment or flavour (*rasa,* see p. 508, note) should be either the erotic (*sringara*) or heroic (*vira*), and in the conclusion (*nirvahana*) the marvellous (*adbhuta*). It should be composed like the end of a cow's tail (*go-puchchhagra*), i.e. so that each of the acts is gradually made shorter. If it also

---

1. These five junctures are, 1. the *mukha* or 'opening;' 2. the *prati-mukha* or 'first development of the germ (*vija*) of the plot;' 3. the *garbha* or 'actual development and growth of the germ;' 4. the *vimarsha* or 'some hindrance to its progress;' 5. the nirvahana or *upa-samhriti,* 'conclusion.'
2. There are four kinds of heroes: 1. high-spirited but firm (*dhirodatta*); 2. firm and haughty (*dhiroddhata*); 3. gay and firm (*dhira-lalita*); 4. firm and mild (*dhira-prasanta*).

contain the four *Pataka-sthanaka* or 'striking points,' and the number of its acts (*anka*) be ten, it is entitled to be called a *Maha-nataka*. An example of the *Nataka* is the Shakuntala, and of the *Maha-nataka* is the Bala-ramayana (see p. 547). 2. The *Prakarana* should resemble the Nataka in the number of its acts as well as in other respects; but the plot must be founded on some mundane or human story, invented by the poet, and have love for its principal sentiment, the hero or leading character being either a Brahman (as in the Mrich-chakatika), or a minister (as in the Malati-madhava), or a merchant (as in the Pushpa-bhushita), of the description called firm and mild (*dhira-prashanta*), while the heroine (*nayika*) is sometimes a woman of good family, sometimes a courtesan, or both. 3. The *Bhana*, in one act, should consist of a variety of incidents, not progressively developed, the plot being invented (see note 2, p. 521). An example is the *Lila-madhukara*. 4. The *Vyayoga*, in one act, should have a well-known story for its plot , and few females in its *dramatis personae*. Its hero should be some celebrated personage of the class called firm and haughty (*virod-dhata*). Its principal sentiments or flavours (*rasa*, see p. 508, note) should be the comic (*hasya*), the erotic (*sringara*), and the unimpassioned (*shanta*). 5. The *Samavakara*, in four acts, in which a great variety of subjects are mixed together (*samavakiryante*); it dramatizes a well-known story, relating to gods and demons. An example is the *Samudra-mathana*, 'Churning of the ocean' (described in Bharata's Shastra IV). 6. The *Dima*, in four acts, founded on some celebrated story; its principal sentiment should be the terrible (*raudra*); it should have sixteen heroes (a god, a Yaksha, a Rakshasa, a serpent, goblin, &c.). An example is the *Tripura-daha*, 'conflagration of Tripura' (described in Bharata's Shastra IV). 7. The *Iha-mriga*, in four acts, founded on a mixed story (*misra-vritta*), partly popular, and partly invented; the hero and rival hero (*prati-nayaka*) should be either a mortal or a god. According to some it should have six heroes. It derives its name from this, that the hero seeks (*ihate*) a divine female, who is as unattainable as a deer (*mriga*). 8. The *Anka* or *Utsrishtikanka*, in one act, should have ordinary men (*prakrita-narah*) for its heroes; its principal sentiment should be the pathetic (*karuna*), and its form (*srishti*) should transgress (*utkranta*) the usual rules. An example is the *Sarmishtha-yayati*. 9. The *Vithi*, in one act, is so called because it forms a kind of garland (*vithi*) of various sentiments, and is supposed to contain thirteen members (*anga*) or peculiar properties. An example is the *Malavika*. 10. The *Prahasana*, properly in one act, is a sort of farce representing reprobate characters (*nindya*), and the story is invented by the poet, the principal sentiment being the comic (*hasya*); it may be either pure (*suddha*), of which the Kandarpa-keli, 'love-sports,' is an example; or mixed (*sankirna*), like the Dhurta-charita, 'adventures of a rogue;' or it may represent characters transformed (*vikrita*) by various disguises.

The eighteen Upa-rupakas need not be so fully described. Their names are as follow:

1. The *Natika*, which is of two kinds — *Natika* pure, and *Prakaranika* differing little from the Nataka and Prakarana. The Ratnavali is an example of the Natika. 2. The *Trotaka*, in five seven, eight, or nine acts; the plot should be founded on the story of a demigod, and the Vidushaka or 'jesting Brahman' should be introduced into every act. An example is the Vikramorvashi. 3. The *Goshti*. 4. The *Sattaka*. 5. The *Natyarasaka*. 6. The *Prasthana*. 7. The *Ullapya*. 8. The *Kavya*. 9. The *Prenkhana*. 10. The *Rasaka*. 11. The *Samlapaka*. 12. The *Shri-gadita*, in one act, dedicated chiefly to the goddess Shri. 13. The *Silpaka*. 14. The *Vilasika*. 15. The *Durmallika*. 16. The *Prakarani*. 17. The *Hallisa*, chiefly consisting in music and singing. 18. The *Bhanika*.

As I have elsewhere stated (see Introduction to translation of the Shakuntala), it is probably that in India, as in Greece, scenic entertainments took place at religious festivals, and especially at the Spring festival (*Vasantotsava*, corresponding to the present Holi) in the month Phalguna. Kalidasa's

Shakuntala seems to have been acted at the commencement of the summer season — a period sacred to Kama-deva, the Indian god of love. We are told that it was enacted before an audience 'consisting chiefly of men of education and discernment.' As the greater part of every play was written in Sanskrit, which was certainly not the vernacular of the country at the time when the dramas were performed, few spectators could have been present who were not of the learned classes (see Introduction to this volume, p. xxxvi). This circumstance is in accordance with the constitution of Hindu society, whereby the productions of literature, as well as the offices of state, were reserved for the privileged castes. The following is a brief account of the construction of an ordinary Hindu Nataka:

Every play with a prologue (*prastavana*), or, to speak more correctly, an introduction, designed to prepare the way for the entrance of the *dramatis personae*. The prologue commences with a benediction (*nandi*) or prayer[1] (pronounced by a Brahman, or if the stage-manager happens to be a Brahman, by the manager himself), in which the poet invokes the favour of his favourite deity in behalf of the audience. The blessing is generally followed by a dialogue between the manager and one or two of the actors, in which an account is given of the author of the drama, a complimentary tribute is paid to the critical acumen of the spectators, and such a reference is made to past occurrences or present circumstances as may be necessary for the elucidation of the plot. At the conclusion of the prologue, the manager, by some abrupt exclamation, adroitly introduces one of the dramatic personages, and the real performance commences. The play

---

1. The fact that scarcely a single work in Sanskrit literature is commenced without a prayer to some god, is, as Professor Banerjea has remarked, a testimony to the universal sentiment of piety animating the Hindu race.

being thus opened, is carried forward in scenes and acts; each scene being marked by the entrance of one character and the exit of another. The *dramatis personae* are divided into three classes — the inferior characters (*nicha*), who are said to speak Prakrit in a monotonous unaccented tone (*anudattoktya*); the middling (madhyama); and the superior (*pradhana*). These latter are to speak Sanskrit with accent and expression (*udattoktya*). The commencement of a new act, like that of the whole piece, is often marked by an introductory monologue or dialogue spoken by one or more of the *dramatis personae,* and called *Vishkambha* or *Praveshaka.* In this scene allusion is made to events supposed to have occurred in the interval of the acts, and the audience is prepared to take up the thread of the story, which is then skilfully carried on to the concluding scene. The piece closes, as it began, with a prayer for national prosperity, addressed to the favourite deity, and spoken by one of the principal personages of the drama.

Although, in the conduct of the plot, and the delineation of character, Hindu dramatists show considerable skill, yet in the plot itself, or, in the story on which it is founded, they rarely evince much fertility of invention. The narrative of Rama's adventures and other well-known fictions of Hindu mythology are constantly repeated. Love, too, according to Hindu notions, is the subject of most of their dramas. The hero and heroine are generally smitten with attachment for each other at first sight, and that, too, in no very interesting manner. By way of relief, however, an element of life is introduced in the character of the *Vidushaka* or 'jester,' who is the constant companion of the hero; and in the young maidens, who are the confidential friends of the heroine, and soon become possessed of her secret. By a curious regulation, the jester is always a Brahman; yet his business is to excite mirth by being ridiculous in person, age, and attire. Strictly he should be represented as grey-haired, hump-backed, lame, and ugly. He is a species of buffoon, who is allowed full liberty of speech, being himself a universal butt. His attempts at wit, which are rarely very successful, and his allusions to the pleasures of the table, of which he is a confessed votary, are absurdly contrasted with the sententious solemnity of the despairing hero, crossed in the prosecution of his love-suit. On the other hand, the shrewdness of the heroine's confidantes never seem to fail them under the most trying circumstances; while their sly jokes and innuendos, their love of fun, their girlish sympathy with the progress of the love-affair, their warm affection for their friend, heighten the interest of the plot, and contribute to vary its monotony.

Let me now introduce a few remarks on certain well-known plays, some of which have been already mentioned. And first with regard to the earliest extant Sanskrit drama — the *Mrich-chakatika* or 'Clay-cart.'

This was attributed (probably out of mere flattery) to a royal author, king Shudraka, who is said to have reigned in the first or second century B.C. Its real author is unknown, and its exact date is, of course, uncertain. According to Professor Weber, so much at least may be affirmed, 'that it was composed at a time in which Buddhism was flourishing in full vigour.' Some, indeed, may be inclined to infer from the fact of its describing a *Shramana* or Bhddhist ascetic as appointed to the head of the Viharas or monasteries, that one hundred years after Christ is too early an epoch to allow for the possibility of representing Buddhism as occupying such a position in India. At any rate, the date of this drama ought not be placed before the first century of our era[1]. The play is in ten acts, and though too long and tedious to suit European theatrical ideas, has nevertheless considerable dramatic merit, the plot being ingeniously developed, and the interest well sustained by a rapid succession of stirring incidents and

---

1. Professor Lassen assigns it to about 150 after Christ.

picturesquely diversified scenes of every-day life. In fact, its pictures of domestic manners, and description of the natural intercourse of ordinary men and women, followed by the usual train of social evils, make it more interesting than other Sanskrit dramas, which, as a rule, introduce too much of the supernatural, and abound in overwrought poetical fancies unsuited to occidental minds.

The hero or leading character (*nayaka*) of the 'Clay-cart' is Charu-datta, a virtuous Brahman, who by his extreme generosity has reduced himself to poverty. The heroine (*nayika*) is Vasanta-sena, a beautiful and wealthy lady, who although, according to the strictest standard of morality, not irreproachable in character, might still be described as conforming to the Hindu conception of a high-minded liberal woman. Moreover, her naturally virtuous disposition becomes strictly so from the moment of her first acquaintance with Charu-datta. Her affections are then concentrated upon him, and she spurns the king's brother-in-law, named Samsthanaka, a vicious dissipated man, whose character is well depicted in striking contrast to that of Caru-data. As the one is a pattern of generosity, so the other stands out in bold relief as a typical embodiment of he lowest forms of depravity. They are both probably drawn to the life, but the latter delineation is the most remarkable as an evidence of the corruption of Oriental courts in ancient times, when it was often possible for a man, more degraded than a brute, to prosecute with impunity the selfish gratification of the worst passions under the shelter of high rank[1].

At the commencement of the second act, a gambler is introduced running away from the keeper of a gaming-house,

---

1. That this sort of personage was commonly found at the courts of Eastern kings is evident from the fact of his forming, under the name of the 'Shkara,' one of the stock characters in the *dramatis personae* of Indian plays. He is a king's brother-in-law through one of his inferior wives, and is required by theatrical rules to be represented as foolish, frivolous, vicious, selfish, proud, and cruel.

named Mathura, and from another gambler. I here translate the scene[1]:

1st *Gambler.* The master of the tables and the gamester are at my heels, how can I escape them? Here is an empty temple, I will enter it walking backwards, and pretend to be its idol.

Mathura. Ho! there! stop thief! a gambler has lost ten Suvarnas, and is running off without paying — Stop him! stop him!

2nd *Gambler.* He has run as far as this point; but here the track is lost.

Math. Ah! I see, the footsteps are reversed; the rogue has walked backwards into this temple which has no image in it.

(They enter, and make signs to each other on discovering the object of their search, standing motionless on a pedestal.).

2nd *Gambler.* Is this a wooden image, I wonder?

Math. No, no, it must be made of stone, I think. (So saying, they shake and pinch him). Never mind, sit we down here and play out our game. (They commence playing.)

1st *Gamber.* (Still acting the image, but looking on, and with difficulty restraining his wish to join in the game — Aside.) The rattling of dice is as tantalizing to a penniless man as the sound of drums to a dethroned monarch; verily it is sweet as the note of a nightingale.

2nd *Gambler.* The throw is mine! the throw is mine!

Math. No, no, it is mine, I say.

1st *Gambler.* (Forgetting himself and jumping off the pedestal) No, I tell you, it is mine.

2nd *Gambler.* We've caught him.

Math. Yes, rascal! you're caught at last. Hand over the Suvarnas.

1st *Gamdbler.* Worthy sir, I'll pay them in good time.

---

1. I have made us to Stenzler's excellent edition, and also consulted Professor H.H. Wilson's free translation. I hope to give an epitome of the whole play in Second Series of Lectures.

Math. Hand them over this very minute, I say. (They beat him).

1st *Gambler.* (Aside to 2nd Gambler.) I'll pay you half, if you will forgive me the rest.

2nd *Gambler.* Agreed.

1st *Gambler.* (Aside to Mathura.) I'll give you security for half if you will let me off the other half.

Math. Agreed.

1st *Gambler.* Then, good morning to you, sirs, I'm off.

Math. Hallo! stop there, where are you going so fast? Hand over the money.

1st *Gambler.* See here, my good sirs; one has taken security for half, and the other has let me off the other half. Isn't it clear I have nothing to pay?

Math. No, no, my fine fellow; my name is Mathura, and I'm not such a fool as you take me for. Don't suppose I'm going to be cheated out of my ten Suvarnas in this way; hand them over, you scoundrel.

Upon that they set to work beating the unfortunate gambler, whose cries for help bring another gamester, who happens to be passing, to his rescue. A general scuffle now takes place, and in the midst of the confusion the first gambler escapes. In his flight he comes to the house of Vasanta-sena, and, finding the door open, rushes in. Vasanta-sena inquires who he is, and what he wants. He then recites his story, and makes known to her that he was once in the service of Charu-datta, who discharged him on account of reduced circumstances. Hence he had been driven to seek a livelihood by gambling. The mention of Charu-datta at once secures Vasanta-sena's aid, and the pursuers having now tracked their fugitive to the door of her house, she sends them out a jewelled bracelet, which satisfies their demands, and they retire. The gambler expresses the deepest gratitude, hopes in return to be of use to Vasanta-sena, and announces his intention of abandoning his disreputable habits, and becoming a Buddhist mendicant.

The following is a soliloquy of which he delivers himself after he has settled down into an ascetical life (Act VIII). I translate somewhat freely:

Hear me, ye foolish, I implore.
Make sanctity your only store;
Be satisfied with meagre fare;
Of greed and gluttony beware;
Shun slumber, practise lucubration,
Sound the deep gong of meditation.
Restrain you appetites with zeal,
Let not these thieves your merit steal;
Be ever storing it anew,
And keep eternity in view.
Live ever thus like me austerely,
And be the home of Virtue merely.
Kill your five senses, murder then
Women and all immoral men.
Whoe'er has slain these evils seven
Has saved himself, and goes to heaven.
Nor think by shaven face and head
To prove your appetites are dead;
Who shears his head and not his heart
Is an ascetic but in part;
But he whose heart is closely lopped,
Has also head and visage cropped.

In the end, Charu-datta and Vasanta-sena are happily married, but not till the Buddhist mendicant has saved the life of both.

I pass on to the greatest of all Indian dramatists, *Kalidasa*. He is represented by some native authorities (though on insufficient grounds) to have lived in the time of a celebrated king, Vikramaditya, whose reign forms the starting-point of the Hindu era called *Samvat*, beginning fifty-seven years B.C. This king had his capital in Ujjayini (Oujein); he was a great patron of literature, and Kalidasa is described as one of the

nine illustrious men called the nine jewels of his court. It is,
however, more probable that Kalidasa lived and composed his
works about the commencement of the third century[1]. His
well-known poems have already been noticed at pp. 502-
504[2]. He only wrote three plays — the *Shakuntala,* the
Vikramorvashi, and the *Malavikagnimitra.* Of these, the
Shakuntala, in seven acts, is by far the most celebrated and
popular. I have endeavoured in my translation of this beautiful
drama (fourth edition, published by W.H. Alllen & Co.)[3] to

---

1. Professor Lassen places Kalidasa about the year 250 after Christ. Dr.
   Bhau Daji assigns him to the reign of a Vikramaditya in the sixth
   century. Kalidasa probably lived at Ujjayini, as he describes it with
   much feeling in the Megha-duta, and to this circumstance may probably
   be traced his supposed connection with the great Vikramaditya.
2. Besides these, he is said to have written a poem called the *Setu-kavya*
   or *Setu-bandha,* describing the building of Rama's bridge, and written
   for Pravara-sena, king of Kashmir. A work on metres, called the
   Shrutha-botha, is also attributed to him. This last may be by another
   Kalidasa. No doubt many works were ascribed to the greatest Indian
   poet, as to the greatest Indian philosopher, Shankaracarya, which they
   neither of them wrote.
3. As every Orientalist knows, Sir. W. Jones was the first to translate the
   Shakuntala, but he had only access to the Bengal (Bengali) recension.
   Two other recensions exist, one in the North-west (commonly called
   the Devanagari) and one in the South of India. The last is the shortest,
   and the Bengal version is the longest. The Devanagari recension,
   translated by me into English, is generally considered the purest.
   Nevertheless Dr. R. Pischel in a learned dissertation maintains that
   the palm belongs to the Bengali, and it must be admitted that in some
   cases the Bengal version contains readings which appear more likely
   to represent the original. Professor Bohtlingk's edition of the Devanagari
   recension is well known. My edition of the same recension, with literal
   translation of the difficult passages and critical notes (published by
   Stephen Austin of Hertford), is now out of print. Dr. C. Burkhard
   has lately published a new edition of this recension with a useful
   vocabulary. A good edition of the Bengal recension was prepared in
   Kolkata by Pandit Prem Chunder Tarkabagish, and brought out in
   1860 under the superintendence of Professor E.B. Cowell.

give some idea of the merits of a work which drew unqualified praise from such a poet as Goethe in the following words (Mr. E.B. Eastwick's translation):

> Wouldst thou the young year's blossoms and the fruits of its decline,
> And all by which the soul is charmed, enraptured, feasted, fed?
> Wouldst thou the earth and heaven itself in one sole name combine?
> I name thee, O Sakoontala! and all at once is said.

I merely extract from my own translation of the *Shakuntala* two passages. The following is the hero Dushyanta's description of a peculiar sensation to which he confesses himself subject, and to which perhaps the minds of sensitive persons, even in Western countries, are not altogether strangers (Act V. Translation, p. 121):

> Not seldom in our happy hours of ease,
> When thought is still, the sight of some fair form,
> Or mournful fall of music breathing low,
> Will stir strange fancies, thrilling all the soul
> With a mysterious sadness, and a sense
> Of vague, yet earnest longing. Can it be
> That the dim memory of events long past,
> Or friendships formed in other states of being,
> Flits like a passing shadow o'er the spirit?

Here is a specimen of the poetical similes which occur constantly throughout the drama (Act. V. Translation, p. 129)[1]:

> The loftiest trees bend humbly to the ground
> Beneath the teeming burden of their fruit;

---

1. This verse occurs also in the Bhartri-hari II. 62. He was the author of 300 moral, political, and erotic verses called *Shringara-shataka, Niti-s°*, and *Vairagya-s°*.

High in the vernal sky the pregnant clouds
Suspend their stately course, and hanging low,
Scatter their sparkling treasures o'er the earth:
And such is true benevolence; the good
Are never rendered arrogant by riches.

The two other dramas composed by Kalidasa are the
Vikramorvashi, 'Urvashi won by valour,' and the
Malavikagnimitra, 'story of Malavika and Agnimitra,' the first
of which is unequalled in poetical beauty by any other Indian
drama except the Shakuntala. The *Vikramorvashi* is in only
five acts, and its subject is easily told[1]:

Urvashi, a nymph of heaven — the heroine of the piece —
is carried off by a demon, and is rescued by the hero, king
Pururavas, who, of course, falls in love with her. The usual
impediments arise, caused by the inconvenient fact that the king
has a wife already; but in the end the nymph is permitted by
the god Indra to marry the mortal hero. Subsequently, in
consequence of a curse, Urvashi becomes metamorphosed into
a plant, and Pururavas goes mad. She is afterwards restored to
her proper form through the efficacy of a magical gem, and her
husband recovers his reason. They are happily reunited, but it
is decreed that when Urvashi's son is seen by his father Pururavas
she is to be recalled to heaven. This induces her to conceal the
birth of her son Ayus, and to intrust him for some years to the
care of a female ascetic. Accidentally father and son meet, and
Urvashi prepares to leave her husband; but Indra compassionately
revokes the decree, and the nymph is permitted to remain on
earth as the hero's second wife.

---

1. Various editions of this play have been published; one by Lenz,
another by myself. By far the best edition is by Dr. Bollensen.
Professor H.H. Wilson's spirited verse translation is well known. A
prose translation was made by Professor E.B. Cowell and published
in 1851.

As to the *Malavikgnimitra*, which is also rather a short play in five acts, the excellent German translation of it by Professor Weber of Berlin, published in 1856, and the scholarlike edition published in 1869 by Shankar P. Pandit of the Deccan College[1], have set at rest the vexed question of its authenticity, by enabling the student to compare it with Kalidasa's acknowledged writings. So many analogies of thought, style, and diction in the Malavikagnimitra have been thus brought to light, that few can now have any doubt about the authorship of the extant drama. According to the statement in its own prologue, it is evidently the veritable production of the author of the Shakuntala and Vikramorvashi. Nevertheless, its inferiority to the two masterpieces of Kalidasa — notwithstanding considerable poetical and dramatic merit, and great beauty and simplicity of style — must be admitted on all hands. Perhaps this may be accounted for by supposing the Malavikagnimitra to have been Kalidasa's first theatrical composition. Or possibly the scenes in which the dramatic action is laid, afforded the poet no opportunity (as in the other two plays) of displaying his marvellous powers of describing the beauties of nature and the habits of animals in rural and sylvan retreats. Its hero, king Agnimitra, is certainly a more ordinary and strictly human character than the semi-mythical Dushyanta and Pururavas, and the same may be said of its heroine Malavika, as compared with Sakuntala and Urvashi; but the plots of the three plays resemble each other in depending for their interest on the successful prosecution of love-intrigues under very similar difficulties and impediments.

In the Malavikagnimitra[2], king Agnimitra (son of Pushpamitra, founder of the Sunga dynasty of Magadha kings) falls in love

---

1. A previous edition was published at Bonn in 1840 by Dr. Tullberg.
2. I have consulted Professor H.H. Wilson's epitome of the play in the appendix to his Hindu Theatre.

with a girl named Malavika — belonging to the train of his queen Dharini's attendants — from accidentally seeing her portrait. As usual, the Vidushaka is employed as a go-between, and undertakes to procure the king a sight of the original. It happens that the principal queen, Dharini, has caused Malavika to be instructed in music, singing, and dancing. Hence in the second act a sort of concert (*Sangita*), or trial of skill, is arranged, at which Malavika executes a very difficult part in a particular musical time — called the *Madhya-laya* — with wonderful brilliancy. This, of course, captivates the king, and destroys his peace of mind. In spite of the opposition of his two queens, Dharini and Iravati, and notwithstanding other hindrances, he contrives to carry on an intrigue with Malavika. Not that he attempts to marry her by unlawful means, nor even against the wishes of his other wives. Polygamy is, of course, held to be legitimate in the household of Oriental Rajas. The difficulty consists in conciliating his two queens. This, however, he contrives in the end to accomplish, and their assent to his union with Malavika is at last obtained. In the course of the plot a *Parivrajika* or Buddhist female mendicant is introduced, which is regarded by Professor Weber as an argument for the antiquity of the drama. In the prologue Bhasa and Saumilla are mentioned as two poets, predecessors of Kalidasa.

I here give an example of a wise sentiment from the prelude. The stage-manager, addressing the audience, says:

All that is old is not on that account
Worthy of praise, nor is a novelty
By reason of its newness to be censured.
The wise decide not what is good or bad,
Till they have tested merit for themselves
A foolish man trusts to another's judgment.

I come now to a more modern Indian dramatist named *Bhavabhuti* and surnamed *Shri-kantha,* 'whose voice is eloquence.' His reputation is only second to that of Kalidasa.

In the prelude to two of his plays he is described as the son of a Brahman named Nilakantha (his mother being Jatukarni), who was one of the descendants of Kasyapa, living in a city called Padma-pura, and a follower of the Black Yajur-veda. He is said to have been born somewhere in the district Berar, and to have flourished at the court of Yashovarman, who reigned at Kanouj (Kanya-kubja) about A.D. 720[1]. Like Kalidasa, he only wrote three plays. There are called the *Malati-madhava, Maha-vira-charita,* and *Uttara-rama-charita*[2]. Of these three the Malati-madhava, in ten acts, is perhaps the best known to English Sanskrit scholars. The style is more laboured and artificial than that of Kalidasa's plays, and some of the metres adopted in the versification are of that complex kind which later Hindu poets delight to employ for the exhibition of their skill[3]. In the prelude the poet is guilty of the bad taste of praising his own composition. Its plot, however, is more interesting than that of Kalidasa's plays; its action is dramatic, and its pictures of domestic life and manners are most valuable, notwithstanding too free an introduction of the preternatural element, from which, as we have seen, the *Mrich-Madhava* has been well epitomized by Colebrooke[4]. I give here but a bare outline:

Two ministers of two neighbouring kings have agreed together privately that their children, Madhava and Malati, shall in due time marry each other. Unhappily for the accomplishment of their project, one of the kings requires the father of Malati to make

---

1. According to Professor Lassen he lived about the year 710. Kanouj, now in ruins, ranks in antiquity next to Ayodhya. It is situated in the North-west, on the Kalinadi, a branch of the Ganges, in the district of Furruckabad.
2. *Charita* is sometimes written *charitra.*
3. Colebrooke especially mentions the Dandaka metre, for an account of which see page 166 of this volume.
4. See Professor E.B. Cowell's edition of his Essays, vol. ii. p. 123.

a match between his daughter and an ugly old court-favourite named Nandana. The minister fearing to offend the monarch, consents to sacrifice his daughter. Meanwhile Madhava is sent to finish his studies under an old Buddhist priestess named Kamandaki, who had been Malati's nurse, and who contrives that she and Madhava shall meet and fall in love, though they do not at that time make known their mutual attachment. Soon afterwards the king prepares to enforce the marriage of Malati with his favourite Nandana. The news, when brought to Malati, makes her desperate. Another meeting takes place in Kamandaki's garden between her and her lover Madhava, who is followed to the garden by a friend, Makaranda. During their interview a great tumult and terrific screams are heard. A tiger has escaped from an iron cage and spreads destruction everywhere. Madayantika, sister of Nandana, happens to be passing and is attacked by the tiger. Madhava and Makaranda both rush to the rescue. The latter kills the animal and thus saves Madayantika, who is then brought in a half-fainting state into the garden. On recovering she naturally falls in love with her preserver Makaranda. The two couples are thus brought together, and Malati affiances herself there and then to Madhavan. At this very moment a messenger arrives to summon Madayantika, Nandana's sister, to be preset at Nandana's marriage with Malati, and another messenger summons Malati herself to the king's palace. Madhava is mad with grief, and in despair makes the extraordinary resolution of purchasing the aid of evil demons by going to the cemetery and offering them living flesh, cut off from his own body, as food. The cemetery happens to be near the temple of the awful goddess Chamunda (a form of Durga), presided over by a sorceress named Kapala-kundala and her preceptor, a terrible necromancer, Aghora-ghanta. They have determined on offering some beautiful maiden as a human victim to the goddess. With this object they carry off Malati, before her departure, while asleep on a terrace, and bringing her to the temple are about to kill her at Chamunda's shrine, when her cries attract the attention of Madhava, who is at that moment in the cemetery, offering his flesh to the demons. He rushes forward, encounters the sorcerer

Aghora-ghanta, and after a terrific hand-to-hand fight kills him and rescues Malati, who is thus restored to her family. The remainder of the story, occupying the five concluding acts, is tediously protracted and scarcely worth following out. The preparations for Malati's marriage to Nandana go on, and the old priestess Kamandaki who favours the union of Malati with her lover Madhava, contrives that, by the king's order, the bridal dress shall be put on at the very temple where her own ministrations are conducted. There she persuades Makaranda to substitute himself for the bride. He puts on the bridal dress, is taken in procession to the house of Nandana, disgusted with the masculine appearance of his supposed bride, leaves Makaranda in the inner apartments, thus enabling him to effect an interview with Nandana's sister Madayantika — the object of his own affections. Makaranda then makes himself known, and persuades her to run away, with him to the place where Malati and Madhava have concealed themselves. Their flight is discovered; the king's guards are sent in pursuit, a great fight follows, but Makaranda assisted by Madhava defeats his opponents. The bravery and handsome appearance of the two youths avert the king's anger, and they are allowed to join their friends unpunished. In the midst of the confusion, however, Malati has been carried off by the sorceress Kapala-kundala in revenge for the death of her preceptor Aghora-ghanta. Madhava is again in despair at this second obstacle to his union, but an old pupil of the priestess Kamandaki, named Saudamini, who has acquired extraordinary magical powers by her penances, opportunely appears on the scene, delivers Malati from the sorceress, and brings about the happy marriage of Malati with Madhava and of Madayantika with Makaranda.

The following description of Madhava's first interview with Malati is from the first act[1]:

---

1. Some expressions in my version have been suggested by Professor H.H. Wilson's but I have endeavoured to make my own close to the original.

One day by curiosity impelled
I sought the temple of the god of love.
There I roved to and fro, glancing around,
Till weary with my wandering I stood
Close to a pool that laved a Vakul tree
In the courtyard and precints of the temple.
The tree's sweet blossoms wooed a swarm of bees
To cull their nectar; and in idleness,
To while away the time, I laid me down
And gathered round me all the fallen flowers
To weave a garland, when there issued forth
From the interior fane a lovely maid.
Stately her gait, yet graceful as the banner
Waved by victorious Love o'er prostrate men;
Her garb with fitting ornaments embellished
Bespoke a youthful princess, her attendants
Moved proudly as became their noble rank;
She seemed a treasury of all the graces,
Or Beauty's store-house, where collected shone
A bright assemblages of all fairest things
To frame a perfect form; or rather was she
The very guardian goddess of love's shrine;
Or did the great Creator mould her charms
From some of Nature's loveliest materials —
The moon, the lotus-stalk, and sweetest nectar?
I looked and in an instant both my eyes
Seemed bathed with rapture and my inmost soul
Was drawn towards her unresistingly,
Like iron by the iron-loving magnet.

The other two plays of Bhava-bhuti, called *Maha-vira-charita* and *Uttara-rama-charita,* form together a dramatic version of the story of the second Rama or Rama-chandra, as narrated in Valimiki's Ramayana and Kalidasas's Raghu-vansa.

The *Maha-vira-charita*[1], in seven acts (often quoted in the Sahitya-darpana under the title *Vira-charita*), dramatizes the history of Rama, the great hero (*maha-vira*), as told in the first six Books of the Ramayana, but with some variations.

The author informs us in the prologue that his object in composing the play was 'to delineate the sentiment (*rasa*) of heroism (*vira*, see note, p. 508) as exhibited in noble characters.' The marvellous (*adbhuta*) sentiment is also said to be depicted, and the style of the action is called *Bharati*[2]. The first five acts carry the story to the commencement of the conflict between Rama and Ravana and between his army and the Rakshasa; but no fighting is allowed to take place on the stage, and no one is killed before the spectators. Indra and his attendant spirits are supposed to view the scene from the air, and they describe its progress to the audience; as, for example, the cutting off of Ravana's heads, the slaughter of the demons, the victory of Rama and recovery of Sita. The seventh and last act represents the aerial voyage of Rama, Lakshmana, Sita, Vibhishana, and their companions in the celestial car Pushpaka (once the property of Ravana) from Lanka back to Ayodhya. As they move through the air, they descry some of the scenes of their previous adventures, and many poetical descriptions are here introduced. The car at one time passes over the Dandaka forest, and even approaches the sun. At length it descends at Ayodhya. Rama and Lakshmana

---

1. Mr. John Pickford, one of my former Boden Scholars, some time Professor at Madras, has made a translation of this play from the Calcutta edition of 1857, and Professor H.H. Wilson has given an epitome of it in the appendix to his Hindu Theatre.
2. The word Bharati may perhaps mean simply 'language.' But we may note here that the Sahitya-darpana enumerates four kinds of style or dramatic action (*vritti*), viz. 1. the *Kaishiki*, vivacious and graceful; 2. the *Satvati* or *Sattvati*, abounding in descriptions of brave deeds and characterized by the marvellous; 3. the *Arabhati*, supernatural and terrible; 4. the *Bharati*, in which the vocal action is mostly in Sanskrit.

are re-united to Bharata and Satrughna, and the four brothers once more embrace each other. Rama is then consecrated king by Vasishtha and Visvamitra.

The *Uttara-rama-charita*[1], in seven acts, continues the narrative and dramatizes the events described in the seventh Book or Uttara-kanda of the Ramayana (see pp. 339-341). I give a brief epitome[2]:

Rama, when duly crowned at Ayodhya, seemed likely to enter upon a life of quiet enjoyment with his wife. But this would not have satisfied the Hindu conception of the impossibility of finding rest in this world (compare p. 459), nor harmonized with the idea of the pattern man Rama, born to suffering and self-denial. We are first informed that the family-priest Vasishtha, having to leave the capital for a time to assist at a sacrifice, utters a few words of parting advice to Rama, thus; 'Remember that a king's real glory consists in his people's welfare.' Rama replies: 'I am ready to give up everything, happiness, love, pity — even Sita herself — if needful for my subjects' good.' In accordance with this promise he employs an emissary (named Durmukha) to ascertain the popular opinion as to his own treatment of his subjects, and is astonished to hear from Durmukha that they approve all his conduct but one thing. They find fault with him for having taken back his wife after her long residence in a stranger's house (*para-griha-vasha*). In short, he is told that they still gossip and talk scandal about her and Ravana. The scrupulously correct and over-sensitive Rama, though convinced of his wife's fidelity after her submission to the fiery ordeal (p. 360), and though she is now likely to become a mother, feels himself quite unable to allow the slightest cause of offence to continue among the citizens. Torn by contending feelings, he steals away from his wife, while asleep,

---

1. The whole of this play is translated in Professor H.H. Wilson's Hindu Theatre.
2. I have consulted the Rev. K.M. Banerjea's article in the 'Indian Antiquary' for May 1872.

and directs Lakshmana to seclude her somewhere in the woods. This is the first act. An interval of twelve years elapses before the second act, during which time Sita is protected by divine agencies. In this interval, too, her twin sons, Kusha and Lava, are born and entrusted to the care of Valmiki, the author of the Ramayana, who educates them in his hermitage. This leads to the introduction at the beginning of the second act of Valmiki's stanza (drawn from him by his *shoka* or sorrow on beholding a bird, one of a pair, killed by a hunter), quoted from the Ramayana (I. ii. 18), where it is said to be the first Shloka ever invented. An incident now occurs which leads Rama to revisit the Dandaka forest, the scene of his former exile. The child of a Brahman dies suddenly and unaccountably. His body is laid at Rama's door. Evidently some national sin is the cause of such a calamity, and an aërial voice informs him that an awful crime is being perpetrated; for a Shudra, named Shambuka, is practising religious austerities instead of confining himself to his proper province of waiting on the twice-born (Manu I. 91). Rama instantly starts for the forest, discovers Shambuka in the sacrilegious act, and strikes off his head. But death by Rama's hand confers immortality on the Shudra, who appears as a celestial spirit, and thanks Rama for the glory and felicity thus obtained. Before returning to Ayodhya, Rama is induced to visit the hermitage of Agastya in the woods. Sita now reappears on the scene. She is herself invisible to Rama, but able to thrill him with emotions by her touch. Rama's distraction is described with great feeling. 'What does this mean?' he says, 'heavenly balm seems poured into my heart; a well-known touch changes my insensibility to life. Is it Sita, or am I dreaming?' This leads on to the last act of the drama. In the end, husband and wife are re-united, but not without supernatural agencies being again employed, and not until Prithivi, the Earth, who, it appears, had taken charge of Sita, restores her to the world. Valmiki then introduces Kusha and Lava to Rama, who recognizes in them his two sons. Happiness is once more restored to the whole family, and the play closes.

We may note as remarkable that at the beginning of the fourth act a dialogue takes place between two young pupils of

Valmiki, who are delighted because some guests, having visited the hermitage, afford hopes of a feast at which flesh meat is to constitute one of the dishes. Manu's rule (V. 41; see p. 280 of this volume) is cited, whereby a *Madhu-parka* or offering of honey to a guest is directed to be accompanied with a dish of beef or veal; for on these occasions householders may kill calves, bulls, and goats (*vatsatarim mahoksham va mahajam va nirvapanti griha-medhinah*).

As a specimen of the poetry of the play, I here give Rama's description of his love for his wife (translated by Professor H.H. Wilson):

> Her presence is ambrosia to my sight;
> Her contact fragrant sandal; her fond arms,
> Twined round my neck, are a far richer clasp
> Than costliest gems, and in my house she reigns
> The guardian goddess of my fame and fortune.
> Oh! I could never bear again to lose her.

Two other well-known plays the *Ratnavali* and the *Mudra-rakshasa* (both translated by Professor H.H. Wilson), ought to be mentioned.

The *Ratnavali,* or 'jewel-necklace,' is a short play in four acts, attributed (like the Mrich-chakatika, see p. 527) to a royal author, king Sri *Harsha-deva*[1].

---

1. This is probably a different Sri Harsha from the author of the *Naishadha* or *Naishadhiya* (at p. 503). The *Nagananda* (see p. 547), a Hindu-Buddhist drama, is attributed to the same author. Hindu poets appear to have been in the habit of flattering kings and great men in this way. Professor E.B Cowell is inclined to assign the Nagananda to a poet named *Dhavaka,* mentioned in the Kavya-prakasha, while he conjectures that *Bana,* the author of the Kadambari, may have written the *Ratnavali,* which would place the date of this play (as shown by Dr. Fitz-Edward Hall) in the seventh century of our era. One native commentator on the Kavya-prakasha asserts that *Dhavaka* wrote the *Ratnavali.*

There is nothing of the supernatural about this drama. It may be called a comedy in which the characters are all mortal men and women, and the incidents quite domestic. The play is connected with what appears to have been a familiar story, viz. the loves and intrigues of a certain king *Udayana*, and *Vasava-datta*, a princess of Ujjayini. This tale is told in the Katha-sarit-sagara. The king is there called Udayana (see the account in Wilson's Essays, Dr. Rost's edition, I. 191), and is said to have carried off Vasava-datta, who is there the daughter of Chanda-mahasena, while in the Ratnavali she is daughter of Pradyota, and is not said to be a princess of Ujjayini. The same story (along with the stories of Sakuntala and Urvasi) is alluded to towards the end of the second act of the Malati-madhava, and according to Professor Wilson is referred to by Kalidasa in the Megha-duta when he speaks of the *Udayana-katha* as frequently recited in Ujjayini (verse 32). Dr. Fitz-Edward Hall has shown in his Preface to Subandhu's *Vasava-datta* that this romance has scarcely any feature in common with the Ratnavali story except the name of its heroine. The plot of the Ratnavali resembles in its love-intrigues that of the Vikramorvasi, Malavikagnimitra, &c., and in like manner presents us with a valuable picture of Hindu manners in medieval times. The poet seems to have had no scruple in borrowing ideas and expressions from Kalidasa. The hero of the piece is generally spoken of as 'the King,' or else as *Vatsa-rajah*, king of Vatsa — a country or people whose capital was *Kausambhi*. He is, however, called *Udayana* at the end of the first act, and before the play commences he is supposed to be already married to *Vasava-datta*. His minister's name is *Yaugandharayana* or *Yogandharayana*, his Vidushaka or jovial companion is called *Vasantaka*, and his general *Rumanvat*.

The first scene introduces a curious description of the sports and practical jokes practised at the Spring festival (now called Holi), when plays were generally acted, and still continue to be performed in some parts of India. *Sagarika* (otherwise called *Ratnavali*, from her jewel-necklace), a princess of Lanka (Ceylon), is accidentally brought to the king's court, falls in love with him, and paints his picture. The king is, of course, equally struck with her. His queen's jealousy is excited by the discovery of the picture. She even succeeds in imprisoning *Sagarika* and putting fetters on her feet, and more than the ordinary impediments threaten to stop the progress of the love-affair. All difficulties, however, are eventually removed, and the play ends, as usual, by the king's conciliating his first wife and gaining a second.

I give one specimen of a sentiment uttered by the hero on hearing of the death of a brave enemy. He says: *Mrityur api tasya slaghyo yasya ripavah purusha-karam varnayanti;* that is,

> How glorious is the death of that brave man
> Whose very enemies applaud his prowess!

The *Mudra-rakshasa,* or 'signet-ring Rakshasa[1],' is by *Visakha-datta,* and is a political drama in seven acts, attributed to the twelfth century.

This play is noteworthy as introducing the well-known Chandra-gupta, king of Pataliputra, who was happily conjectured by Sir W. Jones to be identical with the Sandrakottus described by Megasthenes in Strabo as the most powerful Raja immediately succeeding Alexander's death, and whose date (about 315 B.C.) serves as the only definite starting-point in Hindu chronology. Another celebrated character is his crafty minister Chanakya, the Indian *Macchiavelli,* and writer on Niti or 'rules of government and polity,' and the reputed author of numerous moral and

---

1. If this title *Mudra-rakshasa* is a compound similar to *Vikramorvasi* and *Abhijnana-shakuntalam,* where there is *madhyama-pada-lopa,* it might be translated, 'Rakshasa known by the signet-ring;' but it may possibly be one in which the terms are inverted. Some translate it as a *Dvandva,* 'Rakshasa and the signet-ring.' In the fifth act, Chanakya's emissary Siddhartha enters, bearing a letter marked with the signet-ring of the minister Rakshasa (*amatya-rakshasasya mudra-lanchito lekhah*).

political precepts commonly current in India. He is represented as having slain king Nanda and assisted Chandra-gupta to the throne. The principal design of the play is to describe how this wily Brahman Chanakya (also called Vishnu-gupta) effects a reconciliation between a person named Rakshasa, the minister of the murdered Nanda, and the persons on whose behalf he was killed. At the beginning of act VII. there is a curious scene in which a Chandala or executioner leads a criminal to the place of execution (*badhya-sthana*). The latter bears a stake (*sula*) on his shoulder, and is followed by his wife and child. The executioner calls out,

'Make way, make way, good people! let every one who wishes to preserve his life, his property, or his family, avoid transgressing against the king as he would poison.' (Cf. Mrichchakatika, act X.)

With regard to the interesting Hindu-Buddhist drama called *Nagananda* or 'joy of the snake-world,' I must refer those who wish for an account of its contents to Professor Cowell's Preface prefixed to Mr. Boyd's recent translation (see note, p. 544).

Some other well-known plays have been before noticed:

Thus, for example, the student will find mentioned at p. 411 the *Hanuman-nataka*, a *Maha-nataka* in fourteen acts[1]; the *Bala-ramayana*, a *Maha-nataka* in ten acts, by *Raja-sekhara* (edited by Pandit Govinda Deva Sastri of Benares in 1868); the *Prasanna-raghava* in seven acts (edited by the same in 1869); the *Anargha-raghava;* and the *Veni-samhara* at p. 437, note 3. The *Hasyarnava*, a comic and satirical piece in two acts, is described in the appendix to Professor Wilson's Hindu Theatre.

---

1. I possess an old and valuable MS. of this play, whish I hope may one day be used in editing it. The edition published in Kolkata by Maharaja Kali-krishna Bahadur, in 1840, was not from the purest recension. It was lithographed at Bombay about ten years ago.

Before, however, taking leave of the Hindu Theatre I ought to note a curious allegorical and philosophical play by Krishna-misra, who is supposed to have lived in the twelfth century of our era. The play is called *Prabodha-chandrodaya,* i.e. 'rise of the moon of (true) intelligence or knowledge,' and its *dramatis personae* remind one of some of our old Moralities — acted in England about the time of Henry VIII — in which the Virtues and Vices were introduced as persons for the purpose of inculcating moral and religious truth.

Thus in an old English Morality called *Every-man* some of the personifications are — God, Death, Every-man, Fellowship, Kindred, Good-deeds, Knowledge, Confession, Beauty, Strength, Discretion. In *Hycke-scorner* — Contemplation, Pity, Imagination, Free-will. In *Lusty Juventus* — Good Counsel, Knowledge, Satan, Hypocrisy, Fellowship, Abominable Living, God's Merciful Promises. Similarly in the Hindu Morality *Prabodha-chandrodaya* we have Faith, Volition, Opinion, Imagination, Contemplation, Devotion, Quietude, Friendship, &c. &c., on one side; Error, Self-conceit, Hypocrisy, Love, Passion, Anger, Avarice, on the other. The two sets of characters are, of course, opposed to each other, the object of the play being to show how the former become victorious over the latter, the Buddhists and other heretical sects being represented as adherents of the losing side.

V. *The Puranas*

I must now advert briefly to the eighteen Puranas. They constitute an important department of Sanskrit literature in their connection with the later phases of Brahmanism, as exhibited in the doctrines of emanation, incarnation, and triple manifestation (*tri-murti,* see pp. 359-363), and are, in real fact, the proper Veda of popular Hinduism, having been designed to convey the exoteric doctrines of the Veda to the lower castes and to women. On this account, indeed, they are sometimes called a fifth Veda (see note 1, p. 415). Their name *Purana* signifies 'old traditional story,' and the eighteen ancient narratives to which this name is applied are said to have been compiled by the ancient sage *Vyasa* (also called Krishna-dvaipayana and Badarayana), the arranger of the Vedas and Mahabharata (p. 415, note 1), and the supposed founder of the Vedanta philosophy (p. 120, note 1). They are composed chiefly in the simple Sloka metre (with occasional passages in prose), and are, like the Mahabharata, very encyclopedical in their range of subjects. They must not, however, be confounded with the Itihasas, which are properly the histories of heroic *men*, not *gods*, though these men were afterwards deified. The Puranas are properly the history of the gods themselves, interwoven with every variety of legendary tradition on other subjects. Viewing them as a whole, the theology they teach is anything but simple, consistent, or uniform. While nominally tritheistic — to suit the three developments of Hinduism explained at p. 363 — the religion of the Puranas is practically polytheistic and yet essentially pantheistic. Underlying their whole teaching may be discerned the one grand doctrine which is generally found at the root of Hindu theology, whether Vedic or Puranic — pure uncompromising pantheism. But interwoven with the radically pantheistic and Vedantic texture of these compositions, tinged as it is with other philosophical ideas (especially the Sankhyan doctrine of Prakriti), and diversified as it is with endless fanciful mythologies, theogonies, cosmogonies, and mythical genealogies, we have a whole body of teaching on nearly every subject of knowledge. The Puranas pretend to give the history of the whole universe from the most remote ages, and claim to be the inspired revealers of scientific as well as theological truth. They dogmatize on physical science, geography, the form of the earth (see p. 469), astronomy, chronology; and even in the case of one or two Puranas, anatomy, medicine, grammar, and the use of military weapons. All this cycle of very questionable omniscience is conveyed in the form of leading dialogues (connecting numerous subordinate dialogues), in some of which a well-known and supposed divinely inspired sage, like Parashara, is the principal speaker, and answers the enquiries put to him by his disciples; while in others, Loma-harshana (or Roma-harshana), the pupil of Vyasa, is the narrator, being called Suta, that is, 'Bard' or 'Encomiast,' as one of an order of men to whom the reciting of the Itihasas and Puranas was especially entrusted[1].

Strictly, however, every Purana is supposed to treat of only five topics: 1. The creation of the universe (*sarga*); 2. Its destruction and re-creation (*prati-sarga*); 3. The genealogy of gods and patriarchs (*vansha*); 4. The reigns and periods of the Manus (*manv-antara*); 5. The history of the solar and lunar races of kings (*vanshanucharita*[2]). On this account the oldest

---

1. A Suta was properly the charioteer of a king, and was the son of a Kshatriya by a Brahmani. His business was to proclaim the heroic actions of the king and his ancestors, as he drove his chariot to battle, or on state occasions. He had therefore to know by heart the epic poems and ancient ballads, in which the deeds of heroes were celebrated, and he had more to do with reciting portions of the Mahabharata and Itihasas than with the Puranas. In Maha-bh. I. 1026 it is said that Sauti or Ugra-shravas (son of the Suta Loma-harshana) had learnt to recite a portion of the Mahabharata from his father. Generally it is declared that Loma-harshana learnt to recite it from Vaisampayana, a pupil of Vyasa.

2. Certainly the recounting of royal genealogies is an important part of the Puranas. It consists, however, of a dry chronicle of names. Similar chronicles were probably written by the early Greek historians, called (Thuc. I. 21); but these developed into real histories, which the Indian never did. It was the duty of bards to commit their masters' genealogies to memory, and recite them at weddings, or great festivals, and this is done by Bhats in India to this day. In Ramayana I. lxx. 19, however, it is the family-priest Vasishtha who,

native lexicographer Amara-sinha (see p. 187), whose date was placed by Professor H.H. Wilson at the end of the first century B.C. gives the word *Pancha-lakshana,* 'characterized by five subjects,' as a synonym of Purana. No doubt some kind of Puranas must have existed before his time, as we find the word mentioned in the Grihya-sutras of Ashvalayana (see p. 222 of this volume), and in Manu (see p. 236, note 1, and p. 280 of this volume). The fact that very few of the Puranas now extant, answer to the title Panca-lakshana, and that the abstract given in the Matsya-purana of the contents of all the others, does not always agree with the extant works, either in the subjects described, or number of verses enumerated[1], proves that, like

---

before the marriage of the sons of Dasaratha with the daughters of Janaka, recites the genealogy of the solar line of kings reigning at Ayodhya. This dry genealogy of a race of kings is sometimes called *Anuvansha.* Several similar catalogues of the lunar race (Soma-vansa or Aila-vansha), who first reigned at Pratishthana,and afterwards at Hastina-pura, are found in the Mahabharata (see especially one in prose, with occasional Slokas called *Anu-vansha-shloka* interspersed, Maha-bh. I. 3759 &c.). Professor Lassen gives valuable lists at the end of vol. i. of his Ind. Alt. It must be noted that both the *solar* and *lunar* races have collateral lines or branches. A principal branch of the. *solar* consisted of the kings of *Mithila* or *Videha,* commencing with the bad king *Nimi,* who perished for his wickedness (Manu VII. 41). His son was *Mithi* (who gave his name to the city), and his son was *Janaka* (so called as the real 'father of the race'); the great and good Janaka, learned in Brahmanical lore, being, it appears, a descendant of this first Janaka. The *lunar* race, to which the Pandavas belonged, had two principal branches, that of the *Yadavas* (commencing with *Yadu,* and comprising under it *Arjuna Kartavirya* and *Krishna*), and that of the kings of *Magadha.* The Yadavas had also a collateral line of kings of *Kasi* or *Varanasi.* For the solar and lunar genealogies see pp. 383 and 418 of this volume.

1. Thus the *Bhavishya-purana* ought to consist of a revelation of future events by Brahma, but contains scarcely any prophecies. This work is rather a manual of religious observances; and the commencement, which treats of creation, is little else than a transcript of Manu. We may note, however, that Sankara Acharya often quotes the extant Vishnu-purana.

the Ramayana and Mahabharata, they were preceded by more ancient works. In all probability there were *Mula* or original Puranas, as there once existed also a *Mula* Ramayana and *Mula* Mahabharata. Indeed, in the Bhagavata-purana XII. vii. 7, six *Mula-samhitah* or original collections are specially declared to have been taught by Vyasa to six sages, his pupils; and these six collections may have formed the bases of the present works, which, as we shall presently see, are arranged in three groups of six. At any rate, it appears certain that the Puranas had an ancient groundwork, which may have been in some cases reduced by omissions or curtailments, before serving as a basis for the later superstructures. This groundwork became more or less overlaid from time to time by accretions and incrustations; the epic poems, and especially the Mahabharata, constituting the principal sources drawn upon for each successive augmentation of the original work. Nevertheless, it must always be borne in mind that the mythology of the Puranas is more developed than that of the Mahabharata, in which (as properly an Itihasa, and therefore only concerned with kings and heroic men) Vishnu and Shiva are often little more than great heroes, and are not yet regarded as rival gods. In medieval times, when the present Puranas were compiled, the rivalry between the worshippers of Vishnu and Shiva was in full force — the fervour of their worship having been stimulated by the Brahmans as an aid to the expulsion of Buddhism — and the Puranas themselves were expression and exponent of this phase of Hinduism. Hence the great antiquity ascribed to the present works by the Hindus, although it may have had the effect of investing them with a more sacred character than they could otherwise have acquired, is not supported by either internal or external evidence. The oldest we possess can scarcely date from a period more remote than the sixth or seventh century of our era.

Of course the main object of most of the Puranas is, as I have already hinted, a sectarian one. They aim at exalting one of the three members of the Tri-murti, Brahma, Vishnu, or Shiva; those which relate to *Brahma* being sometimes called *Rajasa* Puranas (from his own peculiar Guna *rajas*); those which exalt *Vishnu* being designated *Shattvika* (from his Guna *Sattva*); and those which prefer *Shiva* being styled *Tamasa* (from his Guna *tamas*). The reason for connecting them with the three Gunas will be understood by referring to p. 359.

I now give the names of the eighteen Puranas according to the above three divisions:

A. The Rajasa Puranas, or those which relate to Brahma, are, 1. *Brahma*, 2. *Brahmanda*, 3. *Brahma-vaivarta*, 4. *Markandeya*, 5. *Bhavishya*, 6. *Vamana*.

B. The Sattvika Puranas, or those which exalt Vishnu, are, 1. *Vishnu*, 2. *Bhagavata*, 3. *Naradiya*, 4. *Garuda*, 5. *Padma*, 6. *Varaha*. These six are usually called Vaishnava Puranas.

C. The Tamasa, or those which glorify Shiva, are, 1. *Shiva*, 2. *Linga*, 3. *Skanda*, 4. *Agni*, 5. *Matsya*, 6. *Kurma*. These six are usually styled Saiva Puranas. For the 'Agni,' an ancient Purana called 'Vayu,' which is probably one of the oldest of the eighteen, is often substituted.

Although it is certainly convenient to group the eighteen Puranas in these three divisions in accordance with the theory of the Tri-murti or triple manifestation, it must not be supposed that the six Puranas in the first, or *Rajasa* group, are devoted to the exclusive exaltation of *Brahma*, whose worship has never been either general or popular (see note 1, p. 363).

Though these six Puranas abound in legends connected with the first member of the Triad, they resemble the other two groups in encouraging the worship of either Vishnu or Shiva, and especially of Vishnu as the lover Krishna. According to Professor H.H. Wilson some of them are even favourites with the Saktas (see p. 563 of this volume), as promoting the adoration of the goddess Durga or Kali, the personified energy of Shiva.

One of their number, the *Markandeya,* is (as Professor Banerjea has shown in the Preface to his excellent edition of this work) quite unsectarian in character.

This *Markandeya-purana* is, therefore, probably one of the oldest — perhaps as old as the eighth century of our era. Part of it seems to be devoted to Brahma, part to Vishnu, and part consists of a *Devi-mahatmya* or exaltation of the female goddess. At the commencement *Jaimini,* the pupil of Vyasa, addresses himself to certain sapient birds (who had been Brahmans in a previous birth) and requests the solution of four theological and moral difficulties, viz. 1. Why did Vishnu, himself being *nirguna* (see p. 102), take human form? 2. How could Draupadi become the common wife of the five Pandavas (see p. 431, with notes)? 3. Why had Bala-rama to expiate the crime of Brahmanicide committed by him while intoxicated (see p. 436)? 4. Why did the five sons of Draupadi meet with untimely deaths, when Krishna and Arjuna were their protectors (see p. 435, note 1, and p. 457-458)?

Another of this group of Puranas, the *Brahma-vaivarta,* inculcates the worship of the young Krishna (*Bala-krishna*) and his favourite Radha, now so popular in India; from which circumstance this work is justly regarded as the most modern of all the Puranas.

Of course it will be inferred from the statement at p. 363-364 that the second group of Puranas — the *Sattvika* or *Vaishnava* — is the most popular. Of these the *Bhagavati* and *Vishnu,* which are sometimes called *Maha-puranas,* 'great Puranas,' are by far the best known and most generally esteemed. The *Bhagavata-purana*[1], in twelve books, is perhaps the

---

1. A magnificent edition was commenced by Euène Burnouf at Paris in the 'Collection Orientale,' but its completion was prevented by that great scholar's death.

most popular of all the eighteen Puranas, since it is devoted to the exaltation of the favourite god Vishnu or Krishna, one of whose names is Bhagavat.

It is related to the Rishis at Naimisharanya by the Suta (see p. 550), but he only recites what was really narrated by the sage Shuka, son of Vyasa, to Parikshit, king of Hastina-pura, and grandson of Arjuna, who in consequence of a curse was condemned to die by the bite of a snake in seven days, and who therefore goes to the banks of the Ganges to prepare for death. There he is visited by certain sages, among whom is Shuka, who answers his inquiry (how can a man best prepare to die?) by relating the Bhagavata-purana as he received it from Vyasa.

Colebrooke believed it to be the work of the grammarian Vopadeva (p. 194 of this volume).

This Purana has been well edited at Bombay with the commentary of Shridhara-svamin.

Its most important Book is the tenth, which gives the early life of Krishna. This Book has its Hindu counterpart in the Prem Sagar, and has been translated into nearly all the languages of India.

An epitome of this part of the work has already been given at p. 370. As an example of the style of the Puranas I here give the text of the story related at p. 373 of this volume. It is condensed in *Bhagavata-purana* X. lxxxix. 1, thus:

Shri-Shuka uvacha | Sarasvatyas tate rajann Rishayah satram asata | Vitarkah samabhut tesham trishv adhisheshu ko mahan || Tasya jijnasaya te vai Bhrigum Brahma-sutam nripa | Taj jnaptyai preshayam-asuh so 'bhyagad Brahmanah sabham || Na Tasmai prahvanam stotram chakre sattva-parikshaya | Tasmai chukrodha Bhagavan prajvalan svena tejasa || Sa atmany utthitam manyum atma-jayatmana prabhuh | Asishamad yatha vahnim sva-yonya varinatmanah || Tatah Kailasam agamat sa tam devo mahesvarah

| Parirabdhum samarebha utthaya bhrataram muda || Naicchat tvam asy utpathaga iti devas chukopa ha | Shulam udyamya tam hantum arebhe tigma-locanah || Patitva padayor Devi santvayamasa tam gira | Atho jagama Vaikuntham yatra devo Janardanah || Shayanam Shriya utsange pada vakshasy atadayat | Tata utthaya Bhagavan saha Lakshmya satam gatih || Sva-talpad avaruhyatha nanama shirasa munim | Ahate svagatam Brahman nishidatrasane kshanam | Ajanatam agatan vah kshantum arhatha nah prabho || Ativa komalau tata charanau te maha-mune | Ity uktva vipra-charanau mardayan svena panina || Punihi sahalokam mam loka-palans-cha mad-gatan | Padodakena bhavatas tirthanam tirtha-karina || Adyaham Bhagaval lakshmya asam ekanta-bhajanam | Vatsyaty urasi me bhutir bhavat-pada-hatanhasah ||

The above story affords a good example of the view taken by the Bhagavata of the comparative excellence of the three members of the Tri-murti.

In VIII. vii. 44, the following sentiment occurs:

When other men are pained the good man grieves —
Such care for others is the highest worship
Of the Supreme Creator of mankind.

Perhaps the *Vishnu-purana* as conforming most nearly to the epithet *Pancha-lakshana* (see p. 551), will give the best idea of this department of Sanskrit literature.

It is in six Books, and is, of course, dedicated to the exaltation of Vishnu, whom it identifies with the Supreme Being. Book I. treats of the creation of the universe; the peopling of the world and the descent of mankind from seven or nine patriarchs[1], sons

---

1. The seven patriarchs or sages (*saptarshayah*, sometimes identified with the seven stars of the Great Bear) were created by Brahma as progenitors of the human race, and are called his mind-born sons; they are, *Marichi, Atri, Angiras, Pulastya, Pulaha, Kratu,* and *Vasishtha.* To these two others are added in Vishnu-purana I. vii, viz. *Daksha* and *Bhrigu.* In Manu I. 35, *Narada* is also added, making ten.

of Brahma; the destruction of the universe at the end of a Kalpa (see p. 368, note 3), and its re-creation (*prati-sarga*); and the reigns of king during the first Manvantara. Book II. describes the various worlds, heavens, hells, and planetary spheres; and gives the formation of the seven circular continents and concentric oceans as described at p. 469 of this volume. Book III. describes the arrangement of the Vedas, Itihasas, and Puranas by Vyasa, and the institution and rules of caste, in which it follows and resembles Manu. Book IV. gives lists of kings and dynasties. Book V. corresponds to Book X. of the Bhagavata-purana and is devoted to the life of Krishna. Book VI. describes the deterioration of mankind during the four ages, the destruction of the world by fire and water, and its dissolution at the end of a Kalpa.

The above is a bare outline of the contents of this Purana. It is encyclopedical, like the others, and is rich in philosophical speculations and curious legends. A passage illustrating the Sankhyan tone of its philosophy will be found quoted at p. 109 of this volume. The great sage Parashara, father of Vyasa (p. 419, note 4), is supposed to relate the whole Purana to his disciple Maitreya. The narrative begins thus[1]:

Having adored Vishnu, the lord of all, and revered Brahma and the rest, and done homage to the Guru, I will relate a Purana, equal to the Vedas [*Pranamya Vishnum vishvesham Brahmadin pranipatya ca | Gurum pranamya vakshyami Puranam Veda-sammitam*, I. 3].

The metre is generally the simple Shloka, with occasional stanzas in the Indra-vajra, Vansha-sthavila, &c.

The following is a metrical version of the prayer of Parashara, addressed to Vishnu, at the beginning of Book I.

---

1. In my translations I have consulted Professor H.H. Wilson's great work, but I have had the text of the Bodleian MS. before me.

2, (with which compare similar descriptions of the Supreme
Being in the Upanishads and Bhagavad-gita, pp. 48, 155-159
of this volume):

> Hail to thee, mighty Lord, all-potent Vishnu!
> Soul of the Universe, unchangeable,
> Holy, eternal, always one in nature,
> Whether revealed as Brahma, Hari, Shiva —
> Creator or Preserver or Destroyer —
> Thou art the cause of final liberation;
> Whose form is one, yet manifold; whose essence
> Is one, yet diverse; tenuous, yet vast;
> Discernible, yet undiscernible;
> Root of the world, yet of the world composed;
> Prop of the universe[1], yet more minute
> Than earth's minutest particles; abiding
> In every creature, yet without defilement;
> Imperishable, one with perfect wisdom.

There is a curious story of the churning of the ocean for
the production of the *Amrita*, 'ambrosial food of immortality,'
in Book I. 9, (compare p. 330 of this volume). It is noteworthy
as differing considerably from that in Ramayana I. xlv. The
passage represents Indra and the gods as having lost all their
strength — in consequence of a curse pronounced on them
by the choleric sage Durvasas — and so becoming subject to
the demons. The gods apply to Vishnu in their distress, and
even Brahma adores him in a long hymn. I give a portion of
the story metrically, changing the order of the text in one or
two places:

> The gods addressed the mighty Vishnu thus —
> 'Conquered in battle by the evil demons

---

1. In the original these three attributes are, *Mula-bhuto jagatah, jagan-
mayah*, and *adhara-bhuto vishvasya.*

We fly to thee for succour, Soul of all,
Pity and by thy might deliver us.'
Hari the lord, creator of the world,
Thus by the gods implored, all graciously
Replied — 'Your strength shall be restored, ye gods;
Only accomplish what I now command;
Unite yourselves in peaceful combination
With these your foes; collect all plants and herbs
Of diverse kinds from every quarter; cast them
Into the sea of milk; take Mandara,
The mountain, for a churning-stick, and Vasuki,
The serpent, for a rope; together churn
The ocean to produce the beverage —
Source of all strength and immortality —
Then reckon on my aid, I will take care
Your foes shall share you toil, but not partake
In its reward or drink th' immortal draught.'
Thus by the god of gods advised, the host
United in alliance with the demons.
Straightway they gathered various herbs and cast them
Into the waters, then they took the mountain
To serve as churning-staff, and next the snake
To serve as cord, and in the ocean's midst
Hari himself, present in tortoise-form,
Became a pivot for the churning-staff.
Then did they churn the sea of milk; and first
Out of the waters rose the sacred Cow,
God-worshipped Surabhi — eternal fountain
Of milk and offerings of butter; next,
While holy Siddhas wondered at the sight,
With eyes all rolling, Varuni uprose —
Goddess of wine. Then from the whirlpool sprang
Fair Parijata, tree of Paradise, delight
Of heavenly maidens, with its fragrant blossoms
Perfuming the whole world. Th' Apsaras

Troop of celestial nymphs, matchless in grace,
Perfect in loveliness, were next produced.
Then from the sea uprose the cool-rayed moon,
Which Maha-deva seized; terrific poison
Next issued from the waters; this the snake-gods
Claimed as their own. Then seated on a lotus
Beauty's bright goddess, peerless Sri, arose
Out of the waves; and with her, robed in white
Came forth Dhanvantari, the gods' physician.
High in his hand he bore the cup of nectar —
Life-giving draught — longed for by gods and demons.
Then had the demons forcibly borne off
The cup, and drained the precious beverage,
Had not the mighty Vishnu interposed.
Bewildering them, he gave it to the gods;
Whereat incensed the demon troops assailed
The host of heaven, but they with strength renewed
Quaffing the draught, struck down their foes, who fell
Headlong through space to lowest depths of hell.

The following is part of the prayer of Muchukunda, Book
V. 23:

Lord of the Universe, the only refuge
Of living beings, the alleviator
Of pain, the benefactor of mankind,
Show me thy favour and deliver me
From evil; O creator of the world,
Maker of all that has been and will be,
Of all that moves and is immoveable,
Thyself composed of what possesses form,
And what is formless; limitless in bulk,
Yet infinitely subtle; lord of all,
Worthy of praise, I come to thee my refuge,
Renouncing all attachment to the world,
Longing for fulness of felicity —
Extinction of myself, absorption into thee.

The following account of the Kali or fourth age of the
world — the age of universal degeneracy — is from Book VI.
1, (compare p. 368, note 3, of this volume):

> Hear what will happen in the Kali age.
> The usages and institutes of caste,
> Of order and of rank, will not prevail,
> Nor yet the precepts of the triple Veda.
> Religion will consist in wasting wealth,
> In fasting and performing penances
> At will; the man who owns most property
> And lavishly distributes it, will gain
> Dominion over others; noble rank
> Will give no claim to lordship; self-willed women
> Will seek their pleasure, and ambitious men
> Fix all their hopes on riches gained by fraud.
> Then women will be fickle and desert
> Their beggared husbands, loving them alone
> Who give them money. Kings instead of guarding
> Will rob their subjects, and abstract the wealth
> Of merchants, under plea of raising taxes.
> Then in the world's last age the rights of men
> Will be confused, no property be safe,
> No joy and no prosperity be lasting.

There are eighteen *Upa-purapnas* or 'secondary Puranas,'
subordinate to the eighteen *Maha* or principal Puranas, but
as they are of less importance I shall do little more than simply
give their names as follow:

1. *Sanatkumara*, 2. *Nara-sinha* or *Nri-sinha*; 3. *Naradiya* or
Vrihan-naradiya[1]; 4. *Siva*; 5. *Durvasasa*; 6. *Kapila*; 7. *Manava*;
8. *Ausanasa*; 9. *Varuna*; 10. *Kalika*; 11. *Samba*; 12. *Nandi*; 13.

---

1. According to Rajendralal Mitra this is called *Vrihat* to distinguish it
   from the Naradiya, one of the Maha-puranas. He gives an abstract
   of it in No. 1021 of his valuable Notices of MSS.

Saura; 14. *Parasara;* 15. *Aditya;* 16. *Mahesvara;* 17. *Bhagavata* (thought to be a misreading for Bhargava); 18. *Vasishtha.* Another list given by Professor H.H. Wilson varies a little, thus: 1. *Sanatkumara;* 2. *Nara-sinha;* 3. *Nanda;* 4. *Shiva-dharma;* 5. *Durvasasa;* 6. *Bhavishya;* 7. *Kapila;* 8. *Manava;* 9. *Aushanasa;* 10. *Brahmanda;* 11. *Varuna;* 12. *Kalika;* 13. *Maheshvara;* 14. *Samba;* 15. *Saura;* 16. *Parashara;* 17. *Bhagavata;* 18. *Kaurma.*

With regard to the second or *Nara-sinha Upa-purana* we have an abstract of its content by Rajendralal Mitra in his Notices of MSS. (No. 1020), whence it appears that the general character of these works is very similar to that of the principal Puranas. For example, Chapters 1-5 give the origin of creation; 6. the story of Vashishtha; 18. the praises of Vishnu; 22. the solar race; 23. the lunar race; 30. the terrestial sphere. That this work was well known at least five hundred years ago is proved by the fact that Madavacharya quotes from it.

The Tantras

I have already alluded to the Tantras, which represent a phase of Hinduism generally later than that of the Puranas, although some of the Puranas and Upa-puranas, such as the Skanda, Brahma-vaivarta, and Kalika, are said to teach Tantrika doctrines, by promoting the worship of Prakriti and Durga.

The Tantras are very numerous, but none have as yet been printed or translated in Europe. Practically they constitute a fifth Veda (in place of the Puranas) for the Shaktas or worshippers of the active energizing will (*shakti*) of a god — personified as his wife, or sometimes as the female half of his essence[1].

---

1. It is remarkable, as noticed by Professor H.H. Wilson, that Kulluka-bhatta in commenting on Manu II. 1, says *Shrutis-cha dvi-vidha vaidiki tantriki cha,* 'revelation is two-fold, Vedic and Tantric.'

It must here be remarked that the principal Hindu deities are sometimes supposed to possess a double nature, or, in other words, two characters, one quiescent, the other active. The active is called his *Sakti*.

Sometimes only eight Shaktis are enumerated and sometimes nine, viz. *Vaishnavi, Brahmani, Raudri, Maheshvari, Narasinhi, Varahi, Indrani, Karttiki,* and *Pradhana.* Others reckon fifty forms of the hakti of Vishnu, besides *Lakshmi;* and fifty of Shiva or Rudra, besides *Durga* or *Gauri. Sarasvati* is named as a Sakti of Vishnu and Rudra, as well as of Braham. According to the Vayu-purana, the female nature of Rudra (Shiva) became two-fold, one half *Asita* or white, and the other half *Sita* or black, each of these again becoming manifold. The white or mild nature includes the Saktis *Uma, Gauri, Lakshmi, Sarasvati,* &c.; the black or fierce nature includes *Durga, Kali, Chandi, Chamunda,* &c.

This idea of personifying the will of a deity may have been originally suggested by the celebration hymn (129) in the tenth Mandala of the Rig-veda, which, describing the creation, says that Will or Desire (*Kama*), the first germ (*prathaman retas*) of Mind, brought the universe into existence (see p. 22 of this volume).

But in all probability, the Tantrika doctrine owes its development to the popularizing of the Sankhya theory of *Purusha* and (as described at p. 104 and p. 109 of this volume). The active producing principle, whether displayed in creation, maintenance, or destruction — each of which necessarily implies the other — became in the later stages of Hinduism a living visible personification. Moreover, as destruction was more dreaded than creation or preservation, so the wife of the god Shiva, presiding over dissolution, and called *Kali, Durga, Parvati, Uma, Devi, Bhairavi,* &c., became the most important personage in the whole Pantheon to that great majority of worshippers whose religion was actuated by superstitious fears. Sometimes the god himself was regarded

as consisting of two halves, representing the male principle
on his right side, and the female on his left[1] — both intimately
united, and both necessary to re-creation as following on
dissolution. It may be easily imagined that a creed like this,
which regarded the blending of the male and female principles,
not only as the necessary cause of production and reproduction,
but also as the source of strength, vigour, and successful
enterprise, soon degenerated into corrupt and superstitious
practices. And, as a matter of fact, the Tantrika doctrines have
in some cases lapsed into a degrading system of impurity and
licentiousness.

Nevertheless the original Tantra books, which simply
inculcate the worship of the active energizing principle of the
deity — full as they are of doubtful symbolism, strange
mysticism, and even directions for witchcraft and every kind
of superstitious rite — are not necessarily in themselves impure.
On the contrary, the best of them are believed to be free from
gross allusions, however questionable may be the tendency
of their teaching. The truth, I believe, is that they have never
yet been thoroughly investigated by European scholars. When
they become more so, their connection with a popular and
distorted view of the Sankhyan theory of creation, and perhaps

---

1. This is the *Ardha-nari* or half male half female form of Shiva. There
are two divisions of the Shaktas: 1. the *Dakshincharins,* 'right-doers,'
'right hand worshippers,' or *Bhaktas,* 'devoted ones,' who worship
the goddess Parvati or Durga, openly, and without impure practices;
2. the *Vamacarins,* 'left-doers,' 'left-hand worshippers,' or *Kaulas,*
'ancestral ones,' who are said to perform all their rites in secret, a
naked woman representing the goddess. The sacred books appealed
to by 1. are called the *Nigamas;* by 2. the *Agamas.* The forms of
worship are said to require the use of some one of the five *Ma-karas,*
'words beginning with the letter *m,*' viz.1. *madya,* wine; 2. *mansa,*
flesh; 3. *matsya,* fish; 4. *mudra,* mystical gestures; 5. *maithuna,*
intercourse of sexes.

with some corrupt forms of Buddhism, will probably be made clear. It is certain that among the Northern Buddhists, especially in Nepal, a kind of worship of the terrific forms of Siva and Durga appears to have become interwoven with the Buddhistic system.

In all probability, too, the mystical texts (*Mantras*) and magical formularies contained in the Tantras will be found to bring them into a closer relationship with the Atharva-veda than has been hitherto suspected.

As so little is known of these mystical writings, it is not possible to decide at present as to which are the most ancient, and still less as to the date to be assigned to any of them. It may, however, be taken for granted that the extant treatises are, like the extant Puranas, founded on older works; and if the oldest known Purana is not older than the sixth or seventh century (see p. 552), an earlier date can scarcely be attributed to the oldest known Tantra[1]. Perhaps the *Rudra-yamala* is one of the most esteemed. Others are the *Kalika, Maha-nirvana* (attributed to Shiva), *Kularnava* (or text-book of the Kaulas, see note, p. 564), *Shyama-rahasya, Sharada-tilaka, Mantra-mahodadhi, Uddisa, Kamada, Kamakhya.*

I now note some of the subjects of which they treat, merely premising that the Tantras are generally in the form of a dialogue between Shiva and his wife Durga or Parvati, the latter inquiring as to the correct mode of performing certain secret ceremonies, or as to the mystical efficacy of various Mantras used as spells, charms, and magical formularies; and the former instructing her.

Properly a *Tantra*, like a Purana, ought to treat of five subjects, viz. 1. the creation; 2. the destruction of the world;

---

1. It has been noted that the oldest native lexicographer, Amara Sinha, does not give the meaning 'sacred treatise' to the word *tantra*, as later writers do.

3. the worship of the gods; 4. the attainment of all objects, especially of six superhuman faculties; 5. the four modes of union with the Supreme Spirit. A great variety of other subjects, however, are introduced, and practically a great number of Tantras are merely handbooks or manuals of magic and witchcraft, and collections of Mantras for producing and averting evils. Such, at least, must be the conclusion arrived at, if we are to judge of them by the bare statement of their contents in the Catalogues published by Rajendralala Mitra and others. I select the following as specimens of what they contain:

Praise of the female energy; spells for bringing people into subjection; for making them enamoured; for unsettling their minds; for fattening; for destroying sight; for producing dumbness, deafness, fevers, &c.; for bringing on miscarriage; for destroying crops; for preventing various kinds of evil; modes of worshipping Kali; methods of breathing in certain rites; language of birds, beasts, &c.; worship of the female emblem, with the adjuncts of wine, flesh-meat, women, &c.

This last is said to be the subject of the Kamakhya-tantra.

VI. The Niti-sastras

This department of Sanskrit literature may be regarded as including, in the first place, Niti-sastras proper, or works whose direct object is moral teaching; and, in the second, all the didactic portion of the epic poems and other works.

The aim of the *Niti-sastras proper* is to serve as guides to correct conduct (*niti*) in all the relations of domestic, social, and political life. They are either, *A.* collections of choice maxims, striking thoughts, and wise sentiments, in the form of metrical stanzas; or, *B.* books of fables in prose, which string together stories about animals and amusing apologues for the sake of the moral they contain, or to serve as frameworks for the introduction of metrical precepts. These latter often represent wise sayings orally current, or are cited from the regular collections and from other sources.

But besides, the Niti-shastras proper, almost every department of Sanskrit literature contributes its share to moral teaching.

Any one who studies the best Hindu writings cannot but be struck by the moral tone which everywhere pervades them. Indian writers, although they do not trouble themselves much about the history of past generations, constantly represent the present condition of human life as the result of actions in previous existences. Hence a right course of present conduct becomes an all-important consideration as bearing on future happiness; and we need not be surprised if, to satisfy a constant longing for *Niti* or guidance and instruction in practical wisdom, nearly all departments of Sanskrit literature — Brahmanas, Upanishads, Law-books, Epic poems and Puranas — are more or less didactic, nearly all delight in moralizing and philosophizing, nearly all abound in wise sayings and prudential rules. Scarcely a book or writing of any kind begins without an invocation to the Supreme Being or to some god supposed to represent his overruling functions, and as each work proceeds the writers constantly suspend the main topic, or turn aside from their regular subject for the purpose of interposing moral and religious reflections, and even long discourses, on the duties of life. This is especially the case in the Mahabharat.

Examples of the religious precepts, sentiments, and aphothegms, scattered everywhere throughout Sanskrit literature, have already been given in this volume (see, for instance, pp. 312-327, 491, 512)[1].

---

1. I need scarcely mention here so well-known and valuable a work as Dr. Bohtlingk's *Indische Spruche,* which contains a complete collection of maxims, &c., in three volumes, and gives the text of each aphothegm critically, with a German translation.

We now, therefore, turn, in conclusion, to the *two divisions of Niti-shastras proper.*

A. With regard to the regular collections of moral maxims, sentiments, &c., these are generally in metrical stanzas, and sometimes contain charming allusions to natural objects and domestic life, with occasional striking thoughts on the nature of God and the immortality of the soul, as well as sound ethical teaching in regard to the various relations and conditions of society. They are really mines of practical good sense. The knowledge of human nature displayed by the authors, the shrewd advice they give, and the censure they pass on human frailties — often in pointed, vigorous, and epigrammatic language — attest an amount of wisdom which, if it had been exhibited in practice, must have raised the Hindus to a high position among the nations of the earth. Whether, however, any entire collection of such stanzas can be attributed to any one particular author is doubtful. The Hindus, for the reasons we have already stated, have always delighted in aphothegms. Numbers of wise sayings have, from time immemorial, been constantly quoted in conversation. Many thus orally current were of such antiquity that to settle their authorship was impossible. But occasional attempts were made to give permanence to the floating wisdom of the day, by stringing together in stanzas the most celebrated maxims and sayings like beads on a necklace; each necklace representing a separate topic, and the authorship of a whole series being naturally ascribed to men of known wisdom, like Bhartri-hari and Chanakya (see p. 546), much in the same way as the authorship of the Puranas and Mahabharata was referred to the sage Vyasa (see p. 414). Among these collections it will be sufficient to note:

1. The three hundred aphothegms, ascribed to *Bharti-hari*[1] (see p. 574), of which the 1st Shataka, or collection of a hundred

---

1. Edited by Von Bohlen, with a Latin translation, in 1833.

verses, is on love (*sringara*), and therefore more lyrical than didactic, the 2nd is on good conduct (*niti*), and the 3rd on the renunciation of worldly desires (*vairagya*). 2. The *Vriddha-chanakya* or *Rajaniti-shastra*. 3. The *Chanakya-shataka* or hundred verses (109 in one collection translated by Weber) of *Chanakya*, minister of Chandra-gupta (see under Mudra-rakshasa, p. 546). 4. The *Amaru-shataka* or one hundred erotic stanzas of Amaru (already described at p. 504). 5. The *Sarngadhara-paddhati*, 'Sarnga-dhara's collection,' an anthology professing to collect sententious verses from various sources and to give the names of most of the authors, to the number of about 247[1]. Some verses, however, are anonymous.

There are numerous other collections of didactic and erotic stanzas, some of which are quite modern, e.g. the *Subhashitarnava*, *Santi-sataka*, *Niti-sankalana*, *Kavitamrita-kupa*, *Kavitarnava*, *Jnana-sudhakara*, *Shloka-mola*, the *Bhamini-vilasa* by Jagan-natha, the *Chaura-panchasika* by Vihlana (edited with Bhartri-hari by Von Bohlen).

B. As to the collections of fables and apologues, these form a class of composition in which the natives of India are wholly unsurpassed.

Sir W. Jones affirmed that the Hindus claimed for themselves three inventions: 1. the game of chess (*chaturanga*, see p. 289 of this volume); 2. the decimal figures (see p. 210); 3. the method of teaching by fables. To these might be added: 4. grammar (p. 189); 5. logic (p. 78).

It is thought that both the Greek fabulist Aesop and the Arabian Lokman[2] (*Lukman*) owed much to the Hindus. Indeed,

---

1. See Professor Aufrecht's article on this anthology in vol. xxvii of the Zeitschrift der Deutschen Morgenändischen Gesellschaft.
2. According to Herodotus and Plutarch, Aesop lived in the latter part of the sixth century B.C, and was once a slave at Samos. On being freed, he travelled about and visited Croesus, &c. As to Lokman, probably such a person once lived, though thought by some to be an imaginary character. He is certainly more likely to have borrowed

in all likelihood, some ancient book of Sanskrit apologues, of which the present representative is the *Pancha-tantra,* and which has been translated or paraphrased into most of the dialects of India, as well as into Hebrew, Arabic, Syriac, Pahlavi, Persian, Turkish, Italian, French, German English, and almost every known language of the literary world, is the original source of all the well-known fables current in Europe and Asia for more than two thousand years since the days of Herodotus (II. 134) [1].

This *Pancha-tantra*[2] — which is itself the original source of a still later work, the well-known class-book *Hito-padesha,*

---

ideas from Indian fabulists than from Job, or Abraham, whose nephew he is said by some Arabic writers to have been. The 31st chap. of the Koran is called after him, God being made to say, 'We have given him wisdom.'

1. A Pahlavi version of the Pancha-tantra was the first real translation. It was made in the time of Nushirvan, about A.D. 570, and perished with much of the Pahlavi literature when the Arabs invaded Persia. Before its destruction it had been translated into Arabic, about A.D. 760, and was called *Kalila wa Damna* (= Sanskrit *Karataka* and *Damanaka,* the names of two jackals) or fables of the Brahman Bidpai. The well-known Persian *Anvar-I-Subhaili,* 'lights of Canopus,' of Husain Va'iz, written about the beginning of the fifteenth century, was also an amplification of the Pancha-tantra. Abu-l Fazl, Akbar's celebrated minister, also translated it into simpler Persian and called it *'Iyar-I-Danish,* 'criterion of knowledge.' An Urdu version, called *Khirad Afroz,* 'illuminator of the understanding,' was made in 1803 by Hafizu'd din Ahmad. The Hebrew version is attributed to one Rabbi Joël. This was translated into Latin by John of Capua at the end of the fifteenth century; and from this various Italian, Spanish, and German translations were made. The English Pilpay's fables is said to have been taken from a French translation. The best of the Turkish versions, called *Humayun Namah,* was made, according to Mr. E.B. Eastwick, in the reign of the Emperor Sulaiman I, by' Ali Chalabi bin Salih.

2. Edited by Kosegarten in 1848, and lately in India by Professors Buhler and Kielhorn. Translated into German, with an elaborate Introduction, by Professor Benfey in 1859.

'friendly instruction' — derives its name from being divided into five chapters (*Tantras*); but it is also commonly called the *Panchopakhyana*, 'five collections of stories.' The date of the extant Pancha-tantra is usually placed about the end of the fifth century. But the fables of which it consists are many of them referable to a period long preceding the Christian era.

It has even been conjectured that the notion of instructing in domestic, social, and political duties by means of stories in which animals figure as the speakers, first suggested itself to Hindu moralists when the doctrine of metempsychosis had taken root in India. We have seen that a most elaborate theory of transmigration of souls through plants, animals, men, and gods was propounded by Manu at least 500 years B.C. to which date we have conjecturally assigned the existing Code of the Manavas (see p. 71, note 2, and p. 309). Accordingly there is evidence that contemporaneously with the rise of Brahmanism in Manu's time, and the consequent growth of antagonistic systems like Buddhism and the Sankhya philosphy, fables were commonly used to illustrate the teaching of these systems. Thus:

In the whole fourth Book of the *Sankhya-pravachana* (see p. 96, note 1) there are constant exemplifications of philosophical truth by allusions to the habits of animals, as recorded in popular stories and proverbs. (For example, *sarpa-vat*, 'like serpent,' IV. 12; *bheki-vat*, 'like the female frog,' IV. 16; *Shuka-vat*, 'like the parrot,' IV. 25, &c.). Again, one of Katyayana's Varttikas or supplements to a rule of the grammarian Panini (IV. 2, 104; cf. IV. 3, 125) gives a name for the popular fable of the crows and owls (*Kakolukika*), the actual title of the fourth Tantra of the Pancha-tantra, *Kakolukiya*, being formed according to another rule of Panini (IV. 3, 88). This fable is also alluded to in the Sauptika-parvan of the Mahabharata (see p. 409 of this volume). In that Epic, too, other well-known fables are related. For example, the story of the three fishes occurring in Hitopadesha, Book IV, is found in Shanti-parvan 4889 &c., and that of Sunda and Upasunda in Adi-parvan 7619.

The fables of the Pancha-tantra and Hitopadesha are supposed to be narrated by a learned Brahman named Vishnu-sharman for the improvement of some young princes, whose royal father had expressed himself grieved by their idle, dissolute habits. Of course, the fables are merely a vehicle for the instruction conveyed. They are strung together one within another, so that before one is finished another is commenced, and moral verses from all sources are interwoven with the narratives.

A still larger collection of tales exists in Sanskrit literature. It is called the *Katha-sarit-sagara*, 'ocean of rivers of stories,' and was compiled by *Soma-deva Bhatta* of Kashmir, towards the end of the eleventh or beginning of the twelfth century, from a still larger work named *Vrihat-katha* (ascribed to *Gunadhya*):

The *Katha-sarit-sagara*[1] consists of eighteen Books (*Lambakas*), containing in all 124 chapters (*Tarangas*). The second and third Books contain the celebrated story of Udayana (see p. 545). A contemporary of Soma-deva was *Kalhana*, who is said to have written the *Rajatarangini*, 'stream of kings' — a chronicle of the kings of Kashmir — about A.D. 1148. This is almost the only work in the whole range of Sanskrit literature which has any historical value. It is mostly composed in the common Shloka metre, and consists of eight chapters (*Tarangas*)[2].

---

1. The whole work has been excellently edited by Dr. Hermann Brockhaus, all but the first five Lambakas being in the Roman character.
2. The first six Books were edited and the whole work translated into French by M. Toyer in 1840, and analysed by Professor. H.H. Wilson. See Dr. Rost's edition of his works.

Other collections of tales and works of fiction — which are not, however, properly Niti-sastras — are the following:

1. The *Dasha-kumara-charita*, 'adventures of ten princes,' a series of tales in prose (but called by native authorities a *Kavya* or poem) by *Dandin*, who lived in the eleventh century. The style is studiously difficult, long compounds and rare grammatical forms being used. It was edited, with a long Introduction, by Professor H.H. Wilson in 1846. 2. The *Vetala-pancha-vinshati*, 'twenty-five tales of a demon,' ascribed to an author named *Jambhala-datta*. It is the original of the well-known Hindi collection of stories called *Baital-pachisi*. The stories are told by a Vetala, or spirit, to king Vikramaditya, who tries to carry off a dead body occupied by the Vetala. 3. The *Sinhasana-dvatrinsat* (sometimes called Vikrama-carita or 'adventures of Vikramaditya'), stories related by the thirty-two images on king Vikramaditya's throne which was dug up near Dhara, the capital of king *Bhoja,* to whom the tales are told, and who is supposed to have flourished in the tenth or eleventh century. It is the original of the Bengali *Batrish Sinhasan.* 4. The *Shuka-saptati* or 'seventy tales of a parrot,' translated into many modern dialects of India (e.g. into Hindustani under the title *Tota-kahani;* several Persian versions called *Tuti-mama* being also extant). 5. The *Katharnava*, 'ocean of stories,' a collection of about thirty-five comparatively modern stories attributed to Shiva-dasa. 6. The *Bhoja-prabandha,* a work by *Ballala,* celebrating the deeds of king Bhoja. 7. The *Kadambari,* a kind of novel by *Vana* or *Bana,* who flourished in the seventh century at the court of Harsha-vardhana or Shiladitya, king of Kanauj. An analysis of this work is given by Professor Weber (vol. i. p. 352 of his Indische Streifen). Good editions have been printed at Calcutta. 8. The *Vasava-datta,* a romance by *Subandhu,* written according to Dr. Fitz-Edward Hall, not later than the early part of the seventh century (see the elaborate Preface to his excellent edition of the work in 1859). This and the previous story, although written in prose, are regarded (like 1) as Kavyas or poems, and are supposed,

like the Raghava-pandaviya (p. 504), to contain numerous words
and phrases which convey a double sense.

I conclude with examples from Bhartri-hari's aphothegms,
from the Pancha-tantra, and from the Hitopadesha.
The following are specimens from *Bhartri-hari:*

Here in this world love's only fruit is won,
When two true hearts are blended into one;
But when by disagreement love is blighted,
'Twere better that two corpses were united (I. 29).

Blinded by self-conceit and knowing nothing,
Like elephants infatuated with passion,
I thought within myself, I all things knew;
But when by slow degrees I somewhat learnt,
By aid of wise preceptors, my conceit,
Like some disease, passed off; and now I live
In the plain sense of what a fool I am (II. 8).

The attribute most noble of the hand
Is readiness in giving; of the head,
Bending before a teacher; of the mouth,
Veracious speaking; of a victor's arms,
Undaunted valour; of the inner heart,
Pureness the most unsullied; of the ears,
Delight in hearing and receiving truth —
These are adornments of high-minded men
Better than all the majesty of Empire (II. 55).

Better be thrown from some high peak,
Or dashed to pieces, falling upon rocks;
Better insert the hand between the fangs
Of an envenomed serpent; better fall
Into a fiery furnace, than destroy
The character by stains of infamy (II. 77).

Now for a little while a child, and now
An amorous youth; then for a season turned
Into the wealthy householder; then stripped

Of all his riches, with decrepit limbs
And wrinkled frame, man creeps towards the end
Of life's erratic course; and, like an actor,
Passed behind Death's curtain out of view[1] (III. 51).

I now give, as an example of an Indian apologue, a nearly
literal translation of a fable in the Pancha-tantra (Book V.
8th story):

The Two-headed Weaver[2]

Once upon a time there lived in a certain place a weaver (*kaulika*)
named Manthara, all the wood-work of whose loom one day
fell to pieces while he was weaving. Taking his axe (*kuthara*),
he set off to cut fresh timber to make a new loom, and finding
a large Sinshapa tree by the sea-side, and thinking to himself,
'This will furnish plenty of wood for my purpose,' began to fell
it. In the tree resided a spirit (*vyantara*), who exclaimed on the
first stroke of the axe, 'Hallo, there! what are you about? this
tree is my dwelling, and I can't allow you to destroy it; for here
I live very happily, inhaling the fresh breezes cooled by the
ocean's spray.' The weaver replied, 'What am I to do? unless I
get wood, my family must starve. Be quick, then, and look out
for another house; for cut your present one down I must, and
that too instantly.' The spirit replied, 'I am really quite pleased
with your candour, and you shall have any boon you like to ask
for; but you shall not injure this tree.' The weaver said he would
go home and consult a friend and his wife; and would then come
back and let the spirit know what gift he would be willing to
take in compensation for the loss of the tree. To this the spirit
assented. When the weaver returned home, he found there a

.1. The parallel in Shakespeare need scarcely be suggested.
2. I have omitted some verses in this story, and taken a few liberties.
   In my translations I have consulted Professor H.H. Wilson, and
   Professor Benfey's German translation.

particular friend of his — the village barber (*napita*). To him he
confided all that had occurred, telling him that he had forced
the spirit to grant him a boon, and consulting his friend as to
what he should demand. The barber said, 'My good fellow, ask
to be made a king; then I'll be your prime minister, and we'll
enjoy ourselves gloriously in this world and gain felicity in the
next. Don't you know the saying? —

> A king by gifts on earth achieves renown
> And, when he dies, in heaven obtains a crown.'

The weaver approved his friend's suggestion, but said he
must first consult his wife. To this the barber strenuously objected,
and reminded him of the proverb,

> 'Give women food, dress, and all that's nice,
> But tell them not your plans, if you are wise.

Beside, the sagacious son of Bhrigu has said as follows:

> If you have ought to do and want to do it,
> Don't ask woman's counsel, or you'll rue it.'

The weaver admitted the justice of his friend the barber's
observations, but insisted that *his* wife was quite a model woman
and wholly devoted to her husband's welfare, and that he felt
compelled to ask her opinion. Accordingly he went to her, and
told her of the promise he had extorted from the spirit of the
tree, and how the barber had recommended his asking to be
made a king. He then requested her advice as to what boon he
should solicit. She replied, 'You should never listen, husband,
to barbers. What can they possibly know about anything? Surely
you have heard the saying,

> No man of sense should take as his adviser
> A barber, dancer, mendicant, or miser.

Besides, all the world knows that royalty leads to a perpetual
round of troubles. The cares of peace and war, marching and
encamping, making allies and quarrelling with them afterwards,

never allow a monarch a moment's enjoyment. Let me tell you then,

> If you are longing to be made a king,
> You've set your heart upon a foolish thing;
> The vase of unction at your coronation
> Will sprinkle you with water and vexation.' (Cf. p. xxxvii, 3.)

The weaver replied, 'What you say, wife, is very just, but pray tell me what I am to ask for.' His wife rejoined, 'I recommend you to seek the means of doing more work. Formed as you now are, you can never weave more than one piece of cloth at a time. Ask for an additional pair of hands and another head, with which you may keep a loom going both before and behind you. The profits of the first loom will be enough for all household expenses, and with the proceeds of the second you'll be able to gain consequence and credit with your tribe, and a respectable position in this world and the next.'

'Capital! Capital!' exclaimed the husband, mightily pleased with his excellent wife's advice. Forthwith he repaired to the tree, and addressing the spirit, said, 'As you have promised to grant me anything I ask for, give me another pair of arms, and an additional head.' No sooner said than done. In an instant he became equipped with a couple of heads and four arms, and returned home, highly delighted with his new acquisitions. No sooner, however, did the villagers see him, than , greatly alarmed, they exclaimed, 'A goblin! a goblin!' and between striking him with sticks and pelting him with stones, speedily put an end to his existence.

The following sentiments are also from the Panca-tantra:

> Praise not the goodness of the grateful man
> Who acts with kindness to his benefactors.
> He who does good to those who do him wrong
> Alone deserves the epithet of good (I. 277).
> The misery a foolish man endures

In seeking riches, is a hundred-fold
More grievous than the suffering of him
Who strives to gain eternal blessedness (II. 127).

Hear thou a summary of righteousness,
And ponder well the maxim: Never do
To other persons what would pain thyself (II. 104).

The little minded ask: Belongs this man
To our own family? The noble-hearted
Regard the human race as all akin (V. 38).

As a conclusion, I subjoin some sentiments from the
Hitopadesha or book of 'friendly advice.' My translations are
from Professor Johnson's excellent edition:

Fortune attends the lion-hearted man
Who acts with energy; weak-minded persons
Sit idly waiting for some gift of fate.
Banish all thought of destiny, and act
With manly vigour, straining all thy nerve;
When thou has put forth all thy energy
The blame of failure will not rest with thee (Introd. 31).

Even a blockhead may respect inspire,
So long as he is suitably attired;
A fool may gain esteem among the wise,
So long as he has sense to hold his tongue (Introd. 40).

A piece of glass may like a jewel glow,
If but a lump of gold be placed below;
So even fools to eminence may rise
By close association with the wise (Introd. 41).

Never expect a prosperous result
In seeking profit from an evil quarter —
When there is taint of poison in the cup,
E'en th' ambrosial draught, which to the gods
Is source of life immortal, tends to death (I. 5).

Subjection to the senses has been called
The road to ruin, and their subjugation

The path to fortune; so by which you please (I. 29).

A combination of e'en feeble things
Is often potent to effect a purpose;
E'en fragile straws, when twisted into ropes,
May serve to bind a furious elephant (I. 35).

A man of truest wisdom will resign
His wealth and e'en his life, for good of others;
Better abandon life in good cause,
When death in any case is sure to happen[1] (I. 45).

He has all wealth who has a mind contented.
To one whose foot is covered with a shoe
The earth appears all carpeted with leather (I. 152).

'Tis right to sacrifice an individual
For a whole household, and a family
For a whole village, and village even
For a whole country's good; but for one's self
And one's own soul, one should give up the world (I. 159).

Make the best use of thy prosperity,
And then of thy reverses when they happen.
For good and evil fortune come and go,
Revolving like a wheel in sure rotation (I. 184).

Strive not too anxiously for a subsistence,
Thy Maker will provide thee sustenance;
No sooner is a human being born
Than milk for his support streams from the breast (I. 190).

He by whose hand the swans were painted white,
And parrots green, and peacocks many-hued,
Will make provision for thy maintenance[1] (I. 191).

How can true happiness proceed from wealth,
Which in its acquisition causes pain;
In loss, affliction; in abundance, folly (I. 192)?
A friend, the sight of whom is to the eyes
A balm — who is the heart's delight — who shares

---

1. Compare St. Mathew vi. 26.

Our joys and sorrows — is a treasure rare.
But other friendly persons who are ready
To share in our prosperity, abound.
Friendship's true touchstone is adversity (I. 226).

Whoever, quitting certainties, pursues
Uncertain things, may lose his certainties (I. 227).

By drops of water falling one by one,
Little by little, may a jar be filled;
Such is the law of all accumulations
Of money, knowledge, and religious merit (II. 10).

That man is sapient who knows how to suit
His words to each occasion, his kind acts
To each man's worth, his anger to his power (II. 48).

Is anything by nature beautiful
Or the reverse? Whatever pleases each,
That only is by each thought beautiful (II. 50).

Disinclination to begin a work
Through fear of failure, is a mark of weakness;
Is food renounced through fear of indigestion (II. 54)?

If glass be used to decorate a crown,
While gems are taken to bedeck a foot,
'Tis not that any fault lies in the gem,
But in the want of knowledge of the setter[1] (II. 72).

A man may on affliction's touchstone learn
The worth of his own kindred, wife, and servants;
Also of his own mind and character (II. 79).

A feverish display of over-zeal
At the first outset, is an obstacle
To all success; water, however cold,
Will penetrate the ground by slow degrees (III. 48).

Even a foe, if he perform a kindness,
Should be esteemed a kinsman; e'en a kinsman,

---

1. 'Is such a thing as an emerald made worse than it was, if it is not
   praised?' Marcus Aurelius. Farrar's 'Seekers after God,' p. 306.

If he do harm, should be esteemed a foe.
A malady, though bred within the body
Does mischief, while a foreign drug that comes
From some far forest does a friendly work (III. 101).

Whither have gone the rulers of the earth,
With all their armies, all their regal pomp,
And all their stately equipages? Earth,
That witnessed their departure, still abides (IV. 68).

E'en as a traveller, meeting with the shade
Of some o'erhanging tree, awhile reposes,
Then leaves its shelter to pursue his way,
So men meet friends, then part with them for ever[1] (IV. 73).

Thou art thyself a stream whose sacred ford
Is elf-restraint, whose water is veracity,
Whose bank is virtue, and whose waves are love;
Here practise thy ablutions; by mere water
The inner man can ne'er be purified (IV. 90).

---

1. Compare p. 441, l. 11, of this volume.
   Many parallels in European writers will naturally suggest themselves
   to the educated reader while perusing the foregoing pages. I have
   purposely avoided cumbering my notes with obvious comparisons.

Index

Abbas, *liii,* 1.
Abbassi Khalifs, *liii,* 1.
Abhava, 83.
Abhidhana-Chintamani, 140; 187.
Abhidhana-ratnamala, 187.
Abhidharma-pitaka, *xl,* 1; 64; 3.
Abhijit, 380, 1.
Abhijnana-Shakuntalam, 546.
Abhimanyu, 435, 1; 445; 452.
Abhiramamani, 410.
Abhisheka, *xlvi* 3; 436.
Abhyasa, 110.
Abhyudayika Sraddha, 228.
Abubakr, *liii,* 1.
Abu-l Fazl, 570, 1.
Achara, 237; 243; 293; 312; 328; 330.
Acharya, 261; 217; 331; 457.
Accent, 179; 276, 1.
Acesines, river, 419; 1.
Achilles, 352; 1; 399, 1.
Action, 61; 522.
Achyuta, 435, 2. .
Achyuta-Chakravartin, 341.
Adbhuta, 508, 1. .
Adhidaivikam, 246.
Adhikara, 191.
Adhimasa, 200.

Adhiratha, 422.
Adhishthana, 226; 3.
Adhiyajnam, 246.
Adho-nivitah, 224.
Adhvaryu (priests) 9, 1; 245.
Adhyapanam, 267.
Adhyatmam, 164.
Adhyatma-ramayana, 411.
Adhyatmika, 246; 312, 1.
Adhyavahanikam, 301.
Adhyayanam, 267.
Adi Grantha, of Sikhs, 363.
Adi-parva, 414, 1; 416.
Adisura, 239, 1 .
Adishvara, 239, 1.
Aditi, 12; 17.
Aditya, 562.
Adityas twelve, 13; 358; 447.
Aditya-vara, 204, 1.
Admetus and Alcestis, 440.
Adrishta, 7, 1; 73; 88; 90; 91 143; 2; 317; 520.
Advaita, 'non-dualism, 121.
Advayam 132; 6.
Aegera, 5, 2.
Aegle marmelos, 493, 2.
Aeneid, 72, 1.
Aesop, 569.
Afghnistan, *xxiv,* 1.

Afghans, xxiv, 2; xxvii, 1.
Agama, xliv, 1; 5; 564.
Agamemnon, 474.
Agastya, xlvi, 1; 264; 1; 394; 543.
Ages, four, 204, 2; 251.
Aghorins, lix.
Aghora-ghanta, 538.
Agneyastra, 451, 2.
Agni, 14; 18; 19; 1; 216; 288; 359; 479; 533.
Agni, a prayer to, 31, 1.
Agni-hotra, 32; 1; 143; 173; 275; 285.
Agnihotra-homah, 246.
Agnihotrin, 216, 1.
Agnimitra, 335.
Agnipurana, 328; 411.
Agnishtoma, 215; 260; 261.
Agni-vesa, 412.
Agrayana, 184.
Ahalya, wife of Gautama, 432; 1.
Ahankara, 69, 1; 100; 101; 103; 136; 164; 250.
Ahavaniya fire, 216, 1; 216, 2; 224; 225.
Ahi, 17.
Ahimsa, 273; 1.
Ahura mazda, 12.
Ahvaya, 293.
Aila, 419.
Aila vamsa, 550, 2.
Airavata, Indra's Elephant, 395; 481, 1.
Aisha, wife of Muhammad, liii, 1.
Aitaraya Aranyaka, 276, 1.
Aitareya Upanishad, 39.
Aitareya Brahmana, 29; 32; 33; 37 198; 276, 1; 368, 1.
Aitihasikas, 184.

Aja, 383; 457, 2.
Ajata Satru, 64, 1.
Ajigarta, 31; 32.
Ajita, 140, 1.
Ajimir, 363, 1.
Akasa, 68, 1; 84; 100; 100, 2.
Akasa-mukhins, lx.
Akbar, Emperor, xxiv, 2; xxvii, 1; 570.
Akhyana, 236, 1; 280; 413, 1.
Akhyata, 177; 186.
Aksha-pada, 82, 1; 96, 1.
Akshapa darsara, 137, 1.
Akshepa, 509.
Alankara-Kaustubha, 521.
Alankaras, 507; 508.
Alankara-sarvasva, 521.
Alankara-sastra, 521.
Albert, king Charles, 375.
Alexander (death of), 546.
Alexander (invasion of), 282; 355.
Alexander the Great, xxii.
Algebra, invention of, 200.
Algebra, Hindu, 207; 208.
Algebraists, Hindu, 208.
Ali, liii, 1.
Ali (descendants, of) liii, 1.
Al-Kadr, night called, 6.
Allah, li, 1.
Allahabad, xxxvii, 2.
Allegory of two birds, 45; 252.
Allen W.H. & Co., 532.
Alliteration, employment of, 505.
Almanacs, 204, 1.
Altai mountains, xxiv, 1.
Amara kosha, 187; 481, 1.
Amara Sinha, 167; 551; 565, 1.
Amaru, 504.

Amaru sataka, 504; 569.
Ambalika, 420.
Ambarish, 31, 1; 403; 1.
Ambashtha, 239, 1; 255.
Ambika, 420.
Amlika, 472, 3.
Amrit (nectar); 365; 538.
Amoolam-moolam 98; 100.
Amurta, 203.
Amyak, 184.
Analysis, 76; 187.
Ananda, 58, 1; 64, 1.
Ananda maya, 133.
Ananda tirtha, 137, 1.
Ananta, 140, 1; 480.
Ananta vijaya, 450.
Anargha raghava, 410; 547.
Anarya, 347.
Anaryas, 346.
Anashrita, 336.
Anasuya, wife of Atri, 402; 1.
Anatha pindada, 58, 3.
Anatomy, 212.
An-anpadhikah sambandhah, 79.
Anaximander, 67, 1.
Anaximenes, 67, 1.
Anda, 250.
Andhakas, 447.
Andromache, 352, 1; 489.
Anga, kingdom of, 379; 466.
Anga-Raga, 402, 1.
Angas, xliv, 1.
Angiras, 9, 1; 232; 245; 265;
    283, 1; 339; 556; 1.
Anglo Saxon, xxxv .
Angushtha-matra, 226, 3.
Anguttara-nikaya, xl, 1.
Anila (wind); 288.
Animals, xxxl, 1; 71; 2; 310.

Anjalika, 453, 1.
Anjana, 481, 1.
Anka, 210; 522; 522; 523.
Ankusha, 211.
Anna-maya, 133.
Anna-prasanna, 220; 262; 269.
Antha-karana, 69; 69, 1; 136.
Antahasanjna, 72, 1.
Anthariksha, 225.
Antar-vedi, 225.
Anthropomorphism, 357.
Antiochus and Eumenes, 282, 3.
Antya, 274.
Anubandha, 189; 189, 3.
Anudattoktya, 526.
Anucramani (indices') 211.
Anumana, 77; 99; 136; 252.
Anumati 184; 199.
Anuplabdhi, 135.
Anuprasa, 508.
Anus or 'atoms', 93.
Anusasanparvam, 417; 459.
Anushtubh metre, 166; 349; 374.
Anusravika, 54, 1.
Anuvansa sloka, 550, 2.
Anuvritti, 191.
Anuyoga dvara sutra, xliv..
Anvaharya, 280.
Anvaharya pacana fire, 216, 2.
Anvar-Suhaili, 570, 1.
Anvashtakya Sraddha, 220.
Anvikshiki, (logic); 249.
Apadava, xl, 1.
Apad-dharma, 417.
Apara, 86.
Apararka, 340.
Aparatava, 85.
Apas, (water), 84; 101.
Apasadah, 274.

Apastamba, 232; 232, 1; 266, 2, 339.
Apastamba Grihya sutra, 214.
Apastamba Shrauta sutra, 171; 214, 1.
Apastrambas, the, 214, 1.
Apavarga, 75; 80.
Aphorisms, 52.
Aphrodite 366, 1.
Apisali, 188, 1.
Apologue, Indian, 575.
A-prakrita, 508.
A-prastuta, 508.
Apsaras, 310; 559.
Apta vachana, 99.
Apya-dikshita, 521.
Apyaya, 521.
Ara, 140.
Arabhati, 541.
Arabs, xxiv, 207, 1.
Arani, 18.
Aranya-kanda, 375; 409.
Aranyakas, 39.
Ararat, xxiv, 1.
Arechery, 211.
Architecture, 212.
Ardha-nari (siva); 107; 361; 564.
Argha, 331; 311, 3.
Arhat, 58, 2; 139.
Arhata darsana, 137, 1.
Arhatas, 138.
Ariman, xxiii, 1.
Aristotle, 67, 1; 73, 1; 78; 84, 1; 87, 1; 102, 2; 121; 135; 450; 1.
Aritra, 256; 1.
Arjuna, 118; 149; 258; 2; 424: 432, 1; 450; 422; 468; 480; 1; 550; 2.

Armenian language, xxii, xxiv, 1.
Armenians, of India, xxiv, 1.
Aropa, 509.
Arian xxiii, 282, 3.
Arsha (revealed knowledge), 243.
Arsha (from of marriage), 217; 274.
Arts poetica, 507.
Artha, 80; 223.
Artha-katha, xl, 1.
Arthalankara, 508.
Arthantaranyasa, 509.
Arthapatti, 136; 509.
Artha vada, 28.
Aruna, 477.
Arundhati, 219.
Arya, xxii; 348.
Arya bhatta, 201.
Aryaman, 217.
Aryans, 5; 1; 9; 349.
Aryashta-sata, 201.
Aryavarta, xx, 2; 256.
A-samavayi karana, 87.
Asana (postures); 111.
Asauca, 9; 1.
Asucam, 337.
Ascetic, Buddhist and Jaina, 61; 140.
Asceticism, 111, 152.
Ashadha, 200; 1.
Ashoka, xl, 1; 64; 1; 414; 1; 519.
Ashoka inscriptions, 141; 1; 351.
Ashramas (orders); 244; 268.
Ashrama Vasika, 459; 1.
Ashramavasika parvan, 418.
Ashtadhyayi 189.
Ashtaka Sradha, 220; 228.
Ashtakam Paniniyam, 189.
Ashtakshara, 180.

Ashtamoorthi, 361; 2.
Ashvin, 408; 1.
Ashvina, 200; 1.
Ashvini, 200; 1; 477; 2.
Ashvini Kumaras, 477; 1.
Ashvins, 14; 184; 424; 432; 1; 470.
Ashvalayana Grihya sutra, 213, 276, 1; 222; 236; 1; 280; 298, 1; 298, 3; 414, 1; 551.
Ashvalavana srauta sutra, 171; 213, 1; 276, 1.
Ashvalayana-Brahmana, 29, 3.
Ashva medha, 32, 1; 379; 214; 418.
Ashvamedha paravan, 418.
Asiatic Researches, 114; 181; 1.
Asi-patra-vana, 463.
Asita, 563.
Assam, xlv.
Assamese language, xxxvi.
Assessors, 332.
Astrologer, 205.
Astrology, 200; 205.
Astronomy, 196; 198; 200.
Asuci, 245.
Asura, 274.
Asura form of marriage, 217.
Asura Charvaka 427; 1.
Asuras, 440; 184.
Asuryam-pasya, 486, 1.
Aswani vikraya, 293.
Asvapati-king of kekaya, 380, 2.
Asvatha holy fig tree, 45; 1.
Asvatthaman 327, 2, 452; 455; 456.
Atala, 480, 1.
Atharvan, 245; 265.
Atharvangiras, 223; 276; 1; 331.

Atharvaveda, 7; 1; 9; 15; 26; 276; 1; 308.
Atharva veda pratisakhya, 176; 176.
Atheists, 56.
Athene temple of, 158, 1.
Athenians, 253, 1.
Atikaya, 427, 1.
Ati-krichra penance, 307.
Atiratra, 380.
Atisayokti, 509.
Atithi, 281.
Atithi bojana, 216.
Ativahika, 226, 3.
Ativyapti, 79.
Atmabodha, 128; 133.
Atman, 80; 84; 92; 250; 251; 326, 2.
Atmane pada, 190; 191.
Atma tushti, 237.
Atmatyagi, 336.
Atmavidya, 249.
Atoms, 88.
Atri, 231; 339; 418; 556, 1.
Aufrecht, Professor, 3, 1; 565, 2; 569, 2.
Aulukya darsana, 137, 1.
Aupamanyava, 184.
Aurangzib xxiv, 2; 363.
Aurelius, Marcus, 50, 1; 167; 168; 580, 1.
Aurnabhava, 184.
Ausanasa, 561.
Austin, Stephen, 532, 3.
Authority of veda, 244.
Auttami Manu, 234, 1.
Avaka, 226, 3.
Avarna, 128.
Avarodha, 486, 1 .

Avasarpini, 140.
Avasathya, fire, 216, 2.
Avasta, 6.
Avayava, (member of an argument, 77; 80.
Avidya, 127.
Avyakta, 99; 250.
Avyakta-ganita 202, 2.
Avyavibhava, 178.
Ayodhya, 31, 1; 355; 373, 1; 393; 401; 536, 1.
Ayodhya kanda, 375; 409.
Ayogava, 255.
Ayurveda, 211.
Ayus, 419.
Azali, without beginning) 66; 3.

Baber, xxiv, 2.
Babhru-vahan, 435.
Badarayana, 119; 276; 548.
Bagdis, 239, 1.
Baghdad, xxiv, 2.
Bahu-janma-bhak, 21, 1.
Bahuprajab, 21, 1.
Bahurupa, 457, 2.
Bahusalin, 426, 3.
Bahuvrihi, 177.
Bahvricha, 246.
Baidya (medical), 239, 1.
Bailee, 296.
Bailments, 296.
Baittal-pacihsi, 573.
Baka, 430.
Bala (power), 55, 1.
Bala (strength); 531; 1.
Baladeva, 531, 2.
Baladeva (nine); 141.
Bala kanda, 375; 409.
Bala krishna, 554; .

Balam-bhatta, 568.
Bala rama, 370; 371; 419; 418; 427; 436; 445; 456; 554.
Bala Ramayana, 410; 547.
Balasore, xxvi, 2.
Bali, 215, 1; 222; 275; 291; 366.
Ballala, 573.
Ballantyne, Dr., 76, 1; 87, 1; 91; 96, 1; 106, 1; 521, 2.
Baha, 410; 573.
Bandyopadhyaya, 239, 1.
Banerjea, Prof. K.M., xlvi, 1; 65; 1; 81; 90; 91; 2; 114; 239, 1; 408, 1.
Banerjea, dialogues, 207.
Banians, 254, 1.
Banias, 254, 1.
Bahijya, 267, 2.
Banik, 254, 1.
Baniyas, 254, 1.
Bapudeva sastri, 201, 2.
Barbarians, xliix, 1.
Bard, 550.
Baroda, xxvii, 1.
Barth, M. Revue Critique, 286, 1.
Batn, 38.
Batrish Sinhasan, 573.
Baudhayana, darsana, 137, 1.
Baudhayana, 231, 1; 232; 339.
Baudhayana Grihya Sutras, 214.
Baudhayana Shrauta Sutras, 171.
Beames Mr.; xxxvi, 1.
Bear, Great, 556.
Bediyas, 239, 1.
Behar xxi, 1; 2; 58; 339.
Benares, xx, 1; 3.
Benares College of xxxvii, 2; 1.
Benares school of 339; 341.
Benfey, Professor, 570, 2; 575; 2.

Bengal, xx, 1; *xxi,* 1; 340.
Bengal school of law, 339.
Bengalis, *xxx.*
Bentinck, Lord William, 283, 2.
Berkeley, 68, 1; 99; 1; 102, 1;
　107, 1.
Bha (in algebra), 209; 210.
Bhadra, 481; 1.
Bhadra, 200; 1; 370, 2.
Bhadrapada, 200, 1.
Bhaga, 204.
Bhagana, 204.
Bhagavad gita, 45, 1; 52, 1; 70,
　3; 108; 108, 3; 111; 118;
　145; 355; 362, 3; 448; 558.
Bhagavat, 58, 2; 554.
Bhagavata puranam, 149, 2; 364,
　2; 369; 434; 2; 554; 556.
Bhagavatas *lx,* 362; 2; 554; 562.
Bhagiratha, 383; 405.
Bhagirathi, 405.
Bhaguri, 341.
Bhaiksha, 430.
Bhakshyabhakshya, 459, 1.
Bhaktas, 564.
Bhaktas, *lix.*
Bhakti (faith); 246; 364.
Bhakti, (later theory of), 149.
Bhalla, 452.
Bhama, 521.
Bhana, 522.
Bhandarkar, Prof., 193, 2; 214,
　2; 266, 2; 276, 1.
Bhanika, 524.
Bhanu-datta, 507.
Bharadvaja, 401; 451, 2.
Bharadvaja (grammarian), 188, 1.
Bharadvaja Grihya Sutra, 214.
Bharadvaja, Shrauta Sutras, 171.

Bharata, 383; 392; 401; 406;
　469; 520.
Bharata, (Sutras); 520.
Bharata, *xxi;* 376, 1; 415, 1.
Bharatam akhyanam, 415, 1.
Bharata mallika, 194.
Bharata sena, 194.
Bharata varsha, xxi; 414; 418.
Bharati, 541, 2.
Bharavi, 437, 2; 502.
Bhartrihari, 193, 1; 504; 568;
　574.
Bhasa, 536.
Bhasha, *xxxv,* 1.
Bhasha paricheda, 76, 1.
Bhashya, *xliv,,* 1.
Bhashya pradipa, 194.
Bhashya pradipoddyota, 194.
Bhaskara, 202; 204; 207; 208.
Bhaskaracharya, 114; 202.
Bhatiyas, 254.
Bhatta, 262.
Bhatta divakara, 242, 2.
Bhatta narayana, 437, 3.
Bhatti kavya, 194; 410; 503; 507.
Bhattoji dikshita, 194.
Bhau Daji Dr., 532.
Bhauma, 205.
Bhava, 457; 2.
Bhavabhuti, 377; 401, 2; 409;
　410; 536.
Bhavana, 457, 2.
Bhavishya, 553; 561.
Bhavishya purana, 551; 1.
Bhavita, 209.
Bhawal pur, *xxvii,* 1.
Bhayanaka, 507, 1.
Bhikshu, 240; 268; 285.
Bhikshua, *xl,* 1; 61, 3; 276, 1.

Bhikshus, 61, 3; 62.
Bhils, 347.
Bhima, 423; 452; 462; 468.
Bhimasena, 426, 3.
Bhishma, 367, 2; 417; 419; 429; 436; 443; 449; 450; 458.
Bhishma parvan, 417.
Bhitis (water bearers); 254.
Bhogavati, 480; 1.
Bhoja, 410; 455; 573.
Bhoja deva (commentary of); 110, 1.
Bhoja prabandha, 573.
Bhopal, xxvii, 1.
Bhotan, xliv, 1.
Bhrigu, 211; 232; 235; 251; 339; 373; 556.
Bhu, 480.
Bhuh, 184.
Bhuki, 333.
Bhumi, (earth), 100.
Bhur, 70, 2; 222.
Bhuta, 211.
Bhutan, xxvii, 1.
Bhuta-yajna, 222; 275.
Bhuvah or Bhuvar, 70, 2; 184; 222; 480, 1.
Bibhatsa, 507.
Bibhatsu, 426, 3; 443.
Bible, xlix, li, 1; 4, 1; 6, 155; 1.
Bibliotheca Indica, 39; 49, 2; 116, 1.
Binary compound, 88.
Bodhi-sattva, 59, 1; 62, 2.
Bohlem Von, 569.
Bohn, 85, 1.
Bohtlingk, Prof., 3, 1; 196, 568, 1.
Bokhara, 10.

Bombay ceded, xxvii, 1.
Bombay population of, xxi, 1.
Bombay school of law, 339.
Bopp, 430.
Borrodaile Mr. H., 343, 1.
Bose, 239, 1.
Bottomry, 296.
Bower, the Rev H., 139, 1.
Brachmanes, 310.
Brahma, 42, see Brahman.
Brahma (world), 480.
Brahma, 25, 3; 36; 44; 68; 100, 2; 109; 363, 1; 382; 477; 480; 553; 557.
Brahma (son of); 96, 1.
Brahma (from marriage); 217.
Brahmanchari,418.
Brahmacharin, 220; 269; 272.
Brahmacharya –vrita, 423; 2.
Brahma-ghosha, 468, 4.
Brahma gupta, 201; 201, 3.
Brahma-ha, 303.
Brahmahatya, 302.
Brahma jijnasa, 122.
Brahma loka, 452.
Brahma-mimansa, 116.
Brahman (Supreme sprit), 12, 1; 99; 123; 123, 2; 216; 247.
Brahman (prayer, veda); 243; 259, 2; 306.
Brahman (portion of veda); 8; 29; 28; 54; 69, 1.
Brahmans (of each veda); 29; 222.
Brahmanda, 553; 562.
Brahmanda purana, 411.
Brahmani, 563.
Brahmanicide, 353.
Brahmanism, xlvii, 4; 4, 1; 262-269.

Brahmanism tyranny of, 56.
Brahmans, *xxv,* 1; 253; 263.
Brahmans, Kshatriyas, and Vaisya, 263.
Brahmans (of Konkan); 267, 1. ·
Brahma pura, 136, 1.
Brahma purana, 283, 2; 553.
Brahma sampradayins, *lix.*
Brahma siddhanta or Brahmas, 201; 202.
Brahmastra, 449, 1.
Brahmavarta, 238.
Brahmavaivarta, 553; 554; 563.
Brahma vidya, 248.
Brahma yajna, 222; 275; 276, 1; 303; 330, 2; 331, 1.
Brahmodyam, 331; 1.
Brahmojjhata, 303.
Brahu-i (language); *xxxvi.*
Brihad aranyaka Upanishad, 40; 41; 134; 157, 4; 384, 2.
Brihat samhita, 201; 205.
Brockhaus, Dr. Hermann, 572; 1.
Brother-in-law, 528; 1.
Buddha, 55; 58; 58; 371.
Buddha vansa, *xl,* 1.
Buddhi, 68, 3; 80; 99; 104; 128; 136; 164; 251.
Buddhindriyani, 101; 1.
Buddhism, *xxxvi, xliii, xxxix,* 4; 32, 1; 58; 235, 1; 527; 552; 565.
Buddhist ascetics, 310, 1; 527; 529.
Buddhist canon, *xl,* 1.
Buddhist council, *xl,* 1.
Buddhist heavens, 62, 2.
Buddhist literature, *xxxvi,* 1.
Buddhist reformation, 56.

Buddhist scriptures, *xl,* 1; 64, 1.
Buddhist philosophy, xliv.
Buddhist skepticism, 352.
Buddhist xliv, 1; *xxix,* 1.
Buddhist Nepal, *xxxvi,* 1.
Budha, 205; 418.
Budha-vara, 204, 1; 570, 2.
Buhler, Dr.; 188, 1.
Bukka, court of king, 137, 1.
Bundelkhand, *xxvii,* 1.
Burgess, E, 201, 2; 202.
Burial in the ground, 336.
Burkhand, Dr. C.; 532, 3.
Burmah, *xxxvi,* 1; *xliv.*
Burmese language, *xxxvi.*
Burnell, Dr., 137, 1; 276, 1.
Burnouf, *xl,* 1.
Bushire, *xxiii,* 1.

Ca hara, 209.
Chitanya (intelligence), 142.
Chitanya (reformer) *lix.*
Chitra, 200; 3; 408; 1.
Chitrayajna, 219.
Chauka, 471, 1.
Chakravarnana, 188.
Chakravartis, 141; 233.
Chakravriddhi, 296.
Chakshurdivyam, 431; 2.
Chakshusha, manu, 235, 1.
Calcutta, xxi, 1; *xxiii,* 1; *xxxvii,* 1.
Calcutta, population of, *xxi,* 1.
Calcutta Review, 374; 1; 377; 2; 379, 1; 398, 2.
Calcutta University, *xxxviii,* 2; 339, 2.
Caldwell Dr., 347, 2.
Campbell, xxi, 1; *xxvi,* 1.
Champu, 412.

Champu ramayana, 411.
Chamunda, 538; 563.
Chanakya, 546; 547; 568.
Chandala, 255; 258, 2; 303.
Chandana, 472, 2.
Chandi, 563.
Chandra, 264, 2; 287; 368, 1; 402.
Chandra gupta, 253, 1; 316; 546; 547.
Chandraloka, 521.
Chandrayana penance, 308.
Chara, 289.
Charaka, 212.
Charana, 214.
Charanavyuha, 214; 2.
Carey, 446, 2.
Chriyapitaka, xl, 1.
Charu, 335.
Charudatta, 528.
Charvaka, 142; 247; 458.
Charvakadarsana, 137, 1.
Charvakas, 137; 142.
Charvakas, doctrine of the, 393.
Caste, xxiv; xxx; 239; 252.
Caste lose of, 306.
Categories, Aristotelian, 83; 1.
Categories of Vaiseshika, 83.
Catharine, Infanta, xxvii, 1.
Chattopadhyaya, 239; 1.
Chaturanga, 233; 392.
Chaturjea, 239, 1.
Chaturmasya, 32, 1.
Chatushtoma, 379, 2.
Chaula, 216; 220; 270.
Causation, theory of, 87.
Cebes, 74, 1.
Chennes pattanam, xxi, 1.
Census of India, xxi, 1.

Centauri, 348, 1.
Central Asia, xxii.
Ceremonies, Sraddha, 223; 298; 479.
Ceylon, xxxvi, 1.
Chala, 80 .
Chaldee translations, 6.
Chalita rama, 344.
Chambers Cyclopaedia, 61, 2; 87, 1; 192, 1.
Chambers (leather cutters); 254; 1.
Chandah-Sastra, 177.
Chandas, 170; 177; 178; 243.
Chandernagore, xxvi, 2.
Chando-go, 246.
Chandogya Upanishad, 40; 42; 43; 55; 120;.
Charles II, xxvii, 1.
Charter, xxvii, 1.
Cheda, 209.
Cheddas, xliii, 1.
Chess, 569.
Childers, Mr. R.C.; xxxvii, 1.
China, xxvi, 2; 199; 2.
Chinese drama, 519.
Chinese language, xxvi, 2; 342; 1.
Chinsura, xxvi, 2.
Chitpavan, 254, 2.
Chittagong, xliii, 1.
Chota Nagpur, xxvii, 1.
Christ, xlix, li, 1; 156, 1.
Christ and other Masters, 32, 1; 75, 2.
Christianity, xlix, 1; li.
Christians Syrian, lx.
Chronicle 550, 2.
Chumbi, xxvi, 2.
Chun-tisu, 4, 1.

Chuterkote, 397, 3.
Cicero, 66, 1; 89, 1; 91, 1; 94, 2; 100, 3.
Cicero, Tusc. Disp., 74, 1; 91, 1; 283, 1.
Chinas, 258, 2.
Chintamani, 139, 1.
Chitra, 250, 1; 506.
Chitrakut, 275, 1; 398; 2 .
Chitrangada, 435.
Chitra ratha, 395.
Chitta, 68, 3 110; 136.
Civil code, 292.
Claughton, Bishop, 59, 1.
Clay cart, 527.
Cochin, xxvi, 2.
Codes, eighteen, after Yajnavalkya, 337.
Colebrooke, xxi, 1; 48, 2; 197, 1; 332, 1; 337; 537.
Colebrooke's Essays, xxxvii, 1; and passim, .
Colebrooke's Indian Algebra, 202.
Colebrooke's Bhaskara, 207.
Comedy, 520.
Compound interest, 297.
Conciliation in religion, 2, 1.
Confidantes, heroine's, 527.
Confucius, 3, 1; 4, 1; 53.
Consumptive persons, 304, 1.
Contract, 295.
Copernicus, 37.
Cornelius, xlii, 1.
Coromandel, xxvi, 2.
Cosmogony (Vaiseshika); 94.
Court of Directors, first, xxvii, 1.
Cow (sacred); 559.
Cowell Prof. E.B. xxxvii, 1; 39,

1; 49, 2; 76; 88; 93; 229, 1; 337; 532, 3.
Cowell, Mr. Herbert, 300, 1.
Cowell's Tagore law lectures, 339.
Creator, 558.
Crimes (great); 303.
Crimes (secondary); 304.
Criminal code, Manus's, 301.
Chuda karman, 216; 220; 270.
Chulavagga, xl, 1.
Cunningham, Major-General, v.
Churni .
Curzon, Mr.; 379, 1.
Cust, Mr. R.N.; 373, 1; 377, 2; 379, 1.
Chuta, 472, 2.
Cyclopes, 348; 1.

Dacca, xxvi, 1.
Dadhi, 469.
Dadima, 472, 2.
Daupathins, lx.
Daiva, 274, 317, 1.
Daiva form of marriage, 218.
Daiva Sraddha, 228.
Daivata, 183.
Daksha, 198; 232; 264, 2; 339; 556, 1.
Daksha-kratu-hara, 458, 2.
Daksheya, 188.
Dakshi, 188.
Dakshina, 226; 266, 2.
Dakshina (fee), 214, 2; 267.
Dakshina (fire), 216, 1.
Dakshina (Hearth), 215, 1.
Dakshinacarins, 564.
Dalton, Colonel, vi.
Daman, xxvi, 2.

Damanaka, 570, 1.
Damaru xlix, 210.
Damascus, xxiv, 1.
Damayanti-katha, 410.
Dam-dupat, 296, 2.
Damodara, 211; 436, 1.
Dana, 63.
Danam, 267.
Dana-samvanana, 394.
Dancing, 212, 518.
Danda, 203; 325, 2.
Dandaka forest, 387, 1; 466; 541.
Dandaka metre, 181.
Dandi, 286.
Dandin, 409, 572.
Danes, xxvi, 2.
Daniel, 161, 4.
Dante, 464.
Darius Hystaspes, xxii.
Darjeeling, xlv.
Darsha, 277.
Darsanas, 52; 73, 1; 75, 1.
Darsa-purnamasa, 32, 1.
Darwinians, 96.
Dasa, 239.
Dasa-gitika, 201.
Dasa-hara, 408.
Dasa-kumara-carita, 289, 2; 572.
Dasama-granth (Sikh); 363, 1.
Dasa pati, 288.
Dasaratha, 368, 373, 1; 376; 383; 386; 476.
Dasaratha-jataka, 355, 1.
Dasaratha's ministers, 378.
Dasarha, 435, 1.
Dasa-rup, Dasa-rupaka, 411; 508.
Dasras, 14.
Dasyus, 348.

Datta, 239.
Dattaka-chanderika, 342.
Dattaka mimansa, 341.
Dattasyanapakarma, 292.
Dattatreya, 363, 1.
Dawn, 19; 20.
Daya, 295; 297.
Daya-bhaga, 300, 1; 341.
Daya-krama-sangrha, 342.
Daya-tattva, 342.
De, 239; 1.
Death, 22; 36; 41; 46; 238, 1.
Debt, 293.
Debts, three, 285.
Decimal figures, 569.
Defendant, 560.
Dekhan xx, 1, xxvii, 1.
Delhi, xxvi,1; 233; 413; 435.
Deluge, tradition of the, 438.
Deposits law of, 296.
Desasth, 254, 1.
Desire, 23; 67; 1.
Destroyer, 547.
Deva, 457, 2.
Deva-bodha, 340.
Devadatta, 59, 2; 450.
Devah, 310.
Devaki, 149; 369; 370; 432, 1.
Devala, 188.
Devalaka, 248.
Devarah, 229.
Devas, 274.
Devata, 272, 310.
Devavrata, 419.
Devayajna, 22; 275.
Devi, 564.
Devimahatmya, 554.
Devrukh, 254.
Dhammapada, xli, 1; 236; 1.

Dhamma sangani, *xli*, 1.
Dhana, 209.
Dhananjaya, 410; 426, 3; 443; 508.
Dhanishtha, 197.
Dhanu-bandha, 506.
Dhanurveda, 212.
Dhanvantari, 559.
Dhar, *xxvii*, 1.
Dhara, 573.
Dharana, 111.
Dharana, 329.
Dharani (glossary); 187.
Dharani-dhara, 340.
Dharanis, 62; 1.
Dharma, 81; 264, 2; 431, 2.
Dharmadharma, 305, 1.
Dharma-jijnasa, 117.
Dharma-moolam, root of law, 328.
Dharma putra, 426, 3.
Dharmaraja, 426, 3.
Dharmaratna, 340, 2.
Dharmasastra, 231; 236, 1; 242.
Dharmasutras, 231.
Dharna, 297.
Dhatu, *xlix*, 1; 189.
Dhatupatha, 189.
Dhaumya, 340; 434.
Dhi, 318.
Dhigvana, 255.
Dhiralalita, 522, 2.
Dhira prasantha, 522, 2.
Dhirodatta, 522, 2.
Dhrishta dyumna, 417; 428; 431, 2; 448; 452; 455; 1; 458.
Dhritarashtra, 417; 418; 420.
Dhurjati, 362.
Dhurtacarita, 524.
Dhyana, 63; 111.

Dialogue dramatic, 520.
Dianus, 478, 2.
Didhishu, 225.
Diet, rules, of, 281.
Digarmbara, 139; 362.
Digha-nikaya, *xlix*, 1.
Dilipa, 382.
Dima, 522.
Dinkard, *xxiii*, 1.
Diodorus, 253, 1; 356.
Diogenes, Siculus, 283; 1; 371, 1.
Diogenes, 67, 1.
Diochrysostomos, 352; 352, 1.
Dionysos, 311.
Diophantus, 208.
Dipaka, 509.
Dipakalika, 341.
Dipali, 363, 2.
Dis, 84.
Diu, *xxvi*.
Divali, 363; 2.
Divasvapna, 220.
Divya, ordeal, 304.
Divyadivya, 408.
Dolayatra, 363.
Domestic manners (Hindu), 486.
Doms, 239, 1.
Dosha, 80, 521, 2.
Dower, 300.
Draco, laws of 301, 1.
Drahyayana Srauta Sutras, 171.
Dramas, 518, 521, xxvi.
Dramas of Greeks, 520.
Draupadi, 408; 416; 429; 453; 456; 554.
Dravatva, 85.
Dravida, 239; 1; 258, 2; 339.
Dravidyans races and languages, *xxxvi, xxxvii*, 347, 1.

Dravidyans school of law, 342.
Dravyan 68, 1; 84; 93.
Drikana, 199; 2.
Drishadvati 233; 238 .
Drishi, 169.
Dristhta, 99.
Drishtanta, 80; 508.
Drona, 417; 426; 433; 436; 451.
Drona parvam ; 410; 416.
Drupada, 428; 436.
Dugdha, 469.
Duhkha, 80; 85 .
Duhsala, 423; .
Dushasana, 429; 437; 453.
Durga, 183; 360, 2; 362, 2; 476; 479; 553; 563; 584.
Durga images of, 408; 1.
Durga puja, 408; 1.
Durmallika, 523.
Durvasa, 421; 558.
Durvasa Upapurana, 562.
Dur-vipaka, 70; 1.
Duryodhana, 417; 423; 425; 429; 443;.452.
Dushyanta, 419; 533.
Dutangada, 411.
Dutch in India, xxvi, 2.
Dvaidha, 334.
Dvaipayan, 419; 4.
Dvaita-vadin, 96.
Dvandva, 178; 287.
Dvapara, 204; 2; 246; 338; 339; 367; 458; 1.
Dvaraka, 371; 456.
Dvesha, 85.
Dvija (twice born); 227; 253; 263; 329.
Dvi jati, 253.

Dvikam satam, 296.
Dvipa, 419; 4; 469.
Dvy-anuka, 88.
Dyaus, 12; 15.
Dyaush-pitar, 12; 12; 2.

Earth, 216.
Earth and the Heaven (union of), 108.
East India Company, xxvii, 1.
Eastwick, Mr. E.B.; 533; 570; 1.
Eclectic School, 108; 3; 137; 145.
Eggeling Prof. J, 196.
Ego, 101.
Egyptians, ancient, 301, 1.
Ekacakra (city of); 430.
Eka jati, 353.
Ekashahara, 111, 1.
Ekam evadvitiyam, 43.
Ekapadi, 219.
Ekoddishta sraddha, 228; 278.
Eleatics, 67, 1.
Elizabeth queen, xxvii, 1.
Elphinstone, Mr., 236, 1.
Elphnstone's India, 106, 2; 259, 1; 287, 2.
Emanation, xxxiii.
Emusha, 366, 2.
Empedocles, 67, 1; 90, 2.
Encomiast, 550.
Entity, 23.
Epic poetry, 344.
Epic poetry, principal, characteristics of, 345.
Epic Indian, compared together and with Homer, 465.
Epictetus, doctrines of, 89.
Epos, 345.

Estoeric Hinduism, *xxxii.*
Ether, 68, 84, 100, 100, 3.
Ethnology of India, *xi, xxi-xxx,*
  347; 1.
Etymologist, 184.
Etymology, 181.
Eurasians, *xxi,* 2.
Every man (morality), 548.
Evidence, law of, 304.
Exoteric Hinduism, *xxxii.*
Expiation, 307; 323.

Fables, 567, 569.
Factory, first Indian, *xxvii,* 1.
Fakir, 112, 1.
False evidence, 304.
Farrar, Dr, 502; 167; 580; 1.
Farrukh siyar, *xxivi,* 1.
Fatima, *liii,* 1.
Female mendicant Buddhist, 536.
Fetish worshippers, *xlii.*
Ficus religiosa, 18, 1.
Finnish language, 347, 2.
Firdausi, 61.
Fish eating of, 281.
Five per cent, 297.
Flesh, eating of, 281; 544.
Food, tradition of, 33.
Food preparations of, *xxxi,* 1.
Frederic the great, 289, 2.
French possessions, *xxxvi,* 2.
Funeral ceremonies, 225; 277;
  336.
Farruckabad, 537; 1.
Future life, belief in a, 36.

Gabr (infidel); *xlii,* 1.
Gabriel, (angel), 6.
Gadayaddha, 456.

Gadya (prose), 412.
Gairs, *xlii,* 1.
Gajasahvaya, 421; 2.
Galava, 188.
Gambler, 528.
Ganaka, 200.
Ganapati, 150, 1.
Ganapatyas, 150; 1; 363, 1.
Gandha, 85.
Gandhamadana, 469, 1.
Gandhara country, 188.
Gandhari, 421; 422.
Gandharva, 309.
Gandharva (marriage), 218.
Gandharvas, 184, 447.
Gandharva-veda, 211.
Gandiva, 150; 443; 450; 461, 1.
Ganesa, 142; 150; 1; 328; 363;
  1; 477; 479.
Ganesa-gita, 150, 1.
Ganesa-parava, 150, 1.
Ganga, 404, 419.
Ganges, xx, 310, 1; 459.
Ganges, story, 404.
Gangeya, 418.
Ganguli, 239, 1.
Ganita, 202.
Garbha, 522, 1.
Garbha Upanishad, 74, 1.
Garbhadhana, 269.
Garbha lambhana, 220; 269.
Garbhikam enas, 269.
Garcin de Tassy M., *xii,* 1.
Garga, 205.
Garga-siddhanta, 201.
Gargi, 488, 1.
Gargya, 186; 187; 188, 1; 339.
Garhapatya fire, 214; 216, 2;
  224; 225.

Garmanes, 311, 1.
Garos (garrows); 312; 1.
Garuda, 479; 480, 1; 533.
Gatha, 59; 1; 222; 336; *xxiii*, 1; *xxxvi*, 1.
Gatha Ahunavait, 155, 2.
Gathikah, 231.
Gauda, 239, 1; 376, 1.
Gauda pada, 99, 1; 106.
Gaur, xxv, 1; 239, 1.
Gauri, 563.
Gautama, 55; 57; 81; 1; 93; 339, 1.
Gavaya, 472; 1.
Gayatri, text, 7, 1; 19; 159, 1; 179; 222; 243; 261; 308.
Gayatri metre, 180.
Genealogies, 550, 2.
Gentiles *xlii.*
Gesticulations, pantomimic, 519.
Ghana arrangement of text, 176, 2; 276, 1.
Ghati, 203.
Ghatika, 203.
Ghatotkcha, 430; 434, 2; 451.
Ghosha, 239, 1.
Ghrana, 89.
Girisha, 457, 2.
Gitagovinda, 410; 412; 504.
Glossaries, 187.
Gnostics, 73, 2.
Goa, *xxvi*, 2.
Go-badhah, 303.
Gobhila's Grihya Sutra, 214; 214, 1.
Godona, 217.
Godavari river, 378, 1; 466.
Goethe, 533.
Gogra river, 378, 2.

Gokarna, 396.
Gokulam, 369.
Goldstucker, Professor, 172, 1; 174, 3.
Gomutrika, 507.
Gonarda, 193.
Gond, *xxvii*, 1; 347, 1.
Gonika, 193.
Gopa, 239; 1.
Gopatha Brahmana, 29.
Gopis, 363, 1; 370; 504.
Gopucchagra, 522.
Gorakhnath, *xxix*, 1.
Gnrakhpur, *xxix*, 1.
Goraksha, *xxix*, 1; 267, 2.
Gorkha, xxixi, 1.
Gorresio, 375, 1; 377; 396; 1; 407, 1; 491.
Gos, 239, 1.
Goshala, 239, 1.
Goshti, 524.
Gotama or Gautama (Buddha); *xl*, 1; 58.
Gotama (of nyaya); 76; 91.
Gotama (of law book); 232.
Gotra (family); 279.
Gough Professor A.E., 76; 78; 79, 2; 84; 193, 1.
Govardhana, 398, 1; 411.
Govind, 362, 1.
Govinda, 435, 2; 504; 507.
Govinda Deva Sastri, 547.
Govinda raja, 329.
Graha-yajna, 329.
Grama (village), 290.
Grammar, 187, 569.
Grantha, 262, 1.
Granthis, 262, 1.
Grasacchadana, 300.

Gravitation, 206.
Greeks, 199, 2; 403; 519.
Greeks and Romans, 38.
Griffith Professor R., 148; 2;
  404; 440; 1.
Griha-prapadana, 221.
Grihastha, 223; 268; 272; 273;
  276, 1.
Grihya (Domestic rites); 213.
Grihya Sutras, 170; 213; 337;
  346.
Grishama 503.
Gudakesha, 426, 3.
Guhyaka, 309.
Guikwar, xxvii, 1.
Gujarat, 139, 2; 266; 2; 371.
Gujrati, xxxvi.
Gujrati native states, xxvii, 1.
Guna (of the Vaiseshika), 83;
  85.
Guna (three), 71; 2; 102; 309,
  553.
Gunadhya, 572.
Gunga, 199.
Gurjara, 239, 1.
Guru, 71, 2; 262; 262, 1; 268;
  271; 272.
Guru Nanak, 363, 1.
Gurumukhi character, lx.
Gurutva, 85.
Guru-vara, 204.
Gurvartha, 429.
Gwalior, xxvii, 1.

Haberlin, Dr., 129.
Hadis, 28.
Hadis, 239, 1.
Hafiz, 3, 1.
Haiderabad, xxvii, 1.

Haituka, 248.
Haj, 275, 1.
Hajji, 275.
Hala, 410.
Halyudha, 187; 271, 1.
Hall Dr. F., xvi; xxxvi, 1; 96,
  1; 201, 2; 283, 2; 573.
Hallisa, 523.
Hanbal, lii, 1.
Hanifa, lii, 1.
Hamsa, 274.
Hanuman, or nataka, 410; 547.
Hanumat, 397; 401; 410; 468;
  4; 474; 476.
Hapta Hendu, xxix, 2.
Hara, 247; 358; 458; 2.
Haravali, 187.
Hardwick, Mr., 32, 1; 75, 2.
Hari, 159, 1; 558.
Haridasa's comment, 93.
Haridvar, 275, 1.
Hari Narayana, 479.
Harinatha, 411.
Harichandra, 30.
Harita, 231; 338.
Hari vansha, 355; 369; 409;
  417; 467; 467, 2.
Hariot, 208.
Hari havardhana, 573.
Hansan, liii, 1.
Hastinapur, 413; 434.
Hastinapura, 149; 416; 417;
  458, 1 550, 2.
Hasya, 507, 1.
Hasyarnava, 547.
Haug, Professor, xxiii, 1, 29.
Heads of law (eighteen), 292.
Heathen, xlii.
Heaven, 216.

Heavens (seven), 246; 480, 1.
Hecter, 352, 1; 472.
Hecuba, 352.
Hellemic languages, *xxii.*
Hells, 246; 469, 1.
Hemachandra, 139; 187.
Hemadri, 194.
Hemakuta, 469, 1.
Hemanta, 503.
Heracleitus, 67, 1.
Herakles, 310, 1.
Hercules, 394, 1; 399, 2. .
Hero, 526.
Herodotus, *xxii,* 253, 1.
Heroes, (four kinds), 522.
Heroine, 526.
Hesiod, 67, 1; 477, 1.
Hetu sastra, 56; 247.
Hetv-abhasa (fallacy), 81.
Hidimba, 430; 434, 2; 452.
Hijra, *liii,* 1.
Hill tribes, *xxi,* 347; 2.
Himalaya, *xx,* 2; *xxvii,* 1.
Himvat, 403; 439; 461.
Hina-yana, 71; 1.
Hindi, *xxxiv, xxxvi.*
Hindu (meaning of word), *xix-xx.*
Hindu Dharma, 57.
Hindu-I, *xxxiv; xxxvi.*
Hindustan, *xix.*
Hindustani *xxxvi,* 1; *xxxviii,* 2.
Hiranya garbha, 107; 134.
Hiranya kasipu, 367; 436, 2.
Hiranyaksha, demon, 366.
History of kings of Kasmir, 572.
Hitopadesa, 3; 1; 419, 2; 459,
    1; 474; 571; 572; 573.
Holi, 525; 545.
Holkar, *xxvii,* 1.

Homa (oblation), 222; 275;
    275, 2.
Homer, 348, 1; 351; 477; 1.
Hora, 199, 2.
Horace, 181.
Horoscope, 204, 1; (of Rama's
    birth), 383, 1.
Hospitality, 282.
Hotri, 245.
Hrishikesa, 435, 1.
Holi, 363.
Hum, 308.
Humayoon, *xxiv,* 1.
Hamayyun Nama, 570.
Hunter, Dr. (Orisa), 239, 1;
    275, 1.
Husain, *liii,* 1.
Hycke-scorner, 548.
Hydaspes, river, 418; 1.
Hydra, 399.

Ichha, 84.
Ida, 418.
Idolatry, 247, 1.
Idols, 15; 247.
Iha-mriga, 523.
Ikshu, 469.
Ikshvaku, 382; 418.
Ila, 418.
Illiad, 344; 351; 399, 1; 448,
    1; 47; 1.
Imams, *liiix,* 1.
Immigrants, *xxi.*
Incarnation, doctrine of, 355; 356.
Incarnation of Vishnu, 364.
India office report, *xxi,* 1.
India (population of); *xxi.*
Indian Antiquary, 139; 254, 1;
    266, 2; 542, 2.

Indian Vedantists, 67, 1.
Indices, to Veda, 211.
Indische Alterthumskunde, 414, 1.
Indische Spruche, Bohtlingk's 568.
Streifen (Weber); *xl*, 1; 410; 573.
Indo-Armenians, *xxiv*, 1.
Indo-Aryans, *xxviii*, 53.
Indra, 13; 16; 17; 19; 1; 216;
  286; 346; 359; 477; 479.
Indra and Vishnu hymns to 31, 1.
Indra, poetical sketch of, 16; 17.
Inderjit 474.
Indrani, 563.
Indra prastha, 435.
Indrasena, 426, 2.
Indra vajra, 181; 432, 1.
Indriya, 80, 89.
Indu, 13.
Indus, *xx*.
Industrial survey of India, *xi*.
Inference, 77.
Inheritance, law of, 297.
Inscriptions, *xxxvi*, 1.
Intercalary month, 200.
Interest on money, 296.
Invaders, *xxi*.
Iravat, 435, 1.
Iravati, 535.
Isa Upanishad, 40.
Isana, 457, 2.
Isavasya Upanishad, 40.
Ishika, 452, 1.
Ishti (preference), 364.
Ishtis (desiderata), 193, 1.
Ishu 452, 1.
Islam, *xxvi*, 1; *xlviii, li, lii, liii*,
  4; 1; 5, 3; 6.
Isvara, 91; 93; 105; 457, 2.
Isvara Chandra Vidyasagara, 142.

Isvara Pranidhana, 110.
Italic (languages); *xxii*.
Itihasa, 42; 222; 236, 1; 281; 330;
  336; 344, 1; 465; 349; 522.
Itivuttakam, *xl*, 1.

Jagadamba, 109.
Jagannath, 239, 1; 275, 1.
Jagati, 180; 374, 1.
Jahandar Shah, *xxiv*, 1.
Jahangir, xxiv, 1; *xxvii*, 1.
Jahnavi, 405.
Jahnu, 405.
Jaimini, 116, 116, 1.
Jaimini (Mimansa), 116; 137, 1;
  276, 1.
Jaiminiya-nyaya-mala-vistara,
  116, 1.
Jainas, *xlivi*, 1; 137.
Jain scriptures, *xliv*, 1.
Jainism, *xlivi*, 1; 63; 2; 138.
Jaipur, *xxvii*, 1.
Jala, 469.
Jaliyas (fishermen); 239, 1.
Jalpa (mere wrangling); 80.
Jamadagni 367, 2.
Jambavat, 474.
Jambhala-datta, 573.
Jambudvipa, *xx*, 2; 469.
Jamshid, 353; 1.
Jana (people); 319.
Janaka, 373; 1; 380, 2; 383;
  550, 2.
Janamejaya, 414; 1; 417; 434; 2.
Janar 70; 2; 480, 1.
Janardana, 435, 1.
Jane-o, 270, 1.
Jangiz Khan, *xxivi*, 1.
Janitva, 224.

Janma patra, 204.
Janmashtami, 370; 2.
Janus, 477, 2.
Japan, 5, 1.
Japa-yajna, 276; 277; 330, 2.
Japyam, 272.
Jarbhari, 145, 2.
Jat, *xxviii*, 239, 1.
Jata, arrangement of text, 177; 276, 1.
Jataka, *xl*, 1.
Jata karman, 220; 270.
Jati (birth), 239, 1.
Jati (futile replies), 80.
Jati (flower), 472, 2.
Jatu, 429.
Jatukarni, 536.
Javali, 54, 143, 1; 351; 353; 392; 406.
Jayadeva, 410; 504; 521.
Jayadratha, 409; 423; 436; 422.
Jester, 526.
Jews, 73, 1.
Jhalla (club fighter); 309.
Jihmayodhin, 456.
Jimutavahana, 340; 341.
Jina, 139; 140, 1.
Jinesvara, 139.
Jjishnu, 426; 3; 443.
Jivatman, 44; 66; 92; 128; 257.
Jnana, 63, 1; 74; 361; 364.
Jnana kanda, 38.
Job, 23; 519.
Johaentgin, Dr., 242; 2; 326, 2; 326, 1.
John of Capua, 570, 1.
Johnson, Prof. F., 503; 578.
Johns Sir W., 3, 1; 40, 2; 49; 2; 99, 1; 276, 1; 545.

Jovian, cycle of sixty years, 205.
Judaism, 4, 4, 1.
Junctures (Sandhi), 466.
Jung, Sir Salar, *xxvii*, 1.
Jupiter (planet), 204.
Jupiter Pluvius, 13, 310, 1.
Justice, administration of, 291.
Jvala-mukhi, 275, 1.
Jyaishtha, 200, 1.
Jyotis (fire, light), 100.
Jyotisha (astronomy), 170, 196.
Jyotishtoma, 214; 261, 1; 271; 379; 2.

Kabandha, 398, 409; 478, 2.
Kabir, *lviii*.
Kabirpanthi, *lviii*.
Kadambari, 411, 573.
Kadru, 480, 1.
Kabirs, *xlii*, 1.
Kaikeyi, 380; 385; 388.
Kailasa, 453.
Kaisiki (style), 541, 2.
Kaiyata, 194.
Kakolukiya, 571.
Kakutstha, 383.
Kala, 7, 1, 79.
Kala, 203, 204.
Kala nirnaya, 137, 1.
Kalapa (grammar), 196.
Kalasoka, 64, 1.
Kaler-ansa, 458.
Kalhana, 572.
Kali, 32; 1; 59, 1; 204, 2; 250, 338; 458; 560.
Kali, 533; 562; 563.
Kalidasa, 401; 2; 410; 502; 531.
Kalidasa's dramas, 410.

Kalika, 561; 562; 563.
Kalikata, *xxi*, 2.
Kalilah Damnah, 570, 1.
Kalindi, 537, 1.
Kaliya (serpent), 484.
Kali yuga, 338; 368, 3.
Kalki, 371; 372, 1.
Kalpa, (period of time), 59, 1; 204; 234; 3; 359; 368, 3; 479; 556.
Kalpa (ceremonial); 170; 171; 222; 261.
Kalpa sutra, 171.
Kalpa sutra, (Jaina); *xliv*, 1.
Kalyana, 282, 3.
Kama, 362, 2.
Kamda, 565.
Kama deva, 479.
Kama dhenu, 403.
Kama-ga, 336.
Kamakhya, 565.
Kamalayataksha, 425, 3.
Kamandaka, 537.
Kambojas, 258, 2; 403.
Kamya Sradda, 228.
Kamayaka forest, 416; 437.
Kanada, 82; 96, 1.
Kanada's Sutra, 87; 91; 276, 1.
Kanarese, *xxxix*, 347, 2.
Kanauj 537; 573.
Kanda (arrow), 453, 1.
Kandahar, 188.
Kandarpa keli, 523.
Kanishka (king), 64, 1.
Kanjalata, 239, 1.
Kanka, 422.
Kanoj, 403.
Kanouj Brahmans, 239, 1; 254; 1.
Kansa, 149; 2; 366; 369; 370.

Kansaris (braziers), 239.
Kanyakubja, 239; 1; 536.
Kanyatva, 422.
Kapala-kundala, 538.
Kapila, 57; 96; 1; 98; 101, 404.
Kapila, 561.
Kapila's Aphorisms, 105.
Kapilavastu, 57.
Karana, 87; 255.
Karana-mala, 509.
Karana-sarira, 68, 2.
Karanas eleven, 204, 1.
Karani, 174, 1.
Karataka, 57, 1.
Karbala, *liii*, 1.
Karical, *xxvi*, 2.
Karkandhu, 472, 2.
Karkata, 383, 1.
Karma dosha, 71, 1.
Karma kanda, 38.
Karmakara, 239, 1.
Karma mimansa, 116.
Karman, 61; 83; 86; 364.
Karama-phala, 238; 241; 242; 308; 312; 324.
Karma vipaka, 70, 1.
Karmendriyani, 101, 1.
Karna, 416; 427; 428.
Karna parvam, 416.
Karnata, 239; 1; 254, 1.
Karna vedha, 270, 1.
Karnikara, 472, 2.
Kartavirya, 550, 2.
Karthika, 200, 1.
Karthikeya, 363, 1; 476, 2; 479, 1; 502.
Karttiki, 563.
Karuna, 507, 1.
Karya, 87, 1.

Karya darsana, 292.
Kashaya vasas, 328.
Kastha, 203.
Kashi 550, 2.
Kashinatha, 362, 2.
Kashyapa, 188, 1; 264, 2; 339; 382; 385; 480; 1.
Kasyapa, xl, 1.
Katantra (grammar), 196.
Kata-putana, 310.
Katha, 44; 2; 46.
Katha Shrauta Sutras, 171.
Katha Upanishad, 25; 2; 40.
Kathaei, 283; 1.
Kathaka Grihya Sutras, 214.
Katharnava, 573.
Katha sarit sagara, 572.
Kathavatthu, xl, 1.
Katthakya, 184.
Katyayana, 175; 192; 571.
Katyayana's law treatise, 231; 339.
Katyayana's Srauta sutra, 170; 173; 379, 2.
Kaulas, 563; 2.
Kaulika (weaver); 563; 2; 574.
Kaunakya, 303.
Kauravas, 416; 426; 443; 455.
Kaurma, 561.
Kausalya, 379; 387; 406; 419; 1.
Kausambhi, 545.
Kaushitaki brahmana, 29.
Kaushitaki-brahmana – Upanishad, 39; 124, 4.
Kaustubha, 446.
Kautsa, 184.
Kavi Karna Puraka, 521.
Kaviraja, 411.
Kavya, 344; 2; 353; 354; 413; 1; 465; 523.

Kavyadarsa, 409; 506.
Kavya lakshana, 503.
Kavyalankara vritti, 521; 507.
Kavya pradipa, 507.
Kavya prakasa, 506.
Kayastha, 239; 1; 254, 1; 255; 322, 1.
Kearns, Rev. I. F.; 129, 2.
Keltic languages, xxii.
Kena Upanishad, 40.
Kendra, 199, 2.
Kern, Professor, 44, 1; 139, 1; 141, 1; 201.
Keshanta, 270.
Keshava, 435, 1.
Ketu, 205, 1, 283, 1.
Kevalatman, 359.
Khadga-bandha, 506.
Khairpur, xxvii, 1.
Khalifs, xxiv, 1.
Khanaka, 430.
Khandana-khanda-khadya, 503.
Khandava-prastha, 434.
Khasias, 347.
Khatri, 254; 1; 283, 1.
Khatvanga, lx.
Khila, 235; 1.
Khirad Afroz, 570, 1.
Khonds, 347, 1.
Khudhaka-nikaya, xl, 1.
Khuddaka-pather, lx, 1.
Kielhorn, Prof. 188, 1; 194, 1; 570, 2.
Kinchit prana, 457.
King, 4, 1.
Kinsuka, 453; 472, 2.
Kirata, 437; 559.
Kirata (mountaineer), 258, 2; 393, 2.

Kiratajuniya, 258, 2; 416; 437; 2; 450, 2; 502; 512.
Kritin, 426, 3; 443.
Kishkindhya kanda, 376.
Kokila, 472, 1.
Kolapur, *xxvii*, 1.
Kole, *xxvii*, 1.
Kolis, 254, 1.
Kols, 347, 1.
Konkanasth, 254, 1.
Korawars, 347, 1.
Kosha, 133; 304, 1; 333.
Kosala, 355; 373, 1.
Kosegarten, 570, 1.
Koshtis, 254, 1.
Kota, 347, 1.
Krama arrangement of text, 276, 1.
Krama text, 176, 2.
Kranti pata, 207.
Kratu, 545, 1.
Krauncha, 412, 1.
Krauncha, dvipa, 469.
Kraya vikrayanusaya, 292.
Kripa, 426; 436; 455; 456.
Kripi, 426, 3.
Krishi, 256; 2; 267, 2.
Krishna, 108; 2; 145; 149; 246; 368; 400, 3; 426; 443, 550; 2; 554.
Krishna (life of); 369; 556.
Krishna (names of), 435, 1.
Krishna (wives of) 350.
Krishna (Draupadi); 428.
Krishna dvaipayana, 548.
Krishna-mishra, 547.
Krishna-tarkalankara, 341.
Krishnau, 435.
Krit affixes, 177; 196.

Krita age, 196, 2; 245; 338; 369; 1.
Kritavarman, 455; 456.
Krittika, 196; 200, 1.
Kshana, 203.
Kshanti, 63.
Kshatra, 258, 1.
Kshatriya, 21; 1; 25, 1; 55; 55; 57; 58; 241; 253; 253, 1.
Kshattari, 419.
Kshetra, 164.
Kshiva, 435.
Kuch Bahar, *xxvii*, 1.
Kuhu (new moon); 184; 199.
Kula, 332; 1.
Kulaka, 239, 1.
Kularnava, 565.
Kulina (noble), 239, 1.
Kulluka, 8; 1; 9, 1; 16; 13; 25, 3; 216; 232; 235; 1; 239; 1; 242; 2; 339; 340; 562, 2.
Kumara, 502.
Kumara sambhava, 116, 1; 359, 1; 362, 2; 502.
Kumarila, 59; 1; 116, 1; 261, 3.
Kumbhara, (potters); 254; 1.
Kumbha-karan, 395.
Kumuda, 480, 2.
Ku-nakhin, 303, 1.
Kung-fu-tsze (Confucius), 4, 1; 5, 1.
Kunthu, 140, 1.
Kunthi, 416; 417; 418, 2; 421; 430; 485.
Kuntibhoja, 421; 436.
Kuran, *xliv, li*, 1; 4, 1; 6; 6, 2; 6, 3, 8; 28; 38; 120, 1.
Kurma, 365; 365; 3; 553.
Kuru kshetra, 416; 448.

Kurus, 346; 427.
Kuruvaka, 472, 2.
Kus or Khonds, 347, 1.
Kusha, 373; 1; 542.
Kusha-dvipa, 469.
Kusha (grass); 22; 224; 306.
Kushida-vriddhi, 296.
Kushika srauta sutras, 171.
Kushi-lavau, 373, 1.
Kusumanjali 76, 1; 88; 1; 93.
Kutasthah, 154, 1.
Kuthumi or Kusthumbi, 339.
Kuttaka, 202, 202, 1.
Kuvalayananda, 521.
Kuvera (God of wealth), 287, 395; 476.
Kymar range of mountains, 398, 1.

Laestrygones, 348, 1.
Laghu-kaumudi, 194.
Lakhima-devi, 342.
Laksha, 210.
Laksha, 428.
Lakshana, 273; 522.
Lakshma, 479.
Lakshmana, 383; 387; 397; 406; 474; 475; 541.
Lakshmi, 363, 1; 366; 400; 411; 431; 2; 562.
Lalita vistara, xxxvi, 1; xl, 1; 59, 1; 631.
Lambadies, 347, 2.
Lambaka, 572.
Languages of India, xxxv.
Lanks, 376; 378, 1; 383, 1; 397; 468, 4; 541.
Lassen, Prof, 149, 2; 329, 1; 351; 378, 1; 414, 1; 536; 550; 2.

Lasya (dance), 518.
Latyayana Shrauta Sutras, 171.
Laugakshi Shrauta Sutras, 171.
Laukika (secular), 312; 1.
Laukikagni, 336.
Lau-tsze, xlvii, 4, 1; 5, 1.
Lava, 373; 1; 542.
Lavana, 469.
Law schools of, 339.
Laya, 110.
Left hand worshippers, 563.
Lekhya, 328.
Lethe, 74; 1.
Lexicographers, 186.
Lex talionis, 301.
Liddon, Cannon, 75, 2.
Lidhu, 195; 1.
Likhita (lawyer); 231; 338; 339.
Liklita (written document); 333.
Li-ki (Chinese book); 4, 1.
Lila Madhukara, 522.
Lilavati, 202; 202, 2; 210.
Linga, 179; 1; 226; 3; 360; 553.
Linga-sarira, 68; 2; 128.
Lingayats, lix.
Lipta, 199, 2.
Loans, Law of, 292.
Locke, 98, 1.
Logic (Hindu), 77; 568.
Logician (Hindu), 77.
Lohars (smiths,); 254, 1.
Lokakshi, 339.
Lokaloka, 469, 1.
Lokas, xlvii, 480.
Lokayatas, 142.
Lokman, 568.
Loma harshana, 349.
Lomapada, 378.
Loharis, 254, 1.

Lorinser, Dr., 149, 2; 155, 2; 160; 1; 162, 1.
Lotus de la bonne loi, *xl,* 1.
Lotus stanza, 506.
Lucretius, 67; 1; 69, 1; 89, 1; 93; 1; 97, 1; 100, 2; 124, 3.
Lunar line of kings, 418; 550, 2.
Luncita kesa, 139, 3.
Luptopama, 507.
Lusty Juventus, 548.

Macchiavelli, 545.
Madayantika, 537.
Madhava, 137, 1; 435, 1; 537.
Madhavacarya, 116, 1; 137; 137, 1; 142; 339; 342; 415, 1; 487; 1; 561.
Madhuparka, 281; 543.
Madhusudana, 435, 1.
Madhusudana Gupta, 211.
Madhvas, *lix.*
Madhyadesa, 256, 1.
Madhyalaya, 535.
Madhyama, 525.
Madhyama-kaumudi, .
Madhy madira, 137, 1.
Madhyandina sakha, 175, 276, 1.
Madhyandinas, 276, 1.
Madras, *xxi,* 1, *xxvii,* 1, 339.
Madreyau, 426, 3.
Madri, 283, 1; 350, 416.
Madya, 280.
Magadha, *xxxvi,* 1, 58; 403.
Magadha, king of, 351.
Magadhi, *xxxvii,* 1, *xliv,* 1.
Madha, 200, 1.
Magha, 16, 2; 200, 1; 503.
Magha, month of, 197.
Magha poem of, 437, 2.

Mahabharata, 36, 233, 276, 1; 344, 404, 1; 409, 413, 453, 1.
Mahabhashya, 110, 1; 193.
Mahabhua, 100, 250.
Mahadeva, 361, 559.
Mahajan, 296, 2.
Maha-kavyas, 503.
Maha-nataka, 410, 522.
Mahaniddesa, *xl,* 1.
Mahanirvana, 565.
Maha-padma, 481, 2.
Maha patakas, 302.
Maha prasthanika parvan, 418.
Maha puranas, 554.
Mahar, 70; 2; 480, 1.
Maharashtra, 239, 1; 339.
Maharashtri, *xxxvii,* 1.
Maharshis, 161; 2; 234, 1; 338.
Mahasingh-gati, 425, 1.
Mahasravakas, 61, 3.
Mahat, 100, 109, 244, 250.
Mahatala, 480, 1.
Mahatmya, 456, 1.
Mahavagga, *xl,* 1.
Mahavira, 140, 1.
Mahavira charita, 377; 401, 1; 402, 1; 409 536; 539; 541.
Mahayajna, 215; 216; 1; 222; 275; 300; 323, 3.
Mahayamaka, 507.
Mahayana, 71, 1.
Mahayuga, 204; 250; 369, 1.
Mahe, *xxvi,* 2.
Mahesvara, 137; 1; 186; 341; 561.
Mahesvari, 563.
Mahisha, 471; 1; 479.
Mahishya, 174; 1; 255.
Mahmud, *xxiv,* 1.

Maithila, 239; 1.
Maithila, school, 341.
Maitra Sruata Sutras, 171.
Maitraksha,-joytika, 310.
Maitrayana, 49, 2.
Maitrayani Upanishad, 49; 40, 2.
Maitrayania Grihya Sutras, 214.
Maitreyi, 488.
Maitri Upanishad, 49, 2.
Majjhima-nikaya, *xl*, 1.
Makamat of Hariri, 519.
Makaranda, 563, 1.
Makaras, 563; 1.
Malabar coast, *xxvii*, 1; 369, 2.
Mala-masa, 200.
Malati, 472, 2; 537.
Malati-madhava, *xliv*, 181; 536.
Malavika, 523; 535.
Malavikagnimitra, 532; 534.
Malayalam, *xxxviiii*, 347; 2.
Malcolm's Persia, 253, 1.
Male-arasars, hill kings, 347, 2.
Mali, 239, 1.
Malik, *lii*, 1.
Malimluch, 200.
Mallah (prize fighters), 309.
Malwa, *xxvii*, 1.
Malayavat, 469, 1.
Mammata, 506.
Manapamana, 286, 2.
Manas, 69; 69; 1; 80; 84; 92;
     100; 128; 136; 249.
Manasara, 211.
Manava Grihya-Sutras, 214; 561.
Manava-Srauta-Sutras, 171.
Manava-kalpa-Sutras, 214; 234, 2.
Manavas, 233; 236; 1.
Manavas, code of, 242; 326.
Mandakini, 392, 2.

Manda kranta, 502.
Mandala, 20, 2.
Mandala of the Rik, ninth, 9, 1.
Mandanis, 325, 2.
Mandara, 399, 3; 559.
Mandochcha, 205.
Mandodari, 486.
Manduki siksha, 174, 2.
Mandukya Upanishad, 40.
Mangala, 206.
Mangala vara, 204.
Mang-tsze, 4; 1.
Mankind, deterioration of, 556.
Manning Mrs, xvi, 1.
Mano-maya, 133.
Mansa bhakshana, 281.
Mansel, Dean, 134.
Manthara, 574.
Mantra-mahodadhi, 565.
Mentra portion of the veda, 8;
     9; 14; 276, 1.
Mantra period, 56.
Mantra-jargaras, 276; 1.
Mantras (texts); 7; 1; 8; 26;
     565; 566.
Manu, 8, 1; 9; 1; 33, 1; 231;
     249; 340; 551, 1.
Manu 's code, 231.
Manushya-loka, 226.
Manushyayajna, 222; 275.
Manvanthara, 234; 1; 250; 369,
     1; 550.
Manv artha muktavali, 340.
Mara (demon), 62, 1.
Marathi, *xxxvi*.
Marathi country, *xxvii*, 1; 266; 2.
Marathi empire, 288, 1.
Margasirsha, 200, 1.
Maricha, 395; 1; 556; 1.

Marichi, 234; 309; 339; 382.
Markandeya, 409.
Markandeya purana, 432; 1; 553.
Markham, Mr. C.R., xi.
Marriage forms of, 274.
Marriage portion, 300.
Marriage rite, 218; 274.
Mars, 204.
Marshman, 375, 1.
Marut (wind) 432, 1.
Maruts, 13; 17; 447.
Marvdi, (merchants), 254; .
Mashaka Srauta Sutras, 171.
Matali, 399.
Materialists, 143, 2; 393.
Mathas (monasteries), 142.
Mathavya, 291, 1.
Mathematical science, 198.
Mathura, 368, 2; 371.
Matsya, 364; 443; 553.
Matsya purana, 551.
Matula, 424; 1.
Mauna-vrata, 285.
Maunji-bhandhana, 271; 329.
Mausala-Parvan, 417; 459, 1.
Maya, 99; 127; 165.
Maya (mother of Buddha), 58, 1.
Mecca, liii, 1.
Mechanical arts, 211.
Medhatithi (lawyers); 232; 340.
Medicine, 211.
Medini, 187.
Megasthenes, xxiii, 236, 1; 253,
  1; 268, 2; 289, 2; 310, 1;
  350; 355; 545.
Megasthenes, caste-divisions of,
  253; 1; 268, 1.
Meghadoot, 401, 2; 411; 436;
  1; 446, 1; 503; 532, 1.

Mekhala, 270.
Menaka, 403.
Mencius, 4; 1.
Mercury, 204.
Meru (mount); 399, 3; 461;
  469, 1.
Metaphor, 509.
Metaphysics, (Hindu), 77.
Metempsychosis, 14, 1; 21; 71,
  1; 73; 1; 571.
Metre, 178; 180.
Mill, J.S.; 83, 1.
MILL'S INDIA, 112; 253, 1;
  287, 2.
Millar, 253, 1.
Milman Dean, 152, 1; 430.
Milton's Satan, 396.
Mimansa, 52; 116; 234, 3;
  248; 262, 1.
Mimansaka, 7; 1; 118; 234, 3.
Mimansa sutra, 116; 1; 118, 1.
Mind-born sons, 556, 1.
Minerva, 397, 1.
Miracles, lix, 1.
Misals of Sikhs, 363, 1.
Misaru-misra, 342.
Mishra, 342, 1.
Mishra-damodara, 410.
Mishra-vritta, 523.
Mitakshara, 326; 240; 341.
Mithi 550, 2.
Mithila, 383; 384, 2; 550, 2.
Mithila (schools of law), 327;
  340; 342.
Mithya-jnana, 123.
Mitra, 13; 19; 239, 1.
Mlecha, xlii, 1; 258, 2; 274;
  309; 451.
Mlechadesa, 258; 2.

Mlechas, 451.
M'Mahon, Rev, J.H., 84, 1; 135, 1.
Modaka, 239, 1.
Modern India, xxvii, 1.
Mogal Empire, xxiv, 1.
Moksha, 75; 141.
Moksha dharma, 417.
Monasteries, 527.
Money lender, 296.
Mongol language, 347, 2.
Mongol tribes, xxiv, 1.
Monks, xl, 1.
Months, names of, 200, 1.
Montriou W.A., 327, 2.
Moor's Hindu Pantheon, 372.
Moral (prohibitions), 62.
Morality, 548.
Mrichakatika, 11, 2; 332, 1; 351; 362, 2; 368, 3; 410; 520; 527.
Mriga-shiras, 200; 1.
Muchakunda, 560.
Mudra-rakshasa, 546; 546, 1.
Mugdha bodha, 196.
Mugha bodhini 196.
Muhammad, l, lii, 1; liii, 5; 6; 7; 275, 1.
Muhammad Kasim, xxiv, 1.
Muhammad Shah, xxivi, 1.
Muhammadans in Bengal xxvi, 1.
Muhammadans, Indian, xxvi, 1.
Muharram liii, 1.
Muhurta 203.
Muhurtas, 197.
Muir, Dr. John, 15, 1; 15, 2.
Muir Sir W.; xxxvii, 2.
Muir University-College, xxvii, 2.
Muka, 438.

Mukha, opening, 522, 1.
Mukhopadhyaya, 239, 1.
Mukhurjea, 239, 1.
Muktambaras, 139, 3.
Mukti, 75.
Mula- Mahabharata, 522.
Mula-prakriti, 99.
Mula-ramayana, 349; 378, 1; 522.
Mula-Samhita, 522.
Mula-Sutra, xliv, 1.
Mullen's Eassy, 74, 1; 106; 1.
Muller, Prof, Max, 4, 1; 12, 2; 15; 2; and passim.
Mumbai, xxi, 1.
Munda, 328.
Mundaka Upanishad, 40; 44; 49, 2; 129; 1.
Muni, 285; 286.
Muraja bandha, 507.
Murari, 401, 2; 410.
Murdha vasikta, 255.
Murshidaba, xxvi, 1.
Murta, 203.
Murtti, 68; 1.
Musala, 417.
Musalin (club-armed), 371, 1.
Musalman invasion, xxvi, 1.
Musalman's, 275.
Mushroom's eating of, 281.
Music, 212.
Muslims, xxvi, 1; xlii, 1; 5; 1; 8; 282; 1.
Muttra, 398, 1.
Mysore, 398, 1.
Mythology (Grecian); 357; 476; 477.
Mythology (Post-vedic), 359; 467; 477-483.

Nachiketas, 46.
Nadi, 203.
Nadika, 203.
Nadir Shah, *xxiv,* 1.
Naga (serpetdemons), *xlvi,* 1
   271, 1; 424; 479; 480; 1.
Nagakanyas, 480, 1.
Nagaloka, 480, 1.
Nagananda, 544, 1; 547.
Nagapanchami, 480, 1.
Nagasahavya, 421, 2.
Nagoji-bhatta, 110, 1; 194.
Nahusha, *xlvi,* 1; 418.
Naigama, 183.
Naigantuka, 182; 183.
Naimittika Sraddha, 228.
Nair tribe, 431, 2.
Nairuktas (etymologists), 184.
Nairuktikas, 182.
Naishadha, 503, 1; 505; 544; 1.
Naishthika, 272.
Naivedya, 247.
Naiyayikas, 78; 81; 83; 90, 1;
   105.
Nakshatra, 198; 198; 1; 204, 1;
   227.
Nakshatra darsa, 200.
Nakula, 432; 1; 449; 462.
Nakulisa, 137, 1.
Nala (Story of) 16, 2; 282, 2.
Nala (king); 383.
Nala (monkey general), 398.
Nalodaya, 503; 504.
Namakarana, 270.
Nama-karman, 270.
Namaz, 275; 1.
Names of India, *xix.*
Nanaka (coin), 296; 328.
Nanak Shah, 363; 1.

Nana Sahib, 254.
Nanda, 370.
Nanda, 561.
Nandana, 537.
Nandapandita, 341; 342.
Nandi, 362, 2; 525; 561.
Nandi-grama, 393.
Nandi sutra, *xliv,* 1.
Napita, 239, 1; 576.
Nara, 426; 3; .
Narabhimani, 522.
Naracha, 453, 1.
Narada, 30; 42; 231; 338; 339;
   458; 476; 556, 1.
Narada-pancharatra, *lx.*
Narada-siddhanta, 201.
Naradiya, 553; 561.
Narakas, 70, 3; 480, 1.
Narasansa, 184.
Narasansi, 223; 331.
Nara-sinha, 253; 561; 562.
Nara-sinha Upa purana, 561.
Narayana, 247; 435; 2; 400;
   446.
Narmada, 378, 2.
Nartaka, 518; 521.
Nasatyau, 14; 184; 432, 1.
Nasik (from nasika), 395, 1.
Nastika, 56; 247.
Nastikyam, 304.
Nathacharya, chadamani, 341.
Nathooboy, Sir Mungoldas,
   xxxiii, 1.
Natika, 523.
Natya, 518.
Natyarasaka, 523.
Nava Sak (nine divisions), 239, 1.
Nayaka, 522; 527.
Nayar, 431, 2.

Nayika 522; 527.
Nearchus, *xxiii.*
Nectar, 560.
Nekyomanteia, 463.
Nemi, 140, 1.
Nepal, *xxvii,* 1; *xlv,* 58; 565.
Nestor, 474.
New Testament, 156, 1.
Nic, 190; 1.
Nicha, 526.
Nicholson, John, 357, 1.
Nidana sutra, 177.
Nidarsana (example), 77.
Nigama, 183; 564, 1.
Nigamana (conclusion), 77.
Nighantu, 182; 185; 276, 1.
Night, 19; 26; 472.
Nigraha-sthana, 81.
Nihilism, 60; 134.
Nihsreyasa, 75.
Nikshepa, 293.
Nila, 469, 1.
Nila-kantha, (Siva), 361.
Nilakantha-bhatta, 343.
Nilgiri hills, 247, 2.
Nimb tree leaves of, 336.
Nimesha, 203; 449.
Nimi, 140; 1; 383; 550, 2.
Nimitta-karana, 87.
Ninda, 29.
Nipa, 472, 3.
Nipata, 176; 186.
Nirgauna, 104; 125; 131, 3; 554.
Nirnaya, 80.
Nirnaya-sindhu, 228.
Nirukta, 145; 1; 170; 183; 246.
Nirvahana, 522; 1.
Nirvana, *xlviii,* 58, 2; 59, 1;
    61; 66, 2; 75.

Nirvikalpa, 131, 4.
Niryukti, *xliv,* 1.
Nishadas, 184; 348, 1.
Nishadha, 469, 1.
Nishadi, 430.
Nishka, 328.
Nishkramana, 270.
Nishphala, 170, 1.
Niti, 566; 567.
Nitisastras, 171; 566.
Niti sastras, proper, 566.
Nitya (Sraddha), 216, 1; 228;
    278.
Nitya-siddha, 141.
Nirvritti, 191.
Niyama, 111.
Nizam, *xxvii,* 1.
Non-Aryan races, 349.
Northern Buddhist, 565.
North-west provinces, *xxvi,* 1.
Notation (in algebra), 208.
Nri-sinha Upapurana, 561.
Nritya, 518.
Nullity, 23.
Numa Pompilius, 5, 2.
Numerations system of, 210.
Nushirvan, 570, 1.
Nyagrodha tree, 456.
Nyarsa-dharin, 296.
Nyaya, 52; 57; 65; 76; 104, 1;
    248.
Nyaya sutra, 76; 1.
Nyayamala vistara, 137; 1.
Nyaya sutra vritti, 76; 1.

Odras, 258; 2.
Odyssey, 344; 397, 1; 434;
    463; 471.
Old and new Testament, 4, 1.

Om, *iii*, 185; 222; 243; 1.
Omar, *xxiii, liii*, 1.
Omens, 211.
Ordeal ten forms of, 304.
Ordeal, trial by 304; 334.
Oriental Congress, *ix*, 1.
Orissa, *xxi*, 1; *xxvii*, 239, 1; 275, 1.
Ormuzd *xxiii*, 1, 12.
Orphic hymns, 125, 1.
Othman, *liii*.
Ottoman, tribe, *xxivi*, 1.
Oudh, *xxvi*, 58, 3.
Ovid's metamorphoses, 368, 3.
Oxus, *xxii*, 10.

Pacittiya *xlii*.
Pada (traditional art), 94.
Pada (text), 175; 176; 276, 1.
Padartha, 68; 1; 83; 98.
Padma, 411; 553.
Padma-bandha, 506.
Padma-pura, 536.
Padma purana, 339.
Padya (verse), 412.
Pahlavas, 403.
Pahlavi, 6; 6; 1; 570; 1.
Paishacha (marriage), 217; 274.
Paitamaham astram, 339; 3.
Paitamaha siddhanta, 201.
Paithinasi, 339.
Pakashasani, 426, 3.
Paka-yajna, 216; 216, 1; 261; 276; 277.
Pala, 203; 296.
Pali, *xxxvi*, 1.
Palibothra, *xxii*, 351; 371, 1.
Palita, 239, 1.
Panchagavya, penance, 306.

Panchagni, 216, 2.
Pancha-janah, 184; 450.
Pachajanya, 450.
Panchakosa, 133.
Panchala, 57; 534.
Pancha-lakshana, 551; 556.
Panchanana, 361; 2.
Panchanga, *xlivi*, 204, 1.
Pancharatras, *lx*.
Panch siddhantika, 201.
Panchatantra, 70; 1; 33, 1; 570, 1; 571; 572; 574; 577.
Pancha tapas, 113; 285.
Panchavti, 396, 1.
Pancha vinsa Brahmana, 29.
Pancha yajna, 215.
Panchi karana, 130, 1.
Panchi krita, 130, 1.
Panchopakhyana, 571.
Pandavas, 385, 1; 416; 448; 554.
Pandits, *xxxvi, xxxvii*.
Pandu, 416; 420.
Pani grahana, 219.
Panigrahanika mantrah, 295.
Panini, 188.
Panini, *xxxv*, 1; 137; 174; 182; 2; 188; 571.
Panini darsana, 137, 1.
Panini's grammar, 177; 187.
Panjab, *xxii, xxvi*, 1; 262, 1; 282, 3.
Panjabi, language, *xxxvi*.
Pantheism *xxxiii*, 39; 120; 129; 134; 549.
Para, 86.
Paradas, 258, 2.
Parajika xl, 1.
Paraka (penance), 307.

Parama-hansa, *lix.*
Paramanu, 203.
Paramarthika (existence), 127.
Paramatman, 66; 69; 92; 252; 361.
Param-itas (Buddhist), 63.
Parasara, 231; 339; 418; 550; 557; 562.
Parashara's Code, 137; 338; 339; 342.
Parashara-siddhanta, 201.
Parashara, smriti-vyakhya, 342.
Parashara's Grihya-sutras, 213; 231, 1; 331, 3.
Parasmai-pada, 190.
Parashurama, 367; 367; 2; 388; 386; 446; 459.
Paratva, 85.
Parda-nishin, 486, 2.
Paribhasha, 189, 2.
Paribhashendu-sekhara, 194, 1.
Parajata, 559.
Parikara, 510.
Parikshit, 435; 555.
Parimanani, 85.
Parishad, 246; 249.
Parisishta (supplements), 221.
Parits (washermen), 254, 1.
Parivara, *xl,* 1.
Parivrajika 62; 268; 286; 536.
Paramenides, 67, 1.
Parsis, *xxiii, xlii,* 5; 6; 6, 1.
Parshv-natha, 140, 1.
Partha, 426, 3.
Partnership, 293.
Parushye, 293.
Parvana, Sraddha, 228; 277.
Parvati, 361; 361, 2; 363, 1; 476; 564, 1.
Paryanaka-bandha, 362, 2; 111, 2.

Pasa, 210.
Pashandin (heretic), 248; 336.
Pasukalpa, 219.
Pashupata (weapon), 438.
Pashupatas, 137, 1.
Pashu pati, 137, 1.
Pashu yajna, 32, 1.
Pata, 205.
Patakas sthanaka, 523.
Patala, 70; 3; 405; 469, 1; 480; 1.
Pataliputra, 193; 2; 253; 1; 545.
Patanjala darsana, 137.
Patanjali, 110; 193; 329.
Pati-ganita, 202; 3.
Patisambhida, *xl,* 1.
Pativrata, 486.
Patriarchs, 556.
Patrin, 453, 1.
Patroclus, 474.
Pathana, *xl,* 1.
Paulastya, 396, 1.
Paulisa-siddhanta, 201.
Pauloma, 414, 1.
Paundra (trumpet), 450.
Paundrakas, 258, 2.
Paurava, 451.
Paurnamasa, 277.
Pausha, 200.
Paushya, 414, 1.
Pavitra, 270, 1.
Payannas, *xliv,* 1.
Pazand, 6, 1.
Pegu, xlv.
Penance, 306; 323.
Penelope, 397, 1.
Perfection (Buddhist), 63.
Persia, *xxii.*
Persia (ancient), 4.

Persi-Armenians, *xxiv,* 1.
Persian language, *xxii.*
Persians, *xix; xxiii; xxiv,* 1; 403.
Pervasion in logic, 78.
Peshwa, 288; 1.
Petavattu, *xl,* 1.
Phaedo of Plato, 74, 1.
Phaedrus, 48, 1.
Phala, 80.
Phalguna, 200, 1; 363, 1; 426, 3; 443; 525.
Phalguni, 200, 1.
Phallus, 360, 2.
Philosophy, common creed, 65.
Philosophy, six system of, 52.
Pickford, Mr. John 541, 1.
Pichala, 472, 3.
Pilpay's fables, 570, 1.
Pinda, 228; 278; 279; 299.
Pingala, 178.
Pingala naga, 178.
Pippala, 45, 1.
Pishacha, 410.
Pischel, Dr. R., 532, 3.
Pisistratus, 414.
Pishuni, 392, 2.
Pitamaha, 447, 2.
Pitris, 9; 1; 22; 184; 272; 279; 309.
Pitri-yajna, 222; 275.
Piyadasi, 64, 1.
Plaintiff, 333.
Plakshadvipa, 469.
Planets, nine, 206.
Plassy (battle); *xxvii,* 1.
Plato, 48; 1; 66; 1; 68; 2; 73; 1; 90; 2; 92; 2; 98; 2; 100; 2; 123; 1; 125; 2; 128; 155; 2; 253, 1.
Plato (Republic), 253; 1.

Plato (Timaeus), 253; 1.
Platonic idealism, 122.
Platonic realism, 86.
Platonists, 68, 2.
Plays Hindu, 517.
Pliny, *xxiii.*
Poems, artificial, 503; 505.
Poems Homeric, 465.
Poison, 559.
Poita, 270, 1.
Polyandry, 431; 2.
Polygamy, 274.
Polyphemus, 478, 2.
Pondicherry, *xxvi,* 2.
Portuguese, *xxvi,* 2.
Porus, 419, 1.
Post-vedi literature, 231.
Prabha kara, 262, 1.
Prabhasa, 435.
Prabhus, 254.
Prabodha-chandrodaya, 548.
Prachanda pandava, 411.
Pradhana, 68; 1; 99; 108, 2; 109; 124, 2; 526; 563.
Pradvivaka, 332, 1.
Prahasana, 525.
Prablada, 366.
Prajapati, 179; 235, 1; 246; 264; 306; 365, 3.
Prajapatis, 235, 1; 274; 338.
Parjapatya (marriage), 217; 274.
Prajapatya penance, 306.
Prajna, 63.
Prakarana, 523.
Prakarani, 524.
Prakaranika, 524.
Parakranta, 508.
Prakrit, *xxi, xxxvii,* 59, 1; 351; 526.

Prakrit of the plays, *xxxvi*, 1.
Prakrita, 508; *xxxvi*.
Prakrita-prakasha, *xxxvii*, 1.
Prakrit, 97; 102; 104; 165; 563.
Prama, 74; 77; 79; 99.
Pramana (Philosophical), 76;
99; 110; 136; 252.
Pramanam 264; 333.
Prameya, 79.
Prana, 42; 203.
Prana-maya, 133.
Pranatman, 134.
Pranava, *iii*.
Pranayama, *iii*.
Pranidhi, 63; 1; 289; 296.
Prasada, *xlvi*, 1.
Prasanna Kumar Thakur, 341;
342, 2.
Prasanna raghava, 410; 547.
Prashna Upanishad, 40.
Prastavana (prologue), 526.
Prasthana, 525.
Prastuta, 508.
Prathamam retas, 563.
Pratibhasika (existence), 127.
Pratigraha, 267; 294.
Pratiyna (Proposition), 77.
Pratima, 247, 1; 272.
Pratima paricharka, 247, 1.
Pratimukha, 521, 2.
Prati nayaka, 523.
Pratipadika, 189.
Pratisakhyas, vedic, 174.
Prati sarga (re-creation), 550; 557.
Pratitakshara, 341.
Prativadin, (defendant), 334.
Prativasudevas, 141.
Pratiyamana, 507.
Pratyabhijna-darsana, 137, 1.

Pratyahara (grammatical), 189,
3; 195, 1.
Pratyahara (restraint), 111.
Pratyaksha, 77; 136; 252; 393.
Praudha Brahmana, 29.
Pravachana, 170.
Pravaha, 205.
Pravahana, 55.
Pravara-sena, 532, 2.
Pravargya, 379; 2.
Praveshaka, 526.
Pravritti, 80.
Prayaga, 401.
Prayas-chitta, 70, 2; 238; 241;
243; 306; 312; 323; 328;
336; 459, 1.
Prayatna, 85.
Prayer, 62, 1, 525.
Prayoga, 449, 1.
Prayojana, (motive), 80.
Precepts (mortal), 3, 1; 312;
490; 512; 573; 577.
Prem Chunder Tarkabagish,
532, 3.
Premiss in logic, 77.
Prem sagar, xxxvi, 1; 149, 2; 555.
Prenkhana, 524.
Preserver, 558.
Presidency, towers, *xxi*, 1.
Pretakaryani (funeral rites), 458.
Pretya bhava, 80.
Priam, 352; 1; 447, 2.
Prinsep's tables, 383, 1.
Prishatka, 453, 1.
Pritha, 416; 419; 2; 421-23;
458.
Prithaktva, 85.
Prithivi, 14; 67, 1; 84; 101;
476; 543.

Privileges, six (of Brahmans), 267, 1.
Priya darsi, 64, 1.
Problem (from Lilavati), 210.
Pronunciation, 174.
Properties (an ga), 522.
Propertius, 282, 3.
Property, law of, 293.
Proposition in logic, 77.
Protagoras, 122, 1; 155; 2.
Prdgala, 141.
Puga, 332; 1.
Puggala, *xl*, 1.
Pukkasa, 244.
Pulaha, 556, 1.
Pulastya, sage, 339; 396, 1; 556, 1.
Pulastya-siddhanta, 201.
Pundarika, 481, 1.
Punsavana, 219; 270.
Purana, 42; 108; 222; 281; 331; 411; 548; 549; 553; 561.
Puri, 239, 1; 275, 1.
Purna-prajna, 137, 1.
Purochana, 430.
Purohita, 289, 2; 310.
Puru, 370; 419.
Purusha, 25; 25, 2; 3; 99; 105; 108, 2; 165; 563.
Purusha-pashu, 102.
Purusha-sukta, 7, 1; 12, 1; 14; 25; 49, 1; 236; 1; 243; 249.
Purushottama, 109, 2; 159, 3; 435, 2.
Purva, 227.
Purva mimansa, 116.
Purva-paksha, 117.
Pushan, 20.
Pushkara, 363, 1; 469.

Pushpa-danta, 140, 1; 481, 1.
Pushpaka, 395; 401; 541.
Pushpamitra, 193, 2.
Pushya, 200, 1.
Put, 280.
Put-tra, 280, 1.
Pythagoras, 53; 73, 1; 99, 1; 767; 208.

Qualities, three, 71, 2; 102; 309; 553.
Qualities, of the Vaiseshika, 85.
Quality, 83.
Queen Elizabeth, *xliii*, 1.

Race (solar and lunar), 550, 2.
Radha, 363, 1; 171; 421.
Radha, 239, 1; 504; 554.
Radheya, 422.
Raffles, Sir Stamford, xxvi, 2.
Raga (musical), 212.
Raghava, 383.
Raghavabhyudaya, 410.
Raghavapandaviya, 412; 504; 574.
Raghava-vilasa, 412.
Gaghu, 383.
Raghunandana, 342; 283, 1.
Raghu-nathabhyudaya, 412; .
Raghu vansa, 258, 1; 383, 1; 410; 502; 510.
Ragini (musical), 212.
Rahasya, 37; 309.
Rahu, 206, 1.
Rahula, 58, 1.
Raivata, Manu, 234, 3.
Raivataka (mountain), 436.
Rajadharma, 417.
Rajaks (washermen), 239, 1.

Rajanya, 26, 1; 173; 1; 258.
Rajarshris, 158, 3.
Rajas (guna), 101; 164; 151; 309; 359.
Rajasa Puranas, 553-554.
Rajsekhara, 410; 547.
Rajasuya, 436; 503.
Raja tharangini, 411; 572.
Raja yakshma, 263, 2.
Rajendralala Mitra, xlivi, 1; 105, 1; 566.
Rajput, 239, 1; 254, 1; 373, 1.
Rajput States, xxvii, 1.
Rajputana, xxvii, 1; 363, 1.
Raka, 184; 198.
Rakshasa (demon), 310; 348; 387, 1; 447.
Rakshasa (marriage),; 217.
Rakshasi, 397.
Rama, 275, 1; 382; 541; 542.
Rama's banishment, 387.
Rama's birth, 383.
Rama (second), 368.
Rama and Lakshamana, 389; 392, 2.
Rama and Ravana, 399.
Ramachandra, 353, 1; 367, 2; 368; 384, 3; 402, 1.
Ramachandra Charita sara, 412.
Ramachandra, 412.
Ramage's Beautiful Thoughts, 168.
Rama gita, 412.
Rama-hridaya, 411.
Ramalila, 408.
Ramananda, lviii.
Ramanavami, 408; 1.
Ramanuja, lviii, 137, 1; 363; 1.
Rama setu, 398, 1.
Ramavats, lix.

Ramavilasa, 412.
Ramayana, 344; 354; 373; 409; 410; 411.
Ramayana (epitome of), 373.
Ramayana (recension of), 374; 375.
Ramayana mahatmya, 411.
Ramzan (month); 6.
Ramdoolal Dey, 280, 2.
Ramesuram 398, 2.
Ramopakhyayana, 409; 409; 1.
Rampur, xxvii, 1.
Ramusies, 347; 2.
Rangaris, (dyers), 254; 1.
Rasa, 85; 507; 522.
Rasaka, 524.
Rasamanjari, 508.
Rasana, 89.
Rasatala, 480; 1.
Rasesvara, 137; 137; 1.
Rasi, 204; 209.
Ratha charya, 427.
Rathakara, 174; 174, 1; 254; 1.
Rathanga, 472; 1.
Rationalism, 248.
Rationalistic Brahmanism, 66.
Ratnavali, 486; 2; 544; 545.
Raudra, lix, 508, 1; 523.
Raudri, 563.
Ravana, 347, 2; 267; 368; 376; 377; 395; 437, 2; 541.
Ravana (description of), 395; 470; 478.
Ravigupta, 3, 1.
Realism, 86.
Reasoning, 77.
Reciters, of the Ramayana, 375.
Recorde, Robert, 208, 1.
Regions, (seven), 480.

Regnier, M. Adolphe, 175, 3.
Religious of the world, *xlvii*, 4, 1.
Retaliation, 301.
Revati, 436.
Revenue, 290.
Rewah, *xxvii*, 1.
Rhetoric (figures of); 521.
Rhyme (employment of); 505.
Ribhus, 17; 17, 1; 174, 1.
Richika, 31; .
Right hand Worshippers, 564; 1.
Rig veda, 90; 23; 25; 27; 118; 278, 1.
Rig veda pratisakhya, 176.
Rigvedi Brahmans, 254, 1; 276, 1.
Riju yodhin, 456.
Rik, 9; 1.
Rina, 209;.
Rinadana, 293.
Rishabha, 140, 1.
Rishi, 7; 7; 1; 31; 219; 272; 274; 418; 446.
Rishyasringa, 379.
Ritu samhara, 503.
Ritv-ji, 260, 2; 261.
Rivalry between sects, 522.
Rock inscriptions, xxxvi, 1.
Röer, Dr., 40, 3; 44, 1; 76, 1; 231, 1; 327, 1; 327, 2.
Rohilkhand, *xxvii*, 1.
Rohini, 264, 2; 370; 432;.
Rihita, 30.
Roma harshana, 550.
Romaka-siddhanta, 201.
Roman alphabet, *xxxvii*, 2.
Rost, Dr.; *lviii*, 282, 3; 545; 572, 2.
Roth, Professor, 9, 1; 43, 1; 183, 1.

Royal Asiatic Society, 184; 205.
Ru (in algebra), 209.
Rudra, 360; 360. 2; 446; 457, 2.
Rudra-bhatta, 508.
Rudraksha berries, 362, 2.
Rudra-yamala Tantra, 565.
Runjit Singh, 363, 2.
Rupa, 85; 209; 432, 1.
Rupaka, 507.
Ryot (cultivator), 257; 2; 290; 1.

Sabaktagin, *xxiv*, 1.
Sabra-svamin, 116, 1.
Sabda (sound), 7.
Sabda (verbal authority), 77; 136; 252.
Sabda-kalpa-druma, 70, 2.
Sabda-lakshana, 504.
Sabdalankara, 508.
Sabha, 292; 436.
Sabha-parvan, 416.
Sabhya (fire), 216, 2.
Sachitananda, 125; 131; 1.
Sacrifice, *xlvi*, 2; 321; 479.
Sadachara, 238; 329.
Sad-dharma-pundarika, *xl*, 1.
Sadhu, 142.
Sadhyas, 161, 2; 310; 447.
Sadi of chiraz, 3; 1.
Sagar, 96, 1; 383; 404.
Sagarika, 545.
Sahadeva, 423; 432, 1; 449.
Sahasa, 293.
Sahitya-darpana, 411; 507.
Sahokti, 510.
Shaiva-darsana, 137.
Shaiva-puranas, 554.
Shaiva sect, *lix*, 112; 362, 2.
Shaka-dvipa, 469.

Shakala, shakha, 175.
Shaklya, 188; 1.
Shakapuni, 184.
Shakara, 528, 1.
Shakas, 259, 1; 403.
Shakatayana, 185; 186; 188, 1.
Shakha, 175; 214.
Shakhanta-ga, 245.
Shakrasyansha, 432, 1.
Sakshinah (witness), 33.
Shaktas, 360, 1; 361, 1; 363, 1; 553.
Shakti, 109; 247; 361, 1; 562.
Shakuni 417; 424; 429; 436; 458.
Shakuntala, 74; 1; 112; 151, 2; 287, 3; 291, 1; 403; 486, 1; 532.
Shakya (Buddha), 58; 58, 2; 62, 2; 64, 1.
Shalatura, Shalaturiya, 188.
Shalis (weavers); 254, 1.
Shalmali-dvipa, 469.
Shalya (king); 422, 436; 453; 454.
Shalya-parvan, 417.
Sama 446.
Samadhi, 111; 362.
Samahara, 195, 1.
Saman, 9; 444.
Samanodaka-bhava, 279.
Samanya, 83; 86.
Samanya-dharma, 508.
Samavakara, 523.
Samavartana, 223; 270; 273.
Samavaya, 83; 86.
Samavayi-karana, 66, 4; 68, 1; 87.
Sama-veda, 7; 1; 9, 1; 29; 276, 1.
Sama-veda priest, 245.

Sama-veda Upanishad, 40.
Samayachara, 170; 213.
Samayachrika Sutra, 170; 213; 230; 231; 237; 242.
Samba, 561.
Shambhu, 210.
Sambhuya samutthana, 293.
Shamhuka, 543.
Samhara (restraint), 449; 1.
Samhit (text), 177.
Samhitas of the veda, 9; 29; 276, 1; 309.
Sami tree, 224.
Samlapaka, 524.
Samoyedic language, 347, 2.
Sampradayin, lviii.
Samsaptka, 453.
Samsaya, 80.
Samsrishti, 510.
Samudra-mathana, 523.
Samvarta's Code, 231; 359.
Samvat, 531.
Samvido vyatikrama, 293.
Samyavastha, 102.
Samyoga, 85.
Shyan (in grammar), 190, 1.
Sanat-kumara, 42; 561.
Sanchayana (of ashes), 227.
Sandhi (juncture in drama), 522, 1.
Sandhi (rules of) 177 .
Sandhyas, 277; 315; 1.
Sandhya-vandana, 276, 1.
Sandilya, Aphorisms of, 148, 2.
Sandrokottos or Sandrakottus, 253, 1; 546.
Sangita, 536.
Sangita-damodara, 212.
Sangita-darpana, 212.

Sangita-ratnakara, 212; 521.
Sagnita- parvan, 413, 1.
Shani (Saturn); 205.
Shani-vara, 204.
Sanjaya, 422; 447; 455, 1.
Sanjna, 189, 2.
Shankara Acharya, or
    Shankaracharya, 45, 1; 52, 1;
    90; 120, 1; 123; 125; 127;
    129; 145; 340, 2; 363, 1;
    504; 532, 2.
Shankara (of figures), 510.
Sankara-jatiyah, 254.
Shankara-mishra, 73; 85.
Sankha, 210; 232; 338; 339.
Sankhayana, 171.
Sankhayana-brahmana, 29.
Sankhayana Grihya Sutras, 213.
Sankhya philosophy, 45; 52; 57;
    65; 90; 96; 104, 1; 137, 1;
    248; 571.
Sankhya-Gunas, 66, 4; 102, 2.
Sankhya Sutras, 56, 1; 96, 1.
Sankhya (synthesis); 76.
Sankhyah (numbers); 85.
Sankhya-karika, 54, 1; 66, 4; 70,
    3; 90, 3; 96, 1; 98, 1; 100, 1.
Sankhya-pravachana, 96, 1;
    250; 326, 1; 571.
Sankhya-pravachana-bhashya,
    96, 1; 102.
Sankirna, 524.
Sannyasin, 268; 286; 340, 1.
Sanskara, (ceremonies), 215;
    220; 261; 268; 269; 270.
Sanskara (quality); 85; 163.
Sanskarana, 187.
Sanskrit (meaning of), xxxv.
Sanskrita, xxxvi, 187.

Santha (rasa), 508; 1.
Santha, Dsaratha's daughter, 379.
Shantanava, 419.
Shantanava's Phit-Sutra, 188; 1.
Shantanu, 419.
Santapana (penance), 307.
Santhals 347, 2.
Santi, 459.
Shanti-parvan, 410; 418; 459.
Sanyutta-nikaya, xl, 1.
Sapindata (sapindaship), 279; 298.
Sapta-bhanga-naya, 142.
Saptapadi-bhava, 218.
Saptarshayah (seven patriarchs),
    556, 1.
Sapta-staka, 411.
Sapta-Sati, 411.
Sapta-Sindhavah, xix, 2.
Sara, 453, 1; 509.
Sarabhanga (an ascetic), 282, 3.
Sharad, 503.
Sharada-tilaka, 565.
Sarama, (sons of), 226.
Sarasvata, 239, 1.
Sarasvati xxii, 234; 238; 456,
    1; 476; 563.
Sarasvati-kanthabharana, 508.
Sarayu, river, 378, 2.
Sardula-vikridita metre, 242, 2.
Sarga (creation), 550.
Sarira, 80; 89.
Sharmishtha-yayati, 524.
Saranga-deva, 212; 521.
Sarangadhara-paddhati, 3; 1; 411.
Sarpari, 480.
Sarpis, 479.
Sarva, 457; 2.
Sarva-darsana-sangraha, 98; 1;
    137; 142; 377.

Sarava-naman, 195.
Sarvato-bhadra, 506.
Sarva-bhauma, 481; 1.
Shastra, 52; 292; 318; 1; 415, 1.
Shastram Aiyar, 139.
Shatanika, 435; 1.
Shapatha-brahmana, 7, 1; 29; 33; 36; 40; 72; 1; 173; 331; 1; 358; 365, 1; 3; 380; 1.
Satara, xxvii, 1.
Shatatapa's Code, 232; 339.
Sati, 224, 1; 230, 1; 275, 1; 282; 283, 2; 350.
Shatru–ghna, 384; 542.
Shatrunjoya-mahatmya, 411.
Sattaka, 524.
Sattva, 102; 165; 309; 359.
Sattvika puranas, 552-555.
Saturn, 204.
Satya (age), 70, 3; 367; 372.
Satyaki, 445; 547.
Satyashadha Srauta Sutras, 171.
Satyavan, 441.
Satyavati, 414, 1; 419.
Saubala, 425, 1.
Saubaleyi, 421.
Saubali, 421, 425, 1.
Sauda, xxxviii, 2.
Saudhanvana, 174, 1.
Saumanas, 481, 1.
Saumitri, 384.
Saunaka, 175.
Saunaka Srauta Sutras, 171.
Saunakiya Caturadhyayika, 175.
Sauptika-pravan, 417; 457, 1.
Saura, 203; 205; 561.
Sauraseni, xxxvii, 1.
Saura-Siddhanta, 201.
Sauti, 550, 1.

Sautramani, 338, 2.
Savala, 403.
Shravana (month), 203; 205.
Savanas (three), 271; 285.
Savitri, 19; 218; 384, 3.
Savitri (Gayatir), 21; 222; 243; 243, 1; 308.
Savya-sachin, 426, 3; 444.
Sayaka (arrow), 452, 1.
Sayana, 45; 137, 1; 179; 182.
Scepticism, 54; 56; 143; 393; 446.
Schlegel Augustus William, 375, 1.
Schools of Hindu, law, 340.
Scythians, 403.
Seclusion of Hindu women, 486, 2.
Sects, Hindu, lviii, 363, 1; 364.
Seekers after God (Farrar's), 167.
Seleukos Nikator, xxiii.
Semitic race, 5, 1.
Sena (tribe); 239, 1.
Senaka (grammarian), 188, 1.
Seneca, 167; 168.
Sentiments, moral, 312; 490; 514; 573.
Serampore, xxvi, 2.
Seamum seed, 228.
Shesha, serpᴇɴᴛ, 266, 1; 371; 1; 480; 480, 1.
Sheshadri, Rev, Narayan, 266, 1.
Seton-Karr, Mr., 283, 1.
Setu, 398, 1.
Setu-bandha, 410; 532; 2.
Setu-kavya, 532, 2.
Shad-vinsa Brahmana, 29.
Shafi, lii, 1.
Shahadat, 275, 1.
Shah'Alam, xxiv, 1.

Shajahan, *xxiv*, 1.
Shakespere, 129, 3; 484.
Shams-ul-Umra, *xxvii*, 1.
Shakar P. Pandit, 535.
Shat-karmani, 267.
Shi (Chinese book), 4; 1.
Shi'as, xxv, 1; *liii*, 1.
Shirk, *li*, 1.
Shir Shash Sur, *xxiv*, 1.
Shu (Chinese book), 4; 1.
Siamese, language, 347, 2.
Siddha (divine being); 161, 2; 559.
Siddhanta (astronomical), 200.
Siddhanta (in logic), 80.
Siddhanta (Jaina), *xliv*, 1.
Siddhanta-kaumudi, 194.
Siddhanta-muktavali, 76, 1.
Siddhanta-siromani, 202.
Sidhartha, 58, 2; 546, 1.
Sighrocha, 204.
Sikalgars, 254, 1.
Sikh chiefs, 363, 1.
Sikhs of Punjab, *xxvii*, 1; 363, 1.
Sikkim, *xxvii*, 1; *xliv*.
Siksha, 170; 171.
Sila, 63; 237.
Shiladitya, 573.
Silara (king), 341.
Shilimukha, 453; 1.
Shilpa (mechanical arts), 212.
Silpaka, 524.
Shilpa-shastra, 211.
Simantonnayana, 219; 270.
Sima-vivada-dharma, 293.
Simla, 431, 2.
Simpis (tailors), 254, 1.
Sinclair, Mr. W. F., 254, 1; 256, 2.
Sindhi language, xxxvi.
Sindhu, *xix*.

Sindia, *xxvii*, 1.
Singapore, *xxvi*, 2.
Singing, 212; 518.
Sinha, *xlviii*, 1; 58, 2; 472, 1.
Sinhala, 383, 2.
Sinhasana-dvatrinsat, 573.
Sinivali, 184; 199.
Sinshapa, 575.
Sipahis, 254, 1.
Shipala, 226, 3.
Sirhind, *xxvii*, 1.
Sisira, 504.
Sishupala-baudha, 503; 516.
Sita (black), 563.
Sita, 373; 1; 394; 475; 542; 543.
Sita (rape of), 276.
Sita-phal, 392, 2.
Sitikantha, 457, 2.
Shiva 12; 1; 66; 310, 1; 359;
    360; 457, 2; 478; 479; 552;
    553; 558; .
Shiva-Dharma, 562.
Shiva-ratri, 363, 1.
Shiva-Sutras, 189, 1.
Shivaji, *xxviii*, 288, 1.
Shivaka, 400.
Six privileges of Brahmans, 267.
Skanda, 411; 476; 553; 562.
Slavonic language, *xxii*.
Shlesha, 509.
Shloka, 181; 242.
Sloka (invention of), 349; 543.
Smartha-bhattacharya, 342, 1.
Smartha Sutras, 170; 213.
Smasana (burning-ground), 224,
    336.
Smith, Mr. G., 439, 1.
Smrith, 8; 1; 56; 118; 169; 237;
    242; 249; 329; 339; 502.

Smrith Chandrika, 342.
Smrith tattva, 342.
Snana, 223; 273.
Snataka, 223; 331.
Sneha, 88.
Socrates, 74, 1.
Soka, 543.
Solar line of kings, 382.
Solomon, Song of, 519.
Soma (ceremonies and sacrifice), 9, 1; 32, 1; 308.
Soma (juice), 308.
Soma (god), 216.
Soma (moon), 264, 2; 418.
Soma (plant), 9; 1; 17.
Soma-deva, 572.
Soma-deva Bhatta, 572.
Soma-rudra, 308.
Soma-Siddhanta, 418; 550, 2.
Soma-Vara, 204, 2.
Sonars, 254, 1.
Soul (universal), 12, 1; 25; 38; 120.
South-Bihar (Magadha), 139; 2.
South Indian school, xxxviii, 1; 342.
Sparasa 85.
Sphotayana, 188, 1.
Spirit (universal), 12, 1; 25; 38; 120.
Spirituous liquor, 281.
Sraddha, 30, 1; 144; 3; 223; 228; 277; 299; 303, 1; 337; 458; 479; 482, 1.
Shraddha, 384, 3.
Srag-bandha, 507.
Shramana, 58, 2; 61; 310, 1; 351, 1; 527.
Shrauta-Sutra, 170; 171; 211; 213.

Shravakas, 61, 3; 142.
Shravana (nakshata); 200, 1.
Shravana (month), 197; 200; 1; 480, 1.
Shravasti (city), 58; 3.
Shravishta, 197.
Shreni, 332, 1; 333.
Shreshtin, 332, 1.
Shri, 476; 559.
Shridhara-sena, 410.
Shridhara-svamin, 555.
Shri-gadita, 524.
Shri-harsha, 503, 1; 544.
Shri-kantha, 536.
Shrinagar, 508, 1; 522; 569.
Shringara-tilaka, 508.
Shringata, 472, 2.
Shringin, 469, 1.
Shri-vatsa, 370.
Shruta, 7, 1; 169.
Shruta-bodha, 177; 532, 2.
Shruta karman, 435.
Shruta sena, 435.
Shruti, 28; 29, 2; 37; 54, 1; 56; 169; 243; 249; 329.
Shruti-dvaidham, 246.
Stage-manager, 525.
Stanzas, fanciful shapes of, 506.
Stenzler, Prof., 214, 1; 216; 231, 1; 232, 1; 327, 2; 338, 3; 529, 1.
Steya, 293, 303.
Sthalipaka, 219.
Sthana, 362; 457, 2.
Sthapati (architect), 212.
Sthapatya-veda, 211.
Sthavara, 71, 2.
Sthula-sarira, 68, 2.
St. Paul, xli.

St. Peter, *xliii.*
St. Thomas, *lxi.*
Starbo, *xxiii,* 250; 253, 1; 282, 3; 289, 2; 291, 1; 301, 1; 310, 1; 313, 1; 347, 1; 356, 546.
Stri-dhana, 300, 300, 1.
Stri-parvan, 417.
Stri-pun-dharma, 293.
Stri-sangrahana, 293.
Subala (king), 421; 436.
Subandhu, 411; 573.
Subhadra, 426, 2; 435, 1; 436.
Shubankara, 212.
Su-bhata, 411.
Subodhini, 341.
Sudatta, 58, 3.
Suddhodana, 58.
Shudra, 241; 253; 489.
Shudraka, 527.
Sufism, *liii,* 1; 38; 120, 2.
Sugata, 58, 2.
Sugriva, 398; 401; 474.
Suicide, 336.
Shuka, 555.
Shuka-saptai, 573.
Sukha, 85.
Shukra, 205; 338; 457, 2.
Shukra-vara, 204, 1.
Sukshama-dharma, 432, 1.
Sukshma-sarira, 68, 2; 226, 3.
Sukti, 129, 4.
Sulaiman I, 570, 1.
Shula-pani, 340.
Sulka, 300.
Sumantu, 339.
Sumatra (island), *xxvi,* 2.
Sumitra, 380.
Sun, 19.
Shunahsepha, 29; 31.

Sundara-kanda, 376; 411.
Sundara-mishra, 410.
Shunga-dynasty, 535.
Sunitha, 437.
Sunnah or Sunna, *liii,* 1; 28.
Sunni, *xxv,* 1; *liii,* 1.
Shunya 100, 3; 124, 3; 209; 210.
Suparna, 310.
Supplements to Veda, 211.
Suppressions of breath three, 271.
Su-prabuddha, 58, 1.
Supratika, 481, 1.
Supreme Being epithets of, 48.
Sura (Yadava king), 421.
Surabhi, 559.
Sura-pana, 303; 469.
Surashtra, 466.
Surat, *xxiii, xxvii,* 1.
Surgery, 212.
Suris (sprit sellers), 239, 1.
Shurpanakha, 395; 409.
Surunga, 430.
Surya, 14; 19; 288; 360; 383.
Surya-Siddhanta, 201; 202; 204.
Surya, 385, 1.
Surya-sukta, 318, 1.
Sushupti, 130, 4.
Suta (charioteer, bard), 422; 550.
Sutala, 480, 1.
Sutars (carpenters), 254, 1.
Sutasoma, 435, 1.
Sutlej, *xx,* 1.
Sutra, *xl,* 1; 77.
Sutra dhara or carpenter, 254, 1.
Sutra-pitaka, 64, 1.
Sutras of Panini, 189; 190.
Sutras (aphorism's), 29; 52; 538.
Sutras (Buddhist), 172, 3.
Sutratman, 66, 2; 134.

Sutta-nipata, *xl,* 1.
Shuvarnas, 329.
Suyodhana, 423.
Sva (in algebra), 209.
Sva-dharma, 333.
Svadhyaya, 222; 276; 276, 1.
Svar, 70, 3; 185; 222; 480, 1.
Svargarohanika-parvan, 418.
Svarochisha (Manu), 234, 3.
Svayam-bhu, 234, 3; 246, 249.
Svayambhuva (Manu), 234,
 250; 368, 3.
Svayamvara, 421; 433; 487, 2;
 488, 3.
Shveta, 145, 3.
Shveta (mountains), 469, 1.
Shveta-dvipa, 149, 2.
Shvetaketu, 55.
Shveta-lohita, 145, 3.
Shvetam baras, 139.
Shveta-shikha, 145, 3.
Shvetasva, 145, 3.
Shvetasvatara Upanishad, 48,
 49, 1; 145.
Shveta-vahana, 426, 3; 444.
Swamy, Sir M.C., xl, 1.
Swinging festival, 363, 1.
Syad-vada and Syad-vadins, 142.
Shyama-rahasya, 565.
Shyan (in grammar), 190, 1.
Syllogism 78.
Synthesis, 76; 98.

Tadaka, 396.
Taddhita affixes, 178; 196.
Tagore, Law Lectures, 300, 1.
Taili (oilman); 239, 1; 254, 1.
Taittiriya (Yajur-veda), 9; 9, 1;
 40; 264, 2.

Taittriyas or Taittiriyakas, 234;
 276, 1; 374, 1.
Taittifriya –brahmana, 29; 336,
 2.
Taittiriyaranyaka, 174.
Taittiriya Upanishad, 39.
Taj-jalan, 120, 2.
Takshaka, 395; 480, 1.
Talatala, 480, 1.
Talava-kara Upanishad, 40, 2.
Talmud, 28.
Tamas, 84; 102; 165; 251; 309;
 359.
Tamasa (Manu), 234, 3.
Tamil *xxxviii,* 347, 2.
Tamistra (hell); 265.
Tamraparni, 384.
Tandava, 518; 518, 1.
Tandula, 304, 1.
Tandya Bhramana, 29.
Tanjore, *xxvi,* 2.
Tan matras, 100; 250.
Tantis (weavers), 239, 1.
Tantra, 108; 361, 1; 561-565; 571.
Tantri, 239, 1.
Tantrika doctrines, 361; 563.
Tapah or tapar (heavenly
 sphere), 70, 3; 480, 1.
Tapas (austerity), 362.
Tapar (theory of), 381, 1.
Tapa-krichahara (penance), 307.
Tapta-masha, 304, 1.
Taraka (a Daitya), 362, 2.
Taranga, 572.
Targam, 6.
Tarka, 80; 249.
Taraka-sangraha, 76, 1; 87; 89;
 91.
Tarka-vidya, 249.

Tarkin, 249.
Tarpana, 272.
Tartar tribes, *xxiv*, 1; 347; 2.
Tatha-gata, 58, 2.
Tatpara (measure of time), 203.
Tatpurusha, 178.
Tattva, 98; 98, 1.
Tattava-jnanam, 122.
Tattva-samasa, 25, 1; 96, 1; 326, 2.
Tattavas, twenty-five, 99; 100; 249.
Tau-te-King, 4, 1.
Tauhid, 275, 1.
Taxation, six head of, 290 .
Taxes, 290.
Te Deum, 161, 2.
Tejas, 84; 101; 432, 1.
Telismachus, 489, 1.
Telinge, 254, 1.
Telis or oilmen, 254, 1.
Telungu, *xxxviii*, 1; 247, 2.
Telung contry, 276, 1.
Term in arithmetic and algebra, 209.
Tertiary compound, 88.
Testamentary, power, 298.
Teutonic language, xxi.
Thales, 67, 1; 131, 2.
Thera-gatha, *xl*, 1.
Their-gath, *xl*, 1.
Thirty-three gods, 360, 1.
Thomson, Mr. 147, 1; 162.
Thracians, 282, 3.
Thunderer, 17.
Tibetan language, 347, 2.
Tika, xliv, 1.
Tila, 228.
Tilaka, *lviii*.

Timaeus, 66, 1; 66, 4; 68, 2; 72, 1; 98; 121.
Time, hymn in praise of, 26.
Timur, *xxxviii*, 2.
Tirhut, 340.
Tirtha, 275, 1; 456, 1.
Tirtha-kara, 139.
Tirthan-kara, 139. .
Tithi, 204.
Tithi-tattva, 342.
Tomara, 453, 1.
Tonk, *xxvii*, 1.
Topics of the Nyaya, 76; 80.
Torana, 212.
Tota Kahani, 573.
Townships, 290.
Toxicology, 212.
Tradition (smriti), 169.
Tragedy, 520.
Trailokya, 247.
Trajan, Emperor, 352.
Tranquebar, *xxvi*, 2.
Transfiguration, 160, 1.
Transmigration, 14, 1; 36; 72; 72, 1; 247; 251; 372; 571.
Trasa-renu, 88.
Travancore, *lx*.
Trayam brahma, 243.
Trayi vidya, 243.
Treasure-trove, 291.
Treta (age), 204; 2; 251; 338; 339; 368, 3.
Trevelyan, Sir C., *xxxviii*.
Triad, 14, 1; 247; 359.
Tribes, aboriginal, *xxii*, 1.
Tri-danda, 144, 1.
Tri-dandin, 156, 1; 325, 3.
Tri-kanda, 187.
Tri-linga, 254, 1.

Trimurti, 14, 1; 247; 359; 548; 553; 556.
Tri-nachiketa, 243, 1.
Tri-pada, 18.
Tri-pitaka, *xl*, 1; 4, 1; 64, 1.
Tripura- daha, 523.
Rrishtubh-metre, 180, 374, 1.
Trisula, 210.
Tri-suparna, 243, 1.
Tri-vikrama, 367, 1.
Tri-vrit, 179.
Trotaka, 524.
Troyer, M.; 572, 2.
Trubner, xxvii, 1.
Truti, 203.
Try-ambaka, 361, 2.
Tuda, 347, 2.
Tukarma, lx.
Tula 304, 1; 334.
Tulasi, 304; 1.
Tulasi dasa or Tulsidas, 412; *xxxvi*, 1.
Tullberg, Dr., 525, 1.
Tulya-yogita, 509.
Mumlung, *xxvii*, 1.
Tungusic (Mantchu) language, 347, 2.
Turanian languages, 347, 2.
Turanian race, *xxxix*, 5, 1; 288.
Turkih language, 347; 2.
Turks, *xxiv*, 1.
Turphari, 145; 1.
Tushita, 62, 2.
Tuti-nama, 573.
Tvashtri, 17; 432, 1.

Uchcha, 205.
Udaharana, 77.
Udaka-dana, 278.

Udana, *xl*, 1.
Udatta-raghava, 410.
Udattokti, 526.
Udayana (king), 545.
Udayana Acharya, 94.
Uddhara, 299.
Uddisa, 565.
Udyatari, 9, 1; 245.
Udyoga-parvan, 417.
Ugra, 457, 2.
Ugra-shravas, 550, 1.
Ujjayini, 201; 368; 3; 531; 532, 1.
Ujjvala-datta, 188, 1.
Ulka-mukh, 267; 310.
Ullapya, 524.
Ulua, 82, 1.
Ulupi, 82, 1.
Ulysses, 474.
Uma, 404, .
Umapati, 457, 2.
Umayyad, Khalif, *liii*, 1.
Unadi-sutras, 188, 1.
Unclean animals, *xxxi*, 1.
Unity of the Godhead, *li*, 1.
Unmarried girls, 301.
Upadana –karana, 68, 1.
Upa-dharma, 278.
Upadhi, 79, 1; 132, 4.
Upadhyaya, 261.
Upali, *xli*, 1.
Upama, 508.
Upamana, 77; 136; 508.
Upameya, 508.
Upanaya, 77.
Upanayana, 217; 220; 270.
Upanyas, *xliv*, 1.
Upanishads, 8; 25, 1; 37; 37, 1; 39; 72, 1; 145; 246.
Upansa, 277.

Upapataka, 304.
Upa-purana, 171; 561.
Upa-rupaka, 522; 524.
Upasad, 380, 1.
Upasaka, 61.
Upa-Samhriti, 522, 1.
Up sarga, 177; 186.
Upavasa, 363, 1.
Upaveda, 211.
Upaya, 63, 1.
Upendra-vajra, 181.
Uposhita ((fasting), 284.
Urdu language, xxxviii, 2.
Uriya language, xxxvi.
Urvshi, 419.
Ushanas, 213; 339.
Ushas, 14; 21; 477.
Usury, 296.
Utkala, 239, 1.
Utpreksha, 509.
Utsarpini, 140.
Utsava, 363, 1.
Utsrishtikarna, 524.
Uttara, 227.
Uttara-kanda, 376; 402; 408, 1.
Uttara-mimansa, 116.
Uttara-paksha, 117.
Uttara-rama-charita, 377; 408, 1;
    409; 537; 540; 542.
Uttarayana, 451.

Vac (word), 243.
Vachyapati Mishra, 110, 1; 342.
Vachya, 509.
Vada (controversy), 80.
Vadhuna Shruta Sutras, 171.
Vadin (plaintiff) 334.
Vag-dandayoh, parushye, 306.
Vashna, 479.

Vaidika, 312; 1.
Vaidika (repeaters of veda), 276,
    1.
Vaidya, 239, 1; 255.
Vaidyanti, 341, 342.
Vaikartana, 422, 2.
Vaikhansa, Shruta Sutras, 171.
Vaikuntha, 373.
Vaimanika, 309.
Vairagya, 110; 569.
Vaisakha, 200, 1.
Vaishampayana, 414, 1; 418;
    550, 1.
Vaiseshika philosophy, 52; 57; 68,
    1; 77; 82; 88; 93; 106; 248.
Vaisheshika Sutras 76, 1; 78;
    81, 1.
Vaishnavas, lviii, 363, 1; 554.
Vaishnavi, 563.
Vaishravana, 395.
Vaisvadeva homa, 216, 1.
Vaisya, 26, 1; 241; 253; 254,
    1; 389, 1.
Vaitanika oblations, 215; 286.
Vaitarani, 463.
Vaivasvata (seventh Manu), 34,
    1; 234, 3; 368, 3; 383.
Vajsaneyins-pratisakhya, 175, 178.
Vajasaneyi-samhita, 29, 40.
Vaka, 430.
Vakovakyam, 331, 331, 1.
Vakula, 472, 3.
Valabhi, 411.
Valabhi, or Ballabhi, 504.
Valabhi-pura, 410.
Vallabyhacharya, 363, 1.
Valli (Katha Upanishad), 47.
Valmiki, 349, 1; 352; 354; 409;
    412 465; 543.

Vamacharins, 564, 1.
Vamadeva, 378.
Vamana (dwarf), 358; 367; 481, 1; 521; 533.
Vamana's Kasika Vritti, 194.
Vana, 453, 1; 573.
Vana parvan, 404, 1; 410; 416.
Vanaprastha, 240, 168; 271; 285; 338.
Vanis, 254, 1.
Vansa (genealogy), 550.
Vansa-brahmana, 137, 1.
Vansanucharita, 550.
Vansa-sthavila, 557.
Vara, 204, 1.
Varada, 457, 2.
Varaha(boar), 366; 422, 1.
Varaha-mihira, 201; 205; 411.
Varaha Shruta Sutras, 171.
Varsahi, (betel –grower), 239, 1.
Varanasi, 550, 2.
Varanavata (city), 429.
Vararachi xxxvii, 1.
Vardhamana, 140, 1.
Vardushika, 297.
Vardhushya, 304.
Varendra, 239, 1.
Varuhaspatya Sutras, 143.
Varna (caste), 239, 1; 253.
Varna-sankarh, 254.
Varsha, 469; 503.
Vartha karma, 267.
Varthika-kara, 192.
Varthikas, 175; 192; 193, 1; 571.
Varuna, 12; 13; 15; 16; 19; 30; 216; 226; 288; 479; 562.
Varuni, 559.
Vasanta (spring), 503.

Vasantaka, 545.
Vasanta-sena, 528; 530.
Vasanthotsava, 524.
Vasava-datta, 411; 545; 573.
Vasishtha, 232; 339; 353, 1; 378; 386; 403; 449, 1; 542; 550, 2; 562.
Vasishtha, 412.
Vasishtha-ramayana, 412.
Vasishtha-siddhanta, 201.
Vastu, 68, 1; 120; 122; 508; 522.
Vastu-pariksha, 221.
Vastu-purusha, 212.
Vasu (king), 239, 1; 414, 1.
Vasu-deva, 350; 369.
Vasudeva, 369; 371; 419; 435, 2.
Vasudevas (nine), 141.
Vasuki (serpent), 365; 395; 480; 1; 559.
Vasus, 446; 447.
Vasu-Shena, 422; 428, 2.
Vata or Banyan (Ficus Indica), 45, 1.
Vatsa, 486, 2.
Vatsalya, 508, 1.
Vatsa-raka, 545.
Vatsayayana, 81.
Vatup (in grammar), 189, 3.
Vayu, 13; 84; 101; 477.
Vayu-purana, 553.
Veda, xxxiv, xlii, 2; 237; 548; 562.
Veda (repetition of), 22; 267; 276; 276, 1; 308.
Vedabhyasa, 267.
Vedanyas (six), 169; 171; 187.
Vedanta, lii, 1; 52; 90; 116; 120; 237.
Vedanta-paribhasha, 128, 1.

Vedanta-sara, 128, 1.
Vedanta-sutras, 52, 1; 276, 1.
Vedantist formula, 43.
Vedantists, 44.
Vedars, 347, 2.
Vedartha-prakasa, 415, 1.
Veda-vahya, 170.
Vedic Nakshatras (twenty-seven), 198, 1.
Vedic prosody, 180.
Veni-samhara, 437, 2; 547.
Venus (planet), 204.
Venacular dialects, *xxxvii*, *xxxvii*, 2.
Vetala, 573.
Vetala-pancha-vinshati, 573.
Vibhaya, 85; 293.
Vibhandaka, 379.
Vibhanga, *xl*, 1.
Vibhishana, 347, 1; 396, 1; 398; 401; 427, 1.
Vichitra-virya, 419.
Vidarbha-raja, 410.
Videha, 373, 1; 466; 550, 2.
Vidhi, 28.
Vidhi-yajna, 277.
Vidura, 420; 430; 437; 446; 458.
Vidushaka or jester, 526; 536.
Vidya, 318, 2; 331.
Vighatika, 203.
Viharas, 527.
Vija, 250, 522, 1.
Vija-ganita, 203; 202; 209.
Vijaya, 426, 3; 444.
Vijaya-nagara, 137, 1.
Vijnana-bhikshu, 96, 1; 110, 1.
Vijnana-maya-kosha, 133.
Vijnanesvara, 327.

Vikala, 204.
Vikara (productions), 100; 165.
Vikarna, 190.
Vikartana, 422, 1.
Vikramadiya, 531; 532, 1; 573.
Vikramorvasi, 532; 534.
Vikrita, 524.
Vikshepa, 128; 132, 1.
Vikukshi, 383.
Vilasika, 524.
Village government, 290.
Vimana-vatthu, *xi*, 1.
Vimarsha (hindrance), 522, 1.
Vinadi, 203.
Vinaya-pitaka, *xl*, 1 64, 1.
Vindhya, *xx*, 2.
Vipatha, 453, 1.
Vira, 140, 1; 508, 1; 522.
Vira-charita, 541.
Viradha, 348; 1.
Viraj, 25; 25, 3; 234, 3; 250.
Vira-mitrodaya, 342.
Virana, 221.
Vira-shayana, 459.
Virata (king), 417.
Virata-parvan, 417.
Virgil, 68, 2; 72, 1; 74, 1; 125, 1.
Virupa, 119.
Virupaksha, 457, 2; 481, 1.
Virya, 63.
Vishaka, 200, 1.
Vishesha, 83; 86; 88.
Visheshokti, 509.
Visha (poison); 212; 304, 1.
Vishaya, 68; 89; 101; 508.
Vishkambha, 526.
Vishnu, 12, 1; 66; 96, 1; 231; 247; 310, 1; 358; 479; 553; 560.

Vishnu (of the Rig-veda), 358; 360.
Vishnu-gupta, 547.
Vishnu-purana, 109; 411; 432, 1; 435, 1; 553; 556.
Vishnu-Sharman, 572.
Vishnu-yashas, 372. 1.
Vishnuvat, 208.
Vishikha, 453, 1.
Vision of the Universal form, 160; 447.
Vishravas, 396, 1.
Vishvadeva, 447.
Vishvakarman, 20, 1; 31, 1; 212; 352, 1; 384; 403; 449, 1; 456, 1.
Vishva-prakasa, 187.
Viisva-rupa, 340; 457, 2.
Visve Devah, 216; 228.
Vitala, 480; 1.
Vitana (heaths), 216; 216, 1.
Vitanda (cavilling), 81.
Vithi, 524.
Vithoba, *lx.*
Viththal, *lx.*
Vidada-Charana, 342.
Vivada-Chintamani, 342.
Vivadh Svanipalayoh, 342.
Vivada-tandava, 342.
Vivaha (marriage), 217; 270; 274.
Vivasana, 139, 3.
Vivasvat, 383.
Vopadeva, 195; 195, 1; 555.
Vow of continence, 423, 2.
Varaja, 370.
Vrata, 141; 284; 362, 2.
Vratyata, 304.
Vriddha yajanavalka, 232; 327.
Vriddhi, 297.

Vriddhi-putra, 228.
Vrihaj-jataka, 201.
Vrihan-nala, 443.
Vrihannaradiya, 561.
Vrihaspati, 205; 231; 339.
Vrihaspati (aphorisms of), 143.
Vrihaspati siddhanta, 201.
Vrihat, katha, 572.
Vrikodara, 425.
Vriksha-bandha, 507.
Vrisha, 422, 1.
Vrishabha, 140, 1.
Vrishnis 446.
Vritra, *ix,* 13; 17; 432, 1; 467, 1.
Vritti, 238; 522.
Vyahritis (three), 222; 243, 1.
Vyaja-Stuti, 509.
Vyakarana (grammar), 170; 175; 187.
Vyakta-ganita, 202, 2.
Vyapaka pervader, 78.
Vyapti, 78; 79, 1.
Vyapaka, 78.
Vyasa, 52; 119; 232; 283, 1; 339; 354; 411; 414; 1; 415, 1; 419; 422; 430; 455, 1; 458; 549; 550, 1; 554.
Vyatireka, 509.
Vyavahara, 238; 287; 312; 320; 328; 332.
Vyavahara chintamani, 342.
Vyavahara-mayukha, 343.
Vyavahara-padam, 333.
Vyavaharika (existeve), 127.
Vyavakalana, 210.
Vyayoga, 523.

Wahabi, *liii,* 1.
Walid, 1; *xxiv,* 1.

Weaver, two headed, 575.
Weber, A., 15, 2; 29, 1; 33;
72, 1; 197, 352, 1; 409, 1;
535.
Weber's Indische Streifen, 35, 1.
Weber's Indische Studien, 48, 2;
368, 3.
Western school, 343.
Wheeler, Mr. Talboys, 242, 2;
280, 2; 355, 1; 412, 1.
Whitney Prof. W.D., xxvi; 9,
10, 1; 43, 1; 176, 2; 197, 1;
199, 2; 201, 2.
Whitney's Oriental Studies, 368,
3; xxvil, 1.
Widows, marriage of, 284; 487, 2.
Wife (Directions of choosing),
273.
Wilkins, Sir C., 298, 2.
Wills Act (Hindu), 298, 2.
Wilson, Professor, H.H., 29, 3;
90, 2.
Wilson's Glossary, 297, 1.
Wilson's Hindu Theatre, 289, 2.
Winking of eyes, 16, 2.
Witness (four or three), 274;
329.
Wives, Character of, 486.
Women and wives duties of,
318.
Women, position of, lvii, 490.
World destruction of, 557.
Wort-spiel, 505.
Written evidence, 276, 1; 329;
333.

Ya (in algebra), 210.
Yadavas, 370; 418; 550, 2.
Yadu, 370; 419.

Yajnam, 267.
Yajna, 358.
Yajna-patra, 224.
Yajnavalkya, 217; 231; 262, 1;
276, 1; 230, 1; 340.
Yajvalkya, code of, 327.
Yajvalkya commentary on, 340.
Yajnavalkya Vrihad, 327.
Yajnika-deva, 173.
Yajnika (ritualist), 184; 276, 1.
Yajnopavita, 220; 222; 262, 3.
Yajur-veda, 9, 1; 29; 48, 2.
Yajur-veda, Black, 9, 1; 49; 276, 1.
Yajur-veda, White, 9; 1; 276, 1.
Yajurvedi, 9, 1.
Yajvan (Sacrificer), 309.
Tak (in grammar), 190, 1.
Taksha, 310; 447.
Yama, 14; 21; 22; 46; 216;
226; 231; 288; 476; 479.
Yama (abode of), 70, 3.
Yama (forbearance), 111.
Yama (hymn to), 22; 336.
Yamak, 426, 3.
Yami, 22.
Yamuna (river), 419, 4; 466.
Yan (in grammar), 190, 1.
Yaska, 19, 1; 182; 182, 1.
Yasoda, 370.
Yasodhara, 58, 1.
Yashovarman, 537.
Yates, Dr., 181; 507.
Yati, 142; 286.
Yatudhanas, 348.
Yaugandharayana, 545.
Yavanas), 258, 2; 355; 403.
Yavat-tavat, 209.
Yayati, 370; 419.
Yazd, xxiii, 1.

Yazid, *liii*, 1.
Yellow garments, 329.
Yi (Chinese book), 4, 1.
Yoga, 52, 1; 110; 111; 154, 3; 178; 246; 329.
Yoga (Sutras of), 110, 1.
Yoga-kshema, 291.
Yogas (twenty seven), 204; 1.
Yoga-vasishtha, 412.
Yogesa, 362, 2.
Yogin, 112; 132, 3; 362, 2.
Yojana (measure) 204.
Yoni (female symbol), 360, 2.
Yuddha-kanta, 376.
Yudhishthisra, 409; 416; 417; 423; 429; 432, 1; 435, 1; 443; 455; 458; 462; 463.
Yuga (Jaina), 140.

Yugas (four), 204; 204, 2; 205; 251.
Yukti, 130, 3.
Yupa, 33; 280, 1.
Yuthika, 472, 3.
Yuva-raja (heir-apparent), 429.

Zahr, 38.
Zakat, 275, 1.
Zamindar, 290, 1.
Zand, *xxii*, 6, 1.
Zanda-Avasta, *xxiii*, 155, 2.
Zarathashtra, 6.
Zeno, 99, 1.
Zeus, 12; 125, 1; 158, 1.
Zodiac (division of), 197.
Zoroaster, *xxiii*, *liii*, 1; 6; 63.
Zoroastrian Persians, *xxiii*, *xlvi*, 1; 4, 1.